DISABILITY DISCRIMINATION

LAW AND PRACTICE

 University of Essex   Library

Date Due Back

Books may be renewed online (or telephone 01206 873187)
Unless they have been recalled.

Form No. L.43 April 2004

DISABILITY DISCRIMINATION
LAW AND PRACTICE

Fifth Edition

Brian J. Doyle LLB, LLM, PhD, *Barrister*
Regional Chairman of the Employment Tribunals

JORDANS

2005

Published by
Jordan Publishing Limited
21 St Thomas Street
Bristol BS1 6JS

British Library Cataloguing-in-Publication Data
A catalogue record for this book is available from the British Library.

ISBN 0 85308 957 4

Typeset by MFK-Mendip, Frome, Somerset
Printed in Great Britain by Antony Rowe Limited

DEDICATION

For my daughter, Natalie

PREFACE

Published in the year of the tenth anniversary of the enactment of the Disability Discrimination Act 1995, this fifth edition continues the pattern of producing a new edition every two years.

A major impetus behind the updated commentary and analysis is the important changes in the employment field effected by the Disability Discrimination Act 1995 (Amendment) Regulations 2003 and the Disability Discrimination Act 1995 (Pensions) Regulations 2003. This has necessitated a complete rewriting of Chapters 3 and 4. In force from 1 October 2004, the changes expand the scope of Part 2 of the Act to embrace not just employees, contract workers and trade organisations, but also office-holders, police officers, partners in firms, barristers and advocates, providers of practical work experience, and qualifications bodies. New rules on occupational pension schemes have been introduced, while most of the previous exemptions from Part 2 (not least for small businesses) have been swept away. The two new supporting codes of practice are integrated into the discussion of these reforms. The changes made by the Disability Discrimination (Employment Field) (Leasehold Premises) Regulations 2004, the Employment Tribunals Rules of Procedure 2004 and the Disability Discrimination (Questions and Replies) Order 2004 are also reviewed.

Case-law continues to develop our understanding of Part 2 of the Act. Among the more important decisions of the higher appellate courts within the last two years which are accounted for in this edition are: *Collins v Royal National Theatre Board Ltd* and *HM Prison Service v Beart* (on the justification defence); *Archibald v Fife Council* and *Electronic Data Systems Ltd v Travis* (on the duty to make reasonable adjustments); *Nottinghamshire County Council v Meikle* (on constructive dismissal and on sick pay); and *Rhys-Harper v Relaxion Group plc* (on relationships that have come to an end).

While the law on the meaning of disability and disabled persons has remained largely unchanged, the Disability Discrimination (Blind and Partially Sighted Persons) Regulations 2003 and the decisions of the

Court of Appeal in *Woodrup v London Borough of Southwark* and *Kirton v Tetrosyl Ltd* are taken on board.

The process of bringing into full force the goods and services provisions of Part 3 of the Act was also completed on 1 October 2004. Those changes were anticipated and dealt with in the last edition. The account of this area of the Act has been brought up to date in this edition, including consideration of the new provisions on employment services and the changes made by the Disability Discrimination (Providers of Services) (Adjustment of Premises) (Amendment) Regulations 2004. Part 3 also deals with the disposal and management of premises, and so the significance of the recent decision of the Court of Appeal in *Council of the City of Manchester v Romano and Samari* is assessed.

The new provisions on disability discrimination in education are now producing their first crop of judicial precedents. This edition considers the decisions in *McAuley Catholic High School v CC and PC* and *R (D) v Governing Body of Plymouth High School for Girls*. The interaction of the Part 5 provisions on transport vehicles and the Part 3 duty to make reasonable adjustments to services was recently considered by the Court of Appeal in *Roads v Central Trains Ltd* and is dealt with here. The amendments made by Private Hire Vehicles (Carriage of Guide Dogs etc) Act 2002 and the Disability Discrimination Act 1995 (Private Hire Vehicles) (Carriage of Guide Dogs etc) (England and Wales) Regulations 2003 are also accounted for.

I have endeavoured to state the law as I understand it to be at 1 January 2005. However, as this edition was going to press, the Disability Discrimination Bill was progressing through Parliament. If enacted, the Bill will make important changes to the meaning of disability and will further amend the provisions on disability discrimination in the employment field, in relation to goods and services and public authorities, and in respect of rail vehicles and disabled persons' parking. Proposals for a Commission for Equality and Human Rights have also been recently published. All these developments are anticipated in this new edition at appropriate points.

As in previous editions, the analysis takes account of the different implementation of the Disability Discrimination Act 1995 in Wales, Scotland and Northern Ireland, as well as in England or across the UK as whole. I have also adopted the modern legislative practice of referring to Parts of the Act in Arabic (rather than Roman) numerals.

BRIAN DOYLE
January 2005

CONTENTS

Dedication		v
Preface		vii
Table of Cases		xix
Table of Statutes		xxix
Table of Statutory Instruments and Circulars		xlvii
Table of Codes of Practice, Guidance etc		lvii
Table of European, UN and International Legislation		lxix
Table of Abbreviations		lxxi
Chapter 1	INTRODUCTION	1
	1.1 Introduction	1
	1.2 Disability Discrimination Act 1995	2
	1.3 Scope and extent	3
	1.4 Northern Ireland	3
	1.5 Disability Discrimination Bill	4
Chapter 2	DISABILITY AND DISABLED PERSON	7
	2.1 Introduction	7
	2.2 Meaning of 'disability' and 'disabled person'	9
	2.3 Impairment	11
	Physical impairment	12
	Mental impairment	13
	Physical impairment or mental impairment?	15
	Sensory and other impairments	16
	2.4 Ability to carry out normal day-to-day activities	17
	2.5 Substantial adverse effect	21
	Meaning of 'substantial'	21
	Recurring conditions	24
	Progressive conditions	25
	Severe disfigurement	27
	Effect of medical treatment	28
	2.6 Long-term adverse effect	30

	Past disability and long-term adverse effect	32
2.7	Persons deemed to be disabled	32
2.8	Past disabilities	33
2.9	Disability Discrimination Bill	35

Chapter 3	THE EMPLOYMENT FIELD: COMMON CONCEPTS	37
3.1	Introduction	37
	Disability Discrimination Act 1995 (Amendment) Regulations 2003	37
	Secondary sources	38
	The scheme of Part 2, as amended	39
3.2	Discrimination	40
	Disability-related discrimination	40
	Direct discrimination	55
	Failure to make reasonable adjustments	58
	Victimisation	61
	Discrimination by association or perception	62
3.3	Harassment	63
3.4	Duty to make reasonable adjustments	63
	The duty illustrated	64
	What are reasonable steps to take?	67
3.5	Relationships which have come to an end	70
3.6	Discriminatory advertisements	71
3.7	Instructions and pressure to discriminate	73
3.8	Disability Discrimination Bill	74
	Discrimantory advertisements	74

Chapter 4	THE EMPLOYEMENT FIELD: UNLAWFUL ACTS	75
4.1	Introduction	75
4.2	Employers	76
	Unlawful acts	76
	Scope of the employment provisions	82
	Employer's duty to make reasonable adjustments	88
	Unfair dismissal and disability discrimination	95
	Performance-related pay	96
	Agricultural wages	97
4.3	Contract workers	97
	Definitions	98
	Unlawful discrimination	99

		Contract work and reasonable adjustments	100
	4.4	Office-holders	102
		Offices or posts	102
		Exclusions	104
		Unlawful acts	105
		Duty to make adjustments	108
	4.5	Occupational pension schemes	109
		Employers' obligations	109
		Trustees and managers of occupational pension schemes	110
		Non-discrimination rule	111
		Unlawful acts	112
		Alterations to a scheme	112
		Duty to make reasonable adjustments	112
		Procedure and remedies	113
	4.6	Insurance benefits	114
	4.7	Partnerships	116
		Unlawful acts	117
		Duty to make reasonable adjustments	117
	4.8	Barristers and advocates	118
		England and Wales	118
		Unlawful acts	119
		Duty to make reasonable adjustments	120
		Scotland	121
		Northern Ireland	122
	4.9	Trade organisations	122
		Trade organisation	123
		Unlawful acts	125
		Duty to make reasonable adjustments	126
	4.10	Qualifications bodies	128
		Qualification bodies	129
		Unlawful acts	129
		Competence standards and justification	130
		Duty to make reasonable adjustments	130
	4.11	Practical work experience	131
		Unlawful acts	132
		Duty to make reasonable adjustments	132
	4.12	Enforcement, remedies and procedures	133
	4.13	Disability Discrimination Bill	133
		Group insurance	134
Chapter 5		GOODS, FACILITIES AND SERVICES	135
	5.1	Introduction	135
		Timetable	136

		Code and regulations	136
		Part 3 of the DDA 1995 outlined	137
	5.2	Provision of services	137
		Services	137
		Goods and facilities	139
		Service providers	140
		Manufacturers and designers	141
		Private members' clubs	141
		To whom the service is provided	142
		Excluded services	142
	5.3	Unlawful discrimination	143
		Refusal to provide goods, facilities or services	143
		Standard or manner of service	143
		Terms on which service is provided	144
		Failure to make reasonable adjustment	144
	5.4	Meaning of discrimination	144
		Less favourable treatment	145
		Indirect discrimination	149
	5.5	Duty to make reasonable adjustments	150
		Introduction	150
		Practices, policies or procedures	153
		Physical features	154
		Auxiliary aids and services	158
	5.6	Justification	159
		Subjective opinion and objective reasonableness	161
		Conditions for justification defence	162
		Insurance services	166
		Guarantees	167
		Deposits	168
	5.7	Employment services	169
	5.8	Enforcement, remedies and procedures	171
	5.9	Disability Discrimination Bill	172
		Public authorities and police	172
		Transport services	172
		Private clubs	173
Chapter 6		PROPERTY, PREMISES AND LEASES	175
	6.1	Introduction	175
	6.2	Discrimination in relation to premises	176
		Unlawful acts of discrimination	176
		Person with power to dispose of any premises	178

Premises and tenancy 179
Exemption for small dwellings 180
Meaning of discrimination 181
Victimisation 185
Enforcement and remedies 186
Judicial consideration of sections 22–24 186
6.3 Alterations to premises 187
The duty to make reasonable adjustments
to premises 187
Building regulations: employment field 188
Building regulations: service providers 189
The problem of leases 191
The effect of the DDA 1995 upon premises
occupied under leases 191
Employment field cases 194
Goods and services cases 198
Management and disposal of premises 204
6.4 Educational institutions and alteration of
leasehold premises 205
6.5 Disability Discrimination Bill 205

Chapter 7 EDUCATION 207
7.1 Introduction 207
7.2 The law pre-September 2002 209
Education and Part 3 of the DDA 1995 209
Exempted educational services 211
Education and policy-making 213
Schools 213
Teacher Training Agency 215
Further education colleges and institutions 215
Further education funding councils 217
Local education authorities 218
Universities and higher education
institutions 219
7.3 The law post-September 2002 222
Special Educational Needs and Disability
Act 2001 222
7.4 Schools and education authorities 223
Disability discrimination duties 224
Discrimination 226
Knowledge of disability 229
Justification 230
Accessibility strategies and plans 230
Residual duty of education authorities 236

		Enforcement	237
	7.5	Further and higher education	238
		Disability discrimination duties	239
		Discrimination	241
		Knowledge of disability	244
		Justification	245
		Other providers of further education or training facilities	246
		Enforcement	247
		Reasonable adjustments and the problem of leases	248
	7.6	Disability Discrimination Bill	255
		General qualifications bodies	255
Chapter 8		PUBLIC TRANSPORT	257
	8.1	Introduction	257
		Transport services and Part 3 of the DDA 1995	257
		Transport employers and Part 2 of the DDA 1995	258
		Public transport and Part 5 of the DDA 1995	259
	8.2	Taxis	259
		Taxi accessibility regulations	260
		Taxis to be covered by the regulations	261
		Exemption regulations	262
		Swivel seat regulations	263
		Duties of taxi drivers towards disabled passengers	264
		Carrying of guide dogs and hearing dogs in taxis	266
		Carrying of assistance dogs in private hire vehicles	268
		Taxi accessibility at designated transport facilities	270
		Application to Scotland and Northern Ireland	271
		Implementation	271
	8.3	Public service vehicles	272
		PSV accessibility regulations	273
		Accessibility certificates	277
		Type approval certificates	278
		Offences and exemptions	279
	8.4	Rail vehicles	280

	Rail vehicle accessibility regulations	281
	Offences	284
	Regulated rail vehicles	284
	Exemptions	286
8.5	Aviation and shipping	287
8.6	Disability Discrimination Bill	288
	Rail vehicles	288
	Disabled persons' parking badges	289

Chapter 9	INSTITUTIONAL FRAMEWORK	291
9.1	Disability Rights Commission	291
	Introduction	291
	Status	292
	Staffing of the Commission	292
	Commissioners	292
	Functions and powers	294
	Assistance in relation to proceedings	296
	Formal investigations	298
	Formal investigation into website accessibility	303
	Non-discrimination notices	304
	Action plans	306
	Agreements in lieu of enforcement action	311
	Persistent discrimination	313
	Disclosure of information	314
	Enforcement of court orders	314
	Offences	315
	Service of notices	316
9.2	Commission for Equality and Human Rights	316
9.3	Codes of practice	317
9.4	Guidance on meaning of disability	319
9.5	Application to the Crown	321
9.6	Application to Parliament	322
9.7	Regulations and orders	323
9.8	Disability Discrimination Bill	324
	Public authorities	324
	Police	325
	Codes of practice	325

Chapter 10	LIABILITY AND REMEDIES	327
10.1	Victimisation	327
10.2	Legal liability	330
	Aiding unlawful acts	330
	Liability of employers	332

	Liability of principals	334
	Statutory authority	335
	National security	337
10.3	Employment cases	338
	Statutory questionnaire	338
	Employment tribunal proceedings	340
	Time-limits	341
	Dispute resolution procedures	343
	ACAS conciliation and arbitration	343
	Compromise contracts	344
	Restriction on publicity	345
	Burden of proof	347
	Remedies	348
	Recommendations	353
10.4	Services and premises cases	354
	Proceedings in the county court or sheriff court	354
	Time-limits	355
	Conciliation	356
	Settlements	357
	Remedies	358
10.5	Education cases: schools	359
	Special Educational Needs and Disability Tribunal	359
	Claims and remedies	361
	Time-limits	363
	Roles of the Secretary of State and the Welsh Assembly	363
	Enforcement in Scotland	364
	Validity and revision of agreements of responsible bodies	365
	Conciliation	366
10.6	Education cases: further and higher education	367
	Time-limits	367
	Remedies	368
	Validity and revision of agreements of responsible bodies	368
	Conciliation	369
10.7	Disability Discrimination Bill	369

Appendix I   DISABILITY DISCRIMINATION ACT 1995   371

Appendix II   DISABILITY RIGHTS COMMISSION ACT
                  1999   511

Index   537

TABLE OF CASES

References are to paragraph numbers.

A v London Borough of Hounslow (2001) EAT/1155/98 (2001) IDS Brief
  B694/3   3.2.25, 3.2.30, 3.2.32
AB v South Western Water Services Ltd, *sub nom* Gibbons v South Western
  Water Services Ltd [1993] QB 507, [1993] 2 WLR 507, [1993] 1 All ER
  609, CA   10.3.26
Abadeh v British Telecommunications plc [2001] ICR 156, [2001] IRLR 23,
  (2000) IDS Brief B675/3, EAT   2.1.3, 2.1.4, 2.4.3, 2.4.5, 2.5.15
Abbey Life Assurance Co Ltd v Tansell [2000] ICR 789, [2000] IRLR 387,
  (2000) IDS Brief 661/5, CA; *sub nom* MHC Consulting Services Ltd v
  Tansell [1999] IRLR 677, (1999) IDS Brief B649/8, EAT   4.3.3
Air Canada and Alpha Catering Services v Basra [2000] IRLR 683, (2000) *The
  Independent*, April 3, EAT   10.1.2
Aldred v Nacanco [1987] IRLR 292, CA   10.2.5
Alexander v Home Office [1988] 1 WLR 968, [1988] 2 All ER 118, [1988]
  IRLR 190, CA   10.3.26
AM v WC and SPV [1999] ICR 1218, [1999] IRLR 410, (1999) IDS Brief
  B641/3, EAT   10.2.2, 10.2.4
Amies v Inner London Education Authority [1977] 2 All ER 100, [1977] ICR
  308, [1977] 1 CMLR 336, EAT   10.3.8
Andrews (Deceased) v Lewisham and Guys Mental Health NHS Trust. *See*
  Harris (Personal Representative of Andrews (Deceased)) v Lewisham and
  Guy's Mental Health NHS Trust
Aniagwu v London Borough of Hackney [1999] IRLR 303, (1999) IDS Brief
  B638/12, EAT   10.3.9
Anya v University of Oxford [2001] EWCA Civ 405, [2001] ICR 847, [2001]
  IRLR 364, [2001] Emp LR 509, CA   3.2.6, 10.3.20
Anyanwu v South Bank Students' Union [2001] UKHL 14, [2001] 1 WLR 638,
  [2001] 2 All ER 353, [2001] ICR 391, [2001] IRLR 305, HL   10.2.2
Apelogun-Gabriels v London Borough of Lambeth [2001] EWCA Civ 1853,
  [2002] IRLR 116, (2002) IDS Brief B704/12, CA   10.3.9
Applin v Race Relations Board [1975] AC 259, [1974] 2 WLR 541, [1974] 2 All
  ER 73, HL   5.2.7
Arboshe v East London Bus & Coach Co Ltd (1999) EAT/877/98   3.4.4
Archibald v Fife Council [2004] UKHL 32, [2004] ICR 954, [2004] 4 All ER
  303, [2004] IRLR 651, HL; [2004] IRLR 197, Ct of Sess   3.2.34, 3.4.1, 3.4.4,
                                                  4.2.43, 4.2.44, 9.3.5, 10.2.10
Armitage, Marsden and HM Prison Service v Johnson [1997] ICR 275, [1997]
  IRLR 162, (1996) *The Times*, December 31, EAT   10.3.26
Ashton v Chief Constable of West Mercia Constabulary [2001] ICR 67, (2000)
  IDS Brief B675/7, (2000) *The Times*, November 14, EAT   2.4.1
Atos Origin IT UK Ltd v Haddock [2005] 1 CR 277, [2005] IRLR 20, EAT   10.3.2

Aziz v Trinity Street Taxis Ltd [1988] 3 WLR 79, [1988] ICR 534, [1988] IRLR
        204, CA   10.1.7

BP Chemicals Ltd v Gillick [1995] IRLR 128, EAT   4.2.17, 4.3.4
Bahl v The Law Society [2004] EWCA Civ 1070, [2004] IRLR 799, (2004) IDS
        Brief B768/3, (2004) *The Times*, 7 October, CA   3.2.6, 10.3.20
Balamoody v United Kingdom Central Council for Nursing, Midwifery and
        Health Visiting [2001] EWCA Civ 2097, [2002] ICR 646, [2002] IRLR 288,
        (2002) IDS Brief B713/9, CA   3.2.5
Balfron Trustees Ltd v Peterson [2001] IRLR 758, (2001) 151 NLJ 1180, (2001)
        The Independent, October 29, ChD   10.2.5
Balgobin and Francis v Tower Hamlets London Borough [1987] ICR 829,
        [1987] IRLR 401, (1987) 84 LS Gaz 2530, EAT   10.2.6
Barclays Bank plc v Kapur [1991] 2 AC 355, [1991] 2 WLR 401, [1991] 1 All
        ER 646, [1991] ICR 208, HL   10.3.8
Barker v Westbridge International Ltd (2000) EAT/1180/98, (2000) *The Times*,
        8 June, EAT   2.1.4
Barton v Investec Henderson Crosthwaite Securities Ltd [2003] ICR 1205,
        [2003] IRLR 332, EAT   3.2.6, 10.3.20
Baynton v Saurus General Engineers Ltd [2000] ICR 375, [1999] IRLR 604,
        (1999) IDS Brief B646/5, EAT   3.2.23, 3.2.29, 3.2.48
Bentwood Bros (Manchester) Ltd v Shepherd [2003] EWCA Civ 380, [2003]
        ICR 1000, [2003] IRLR 36, CA   10.3.27
Boddington v Lawton [1994] ICR 478, (1994) *The Times*, February 19   4.9.4
Bradford City Metropolitan Borough Council v Arora [1991] 2 QB 507, [1991]
        2 WLR 1377, [1991] 3 All ER 545, [1991] IRLR 165, CA; [1989] IRLR 442,
        EAT   10.3.1, 10.3.26
Bradford Hospitals NHS Trust v Al-Shabib [2003] IRLR 4, EAT   10.1.1
British Airways Engine Overhaul Ltd v Francis [1981] ICR 278, [1981] IRLR 9,
        EAT   10.1.7
British Gas plc v Sharma [1991] ICR 19, [1991] IRLR 101, (1990) *The Times*,
        October 11, EAT   10.3.34
British Gas Services Ltd v McCaull [2001] IRLR 60, (2001) IDS Brief 679/7,
        EAT   3.2.4, 3.2.12, 3.2.47, 4.2.1, 4.2.40, 4.2.41, 4.2.42, 10.3.8
British Sugar plc v Kirker [1998] IRLR 624, [1999] Disc LR 87, EAT   3.2.5, 3.2.6,
                                                                    3.2.11, 4.2.8, 4.2.45
British Telecommunications plc v Reid [2003] EWCA Civ 1675, [2004] IRLR
        327, (2004) IDS Brief B751/7, CA   10.3.26
Broadbent v Crisp [1974] 1 All ER 1052, [1974] ICR 248, [1974] ITR 147   4.9.4
Bruce v Addleshaw Booth & Co EAT/0404/03 (2004) IDS Brief B761/6, EAT   3.2.49,
                                                                                 10.1.2
Burton v Higham (t/a Ace Appointments) [2003] IRLR 257, EAT   4.2.17, 4.2.20
Butterfield v Rapidmark Ltd t/a 3 MV (1998) EAT 131/98, 9 September 1998   3.2.46
Buxton v Equinox Designs Ltd [1999] ICR 269, [1999] IRLR 158, [1999] Disc
        LR 133, EAT   10.3.23

Calder v James Finlay Corporation Ltd [1989] ICR 157n, [1989] IRLR 55, EAT   10.3.8
Callagan v Glasgow City Council [2001] IRLR 724, EAT   3.2.25, 3.2.35, 3.2.47, 3.4.5
Canniffe v East Riding of Yorkshire Council [2000] IRLR 555, (2000) IDS Brief
        B668/12, EAT   10.2.6

Carrington v Helix Lighting [1990] ICR 25, [1990] IRLR 6, (1990) 87(1) LSG
    30, EAT   10.3.1,
Catherall v Michelin Tyre plc [2003] ICR 28, [2003] IRLR 61, EAT   4.2.9
Cave v Goodwin [2001] All ER (D) 163 (Mar), (2001) IDS Brief B687/3, CA   4.2.38
Chamberlin Solicitors v Emokpae [2004] ICR 1476, [2004] IRLR 592, EAT   3.2.6,
      10.3.20
Charter v Race Relations Board [1973] AC 868, [1973] 2 WLR 299, [1973] 1
    All ER 512, HL   5.2.7
Chief Constable of Lincolnshire Police v Stubbs [1999] ICR 547, [1999] IRLR
    81, (1999) IDS Brief B630/3, EAT   10.2.5
Chief Constable of West Yorkshire Police v Khan [2001] UKHL 48, [2001] 1
    WLR 1947, [2001] 4 All ER 834, [2001] ICR 1065, [2001] IRLR 830, HL;
    [2000] ICR 1169, [2000] IRLR 324, (2000) 150 NLJ 308, CA,   10.1.7, 10.3.25,
      10.3.26
Chief Constable of West Yorkshire v Vento [2001] IRLR 124, EAT   3.2.5
Chief Constable of West Yorkshire v Vento (No 2) [2003] EWCA Civ 1871,
    [2003] ICR 318, [2003] IRLR 102, CA; [2001] IRLR 177, EAT   10.3.25, 10.3.26,
      10.3.32
Clark v Novacold Ltd [1999] 2 All ER 977, [1999] ICR 951; *sub nom* Clark v
    TGD Ltd t/a Novacold [1999] IRLR 318, CA; [1998] IRLR 420, EAT   3.1.3,
      3.2.9, 3.2.11, 3.2.19, 3.2.21, 3.2.37, 3.2.46, 4.2.8, 4.2.36, 5.1.2, 5.4.5, 5.4.6,
      5.4.8, 6.2.20, 7.4.5, 9.3.5
College of Ripon & York St John v Hobbs [2002] IRLR 185, (2002) IDS Brief
    B706/10, EAT   2.3.8
Collins v Royal National Theatre Board Ltd [2004] EWCA Civ 144, [2004] 2 All
    ER 851, [2004] IRLR 395, (2004) IDS Brief B753/10, CA   3.2.34, 3.2.47
Colt Group Ltd v Couchman [2000] ICR 327, EAT   4.2.20
Commissioner of Police of the Metropolis v Harley [2001] ICR 927, [2001]
    IRLR 263, (2001) IDS Brief B684/11, EAT   4.2.9
Conservative and Unionist Central Office v Burrell [1982] 1 WLR 522, [1982]
    2 All ER 1, [1982] STC 317, CA   4.9.5
Construction Industry Training Board v Labour Force Ltd [1970] 3 All ER 220,
    [1970] ITR 290, (1970) 9 KIR 269, DC   4.3.2
Cornelius v University College of Swansea [1987] IRLR 141, (1987) 131 SJ 359,
    (1987) 84 LS Gaz 1141, CA   10.1.7
Cosgrove v Caesar & Howie [2001] IRLR 653, (2001) IDS Brief B698/5, EAT   3.2.11,
      3.2.47, 4.2.40, 4.2.41
Council of the City of Manchester v Romano and Samari [2004] EWCA
    Civ 834   5.4.9, 6.2.6, 6.2.14, 6.2.15, 6.2.19–6.2.21
Croydon London Borough Council v Moody (1998) 31 HLR 738, CA   6.2.19
Cruickshank v VAW Motorcast Ltd [2002] ICR 729, [2002] IRLR 24, (2002)
    IDS Brief B703/5, EAT   2.4.3, 2.6.4

Daley v Allied Suppliers Ltd [1983] ICR 90, [1983] IRLR 14, (1983) 80 LS Gaz
    213, EAT   4.3.2
De Keyser Ltd v Wilson [2001] IRLR 324, (2001) IDS Brief B685/3, EAT   2.2.2,
      10.3.23
Deane v London Borough of Ealing [1993] ICR 329, [1993] IRLR 209, EAT   10.3.26
Del Monte Foods Ltd v Mundon [1980] ICR 694, [1980] IRLR 224, EAT   3.2.18
Derby Specialist Fabrication Ltd v Burton [2001] 2 All ER 840, [2001] ICR 833,
    [2001] IRLR 69, (2001) IDS Brief B679/17, EAT   10.3.27
Dockers' Labour Club and Institute Ltd v Race Relations Board [1976] AC 285,
    [1974] 3 WLR 533, [1974] 3 All ER 529, HL   5.2.7

Doshoki v Draeger Ltd [2002] IRLR 340, (2002) IDS Brief B710/12, [2002] All
    ER (D) 139 (Mar), EAT   10.3.26
DPP v Marshall [1998] ICR 518, [1999] IRLR 494, EAT   10.3.9

Edmonds v Lawson [2000] QB 501, [2000] 2 WLR 1091, [2000] ICR 567,
    (2000) *The Times*, 16 March, CA   4.8.2
Edwards v Mid Suffolk District Council [2001] ICR 616, [2001] IRLR 190,
    (2001) IDS Brief B684/9, EAT   3.2.13
Ekpe v Commissioner of Police of the Metropolis [2001] ICR 1084, [2001]
    IRLR 605, [2001] Emp LR 741, EAT   2.4.1, 2.4.2, 2.4.5, 2.5.3
Electronic Data Systems Ltd v Travis [2004] EWCA Civ 1256, (2004) 26 August,
    CA   3.4.4
Enterprise Glass Co Ltd v Miles [1990] ICR 787, EAT   10.2.4
Essa Ltd v Laing [2003] IRLR 346, EAT   10.3.26
Executors of Soutar v James Murray and Co (Cupar) Ltd and Scottish
    Provident Institution [2002] IRLR 22, (2002) IDS Brief B704/11, EAT   10.3.6

Fennelly v Connex South Eastern Ltd [2001] IRLR 390, (2001) *The Independent*,
    January 22, CA   10.2.5
Foster v Hampshire Fire and Rescue Service [1999] Disc LR 1, (1998) 43
    BMLR 186, EAT   2.1.4
Foster v South Glamorgan Health Authority [1988] ICR 526, [1988] IRLR 277,
    EAT   10.3.9
Fu v London Borough of Camden [2001] IRLR 186, (2001) IDS Brief B685/5,
    EAT   3.2.47, 3.4.11

Garry v London Borough of Ealing [2001] EWCA Civ 1282, [2001] IRLR 681,
    [2001] Emp LR 1165, (2001) IDS Brief B693/5, CA   4.2.10
General Medical Council v Cox EAT 76/01, [2003] 70 BMLR 31, [2002] TLR
    165, [2002] All ER (D) 383 (Mar), (2002) *The Times*, April 16, EAT   4.10.1
General Medical Council v Goba [1988] ICR 885, [1988] IRLR 425, EAT   4.10.1
Gibbons v South Western Water Services Ltd. *See* AB v South Western Water
    Services Ltd
Gilbert v Kembridge Fibres Ltd [1984] ICR 188, [1984] IRLR 52, (1984) 134
    NLJ 256, EAT   10.3.13
Gittins v Oxford Radcliffe NHS Trust (2000) EAT/193/99, EAT   2.3.9
Glasgow City Council v Zafar. *See* Zafar v Glasgow City Council
Goodwin v The Patent Office [1999] ICR 302, [1999] IRLR 4, [1999] Disc LR
    104, EAT   2.1.2, 2.2.2, 2.3.6, 2.4.2, 2.5.3, 2.5.16, 9.3.5
Greater Glasgow Health Board v Carey [1987] IRLR 484, EAT   10.3.1
Greater Manchester Fire & Civil Defence Authority v Bradley (2001) 27 April
    (unreported), EAT   3.2.47
Greenwood v British Airways plc [1999] ICR 969, [1999] IRLR 600, (1999) IDS
    Brief B647/5, EAT   2.1.1, 2.6.4

Hall v Woolston Hall Leisure Ltd [2001] 1 WLR 225, [2000] 4 All ER 787,
    [2001] ICR 99, [2000] IRLR 578, CA   4.2.17
Hallam v Cheltenham Borough Council [2001] UKHL 15, [2001] 1 WLR 655,
    [2001] ICR 408, [2001] IRLR 312, HL   10.2.2
Hampson v Department of Education and Science [1991] AC 171, [1990] 3
    WLR 42, [1990] 2 All ER 513, [1990] IRLR 302, HL, [1989] IRLR 69, CA   10.2.9

Hanlon v Kirklees Metropolitan Council EAT 0119/04 (2004) IDS Brief
    B767/13, EAT   2.1.4
Hanlon v University of Huddersfield [1999] Disc LR 82, (1998) EAT 166/98   4.2.30
Hardie v CD Northern Ltd [2000] ICR 207, [2000] IRLR 87, (2000) IDS Brief
    655/3, EAT   4.2.20
Harris (Personal Representative of Andrews (Deceased)) v Lewisham and
    Guy's Mental Health NHS Trust; *sub nom* Andrews (Deceased) v Lewisham
    and Guys Mental Health NHS Trust; Lewisham and Guys Mental Health
    NHS Trust v Andrews (Deceased) [2000] 3 All ER 769, [2000] ICR 707,
    [2000] IRLR 320, (2000) IDS Brief B660/7, CA   10.3.6
Harrods Ltd v Remick [1998] 1 All ER 52, [1998] ICR 156, [1997] IRLR 583,
    (1997) *The Times,* July 22, CA   4.3.2
Hawkins v Ball and Barclays Bank plc [1996] IRLR 258, EAT   10.3.9
Hawkins v Nigel Darken t/a Sawbridgeworth Motorcycles [2004] EWCA Civ
    1755, [2004] All ER (D) 186 (Dec), CA
Heasmans (a firm) v Clarity Cleaning Co Ltd [1987] ICR 949, [1987] IRLR
    286, (1987) 137 NLJ 101, CA   10.2.5
Heggison v A & W Bernard (2000) EAT/1276/99   3.2.21
Heil v Rankin [2001] QB 272, [2000] 2 WLR 1173, [2000] 3 All ER 138, [2000]
    IRLR 334, [2000] TLR 224, CA   10.3.26
Heinz (HJ) & Co Ltd v Kenrick [2000] ICR 491, [2000] IRLR 144, (2000) IDS
    Brief 657/3, EAT   3.2.20, 3.2.21, 3.2.30, 3.2.35, 3.2.48, 4.2.45, 5.4.8, 9.3.5
Hendricks v Commissioner of Police for the Metropolis [2002] EWCA Civ
    1686, [2003] ICR 615, [2003] IRLR 96, CA   10.3.8
Hewett v Motorola Ltd [2004] IRLR 545, (2004) IDS Brief B762/12, EAT   2.4.1
Hillingdon London Borough Council v Commission for Racial Equality. *See* R v
    Commission for Racial Equality ex parte Hillingdon London Borough
    Council
HM Prison Service v Beart [2003] EWCA Civ 119, [2003] ICR 1068, [2003]
    IRLR 238, CA; (2002) IDS Brief B713, EAT   3.2.47, 3.4.5, 3.4.11, 4.2.40
HM Prison Service v Beart (No 2) [2005] IRLR 171, EAT   10.3.28
HM Prison Service v Salmon [2001] IRLR 425, (2001) IDS Brief B689/9,
    EAT   10.3.26
Home Office v Evans 18 November 1993 (unreported), DC   4.9.4
Humphreys v Environment Agency (1999) EAT/24/95   3.4.3
Hutchinson v Westward Television Ltd [1977] ICR 279, [1977] IRLR 69,
    (1976) 12 ITR 125, EAT   10.3.9

ICTS (UK) Ltd v Tchoula [2000] ICR 1191, [2000] IRLR 643, EAT   10.3.26
Igen Ltd v Wong; Chamberlain Solicitors v Emokpae; Brunel University v
    Webster (EOC, CRE and DRC intervening) [2005] EWCA Civ 142, CA
Irving and Irving v Post Office [1987] IRLR 289, CA   10.2.5

Jiad v Byford [2003] EWCA Civ 135, [2003] IRLR 232, CA   10.1.1
Johnson & Johnson Medical Ltd v Filmer [2002] ICR 292, EAT   3.2.35, 3.2.47, 3.4.11,
                                                                         4.2.40, 4.2.42
Jones v Post Office [2001] EWCA Civ 558, [2001] ICR 805, [2001] IRLR 384,
    [2001] Emp LR 527, CA   3.2.31, 3.2.32, 3.2.33, 3.2.34, 3.2.48, 7.4.11, 10.2.9
Jones v Tower Boot Co Ltd [1997] 2 All ER 406, [1997] ICR 254, [1997] IRLR
    168, CA   10.2.5

Kapadia v London Borough of Lambeth [2000] IRLR 699, (2001) 57 BMLR
    170, (2000) IDS Brief B670/3, CA; [2000] IRLR 14, (1999) IDS Brief
    B645/11, EAT   2.1.4, 2.5.14, 2.5.16
Kenny v Hampshire Constabulary [1999] ICR 27, [1999] IRLR 76, [1999] Disc
    LR 118, EAT   4.2.36
Kent County Council v Mingo [2000] IRLR 90, (2000) IDS Brief 657/5, EAT   4.2.44,
                                                                      4.2.45
King v The Great Britain–China Centre [1992] ICR 516, [1991] IRLR 513,
    (1991) *The Times*, October 30, CA   3.2.6, 10.3.1, 10.3.20
Kirby v Manpower Services Commission [1980] 1 WLR 725, [1980] 3 All ER
    334, [1980] IRLR 229, EAT   10.1.7
Kirton v Tetrosyl Ltd [2003] EWCA Civ 619, [2003] IRLR 353, CA; [2002]
    IRLR 840, EAT   2.4.1, 2.5.7
Kuddus v Chief Constable of Leicestershire Constabulary [2001] UKHL 29,
    [2001] 2 WLR 1789, [2001] 3 All ER 193, (2001) IDS Brief B690/16, HL   10.3.26

Lana v Positive Action Training in Housing (London) Ltd [2001] IRLR 501,
    (2001) IDS Brief B694/7, (2001) *The Independent*, July 16, EAT   10.2.7
Lancashire County Council v Mason [1998] ICR 907, EAT   4.2.16, 10.2.7
Lane Group plc v Farmiloe EAT 0352/03, 0357/03 (2004) IDS Brief B759/11 10.2.10
Latchman v Reed Business Information Ltd [2002] ICR 1453, EAT   2.5.6
Law v Pace Micro Technology plc [2004] EWCA Civ 923, CA   3.2.34
Law Hospital NHS Trust v Rush [2001] IRLR 611, (2001) IDS Brief B693/7,
    2001 GWD 21–810, Ct of Sess; (2000) EAT/842/99   2.4.3, 2.4.7
Leonard v Southern Derbyshire Chamber of Commerce [2001] IRLR 19,
    (2001) IDS Brief B678/9, EAT   2.1.2, 2.4.2
Lewisham and Guys Mental Health NHS Trust v Andrews (Deceased). *See*
    Harris (Personal Representative of Andrews (Deceased)) v Lewisham and
    Guy's Mental Health NHS Trust
Lister v Hesley Hall Ltd [2001] UKHL 22, [2002] 1 AC 215, [2001] ICR 665,
    [2001] IRLR 472, HL   10.2.5
Littlewoods Organisation plc v Traynor [1993] IRLR 154, EAT   10.3.8
London Borough of Hammersmith and Fulham v Farnsworth [2000] IRLR
    691, EAT   3.2.21, 3.2.22, 3.2.35, 4.2.15, 4.2.31, 10.2.2, 10.2.7
London Borough of Hillingdon v Morgan EAT/1493/98, (1999) IDS Brief
    B649/10, EAT   3.4.4, 3.4.5, 4.2.44, 9.3.5
London Borough of Southwark v Afolabi [2003] EWCA Civ 15, [2003] ICR
    800, [2003] IRLR 220, CA   10.3.9
London Clubs Management Ltd v Hood [2001] IRLR 719, (2001) IDS Brief
    B696/14, EAT   3.2.14, 3.4.5, 4.2.38
London Underground Ltd v Bragg (1999) EAT/847/98   2.1.4, 2.4.3, 2.5.2, 2.5.7

M and M v SW School and the Special Educational Needs and Disability
    Tribunal [2004] EWHC Admin 2587   2.5.2
MHC Consulting Services Ltd v Tansell. *See* Abbey Life Assurance Co Ltd v
    Tansell
McAuley Catholic High School v (1) CC; (2) PC; and (3) Special Educational
    Needs and Disability Tribunal [2003] EWHC 3045 (Admin), [2004] ICR
    1563, QBD   7.4.2, 7.4.5, 7.4.7, 10.5.5
McNicol v Balfour Beatty Rail Maintenance Ltd [2002] EWCA Civ 1074, [2002]
    IRLR 711, [2002] TLR 362, (2002) IDS Brief B716/3, (2002) *The Times*,
    August 26, CA   2.2.2, 2.3.2, 2.3.8, 9.1.7

Madden v Preferred Technical Group Cha Ltd [2004] EWCA Civ 1178, [2005]
    IRLR 46, CA   10.3.20
Medical Protection Society v Sadek [2004] EWCA Civ 865, [2004] ICR 1263,
    [2005] IRLR 57, (2004) IDS Brief B767/14, CA   4.9.4
Midland Cold Storage Ltd v Turner [1972] 3 All ER 773, [1972] ICR 230, 116
    SJ 783, NIRC   4.9.5
Mid-Staffordshire General Hospitals NHS Trust v Cambridge [2003] IRLR 566,
    EAT   3.2.32
Mingeley v Pennock and Ivory t/a Amber Cars [2004] IRLR 373, (2004) IDS
    Brief B756/8, CA   4.2.17
Mirror Group Newspapers v Gunning [1986] 1 WLR 546, [1986] 1 All ER 385,
    [1986] ICR 145, CA   4.2.17, 4.3.2
Morgan v Staffordshire University [2002] ICR 475, [2002] IRLR 190, (2002)
    IDS Brief B706/7, EAT   2.1.4, 2.2.2, 2.3.6
Morganite Electrical Carbon Ltd v Donne [1988] ICR 18, [1987] IRLR 363,
    EAT   10.3.30
Morse v Wiltshire County Council [1998] ICR 1023, [1998] IRLR 352, (1998)
    44 BMLR 58, [1999] Disc LR 40, EAT   3.4.7, 4.2.40, 4.2.42
Motherwell Railway Club v McQueen [1989] ICR 418, EAT   10.3.30
Mowat-Brown v University of Surrey [2002] IRLR 235, [2001] All ER (D) 115
    (Dec), (2002) IDS Brief B708/3, EAT   2.5.7
Mulligan v Commissioner for Inland Revenue (1999) EAT/691/99   3.4.3
Murphy v Sheffield Hallam University (2000) EAT/6/99   3.2.13
Murphy v Slough Borough Council [2005] EWCA Civ 122, CA; [2004] ICR
    1163, EAT   3.2.15, 4.2.16, 10.2.7
Murray v Newham Citizens Advice Bureau Ltd [2003] IRLR 340, EAT   2.3.4, 3.2.34
Murray v Powertech (Scotland) Ltd [1992] IRLR 257, EAT   10.3.26

Nagarajan v London Regional Transport [2000] 1 AC 501, [1999] 3 WLR 425,
    [1999] 4 All ER 65, [1999] ICR 877, [1999] IRLR 572, HL   3.2.13, 10.1.7, 10.3.20
Nelson v Tyne and Wear Passenger Transport Executive [1978] ICR 1183,
    (1978) 122 SJ 642, EAT   10.3.35
Noon v North West Thames Regional Health Authority (No 2) [1988] ICR 813,
    [1988] IRLR 530, CA   10.3.34
North Devon Homes Ltd v Brazier [2003] EWHC 574, [2003] HLR 59, QBD   6.2.19
Nottinghamshire County Council v Meikle [2004] EWCA Civ 859, [2004] 4 All
    ER 97, [2004] IRLR 703, CA   3.2.14, 3.2.45, 3.4.5, 4.2.9, 10.3.8

O'Donoghue v Redcar and Cleveland Borough Council [2001] EWCA Civ 701,
    [2001] IRLR 615, [2001] Emp LR 711, (2001) IDS Brief B689/11, CA   10.3.26
O'Neill v Symm & Co Ltd [1998] ICR 481, [1998] IRLR 233, [1999] Disc LR
    59, EAT   2.3.9, 3.2.19, 3.2.21, 5.4.8
Orthet Ltd v Vince-Cain [2005] ICR 394, [2004] IRLR 857, (2004) IDS Brief
    B770/7, EAT   10.3.26
O'Shea (CJ) Construction Ltd v Bassi [1998] ICR 1130, EAT   4.3.2

Paul v National Probation Service Ltd [2004] IRLR 190, EAT   3.2.34, 4.2.34, 4.2.35
Paul Higham of 1 Pump Court Chambers v Horton [2004] EWCA Civ 941, CA;
    (2004) IDS Brief B754/11, EAT   4.8.2
Pearce v Governing Body of Mayfield Secondary School [2000] ICR 920,
    [2000] IRLR 548, [2000] ELR 1, (2000) IDS Brief B663/9, EAT   10.2.6

Photis and Bruce v (1) KMC International Search & Selection and (2)
    Department of Trade and Industry; Heyes v Lord Chancellor's
    Department (EAT/732/00, 766/00, 960/00) 6 December 2001
    (unreported), EAT   4.2.21, 4.4.2, 9.5.2
Post Office v Jones [2000] ICR 388, EAT   3.2.31, 3.2.48, 10.2.9, 10.3.33
Power v Panasonic UK Ltd [2003] IRLR 151, EAT   2.3.3
Prestige Group plc, Re; Commission for Racial Equality v Prestige Group plc
    [1984] 1 WLR 335, [1984] ICR 483, [1984] IRLR 166, HL   9.1.16
Purves v Joydisk Ltd [2003] Scot SC 16, [2003] IRLR 420, Sh Ct   10.4.10

Quinlan v B & Q plc [1999] Disc LR 76, (1998) IDS Brief 614, EAT 1386/97   2.1.4
Quinn v Schwarzkopf Ltd [2002] IRLR 602; *sub nom* Schwarzkopf Ltd v Quinn
    (2002) IDS Brief B715/7, Ct of Sess; [2001] IRLR 67, (2001) IDS Brief
    B679/9, EAT(S)   3.2.35, 3.2.47, 3.4.7
Quinnen v Hovells [1984] IRLR 227, EAT   4.2.17
Qureshi v London Borough of Newham [1991] IRLR 264, CA   3.2.6

R v Commission for Racial Equality ex parte Hillingdon London Borough
    Council [1982] AC 779, [1982] 3 WLR 159, [1982] IRLR 424, HL   9.1.16
R v Entry Clearance Officer Bombay ex parte Amin [1983] 2 AC 818, [1983] 3
    WLR 258, [1983] 2 All ER 864, HL   5.2.2
R v Powys County Council ex parte Hambidge (No 2) [2000] 2 FCR 69, (2000)
    2 LGR 926, [2000] TLR 196, CA   5.4.6
R v Secretary of State for Employment ex parte Equal Opportunities
    Commission [1995] 1 AC 1, [1994] 2 WLR 409, [1994] 1 All ER 910,
    [1994] ICR 317, [1994] IRLR 176, HL   9.1.7
R (ota A and B, X and Y) v East Sussex County Council and Disability Rights
    Commission [2003] EWHC 167 (Admin), (2003) 6 CCLR 194   9.1.7
R (ota D) v Governing Body of Plymouth High School for Girls [2004] EWHC
    1923   7.4.2. 7.4.5, 7.4.7
Read v Tiverton District Council and Bull [1977] IRLR 202, IT   10.2.4
Rhys-Harper v Relaxation Group plc; D'Souza v Lambeth London Borough
    Council; Jones v 3M Healthcare Ltd [2003] UKHL 33, [2003] ICR 867,
    [2003] IRLR 484, HL   3.5.1, 4.2.11
Rice v Fon-A-Car [1980] ICR 133, EAT   4.3.2
Ridout v TC Group [1998] IRLR 628, [1999] Disc LR 8, EAT   4.2.33, 9.3.5
Rihal v London Borough of Ealing [2004] EWCA Civ 623, [2004] IRLR 642,
    CA   3.2.6
Roads v Central Trains Ltd [2004] EWCA Civ 1541   8.1.2
Robertson v Bexley Community Centre [2003] EWCA Civ 576, [2003] IRLR
    434, CA   10.3.8
Robinson v Post Office [2000] IRLR 804, EAT   10.3.9
Rose v Bouchet [1999] IRLR 463, 2000 SLT (Sh Ct) 170, 1999 SCLR 1004   5.6.4,
                                                       5.6.5, 6.2.14, 6.2.20
Ross v Ryanair Ltd and Stansted Airport Ltd [2004] EWCA Civ 1751, [2005]
    TLR 20, CA   5.2.9, 5.5.4, 5.5.13, 8.5.2
Rowden v Dutton Gregory (a firm) [2002] ICR 971, (2002) IDS Brief B718/3,
    EAT   3.2.6, 3.2.13, 3.2.15, 3.2.46, 7.4.5, 10.3.20
Rugamer v Sony Music Entertainment UK Ltd; McNicol v Balfour Beatty Rail
    Maintenance Ltd [2002] ICR 381, [2001] IRLR 644, [2001] Emp LR 1318,
    (2001) IDS Brief B697/9, EAT   2.2.2, 2.3.8

St Helens MBC v Derbyshire [2004] IRLR 851, (2004) IDS Brief B766/7, EAT   10.1.1
Schwarzkopf Ltd v Quinn. *See* Quinn v Schwarzkopf Ltd
Scott v Commissioners of Inland Revenue [2004] EWCA Civ 400, [2004] ICR
   1410, [2004] IRLR 713, CA   10.3.26
Shamoon v Chief Constable of the Royal Ulster Constabulary [2003] UKHL 11,
   [2003] ICR 337, [2003] IRLR 285, HL   3.2.40
Sheehan v Post Office Counters Ltd [1999] ICR 734, EAT   4.2.17
Sheriff v Klyne Tugs (Lowestoft) Ltd [1999] ICR 1170, [1999] IRLR 481,
   (1999) IDS Brief B645/3, CA   10.3.26
Sidhu v Aerospace Composite Technology Ltd [2001] ICR 167, [2000] IRLR
   602, (2000) IDS Brief B665/3, CA   10.2.5
Simon v Brimham Associates [1987] ICR 596, [1987] IRLR 307, CA   3.2.18
Sinclair Roche & Temperley v Heard [2004] IRLR 763, EAT   3.2.6, 10.3.20
Sougrin v Haringey Health Authority [1991] ICR 791, [1991] IRLR 447, EAT   10.3.8
South East Sheffield Citizens Advice Bureau v Grayson [2004] IRLR 354,
   EAT   4.2.17, 4.2.20
Surrey Police v Marshall [2002] IRLR 843, EAT   3.2.34
Swift v Chief Constable of Wiltshire Constabulary [2004] ICR 909, [2004] IRLR
   540, EAT   2.5.6
Swithland Motors plc v Clarke [1994] ICR 231, [1994] IRLR 275, EAT   10.3.8

Tanna v Post Office [1981] ICR 374, EAT   4.3.2
Taylor v Lifesign Ltd (2000) EAT/147/98, (2000) 10 February, EAT   4.2.20
Thornhill v London Central Bus Co Ltd (2000) EAT/463/99   2.4.1
Tyagi v BBC World Service [2001] EWCA Civ 549, [2001] IRLR 465, (2001)
   IDS Brief B690/14, CA   10.3.8

University of Huddersfield v Wolff [2003] ICR 828, [2004] IRLR 534, (2004)
   IDS Brief B761/9, EAT   3.2.6, 10.3.20

VK v Norfolk County Council and the Special Educational Needs and Disability
   Tribunal [2004] EWMC 2921, [2005] TLR 12, QBD   7.4.5, 7.4.11
Vicary v British Telecommunications plc [1999] IRLR 680, (1999) IDS Brief
   B650/7, EAT   2.1.2, 2.2.1, 2.4.3, 2.5.2, 2.5.4, 2.5.14
Visa International Service Association v Paul [2004] IRLR 42, (2004) IDS Brief
   B752/6, EAT   10.1.1

Waters v Commissioner of Police of the Metropolis [2000] 1 WLR 1607, [2000]
   4 All ER 93, [2000] ICR 1064, [2000] IRLR 720, HL   10.2.4
Waters v Metropolitan Police Commissioner [1997] ICR 1073, [1997] IRLR
   589, (1997) *The Times,* July 21, CA   10.1.7
West Midlands Passenger Transport Executive v Singh [1988] IRLR 186, CA   3.2.6
White v Clitheroe Royal Grammar School (2002) EO Rev 106, 26–28, Preston
   Cty Ct   5.2.9, 5.6.5, 5.6.7, 7.2.3, 10.4.10
Wilding v British Telecommunications plc [2002] EWCA Civ 349, [2002] ICR
   1079, [2002] IRLR 524, [2002] Emp LR 627, (2002) IDS Brief B709/14,
   CA   10.3.25
Williams v J Walter Thompson Group Ltd [2005] EWCA Civ 133, CA   3.4.1, 4.2.11
Wiltshire Police Authority v Wynn [1981] QB 95, [1980] 3 WLR 445, [1980]
   ICR 649, CA   4.9.4

Woodrup v London Borough of Southwark [2002] EWCA Civ 1716, [2003]
    IRLR 111, CA   2.2.2, 2.5.16
Wright v Governors of Bilton High School and Warwickshire County Council
    (2002) EAT/113/01, [2002] ICR 1463, (2002) IDS Brief B711/11, EAT   3.2.35,
                                                                          3.2.47
Writers' Guild of Great Britain v British Broadcasting Corporation [1974] 1 All
    ER 574, [1974] ICR 234, NIRC   4.9.4

X v Stevens [2003] ICR 1031, [2003] IRLR 411, EAT   10.3.16

Yeboah v Crofton [2002] EWCA Civ 794, [2002] IRLR 634, (2002) *The Times*,
    June 20, CA   10.2.2, 10.2.4

Zafar v Glasgow City Council; *sub nom* Glasgow City Council v Zafar [1997] 1
    WLR 1659, [1998] ICR 125, [1998] IRLR 36, HL   3.2.6, 10.3.20
Zaiwalla & Co v Walia [2002] IRLR 697, (2002) IDS Brief B717/3, (2002) *The
    Times*, August 1, EAT   10.3.26

TABLE OF STATUTES

References are to paragraph numbers.

Access to Justice Act 1999
Pt I — 9.1.12
s 10(7) — 9.1.12
s 24 — 9.1.12
Sch 4, para 56 — 9.1.12
Adults with Incapacity (Scotland)
  Act 2000
s 88(2) — 5.6.9
Sch 5, para 1 — 5.6.9
Agricultural Wages Act 1948
s 5 — 4.2.47
Agricultural Wages (Scotland)
  Act 1949
s 5 — 4.2.47
Anti-terrorism, Crime and
  Security Act 2001
s 17 — 9.1.38
Sch 4, Pt 1, para 46 — 9.1.38
Arbitration Act 1996
Pt 1 — 10.5.2

British Transport Commission
  Act 1949
s 53 — 9.5.3
Broadcasting Act 1990 — 5.2.2
Broadcasting Act 1996 — 5.2.2
Building Act 1984
s 122 — 6.3.3

Charities Act 1993 — 4.2.24
Charities Act (Northern Ireland)
  1964 — 4.2.24
Chronically Sick and Disabled
  Persons Act 1970 — 1.5.3, 8.6.5
s 2(1) — 5.4.6
Civic Government (Scotland) Act
  1982 — 8.2.21
s 20 — 8.2.2
(2A) — 8.2.19

Companies Act 1985 — 5.2.2
Contempt of Court Act 1981
s 15 — 9.1.39
County Courts Act 1984
s 55 — 9.1.39
(1)–(4) — 9.1.39
Courts Act 2003 — 8.2.11
Courts and Legal Services Act
  1990 — 10.3.15
Criminal Justice and Public
  Order Act 1994
s 126 — 4.9.4
Crown Proceedings Act 1947
Pts II–V — 9.5.1
s 20 — 9.5.1
s 23 — 9.5.1
s 44 — 9.5.1

Disability Discrimination Act
  1995 — 1.1.1, 1.1.2, 1.2.1, 1.2.2, 1.3.1,
    1.4.1, 1.5.3, 1.5.7, 2.1.1,
    2.1.4, 2.2.2, 2.3.1, 2.3.6,
    2.3.8, 2.3.9, 2.3.10, 2.3.11,
    2.4.3, 2.4.4, 2.4.7, 2.5.3,
    2.5.9, 2.5.14, 2.6.2, 2.7.3,
    2.9.1, 2.9.2, 2.9.3, 2.9.4,
    2.9.5, 3.1.3, 3.2.13, 3.2.32,
    3.2.36, 3.2.37, 3.2.43,
    3.2.51, 4.2.45, 4.4.1,
    4.9.5, 4.9.13, 4.9.14, 4.10.2,
    5.2.5, 5.4.3, 5.4.4, 5.4.10,
    6.4.1, 7.1.3, 7.2.24, 8.2.1,
    8.3.8, 8.5.2, 9.1.4, 9.8.1,
    9.8.2, 10.2.1, 10.2.9, 10.2.10,
    10.3.23, 10.3.26, 10.3.28,
    10.3.29, 10.3.30, 10.3.31,
    10.3.34, 10.7.1
Pt 1 — 1.3.1, 1.5.7, 2.1.2, 10.1.5

Disability Discrimination Act
    1995 – *cont*
    Pt 2   1.3.1, 1.5.2, 1.5.5, 1.5.6, 2.5.2,
             2.5.7, 2.6.4, 2.8.1, 3.1.1,
             3.1.2, 3.1.3, 3.1.4, 3.1.5,
             3.2.1, 3.2.3, 3.2.6, 3.2.44,
             3.2.45, 3.3.2, 3.4.1, 3.5.1,
             3.5.2, 3.6.2, 3.7.1, 4.1.2,
             4.2.7, 4.2.9, 4.2.20, 4.2.22,
             4.2.23, 4.2.24, 4.2.25, 4.3.1,
             4.4.2, 4.5.1, 4.5.2, 4.5.8,
             4.5.9, 4.6.3, 4.7.1, 4.8.1,
             4.9.1, 4.9.2, 4.9.3, 4.9.7,
             4.9.9, 4.11.1, 4.13.1, 4.13.2,
             4.13.4, 5.4.1, 5.4.5, 5.4.6,
             5.4.8, 5.5.3, 5.6.3, 5.6.4,
             5.7.2, 6.1.2, 6.3.1, 6.3.3,
             6.3.9, 6.3.25, 7.1.2, 7.2.2,
             7.4.5, 7.4.10, 7.4.11, 7.5.6,
             7.5.12, 7.5.13, 7.6.1, 7.6.2,
             8.1.4, 9.1.7, 9.1.10, 9.1.16,
             9.1.21, 9.1.22, 9.1.27, 9.1.34,
             9.1.37, 9.3.2, 9.3.5, 9.5.2,
             9.5.3, 9.6.2, 10.1.1, 10.1.2,
             10.1.3, 10.2.12, 10.3.1,
             10.3.5, 10.3.6, 10.3.20,
             10.3.21, 10.3.24, 10.6.1,
             10.7.2
    Pt 3   1.3.1, 1.5.2, 1.5.3, 1.5.6, 2.8.1,
             3.5.2, 3.6.2, 3.7.1, 4.2.7, 4.3.6,
             4.6.3, 4.6.4, 4.8.1, 4.9.2, 4.9.9,
             4.10.1, 4.11.1, 4.13.4, 5.1.2,
             5.1.3, 5.1.4, 5.2.2, 5.2.4,
             5.2.6, 5.2.7, 5.2.8, 5.2.9,
             5.3.1, 5.4.1, 5.4.2, 5.4.5,
             5.4.6, 5.4.7, 5.4.9, 5.5.2,
             5.5.3, 5.6.2, 5.6.3, 5.6.4,
             5.6.5, 5.6.6, 5.7.1, 5.7.6,
             5.8.1, 5.8.2, 5.9.1, 5.9.2,
             5.9.3, 5.9.5, 6.1.1, 6.1.2,
             6.2.13, 6.2.17, 6.3.2, 6.3.4,
             6.3.9, 6.3.25, 7.1.2, 7.1.4,
             7.2.1, 7.2.2, 7.2.3, 7.2.4,
             7.2.5, 7.2.6, 7.2.7, 7.2.12,
             7.3.1, 7.4.10, 7.5.2, 7.5.3,
             7.5.12, 7.5.26, 8.1.2, 8.1.3,
             8.1.4, 8.5.1, 9.1.7, 9.1.10,
             9.1.16, 9.1.21, 9.1.22, 9.1.27,
             9.1.34, 9.1.37, 9.3.2, 9.3.5,
             9.6.2. 9.8.4, 10.1.1, 10.1.2,
             10.1.3, 10.2.11, 10.2.12,10.3.1,
             10.3.5, 10.3.6, 10.3.7, 10.4.1,
             10.4.2, 10.4.4, 10.4.6, 10.4.7,
             10.4.9, 10.4.10, 10.4.11

    Pt 4   1.3.1, 2.5.2, 2.8.1, 4.10.3, 4.11.1,
             6.4.1, 7.1.2, 7.2.8, 7.2.13,
             7.3.1, 7.4.10, 7.5.2, 7.5.3,
             7.5.5, 7.5.12, 7.5.26, 7.6.1,
             9.1.7, 9.1.10, 9.1.16, 9.1.22,
             9.1.27, 9.1.34, 9.1.37, 9.3.2,
             9.3.5, 9.4.1, 10.1.1, 10.1.2,
             10.1.3, 10.2.11, 10.2.12,
             10.5.10, 10.6.1
    Pt 4 Ch 1   7.3.1, 7.4.1, 7.4.16, 7.4.19,
             7.5.2, 10.1.3, 10.2.2, 10.5.1,
             10.5.2, 10.5.3, 10.5.4, 10.5.5,
             10.5.6, 10.5.10, 10.5.11,
             10.5.12
       Ch 2   7.3.1, 7.5.1, 7.5.17,
             10.5.12, 10.6.1, 10.6.3
    Pt 5   1.3.1, 1.5.3, 1.5.4, 8.1.1, 8.1.5,
             8.2.6, 8.2.12, 8.2.20, 8.2.22,
             8.5.1
    Pt 6   9.1.1
    s 1   2.1.2, 2.2.1, 2.8.3, 2.9.4, 7.2.14,
             7.4.2, 7.5.3, 8.2.13
       (1)   2.1.2, 2.4.1, 2.5.1
       (2)   2.1.2
    s 2   2.1.2, 2.7.2, 7.2.14, 7.4.2, 7.5.3
       (1)   2.8.1
       (2)   2.6.5, 2.8.1, 4.2.38
       (4), (5)   2.8.2
    s 3   2.1.2, 2.9.4, 9.7.1
       (1)   9.4.1
       (2)   9.4.2
       (3)   2.1.2, 9.4.1
       (3A)   9.4.1
       (4), (5)   9.4.3
       (6)   9.4.4
       (7), (8)   9.4.4
       (9)   9.4.4, 9.7.1
       (10)   9.4.4
       (11)(a), (b)   9.4.1
       (12)   9.4.1, 9.4.4
    s 3A   3.1.5, 3.2.1, 4.3.4, 4.10.5
       (1)   3.2.3, 3.2.45, 3.2.48, 3.4.1,
                            4.2.27, 5.4.8
          (a)   3.2.4, 3.2.5, 3.2.9, 3.2.12,
                                    3.2.24
          (b)   3.2.10, 3.2.23, 4.10.5
       (2)   3.2.45, 3.4.1, 4.2.27, 4.10.9
       (3)   3.2.3, 3.2.23, 3.2.27, 3.2.48,
                            4.2.27, 4.10.5
       (4)   3.2.3, 3.2.36, 3.2.41
       (5)   3.2.3, 3.2.36, 5.7.4
       (6)   3.2.3, 3.2.23, 3.2.29, 3.2.45,
                   3.2.48, 3.4.1, 4.2.27, 4.10.9

Disability Discrimination Act
   1995 – *cont*
s 3B   3.1.5, 3.7.1, 4.2.10, 4.3.4, 5.7.2
   (1), (2)   3.3.2
ss 4–7   3.1.1
s 4   3.2.49, 3.2.50, 4.2.1, 4.2.16, 4.2.27,
          4.3.5, 4.4.2, 10.1.5, 10.2.4,
          10.2.7, 10.2.10
s 4(1)   4.2.27
   (a)   4.2.2, 4.2.15
   (b)   4.2.3
   (c)   4.2.3
   (2)   4.2.27, 4.5.1
     (a)   4.2.4, 4.6.1
     (b), (c)   4.2.5, 4.6.1
     (d)   4.2.8, 4.2.10
   (3)   4.2.10, 4.2.12
   (4)   4.2.6, 4.3.6, 4.9.9
     (a)–(c)   4.2.6
   (5)(a)   4.2.8
     (b)   4.2.9
   (6)   4.2.16
s 4A   4.3.8, 10.2.10
   (1)   4.2.38, 4.2.41
     (a), (b)   4.2.28
   (2)(a), (b)   4.2.29
   (3)(a), (b)   4.2.30
s 4B   3.2.50, 4.3.1, 4.4.2, 10.1.5, 10.2.4
   (1)(a)–(d)   4.3.4
   (2)   4.3.4
   (3)   4.3.6
   (4)(a), (b)   4.3.7
   (5)–(7)   4.3.8
   (8)   4.3.2
   (9)   4.3.2
ss 4C-4F   9.5.2
s 4C   4.4.1
   (1), (2)   4.4.2
   (3)(a), (b)   4.4.3
     (c)   4.4.3, 4.4.7, 4.4.10
   (4)(a)   4.4.3
     (b)(i), (ii)   4.4.3
   (5)   4.4.2, 4.4.4
s 4D   3.2.50, 3.6.2, 4.4.1, 4.4.2, 4.4.5,
          10.1.5, 10.2.4, 10.2.10
   (1)(a)–(c)   4.4.6
   (2)   4.4.7
     (a), (b)   4.4.7
   (3)(a), (b)   4.4.8
     (c), (d)   4.4.9
   (4)   4.4.10
     (c)   4.4.10

s 4D(5)   4.4.8
   (6)   4.4.9
   (7)(a)   4.4.7
     (b)   4.4.6, 4.4.7
s 4E   4.4.1, 4.4.2, 10.2.10
   (1)(a), (b)   4.4.11
   (2)(a)(i), (ii)   4.4.13
     (b)(i), (ii)   4.4.13
   (3)(a)(i), (ii)   4.4.14
     (b)   4.4.14
s 4F   4.4.1
   (1)   4.4.5
   (2)   4.4.12
     (a)   4.4.6
     (b)   4.4.7
     (c)   4.4.8
     (d)   4.4.8, 4.4.12
     (e)   4.4.9
     (f)   4.4.9, 4.4.10
   (3)(a)   4.4.8
     (b)   4.4.12
s 4G   3.2.50, 4.5.3, 4.5.4, 10.1.5, 10.2.4
   (1)   4.5.4
     (a)   4.5.4
   (2)   4.5.4
   (3)   4.5.5
   (4)   4.5.4
   (5)(a), (b)   4.5.6
   (6)   4.5.6
s 4H   4.5.3, 4.5.4
   (1)(a), (b)   4.5.7
   (2)   3.4.2, 4.5.7
   (3)   4.5.7
s 4I   4.5.3, 4.5.4
s 4J   4.5.3, 4.5.4
   (1)(a)   4.5.9
     (b)   4.5.9
       (i), (ii)   4.5.9
     (c), (d)   4.5.9
   (2)   4.5.9
   (3)(a), (b)   4.5.9
   (4)   4.5.9
s 4K   4.5.3, 4.5.4
   (1), (2)   4.5.4
s 5   5.4.1, 6.2.20, 9.1.34
   (2)   3.2.34
     (b)   3.2.47
   (4)   3.2.34, 3.2.47
   (5)   5.6.3
s 6   3.2.47, 8.1.4,
   (1)(a)   4.2.34

Disability Discrimination Act
  1995 – *cont*
s 6(1)(b)   6.3.1
   (2)   4.2.34
   (4)   5.5.3
s 6A   3.6.2, 4.4.2, 4.7.1, 10.1.5, 10.2.4
   (1)(a)–(c)   4.7.2
      (d)(i)   4.7.2
         (ii)   4.7.3
   (2)   4.7.3
   (3)   4.7.2
   (4)   4.7.3
s 6B   4.7.1, 4.7.4
   (1)   4.7.4
   (2)(a), (b)   4.7.5
   (3)(a), (b)   4.7.5
   (4)   4.7.6
s 6C   4.7.1
   (1)   4.7.1, 4.7.2, 4.7.3, 4.7.4
   (2), (3)   4.7.1
s 7(1)   4.2.20
s 7A   3.2.50, 3.6.2, 4.4.2, 4.8.1, 10.1.5,
                                             10.2.4
   (1)   4.8.4
   (2)   4.8.5
   (3)   4.8.6
   (4)   4.8.6
   (5)   4.8.3
s 7B   4.8.1
   (1), (2)   4.8.7
   (3)(a), (b)   4.8.8
   (4)(a), (b)   4.8.8
s 7C   3.2.50, 3.6.2, 4.4.2, 4.8.1, 4.8.9,
                                    10.1.5, 10.2.4
   (5)   4.8.9
s 7D   4.8.1, 4.8.9
s 8   3.1.1
s 9   3.1.1,
s 10   3.1.1
   (1)   4.2.24
s 11   3.1.1, 3.6.1
s 12   3.1.1, 4.3.1
ss 13–15   3.1.1, 4.8.2, 4.9.1, 5.2.2, 5.2.7
s 13   3.2.50, 3.6.2, 4.10.1, 4.10.3,
                                    10.1.5, 10.2.4
   (1)   4.9.8
   (2)   4.9.9
   (3)   4.9.10
   (4)   4.9.3
s 14   4.10.3, 5.4.1
   (1)   4.9.11
   (2)(a), (b)   4.9.12

s 14(3)(a), (b)   4.9.12
s 14A   3.2.50, 3.6.2, 4.9.3, 4.10.2,
                          4.10.3, 10.1.5, 10.2.4
   (1), (2)   4.10.4, 10.3.6
   (3)   4.10.5
   (4)(a)   4.10.9
      (b)   4.10.5
   (5)   4.10.3, 4.10.5
s 14B   4.9.3, 4.10.2, 4.10.3
   (1)   4.10.5
   (2)(a), (b)   4.10.7
   (3)(a), (b)   4.10.8
s 14C   3.2.50, 3.6.2, 4.4.2, 4.11.1,
                                    10.1.5, 10.2.4
   (1), (2)   4.11.2
   (3)–(5)   4.11.1
s 14D   4.11.1
   (1)   4.11.3
   (2)(a), (b)   4.11.4
   (3)(a), (b)   4.11.5
s 16   3.1.1, 6.3.9
s 16A   3.1.5, 3.2.50, 3.5.1, 5.7.4, 10.1.5,
                                             10.2.4
   (1)   3.5.2, 4.2.11
   (2)(a), (b)   3.5.2
   (3)   3.5.2
   (4)(a), (b)   3.5.3
   (5)   3.5.3
   (6)   3.5.3
   (7)   3.5.2
s 16B   3.1.5, 4.2.2, 5.7.4, 10.2.4
   (1)   3.6.2
      (a)   3.6.2
      (b)(i), (ii)   3.6.2
   (2)   3.6.2
   (3)   3.6.2
   (4)   3.6.2
s 16C   3.1.5, 5.7.4, 10.2.4
   (1)   3.7.1
   (2)   3.7.1
      (a)   3.7.1
      (b)   3.7.1, 4.2.10
   (3)   3.7.1
s 17   3.1.1
   (1)   4.5.2
s 17A   4.5.8, 9.1.10, 9.1.37, 10.2.11
   (1)   5.8.2, 10.3.6
   (1A)–(7)   5.8.2
   (1A), (1B)   10.3.6
   (1C)   3.2.6, 4.5.3, 10.3.20
   (2)   10.3.21
      (a)   4.5.9, 10.3.22

Disability Discrimination Act
   1995 – *cont*

s 17A(2)(b)	4.5.9, 10.3.24
(c)	10.3.32
(3)	10.3.24
(4)	10.3.26
(5)	4.5.9, 10.3.35
(6)	10.3.27
s 17B(1), (2)	3.6.3, 3.7.2
(3)–(9)	3.6.3
s 17C	10.3.13, 10.3.14
s 18	3.1.1, 4.6.1, 4.13.4, 10.2.4
(1)(a), (b)	4.6.2
(2)	4.6.3
(3)	4.6.3, 4.6.5
(4)	4.6.3
s 18A	6.3.9, 6.3.11, 6.3.15, 6.3.18
(1)	6.3.10
(a)	6.3.9
(b), (c)	6.3.10
(2)	6.3.12
(a)–(b)	6.3.10
(c)–(d)	6.3.10, 6.3.15
(2A)	6.3.11
(3)	6.3.9
(4)(a), (b)	6.3.10
s 18B	3.1.5, 4.3.8
(1)	3.4.9, 4.2.42
(2)	3.4.2, 4.2.36, 4.2.41, 4.3.6, 4.5.7
(3)–(5)	6.3.14
(6)	3.2.45
s 18C(1)	4.2.24
(a), (b)	4.2.24
(2)(a), (b)	4.2.25
(3)	4.2.24, 4.2.25
(4), (5)	4.2.24
s 18D(2)	3.7.1, 4.2.2, 4.2.5, 4.2.10, 4.2.34, 4.2.37, 4.5.4, 4.9.9
ss 19–21	4.6.3, 5.1.2, 5.4.1, 5.7.2, 6.2.8, 6.2.13, 7.1.2, 7.2.1, 7.2.4, 8.1.2, 8.1.3
s 19	5.7.4, 10.1.5, 10.2.4
(1)	5.1.2, 5.3.5, 5.4.1, 5.5.2
(a)	5.1.4, 5.3.2, 5.6.10
(aa)	5.7.3
(b)	5.1.2, 5.1.4, 5.3.5, 5.5.2, 5.5.4, 5.5.13, 5.7.3, 8.5.2
(c)	5.1.4, 5.3.3, 5.6.11
(d)	5.1.4, 5.3.4, 5.4.6, 5.6.11, 5.6.12
(2)	5.7.3

s 19(2)(a)	5.1.4, 5.2.1, 8.5.2
(b)	5.2.4, 5.2.7
(c)	5.2.1, 5.4.6
(3)	5.2.1, 5.2.3
(h)	5.4.6, 7.2.3
(4)	5.4.1, 10.1.5
(5)	4.10.1, 7.1.2, 7.1.4
(a)–(ab)	5.2.9, 7.1.4
(a)	7.2.1, 7.2.4
(i)	7.2.1
(ii)	7.2.1, 7.2.6
(aa), (ab)	7.2.1
(b)	5.2.9, 8.1.2, 8.5.1, 8.5.2
(c)	5.1.3, 5.2.9, 7.2.4
(5A)	5.2.9, 7.1.4
(6)	4.10.1, 5.2.9, 7.1.4, 7.2.1, 7.2.6
s 20	5.4.1, 5.6.14, 6.2.15, 6.3.2
(1)	5.1.2, 5.4.2, 5.4.8, 5.4.9, 5.5.1, 5.5.2
(a)	5.4.2, 5.4.6, 5.6.2
(b)	5.4.9, 5.6.1
(1A)	5.7.4
(2)	5.1.2, 5.5.2, 5.5.4
(a)	5.7.4
(b)	5.6.1
(3)	5.4.9, 5.6.1, 5.7.4
(a)	5.6.1, 5.6.5
(b)	5.6.1, 5.6.5
(3A)	5.7.4
(4)	5.4.9, 5.6.1, 5.6.6, 6.2.15
(a)	5.4.9, 5.6.7
(b)	5.6.8
(c)	5.4.9, 5.6.10
(d)	5.4.9, 5.6.11
(e)	5.6.12
(5)	5.6.13
(7)	5.1.3, 5.6.9
(8)	5.1.3, 5.6.1, 5.6.14
(9)	5.5.2, 5.6.1
s 21	5.1.2, 5.1.4, 5.3.5, 5.5.2, 5.5.4, 5.5.7, 5.5.8, 5.5.11, 5.6.1, 5.6.5, 6.3.2, 6.3.23, 6.3.24
(1)	3.6.2, 5.5.5, 5.5.6, 5.5.13, 5.7.3, 5.7.4, 5.7.5
s 21(1A)	5.7.5
(2)	5.5.7, 5.5.9, 5.5.10, 5.5.11, 5.5.13, 5.7.3, 5.7.4
(a)	5.1.2, 5.5.7, 5.5.15, 8.1.3
(b)	5.1.2, 5.5.7, 5.5.15, 8.1.3
(c)	5.1.2, 5.5.7, 5.5.15, 8.1.3
(d)	5.5.7, 8.5.2
(3)(a)	5.5.7

Disability Discrimination Act
1995 – *cont*

s 21(3)(b)	5.5.11
(4)	5.5.6, 5.5.14, 5.7.3, 5.7.4
(a)	5.5.13
(b)	5.5.13, 8.5.2
(5)(a), (b)	5.1.3, 5.5.7
(a)–(d)	5.5.5
(e)	5.1.3, 5.5.9
(f)	5.5.9
(g)	5.5.14
(h)	5.1.3, 5.5.14
(6)	5.5.3
(7)–(9)	5.5.3, 5.5.13
(10)	5.5.2
s 21A	5.7.1, 5.7.3, 5.8.2
(1)	5.7.1
(2)	, (3)5.7.2
(4)(a)–(c)	5.7.3
(5)(a)–(c)	5.7.4
(6)	3.6.2
(a), (b)	5.7.5
ss 22–24	6.1.1, 6.2.8, 6.2.13, 6.2.17, 6.2.19, 6.2.21, 6.3.2, 6.3.30
s 22	6.2.10, 6.2.13, 6.2.14, 6.2.17, 10.1.5, 10.2.4
(1)	6.2.1, 6.2.8, 6.2.9, 6.2.11, 6.2.12
(a)	6.2.2
(b)	6.2.3
(c)	6.2.4
(2)	6.2.9
(3)	6.2.1, 6.2.11
(a), (b)	6.2.5, 6.2.15
(c)	6.2.6
(4)	6.2.1, 6.2.7, 6.2.11, 6.2.12
(5)	6.2.7
(6)	6.2.8, 6.2.9, 6.2.10
(7)	6.2.17, 10.1.5
(8)	6.2.10
s 23(1)	6.2.11
(2)(a)–(c)	6.2.12
(d)	6.2.11
(3)–(5)	6.2.11
(6), (7)	6.2.12
s 24	5.6.4, 6.2.1, 6.2.6, 6.2.13, 6.2.14, 6.2.15, 6.2.16, 6.2.20
(1)	6.2.13
(a), (b)	6.2.14
(2)	6.2.14, 6.2.20
(a), (b)	6.2.14
(3)	6.2.15
(a)–(d)	6.2.15

s 24(4)	6.2.14
(5)	5.1.3, 6.2.15, 6.2.16, 6.2.21
ss 25–28	5.1.2, 6.2.18
s 25	5.8.1, 6.3.25, 9.1.10, 9.1.37, 10.2.11
(1)	5.8.1, 10.4.1
(2)	5.8.1, 10.4.10
(3), (4)	5.8.1, 10.4.1
(5)	5.8.1, 10.4.11
(7), (8)	5.8.2, 10.3.6, 10.4.1
(9)	5.8.2, 10.3.6
s 26	6.3.30
(1)	5.7.6, 10.4.7
(1A)	5.7.6, 10.4.7
(2)	10.4.9
(3)–(6)	10.4.8
s 27	5.5.8, 6.3.9, 6.3.11, 6.3.25, 6.3.26, 6.3.30, 7.5.26
(1)	6.3.9, 6.3.10
(1)(a)	6.3.9
(b), (c)	6.3.10
(2)	6.3.9, 6.3.12, 6.3.26
(a)	6.3.10
(b)	6.3.10, 6.3.21
(c)	6.3.10, 6.3.21, 7.5.22
(d)	6.3.10, 6.3.21
(2A)	6.3.11, 6.3.26
(3)	5.1.3, 6.3.9
(4)	6.3.9
(a), (b)	6.3.10
(5)	6.3.9
s 28(1)–(8)	10.4.4
ss 28A–28G	7.4.19
ss 28A–28Q	7.4.16
ss 28A–28S	7.1.4
ss 28A–28X	7.2.4
s 28A	5.2.9, 7.1.4, 10.1.5, 10.2.4
(1)–(4)	7.4.2
(5)	7.4.3, 7.4.14
(6)	7.4.2, 10.1.5
s 28B	7.4.4, 7.4.16
(1)	7.4.5, 7.4.17
(3), (4)	7.4.10, 7.4.18
(5), (6)	7.4.5, 7.4.11, 7.4.17
(7)	7.4.5, 7.4.6, 7.4.11, 7.4.17
(8)	7.4.11, 7.4.17
s 28C	7.4.5, 7.4.6, 7.4.7, 7.4.11
(1)(a), (b)	7.4.7
(2)	7.4.7
(3), (4)	7.4.8
(5), (6)	7.4.9
(7)	7.4.9

Disability Discrimination Act
1995 – *cont*

s 28C(7)(a), (b)		7.4.9
(8)		7.4.7
s 28D	7.1.4, 7.4.12, 7.4.15, 9.3.2,	
		10.5.8
(1)(a), (b)		7.4.13
(2)		7.4.13
(a)–(c)		7.4.13
(3), (4)		7.4.13
(5)		7.4.13
(6)		7.4.13, 7.4.14
(7)		7.4.14
(c)		7.4.14
(8)		7.4.14
(a), (b)		7.4.14
(9)		7.4.14
(a)–(c)		7.4.14
(10)–(12)		7.4.14
(13)		7.4.13, 7.4.14
(14)		7.4.14
(15)		7.4.13, 7.4.14
(16)		7.4.12
(17)		7.4.13, 7.4.14
(18)		7.4.12
(19)		7.4.14
s 28E	7.1.4, 7.4.12, 9.3.2, 10.5.8	
(1)(a), (b)		7.4.13
(2), (3)		7.4.13
(4)		7.4.14
(5), (6)		7.4.13, 7.4.14
(7)		7.4.13
(8)		7.4.14
s 28F	5.2.9, 7.1.4, 7.4.16, 7.4.18,	
		10.1.510.2.4
(1)(a), (b)		7.4.16
(2)–(4)		7.4.16
(5)		7.4.16, 10.1.5
(6)–(8)		7.4.16
s 28G		7.4.16
(1)		7.4.16
(1)(b)		7.4.17
(2)		7.4.17, 7.4.18
(2)(a), (b)		7.4.18
(3)		7.4.17, 7.4.18
(4)		7.4.17, 7.4.18
(7)		7.4.17
s 28H		7.4.19, 10.5.1
s 28I	7.4.19, 9.1.10, 9.1.37, 10.2.11,	
	10.5.3, 10.5.4, 10.5.5, 10.5.6,	
	10.5.7, 10.5.10, 10.5.11	
(1)		10.5.3

s 28I(2)		10.5.3, 10.5.4, 10.5.5
(3)		10.5.3, 10.5.9
(4)		10.5.3
s 28J		10.5.1
(1), (2)		10.5.1
(3)		10.5.1, 10.5.2
(5), (6)		10.5.2
(7)		10.5.2
(8)		10.5.1, 10.5.2
(9)–(11)		10.5.1
s 28K	9.1.10, 9.1.37, 10.2.11, 10.5.3,	
	10.5.4, 10.5.6, 10.5.10,	
		10.5.11
(1)–(5)		10.5.4
s 28L	9.1.10, 9.1.37, 10.2.11, 10.5.3,	
	10.5.5, 10.5.6, 10.5.10,	
		10.5.11
(1)–(7)		10.5.5
s 28M		7.4.19, 10.5.8
(1)–(4)		10.5.8
(5), (6)		10.5.9
(7)		10.5.8, 10.5.9
(8)		10.5.8
(9)		10.5.8, 10.5.9
s 28N	7.4.19, 9.1.10, 9.1.37, 10.5.10,	
		10.5.11
(1)–(5)		10.5.10
s 28P	7.5.21, 10.5.11, 10.6.4	
(1)–(6)		10.5.11
s 28Q(2), (3)		7.4.2
(4)		7.4.3
(5)	7.4.3, 7.4.14, 10.5.5	
(6)		7.4.3
(7)		7.4.3
(8)		7.4.9
(9)–(11)		7.4.5
(12)		7.4.14
(13)		7.4.12
(14)		7.4.13
ss 28R–28U		7.5.17
ss 28R–28X		7.5.1
s 28R	5.2.9, 7.1.4, 7.5.14, 7.5.15,	
	7.5.18, 10.1.5, 10.2.4	
(1)		7.5.3, 7.5.15
(2)		7.5.3
(3)		7.5.3, 7.5.15
(4)	7.5.3, 7.5.15, 10.1.5	
(5)		7.5.4, 7.5.15
(6)		7.5.4, 7.5.16
(7)		7.5.4, 7.5.15
(8)		7.5.15
(9)		7.5.4, 7.5.15

Disability Discrimination Act
   1995 – *cont*
   s 28R(10)   7.5.4, 7.5.15
      (11)   7.5.3, 7.5.15
   s 28S   7.5.5, 7.5.16
      (1)   7.5.6
      (2)   7.5.7
      (3), (4)   7.5.12
      (5)   7.5.6, 7.5.7, 7.5.13
      (6)   7.5.6, 7.5.13
      (7)   7.5.6, 7.5.13
      (8)   7.5.6, 7.5.7, 7.5.13
      (9)   7.5.6, 7.5.13
   s 28T   7.1.4, 7.5.6, 7.5.7, 7.5.8, 7.5.9,
            7.5.13, 7.5.14, 7.5.16, 7.5.18,
            7.5.19, 7.5.24, 7.5.25
      (1)   7.1.4, 7.5.16
         (a), (b)   7.5.8
      (2)   7.5.9
      (3)–(5)   7.5.11
      (6)   7.5.8
   s 28U   7.1.4, 7.5.15
      (1), (2)   7.5.14
   s 28V   7.1.4, 7.5.17, 7.5.29, 9.1.10,
            9.1.37, 10.2.11, 10.6.1, 10.6.2
      (1)   10.6.1
      (2)   10.6.3
      (3), (4)   10.6.1
      (5)   10.6.3
      (6), (7)   10.6.1
   s 28W   7.5.18
      (1)   7.5.19
         (a)   7.5.18
         (b), (c)   7.5.19
      (2)   7.5.21
         (a)   7.5.19
         (b)–(d)   7.5.19, 7.5.22
      (2A)   7.5.20, 7.5.27
      (3)   7.5.18
      (4)   7.5.19
         (a), (b)   7.5.19
   s 28X   7.1.4, 7.5.21, 10.6.4
   ss 29–31   7.2.8
   s 29   7.2.11
      (1)   7.2.9
      (2)   7.2.10, 7.4.15
      (3)   7.2.11
   s 30   7.2.15
      (1)   7.2.13
      (2), (3)   7.2.14
      (4)   7.2.17
      (5)   7.2.19

   s 30(6)   7.2.20, 7.2.25
      (7), (8)   7.2.18
   s 31(1), (2)   7.2.19
      (3)   7.2.20, 7.2.25
   ss 31A–31C   7.1.4
   s 31A   7.5.1
      (2), (3)   7.5.3
      (4)   7.5.4
   s 31B   10.5.7, 10.5.12, 10.5.13, 10.6.2,
                                 10.6.5
      (1), (2)   10.5.12
      (3)–(7)   10.5.13
      (8)–(10)   10.5.12
   ss 32–39   8.2.20, 8.2.22
   s 32   8.2.5, 8.2.7, 8.2.9, 8.2.10
      (1)   8.2.2
      (2)(a)–(c)   8.2.3
      (3), (4)   8.2.3
      (5)   8.2.3, 8.2.4
   s 33(1)–(4)   8.2.19
   s 34   8.2.5, 8.2.7, 8.2.8, 8.2.9
      (1)   8.2.5, 8.2.8
      (2), (3)   8.2.5   (4)8.2.5, 9.7.1
   s 35   8.2.7, 8.2.8, 8.2.9
      (1)–(4)   8.2.7
      (5), (6)   8.2.8
      (7)   8.2.7, 8.2.8
   s 36   8.2.9, 8.2.11, 8.2.15
      (1), (2)   8.2.9
      (3)   8.2.11
         (a)–(e)   8.2.9
      (4)(a), (b)   8.2.10
      (5)   8.2.9
      (6)   8.2.10
      (7)(a), (b)   8.2.11
      (8), (9)   8.2.11
   s 37   8.2.11, 8.2.12, 8.2.13, 8.2.15
      (1)(a), (b)   8.2.13
      (2)   8.2.13
      (3), (4)   8.2.14
      (5)–(8)   8.2.15
      (9)–(11)   8.2.13
   s 37A   8.2.11, 8.2.16
      (1), (2)   8.2.17
      (3)   8.2.17, 8.2.18
      (4)   8.2.16
      (5)–(8)   8.2.18
      (9)   8.2.16, 8.2.17, 8.2.18
   s 38(1)–(3)   8.2.11
   s 39   8.2.21
   ss 40–45   8.3.2
   ss 40–48   8.3.1

Disability Discrimination Act
1995 – *cont*
s 40 8.3.10, 8.3.11, 8.3.18, 8.3.19, 9.7.1
   (1) 8.3.3
     (a), (b) 8.3.4
   (2) 8.3.6
   (3)(a)–(c) 8.3.9
   (4) 8.3.9
   (5) 8.3.2, 8.3.4
   (6) 8.3.4, 9.7.1
   (7) 8.3.3, 8.3.12, 8.3.15
s 41 8.3.16, 8.3.17, 8.3.18, 8.3.19, 9.7.1
   (1) 4.5.8, 8.3.17
     (a), (b) 8.3.11
   (2) 8.3.12
   (3) 8.3.11, 8.3.17
   (4) 8.3.11
s 42 8.3.11, 8.3.13, 8.3.17, 8.3.18,
8.3.19, 9.7.1
   (1) 8.3.13, 8.3.14
   (2) 8.3.13
   (3), (4) 8.3.15
   (5) 8.3.15
     (a) 8.3.13
   (6) 8.3.13, 8.3.16
   (7)(a), (b) 8.3.16
   (8) 8.3.15
s 43 8.3.18, 8.3.19
   (1)–(3) 8.3.18
s 44 8.3.14
   (1), (2) 8.3.14
   (3)–(6) 8.3.11, 8.3.15
s 45 8.3.11, 8.3.14, 8.3.15
   (1)(a) 8.3.13
     (b) 8.3.11
s 46 8.4.1, 8.4.2, 8.4.6, 8.4.9
   (1) 8.4.2, 8.4.7
     (a), (b) 8.4.2
   (2) 8.4.2, 8.4.3
     (a)–(g) 8.4.3
   (3), (4) 8.4.6
   (5) 8.4.2, 9.7.1
     (a)–(c) 8.4.5
   (6) 8.4.3, 8.4.5, 8.4.6, 8.4.7, 8.4.8,
8.4.9
   (7) 8.4.8
   (8), (9) 8.4.9
   (10) 8.4.6
   (11) 8.4.2
s 47 8.4.1, 8.4.10, 8.4.11
   (1)–(5) 8.4.10
s 48 8.3.10, 8.4.6

s 48(1)–(3) 8.3.10, 8.4.6
s 49 8.2.11, 8.2.15, 8.2.18, 8.3.11,
8.3.15
ss 50–52 9.1.1
ss 51–54 9.3.1
s 53A 3.1.4, 5.1.3, 7.4.1, 7.4.8, 7.5.2,
7.5.9, 9.3.1
   (1) 9.3.2
   (1A), (1B) 9.3.2
   (2) 9.3.2
   (3) 9.3.3
   (4), (5) 9.3.4
   (6)(a) 9.3.4, 9.7.1
     (b), (c) 9.3.4
   (7) 9.3.4
   (8) 3.1.4, 5.1.3, 9.3.5
   (8A) 5.1.3, 9.3.5
   (9) 9.3.2
s 54A 9.3.2
s 55 3.2.1, 5.4.1, 5.7.4, 7.4.2, 7.4.16,
7.5.3, 9.1.10, 10.1.1
   (1) 3.2.49, 6.2.17, 10.1.3
   (2) 6.2.17, 10.1.3
     (a)(i)–(iv) 3.2.50
     (b) 3.2.50
   (3), (4) 3.2.50, 10.1.4
   (3A) 10.1.3
   (5) 3.2.50, 10.1.5
   (6) 3.2.50
s 56 10.3.1, 10.7.2
   (1) 10.3.1
   (2) 10.3.2
   (3)(a) 10.3.4
     (b)(i), (ii) 10.3.5
   (4) 10.3.2
   (5) 10.3.4, 10.3.5
s 57 4.2.16, 10.2.2, 10.2.4, 10.2.7,
10.3.6, 10.6.1
   (1) 10.2.2
   (2) 10.2.2, 10.2.4, 10.2.7
   (3) 10.2.3
   (4) 10.2.3, 10.2.4
   (5) 10.2.3
   (6) 10.2.2
s 58 4.2.16, 4.2.22, 10.2.2, 10.2.4,
10.2.7, 10.3.6, 10.5.3, 10.5.4,
10.5.5, 10.6.1
   (1) 10.2.4
   (2), (3) 10.2.7
   (4) 10.2.3, 10.2.4
   (5) 10.2.2, 10.2.6, 10.2.7
s 59 5.2.2, 5.5.11, 5.6.7, 6.3.20, 10.2.10

Disability Discrimination Act		(5A), (5B)	4.8.9
1995 – *cont*		(6)	1.4.1, 4.2.16
s 59(1), (2)	10.2.8	Sch 1	2.1.2, 2.2.1, 2.8.3, 2.9.4, 7.2.14,
(2A)	10.2.12		7.4.2, 7.5.3, 9.4.2
(3)	10.2.12	para 1(1)	2.3.4, 2.3.5
s 62(1)	10.3.16	(2)	2.1.2, 2.3.4
s 63	10.3.19	(a)	2.3.3
s 64(1)–(2A)	4.2.21	(3)	2.3.3, 2.3.4
(1)	9.5.3	para 2(1)	2.6.1, 2.6.5
(a), (b)	9.5.1	(2)	2.5.5, 2.6.3, 2.6.5
(2)	9.5.3	(3)	2.5.5, 2.6.5
(a)	9.5.2	(4)	2.1.2, 2.6.1
(b)	9.5.2	para 3	2.3.3
(3), (4)	9.5.1	(1)	2.5.10
(5)	4.2.21, 9.5.3	(2)	2.1.2
(6)	4.2.21	(3)	2.1.2, 2.5.11
(7)	4.2.21, 9.5.3	para 4	2.5.8
(8)	4.2.21, 9.5.1, 9.5.2	(1)	2.4.1
s 64A	9.5.3, 10.2.4	(2)	2.4.1
s 65(1)	9.6.1	(a)	2.1.2
(2)–(4)	9.6.2	para 5	2.5.2
s 66	9.5.2	(a)	2.1.2
s 67(1)	5.1.3, 8.3.19, 9.7.1	para 6	2.3.2
(2)	5.1.3, 8.2.5, 8.3.4, 8.4.5, 9.7.1	(1), (2)	2.5.13
(3)	5.1.3, 8.2.5, 8.3.4, 8.4.5, 9.7.1	(3)(a), (b)	2.5.17
(a), (b)	9.7.1	para 7	2.1.3, 2.7.1
(5)	9.7.1	(2)(a)	2.7.1, 2.7.2
(6)	8.3.19, 9.7.1	(b)	2.7.2
(7)	8.2.5, 8.3.4, 8.4.5	(3)–(6)	2.7.1
s 68	4.3.2	(7)	2.7.1, 2.7.2
(1)	2.3.7, 4.2.17, 4.2.18, 4.3.2,	para 8(1)	2.5.7
	4.9.3, 4.9.7, 5.1.3, 6.2.10,	(a)	2.5.7
	8.2.5, 9.5.1, 9.7.1, 10.2.8,	(2)	2.5.7
	10.3.8, 10.4.2	para 49	2.7.1
(2)–(4A)	4.2.18	Sch 2	2.1.2, 2.7.2, 7.2.14, 7.4.2, 7.5.3
(2)	4.2.18, 4.2.19	para 2	2.6.5, 2.8.1
(a), (b)	4.2.18	para 2C	3.2.36
(2A)	4.2.18	para 3	4.2.38
(2B)	4.2.19	para 5	2.6.5
(2C)(a), (b)	4.2.19	Sch 3, Pt 1	3.1.1
(2D)	4.2.19	Pt 2	6.2.18
(4)	4.2.19	Pt 3	7.1.4, 10.5.1, 10.5.10
(4A)	4.2.19	Pt 4	10.6.1
s 68A(1)(a), (b)	4.2.22	para 1	10.3.12
(2)(a), (b)	4.2.22	para 2	10.3.6
(3)(a), (b)	4.2.23	paras 3–4	5.8.2
(4)	4.2.22	para 3	10.3.4
(5)	4.2.23	(1)	3.6.3, 10.3.8
(6)	4.2.22	(2)	10.3.9
(7)	4.2.22, 4.2.23	(3)	3.6.3
(8)	4.2.22	(a)–(c)	10.3.8
s 70(3)	9.7.1	(4)	3.6.3, 10.3.8

Disability Discrimination Act
1995 – *cont*

Sch 3, para 4(1)(a)		10.2.11
(b)		10.2.12
(2)		10.2.11
para 5(1), (2)		10.4.1
paras 6–8		5.8.2
para 6(1)		10.4.2, 10.4.6
(2)		10.4.6
(3)		10.4.2
(4)(a)–(c)		10.4.3
(5)		10.4.3
para 7		5.8.1, 10.4.10
para 8(1)(a)		10.2.11
(b)		10.2.12
(2)		10.2.11, 10.2.12
para 9		10.5.6
para 10(1)–(4)		10.5.7
(3)		10.5.1
(5)(a)–(c)		10.5.7
(6)		10.5.7
para 11		10.2.11
para 12		10.6.1
para 13(1), (2)		10.6.2
(3)		10.6.2
(a)		10.6.2
(c)		10.6.2
(4)		10.6.2
para 14		10.6.3
para 15		10.2.11
Sch 3A, para 1		10.3.13, 10.3.14
para 2(1)(a)		10.3.13
(b)		10.3.14
(2)		10.3.14
(3)	, (4)	10.3.15
(5)		10.3.15
(7)		10.3.15
(8)		10.3.13
Sch 4		7.5.18
Pt 1		3.1.1, 6.3.9, 6.3.15, 6.3.18
Pt 2		5.5.8, 6.3.9, 6.3.25, 6.3.30, 7.5.26
Pt 3		7.1.4, 7.5.18
para 1		6.3.9, 6.3.18
para 2(1)–(4)		6.3.19
(5)(a), (b)		6.3.19
(6)		6.3.19
(a)–(c)		6.3.19
(7)		6.3.19
(8)		6.3.19
(9)		6.3.19
para 5		6.3.9, 6.3.25

Sch 4, para 6		6.3.9
(1)		6.3.9, 6.3.25
(2)		6.3.25
(1A)		6.3.26
(3), (4)		6.3.9, 6.3.27
(5)		6.3.27
para 7		6.3.9
(1)–(4)		6.3.28
(5)(a), (b)		6.3.29
(6)(a)–(c)		6.3.29
(7), (8)		6.3.29
para 8		5.1.3, 6.3.9, 6.3.29
para 9		5.1.3, 6.3.9
paras 10–12		7.5.18
para 10		7.5.26, 7.5.27
para 11		7.5.27
(1)		7.5.26
(a), (b)		7.5.26
(1A)		7.5.27
(2)–(4)		7.5.28
para 12(1)–(4)		7.5.29
(5)(a), (b)		7.5.30
(6), (7), (8)		7.5.30
para 14		7.5.18
Sch 4A		7.1.4, 7.4.3, 7.4.14
Sch 4B		7.1.4, 7.5.4
Sch 4C		7.1.4, 7.5.15
Pts 1, 2		7.5.14
para 3		7.5.18
Sch 5		9.1.1
paras 5–7		6.3.26
Sch 6		7.5.18
paras 13, 14		7.5.18
Sch 8		1.4.1
Sch 8, para 3		4.2.16
para 7		4.2.25
(2)		4.2.25
(3), (4)		4.2.24
para 9(1)		5.2.1
(2), (3)		7.2.1
para 12		5.8.1, 10.4.1
paras 16–23		8.2.21
para 16(2)		8.2.4
para 18		8.2.5
para 19		8.2.7
para 20		8.2.11
para 21		8.2.15
para 24(1)		8.3.3
(2)		8.3.2
(3)		8.3.3
para 25(1)		8.3.12
(2)		8.3.11

Disability Discrimination Act
1995 – *cont*
 Sch 8, para 26 8.3.13
   para 27 8.3.18
   paras 28, 29 8.3.14
   para 30(1) 8.4.2
    (2), (3) 8.4.8
    (4) 8.4.2
   paras 33–35 9.1.1
   para 38 10.3.2
   para 42(2) 10.3.17
   para 44 9.5.1, 9.5.2
    (1) 9.5.1
    (4)(b) 9.5.1
   para 47 4.2.17
    (1) 10.2.8
    (2) 4.2.18
   para 50(1) 10.3.12
    (2) 10.2.12
    (4) 10.2.11
Disability Rights Commission Act
 1999 1.2.2, 9.1.1, 9.1.2, 9.1.3
 s 1(1) 9.1.1
  (2) 9.1.3
  (3), (4) 9.1.1
 s 2(1) 2.9.3, 5.2.7, 9.1.7, 9.1.13
   (a)–(c) 9.1.9
  (2)–(5) 9.1.8
 s 3(1), (2) 9.1.13
  (3) 9.1.13, 9.1.34
  (4)(a), (b) 9.1.14
  (5) 9.1.13, 9.1.14
 s 4 9.1.13, 9.1.16
  (1) 9.1.22
   (a) 9.1.23, 9.1.25
   (b) 9.1.23, 9.1.24, 9.1.25, 9.1.26,
      9.1.27
  (2) 9.1.23, 9.1.25
  (3) 9.1.24
   (a) 9.1.27
   (b) 9.1.27, 9.1.32
  (4)(a), (b) 9.1.27
  (5) 9.1.27
  (6) 9.1.22, 9.1.27
 s 5 9.1.13, 9.1.34
  (1) 9.1.34
  (2)(a) 9.1.35
   (b) 9.1.36
    (i), (ii) 9.1.35
  (3) 9.1.36
  (4)(a)–(c) 9.1.35
  (5)(a), (b) 9.1.35

s 5(6), (7) 9.1.36
 (8) 9.1.36, 9.1.39, 9.1.40
 (9) 9.1.36
 (10) 9.1.35
 (11), (12) 9.1.34
s 6(1)(a)–(c) 9.1.37
 (2)–(5) 9.1.37
s 7 9.1.10
 (1)(a), (b) 9.1.10
 (2)–(5) 9.1.11
s 8 9.1.12
 (1)–(5) 9.1.12
s 9 9.3.1
 (2) 9.3.3
 (3) 9.3.2
s 10 10.4.4
s 13(2) 9.1.7
s 14(2) 9.3.1
s 15 9.1.2
s 16(1) 9.1.1
 (4), (5) 9.1.1
Sch 1 9.1.1
 para 1 9.1.2
 para 2 9.1.4
  (1)–(3) 9.1.4
  (1A) 9.1.4
 para 3(1), (2) 9.1.5
 para 4 9.1.5
 para 5(a)–(c) 9.1.5
 para 6(1), (2) 9.1.6
 para 7 9.1.6
 para 8 9.1.4
 para 9 9.1.5
 para 10 9.1.3
  (2) 9.1.3
 para 11 9.1.3
 para 12(1), (2) 9.1.8
 para 13 9.1.8
 para 14(1), (2) 9.1.8
 para 15 9.1.3, 9.1.9
 para 16 9.1.9
 para 17(1)–(4) 9.3.3
Sch 2 9.1.14
 para 1(1), (2) 9.1.14
 para 2(1), (2) 9.1.14
 para 3 9.1.14
 para 4(1) 9.1.14
  (2)(a)–(c) 9.1.14
  (3) 9.1.14
 para 5 9.1.14
Sch 3 9.1.34, 9.1.39, 9.1.40
 Pt I 9.1.13

Disability Rights Commission Act
  1999 – *cont*
Sch 3, Pt II   9.1.16, 9.1.22
       Pt III   9.1.16, 9.1.27
       para 1(1)   9.1.13
       para 2   9.1.15, 9.1.19
            (1)(a), (b)   9.1.15
            (2)   9.1.15
            (3) 9.1.15, 9.1.17, 9.1.19
            (4)   9.1.15, 9.1.19
            (5)   9.1.15
       para 3   9.1.13
            (1)   9.1.17
               (a)   9.1.16
               (b), (c)   9.1.16, 9.1.17
            (2)   9.1.16
            (3)(a), (b)   9.1.16
            (4)–(9)   9.1.17
            (10)   9.1.16
       para 4   9.1.40
            (1)   9.1.18, 9.1.19
            (2)   9.1.18
            (3)(a), (b)   9.1.18
       para 5   9.1.40
            (1), (2)   9.1.18
       para 6(1)   9.1.20
            (2)(a), (b)   9.1.20
            (3)   9.1.20
       para 7   9.1.19
            (1)–(5)   9.1.20
       para 8   9.1.22
            (1)–(5)   9.1.22
       para 9   9.1.23
       para 10(1), (2)   9.1.24
            (3)(a), (b)   9.1.24
            (4)   9.1.25
            (5)(a), (b)   9.1.25
            (6), (7)   9.1.25
       para 11(a), (b)   9.1.26
       para 12(1)–(3)   9.1.26
       para 13   9.1.26
       para 14(1)   9.1.28
            (2)   9.1.27
       para 15(1)   9.1.28
            (2)   9.1.28, 9.1.30
            (3)   9.1.28
       para 16   9.1.28, 9.1.30
            (1)   9.1.29
               (b)   9.1.30
            (2)–(4)   9.1.29
       para 17   9.1.29
            (1)–(4)   9.1.30

Sch 3, para 18(1), (2)   9.1.31
            (3)(a), (b)   9.1.31
       para 19   9.1.28
       para 20   9.1.32
       para 21   9.1.40
Sch 3, para 21(1)   9.1.33
               (a)   9.1.28, 9.1.29,
                                    9.1.31
            (2)   9.1.33
            (3)   9.1.33, 9.1.40
            (4)   9.1.33
       para 22(1)   9.1.38
            (2)   9.1.38
               (f)   9.1.38
            (3)   9.1.38
       para 23(1)   9.1.39
            (2)(a)–(c)   9.1.39
            (3), (4)   9.1.39
       para 24(1), (2)   9.1.40
       para 25(1)–(3)   9.1.41
       para 26   9.1.13, 9.1.22, 9.1.27
Sch 5   9.3.1
Disabled Persons (Employment)
   Act 1944   2.1.3, 2.7.1, 2.7.2, 4.2.25
   s 15   4.2.25
Disabled Persons (Employment)
   Act (Northern Ireland)
   1945   2.7.1, 4.2.25
   s 15   4.2.25

Education Act 1944
   s 41   7.2.18
      (2A), (2B)   7.2.18
Education Act 1993   7.2.9
   s 161(5)   7.2.9
      (6)   7.2.10, 7.4.15
      (7)   7.2.10
   Sch 6, para 8   7.2.10
Education Act 1994
   s 1(4)   7.2.11
Education Act 1996
   Pt 4   7.4.8, 10.5.1, 10.5.2
   s 2   7.2.5, 7.2.18
      (3)   7.5.15
   s 3(1)   7.4.2
   s 4(1), (2)   7.2.1
   s 12   7.4.12, 7.4.16, 7.5.15
   s 15   7.2.18
   s 19(2)   7.4.3
   s 317(5)   7.2.9
      (6), (7)   7.2.10, 7.4.15
      (7A)   7.4.15

Education Act 1996 – *cont*
 s 342   7.4.3, 7.4.14, 10.5.8
 s 463   7.4.3, 7.4.14
 s 482   10.5.4, 10.5.5
      (3), (3A)   7.4.14
 s 508   7.2.5
      (1)   7.5.15
      (1A)   7.5.15
 s 528   7.2.18
 s 576   7.4.9
 s 578   7.4.16
 s 579   7.4.3
      (1)   7.5.15
 s 582(1)   7.1.4, 7.2.1
      (2)   7.2.9, 7.2.10, 7.2.18, 7.4.15
 Sch 37, para 129   7.1.4, 7.2.1
 Sch 38, Pt I   7.2.9, 7.2.10, 7.2.18,
                                   7.4.15
Education Act 1997
 s 38   7.4.13
Education Act 2002   7.4.3, 7.4.14
 s 16   10.5.4
 s 19   7.4.3, 10.5.5
 s 52(3)(c)   10.5.5
 s 195   10.5.1
 s 215   10.5.5
      (1)   7.4.14
 Sch 7   10.5.4
 Sch 18   10.5.1
 Sch 21   10.5.5
      para 26   7.4.14
Education (Disability Strategies
   and Pupils' Records)
   (Scotland) Act 2002   7.4.12
 ss 1–3   7.4.12
 s 1   7.4.13, 7.4.14
      (1)   7.4.14
      (2)   7.4.13, 7.4.14
      (a)–(c)   7.4.13, 7.4.14
      (3)–(5)   7.4.13, 7.4.14
      (6)   7.4.13, 7.4.14
 s 2   7.4.13
 s 3(1)(a)–(c)   7.4.13
      (2)–(5)   7.4.13
      (5)(b)   7.4.13
      (6)   7.4.13
 s 6(1)   7.4.12, 7.4.13, 7.4.14
Education (No 2) Act 1986
 s 30   7.2.10
Education Reform Act 1988
 s 120   7.5.15

Education (Scotland) Act 1980   7.4.16
 s 1(3)   7.2.5
      (5)   7.5.15
      (b)(ii)   7.5.4
 ss 60–65G   7.4.8
 s 73(c), (d)   7.4.3
 s 135   7.5.4
      (1) 7.2.1, 7.4.2, 7.4.3, 7.4.5, 7.4.9,
                             7.4.16, 7.5.15
Education (Scotland) Act 1996   7.4.16
Employment Act 2002
 ss 29–40   10.3.10
 s 31   10.3.31
 s 32   10.3.11
 Sch 2   10.3.10, 10.3.11
 Sch 3   10.3.10, 10.3.31
 Sch 4   10.3.10, 10.3.11
 Sch 5   10.3.10
Employment and Training Act
   1973
 s 2   5.2.1
Employment and Training Act
   (Northern Ireland) 1950
 ss 1, 2   5.2.1
Employment Rights Act 1996
 s 94   4.2.45
 s 98   3.2.32, 4.2.45
 s 104   10.1.1
 s 108   4.2.45
 s 113   10.3.30
 s 117(3)   10.3.30
      (4)(a)   10.3.30
      (5)(a), (b)   10.3.30
      (6)(c)   10.3.30
      (7), (8)   10.3.30
 ss 118–127   10.3.30
 s 126   10.3.28
 s 195   9.6.2
Employment Tribunals Act 1996
 ss 10–10B   10.2.12
 s 12(1)   10.3.16
      (2)   10.3.16
      (a)   10.3.18
      (3)(a)–(c)   10.3.18
      (4)–(6)   10.3.18
      (7)   10.3.16, 10.3.17
 s 18   10.3.12
      (1)(c)   10.3.12
      (2), (3)   10.3.12
 s 32   10.3.19
 s 42(1)   10.3.12
European Communities Act 1972
 s 2(2)   1.2.2

Further and Higher Education
    Act 1992   7.2.13
  s 5   7.2.14
    (6)(b)   7.2.14
    (7A)   7.2.14, 7.2.15
    (7B)   7.2.14, 7.2.15
  s 8(6), (7)   7.2.17
  s 62(7A), (7B)   7.2.19
  s 65(4A)   7.2.20, 7.2.25
    (4B)   7.2.20, 7.2.25
  s 89(4)   7.2.15
  ss 90, 91   7.5.4
Further and Higher Education
    (Scotland) Act 1992
  s 7(1)   7.2.1
  s 22   7.2.13
  s 36   7.5.4
  s 37(4A), (4B)   7.2.19
  s 40(5)   7.2.20, 7.2.25
    (6)   7.2.20, 7.2.25
  s 56(2)   7.5.4

Health and Safety at Work etc
    Act 1974
  s 12   10.2.10
Health and Social Services and
    Social Security Adjudications
    Act 1983
  s 17(2)   5.4.6
House of Commons
    Disqualification Act 1975
  Sch 2   4.4.4, 9.5.2
Housing Act 1985   6.2.19
Housing Act 1988   6.2.19
Human Rights Act 1998   3.2.30, 6.2.19,
              7.4.1, 7.5.2, 9.1.8
  s 3   6.2.15
  s 6   9.1.16, 9.1.22, 9.1.34

Insurance Companies Act 1982   5.6.14
Interpretation Act 1978
  s 21   10.2.8
  Sch 1   10.3.6
Interpretation Act (Northern
    Ireland) 1954
  s 1(f)   10.2.8

Law Reform (Miscellaneous
    Provisions) Act 1934
  s 1(1)   10.3.6

Law Reform (Miscellaneous
    Provisions) (Scotland) Act
    1990
  Pt I   4.2.24
Learning and Skills Act 2000
  s 1   7.2.17
  s 6(4)   7.2.17
    (6)   7.2.17
  s 30   7.2.17
  s 35(4)   7.2.17
    (6)   7.2.17
  s 149   7.1.4, 7.2.1
  s 153   7.1.4, 7.2.1
  Sch 9, para 1   7.1.4, 7.2.1
      para 49   7.1.4, 7.2.1
  Sch 11   7.1.4, 7.2.1
Legal Aid (Scotland) Act 1986   9.1.12
Life Peerages Act 1958   4.4.4
Limited Partnerships Act 1907
  s 3   4.7.1
Local Government
    (Miscellaneous Provisions)
    Act 1976
  s 48   8.2.16
  s 51   8.2.17
  s 55   8.2.17
Local Government (Scotland)
    Act 1973
  s 51   4.4.4
Local Government etc
    (Scotland) Act 1994
  s 2   4.4.4
Local Government and Housing
    Act 1989
  s 7   10.2.10

Medical Act 1983
  s 1(1)   4.10.1
Mental Health Act 1983
  Pt VII   5.6.9
  s 1(2)   2.3.7
Metropolitan Public Carriage Act
    1869   8.2.7
  s 6   8.2.4
Ministerial and Other Salaries
    Act 1975   4.4.4
Ministry of Defence Police Act
    1987
  s 1   9.5.3

National Health Service
  Community Care Act 1990
  s 47   5.4.6
Northern Ireland Act 1998
  ss 73–78   9.1.1
  s 73   9.1.2
  s 74   9.1.1
  Sch 8   9.1.1, 9.1.3, 9.1.4, 9.1.9

Parks Regulation Act 1872   9.5.3
Partnerships Act 1890
  s 4   4.7.1
Pensions Act 1995
  s 124(1)   4.5.4, 4.5.8
Private Hire Vehicles (Carriage
  of Guide Dogs etc) Act 2002   8.2.11,
                                               8.2.16
  s 1(1)   8.2.16
Private Hire Vehicles (London)
  Act 1998
  s 3   8.2.17
  s 6   8.2.16
  s 13   8.2.17
Public Passenger Vehicles Act
  1981   8.3.2, 8.3.11

Race Relations Act 1968   5.2.7
Race Relations Act 1976   3.1.3, 4.2.10,
                        5.2.2, 5.4.10, 9.1.16, 9.8.2
  Pt III   7.1.2
  s 2   10.1.1
  s 12   4.10.2
  ss 20–27   5.1.2
  ss 21–24   6.1.1
  s 25   5.2.7
  s 32   10.2.4
    (3)   10.2.2, 10.2.4
  s 33(1), (2)   10.2.2, 10.2.4
  s 41   10.2.9
  s 65   10.3.1
Railways Act 1993
  s 71B   8.4.1
Representation of the People Act
  1983
  s 18   7.2.3
Road Traffic Act 1988
  s 66A   8.3.11

Sale of Goods Act 1979
  s 61   5.2.3

School Standards and
  Framework Act 1998
  s 20(7)   7.4.3, 7.4.14
  s 22(8), (9)   7.4.3
  s 42(1)   7.4.15
  s 80   7.5.15
    (1)   7.5.15
  s 94   10.5.4
    (1), (2)   10.5.4
  s 99(2)   7.4.5
    (4)   7.4.5
  s 104   7.4.5
  s 140(3)   7.1.4, 7.2.1
  Sch 31   7.1.4, 7.2.1
Schools Inspection Act 1996   7.4.14
Scotland Act 1998   8.2.19
  s 44   4.4.4
  s 49   4.4.4
Sex Discrimination Act 1975   3.1.3,
                              5.4.10, 10.2.4
  Pt III   7.1.2
  s 4   10.1.1
  s 10(1)   4.2.19
    (5)   4.2.19
  s 13   4.10.2
  ss 29–36   5.1.2
  ss 30–32   6.1.1
  s 41   10.2.4
    (2)   10.2.7
    (3)   10.2.6
  s 74   10.3.1
Special Constables Act 1923
  s 3   9.5.3
Special Educational Needs and
  Disability Act 2001   1.2.2, 4.10.1,
                   6.4.1, 7.1.4, 7.1.5, 7.2.16,
                   7.2.17, 7.3.1, 7.4.1, 9.1.1
  Pt 1   7.3.1
  Pt 2   7.2.4, 7.3.1
    Ch 2   7.5.1
    Ch 3   7.3.1
  s 11   5.2.9, 7.1.4
  s 14(2)   7.2.10, 7.4.15
  s 16   5.2.9, 7.1.4
  s 17(1)   10.5.1
  s 18   10.5.3
  s 19(1)   10.5.1
    (2)   10.5.6
  s 20   10.5.4
  s 21   10.5.5
  s 22   10.5.8
  s 23   10.5.10

Special Educational Needs and
  Disability Act 2001 – *cont*

s 24	10.5.11, 10.6.4
s 26	5.2.9, 7.1.4
(1), (2)	10.6.1
s 34(1), (2)	7.2.20, 7.2.25
(3)	7.2.18
(5), (6)	7.2.25
(7)–(8)	7.2.17
s 35	9.1.7
s 36	7.5.9
s 37	10.5.12, 10.6.5
s 38(1)	5.2.9, 7.1.4
(5)(a), (b)	5.2.9, 7.1.4
(6)	5.2.9, 7.1.4
s 40(1), (2)	7.2.11
s 42(6)	5.2.9, 7.1.4
s 43(6)(d)	7.1.4
Sch 3, para 1	10.5.6
para 2	10.2.11
Sch 6	7.5.18
Sch 7, para 1	9.1.7
para 2	9.1.7
Sch 8, para 5	7.2.9
Sch 9	5.2.9, 7.1.4

Standards in Scotland's Schools
  etc Act 2000   7.4.16

Superannuation Act 1972	
s 1	9.1.3
Sch 1	9.1.3
Supreme Court Act 1981	
s 31	10.5.8, 10.5.9

Teaching and Higher Education
  Act 1998

s 38	7.1.4, 7.2.1
Town Police Clauses Act 1847	
s 37	8.2.4

Trade Union and Labour
  Relations (Consolidation)
  Act 1992   4.9.13

Pt I, ch IV	4.9.13
s 1	4.9.4
s 47	4.9.13
s 48	4.9.13
s 51	4.9.14
s 122(1)(a), (b)	4.9.6
s 296	4.9.4
Transport and Works Act 1992	8.4.7, 8.4.8

TABLE OF STATUTORY INSTRUMENTS
AND CIRCULARS

References are to paragraph numbers.

Agricultural Wages Order 2004 (No 1)	4.2.47
Agricultural Wages (Abolition of Permits to Incapacitated Persons) Regulations 2004, SI 2004/2178	4.2.47
Agricultural Wages (Permits to Infirm and Incapacitated Persons) (Repeals) (Scotland) Regulations 2004, SSI 2004/384	4.2.47
Building Regulations 1991, SI 1991/2768	6.3.4
Building Regulations 2000, SI 2000/2531	6.3.4
Sch 1	6.3.3
Pt M	6.3.3, 6.3.4
Building (Scotland) Amendment Regulations 1997, SI 1997/2157	6.3.3, 6.3.5
Building Standards (Scotland) Regulations 1990, SI 1990/2179	6.3.3, 6.3.5
Building Standards (Scotland) Amendment Regulations 1993, SI 1993/1457	6.3.3, 6.3.5
Building Standards (Scotland) Amendment Regulations 1994, SI 1994/1266	6.3.3, 6.3.5
Building Standards (Scotland) Amendment Regulations 1996, SI 1996/2251	6.3.3, 6.3.5
Building Standards (Scotland) Amendment Regulations 2001, SSI 2001/320	6.3.3, 6.3.5
Building Standards and Procedure Amendment (Scotland) Regulations 1999, SSI 1999/173	6.3.3, 6.3.5
Civil Procedure Rules 1998, SI 1998/3132	
Pt 35 Experts and Assessors	2.2.2
Pt 35 Practice Direction – Experts and Assessors	2.2.2
Companies Act 1985 (Electronic Communications) Order 2000, SI 2000/3373	5.2.2
DfEE Circular 11/96	7.2.10, 7.4.15
DfEE Circular 12/96	7.2.10, 7.4.15
Departments (Northern Ireland) Order 1999, SI 1999/283 (NI 1)	1.4.1
Departments (Transfer and Assignment of Functions) Order 1999, SI 1999/481	1.4.1
Disability Discrimination (Blind and Partially Sighted Persons) Regulations 2003, SI 2003/712	2.3.11, 2.7.3
Disability Discrimination (Description of Insurance Services) Regulations 1999, SI 1999/2114	4.6.5

Disability Discrimination (Designation of Educational Institutions) Order
  2002, SI 2002/1459   7.5.4
Disability Discrimination (Educational Institutions) (Alteration of Leasehold
  Premises) Regulations 2002, SI 2002/1458   7.5.22
  reg 2   7.5.23
  reg 3(1)   7.5.23
    (2)(a), (b)   7.5.23
    (3)   7.5.23
    (4)(a), (b)   7.5.23
  reg 3(5)   7.5.24
    (6)   7.5.23, 7.5.24
    (7)   7.5.24
    (7)(b)   7.5.23
  reg 4   7.5.25
  reg 5   7.5.25
    (1)   7.5.25
    (2)(a), (b)   7.5.25
  reg 6(1)   7.5.25
    (2)(a)–(e)   7.5.25
  reg 7   7.5.18
    (1)   7.5.18
    (2)   7.5.20, 7.5.27
    (3)   7.5.18
    (4)   7.5.18, 7.5.27, 7.5.28
    (5)   7.5.27
    (6)   7.5.18
      (a), (b)   7.5.29
Disability Discrimination (Employment Field) (Leasehold Premises)
  Regulations 2004, SI 2004/153   3.1.4, 4.2.46, 4.2.47
  reg 2   6.3.15, 6.3.16
  reg 4   6.3.16
    (1)–(4)   6.3.15
  reg 5(1)–(4)   6.3.16
  reg 6(1), (2)   6.3.16
  reg 7(1)(a)–(d)   6.3.17
    (2)   6.3.16
  reg 8   6.3.9
  reg 9   6.3.9
    (b)   6.3.11
Disability Discrimination (Employment Field) (Leasehold Premises)
  Regulations (Northern Ireland) 2004, SR 2004/374   3.1.4, 4.2.46, 4.2.47
Disability Discrimination (Employment) Regulations 1996, SI 1996/1456   3.1.4,
                                        4.2.46, 4.2.47, 6.3.11
  reg 2   6.3.3, 6.3.14
  reg 3(2)   4.2.39
  reg 4(3)   4.5.1
  reg 6(a)   4.2.47
    (b)   4.2.47
  reg 7   4.3.7
  reg 8   6.3.3
  reg 9   4.2.37
  reg 10   6.3.14
  reg 15   6.3.13

Disability Discrimination (Employment) Regulations (Northern Ireland)
    1996, SR 1996/419   3.1.4, 4.2.37, 4.2.39, 4.2.46, 4.2.47, 4.3.7, 4.5.1
Disability Discrimination (Exemption for Small Employers) Order 1998,
    SI 1998/2618   4.2.20
Disability Discrimination (Guidance and Code of Practice) (Appointed Day)
    Order 1996, SI 1996/1996
    art 2   9.4.5
Disability Discrimination (Meaning of Disability) Regulations 1996,
    SI 1996/1455   2.1.2, 2.2.1
    reg 2   2.3.3
    reg 3(1), (2)   2.3.3
    reg 4(1)   2.3.4
      (2), (3)   2.3.3
    reg 5   2.5.2, 2.5.11
    reg 6   2.4.6, 2.5.2
Disability Discrimination (Meaning of Disability) Regulations (Northern
    Ireland) 1996, SR 1996/421   2.1.2
Disability Discrimination (Pensions) Regulations 2003, SI 2003/2770   4.5.3
Disability Discrimination (Prescribed Periods for Accessibility Strategies and
    Plans for Schools) (Wales) Regulations 2003, SI 2003/2531 (W 246)   7.4.13,
                7.4.14
Disability Discrimination (Prescribed Periods for Accessibility Strategies and
    Plans for Schools) (England) Regulations 2002, SI 2002/1981
    regs 1, 2   7.4.13, 7.4.14
    reg 3   7.4.14
Disability Discrimination (Providers of Services) (Adjustment of Premises)
    Regulations 2001, SI 2001/3253   5.1.3, 5.5.7, 5.5.8, 5.5.11, 6.3.2
    reg 2   6.3.20
    reg 3(2)   6.3.20
      (3)   6.3.4, 6.3.6
      (4)   6.3.6
    reg 4   6.3.9
    reg 5   6.3.21
      (2)(a), (b)   6.3.22
      (3)   6.3.22
      (4)(a), (b)   6.3.22
      (5)   6.3.23
      (6)   6.3.22, 6.3.23
      (7)   6.3.23
        (b)   6.3.22
    reg 6   6.3.24
    reg 7   6.3.24
      (2)(a), (b)   6.3.24
    reg 8(1)   6.3.24
      (2)(a)–(e)   6.3.24
    reg 9(1)   6.3.9, 6.3.11, 6.3.26
      (2)   6.3.9, 6.3.26
      (3)   6.3.11, 6.3.26
      (4)   6.3.9
      (5)   6.3.26
      (6)   6.3.9, 6.3.27
      (7)(a), (b)   6.3.28
    Sch, para 1(1)–(3)   6.3.6

Disability Discrimination (Providers of Services) (Adjustment of Premises)
    Regulations 2001, SI 2001/3253 – *cont*
        para 2   6.3.6
            (1)(a)   6.3.4
        para 3   6.3.6
Disability Discrimination (Providers of Services) (Adjustment of Premises)
    (Amendment) Regulations 2004, SI 2004/1429   5.1.3, 5.5.7, 5.5.8, 5.5.11, 6.3.2,
              6.3.4, 6.3.6, 6.3.9, 6.3.20, 6.3.21, 6.3.22, 6.3.23, 6.3.24, 6.3.26, 6.3.27,
                          6.3.28
Disability Discrimination (Questions and Replies) Order 2004, SI 2004/1168   10.3.3
    reg 3   10.3.3
    reg 4(a), (b)   10.3.4
    reg 5(a)–(d)   10.3.3
    Sch 1   10.3.3
    Sch 2   10.3.3
Disability Discrimination (Services and Premises) Regulations 1996,
    SI 1996/1836   5.1.3
    reg 1(2)   5.6.14
    reg 2   5.6.14
        (1)   5.6.14
        (2)(a)–(c)   5.6.14
    reg 3(2)–(4)   5.6.14
    reg 4   5.6.14
    reg 5(1)   5.6.15
        (2)(a)–(c)   5.6.15
        (3)   5.6.15
    reg 6   5.6.16
        (1)   5.6.16
        (2)(a)–(c)   5.6.16
    reg 7(1)   6.2.16
        (2)(a)–(d)   6.2.16
    reg 8   5.6.9, 6.2.15
    reg 9   5.2.9, 7.2.4
        (1)(a)   7.2.5
          (b)   7.2.6, 7.2.7
          (c)   7.2.6
          (d)(i), (ii)   7.2.6
        (2)   7.2.6
          (a), (b)   7.2.6
Disability Discrimination (Services and Premises) Regulations 1999,
    SI 1999/1191   5.1.3
    regs 2, 3   5.5.9
    reg 4   5.5.15
Disability Discrimination (Services and Premises) (Amendment) Regulations
    2002, SI 2002/1980
    reg 2   7.2.4
    reg 4   7.2.4
Disability Discrimination (Sub-leases and Sub-tenancies) Regulations 1996,
    SI 1996/1333   3.1.4, 6.3.11
Disability Discrimination (Sub-leases and Sub-tenancies) Regulations
    (Northern Ireland) 1996,
    SI 1996/420   3.1.4

Disability Discrimination Act 1995 (Amendment) Regulations 2003, SI 2003/
   1673 1.2.2, 2.1.2, 2.6.5, 2.8.1, 3.1.2, 4.1.2, 4.2.1, 4.2.18, 4.2.20, 4.2.21, 4.4.1, 4.7.1,
                                                4.8.1, 4.10.2, 9.1.1
reg 3(1)   5.7.1, 5.7.6
reg 19(1)   5.7.1
   (3)   5.7.6
Disability Discrimination Act 1995 (Amendment) (Northern Ireland)
   Regulations 2004, SR 2004/55   1.2.2, 3.1.2, 4.1.2, 9.1.1
Disability Discrimination Act 1995 (Commencement No 3 and Saving and
   Transitional Provisions) Order 1996, SI 1996/1474   5.1.2
Disability Discrimination Act 1995 (Commencement No 6) Order 1999,
   SI 1999/1190   5.1.2
Disability Discrimination Act 1995 (Commencement No 7) Order 2000,
   SI 2000/1969   8.3.2
Disability Discrimination Act 1995 (Commencement No 7) Order (Northern
   Ireland) 2001, SR 2001/163   8.2.12
Disability Discrimination Act 1995 (Commencement No 8) Order 2000,
   SI 2000/2989   8.2.12
Disability Discrimination Act 1995 (Commencement No 8) Order (Northern
   Ireland) SR 2001/439   5.1.2, 5.5.7, 6.3.9
Disability Discrimination Act 1995 (Commencement No 9) Order 2001,
   SI 2001/2030   5.1.2, 5.5.7, 6.3.9
Disability Discrimination Act 1995 (Commencement No 10) (Scotland)
   Order 2003, SI 2003/215   8.2.21
Disability Discrimination Act 1995 (Taxis) (Carrying of Guide Dogs etc)
   (England and Wales) Regulations 2000, SI 2000/2990   8.2.12
   reg 2   8.2.15
   reg 3(1)   8.2.13
      (2)(a), (b)   8.2.13
      (3)   8.2.13
   Schs 1, 2   8.2.15
Disability Discrimination Act 1995 (Taxis) (Carrying of Guide Dogs etc)
   (Northern Ireland) Regulations 2001, SR 2001/169   8.2.12
   reg 2   8.2.15
   reg 3(1)   8.2.13
      (2)(a), (b)   8.2.13
      (3)   8.2.13
   Sch   8.2.15
Disability Discrimination Code of Practice (Goods, Facilities, Services and
   Premises) (Appointed Day) Order 2002, SI 2002/720   5.1.3
Disability Discrimination Code of Practice (Goods, Facilities, Services and
   Premises) Revocation Order 2002, SI 2002/721   5.1.3
Disability Rights Commission (Expenses) (Scotland) Regulations 2000,
   SI 2000/1888   9.1.12
Disability Rights Commission (Time Limits) Regulations 2000, SI 2000/879   9.1.13,
                                          9.1.19, 9.1.22, 9.1.27
   reg 1(2)   9.1.19
   reg 2(1)   9.1.19
      (2)(a), (b)   9.1.19
      (3)–(7)   9.1.19
   reg 3(1)   9.1.28
      (2)–(4)   9.1.29
      (5)(a), (b)   9.1.30
      (6)–(8)   9.1.31

Disability Rights Commission (Time Limits) Regulations 2000, SI 2000/879 –
   cont
  reg 3(9)   9.1.28, 9.1.29, 9.1.31
    (10)   9.1.30, 9.1.31

Education (Disability Statements for Further Education Institutions)
  Regulations 1996, SI 1996/1664   7.2.15
  reg 2   7.2.15
Education (Disability Strategies) (Scotland) Regulations 2002, SI 2002/391   7.4.12
  regs 2, 3   7.4.13
Education (Disability Strategies and Pupils' Records) (Scotland) Act 2002
  (Commencement) Order 2002, SI 2002/367   7.4.12
Education (Modification of Enactments Relating to Employment) Order
  1999, SI 1999/2256   10.2.7
  art 2(2)   3.2.15
  art 6   3.2.15
Education (Modification of Enactments Relating to Employment) Order
  2003, SI 2003/1964   3.2.15, 4.2.16
Education (Modification of Enactments Relating to Employment) (England)
  (Amendment) Order 2004, SI 2004/2325   4.2.16, 10.1.5, 10.2.1, 10.2.7
Education and Libraries (Northern Ireland) Order 1986, SI 1986/594   7.2.1
Employment Act 2002 (Dispute Resolution) Regulations 2004, SI 2004/752   10.3.10,
                                                                         10.3.11
  reg 15   10.3.4
Employment Appeal Tribunal Rules 1993, SI 1993/2854
  r 23A   10.3.19
Employment Equality (Religion or Belief) Regulations 2003, SI 2003/1660   3.1.3
Employment Equality (Sexual Orientation) Regulations 2003, SI 2003/1661   3.1.3
Employment Tribunals (Constitution and Rules of Procedure) Regulations
  2004, SI 2004/1861   4.5.8, 10.3.7
  rr 1–3   10.3.10, 10.3.11
  rr 4–9   10.3.10
  r 10(2)(r)   9.1.7
  r 18(7)(g)   10.3.16
  rr 22–24   10.3.12
  r 50   10.3.16
Employment Tribunals (Constitution and Rules of Procedure) (Amendment)
  Regulations 2004, SI 2004/2351   10.3.7
Employment Tribunals (Interest on Awards in Discrimination Cases)
  Regulations 1996, SI 1996/2803   10.3.27
Employment Tribunals (National Security) Rules of Procedure 2004   10.2.12
Equality Commission (Time Limits) Regulations (Northern Ireland) 2001,
  SR 2001/6   9.1.13, 9.1.19, 9.1.27, 9.1.28, 9.1.29, 9.1.30, 9.1.31
Equality (Disability, etc) (Northern Ireland) Order 2000, SI 2000/1110
  (NI 2)   9.1.1
  art 4   9.1.7
  art 5   9.1.13
  art 6   9.1.22, 9.1.27
  art 7   9.1.34
  art 8   9.1.37
  art 9   9.1.10
  art 10   9.1.12

Equality (Disability, etc) (Northern Ireland) Order 2000, SI 2000/1110
  (NI 2) – *cont*
  art 11   9.3.2
    (1)   9.3.2
  art 16   9.3.1
  art 17   9.1.2
  art 18   9.1.14
  art 19   9.1.9
  Sch 1, Pt I   9.1.13
         Pt II   9.1.22
         Pt III   9.1.27
         Pt IV   9.1.38, 9.1.39, 9.1.40, 9.1.41
  Sch 2   9.3.1

Fixed-term Employees (Prevention of Less Favourable Treatment)
  Regulations 2002, SI 2002/2034   3.1.3

HEFCE Circular 8/96   7.2.20
  paras 8–10   7.2.21
  paras 12, 13   7.2.22
  para 14   7.2.23
  para 14.b   7.2.23
  paras 15–17   7.2.23
  para 18   7.2.20
  paras 20–21   7.2.20
HEFCW Circular W96/43HE   7.2.20
  para 8   7.2.22

Industrial Tribunals (Constitution and Rules of Procedure) Regulations
  (Northern Ireland) 2004, SR 2004/165   10.3.7
National Assembly for Wales (Transfer of Functions) Order 2000, SI 2000/
  253
  art 3   9.1.4
  Sch 2   9.1.4

Part-time workers (Prevention of Less Favourable Treatment) Regulations
  2000, SI 2000/1551   3.1.3
Pensions (Northern Ireland) Order 1995, SI 1995/3213 (NI 22)
  art 121(1)   4.5.4, 4.5.8
Police (Appointments) Regulations (Northern Ireland) 2004, SR 2004/379 4.2.22
Private Hire Car Drivers' Licences (Carrying of Guide Dogs and Hearing
  Dogs) (Scotland) Regulations 2004, SI 2004/88   8.2.21
Private Hire Vehicles (Carriage of Guide Dogs etc) Act 2002
  (Commencement No 1) Order 2003, SI 2003/3123   8.2.16
Private Hire Vehicles (Carriage of Guide Dogs etc) (England and Wales)
  Regulations 2003, SI 2003/3122
  reg 2   8.2.18
  reg 3   8.2.16
Public Service Vehicles Accessibility Regulations 2000, SI 2000/1970   8.3.3, 8.3.5,
                                                               8.3.6, 8.3.7, 8.3.8
  reg 3   8.3.5, 8.3.7

Private Hire Vehicles (Carriage of Guide Dogs etc) (England and Wales)
   Regulations 2003, SI 2003/3122 – *cont*
   reg 4   8.3.5
   reg 5   8.3.5
   regs 6–8   8.3.12
   regs 9–12   8.3.13
   regs 13–17   8.3.15
   reg 19   8.3.14
      (3)   8.3.14, 8.3.15
   Sch 1   8.3.5
     paras 1–10   8.3.7
   Sch 2   8.3.5
     paras 1–8   8.3.7
   Sch 3   8.3.5
     paras 1–7   8.3.7
   Sch 4   8.3.12
   Schs 5, 6   8.3.15
Public Service Vehicles Accessibility (Amendment) Regulations 2000, SI
   2000/3318   8.3.3
Public Service Vehicles Accessibility (Amendment) Regulations 2002, SI
   2002/2981   8.3.3
Public Service Vehicles Accessibility (Amendment) Regulations 2004, SI
   2004/1881   8.3.3
Public Service Vehicles (Conditions of Fitness, Equipment, Use and
   Certification) Regulations 1981, SI 1981/257   8.3.8
Public Service Vehicles (Conditions of Fitness, Equipment, Use and
   Certification) (Amendment) Regulations 2002, SI 2002/335   8.3.8
Public Service Vehicles (Conduct of Drivers, Inspectors, Conductors and
   Passengers) Regulations 1990, SI 1990/1020   8.3.8
Public Service Vehicles (Conduct of Drivers, Inspectors, Conductors and
   Passengers) (Amendment) Regulations 2002, SI 2002/1724   8.3.8
Rail Vehicle Accessibility Regulations 1998, SI 1998/2456   8.4.2, 8.4.4, 8.4.5, 8.4.9
   reg 2(1)   8.4.7
   reg 3(1)   8.4.7
   regs 4–8   8.4.4
   reg 9   8.4.4, 8.4.5
   reg 10   8.4.4
   reg 11   8.4.4, 8.4.5
   regs 12–14   8.4.4
   reg 15   8.4.4, 8.4.5
   regs 16–24   8.4.4
   reg 20A   8.4.4

Rail Vehicle Accessibility (Amendment) Regulations 2000, SI 2000/3215   8.4.2
Rail Vehicle Accessibility Regulations (Northern Ireland) 2001, SR 2001/264 8.4.2
Rail Vehicle (Exemption Application) Regulations 1998, SI 1998/2457   8.4.11
   regs 3, 4   8.4.11
   Sch   8.4.11
   Sch, para 11   8.4.11
Rail Vehicle (Exemption Application) Regulations (Northern Ireland) 2001,
   SR 2001/265   8.4.11

Road Traffic (Northern Ireland) Order 1981   8.3.2
   art 61   8.2.4

SHEFC Circular 47/96   7.2.20
SHEFC Circular 9/99   7.2.20
Scotland Act 1998 (Consequential Modifications) Order 2000, SI 2000/2040   10.2.8
Scotland Act (Modification of Functions) Order 2000, SI 2000/1458
   art 2   9.1.4
Scotland Act (Transfer of Functions to the Scottish Ministers etc) Order
   2000, SI 2000/1563
   art 5(1)   9.1.4
Scottish Executive Guidance on Planning to Improve Access to Education for
   Pupils with Disabilities   7.4.12
Sex Discrimination and Equal Pay (Offshore Employment) Order 1987,
   SI 1987/930   4.2.19
Special Educational Needs and Disability Act 2001 (Commencement No 2)
   (Wales) Order 2003, SI 2003/2532 (W 247)   7.1.4, 7.4.12
Special Educational Needs and Disability Act 2001 (Commencement No 5)
   Order 2002, SI 2002/2217   7.1.4, 10.5.1
   art 3   7.5.1
   art 4   7.4.12
   arts 5, 6   7.5.1
   Sch 1, Pt 1   7.5.1
      Pt 2   7.4.12
   Sch 2   7.5.1
Special Educational Needs and Disability Tribunal (General Provisions and
   Disability Claims Procedure) Regulations 2002, SI 2002/1985   10.5.1

Taxi Drivers' Licences (Carrying of Guide Dogs and Hearing Dogs)
   (Scotland) Regulations 2003, SI 2003/73   8.2.21
Transfer of Functions to the Scottish Ministers etc Order 1999, SI 1999/1750
   art 2   8.2.19
   Sch 1   8.2.19
Transport and Works (Guided Transport Modes) Order 1992, SI 1992/3231   8.4.7

TABLE OF CODES OF PRACTICE, GUIDANCE ETC

References are to paragraph numbers.

Bar Code of Conduct
    para 305   4.8.1
    para 403   4.8.1
Bar Equality and Diversity Code (revised 2004)   4.8.1
British Standard 8300:2001 Design of Buildings and their Approaches to
    Meet the Needs of Disabled People – Code of Practice   6.3.3

Code of Practice: Duties of trade organisations to their disabled members
    and applicants (1999)   4.9.1
Code of Practice for the elimination of discrimination in the field of
    employment against disabled persons or persons who have had a
    disability (1996)   3.1.4
    para 4.6   3.2.28
    paras 4.21–4.32   5.5.3
    para 7.6   4.3.10
Code of Practice: Employment and Discrimination (2004)
    paras 9.7–9.13   4.3.7
Code of Practice: Employment and Occupation (2004)   3.1.4, 9.3.5
    para 3.8   4.2.17
    para 3.9   4.2.21
    para 3.11   4.2.22
    paras 3.15–3.21   4.2.1
    para 3.22   3.7.1
    para 3.23   10.2.4
    paras 3.24–3.25   10.2.2
    para 4.5–4.23   3.2.37
    para 4.7   3.2.38
    para 4.8   3.2.38
    para 4.9   3.2.38
    para 4.10   3.2.38
    para 4.11   3.2.38
    para 4.12   3.2.39
    para 4.13   3.2.39
    paras 4.14–4.16   3.2.40
    para 4.17   3.2.40
    para 4.18   3.2.39
    para 4.19   3.2.37
    paras 4.20–4.22   3.2.40
    para 4.23   3.2.41

Code of Practice: Employment and Occupation (2004) – *cont*

paras 4.24–4.26	3.2.45, 3.4.1
paras 4.27–4.32	3.2.3
para 4.30	3.2.8
paras 4.30–4.31	3.2.4
paras 4.33–4.36	3.2.49, 10.1.6
para 4.37	3.2.37
paras 4.38–4.39	3.3.2
para 4.40	10.2.8
paras 4.41–4.43	3.2.6
para 5.3	4.2.28
para 5.4	4.2.38
paras 5.5–5.7	4.2.29
para 5.8	4.2.34
para 5.9	4.2.37
para 5.10	4.2.37
para 5.11	4.2.39
paras 5.12–5.16	4.2.31
para 5.18	3.4.2
para 5.19	3.4.3
para 5.20	3.4.3, 4.2.44, 4.2.46
para 5.22	4.2.32
para 5.24	4.2.41
para 5.25	3.4.9
para 5.26	3.4.9
para 5.27	3.4.10
paras 5.28–5.41	3.4.9
paras 5.32–5.35	3.4.9
para 5.42	3.4.10
paras 5.43–5.44	3.2.47
Ch 6	3.2.23
para 6.3	3.2.28, 3.2.41
paras 6.4–6.6	3.2.29
para 6.7–6.13	3.2.25
para 6.7–6.16	3.2.24
para 6.7	3.2.38
paras 6.8–6.13	3.4.13
paras 6.14–6.16	4.2.15
para 7.4	4.2.2
paras 7.6–7.8	4.2.2
para 7.9	4.2.15
paras 7.10–7.14	4.2.2
paras 7.11–7.15	3.6.2
paras 7.16–7.31	4.2.2
paras 7.27–7.31	4.2.15
para 7.32	4.2.3
paras 8.4–8.7	4.2.4
paras 8.5–8.6	4.2.39, 4.2.46
paras 8.8–8.11	4.2.5
para 8.12	4.2.6
paras 8.13–8.14	4.2.5
paras 8.15–8.27	4.2.8

Code of Practice: Employment and Occupation (2004) – *cont*

paras 8.28–8.32	3.5.1, 4.2.11
para 9.3–9.13	4.3.1
para 9.5	4.3.2
para 9.6	4.3.1
paras 9.8–9.12	4.3.9
para 9.13	4.3.1
para 9.14	4.4.2
paras 9.15–9.20	4.4.5
para 9.21	4.4.11
para 9.22	4.4.5
paras 9.23–9.24	4.2.22
paras 9.25–9.31	4.7.1
para 9.27	4.7.1
para 9.30	4.7.4
para 9.31	4.7.4, 4.7.6
para 9.32–9.41	4.8.1
para 9.33	4.8.5
para 9.35	4.8.3
para 9.36	4.8.9
para 9.37	4.8.6
para 9.39	4.8.6
para 9.40	4.8.7
para 9.41	4.8.9
paras 10.2–10.5	4.5.1
paras 10.6–10.15	4.5.3
para 10.8	4.5.4, 4.5.6
para 10.10	4.5.4
para 10.12	4.5.8
para 10.15	4.5.8
para 10.16	4.6.6
paras 10.17–10.21	4.6.3
Ch 11	5.7.1
para 11.4	5.7.1
paras 11.5–11.7	5.7.3
para 11.8	5.7.2
paras 11.10–11.14	5.7.4
paras 11.15–11.19	5.7.5
paras 11.20–11.22	5.7.4
para 11.23	5.8.2
paras 12.3–12.5	6.3.3
paras 12.6–12.11	6.3.3
para 12.12	6.3.14
paras 12.13–12.31	6.3.9
para 12.13	6.3.10
para 12.14	6.3.18
paras 12.15–12.16	6.3.11
paras 12.17–12.21	6.3.15
paras 12.22–12.25	6.3.16
paras 12.26–12.27	6.3.17
paras 12.28–12.30	6.3.19
para 12.31	6.3.25

Code of Practice: Employment and Occupation (2004) – *cont*
  App C   4.5.8
Code of Practice: Trade Organisations and Qualifications Bodies (2004)   3.1.4, 4.9.1,
                                                                         9.3.5
  Ch 3   4.10.2
  para 3.8   4.9.7
  paras 3.9–3.11   4.10.3
  para 3.11   4.9.3
  para 3.18   4.9.9
  para 3.21   3.7.1
  paras 3.22–3.25   3.6.2
  paras 3.26–3.27   10.2.4
  paras 3.28–3.29   10.2.2
  para 4.5–4.22   3.2.37
  para 4.7   3.2.38
  para 4.8   3.2.38
  para 4.9   3.2.38
  para 4.10   3.2.38
  para 4.11   3.2.38
  para 4.12   3.2.38, 3.2.39
  para 4.13   3.2.39
  paras 4.14–4.16   3.2.40
  para 4.17   3.2.40
  para 4.18   3.2.39
  para 4.19   3.2.37
  para 4.20   3.2.40
  para 4.21   3.2.40
  para 4.22   3.2.41
  paras 4.23–4.25   3.2.45, 3.4.1
  paras 4.26–4.31   3.2.3
  paras 4.29–4.30   3.2.4
  para 4.29   3.2.8
  paras 4.32–4.35   3.2.49, 10.1.6
  para 4.36   3.2.37
  paras 4.37–4.38   3.3.2, 4.9.10
  para 4.39   10.2.8
  paras 4.40–4.42   3.2.6
  paras 5.2–5.3   4.9.11
  paras 5.4–5.5   4.9.12
  paras 5.6–5.10   4.9.11
  para 5.11   4.9.12
  para 5.12   3.4.2, 3.4.3
  paras 5.12–5.25   4.9.13
  para 5.13   3.4.3
  paras 5.14–5.25   3.4.9
  para 5.17   3.4.9
  para 5.18   3.4.10
  para 5.21   3.4.9
  paras 5.26–5.27   3.2.47
  Ch 6   3.2.23
  para 6.3   3.2.28, 3.2.41
  paras 6.5–6.7   3.2.29

Code of Practice: Trade Organisations and Qualifications Bodies (2004) –
   cont
  paras 6.8–6.15   3.2.25
  paras 6.8–6.17   3.4.13
  paras 6.8–6.18   3.2.24
  para 6.8   3.2.38
  paras 7.3–7.4   4.9.3
  paras 7.5–7.14   4.9.8
  paras 7.10–7.14   4.9.11
  paras 7.15–7.29   4.9.9
  para 7.16   4.9.9
  paras 7.19–7.21   4.9.11
  para 7.23   3.5.1
  paras 7.27–7.29   4.9.11
  paras 7.30–7.36   4.9.12
  paras 7.28–7.29   3.5.1
  Ch 8   4.10.2
  paras 8.5–8.8   4.10.3
  para 8.13   3.5.1
  paras 8.15–8.26   4.10.6
  paras 8.18–8.19   3.5.1
  paras 8.27–8.31   4.10.5
  paras 8.32–8.41   4.10.5, 4.10.9
  paras 9.3–9.5   6.3.3
  paras 9.6–9.10   6.3.3
  para 9.11   6.3.14
  paras 9.12–9.30   6.3.9
  para 9.12   6.3.10
  para 9.13   6.3.18
  paras 9.14–9.15   6.3.11
  paras 9.16–9.20   6.3.15
  paras 9.21–9.24   6.3.16
  paras 9.25–9.26   6.3.17
  paras 9.27–9.29   6.3.19
  para 9.30   6.3.25
  paras 9.42, 9.43   4.11.2
  paras 9.44, 9.45   4.11.1
  paras 9.47–9.50   4.11.3
Code of Practice: Rights of Access: Goods, Facilities, Services and Premises
  (1996)   5.1.3
Code of Practice: Rights of Access: Goods, Facilities, Services and Premises
  (1999)   5.1.3
Code of Practice: Rights of Access: Goods, Facilities, Services and Premises
  (2002)   5.1.3, 5.5.3, 5.5.4, 5.6.6,
     9.3.5
  Ch 1   5.1.3
  Ch 2   5.1.4
  Chs 2–4   5.3.1
  paras 2.4–2.8   5.4.2
  para 2.14   5.2.1, 5.2.2
  para 2.15   5.2.4

Code of Practice: Rights of Access: Goods, Facilities, Services and Premises
(2002) – *cont*

para 2.16	5.2.8
para 2.17	5.2.4
para 2.18	5.2.1
para 2.19	5.2.1
paras 2.20–2.30	5.2.4
paras 2.31–2.35	7.1.4
paras 2.31–2.37	5.2.9
paras 2.36–2.37	8.1.2, 8.1.3
para 2.33	7.2.4
para 2.34	7.2.4, 7.2.7
para 2.36	8.5.2
paras 2.38–2.39	5.2.7
paras 2.40–2.41	5.2.6
paras 3.3–3.10	5.4.3
paras 3.3–3.13	5.4.2
paras 3.8–3.10	5.4.4
paras 3.11–3.13	5.4.9
para 3.16	5.4.9
paras 3.17–3.19	5.3.2
paras 3.20.–3.21	5.3.3
paras 3.22	5.3.4
paras 3.23	5.4.2
Chs 4, 5	5.5.3
paras 4.1–4.8	5.5.2
paras 4.13– 4.14	5.5.4
paras 4.17–4.18	5.5.4
paras 4.15–4.16	5.4.9
paras 4.19–4.20	5.5.4
paras 4.21–4.24	5.5.3
paras 4.28–4.29	5.5.3
para 4.29	5.6.3
paras 4.30–4.31	5.6.13
paras 4.32–4.33	5.5.3
para 4.34	5.5.2
paras 5.4–5.9	5.5.5, 5.5.6
para 5.3	5.5.7
para 5.6	5.5.6
paras 5.10–5.30	5.5.14
para 5.15	5.5.15
paras 5.31, 5.32	5.5.7
paras 5.33–5.35	5.5.8
paras 5.36–5.41	5.5.10
paras 5.42–5.43	5.5.8
paras 5.44–5.47	5.5.9
paras 5.48–5.52	5.5.12
paras 5.51–5.52	5.5.10
Ch 6	6.3.2
paras 6.1–6.25	5.5.11
paras 6.2–6.25	6.3.4
paras 6.9–6.11	6.3.5
para 6.11	6.3.5

Code of Practice: Rights of Access: Goods, Facilities, Services and Premises
   (2002) – *cont*

paras 6.12–6.25	6.3.6
para 6.15	5.6.9
paras 6.26–6.49	6.3.9
para 6.27–6.49	5.5.7, 5.5.8
para 6.27	6.3.20
paras 6.28–6.30	6.3.20
para 6.31	6.3.20
para 6.32–6.33	6.3.25
para 6.32	6.3.10
para 6.34–6.35	6.3.11, 6.3.26
paras 6.36–6.40	6.3.21
paras 6.41–6.46	6.3.24
para 6.47	6.3.25
paras 6.48–6.49	6.3.28
paras 7.4–7.7	5.6.1
para 7.8	5.6.4, 6.2.20
paras 7.8–7.10	5.6.5, 6.2.14
para 7.9	6.2.20
paras 7.10–7.13	5.6.7
para 7.13	5.6.3
paras 7.14–7.17	5.6.8
para 7.17	5.6.3
paras 7.18–7.20	5.6.10
para 7.20	5.6.3
paras 7.21–7.23	5.6.11
para 7.23	5.6.3
paras 7.24–7.25	5.6.12
para 7.25	5.6.13
paras 8.2–8.8	5.6.14
paras 8.9–8.13	5.6.15
paras 8.14–8.19	5.6.16
Ch 9	6.1.1
paras 9.1–9.5	6.2.1
para 9.5	6.2.14
para 9.6	6.2.13
para 9.7	6.2.8
para 9.8	6.2.10
para 9.9	6.2.10
paras 9.10–9.11	6.2.9
paras 9.12–9.13	6.2.2
para 9.14	6.2.3
para 9.15	6.2.4
paras 9.16–9.22	6.2.11
paras 9.23–9.25	6.2.5
paras 9.26–9.27	6.2.6
para 9.28	6.2.11
para 9.29	6.2.7
para 9.30	6.2.11
paras 9.31–9.34	6.2.14

Code of Practice: Rights of Access: Goods, Facilities, Services and Premises
    (2002) – *cont*
  paras 9.35–9.37   6.2.15
  paras 9.38–9.43   6.2.16
  paras 10.2–10.5   6.2.17, 10.1.6
  paras 10.6–10.7   10.2.2
  paras 10.8–10.10   10.2.4
  para 10.12   10.2.8

DfES Code of Practice on School Admissions (1999)   7.4.5
DfES Finding Out About People's Disability: A Good Practice Guide for
    Further and Higher Education Institutions (DfES/0024/2002)   7.5.12
DfES Guidance: Accessible Schools: Planning to Increase Access to Schools
    for Disabled Pupils (LEA/0168/2002)   7.4.1
DfES Guidance for LEAs and Adult Education Providers on the
    Implementation of the Disability Discrimination Act Part 4   7.5.2
DfT Code of Practice: Access to Air Travel for Disabled People (2003)   8.5.1
  para 2.14   8.5.2
DfT Conduct of Drivers, Inspectors and Conductors – A Guide for Bus and
    Coach Staff (October 2003)   8.3.8
DfT Guidance: Public Service Vehicles Accessibility Regulations 2000   8.3.3
DfT Guidance on the Public Service Vehicles (Conduct of Drivers, Inspectors,
    Conductors and Passengers) (Amendment) Regulations 2002
    (December 2002)   8.3.8
DfT Guidance: Rail Vehicle Accessibility Regulations 1998   8.4.2
Disability Discrimination Act 1995 Part 4 Code of Practice for Providers of
    Post–16 Education and Related Services (Post-16 Code of Practice)   7.5.2, 9.3.5
  Ch 1   7.5.2
  paras 1.1–1.7   7.5.2
  paras 2.1–2.6   7.5.3
  para 2.7   7.5.2
  para 2.8   7.5.2
  para 2.9   7.5.4
  para 2.17   7.5.5
  paras 3.1–3.4   7.5.2
  paras 3.9, 3.10   7.5.3
  paras 3.11–3.16   7.5.3
  para 3.14   7.5.3, 7.5.15
  para 3.17   7.5.3
  para 3.20   7.5.3
  Ch 4   7.5.6
  paras 4.3–4.10   7.5.6
  paras 4.11–4.15   7.5.3
  para 4.16   7.5.5
  paras 4.17–4.21   7.5.12
  paras 4.22–4.31   7.5.6
  Ch 5   7.5.7
  para 5.2   7.5.8
  paras 5.3, 5.4   7.5.9
  paras 5.5–5.7   7.5.8
  para 5.8   7.5.9

Disability Discrimination Act 1995 Part 4 Code of Practice for Providers of
    Post-16 Education and Related Services (Post-16 Code of Practice) – *cont*
para 5.9   7.5.8
paras 5.10–5.15   7.5.12
para 5.16   7.5.7, 7.5.13
Ch 6   7.5.10
paras 6.1–6.17   7.5.10
paras 6.18–6.20   7.5.11
Ch 7   7.5.22
paras 7.1–7.5   7.5.18
paras 7.6–7.11   7.5.23
paras 7.12–7.18   7.5.25
paras 7.19–7.25   7.5.26
paras 8.1–8.4   7.5.3, 10.1.6
paras 8.5–8.7   10.2.4
paras 8.8–8.10   10.2.2
paras 8.11–8.12   10.6.4
Ch 9   10.6.1
paras 9.3–9.4   10.6.5
para 9.5   10.6.3
para 9.6   10.6.1
Ch 10   7.5.2, 10.2.8
App 2   7.5.4
Disability Discrimination Act 1995 Part 4 Code of Practice for Schools
    (Schools Code of Practice) (2002)   7.4.1, 7.5.2, 9.3.5
paras 1.2–1.10   7.4.1
Ch 2   7.4.1
para 2.8   7.4.7
Ch 3   7.4.1
para 3.8   7.4.7
Ch 4   7.4.2, 7.4.3
paras 4.22–4.27   7.4.2
Ch 5   7.4.5
paras 5.7–5.23   7.4.5
Ch 6   7.4.6
paras 6.9–6.27   7.4.7
paras 6.28–6.34   7.4.8
paras 6.35–6.36   7.4.6
paras 7.4–7.12   7.4.10
paras 7.13–7.17   7.4.9
Ch 8   7.4.19, 10.5.10
paras 8.7–8.9   10.5.10
paras 8.10–8.12   10.5.12
Ch 9   7.4.19, 10.5.1
paras 9.9–9.10   10.5.2
para 9.11   10.5.3
paras 9.14–9.20   10.5.4
paras 9.21–9.27   10.5.5
paras 9.28–9.31   10.5.12
Ch 10   7.4.1
paras 10.1–10.6   7.4.16

Disability Discrimination Act 1995 Part 4 Code of Practice for Providers of
    Post-16 Education and Related Services (Post-16 Code of Practice) – *cont*
    paras 10.7–10.9   7.3.1
    paras 10.10–10.14   7.4.2, 10.1.6
    paras 10.15–10.19   10.2.4
    paras 10.20–10.21   10.5.11
    Ch 11   10.2.8
Disability Rights Commission *A Guide for Schools in England*   7.4.1
Disability Rights Commission *A Guide for Schools in Scotland*   7.4.1
Disability Rights Commission *Information for School Governors in England*   7.4.1
DPTAC Design of Large Passenger Ships and Passenger Infrastructure:
    Guidance on Meeting the Needs of Disabled People   8.5.1

Education and Learning Wales *Disability Across Planning* (NC/C/01/11LL)   7.5.2

Guidance on matters to be taken into account in determining questions
    relating to the definition of disability (1996)   2.1.2, 2.1.4, 2.2.1, 2.2.2, 2.4.3, 9.4.5
    Pt I, para 10 *et seq*   2.3.2
    Pt I, para 11   2.3.3
    Pt I, para 12   2.3.10
    Pt I, para 13   2.3.4
    Pt I, para 14   2.3.6
    Pt II
    Pt II, para A1   2.5.2
        paras A2–A6   2.5.3
        paras A7–A9   2.5.4, 2.5.6, 2.5.14
    Pt II, para A10   2.5.3
        paras A12, A13   2.5.16
        para A14   2.5.17
        para A17   2.5.10
    Pt II, para B1   2.6.3
    Pt II, para B2   2.6.3
    Pt II, para B3   2.5.6
    Pt II, para B4   2.5.6
        para B5   2.5.6, 2.6.3
        para B7   2.5.6, 2.6.3
        para B8   2.6.3, 2.6.4
    Pt II, para B9   2.6.5
    Pt II, para C2   2.4.5
        para C3   2.4.4, 2.4.7
        paras C5–C21   2.5.1
        paras C6–C7   2.4.2
        paras C14–C21   2.4.1

Law Society – Solicitors' Anti–Discrimination Rules 2004   4.8.1
Learning and Skills Council *Special Educational Needs and Disability Act 2001*
    (Equality and Diversity Guidance 02/2002)   7.5.2

Strategic Rail Authority: Guidance on Disabled Persons' Protection Policies
　　(April 2002)　　　　　8.4.1
Strategic Rail Authority: Train and Station Services for Disabled Passengers: A
　　Code of Practice (February 2002)　　　　　8.4.1

Welsh Office: School Admissions Code of Practice (1999)　　　　　7.4.5

TABLE OF EUROPEAN, UN AND INTERNATIONAL LEGISLATION

References are to paragraph numbers.

EC Employment Framework Directive 2000/78/EC – establishing a general
    framework for equal treatment in employment and education, OJ (2000)
    L303/16 1.2.2, 3.1.2, 3.1.2, 3.1.3, 3.2.43, 3.2.51, 4.1.1, 4.4.1, 4.10.2, 9.2.1, 10.3.20

Art 1	3.1.2
Art 2(1)	3.2.36, 3.2.42
(2)(a)	3.2.36
(b)	3.2.42
(i), (ii)	3.2.42
(3)	3.3.1
(4)	3.7.1
Art 3(1)	4.1.1
(4)	4.1.1
Art 5	3.2.42
Art 7(1)	3.2.24
Art 10	3.2.6, 10.3.20

EC Race Directive 2000/43/EC – implementing the principle of equal
    treatment between persons irrespective of racial or ethnic origin, OJ
    (2000) L180   9.2.1

EC Treaty (Treaty of Rome)

Art 13	1.2.2

European Convention for the Protection of Human Rights and Fundamental
    Freedoms 1950

Art 6	2.1.4
Art 8	2.1.4, 3.2.30
Art 14	3.2.30
First Protocol, Art 1	3.2.30

TABLE OF ABBREVIATIONS

1994 Green Paper	*A Consultation on Government Measures to Tackle Discrimination Against Disabled People* (July 1994)
1995 White Paper	*Ending Discrimination Against Disabled People,* Cm 2729 (January 1995)
ACAS	Advisory, Conciliation and Arbitration Service
CEHR	Commission for Equality and Human Rights
CRE	Commission for Racial Equality
DARAS	Disability Access Rights Advisory Service
DDA 1995	Disability Discrimination Act 1995
DPTAC	Disabled Persons' Transport Advisory Committee
DRC	Disability Rights Commission
DRCA 1999	Disability Rights Commission Act 1999
DRTF	Disability Rights Task Force
DRTF Report	*From Exclusion to Inclusion: A Report of the Disability Rights Task Force for Disabled People* (1999, London: DfEE)
EA 2002	Employment Act 2002
EAT	Employment Appeal Tribunal
EC Framework Employment Directive	Council Directive 2000/78/EC of 27 November 2000, establishing a general framework for equal treatment in employment and occupation
ECHR	European Convention for the Protection of Human Rights and Fundamental Freedoms 1950
Employment Code of Practice	*Code of practice for the elimination of discrimination in the field of employment against disabled persons or persons who have a disability* (1996, London: HMSO)
EOC	Equal Opportunities Commission
ERA 1996	Employment Rights Act 1996
ERA 1999	Employment Relations Act 1999
ETA 1996	Employment Tribunals Act 1996
EU	European Union
FEFCE	Further Education Funding Council for England

FEFCs	further education funding councils
GMC	General Medical Council
Government Response to DRTF Report	*Towards Inclusion – Civil Rights for Disabled People: Government Response to the Disability Rights Task Force* (2001, London: DfEE)
Guidance	*Guidance on matters to be taken into account in determining questions relating to the definition of disability* (1996, London: HMSO)
HEFCE	Higher Education Funding Council for England
HEFCW	Higher Education Funding Council for Wales
ILO	International Labour Organization
LEA	local education authority
NACEDP	National Advisory Council on the Employment of Disabled People
NDC	National Disability Council
NIDC	Northern Ireland Disability Council
Post-16 Code of Practice	*Disability Discrimination Act 1995 Part 4 Code of Practice for Providers of Post-16 Education and Related Services* (2002: Disability Rights Commission)
PSV	public service vehicle
Rights of Access Code of Practice 2002	*Code of Practice: Rights of Access: Goods, Facilities, Services and Premises* (2002, London: HMSO)
RRA 1976	Race Relations Act 1976
Schools Code of Practice	*Disability Discrimination Act 1995 Part 4 Code of Practice for Schools* (2002: Disability Rights Commission)
SDA 1975	Sex Discrimination Act 1975
SEN	special educational needs
SENDA 2001	Special Educational Needs and Disability Act 2001
SENDIST	Special Educational Needs and Disability Tribunal
SHEFC	Scottish Higher Education Funding Council
TULR(C)A 1992	Trade Union and Labour Relations (Consolidation) Act 1992
UN	United Nations
WHO	World Health Organization

Chapter 1

INTRODUCTION

1.1 INTRODUCTION

1.1.1 It is now a decade since the Disability Discrimination Act 1995 (DDA 1995) received the Royal Assent. In the nearly nine years since the first provisions of the Act were brought into force, it has begun, slowly but surely, to provide disabled people in the UK with legal processes and remedies to challenge disability discrimination. There is no general agreement on the size of the population of disabled persons in the UK, although the Disability Rights Commission (DRC) presently estimates it at approximately 10 million persons – more than one in five of the general population. Research has long-established evidence that disabled people face discrimination and barriers to equal participation and opportunity in education, employment, health and social services, housing, transport, the built environment, leisure and social activities, and civic rights.[1]

1.1.2 The Employers' Forum on Disability, extrapolating from a variety of sources, estimates that there are approximately 8.6 million disabled people in the UK covered by the DDA 1995 (about 15 per cent of the population).[2] As it notes, most disabled people acquire their disability during or after their working life, and over 5.5 million disabled people are of working age (about 16 per cent of the working population). In contrast, only 50 per cent of disabled people of working age are in employment compared to 87 per cent of non-disabled people of working age, while disabled people are nearly five times as likely as non-disabled people to be out of work and claiming benefits. Of the 2.8 million disabled people on state benefits and not in work, nearly a million would like to work. The stereotypical image of the disabled person is the wheelchair-user, yet fewer than 8 per cent of disabled

---

1   See the references in previous editions of this book. I have reduced or eliminated the contextual, comparative and international material in this chapter in this edition, in order to make space for the enlarged commentary of the DDA 1995 that follows in subsequent chapters.

2   I acknowledge the source of this paragraph as *www.employers-forum.co.uk.*

people use wheelchairs. At least one in four customers either has a disability or is close to someone who is disabled. The estimated annual purchasing power of people with disabilities is £40–£50 billion.

1.2 DISABILITY DISCRIMINATION ACT 1995

1.2.1 Moving the Third Reading of the Disability Discrimination Bill in the House of Commons on 28 March 1995,[1] the then Minister for Social Security and Disabled People, Mr William Hague, claimed:

> 'It is a landmark Bill. It is the only comprehensive Bill for disabled people ever introduced by a British Government. It will mark the United Kingdom out as one of the world leaders and the leader in Europe in the move towards comprehensive anti-discrimination legislation for disabled people. It is a profound measure with significant implications for every part of the economy …. It sets this country on a clear, workable and unambiguous course to ending discrimination against disabled people. It will make a genuine difference to the opportunities and lives of millions of our fellow citizens …'[2]

A decade, and a change of government, later, the DDA 1995 – as amended on more than one occasion – remains the foundation stone of disability discrimination law.

1.2.2 The present Labour Government promised comprehensive civil rights legislation for disabled people and established the Disability Rights Task Force to examine the question. It reported in December 1999 and received a mainly positive response from the Government.[3]

---

1   The complete legislative history of the Bill is as follows. House of Commons: 1st Reading (12 January 1995); 2nd Reading (24 January 1995: HC Deb, vol 253, cols 147–239); Committee (31 January 1995–28 February 1995: HC Deb, Standing Committee E); Report (27 and 28 March 1995: HC Deb, vol 257, cols 697–799 and 840–904); 3rd Reading (28 March 1995: HC Deb, vol 257, cols 904–928). House of Lords: 1st Reading (29 March 1995); 2nd Reading (22 May 1995: HL Deb, vol 564, cols 800–815 and 830–892); Committee (13, 15 and 27 June 1995: HL Deb, vol 564, cols 1640–1718, 1723–1784, 1895–1954 and 1975–2054; HL Deb, vol 565, cols 608–680 and 686–744); Report (18 and 20 July 1995: HL Deb, vol 566, cols 114–141, 168–186, 205–280 and 386–476); 3rd Reading (24 October 1995: HL Deb, vol 566, cols 969–1080). The Bill, as amended, was further considered by the House of Commons (31 October 1995: HC Deb, vol 265, cols 109–179) and the House of Lords (6 November 1995: HL Deb, vol 566, cols 1581–1602). The Bill received Royal Assent on 8 November 1995.

2   HC Deb, vol 257, cols 904 and 928; HL Deb, vol 566, col 1070. The Bill had been preceded by a Green Paper and a White Paper: *A Consultation on Government Measures to Tackle Discrimination Against Disabled People* (1994, London: Department of Social Security); *Ending Discrimination Against Disabled People*, Cm 2729 (1995, London: HMSO).

3   Disability Rights Task Force, *From Exclusion to Inclusion: A Report of the Disability Rights Task Force on Civil Rights for Disabled People* (1999, London: DfEE); Better Regulation Task Force, *Anti-Discrimination Legislation* (May 1999); *Interim Government Response to the Report of the Disability Rights Task Force* (March 2000, DfEE); *Towards Inclusion – Civil Rights for Disabled People: Government Response to the Disability Rights Task Force* (March 2001, DfEE).

As a result, the DDA 1995 has been extensively amended by the Disability Rights Commission Act 1999 (DRCA 1999), the Special Educational Needs and Disability Act 2001 and the Disability Discrimination Act 1995 (Amendment) Regulations 2003.[1] This last enactment is a result of the requirement to amend the provisions of the DDA 1995 in the employment field in order to comply with the EC Framework Employment Directive.[2]

1.3 SCOPE AND EXTENT

1.3.1 With the exception of some of the provisions on public transport and education, the DDA 1995 (as amended) is largely in force. Part 1 of the DDA 1995 defines the meanings of 'disability' and 'disabled person' and is dealt with in Chapter 2. Part 2 deals with discrimination and harassment in the employment field. This is addressed in Chapters 3 and 4. Part 3 deals with disability discrimination in relation to goods, facilities and services, and is described in Chapter 5. Part 3 also addresses the disposal and management of premises. These sections, together with the provisions on leases and adjustments to buildings, are considered in Chapter 6. Education is dealt with in Part 4 of the Act (see Chapter 7). The Part 5 measures on public transport are examined in Chapter 8. The institutional framework that supports the Act (not least the DRC) is surveyed in Chapter 9, while general questions of liability and remedies are approached in Chapter 10.

1.4 NORTHERN IRELAND

1.4.1 The DDA 1995 is expressed to apply only to England, Wales and Scotland. However, its provisions also extend to Northern Ireland, with

---

1   SI 2003/1673, made under the European Communities Act 1972, s 2(2). In Northern Ireland, see Disability Discrimination Act 1995 (Amendment) (Northern Ireland) Regulations 2004, SR 2004/55. See also *(Draft) Disability Discrimination Act 1995 (Amendment) Regulations 2003 Explanatory Notes and Supplementary Questions* (2002, Department for Work and Pensions).

2   2000/78/EC made under the EC Treaty, art 13 (as amended). See *Towards Equality and Diversity: Implementing the Employment and Race Directives: Consultation Document* (Cabinet Office, 2001); *Equality and Diversity – The Way Ahead* (2002, Department of Trade and Industry).

certain modifications and exceptions.[1] The application of the DDA 1995 in Northern Ireland has effect to the extent of and subject to the textual modifications set out in Sch 8 to the Act.[2] Where appropriate, these are indicated in the text.[3]

1.5 DISABILITY DISCRIMINATION BILL

1.5.1 In December 2003, the Government published the *Draft Disability Discrimination Bill* for general consultation.[4] The Draft Bill was subject to scrutiny by a joint parliamentary committee, which reported in April 2004 and to which the Government responded in July 2004.[5] That process has led to the Disability Discrimination Bill, which has been considerably re-drafted and expanded. It was given its First Reading in the House of Lords on 25 November 2004.[6] At the time of writing, it is not certain whether the Bill will complete its parliamentary progress in time for the likely General Election some time in 2005. If it does not, it is possible (but not guaranteed) that it will be held over to the new Parliament. The Bill's proposals are summarised here, but are given relatively more consideration in the relevant chapters that follow.

1.5.2 If enacted, the Bill will bring councillors and members of the Greater London Authority within the scope of Part 2 of the DDA 1995. Subject to some exceptions, it will ensure that functions of public authorities not already covered by Part 3 of the Act are brought within its scope. It would become unlawful for a public authority to discriminate against a disabled person without justification when exercising its functions. A new duty would be placed on public authorities, requiring them to have due regard to the need to eliminate unlawful discrimination against (and harassment of) disabled persons when exercising their functions. Public authorities will also be required to promote equality of opportunity between disabled persons and others. The Act

---

1   DDA 1995, s 70(6).

2   DDA 1995, Sch 8, as amended by Northern Ireland Act 1998, Sch 13, para 16.

3   Note the effect of the Departments (Northern Ireland) Order 1999, SI 1999/283, and the Departments (Transfer and Assignment of Functions) Order (Northern Ireland) 1999, SR 1999/481. This is reflected in the text.

4   Department for Work and Pensions, *Draft Disability Discrimination Bill*, Cm 6058 (December 2003); *Explanatory Notes* Cm 6058-ii; *Draft Regulatory Impact Assessment*, Cm 6058-iii; *Draft Disability Discrimination Bill Clause 15: Relationships Between Locally-electable Authorities and their Members*, Cm 6126 (February 2004).

5   Joint Committee on the Draft Disability Discrimination Bill, *First Report* (April 2004); Department for Work and Pensions, *The Government's Response to the Report of the Joint Committee on the Draft Disability Discrimination Bill*, Cm 6276 (July 2004).

6   HL Bill 6 of 2004–2005. See also the Explanatory Notes to the Bill upon which this account draws: HL Bill 6-EN.

would also be amended to clarify who is the correct defendant in the case of a claim of discrimination being made against a police officer under Part 3 of the DDA 1995 and to authorise payment of compensation from the police fund in relation to such a claim.

1.5.3 By far the largest reforms made to the DDA 1995 by the Bill concern the transport provisions. This will affect both Part 3 and Part 5 of the Act. So far as Part 3 is concerned, the current exemption for transport services from the anti-discrimination provisions dealing with the provision of goods, facilities and services to the public will be clarified and narrowed. It will be made clear that the exemption extends only to transport vehicles themselves, and a power would be created to enable that exemption to be lifted for different vehicles at different times. The Chronically Sick and Disabled Persons Act 1970 will be amended so as to provide for the recognition in England and Wales of disabled persons' parking badges issued outside Great Britain.

1.5.4 In Part 5, the definition of 'rail vehicle' will be amended to enable rail vehicle accessibility regulations to be applied to all rail vehicles. This will also enable the regulations to be applied to the refurbishment of all rail vehicles. The amendment would further clarify and extend the current power to grant exemptions from the requirements and would simplify the exemption process. The Bill seeks to introduce new provisions requiring rail vehicle accessibility compliance certificates to be obtained for prescribed rail vehicles. It will also replace the existing criminal offence for the use of a rail vehicle which does not conform to the rail vehicle accessibility regulations with a civil enforcement system. The Bill sets out the procedure for imposing civil penalties, including a right of appeal to a court.

1.5.5 In Part 2, the Bill proposes to amend the new provisions on discriminatory advertisements, with the result that liability would also be imposed on a third party who publishes a discriminatory advertisement, as well as the person placing the advertisement. The Act's provisions as they affect group insurance arrangements are also in line for amendment.

1.5.6 Important changes are made to Part 3 so as to bring within its scope private clubs with 25 or more members. The Bill will also impose on landlords (and others who manage rented premises) a duty to provide reasonable adjustments and will confer a power to modify or end the current small-dwellings exemption. It will also become unlawful for general qualifications bodies to discriminate against disabled persons in relation to the award of prescribed qualifications. A procedure for questions and replies will be extended to Part 3 claims (and not just claims under Part 2, as at present).

1.5.7 The definition of 'disability' in Part 1 in respect of people with mental illnesses will be amended so as to deem people with HIV infection, multiple sclerosis or cancer to be disabled for the purposes of the DDA 1995 and to clarify that there is no implied limitation to the scope of the regulation-making power which enables people to be deemed to be disabled. The Bill also makes numerous minor and consequential amendments and repeals throughout the Act.

Chapter 2

DISABILITY AND DISABLED PERSON

2.1 INTRODUCTION

2.1.1 The twin concepts of 'disability' and 'disabled person' are central to the operation of disability discrimination law. These are the terms that determine who has rights and expectations under the DDA 1995. Only someone who can satisfy the definition of a disabled person within the meaning of the legislation can enjoy the protection of its framework. This will often be treated as an issue to be determined at a preliminary hearing.[1]

2.1.2 Part 1 of the DDA 1995 (ss 1–3) and Schs 1 and 2 to the Act furnish definitions of 'disability' and 'disabled person' for the purposes of the statute. A 'disabled person' is defined as 'a person who has a disability'.[2] A person has a disability if he or she has a physical or mental impairment which has a substantial and long-term adverse effect on his or her ability to carry out normal day-to-day activities.[3] These provisions are supplemented by regulations[4] and by the statutory guidance issued by the Secretary of State under s 3 (referred to hereafter as the 'Guidance').[5] The Guidance does not impose any legal obligations in itself and is not designed to be an authoritative statement of law. Nevertheless, an employment tribunal or court is required to take

---

1 *Greenwood v British Airways plc* [1999] IRLR 600, EAT. In employment cases, application may be made to the Employment Tribunals Service for funding a medical report addressing the preliminary issue.

2 DDA 1995, s 1(2).

3 Ibid, s 1(1). Note that the definition is also extended to include persons who had such a disability in the past (s 2 and Sch 2, as amended by the Disability Discrimination Act 1995 (Amendment) Regulations 2003, SI 2003/1673). See **2.8**.

4 Disability Discrimination (Meaning of Disability) Regulations 1996, SI 1996/1455, which came into force on 30 July 1996 and were made under the authority of Sch 1, paras 1(2), 2(4), 3(2)–(3), 4(2)(a) and 5(a). See also the Disability Discrimination (Meaning of Disability) Regulations (Northern Ireland) 1996, SR 1996/421.

5 *Guidance on Matters to be Taken into Account in Determining Questions Relating to the Definition of Disability* (1996, London: HMSO). A separate edition of the Guidance has been issued in Northern Ireland.

account of the Guidance, where relevant, when determining certain questions arising from the statutory definition of disability.[1] The Guidance is likely to be of assistance in marginal cases. It is not to be used in a literal fashion to reach conclusions that overturn the obvious impression of someone as being disabled within the meaning of the Act.[2]

2.1.3 Considerable care must be exercised in any attempt to use existing definitions of disability employed in other legal contexts (such as social welfare or social security law) as a means of identifying disabled persons protected under the DDA 1995. In order to enjoy protection from disability discrimination, claimants must bring themselves fairly and squarely within the definitional provisions of the 1995 legislation and the statutory guidance. However, with that necessary caveat, it is likely that many (but not all) individuals who satisfy the definition of disability or disabled person in other statutory contexts will be able to do so under disability discrimination law. Indeed, in one particular case – that of a person registered as disabled under the Disabled Persons (Employment) Act 1944 at specified times – there was a deeming provision by which the existing status of an individual as a legally recognised disabled person was preserved for that purpose.[3] In any event, the fact that a person has been assessed as disabled for some other statutory purpose may be relevant evidence to be taken into account as part of the evidence that the person is disabled for the purposes of the DDA 1995. It is then a question of the weight to be attached to that evidence.[4]

2.1.4 The burden of proof that a claimant was a disabled person at the time of the alleged act of discrimination lies with the claimant on the conventional balance of probabilities.[5] A claimant in tribunal or court proceedings under the DDA 1995 will be expected to lead evidence

---

1   See s 3(3), and *Goodwin v The Patent Office* [1999] IRLR 4, EAT. As to the legal status of the Guidance, see **9.4**.

2   *Vicary v British Telecommunications plc* [1999] IRLR 680, EAT; *Leonard v Southern Derbyshire Chamber of Commerce* [2001] IRLR 19, EAT.

3   DDA 1995, Sch 1, para 7. See **2.7**.

4   *Abadeh v British Telecommunications plc* [2001] IRLR 23, EAT (the fact that a medical appeal tribunal had assessed the person as having an 18 per cent disablement for the purposes of statutory benefits could not be disregarded as wholly irrelevant in determining whether that person was disabled under the DDA 1995).

5   *Morgan v Staffordshire University* [2002] IRLR 190, EAT. While a tribunal or court cannot order a claimant to disclose his or her medical records, it can order that the claimant consent to such disclosure. If the claimant fails to do so, the tribunal or court might stay the proceedings or strike them out. To do so would not offend the right to privacy under Art 8 of the European Convention on Human Rights when balanced against the respondent's right to a fair trial under Art 6: *Hanlon v Kirkless Metropolitan Council* EAT 0119/04 (IDS Brief 767).

which relates to his or her status at the time of the events which have given rise to the complaint. This is a question of fact. Provided the tribunal or court directs itself carefully as to the statutory definition, considers the Guidance, and weighs the evidence appropriately, it is unlikely that its decision on this question will be interfered with on appeal, unless on grounds of perversity.[1] However, a tribunal (or court) cannot simply ignore uncontested medical evidence, unless it rejects the evidence on the basis of which the medical opinion has been formed or where it is clear that the medical witness has misunderstood that evidence.[2] On the other hand, it is not the task of the medical expert to tell the tribunal (or court) whether the claimant satisfies the statutory definition. That is a matter for the tribunal (or court) to decide in the light of the medical evidence.[3] Equally, it is inadvisable for a tribunal to conduct its own tests of the status or extent of an applicant's disability.[4] Knowledge of the disability by the respondent or defendant is not an ingredient of the test of whether there is a disability or not.[5]

2.2 MEANING OF 'DISABILITY' AND 'DISABLED PERSON'

2.2.1 As already noted, a 'disabled person' is a person who has a 'disability'. A person has a 'disability' if he or she has a physical or mental impairment which has a substantial and long-term adverse effect on his or her ability to carry out normal day-to-day activities.[6] It might be useful to take account of what the legislature hoped to achieve in defining the protected class in this way. The apparent intention was to create a common-sense definition which fitted the generally accepted perception of what is a disability and who is a disabled person, and which provided certainty and avoided vagueness.[7] It was thought that the

---

1   See *Quinlan v B & Q plc* [1999] Disc LR 76, EAT, and *Foster v Hampshire Fire and Rescue Service* (1998) 43 BMLR 186, EAT.

2   *Kapadia v London Borough of Lambeth* [2000] IRLR 14, EAT, and [2000] IRLR 699, CA. Once a claimant consents to a medical examination in the course of litigation no further consent is required for the resultant medical report to be disclosed as part of the proceedings.

3   *Abadeh v British Telecommunications plc* [2001] IRLR 23, EAT. The medical report should address the medical diagnosis of the impairment, the expert's observations of the person carrying out normal day-to-day activities (and the ease with which the person is able to perform those functions), together with any relevant opinion as to prognosis and the effect of medication.

4   *London Underground Ltd v Bragg* (1999) EAT/847/98.

5   *Barker v Westbridge International Ltd* (2000) EAT/1180/98.

6   DDA 1995, s 1 (subject to the provisions of Sch 1, the statutory guidance and the Disability Discrimination (Meaning of Disability) Regulations 1996, SI 1996/1455).

7   HC Deb Standing Committee E, col 73. However, tribunals and courts must be aware that a relatively small proportion of disabled people are visibly disabled and should avoid

definition, and the legislation which it underpins, would not be credible if it embraced individuals who were not fairly or generally recognised as disabled. The government of the day believed that the definition would cover the vast majority of the 6.5 million disabled persons in Britain identified by the 1988 Office of Population Census and Surveys report.[1]

2.2.2   The Employment Appeal Tribunal (EAT) in *Goodwin v The Patent Office*[2] has set out the correct approach to the question of whether a claimant is a disabled person within the meaning of the DDA 1995. This is a decision equally relevant in non-employment cases. The tribunal (or court) should look carefully at what the parties say in the documents setting out the claim and the defence. Whether the issue of disability is in contention should be identified before the hearing. Standard directions or a case management hearing will often be appropriate. Where expert evidence is to be called, advance notice should be given to the other party and a copy of any expert report provided.[3] Above all, the tribunal (or court) should adopt an inquisitorial or interventionist approach to the question of disability,[4] while a purposive approach to the construction of the statute should be taken so as to construe the language of the Act in a way which gives effect to Parliament's intention. Explicit reference should always be made to any relevant provision of the Guidance or the relevant Code of Practice, but

---

approaching this issue with a stereotypical image of a disabled person as someone who uses a wheelchair or has severely impaired mobility: *Vicary v British Telecommunications* [1999] IRLR 680, EAT.

1   Martin, Meltzer and Elliott, *The Prevalence of Disability Among Adults: OPCS Surveys of Disability in Great Britain Report 1* (1988, London: HMSO). More recently, it has been estimated that approximately 11.7 million adults (20 per cent of the population) are covered by the Act: Whitfield, *The Disability Discrimination Act: Analysis of Data from an Omnibus Survey* (1997, London: Department of Social Security). See further the Disability Rights Commission's Disability Briefing at *www.drc-gb.org/drc* (Information and Legislation) and the statistical overview prepared by the Employers' Forum on Disability at *www.employers-forum.co.uk* (Information).

2   [1999] IRLR 4, EAT.

3   In employment cases, see the judicial guidance on the use of expert evidence provided in *De Keyser v Wilson* [2001] IRLR 324, EAT. See further *Morgan v Staffordshire University* [2002] IRLR 190, EAT. In non-employment proceedings, account will be taken of Civil Procedure Rules 1998 (CPR 1998), Part 35 and the associated Practice Direction on expert evidence.

4   This has been interpreted as meaning that the tribunal is obliged to conduct the hearing in a fair and balanced manner, intervening and making its own inquiries of the parties and witnesses in the course of the hearing as it considers appropriate: *Rugamer v Sony Music Entertainment UK Ltd; McNicol v Balfour Beatty Rail Maintenance Ltd* [2001] IRLR 644, EAT; upheld on appeal, *McNicol v Balfour Beatty Rail Maintenance Ltd* [2002] EWCA Civ 1074, [2002] IRLR 711, CA (the Court of Appeal rejecting a contention that the tribunal should take a more inquisitorial and proactive role other than to adjudicate on the issues of fact and law). It is not its duty to conduct a free-standing inquiry of its own or to attempt to obtain further evidence beyond that adduced by the parties. Its inquisitorial role is limited to the consideration of the issues raised by the parties. See also *Morgan v Staffordshire*

without creating an extra hurdle over which the claimant must jump. The tribunal (or court) should look at the evidence by reference to four different conditions:

(1) Does the claimant have an impairment?
(2) Does it have an adverse effect on the ability to carry out normal day-to-day activities?
(3) Is the adverse effect substantial?
(4) Is the adverse effect long-term?

Each of these elements of the definition of disability is considered in turn below.

2.3 IMPAIRMENT

2.3.1 The term 'impairment' is vital to an understanding of the concept of disability. Yet it is not defined in the legislation. A literal interpretation of the word would suggest a condition of weakness, injury or damage, but the term has a more precise meaning in medical circles. The World Health Organization (WHO) 1980 classification of impairment, disability and handicap defined impairment as 'any loss or abnormality of psychological, physiological, or anatomical structure or function'.[1] The tenor of the parliamentary debates on the DDA 1995 suggests that the intention was to base the framework of disability discrimination law upon a medical model of disability. In that regard, the WHO definition may be a helpful one (although not necessarily one that would be embraced by disabled people themselves).

2.3.2 The Guidance anticipates that in many cases there will be no dispute over whether or not a person has an impairment. It makes clear that the question of how an impairment was caused is not a relevant consideration. However, the Guidance does not go any further in explaining the term 'impairment'.[2]

University [2002] IRLR 190, EAT; *Woodrup v London Borough of Southwark* [2002] EWCA Civ 1716, [2003] IRLR 111, CA.

1 World Health Organization, *International Classification of Impairments, Disabilities and Handicaps: A Manual of Classification Relating to the Consequences of Disease* (1980, Geneva: WHO). This has now been revised and superseded by WHO, *International Classification of Functioning, Disability and Health* (2001, Geneva: WHO), which gives greater recognition to the social and environmental model of disability. It complements the ICD-10: WHO, *International Statistical Classification of Diseases and Related Health Problems* (10th Revision) (1990, Geneva: WHO).

2 Guidance, Part I, para 10 et seq. Note that an impairment includes one which is controlled or corrected by medical treatment, medication, prosthesis, auxiliary devices or other aids: DDA 1995, Sch 1, para 6. See **2.5.12** et seq. The Court of Appeal has held that the term 'impairment' should be given its ordinary and natural meaning: *McNicol v Balfour Beatty*

Physical impairment

2.3.3 The term 'physical impairment' is also not defined or further explained in the DDA 1995.[1] However, an addiction to (including dependency upon) alcohol, nicotine or any other substance does not amount to an impairment for the purposes of the Act.[2] That does not prevent, for example, liver disease resulting from alcohol dependency or abuse from counting as an impairment, even though alcoholism itself would not be so treated.[3] This exclusion also does not prevent an addiction which was originally the result of administration of medically prescribed drugs or other medical treatment from amounting to an impairment, all other things being equal.[4] So, for example, an addiction to pain-killers, to sedatives or to a mood-altering drug may amount to an impairment provided that the drug in question was *medically prescribed* and not simply bought over-the-counter without prescription or otherwise acquired. Seasonal allergic rhinitis (a form of severe hay fever) is also treated as not amounting to an impairment.[5] In this case, however, account might be taken of the condition so far as it aggravates the effect of another condition which does amount to an impairment (for example, a breathing impairment, such as asthma).[6]

Rail Maintenance Ltd [2002] EWCA Civ 1074, [2002] IRLR 711 (noting that an impairment may result from or consist of an illness and that it is not necessary to consider how the impairment has been caused).

1 Although note that the Act treats a severe disfigurement as a relevant impairment in defined circumstances (see Sch 1, para 3 and the more detailed discussion of this provision at **2.5.10**). Many commonly accepted conditions (such as orthopaedic impairments, cerebral palsy, epilepsy, muscular dystrophy, multiple sclerosis, cancer, heart disease, diabetes and tuberculosis) will almost invariably qualify as impairments.

2 Disability Discrimination (Meaning of Disability) Regulations 1996, SI 1996/1455, regs 2 and 3(1), made under DDA 1995, Sch 1, para 1(2)(a) and (3). This regulation-making power provides flexibility to deal with future medical developments and to resolve problems of interpretation that arise through case-law or medically disputed or controversial conditions: HC Deb Standing Committee E, cols 105 and 109.

3 Guidance, Part I, para 11. See *Power v Panasonic UK Ltd* [2003] IRLR 151, EAT (depression caused by alcoholism capable of amounting to a disability).

4 Disability Discrimination (Meaning of Disability) Regulations 1996, SI 1996/1455, reg 3(2).

5 Ibid, reg 4(2).

6 Ibid, reg 4(3).

Mental impairment

2.3.4 The term 'mental impairment' is only partly defined in the DDA 1995 and then not in a particularly helpful way.[1] The Guidance is of little further assistance, indicating that the term refers to 'a wide range of impairments relating to mental functioning, including what are often known as learning disabilities (formerly known as "mental handicap")'.[2] Clearly, it is intended that learning, psychiatric and psychological impairments are to be included,[3] but regulation-making powers have been used to exclude certain anti-social disorders and addictions.[4] To that end, the conditions of a tendency to set fires, to steal or to physical or sexual abuse of other persons, together with the conditions of exhibitionism and voyeurism, are treated as not amounting to impairments.[5]

2.3.5 A mental impairment *includes* 'an impairment resulting from or consisting of a mental illness' – but only if 'the illness is a *clinically well-recognised* illness'.[6] What amounts to a clinically well-recognised illness will be a question of fact for the decision of a tribunal or court. This will clearly call for expert medical evidence in tribunal or court proceedings where there is any doubt about whether or not an apparent mental illness is well-recognised by medical opinion. In difficult cases, tribunals may be called upon to choose between opposing medical expert evidence. Clearly, merely *some* degree of recognition in *some* quarters of medical opinion will not be sufficient. General medical recognition of the condition as a mental illness will be called for and there is room for lengthy medical and legal dispute about whether a claimant is clinically mentally impaired.

2.3.6 The EAT in *Goodwin v The Patent Office* recommended that, where there is doubt as to whether a mental illness counts as a disability or not, reference should be made to the WHO *International Classification*

---

1   See DDA 1995, Sch 1, para 1(1) discussed below.

2   Guidance, Part I, para 13.

3   Although, as already noted, addiction to alcohol, nicotine or any other substance has been excluded (whether this amounts to a mental or a physical impairment). See **2.3.3**.

4   HC Deb Standing Committee E, cols 72 and 105.

5   Disability Discrimination (Meaning of Disability) Regulations 1996, SI 1996/1455, reg 4(1), made under DDA 1995, Sch 1, para 1(2)–(3). See HC Deb Standing Committee E, col 109. However, in *Murray v Newham Citizens Advice Bureau Ltd* [2003] IRLR 340, the EAT held that a person with a past history of violence resulting from paranoid schizophrenia was a disabled person within the DDA 1995, even though a tendency to violence was an excluded condition. It held that the tendency to violence was a consequence of a recognised illness and thus a manifestation of a disability, rather than a free-standing condition as contemplated by the exclusion in the regulations.

6   DDA 1995, Sch 1, para 1(1) (emphasis added).

of Diseases.[1] Another division of the EAT has gone further in *Morgan v Staffordshire University.*[2] In ruling that simple references to 'anxiety', 'stress' and 'depression' in an applicant's medical notes did not amount to proof of a mental impairment under the DDA 1995,[3] the EAT set out the possible ways of establishing proof of the existence of a mental impairment by reference to:

(1) a mental illness specifically mentioned as such in the WHO classification;

(2) a mental illness referred to in some other classification of very wide professional acceptance;

(3) a mental illness[4] otherwise recognised by a respected body of medical opinion;

(4) substantial and specific medical evidence of a mental impairment which neither results from nor consists of a mental illness.

It then goes on to make a number of useful observations about the approach to be taken by parties and a tribunal when addressing a claim to be disabled by reference to a mental impairment.[5] Those observations are not reproduced here.

2.3.7   The definition of 'mental impairment' used in the DDA 1995 is not the same as that used in other mental health legislation.[6] The fact that an impairment would be a mental impairment for other purposes does not prevent it from being a mental impairment under the Act, but it is not to be treated as automatically so. Nevertheless, mental impairments (including learning disabilities) that are not mental illnesses are covered by the disability discrimination legislation. Similarly, persons with recognised mental illnesses are treated as disabled persons under the DDA 1995. This will include individuals experiencing schizophrenia, manic depression, severe and extended depressive psychoses and a range of other conditions recognised by clinical psychiatrists and psychologists. However, the Act is not intended to cover 'moods or mild eccentricities', 'obscure conditions unrecognised by reputable clinicians' and 'mild or tendentious' conditions. At the same time, 'arrested or incomplete development of the mind, psychopathic disorder and any other disorder or disability of mind' do fall

---

1   [1999] IRLR 4, EAT. See also Guidance, Part I, para 14 to the same effect.

2   [2002] IRLR 190, EAT.

3   For example, 'clinical depression' (without further detail) is not a recognised WHO classification of mental illness.

4   Both the law report and the original judgment use the term 'medical illness' but it is suggested that that is a simple typographical error.

5   [2002] IRLR 190 at para 20.

6   DDA 1995, s 68(1). See eg Mental Health Act 1983, s 1(2).

within the DDA 1995's definition of mental impairment, provided they are conditions which have attracted clinical recognition,[1] and unless otherwise excluded by regulation.[2]

Physical impairment or mental impairment?

2.3.8 Just as the term 'impairment' is not defined, the distinction between a physical and a mental impairment might not always be clear. In two cases,[3] the applicants relied upon a condition described in medical terms as 'functional or psychological overlay'. The applicants claimed to have a physical injury. The medical evidence suggested that their symptoms were not the manifestation of any organic physical pathology, but were a manifestation of each individual's psychological state. In both cases, the applicants relied upon a physical impairment (rather than mental impairment) as the basis of their claim to be disabled persons. The EAT held that functional or psychological overlay was not a physical impairment for the purposes of the DDA 1995. In the EAT's view, the dividing line between physical and mental impairment depended upon whether the nature of the impairment was physical or mental. The distinction did not depend upon whether a physical or mental function or activity was affected. As there was no evidence in the cases that the applicants had a clinically well-recognised illness, and as they had not relied upon a mental impairment in any event, their cases could not succeed. In contrast, in a later case,[4] the applicant claimed to have experienced slow, progressive muscle weakness and wasting. The medical evidence suggested that there was no organic disease process causing the symptoms described. The applicant did not rely upon a mental impairment. The EAT held that an employment tribunal was entitled to conclude that the applicant had a physical impairment. There was no requirement to draw a distinction between an underlying fault, shortcoming or defect of or in the body and evidence of the manifestations or effects thereof. The Act contemplated that an impairment can be something that results from an illness as opposed to

---

1   HC Deb Standing Committee E, cols 103–105.

2   See **2.3.3**.

3   *Rugamer v Sony Music Entertainment UK Ltd; McNicol v Balfour Beatty Rail Maintenance Ltd* [2001] IRLR 644, EAT. The decision is a controversial one as it appears to require an applicant to prove the cause of the impairment, thus adding an additional hurdle to the test of disability. The decision has been upheld on appeal: *McNicol v Balfour Beatty Rail Maintenance Ltd* [2002] EWCA Civ 1074, [2002] IRLR 711, CA. The Court of Appeal stressed the importance of the applicant making clear the nature of his or her claim to be a disabled person, and for both parties to obtain relevant medical evidence on the issue of impairment.

4   *College of Ripon & York St John v Hobbs* [2002] IRLR 185, EAT. On appeal in *McNicol v Balfour Beatty Rail Maintenance Ltd* (above), the Court of Appeal agreed with the EAT in *Hobbs* that an impairment can result from an illness rather than being an illness itself.

itself being an illness, ie an impairment may be cause or effect. The three cases are difficult to reconcile. It is suggested that the reasoning in the later case is to be preferred.

2.3.9 This debate aside, there remains some ground for doubt and argument about what impairments are of a physical or mental nature. Undoubtedly there will be difficult cases where the point will be taken in litigation. For example, the condition of chronic fatigue syndrome (so-called 'ME') is one which is not universally recognised in medicine. Where it is, there is doubt about whether its origins are physical, viral or psychological.[1] Similarly, there is disagreement about whether epilepsy is a physical disability (because of its physical manifestations) or a mental disability (because of its origins as a disturbance in the brain). It cannot be imagined that the legislation will not afford protection against discrimination to persons with epilepsy, despite this dichotomy, whereas doubt will almost certainly be cast upon whether individuals with other conditions (such as 'stress', pre-menstrual tension, obesity and so-called 'repetitive strain injury') are within the protected class. It is important to note that the DDA 1995 does not recognise the concept of a generic disability. In each case, the individual will have to show how his or her condition and its effects fit into the definitional framework erected by the statute.[2]

Sensory and other impairments

2.3.10 Are individuals with sensory impairments embraced by the definition of physical or mental impairment used in the DDA 1995? Sensory impairments include deafness, other hearing impairments or loss, blindness, partial sightedness and dual sensory impairments (such as combined loss of speech and hearing). The legislature intended that persons with sensory impairments should be covered by the legislation:

> 'The terms physical and mental are intended to be seen in their widest sense and should comprehensively cover all forms of impairment ... [A] third category, in addition to physical and mental impairment, might imply that those categories are not all-embracing ... Sensory conditions would generally be covered as physical conditions or, exceptionally, in cases such as hysterical deafness, as mental conditions.'[3]

---

1   The condition was recognised as amounting to a disability for the individual applicant in *O'Neill v Symm & Co Ltd* [1998] IRLR 233, EAT, where the tribunal at first instance placed reliance upon expert evidence and the WHO *International Classification of Diseases.*

2   See eg *Gittins v Oxford Radcliffe NHS Trust* (2000) EAT/193/99 (bulimia is not a generic disability; it is the effects of bulimia on the individual applicant which are in issue).

3   HC Deb Standing Committee E, col 71.

That is as clear an expression of legislative intention as one could hope to receive and, should there be any doubt whether or not an individual who has a sensory impairment is entitled to bring proceedings under the Act, reference should be made to the legislative history of the measure. In any event, the Guidance makes it plain that the concept of a physical or mental impairment includes sensory impairments, such as those affecting sight or hearing.[1]

2.3.11 The Disability Discrimination (Blind and Partially Sighted Persons) Regulations 2003 came into force on 14 April 2003.[2] They state that a person who is certified as blind or partially sighted by a consultant ophthalmologist is deemed to be a disabled person for the purposes of the DDA 1995. A person registered as blind or partially sighted in a register maintained by or on behalf of a local authority is also covered by this deeming provision. The regulations provide for conclusive evidence of certified status by the production of a certificate signed by the consultant ophthalmologist. Alternatively, a person's registered status is presumed by a certificate issued by (or on behalf of) the local authority stating that the person is registered as blind or partially sighted with that authority.

2.4 ABILITY TO CARRY OUT NORMAL DAY-TO-DAY ACTIVITIES

2.4.1 A person is a disabled person only if possessing an impairment that has an adverse effect, of the degree required, upon that person's 'ability to carry out normal day-to-day activities'.[3] An impairment is treated as affecting the ability of the person concerned to carry out normal day-to-day activities *only* if it affects one of the following:[4]

- mobility;[5]
- manual dexterity;
- physical co-ordination;
- continence;[6]

---

1   Guidance, Part I, para 12.

2   SI 2003/712.

3   DDA 1995, s 1(1).

4   Ibid, Sch 1, para 4(1). Note the power to make regulations under Sch 1, para 4(2). No regulations have been made at the time of writing.

5   In *Ashton v Chief Constable of West Mercia Constabulary* [2001] ICR 67, EAT, the personal choice of a person with gender identity dysphoria not to socialise outside work did not result in her condition having a substantial adverse effect on her mobility.

6   A rare example is *Thornhill v London Central Bus Co Ltd* (2000) EAT/463/99 (an unduly frequent desire to urinate, which did not lead to incontinence, was not a disability). See

- ability to lift, carry or otherwise move everyday objects;
- speech,[1] hearing or eyesight;
- memory or ability to concentrate, learn or understand;[2]
- perception of the risk of physical danger.

The Guidance explains what is meant by the scope of the eight listed activities.[3] It is not intended to reproduce this here. The focus is upon whether an impairment affects *any* of the abilities or capacities listed above. If it does, then it will be almost inevitable that there will be some adverse effect upon normal day-to-day activities.[4]

2.4.2 It is clear that it is the effect upon the claimant (and not persons generally) that matters. The EAT in *Goodwin v The Patent Office* has given important guidance on this question:

> 'What the Act is concerned with is an impairment on the person's *ability* to carry out activities. The fact that a person can carry out such activities does not mean that his ability to carry them out has not been impaired ... In order to constitute an adverse effect, it is not the doing of the acts which is the focus of attention but rather the ability to do (or not do) the acts ... The focus of attention required by the Act is on the things that the applicant either cannot do or can only do with difficulty, rather than on the things the person can do.'[5]

The tribunal (or court) should consider matters in the round and make an overall assessment of whether the adverse effect is substantial. However, it is not a question of weighing in the balance things which a person can do against things that person cannot do.[6] This should mean that, contrary to trends in some of the early first instance decisions, a claimant should find it relatively easier to establish his or her status as a

---

also *Kirton v Tetrosyl Ltd* [2003] EWCA Civ 619, [2003] IRLR 353, CA (an impairment of urinary incontinence as a result of surgery for cancer was a disability).

1   In *Ashton* (above) there was no evidence that the applicant's ability to speak was affected by her decision to alter the way in which she spoke (as part of preparation for gender reassignment).

2   An 'ability to understand' is not limited to an ability to understand information, knowledge or instructions. A broad approach to 'understanding' is required. See *Hewett v Motorola Ltd* [2004] IRLR 545, EAT (a person who has difficulty in understanding normal social interaction among people or the subtleties of human non-factual communication – for example, as may be the case of a person with Asperger's Syndrome – can be regarded as having his or her understanding affected).

3   Guidance, Part II, paras C14–C21.

4   *Ekpe v Commissioner of Police of the Metropolis* [2001] IRLR 605, EAT.

5   [1999] IRLR 4, EAT. See also *Leonard v Southern Derbyshire Chamber of Commerce* [2001] IRLR 19, EAT; *Ekpe v Commissioner of Police of the Metropolis* [2001] IRLR 605, EAT.

6   *Leonard v Southern Derbyshire Chamber of Commerce* [2001] IRLR 19, EAT. In cases of mental impairment, Guidance, Part II, paras C6–C7 should be taken into particular account, so that effects of fatigue or the ability to sustain an activity are properly considered.

disabled person, despite having adopted means of neutralising the effects of a disabling condition or environment.

2.4.3 Expert evidence of what the claimant can and cannot do (and the circumstances of that capability) will be important. Often this will be in the form of a report or evidence from a medical specialist (such as a consultant or occupational health professional). However, the tribunal (or a court) must not delegate the decision as to what are normal day-to-day activities to the expert witness. That is a judicial decision, to be arrived at using basic common sense, and in the light of the evidence, the statute and the Guidance.[1] But there is a 'Catch-22' for many claimants in arguing that they are sufficiently disabled to be covered by the DDA 1995, but not so disabled as to be prevented from carrying out, for example, the duties of employment.[2] Yet, as a matter of principle, evidence of the nature of a claimant's duties at work and the way in which they are performed can be relevant to the assessment of whether the claimant is a disabled person.[3] Duties while at work will often encompass normal day-to-day activities. At the very least, evidence of ability or inability to carry out normal day-to-day activities while at work goes to the credibility of any evidence that those activities cannot be carried on outside work (or can only be done so with difficulty).

2.4.4 The reference to the effect which an impairment has upon the ability to carry out normal day-to-day activities is designed to exclude mild or trivial conditions from the scope of the DDA 1995. For example, individuals with temporary and non-chronic conditions, such as sprains or influenza, most obviously fall outside the boundaries of the statute.[4] Moreover, a person who, because of some physical or mental limitation, is effectively excluded from participating in a specialised activity or pursuit – which the majority of people would be incapable of enjoying in any event – enjoys no protection under the Act. Thus, a person with colour blindness, who is disqualified from being a commercial airline pilot, cannot usually be said to experience adverse effects on his or her ability to carry out normal day-to-day activities. A person who is left-handed will be disabled in using industrial machinery designed for right-handed use, but left-handedness is not usually recognised as a

---

1   *Vicary v British Telecommunications plc* [1999] IRLR 680, EAT; *Adabeh v British Telecommunications plc* [2001] IRLR 23, EAT.

2   See *London Underground Ltd v Bragg* (1999) EAT/847/98.

3   *Law Hospital NHS Trust v Rush* [2001] IRLR 611, Ct of Sess; *Cruickshank v VAW Motorcast Ltd* [2002] IRLR 24, EAT (a case where the adverse effects of the claimant's medical condition or impairment – occupational asthma – on his normal day-to-day activities were exacerbated by his working conditions or environment).

4   This is also be underlined by the 'substantial and long-term adverse effect' formula discussed at **2.5–2.6**.

disability. An individual with a poor educational record because of comparatively low or average intelligence will be effectively disqualified from aspiring to the position of heart surgeon, but the majority of the population can be said to be 'disabled' to that extent also. It is not thought that colour blindness, left-handedness or indifferent educational attainment are within the scope of the Act.[1]

2.4.5 It is also not intended that activities which are normal only for a particular person or group of people should be included.[2] Account must be taken of how far the activity is normal for most people and carried out by most people on a daily or frequent and fairly regular basis.[3] However, it is equally the case that what is normal does not depend on whether the majority of people do it.[4] Thus travelling on the London Underground or by plane is a normal day-to-day activity, but if the individual does not use these modes of transport in practice, it will be difficult to show that an inability to use them can be regarded as a substantial adverse effect.[5]

2.4.6 Where a child under six years of age has an impairment which does not have an effect on the child's ability to carry out one of the listed normal day-to-day activities, the impairment is nevertheless to be taken to have a substantial and long-term adverse effect on the child's ability to carry out normal day-to-day activities if it would normally have such an effect on the ability of a person aged six years or over.[6]

2.4.7 Although the DDA 1995 covers clinically well-recognised mental illnesses, it might be difficult for persons with such illnesses to be able to show that they have an adverse effect on normal day-to-day activities, as those activities are defined in the Act. In the employment sphere, many mental illnesses might have an adverse effect upon a person's full working capacity, but work is not one of the listed normal day-to-day activities.[7]

---

1   See Guidance, Part II, para C3.

2   *Abadeh v British Telecommunications plc* [2001] IRLR 23, EAT (what is a normal day-to-day activity must be addressed without regard to whether it is normal to the particular applicant).

3   See Guidance, Part II, para C2.

4   *Ekpe v Commissioner of Police of the Metropolis* [2001] IRLR 605, EAT (what is normal is anything which is not abnormal or unusual, judged by an objective population standard).

5   *Abadeh v British Telecommunications plc* [2001] IRLR 23, EAT.

6   Disability Discrimination (Meaning of Disability) Regulations 1996, SI 1996/1455, reg 6.

7   See Guidance, Part II, para C3. However, see *Law Hospital NHS Trust v Rush* [2001] IRLR 611, Ct of Sess, discussed at **2.4.3**.

2.5 SUBSTANTIAL ADVERSE EFFECT

2.5.1 To satisfy the definition of a disability, the putative disabled person must demonstrate that he or she has a physical or mental impairment 'which has a substantial and long-term adverse effect' on the ability to carry out normal day-to-day activities.[1] The statutory guidance specifically refers to the matters which a court or tribunal ought to take into account when determining whether an impairment has a substantial adverse effect on a person's ability to carry out normal day-to-day activities or whether such an impairment has a long-term adverse effect. Without intending to weaken the definition of disability or to exclude particular impairments,[2] it gives examples in four particular circumstances:[3]

(1) effects which it would be reasonable to regard as substantial adverse effects in relation to particular activities;
(2) effects which it would not be reasonable to regard as substantial adverse effects in relation to particular activities;
(3) substantial adverse effects which it would be reasonable to regard as long-term;
(4) substantial adverse effects which it would not be reasonable to regard as long-term.

By these means, the Guidance assists the present discussion by illustrating and exemplifying how the statutory definition works in practice.

Meaning of 'substantial'

2.5.2 Whether an impairment has a substantial adverse effect upon a person is not explained in the DDA 1995.[4] It was intended that minor impairments should not provide a cause of action. The use of the word 'substantial' is designed to ensure that trivial conditions are beyond the scope of the legislation.[5] For example, persons with a minor vision impairment (such as 20/40 vision) might find it difficult to show that their impairment has a substantial adverse effect of the kind required by the statute. Someone whose hearing impairment merely requires them to view television with the volume up and results in occasional difficulty

---

1   DDA 1995, s 1(1).

2   See the assurance given at HC Deb Standing Committee E, col 124.

3   See Guidance, Part II, paras C5–C21. It is not proposed to replicate those examples here.

4   The word 'substantial' is also used, for example, in the employment provisions of Part 2, and there is no suggestion that this should be interpreted in different ways in different contexts. See the discussion of this question in Chapter 3.

5   HC Deb Standing Committee E, col 114; HC Deb, vol 566, col 174.

in hearing speech may have difficulty in showing substantial adverse effect.[1] The Guidance confirms that a substantial effect is one that is more than minor or trivial. It indicates that the requirement that an adverse effect be substantial is designed to reflect the general under-standing of disability as being a limitation going beyond the normal differences in ability between people.[2] The word 'substantial' is not to be given its ordinary dictionary definition. The Guidance is to be followed so that, for example, the ability to prepare vegetables, cut up meat and carry a tray are all examples of normal day-to-day activities, as would be various DIY and household tasks. An inability to carry out these functions was regarded as 'obviously' amounting to a substantial adverse effect on the ability to carry out normal day-to-day activities.[3] However, it is for the tribunal (or the court) to assess what adverse effects are substantial or not. In the final analysis, what is and what is not a 'substantial' adverse effect will be a matter for judicial interpretation of the statutory language, albeit assisted by the provisions of the Guidance and any appropriate regulations.[4]

2.5.3   The Guidance states that, in judging whether the adverse effects of an impairment upon a normal day-to-day activity are substantial, account should be taken of the time taken to carry out the activity and the way in which the activity is carried out.[5] If the impairment adversely affects the speed or manner in which that person can perform a particular activity in comparison with other persons, that is a relevant consideration. Environmental considerations will also be important (for example, the effect which temperature or stress has upon the

---

1   See the *obiter dicta* in *London Underground Ltd v Bragg* (1999) EAT/847/98.

2   Guidance, Part II, para A1. An example of a tribunal applying the wrong test on substantial effect (under the Part 4 provisions on education) can be seen in *M and M v SW School and the Special Educational Needs and Disability Tribunal* [2004] EWHC Admin 2587.

3   *Vicary v British Telecommunications plc* [1999] IRLR 680, EAT.

4   DDA 1995, Sch 1, para 5 provides that regulations may be made to provide for an effect of a prescribed kind on the ability of a person to carry out normal day-to-day activities to be treated as being (or, alternatively, as not being) a substantial adverse effect. No general regulations have been made under this power; but see Disability Discrimination (Meaning of Disability) Regulations 1996, SI 1996/1455, reg 5 (on tattoos and body piercing, discussed at **2.5.11**) and reg 6 (on babies and young children under six years of age, discussed at **2.4.6**).

5   Guidance, Part II, paras A2–A3.

impairment).[1] The EAT has said that, in judging whether an impairment has a *substantial* adverse effect, a tribunal may take into account how the claimant appears to the tribunal to manage, 'although tribunals will be slow to regard a person's capabilities in the relatively strange adversarial environment as an entirely reliable guide to the level of ability to perform normal day-to-day activities'.[2] It will also be appropriate to take account of the cumulative effects of an impairment.[3] For example, someone with mild cerebral palsy may experience only minor effects upon any of a number of the listed normal day-to-day activities, but the aggregate effect may be quite disabling and should be treated as so under the DDA 1995.[4] The cumulative effect of two or more impairments might also produce the adverse substantial adverse effect on normal day-to-day activities called for by the statute – even if, in isolation, each impairment could not be said to have such an effect.[5]

2.5.4   Account should also be taken of how far a person might reasonably be expected to modify his or her behaviour so as to prevent or reduce the adverse effects of an impairment on normal day-to-day activities.[6] For example, a person with a condition which manifests itself as an allergic reaction to certain substances might reasonably be expected to take steps to avoid those substances. To that extent, that person could not be said to experience a substantial adverse effect upon his or her normal day-to-day activities and would no longer satisfy the definition of disability. However, such avoidance or coping strategies must be subject to a test of reasonableness and might produce second order disabling effects in themselves. In any event, it must be recognised that such strategies might break down at times of stress and that must be weighed in the balance.[7] The fact that a person is able to mitigate the effects of a disability does not mean that they are not disabled within the meaning of the legislation.[8]

---

1   Guidance, Part II, para A10.

2   *Goodwin v The Patent Office* [1999] IRLR 4, EAT. See also *Ekpe v Commissioner of Police of the Metropolis* [2001] IRLR 605, EAT (a tribunal considering whether to draw any conclusions from a party's behaviour during the hearing would be expected to raise it at the hearing).

3   Guidance, Part II, para A4.

4   Ibid, Part II, para A5, and see the examples provided there.

5   Ibid, Part II, para A6.

6   Ibid, Part II, paras A7–A9.

7   Ibid, Part II, para A8. Note also para A9 discussed at **2.5.14**.

8   *Vicary v British Telecommunications plc* [1999] IRLR 680, EAT.

Recurring conditions

2.5.5 The DDA 1995 provides that if an impairment is one which has had a substantial adverse effect on a person's ability to carry out normal day-to-day activities, but subsequently ceased to have that effect, it will be treated as continuing to have such a substantial adverse effect (that is, during any intervening period of remission or good health) 'if that effect is likely to recur'.[1] This is an essential provision which recognises that there are many impairments whose effects upon day-to-day activities fluctuate. In the case of epilepsy or multiple sclerosis, for example, the underlying condition is constant, but the adverse effects of the condition are variable, with periods of impairment or disability alternating with periods of good health and normal activity. Such conditions are within the Act.[2] Nevertheless, seasonal allergic rhinitis, a condition whose effects are recurring and can be substantial for a brief time, has been excluded by regulation.[3]

2.5.6 In respect of an impairment or condition with recurring effects, the Guidance states that an effect is likely to recur if 'it is more likely than not that the effect will recur'.[4] If the effects are likely to recur beyond 12 months after the first occurrence, then they are to be treated as long term.[5] However, in judging the likelihood of recurrence, account should be taken of all the circumstances, including any reasonable expectation that the person concerned should take steps to prevent the recurrence.[6] The EAT in *Swift v Chief Constable of Wiltshire Constabulary* suggests that, when considering the recurring conditions provisions, a tribunal should ask itself the following questions.[7] First, at some stage was there an impairment which had a substantial adverse effect on the claimant's ability to carry out normal day-to-day activities? Secondly, did the impairment cease to have that effect and, if so, when?

---

1   DDA 1995, Sch 1, para 2(2). The likelihood of an effect recurring shall be disregarded in circumstances which may be prescribed in regulations (ibid, Sch 1, para 2(3)). No such regulations have been made to date.

2   HC Deb Standing Committee E, col 113.

3   See **2.3.3**.

4   Guidance, Part II, para B3. It is likely an event will happen if it is more probable than not that it will happen: ibid, para B7. That is to be assessed at the time at which the discriminatory behaviour occurred: *Latchman v Reed Business Information Ltd* [2002] ICR 1453, EAT (it is not what had actually later occurred but what could earlier have been expected to occur that was to be judged and the relevant time to examine the likelihood of a recurrence was at the point at which the impairment had ceased to have a substantial adverse effect).

5   Guidance, Part II, para B4.

6   Ibid, Part II, para B5, applying much the same behavioural expectations as were discussed at **2.5.4** (and see Guidance, Part II, paras A7–A9).

7   [2004] IRLR 540.

Thirdly, what was the substantial adverse effect? Fourthly, is that substantial adverse effect likely to recur (ie is it more probable than not that the effect will recur)? The tribunal must be satisfied that the same effect is likely to recur and will again amount to a substantial adverse effect on the claimant's ability to carry out normal day-to-day activities. The question for the tribunal is whether the substantial adverse effect is likely to recur (and not simply whether the impairment or illness is likely to recur). The effect is that the impairment is treated as continuing for as long as its substantial adverse effect is likely to recur.

Progressive conditions

2.5.7 Special provision is made for persons with progressive conditions. Progressive conditions include 'cancer, multiple sclerosis, muscular dystrophy or infection by the human immunodeficiency virus',[1] but this list is not exhaustive. Where a person has a 'progressive condition' and, as a result of that condition,[2] he or she has an impairment which has (or had) an effect on his or her ability to carry out normal day-to-day activities, but that effect is not (or was not) a *substantial* adverse effect, such a person is treated as having an impairment which has such a substantial adverse effect if the condition is likely to result in that person having such an impairment in the future.[3] However, the double-edged nature of this sword is that a degenerative condition might be seen as undermining a claimant's claim in a Part 2 case to be employable (with or without adjustments) for the future.[4] The answer must be that this is a question that goes to remedy rather than to establishing disability or liability for discrimination. In any event, in order to rely upon the progressive condition provision, the claimant must establish that the condition in his or her

---

1   DDA 1995, Sch 1, para 8(1)(a). Regulations may provide (for the purposes of this provision only) that conditions of a prescribed description are to be treated as being or not being progressive conditions (Sch 1, para 8(2)). No such regulations have been made to date.

2   Because of this phrase, this provision does not embrace a progressive condition (such as cancer) which has been treated – and is thus asymptomatic – but does cover the situation where the treatment itself has resulted in an impairment having an adverse effect upon a person's ability to carry out normal day-to-day activities: *Kirton v Tetrosyl Ltd* [2003] EWCA Civ 619, [2003] IRLR 353, CA (an impairment of urinary incontinence as a result of surgery for cancer was a disability and fell within the progressive conditions provisions – the words 'as a result of that condition' are not to be interpreted narrowly). The adverse effects (if any) arising from the impairment resulting from the treatment have to be judged on their own merits.

3   DDA 1995, Sch 1, para 8(1).

4   See *London Underground Ltd v Bragg* (1999) EAT/847/98.

case is likely to have a substantial adverse effect, usually by medical evidence as to the likely prognosis or by the use of statistical evidence.[1]

2.5.8   It is apparent from the parliamentary debates that the legislature did not intend that this provision should protect individuals from discrimination where they possess asymptomatic conditions (for example, a person diagnosed as HIV positive but without manifest symptoms of the virus or a related illness):[2]

> 'We recognise that there is a need to protect people where the effect of the condition is not yet substantial but is expected to be so in the future. That is why the [Act] specifically includes people with progressive conditions as soon as there are any effects on their ability to carry out normal day-to-day activities. However, we do not believe that it would be right to include people with conditions which may remain latent, possibly for a considerable number of years ... The Disability Discrimination [Act] is designed to protect people who have, or ... have had, an actual disability. It is not a general anti-discrimination [Act] nor a general health discrimination [Act]. If we extend it to cover people who may develop a disability at some unspecified time in the future we will undermine the effectiveness of the [Act] by creating uncertainty about who is covered.'[3]

A symptomless illness or condition is not an impairment which has yet affected one of the designated normal day-to-day activities.[4]

2.5.9   Despite the inclusive tone of the statute's treatment of progressive conditions, the wording of the DDA 1995 makes it plain that it is to be the *future* effects of a *presently existing* progressive condition only which the law intends to embrace. A person whose medical status or condition merely indicates that it is likely that he or she might suffer from a progressive condition *in the future* is not treated as having an impairment with substantial adverse effects on ability to carry out normal day-to-day activities. Thus the 'progressive conditions' provision does not include within the protection of the Act individuals who merely have a genetic or other predisposition to (or risk of) a progressive condition in the

---

1   *Mowat-Brown v University of Surrey* [2002] IRLR 235, EAT (the fact that the applicant had multiple sclerosis was not in itself sufficient to bring him within the progressive condition provision without evidence of the future likely effects of his condition upon him).

2   HL Deb, vol 566, col 1061.

3   HL Deb, vol 564, col 1682.

4   DDA 1995, Sch 1, para 4. Persons with asymptomatic conditions or conditions where it is unclear whether substantial adverse effects are likely to recur or initial effects are likely to worsen (such as some cancers during or after treatment) may have difficulty in satisfying the definition of disability used in the DDA 1995. See **2.9**.

future.[1] Individuals who have undergone a medical test which indicated that they have a predictive propensity to develop an impairment at a later date (such as Usher syndrome, Huntingdon's chorea, Alzheimer's disease or multiple sclerosis) are not protected from disability discrimination at this point. The Act also does not protect individuals who have a mistaken or erroneous reputation as a person who has (or had) a disability or might do so in the future.

Severe disfigurement

2.5.10 An impairment which consists of a severe disfigurement is treated as having a substantial adverse effect on the ability of the person concerned to carry out normal day-to-day activities.[2] The assessment of the severity of a disfigurement is a matter of degree and account may be taken of where on the body the feature in question is to be found.[3] The implication is that a facial disfigurement is more likely to pass the test of severity than one hidden by a person's clothing. The inclusion of severe disfigurements within the definition of disability for the purposes of the DDA 1995 is important. Persons with facial port wine stains, other birth marks, severe burns or scalds, and other disfiguring signs face discrimination based upon aesthetic appearance. The Guidance also refers to scars, limb or postural deformation and diseases of the skin.[4] Such impairments are rarely disabling in themselves. Rather, the disability experienced by disfigured individuals is as a result of society's reaction to perceived imperfection. This is a rare example of the legislation acknowledging a social model of disability rather than a purely medical one.

2.5.11 While the DDA 1995 does not automatically exclude deliberately acquired severe disfigurements, it does provide for their potential exclusion by regulations.[5] Regulations stipulate that a severe disfigurement is not to be treated as having a substantial adverse effect on the ability of the person concerned to carry out normal day-to-day activities if it consists of a tattoo (which has not been removed) or body piercing for decorative or other *non-medical purposes* (including any object attached through the piercing for such purposes).[6] The present writer

---

1   See the recommendations to control the use of genetic testing in Human Genetics Commission, *Inside Information: Balancing Interests in the Use of Personal Genetic Data* (May 2002).

2   DDA 1995, Sch 1, para 3(1).

3   Guidance, Part II, para A17.

4   Guidance, Part II, para A17.

5   DDA 1995, Sch 1, para 3(3).

6   Disability Discrimination (Meaning of Disability) Regulations 1996, SI 1996/1455, reg 5.

suggests that a severe disfigurement resulting from an attempt to remove a tattoo would not be so excluded. For the moment, the regulations do not make any further exclusions. It should be noted that there is no general exclusion of deliberately acquired disfigurements (such as facial or bodily scarring caused by self-mutilation or self-administered injury).[1]

Effect of medical treatment

2.5.12   Does a person whose disability is controlled, corrected or adjusted by medical treatment, or by the use of medication, auxiliary devices or other aids, remain a person with an impairment for the purpose of protection against disability-related discrimination? In a strict sense, such a person might no longer be said to have an impairment which has an adverse effect on normal day-to-day activities. Yet, at the same time, the underlying condition or impairment remains and the person is disabled to the extent that the method of control or correction will involve residual or second order effects and inconveniences. Equally, such a person might experience continuing adverse treatment at the hands of others who might continue to regard the individual as disabled. That might be the case illustratively where an individual walks with the aid of a prosthesis or is mobile with the assistance of a motorised wheelchair.

2.5.13   The DDA 1995 provides that an impairment which would be likely to have a substantial adverse effect on the ability of the person concerned to carry out normal day-to-day activities – but for the fact that measures are being taken to treat or correct it – is nevertheless to be treated as continuing to be an impairment amounting to a disability.[2] The legislation gives examples of measures treating or correcting an impairment as including 'medical treatment and the use of a prosthesis or other aid'.[3]

2.5.14   The DDA 1995 does not define what is meant by an 'aid', but the EAT has offered the *obiter* view that this refers 'to aids such as zimmer frames or sticks or wheelchairs and not to household objects' (such as automatic can-openers).[4] Similarly, the term 'medical treatment' is not defined. The EAT has held that counselling sessions with a consultant clinical psychologist constitute such treatment.[5] If a disabled person is advised by a medical practitioner to behave in a certain

---

1   HC Deb Standing Committee E, cols 110–111.

2   DDA 1995, Sch 1, para 6(1).

3   Ibid, Sch 1, para 6(2).

4   *Vicary v British Telecommunications* [1999] IRLR 680, EAT.

5   *Kapadia v London Borough of Lambeth* [2000] IRLR 14, EAT, and [2000] IRLR 699, CA.

way in order to reduce the impact of a disability, that might count as treatment to be disregarded under this provision.[1] Provided that the impairment would have had a substantial adverse effect on a person's ability to carry out normal day-to-day activities *but for* the fact that it has been treated or controlled or corrected in the manner described, then it is also to be treated as continuing to have such a substantial adverse effect even though no such effect is actually experienced because of such treatment or control or correction. An example of such an impairment might include insulin-controlled diabetes or medication-regulated epilepsy. A further illustration would be hearing loss improved by a hearing aid.

2.5.15 The EAT has said that only continuing medical treatment (and not concluded treatment) is relevant.[2] Where the treatment has ceased the effects of that treatment should be taken into account in assessing the disability. If the medical evidence is that the treatment has created a permanent improvement then the effects of that treatment should be taken into account when assessing the disability. In contrast, where the treatment is continuing, it must be disregarded if the final outcome of the treatment cannot be determined or it is known that ceasing the treatment would result in a relapse of worsened condition.

2.5.16 The Guidance states that this provision applies even if the measures in question result in the effects being completely under control or not at all apparent.[3] The question of whether or not a person has an impairment which has a substantial adverse effect upon the ability to carry out normal day-to-day activities is to be answered by reference to what would be the effect of the impairment or condition but for the treatment, aid or medication.[4] A tribunal (or court) should examine how a claimant's abilities have been affected whilst on medication (or, by analogy, whilst receiving any other medical treatment). It should then consider the 'deduced effects': that is, what effects there would have been *without* the medication (or other medical intervention) and whether those effects are clearly more than minor or trivial.[5] Medical evidence as to what the deduced effects would be is essential.[6]

---

1   Guidance, Part II, para A9, and thus that behaviour should not be taken into account at all under paras A7–A8 (see **2.5.4**).

2   *Abadeh v British Telecommunications plc* [2001] IRLR 23, EAT.

3   Guidance, Part II, para A12.

4   Ibid, Part II, para A13.

5   See *Goodwin v The Patent Office* [1999] IRLR 4, EAT, *Kapadia v London Borough of Lambeth* [2000] IRLR 14, EAT, and [2000] IRLR 699, CA.

6   *Woodrup v London Borough of Southwark* [2002] EWCA Civ 1716, [2003] IRLR 111, CA (the burden of proof is with the claimant).

2.5.17   However, this provision does not extend to the impairment of a person's sight, to the extent that the impairment is, in the particular person's case, 'correctable by spectacles or contact lenses'.[1] Individuals with spectacles or contact lenses which compensate for an impairment to their sight do not usually regard themselves as disabled and are not treated as such for the purposes of the DDA 1995. The use of the word 'correctable' seems to suggest also that an individual who has a sight impairment, but does not use spectacles or contact lenses that might otherwise correct the sight loss, would not qualify as a 'disabled person'. In other words, this provision of the Act only embraces involuntary disabilities. This might mean that a person who chooses not to take basic, non-surgical remedial action to correct a vision impairment cannot claim protection of the Act. The statute does not suggest that a sight impairment correctable by surgical techniques is presently excluded from the coverage of the legislation. However, the Guidance states that the only effects on ability to carry out normal day-to-day activities to be considered are *those which remain* when spectacles or contact lenses are used (or would remain if they were used).[2] There would seem to be some room for confusion here which will call for judicial resolution.

2.6   LONG-TERM ADVERSE EFFECT

2.6.1   The DDA 1995 is more expansive in its explication of what amounts to long-term effects of an impairment. It provides that the effect of an impairment is 'long-term' if:

- it has lasted for at least 12 months; or
- the period for which it lasts is likely to be at least 12 months; or
- it is likely to last for the rest of the life of the person affected.[3]

The intention is to exclude from the protection of the anti-discrimination principle those persons whose impairment or disability is merely short-term or temporary.[4]

---

1   DDA 1995, Sch 1, para 6(3)(a). Regulations may also provide that this exception be extended to other impairments: ibid, Sch 1, para 6(3)(b). No such regulations have been made to date.

2   Guidance, Part II, para A14.

3   DDA 1995, Sch 1, para 2(1). Regulations may prescribe circumstances in which an effect which would not otherwise be long term is to be treated as a long-term effect or an effect which would otherwise be long term is not to be treated as a long-term effect (ibid, Sch 1, para 2(4)). No such regulations have been made to date.

4   HC Deb Standing Committee E, col 70.

2.6.2   Suppose that an employee suffered a sudden onset of deafness and was dismissed within six months of medical diagnosis. Would the employee have redress under the law, all other things being equal? Even though at the time of dismissal the impairment had not lasted at least 12 months, nevertheless the employee should be able to show that the period for which the hearing impairment is likely to last is at least 12 months, and so the employee would be enabled to seek a remedy. However, a person refused access to a restaurant because he has a broken leg in plaster, or because she exhibits obvious signs of German measles, would not have redress because the impairments or conditions in question do not have, or are not likely to have, long-term effects.[1] How does the DDA 1995 treat a person diagnosed as having a terminal illness with a prognosis that he or she will not live for more than a few months and less than 12 months?[2] Could such a person be lawfully refused, for example, provision of goods or services in a shop or restaurant? Terminal illnesses are within the definition and, in this case, the impairment can reasonably be expected to last for the rest of the life of the person affected.

2.6.3   The Guidance states that, in judging whether the adverse effects of an impairment are long-term, it is not necessary for the effect to be the same throughout the period in question. The effect may be variable or progressive. Provided the impairment continues to have (or is likely to have) an adverse effect on ability to carry out normal day-to-day activities throughout the period, there is a long-term effect.[3] The Guidance also states:

> 'In assessing the likelihood of an effect lasting for any period, account should be taken of the total period for which the effect exists. This includes any time before the point when the discriminatory behaviour occurred as well as time afterwards. Account should also be taken of both the typical length of such an effect on an individual, and any relevant factors specific to this individual (for example, general state of health, age).'[4]

Note, however, that provision is also made for recurring effects.[5] If the adverse effects are likely to recur beyond 12 months after the first occurrence, they are to be treated as long-term.[6] It is likely that an event will happen if it is more probable than not that it will happen.[7]

---

1   See further HC Deb Standing Committee E, cols 77–78.

2   Ibid, col 78.

3   Guidance, Part II, paras B1–B2.

4   Ibid, Part II, para B8.

5   See DDA 1995, Sch 1, para 2(2), and the discussion at **2.5.5–2.5.6**.

6   Guidance, Part II, para B5.

7   Ibid, Part II, para B7.

2.6.4 In an early case, it was held that an employment tribunal in a Part 2 case should consider the adverse effects of the applicant's condition up to and including the date of the hearing.[1] That was a curious case where it would seem that the act of disability discrimination complained of triggered a recurrence of the applicant's disability which had appeared to have been successfully treated or at least under control. It is suggested that the proper approach is to judge whether the applicant or claimant satisfied the definition of a disabled person as at the date of the alleged act of unlawful discrimination, even though that judgment may be made with the benefit of hindsight as at the date of the hearing.[2]

Past disability and long-term adverse effect

2.6.5 Some modification of the meaning of 'long-term effect' is necessary in order to accommodate the inclusion of past disabilities.[3] When dealing with the question of whether a person with a past disability has experienced a long-term adverse effect on ability to carry out normal day-to-day activities, the effect of an impairment is a long-term effect if it has lasted for at least 12 months.[4] Where an impairment ceases to have a substantial adverse effect on a person's ability to carry out normal day-to-day activities, it is to be treated as continuing to have that effect if that effect recurs.[5]

2.7 PERSONS DEEMED TO BE DISABLED

2.7.1 There is no implicit assumption that a court or tribunal will regard a certification of a person as disabled under other disability legislation as conclusive or persuasive of their status under the DDA 1995. However, the Act contains one exceptional case in respect of a person who was a 'registered disabled person' under the Disabled Persons (Employment) Act 1944 (or its Northern Ireland equivalent).[6] A person who was on the register maintained under the 1944 Act on

---

1   *Greenwood v British Airways plc* [1999] IRLR 600, EAT, purporting to rely upon Guidance, Part II, para B8.

2   *Cruickshank v VAW Motorcast Ltd* [2002] IRLR 24, EAT.

3   By virtue of DDA 1995, s 2(2) and Sch 2, para 2. Note the amendments made by the Disability Discrimination Act 1995 (Amendment) Regulations 2003, SI 2003/1673.

4   DDA 1995, Sch 2, para 5, modifying Sch 1, para 2(1)–(3).

5   See Guidance, Part II, para B9.

6   DDA 1995, Sch 1, para 7. For the modification of these provisions in the Northern Ireland context, see Sch 1, para 49. Prescribed descriptions of persons might also be deemed to have disabilities and to be disabled persons for the purposes of the Act: Sch 1, para 7(5)–(6). No such prescription has been made to date.

12 January 1995, and who remained registered on 2 December 1996, was 'deemed to have a disability'. That person was treated as a disabled person for the purpose of the application of any provision of the DDA 1995 for 'the initial period'.[1] The certificate of registration was treated as conclusive evidence, in relation to the person with respect to whom it was issued, in respect of the matters certified and, unless the contrary was shown, its validity was entitled to be taken at face value.[2]

2.7.2 However, this deemed status only lasted for the so-called 'initial period'.[3] This was a period of three years beginning on 2 December 1996 (and thus ending on 1 December 1999).[4] Such a person will now need to meet the statutory definition of 'disabled person' contained in all its detail in the DDA 1995 and any accompanying guidance and regulations. In practice, that might not be an insurmountable task for a person who qualified under the Disabled Persons (Employment) Act 1944 and whose conditions and circumstances remain unchanged or comparable. In any event, such a person will be regarded as being a person who *had* a disability, and thus to have been a disabled person, during the initial period.[5] This means that he or she will be able to rely upon the extension of the DDA 1995 to include persons who have had a disability in the past.[6]

2.7.3 The Disability Discrimination (Blind and Partially Sighted Persons) Regulations 2003 provide that a person who is certified as blind or partially sighted by a consultant ophthalmologist, or registered as blind or partially sighted in a register maintained by or on behalf of a local authority, is deemed to be a disabled person for the purposes of the DDA 1995.[7]

2.8 PAST DISABILITIES

2.8.1 Parts 2, 3 and 4 of the DDA 1995 (discrimination in relation to the employment field, goods, facilities and services, premises and education) apply *pari passu* in relation to a person 'who has had a disability' as if that person is a person who has that disability at the

---

1 DDA 1995, Sch 1, para 7(2)(a).

2 Ibid, Sch 1, paras 7(3)–(4) and 7(7).

3 Ibid, Sch 1, para 7(2)(a).

4 Ibid, Sch 1, para 7(7).

5 Ibid, Sch 1, para 7(2)(b).

6 Ibid, s 2 and Sch 2 as discussed at **2.8**.

7 See **2.3.11**.

present or relevant time.[1] The thinking behind this provision is as follows:

> 'It has become clear that people who have had a disability, although they may be no longer disabled as such, share with people who are currently disabled, a need for protection against discrimination in relation to their disability ... It is clearly a very important part of the whole process of recovery that someone who has been disabled is able not only to participate fully in employment and social activities but to feel confident in doing so ... In addition, we have been persuaded that it is not always possible to tell when a person has fully recovered from a disability and when the condition is no longer likely to recur.'[2]

It ensures consistency of treatment between persons who are presently disabled and those individuals who have recovered from the same condition.[3]

2.8.2 In a case of alleged discrimination against a person who complains of an act based upon that person's past disability, it does not matter that the relevant provisions of the DDA 1995 were not in force when that person was actually experiencing the disability in question. The question as to whether a person had a disability at a particular time is determined as if the relevant provisions of the DDA 1995 which were in force at the time of the discriminatory act had been in force at the relevant time (ie when the person had the disability in issue).[4] Furthermore, the past disability in question might have been experienced at a time before the passing of the new legislation.[5]

2.8.3 The inclusion of past disabilities within the protection of the DDA 1995 is an important concession. It provides a potential remedy for those persons who are discriminated against because of their history or record of disability. For example, a person with a history of depression or mental or emotional illness might be unreasonably excluded from employment opportunity. That person would otherwise have no cause of action unless the depression or mental or emotional illness was a clinically recognised condition which the individual had at the time the employment opportunity was denied. However, it is important to note that, where a person seeks to rely upon the status of being 'a person who

---

1   DDA 1995, s 2(1). The substantive provisions of the Act are appropriately modified (s 2(2) and Sch 2, as amended by the Disability Discrimination Act 1995 (Amendment) Regulations 2003, SI 2003/1673). In particular, references in Parts 2 to 4 of the Act to a disabled person are also to be read as references to a person who has had a disability (Sch 2, para 2).

2   HL Deb, vol 564, col 1655.

3   Ibid, vol 564, col 1656.

4   Ibid, s 2(4).

5   Ibid, s 2(5).

has had a disability', it will still be necessary for that person to show that, at the relevant time in the past, he or she had a physical or mental impairment which had a substantial and long-term adverse effect on his or her ability to carry out normal day-to-day activities.

2.9   DISABILITY DISCRIMINATION BILL

2.9.1   The Disability Discrimination Bill will make important changes to the definition of disability.[1] If enacted, the Bill will remove the requirement that a mental illness must be clinically well recognised before it can amount to a mental impairment. People with a mental illness will still need to demonstrate that they have an impairment which has a long-term and substantial adverse effect on their ability to carry out normal day-to-day activities. The Bill will also deem people with HIV, cancer or multiple sclerosis to be disabled before they experience any adverse effects of their condition. The Bill will define HIV infection in recognition of the fact that there are two strains of the Human Immunodeficiency Virus recognised as capable of causing AIDS in human beings. Regulations may exclude persons who have cancer of a prescribed description from these proposed provisions (for example, they may exclude types of cancer which do not require substantial treatment). The existing power to deem a person to have a disability in prescribed circumstances (and thus to be treated as a disabled person for the purposes of the DDA 1995) will be clarified to ensure that there are no implied limitations on the power. Regulations will then be able to deem any group of people to be disabled.[2]

2.9.2   The Government has not agreed to add to the list of normal day-to-day activities, but has undertaken to amend the Guidance in this area. The Joint Committee recommended that eligibility for certain disability benefits should automatically provide coverage for a disabled person under the DDA 1995. The Government has not accepted that

---

1   For the pre-history of the Bill, see Disability Rights Task Force, *From Exclusion to Inclusion: A Report of the Disability Rights Task Force for Disabled People* (1999, London: DfEE), Chapter 3; *Towards Inclusion – Civil Rights for Disabled People: Government Response to the Disability Rights Task Force* (DfEE, March 2001), paras 3.4–3.20; *Interim Government Response to the Report of the Disability Rights Task Force* (DfEE, March 2000); *Legislative Review: First Review of the Disability Discrimination Act 1995: Consultation* (Disability Rights Commission, May 2002), pp 26–27 and 74–93; Department for Work and Pensions, *Draft Disability Discrimination Bill*, Cm 6058 (December 2003); Joint Committee on the Draft Disability Discrimination Bill, *First Report* (April 2004); Department for Work and Pensions, *The Government's Response to the Report of the Joint Committee on the Draft Disability Discrimination Bill*, Cm 6276 (July 2004).

2   See Department of Work and Pensions, *Disability Discrimination Bill: Consultation on private clubs; premises; the definition of disability; and the questions procedure*, Cm 6402 (December 2004).

recommendation. Finally, the Government has rejected the Joint Committee's recommendation that the Act should prohibit direct discrimination and harassment against people who are associated with a disabled person or who are perceived to be disabled.

Chapter 3

THE EMPLOYMENT FIELD: COMMON CONCEPTS

3.1 INTRODUCTION

3.1.1 Part 2 of the Disability Discrimination Act 1995, as originally enacted, was concerned with disability discrimination in employment. That embraced discrimination by employers, against contract workers and by trade organisations.[1] Provision was also made in respect of charities and supported employment, discriminatory advertisements, occupational pension schemes and insurance services.[2] Part 2 contained its own measures for enforcement, remedies and procedure, the validity of certain agreements and the alteration to premises occupied under leases.[3]

Disability Discrimination Act 1995 (Amendment) Regulations 2003

3.1.2 These provisions have been amended by the Disability Discrimination Act 1995 (Amendment) Regulations 2003, with effect from 1 October 2004.[4] The amendments give effect to the EC Framework Employment Directive.[5] The purpose of the Directive is to lay down a general framework for combating discrimination on the ground (among others) of disability as regards employment and occupation, with a view to putting into effect in the Member States the principle of equal treatment.[6] As amended, Part 2 now addresses the problem of discrimination against disabled persons in the employment field at

---

1   DDA 1995, ss 4–7, 12 and 13–15, respectively.

2   Ibid, ss 10, 11, 17 and 18, respectively.

3   Ibid, ss 8 (and Sch 3, Part 1), 9 and 16 (and Sch 4, Part 1), respectively.

4   SI 2003/1673. In Northern Ireland, see the Disability Discrimination Act 1995 (Amendment) (Northern Ireland) Regulations 2004, SR 2004/55.

5   Council Directive 2000/78/EC of 27 November 2000, establishing a general framework for equal treatment in employment and occupation: OJ (2 December 2000) L 303/16.

6   Ibid, Art 1.

large. In particular, it covers applicants for employment, employees, contract workers, office-holders, police officers, partners in firms, barristers and advocates, practical work experience, occupational pensions and group insurance services. It also deals with discrimination in the provision of employment services.[1] The discussions in this chapter and the next are concerned with the relevant law, as in force from 1 October 2004.

3.1.3 To a large extent, the amended provisions in Part 2 are modelled after similar provisions in other employment discrimination legislation,[2] especially following the changes effected in discrimination law generally by the EC Framework Employment Directive. Where the statutory language is common or identical, case-law under related discrimination legislation will be instructive. However, there are important differences between the 1995 Act and the other legal provisions, although those differences are less marked now than they once were. In particular, the 1995 Act deals with direct and indirect forms of discrimination in a unique fashion, it uses a different comparative basis for detecting discrimination, it contains a limited but distinctive justification defence in particular circumstances and it imposes a positive duty upon employers to accommodate disabled persons. The Court of Appeal has expressly warned against approaching the 1995 Act with assumptions and concepts familiar from experience of the earlier equal opportunities statutes.[3]

Secondary sources

3.1.4 Part 2 of the Act, so far as it originally affected employment and contract work, first came into force on 2 December 1996. It has been the subject of regulations amplifying (and sometimes narrowing) the provisions on employment discrimination.[4] Two updated Codes of Practice have been issued by the DRC to support the amended law, with

---

1 See Chapter 5 at **5.7**.

2 See, in particular: Sex Discrimination Act 1975 (as amended); Race Relations Act 1976 (as amended); Part-time Workers (Prevention of Less Favourable Treatment) Regulations 2000 (as amended); Fixed-term Employees (Prevention of Less Favourable Treatment) Regulations 2002; Equality (Religion or Belief) Regulations 2003 (as amended); Employment Equality (Sexual Orientation) Regulations 2003 (as amended).

3 *Clark v TDG Ltd t/a Novacold* [1999] IRLR 318, CA.

4 Disability Discrimination (Employment) Regulations 1996, SI 1996/1456, and Disability Discrimination (Employment) Regulations (Northern Ireland) 1996, SR 1996/419. From 1 October 2004, these regulations are revoked and replaced in part by the Disability Discrimination (Employment Field) (Leasehold Premises) Regulations 2004, SI 2004/153,

effect from 1 October 2004.[1] They provide guidance and assistance in respect of the rights and obligations under Part 2. They do not impose legal obligations and are not intended to be an authoritative statement of the law. However, they are admissible in proceedings before an employment tribunal or court, which must take into account any provision of a Code of Practice which appears to be relevant to the determination of a question in those proceedings.[2]

The scheme of Part 2, as amended

3.1.5 The amendments made to the scheme of Part 2 call for a different treatment of the analysis of discrimination in the enlarged employment field than was adopted in previous editions of this book. Part 2 now contains a number of sections that deal with legal concepts that are common across the employment field, regardless of the identity of the respondent. These common concepts are: (1) the meaning of discrimination; (2) the meaning of harassment; (3) general provisions on reasonable adjustments; (4) relationships which have come to an end; (5) discriminatory advertisements; and (6) instructions and pressure to discriminate.[3] In the litigation process, the natural starting-point is to identify the particular cause of action that arises on the alleged facts. However, to do so presupposes an understanding of the common concepts that underpin those causes of action, such as the meaning of discrimination or the scope of the duty to make reasonable adjustments.

3.1.6 Accordingly, in this chapter, the common concepts are described and explained. In Chapter 4, the individual causes of action are then examined. Enforcement, remedies and procedure will be dealt with in Chapter 10, as will the revised provisions on validity of contracts, collective agreements and rules of undertaking. Alterations to premises occupied by employers and others under leases are dealt with in Chapter 6.

---

and the Disability Discrimination (Employment Field) (Leasehold Premises) Regulations (Northern Ireland) 2004, SR 2004/374. They in turn revoke and replace in full the Disability Discrimination (Sub-leases and Sub-tenancies) Regulations 1996, SI 1996/420, and the Disability Discrimination (Sub-leases and Sub-tenancies) Regulations (Northern Ireland) 1996,

1   SR 1996/420. See *Code of Practice: Employment and Occupation* (2004); *Code of Practice: Trade Organisations and Qualifications Bodies* (2004). They replace the *Code of Practice for the Elimination of Discrimination in the Field of Employment Against Disabled Persons or Persons Who Have Had a Disability* (1996). Separate (but essentially identical) Codes of Practice apply in Northern Ireland, reflecting the different institutional context of the province.

2   DDA 1995, s 53A(8). See generally **9.3**.

3   Ibid, ss 3A, 3B, 18B, 16A, 16B and 16C, respectively.

3.2 DISCRIMINATION

3.2.1   For the purposes of establishing the unlawfulness of an act under Part 2 of the DDA 1995, as amended, a person might 'discriminate' against a disabled person in one of four ways.[1] In shorthand terms, these might be termed as: (1) disability-related discrimination; (2) direct discrimination; (3) failure to make reasonable adjustments; and (4) victimisation. Victimisation is a concept which is common to other parts of the Act and is dealt with in more detail in Chapter 10. Account will also be taken shortly of the provisions dealing with harassment. Consideration will also be given to discrimination by association and perceived discrimination.

3.2.2   In the account which follows, the 'person' who discriminates will be – as the case may be: an employer; the relevant person in relation to an appointment to an office or post; the trustees or managers of an occupational pension scheme; a firm (or partnership); a barrister or barrister's clerk or an advocate; a person instructing a barrister or an advocate; a trade organisation; a qualifications body; or a person providing practical work experience. The statutory language refers to the person as 'he', but that person can equally be 'she' or 'it'. In many cases, the person will be a legal person, such as a limited company, a statutory body or an unincorporated association. Wherever appropriate, the term 'respondent' will be used in the analysis below to avoid confusion, unless a particular kind of respondent (such as an employer) needs to be identified in context.

Disability-related discrimination

3.2.3   For the purposes of Part 2, a person discriminates against a disabled person if, for a reason which relates to the disabled person's disability, the person treats the disabled person less favourably than the person treats (or would treat) others to whom that reason does not (or would not) apply and the person cannot show that the treatment in question is justified.[2] Treatment is justified for this purpose if, but only if, the reason for it is both material to the circumstances of the particular case and substantial.[3] However, treatment of a disabled person cannot be justified in this way if it amounts to direct discrimination.[4] Moreover,

---

1   DDA 1995, ss 3A and 55.

2   DDA 1995, s 3A(1); *Code of Practice: Employment and Occupation* (2004), paras 4.27–4.32 (and examples); *Code of Practice: Trade Organisations and Qualifications Bodies* (2004), paras 4.26–4.31 (and examples).

3   DDA 1995, s 3A(3).

4   Ibid, s 3A(4). Direct discrimination is discrimination that falls within s 3A(5) and will be discussed below.

if a person is under a duty to make reasonable adjustments in relation to the disabled person, but fails to comply with that duty, the treatment of the disabled person cannot be justified unless it would have been justified even if that duty had been complied with.[1] This definition of 'disability discrimination' has been part of the statute since it was first enacted.

Less favourable treatment

3.2.4 The key concept is that of less favourable treatment. It is for the claimant to identify the less favourable treatment complained of.[2] A person only discriminates against a disabled person if he or she treats the disabled person 'less favourably than' the person 'treats or would treat others' to whom the reason which relates to the disabled person's disability does not or would not apply.[3] This concept of less favourable treatment calls for a comparative approach. The question is: how has the disabled person been treated in comparison with other persons to whom the reason relating to the disabled person's disability does not apply? If the treatment of the comparator is more favourable than the treatment of the claimant, one of the necessary (but not sufficient) criteria for establishing unlawful discrimination is in place. A number of points should be noted about this definition of 'discrimination'.

3.2.5 First, a disabled person could seek to show that he or she has been treated less favourably than a hypothetical (rather than an actual) comparator. The double use of the word 'would' supports that reasoning.[4] This is especially important where a disabled person has been refused or denied opportunities in the employment field in a context which is not an immediately competitive one. For example, a disabled employee denied promotion would not need to show that a colleague was actually promoted instead. It might be sufficient to show that a similarly situated employee without a disability would have been promoted in those circumstances. A hypothetical comparator can be constructed by having regard to actual comparators whose circumstances were similar but not identical to those of the claimant.[5] Where a claimant can show that he or she was disadvantaged by reason of his or

---

1   DDA 1995, s 3A(6).

2   *British Gas Services Ltd v McCaull* [2001] IRLR 60, EAT.

3   DDA 1995, s 3A(1)(a); *Code of Practice: Employment and Occupation* (2004), paras 4.30–4.31 (and examples); *Code of Practice: Trade Organisations and Qualifications Bodies* (2004), paras 4.29–4.30 (and examples).

4   DDA 1995, s 3A(1)(a).

5   The case-law in race and sex discrimination is instructive: *Chief Constable of West Yorkshire v Vento* [2001] IRLR 124, EAT; *Balamoody v United Kingdom Central Council for Nursing, Midwifery and Health Visiting* [2001] EWCA Civ 2097, [2002] IRLR 288, CA.

her disability, it may not be necessary at all to identify other comparators with whom to compare the treatment of the disabled person.[1]

3.2.6   Secondly, there will often be no 'smoking gun' or direct evidence of discrimination. Prior to 1 October 2004, an employment tribunal may have been able to draw inferences of discrimination from the primary facts.[2] The outcome in disability discrimination cases was often dependent upon the propriety of drawing inferences from primary facts in relation to the question of whether there has been less favourable treatment for a reason related to disability. If an employer gave an unsatisfactory explanation for the detrimental treatment of a disabled person (eg a dismissal), it was open to the tribunal to infer disability discrimination.[3] From 1 October 2004, where the claimant proves facts from which the tribunal could conclude, in the absence of an adequate explanation, that the respondent has acted in a way which is unlawful under Part 2, the tribunal shall uphold the complaint, unless the respondent proves that it did not so act.[4]

3.2.7   Thirdly, a disabled person can seek to show that he or she has been treated less favourably than another disabled person has been or would be. The provision does not necessarily call for an analysis of discriminatory behaviour which distinguished between disabled and non-disabled individuals. For example, two equally well-qualified applicants might be in competition for an employment vacancy. One has a physical disability and the other a mental disability. If, without interviewing both candidates and considering their respective merits, the employer automatically rejects the applicant with a mental disability, that action could form the basis of a complaint of disability-related discrimination brought by the rejected applicant. Again, the employer might be able to justify the differential treatment, but the

---

1   *British Sugar plc v Kirker* [1998] IRLR 624, EAT (but for his or her disability, would the disabled person have been treated in that way?).

2   *West Midlands Passenger Transport Executive v Singh* [1988] IRLR 186, CA; *King v Great Britain-China Centre* [1991] IRLR 513, CA; *Qureshi v London Borough of Newham* [1991] IRLR 264, CA; *Zafar v Glasgow City Council* [1998] ICR 125, HL; *Anya v University of Oxford* [2001] IRLR 364, CA; *Rihal v London Borough of Ealing* [2004] IRLR 642, CA; *Bahl v The Law Society* [2004] IRLR 799, CA.

3   *British Sugar plc v Kirker* [1998] IRLR 624, EAT; *Rowden v Dutton Gregory (a firm)* [2002] ICR 971, EAT.

4   DDA 1995, s 17A(1C), implementing Council Directive 2000/78/EC, Art 10; *Barton v Investec Henderson Crosthwaite Securities Ltd* [2003] IRLR 332, EAT; *University of Huddersfield v Wolff* [2004] IRLR 534, EAT; *Chamberlin Solicitors v Emokpae* [2004] IRLR 592, EAT; *Sinclair Roche & Temperley v Heard* [2004] IRLR 763, EAT; *Code of Practice: Employment and Occupation* (2004), paras 4.41–4.43 (and examples); *Code of Practice: Trade Organisations and Qualifications Bodies* (2004), paras 4.40–4.42 (and examples).

individual with a mental disability was entitled to be given due consideration.[1]

3.2.8 Fourthly, the actual or hypothetical comparison is between the disabled person and a comparator to whom the reason relating to the disabled person's disability does not or would not apply. The definition of disability-related discrimination does not call for a simplistic comparison between a disabled person and a person who is not disabled or who does not have the disability in question. During the parliamentary debates, the Minister gave the example of two employees who cannot type: one because he or she is disabled with arthritis and the other (who is not disabled) because he or she has never been taught to type. If the disabled person with arthritis is refused employment as a typist, that is not discriminatory treatment, provided the non-disabled person (who has never been taught to type) is also refused employment in such a position.[2] The disabled person has been refused employment because of a reason related to disability (the inability to type being due to arthritis). However, he or she has not been treated less favourably in comparison with the other person if the employer has rejected all candidates who cannot type. If the employer offers the position to someone who is able to type, that may be less favourable treatment of the person with arthritis for a reason related to his or her disability. Nevertheless, subject to the duty to make adjustments, the employer will probably be able to explain the treatment if typing skills are a requirement of the position applied for.

3.2.9 Fifthly, is the basis of the comparison to be drawn widely or narrowly? This depends upon the interpretation to be placed upon the phrase 'that reason'.[3] Take, for example, a disabled employee who is dismissed for absenteeism, including disability-related absences. With whom should the employee be compared for the purpose of establishing less favourable treatment? One possibility is to compare how the disabled employee has been treated relative to an employee also absent from work for the same length of time, but for a reason which is not related to disability. This would reflect the usual expectation in discrimination cases that like should be compared with like.[4]

3.2.10 However, disability-related discrimination (unlike direct discrimination) does not require the comparison to be based upon a

---

1   It is also likely to be direct discrimination but, if so, that cannot be justified.

2   HL Deb, vol 566, col 1200; *Code of Practice: Employment and Occupation* (2004), para 4.30 (example); *Code of Practice: Trade Organisations and Qualifications Bodies* (2004), para 4.29 (example).

3   DDA 1995, s 3A(1)(a).

4   *Clark v Novacold Ltd* [1998] IRLR 420, EAT.

consideration of the comparators in relevant circumstances which are the same or not materially different. Thus, a second possibility is to compare how the disabled employee (who is unable to perform the functions of his or her job) has been treated in comparison with other employees who were not absent from work at all (ie who are performing the main functions of their jobs). This focuses upon the reason for the treatment (ie the reason for the dismissal) and not the reason for the absence which led to the dismissal. The disabled employee has been dismissed for absenteeism. Some of those absences are related to his or her disability, so the dismissal is for a reason (ie absenteeism) which relates to the disabled person's disability. For the purposes of establishing less favourable treatment, the comparison must be with others to whom that reason (ie absenteeism) does not (or would not) apply. Attention would then switch to the employer's justification defence.[1]

3.2.11   That is the approach favoured by the Court of Appeal in *Clark v TDG Ltd t/a Novacold* and is now the authoritative one.[2] It has been explained as requiring the tribunal to determine the material reason for the treatment complained of; then to ask whether that material reason related to the disability in question; and finally to consider whether the respondent would have treated in the same way some other person to whom that material reason would not apply.[3]

Reason related to disability

3.2.12   The less favourable treatment of a disabled person must be 'for a reason which relates to the disabled person's disability'.[4] The intention, purpose or motive for so acting is not relevant. However, there must be a nexus or causal connection between the less favourable treatment and the claimant's disability.[5] The Act does not prohibit an employer from appointing the best person for the job. Equally, it does not prevent employers or others in the employment field from treating disabled people more favourably than those without a disability. A disabled person who is refused or denied an opportunity in the employment field because he or she does not have the necessary vocational qualifications, or is not the best person on merit, has not been discriminated against. That person has been treated less favourably than the person who was awarded the opportunity, at least in the

---

1   DDA 1995, s 3A(1)(b), subject to the duty to make reasonable adjustments.

2   [1999] IRLR 318, CA. The Court of Appeal did not comment upon the EAT's approach in *Kirker v British Sugar plc* [1998] IRLR 624. The 'but for' test in *Kirker* is not without the attraction of simplicity, but *Novacold* navigates the statutory language more assuredly.

3   *Cosgrove v Caesar & Howie* [2001] IRLR 653, EAT.

4   DDA 1995, s 3A(1)(a).

5   *British Gas Services Ltd v McCaull* [2001] IRLR 60, EAT.

sense that his or her employment aspirations have been disappointed. Nevertheless, the reason for the apparently less favourable treatment is not that person's disability, but rather a reason which is unrelated to disability, namely merit or qualification.

3.2.13 The test of causation under the DDA 1995 appears to be the same as that under the other discrimination statutes – was the person's disability the effective and predominant cause or the real and efficient cause of the less favourable treatment?[1] If an employment tribunal is to conclude that there is no connection between the disability and the discriminatory treatment, this must be explained by reference to the evidence (including medical evidence) and its findings of fact.[2] It is equally important for the tribunal to identify correctly what is the treatment that is the subject of the complaint.

3.2.14 For example, in one case, the payment of contractual sick pay was discretionary.[3] The claimant previously had been paid contractual sick pay during disability-related absences. However, due to high sickness levels among its workforce, the employer then exercised its discretion not to pay sick pay generally. It refused to pay sick pay to the claimant when he experienced further disability-related absences. He would be treated no differently from other employees in this respect. The EAT said that the treatment complained of was not the non-payment of wages ordinarily due, but rather the non-payment of discretionary sick pay. The claimant had not been refused sick pay for a reason related to his disability. The reason was the employer's application of its revised policy on discretionary sick pay and that was not a reason related to the claimant's disability (nor, it might be added, was he being treated less favourably than comparable other employees). However, in another case, an employer who reduced a disabled person's sick pay to half pay in accordance with its sickness absence policy was held to have failed to comply with its duty to make reasonable adjustments and committed unjustified disability-related discrimination.[4]

3.2.15 The concept of 'a reason which relates to the disabled person's disability' is a deliberately wide one and should be interpreted broadly. It is noticeably wider and more inclusive than the phrases 'on the ground of' or 'by reason of' which are found elsewhere in discrimination law. It is permissible to adopt a width to the expression 'which

---

1   *Nagarajan v London Regional Transport* [1999] IRLR 572, HL; *Murphy v Sheffield Hallam University* (2000) EAT/6/99; *Rowden v Dutton Gregory (a firm)* [2002] ICR 971, EAT.

2   *Edwards v Mid Suffolk District Council* [2001] IRLR 190, EAT.

3   *London Clubs Management Ltd v Hood* [2001] IRLR 719, EAT.

4   *Nottinghamshire County Council v Meikle* [2004] IRLR 703, CA.

relates to' which is inclusive of causative links beyond those which would fall within phrases such as 'on the ground of disability' or 'by reason of disability'.[1] For example, a disabled employee whose disability worsens, creating difficulty in carrying out his or her work, might have been dismissed by an employer for incompetence or poor performance. However, although the reason for dismissal is a performance-related reason, it is also a reason related to the employee's disability. But for the employee's disability, his or her work performance would not have deteriorated and dismissal would not have resulted. The question will then arise as to whether the disabled employee has been treated less favourably than others to whom that reason does not apply and, if so, whether the employer can justify the treatment. In one case,[2] a teacher had a congenital heart disorder which meant that pregnancy would endanger her life. She had a child by a surrogate mother, but the school refused her paid post-natal leave because of a budget deficit. The EAT held that the refusal amounted to disability-related less favourable treatment. Her comparators were others who gave birth to their own children. The reason for the treatment was her inability to have children. That was a reason that related to her disability. However, the school succeeded in justifying the treatment on the ground of its financial position.

Knowledge of disability

3.2.16   Although the concept of 'a reason which relates to the disabled person's disability' may be at large, is it essential to be able to show that the respondent was aware of the disability? The issue of knowledge is a separate one from the issues of motive and intention (which are irrelevant). There are two possible views.

3.2.17   The first view is that the respondent's knowledge of the disability is irrelevant. The test is whether, with the benefit of hindsight, it can be seen that the disabled person has been treated less favourably for a reason which is related to disability, as a matter of fact. The relevant statutory provision is silent on the question of knowledge. In contrast, in the context of the duty to make reasonable adjustments, there is an express requirement that the respondent must know (or, at least, have reasonable means of knowing) that the claimant is a disabled person. If the statute in one context has made knowledge of disability relevant by

---

1   *Rowden v Dutton Gregory (a firm)* [2002] ICR 971, EAT.

2   *Murphy v Slough Borough Council* [2004] ICR 1163, EAT. The case also decided that a governing body of a school, rather than the local education authority, was the correct respondent by virtue of Education (Modification of Enactments Relating to Employment) Order 1999, SI 1999/2256, arts 2(2) and 6. See now: Education (Modification of Enactments Relating to Employment) Order 2003, SI 2003/1964.

express provision, then the statute must have intended, by its silence, in another context that knowledge of disability should be irrelevant. The question of the respondent's knowledge or ignorance of the claimant's disability then goes to justification rather than to the issue of *prima facie* discrimination.

3.2.18 The second view is that the respondent's knowledge (actual or constructive) is relevant. Can a respondent be said to have treated a person less favourably 'for a reason which relates to' that person's disability if the respondent did not know that the person was disabled? How can someone be said to have acted for a particular reason unless they are aware of the ingredients which inform that reason? A respondent cannot deliberately ignore the available evidence or facts and thereby argue that it did not know that the person was disabled. Equally, the fact that the respondent did not believe the person to be disabled, or did not understand the significance of the statutory definition, may not be an excuse. However, this second view does require the respondent to have some knowledge that the person is disabled before there is disability-related discrimination.[1]

3.2.19 How are these conflicting views to be reconciled? One division of the EAT has ruled in *O'Neill v Symm & Co Ltd* that the respondent's actual or constructive knowledge of the disability is relevant.[2] It reasoned that a respondent cannot be said to have treated a person less favourably *for a reason which relates to* that person's disability if the respondent did not know that the person was disabled. Knowledge of the material features of the disability will be enough, but not simply knowledge of one or other equivocal symptom. This approach might discourage employers from seeking information from employment applicants and employees that might lead to a disclosure of disability. It is doubtful whether this view – that the word 'reason', as a matter of causation, involves knowledge of the matter which is material – was compatible with *Clark v TDG Ltd t/a Novacold*.[3]

3.2.20 Subsequently, another division of the EAT has reconsidered the position in *H J Heinz & Co Ltd v Kenrick*.[4] The EAT rejected the view that the respondent is required to have knowledge of the disability or its material features. It casts doubt upon whether the earlier decision is correct. The EAT ruled that the test of the relationship between the alleged less favourable treatment and a disability is objective (does the

---

1   See, in an analogous context: *Del Monte Foods Ltd v Mundon* [1980] ICR 694, EAT; *Simon v Brimham Associates* [1987] IRLR 307, CA.

2   [1998] IRLR 233, EAT.

3   [1999] IRLR 318, CA.

4   [2000] IRLR 144, EAT.

relationship exist?) rather than subjective (did the respondent know that the relationship existed?). Furthermore, a reason related to disability is a broad concept, which can include a reason which derives from how the disability manifests itself.

3.2.21   The reasoning in *Kenrick* is preferable to that in *O'Neill.* That view is supported by *London Borough of Hammersmith and Fulham v Farnsworth,*[1] where the EAT stated that the approach in *O'Neill* was no longer good law in the light of the decision of the Court of Appeal in *Clark.* The effect is that, for example, employers should pause to consider whether a proposed dismissal might be connected with a reason related to a disability (of which the employer might otherwise be unaware). As soon as factors exist which put the employer on guard (such as the employer's awareness that the employee had been receiving medical treatment), the employer must pause to determine whether a disability exists which requires to be addressed by the duty to make reasonable adjustments (eg by not dismissing or by taking other steps). The employer cannot rely upon its ignorance of the circumstances unless that is rationally based. If, at the relevant time, it would have been reasonable to have undertaken further investigation to discover the actual situation and to assess it in the light of the relevant law, the employer would be expected to do so.[2]

3.2.22   Furthermore, a respondent might be treated as being possessed of knowledge by virtue of what was known to an employee or agent of the respondent (such as a line manager, a personnel officer or an occupational health practitioner) at the relevant time. For example, an occupational health physician was treated as the relevant decision-maker as to whether an employment applicant should be employed where, following a provisional offer of employment, the employer acted upon the physician's medical report as to that person's employability and withdrew the offer.[3] The question of what the respondent knew of the disability may still be relevant to the issue of justification and the duty to make reasonable adjustments.

Justification

3.2.23   A person discriminates against a disabled person if there is less favourable treatment of a disabled person for a reason related to the disabled person's disability *and* the alleged discriminator cannot show that the less favourable treatment is justified.[4] The burden of proof will

---

1   [2000] IRLR 691, EAT.

2   *Heggison v A & W Bernard* (2000) EAT/1276/99.

3   *London Borough of Hammersmith and Fulham v Farnsworth* [2000] IRLR 691, EAT.

4   DDA 1995, s 3A(1)(b).

be upon the person who relies upon the justification defence. Less favourable treatment is justified if, *but only if*, the reason for it is *both* material to the circumstances of the *particular* case *and* substantial.[1] However, the treatment of a disabled person cannot be justified if the respondent is under a duty to make reasonable adjustments in relation to the disabled person, but fails to comply with that duty, unless the treatment would have been justified even if the respondent had complied with the duty.[2] This is a novel defence in the context of discrimination law. The EAT has described the statutory test of justification in the 1995 Act as 'unique'.[3]

3.2.24 The justification defence goes beyond merely showing that a disabled person was treated less favourably than others for a reason unconnected with or unrelated to his or her disability. A respondent will always be able to defend a discrimination complaint of this kind by proving that the alleged discriminatory act was not for a reason which related to the disabled person's disability.[4] The justification defence clearly only applies where a respondent *has* treated a disabled person less favourably for a disability-related reason. In other words, the Act envisages that there will be cases where, despite the merit principle, a respondent could take lawful account of a person's disability. Two especially difficult areas are health and safety concerns and medical information.[5] The EC Framework Employment Directive explicitly anticipates that, with regard to disabled persons, the principle of equal treatment shall be without prejudice to the right of Member States to maintain or adopt provisions on the protection of health and safety at work or to measures aimed at creating or maintaining provisions or facilities for safeguarding or promoting their integration into the working environment.[6]

3.2.25 For example, the disabled person might be otherwise well qualified for an employment position. However, the evidence might support a real fear (as opposed to a stereotypical assumption) of a clear and unacceptable health and safety risk to the disabled person or others, or that the disability will prevent the disabled person from

---

1   DDA 1995, s 3A(3); *Code of Practice: Employment and Occupation* (2004), chapter 6; *Code of Practice: Trade Organisations and Qualifications Bodies* (2004), chapter 6.

2   DDA 1995, s 3A(6).

3   *Baynton v Saurus General Engineers Ltd* [1999] IRLR 604, EAT.

4   That is implicit in the wording of s 3A(1)(a).

5   See *Code of Practice: Employment and Occupation* (2004), paras 6.7–6.16; *Code of Practice: Trade Organisations and Qualifications Bodies* (2004), paras 6.8–6.18.

6   Council Directive 2000/78/EC, Art 7(1).

attending work regularly and predictably.[1] In one case, a school was held
to be justified in dismissing an employee with schizophrenia because he
was not taking medication prescribed to control his condition, and
other staff or pupils could have been at risk if he had an acute relapse.[2]
In another case, the dismissal of an employee was held to be justified in
circumstances where the employee had a poor sickness and attendance
record, failed to comply with sickness reporting procedures, failed to
respond to the employer's attempts to accommodate him and was not fit
to return to work within a predictable timescale.[3] Such conclusions must
be based upon hard evidence and not merely assumptions or
stereotypes.

3.2.26   The justification defence is a particular, rather than general,
defence. The use of the phrase 'if, but only if' clearly limits the scope for
justifying less favourable treatment of a disabled person for a reason
related to disability. A respondent might have no difficulty in subjectively justifying to itself or to others the discriminatory treatment of
disabled persons, but that is not enough to satisfy the test of justification.
Furthermore, where the respondent is under a statutory duty to make
reasonable adjustments, the justification defence must take account of
that duty. This is considered further below.

3.2.27   The statutory defence requires the respondent to show that the
reason for the less favourable treatment of a disabled person, for a
reason related to that person's disability, is both 'material' to the
circumstances of the particular case and 'substantial'.[4] The defence of
justification must take account of the circumstances of the particular
case.[5] The proper interpretation of the terms 'material' and 'substantial' is crucial to an understanding of the justification defence. The word
'material' conveys a sense that the reason for the discriminatory
treatment must be important, essential or relevant in the circumstances
of the case. The word 'substantial' is also used in the 1995 Act to
measure the adverse effect that a person's disability has upon normal
day-to-day activities. In that context, 'substantial' denotes something
which is more than minor or trivial. The term is also used to qualify the
disadvantage that must be faced by a disabled person before a
respondent's duty to make reasonable adjustments is triggered.

---

1   *Code of Practice: Employment and Occupation* (2004), paras 6.7–6.13 (and examples); *Code of
     Practice: Trade Organisations and Qualifications Bodies* (2004), paras 6.8–6.15 (and examples).

2   *A v London Borough of Hounslow* (2001) EAT/1155/98, IDS Brief 694.

3   *Callagan v Glasgow City Council* [2001] IRLR 724, EAT.

4   DDA 1995, s 3A(3).

5   HL Deb, vol 566, cols 118–119.

3.2.28 The Employment Code of Practice (1996) stated that the justification defence 'means that the reason has to relate to the individual circumstances in question and *not just be trivial or minor*'.[1] That suggests that the term 'substantial' should be interpreted consistently wherever it appears in the Act and simply denotes something that is more than minor or trivial. The 2004 versions of the Codes of Practice make it clear that the test is an objective one. It is stated that 'material' means that there must be a reasonably strong connection between the reason given for the treatment and the circumstances of the particular case, while 'substantial' means that the reason must carry real weight and be of substance.[2]

3.2.29 In *Baynton v Saurus General Engineers Ltd*,[3] the EAT noted the statutory sequence for establishing justification as follows:

- the disabled person shows less favourable treatment for a reason related to disability;
- that less favourable treatment is shown to amount to a potentially unlawful act;
- the respondent shows that the treatment is justified if the reason for the treatment is both material to the circumstances of the particular case and substantial:
  - *unless* the respondent is also under a statutory duty to make a reasonable adjustment in relation to the disabled person;
  - *and* the respondent fails to comply with that duty;[4]
- *subject to* the treatment being justified, *even if* the respondent had complied with that duty.[5]

The EAT held that, in applying the test of justification, the interests of the disabled person and the interests of the respondent must be weighed in the balance. All the circumstances of the case must be considered (including both those of the disabled person and those of the respondent) and not simply the justificatory reason offered by the respondent. This appears to emphasise not merely the objective nature of the justification defence, but also its even-handedness.

---

1 *Employment Code of Practice* (1996), para 4.6 (emphasis added).

2 *Code of Practice: Employment and Occupation* (2004), para 6.3 (and example); *Code of Practice: Trade Organisations and Qualifications Bodies* (2004), para 6.3.

3 [1999] IRLR 604, EAT.

4 A failure to comply with a duty to make reasonable adjustments can no longer be justified under the post-1 October 2004 law.

5 DDA 1995, s 3A(6). See *Code of Practice: Employment and Occupation* (2004), paras 6.4–6.6 (and example); *Code of Practice: Trade Organisations and Qualifications Bodies* (2004), paras 6.5–6.7.

3.2.30 Subsequently, however, another division of the EAT re-examined the justification defence in *H J Heinz & Co Ltd v Kenrick*.[1] The EAT agreed that the relevant circumstances include the circumstances of both the claimant and the respondent. Whilst not ruling out the balancing exercise between the interests of the two parties, the EAT pointed to the comparatively limited requirements of the statutory provision that provides both a necessary and sufficient condition for the operation of the defence. The EAT said that the justification defence is not a general test of reasonableness. In fact, the threshold for justification of disability-related less favourable treatment is a very low one, although apparently compatible with the Human Rights Act 1998.[2] The treatment *is* justified (not merely *can* or *may be* justified) if the reason for it is both material to the circumstances of the case and substantial (in the sense of being more than minor or trivial). On the facts of *Kenrick*, the employer's treatment of the disabled employee was held not to be justified because there had not been an adequate consideration of alternative employment or shorter hours before he was dismissed for a disability-related period of absence. The EAT in *Kenrick* recognised that where there was also a duty to make reasonable adjustments, there may be a necessary but *not* sufficient condition for justification, because the test of whether a reasonable adjustment would have made any difference also has to be satisfied. The EAT suggested that whenever a tribunal is moving towards a view that less favourable treatment is justified, it should reflect upon whether the respondent was also under a duty to make reasonable adjustments. If so, and if the respondent has failed to comply with that duty, then the tribunal should consider whether the less favourable treatment would still have been justified *even if* the employer had complied with the duty to make reasonable adjustments.

3.2.31 The substance of the test of justification is now explained more fully and authoritatively by the Court of Appeal in *Jones v Post Office*.[3] The claimant had developed insulin-dependent diabetes. He was removed from driving duties in accordance with the employer's medical fitness standards for its drivers, which required insulin-dependent employees to cease driving duties. The employer conceded that this amounted to disability-related less favourable treatment, but sought to argue that it was justified. The employment tribunal approached the case on the basis that the decision as to what was justified was for it to

---

1   [2000] IRLR 144, EAT.

2   *A v London Borough of Hounslow* (2001) EAT/1155/98, IDS Brief 694 (in particular, Arts 8 and 14 of the European Convention on Human Rights and Art 1 of the First Protocol to the Convention).

3   [2001] EWCA Civ 558, [2001] IRLR 384, CA.

make. It re-examined the medical evidence and concluded that he was not a safety risk when driving. It held that the employer had not established a material and substantial reason for removing the claimant from driving duties. The EAT allowed the employer's appeal, reasoning that the tribunal had misdirected itself when preferring the claimant's medical evidence at the hearing to that of the employer's own doctor considered at the time.[1]

3.2.32 The Court of Appeal in *Jones* dismissed a further appeal.[2] Its view was that the tribunal had been wrong to find that the employer's reason was not material or substantial simply because it preferred the claimant's medical evidence to that relied upon by the employer at the time of the risk assessment. The task of the tribunal is a limited one. The question is whether the reason given for less favourable treatment can properly be described as both material to the circumstances of the particular case and substantial. The employer has to satisfy the statutory criteria. That involves the tribunal investigating the facts and assessing whether there was evidence on the basis of which the employer's decision could properly be taken. For example, if the employer had not carried out a risk assessment,[3] or if the decision was taken without appropriate medical evidence, the tribunal could decide that the employer's reason was insufficient and the treatment unjustified. The tribunal could also so decide if the employer's decision was an irrational one, going beyond the range of reasonable responses open to a reasonable decision-maker. It was not the function of the tribunal to decide whether the employer's assessment of the risk was correct, provided it had been conducted properly, was based upon appropriate evidence and was not irrational.[4] It did not matter that the tribunal might have come to a different conclusion itself. It was not its function to make up its own mind based upon its own appraisal of the evidence. Its role is said to be not very different from that which it has under s 98 of the Employment Rights Act 1996 in unfair dismissal cases (the so-called 'band of reasonable responses' test).

---

1 *Post Office v Jones* [2000] ICR 388, EAT.

2 [2001] EWCA Civ 558, [2001] IRLR 384, CA.

3 A risk assessment might be a reasonable adjustment made as part of a pro-active approach to the DDA 1995: *Mid-Staffordshire General Hospitals NHS Trust v Cambridge* [2003] IRLR 566, EAT.

4 *A v London Borough of Hounslow* (2001) EAT/1155/98, IDS Brief 694 (a school was justified in dismissing an employee with schizophrenia because he was not taking the medication prescribed to control his condition, and other staff or pupils could have been at risk if he had an acute relapse. The employer had sufficient information on which to assess the risk and its medical adviser had been properly qualified to carry out the risk assessment).

3.2.33   The test propounded by the Court of Appeal in *Jones* is thus very different from the objective justification test which applies in sex and race discrimination cases. EC law adopts an objective justification standard in relation to indirect discrimination. For that reason, the decision in *Jones* is a controversial one. From 1 October 2004, following the amendments made to the DDA 1995 to implement the disability discrimination provisions of the EC Framework Employment Directive, it may be necessary to revisit the justification test in *Jones*.

3.2.34   Prior to 1 October 2004, it was possible to justify a failure to comply with a duty to make reasonable adjustments.[1] The applicability of *Jones* in justifying a failure to make reasonable adjustments was questioned judicially in *Collins v Royal National Theatre Board Ltd*.[2] Subsequently, the EAT has held that there is nothing in *Jones* that prevents a tribunal from making findings of fact on medical evidence obtained after an employer had rejected an employment applicant.[3] That evidence was relevant as to whether there was material to hand at the time at which the decision was made upon which such a decision could properly be made and was one open to a reasonable decision-maker. In another case, the EAT emphasised that the respondent must have sufficient material and must have carried out adequate inquiries to justify a decision to reject an employment applicant on grounds of disability.[4] In a further case, the EAT said that the nature and quality of medical evidence would be in issue for the tribunal where the medical practitioner had never treated the disabled person for his condition, did not know him well and did not comment in his report on the disabled person's fitness for the post or his ability to cope with stress.[5]

3.2.35   Is knowledge of a claimant's disability an ingredient of the test of justification of disability-related less favourable treatment? One division of the EAT took the view that a respondent cannot discharge the onus of justifying disability discrimination where it maintained that it did not know that the claimant was disabled (and thus did not apply its mind to what reasonable adjustments should be made).[6] In other words, a respondent could not deploy an *ex post facto* justification

---

1   DDA 1995, s 5(2) and (4), now repealed.

2   [2004] EWCA Civ 144, [2004] IRLR 395, CA (a factor that has already been considered in relation to the reasonableness of an adjustment cannot also be relied upon as part of a justification of a failure to make a reasonable adjustment). See also: *Law v Pace Micro Technology plc* [2004] EWCA Civ 923, CA (noting that *Collins* was implicitly approved in *Archibald v Fife Council* [2004] UKHL 32, [2004] IRLR 651, HL).

3   *Surrey Police v Marshall* [2002] IRLR 843, EAT.

4   *Murray v Newham Citizens Advice Bureau Ltd* [2003] IRLR 340, EAT.

5   *Paul v National Probation Service Ltd* [2004] IRLR 190, EAT.

6   *Quinn v Schwarzkopf Ltd* [2001] IRLR 67, EAT.

defence. However, that view has now been resiled from.[1] The fact that the respondent did not know that the disabled person was disabled might affect the justification issue but does not preclude it. Whether a person knew or did not know that the claimant was a disabled person is not an issue.[2] A person can rely upon a justification defence regardless of what he or she knew of the claimant's disability. The fact that the person did not know that the claimant was a disabled person may itself be capable of forming the substance of the justification.[3]

Direct discrimination

3.2.36 From 1 October 2004, a new form of discrimination is introduced into the 1995 Act in order to implement the EC Framework Employment Directive. This is direct discrimination. For the purposes of the Directive, the principle of equal treatment means that there shall be no direct discrimination whatsoever on the ground of disability.[4] Direct discrimination is taken to occur where one person is treated less favourably than another is (or has been or would be) treated in a comparable situation on the ground of disability.[5] The amended Act provides that a person directly discriminates against a disabled person if, on the ground of the disabled person's disability, the person treats the disabled person less favourably than the person treats (or would treat) a person not having that particular disability (and who has not had that particular disability) whose relevant circumstances (including his or her abilities) are the same as (or not materially different from) those of the disabled person.[6] Less favourable treatment of a disabled person for a reason related to disability cannot be justified if it amounts to direct discrimination.[7]

3.2.37 Direct discrimination is concerned with discrimination that is *on the ground of* a disabled person's disability, as opposed to a *reason related to* that disability. It reflects the definition of direct discrimination to be found in existing discrimination law. It remains to be seen what significance this new form of discrimination will assume in the context

---

1   *Callagan v Glasgow City Council* [2001] IRLR 724, EAT; *Quinn v Schwarzkopf Ltd* [2002] IRLR 602, Ct of Sess.

2   *London Borough of Hammersmith & Fulham v Farnsworth* [2000] IRLR 691, EAT.

3   *H J Heinz & Co Ltd v Kenrick* [2000] IRLR 144, EAT. See also *Johnson & Johnson Medical Ltd v Filmer* [2002] ICR 292, EAT; *Wright v Governors of Bilton High School and Warwickshire County Council* [2002] ICR 1463, EAT.

4   2000/78/EC, Art 2(1).

5   Ibid, Art 2(2)(a).

6   DDA 1995, s 3A(5) and Sch 2, para 2C (as amended).

7   Ibid, s 3A(4).

of the DDA 1995.[1] The DRC places direct discrimination at the top of its analysis of the meaning of discrimination.[2] Direct disability discrimination is likely to be a narrower concept than disability-related discrimination. However, direct disability discrimination cannot be justified (unlike disability-related discrimination). The comparator required to establish direct disability discrimination is also obviously different. The comparison is with the way in which a person not having the particular disability of the disabled person is or would be treated. That does not call for the same approach as is taken in disability-related discrimination following *Clark v TDG Ltd t/a Novacold.*[3]

On the ground of disability

3.2.38   The first point to note is that the less favourable treatment must be 'on the ground of' the disabled person's disability. This is a question of causation.[4] Was the treatment caused by the fact that the disabled person is disabled or has a particular disability? But for the disability, would the disabled person have been treated in the way that he or she was treated? Was the disability the effective (even if not the sole) cause of the treatment, judged objectively? Direct discrimination is likely to tackle discrimination based upon assumptions about and stereotypes of disabled people (such as unfounded health and safety concerns).[5] It will also deal with less favourable treatment that is disability-specific or based upon prejudice, especially where there is an apparently neutral reason for the treatment, but which is a pretext for discrimination.[6] Knowledge that the person has a disability or is a disabled person does

---

1   See the DRC's illustration of how direct discrimination is to be distinguished from disability-related discrimination and discrimination by way of a failure to make reasonable adjustments: *Code of Practice: Employment and Occupation* (2004), para 4.37 (and examples); *Code of Practice: Trade Organisations and Qualifications Bodies* (2004), para 4.36 (and examples).

2   *Code of Practice: Employment and Occupation* (2004), paras 4.5–4.23 (and examples); *Code of Practice: Trade Organisations and Qualifications Bodies* (2004), paras 4.5–4.22 (and examples).

3   [1999] IRLR 318, CA; *Code of Practice: Employment and Occupation* (2004), para 4.19; *Code of Practice: Trade Organisations and Qualifications Bodies* (2004), para 4.19.

4   *Code of Practice: Employment and Occupation* (2004), para 4.7; *Code of Practice: Trade Organisations and Qualifications Bodies* (2004), para 4.7.

5   *Code of Practice: Employment and Occupation* (2004), paras 4.8 and 6.7 (and examples); *Code of Practice: Trade Organisations and Qualifications Bodies* (2004), paras 4.8 and 6.8 (and examples).

6   *Code of Practice: Employment and Occupation* (2004), paras 4.9–4.10 (and examples); *Code of Practice: Trade Organisations and Qualifications Bodies* (2004), paras 4.9–4.10 (and examples).

not appear to be required and the treatment in question might not be conscious.[1]

The comparator

3.2.39 The second point to make is that direct discrimination is concerned with the less favourable treatment of a disabled person compared with the treatment of a person not having that particular disability. The comparator may be actual or hypothetical.[2] The comparator must be a person who does not have a disability at all or a person who has another kind of disability.[3] Where a hypothetical comparator is selected, it may be necessary to construct such a comparator from evidence of other persons who have been treated differently in broadly similar circumstances.[4]

The relevant circumstances

3.2.40 The third issue to address is the relevant circumstances of the comparison. The comparator's relevant circumstances must be the same as, or not materially different from, those of the disabled person. Those relevant circumstances will include the respective abilities of the comparator and the disabled person. It is clear that the relevant circumstances do not have to be identical, provided that they are not materially different.[5] The identification of a comparator in direct discrimination is an exercise that is a familiar one in discrimination law generally.[6] Nevertheless, difficulty may arise in identifying the circumstances that are relevant to the comparison. The fact that the disabled person has a disability is not a relevant circumstance, although the effects of the disability might be.[7] However, the disabled person's circumstances and abilities are to be considered as they actually are.

---

1   *Code of Practice: Employment and Occupation* (2004), para 4.11 (and example); *Code of Practice: Trade Organisations and Qualifications Bodies* (2004), paras 4.11–4.12.

2   *Code of Practice: Employment and Occupation* (2004), para 4.12: *Code of Practice: Trade Organisations and Qualifications Bodies* (2004), para 4.12.

3   *Code of Practice: Employment and Occupation* (2004), para 4.13 (and example); *Code of Practice: Trade Organisations and Qualifications Bodies* (2004), para 4.13.

4   *Code of Practice: Employment and Occupation* (2004), para 4.18 (and example); *Code of Practice: Trade Organisations and Qualifications Bodies* (2004), para 4.18 (and example).

5   *Code of Practice: Employment and Occupation* (2004), paras 4.14–4.16 (and examples); *Code of Practice: Trade Organisations and Qualifications Bodies* (2004), paras 4.14–4.16 (and examples).

6   *Code of Practice: Employment and Occupation* (2004), para 4.17; *Code of Practice: Trade Organisations and Qualifications Bodies* (2004), para 4.17. See *Shamoon v Chief Constable of the Royal Ulster Constabulary* [2003] IRLR 285, HL.

7   *Code of Practice: Employment and Occupation* (2004), paras 4.20–4.21 (and examples); *Code of Practice: Trade Organisations and Qualifications Bodies* (2004), para 4.20 (and example).

That means that if any reasonable adjustments are already in place, it is the disabled person's circumstances or abilities as measured with the assistance of reasonable adjustments that are relevant. However, if no reasonable adjustments have yet been made, the comparison is to be made without consideration of what effect any reasonable adjustments might have on the disabled person's circumstances or abilities.[1]

Justification

3.2.41   Finally, direct discrimination cannot be justified.[2] There is no justification defence contained within the definition of 'direct discrimination'. Furthermore, less favourable treatment of a disabled person for a reason related to disability cannot be justified if it amounts to direct discrimination.[3]

Failure to make reasonable adjustments

3.2.42   The EC Framework Employment Directive requires that the principle of equal treatment shall mean that there shall be no indirect discrimination whatsoever on the ground of disability.[4] Indirect discrimination shall be taken to occur where an apparently neutral provision, criterion or practice would put persons having a particular disability at a particular disadvantage compared with other persons.[5] However, there is no indirect discrimination where that provision, criterion or practice is objectively justified by a legitimate aim and the means of achieving that aim are appropriate and necessary.[6] In addition, there is no indirect discrimination where, as regards persons with a particular disability, a person to whom the Directive applies is obliged under national legislation to take appropriate measures to eliminate disadvantages entailed by such provision, criterion or practice.[7] That anticipates reasonable accommodation for disabled persons. In order to guarantee compliance with the principle of equal treatment in relation to disabled persons with disabilities, reasonable accommodation shall be provided. This means that employers shall take appropriate measures, where needed in a particular case, to enable a

---

1   *Code of Practice: Employment and Occupation* (2004), para 4.22 (and examples); *Code of Practice: Trade Organisations and Qualifications Bodies* (2004), para 4.21 (and example).

2   *Code of Practice: Employment and Occupation* (2004), para 4.23; *Code of Practice: Trade Organisations and Qualifications Bodies* (2004), para 4.22.

3   DDA 1995, s 3A(4); *Code of Practice: Employment and Occupation* (2004), para 6.3; *Code of Practice: Trade Organisations and Qualifications Bodies* (2004), para 6.3.

4   Council Directive 2000/78/EC, Art 2(1).

5   Ibid, Art 2(2)(b).

6   Ibid, Art 2(2)(b)(i).

7   Ibid, Art 2(2)(b)(ii).

person with a disability to have access to, participate in or advance in employment, or to undergo training, unless such measures would impose a disproportionate burden on the employer.[1]

3.2.43 What distinguishes disability discrimination legislation from other discrimination law is the explicit duty that the 1995 Act places upon employers and others in the employment field to make reasonable adjustments to their arrangements and physical environment so as to accommodate disabled persons. The DDA 1995 does not contain a definition of 'indirect discrimination'. However, the statutory provisions:

> 'already firmly cover – and are intended to cover – the use of standards, criteria, administrative methods, work practices or procedures that adversely affect a disabled person. That applies whether determining who should be employed or dismissed or establishing terms on the basis of which people are employed and their access to opportunities is structured.'[2]

This addresses work practices and procedures which have an indirectly adverse effect upon the employment opportunities of disabled persons. It was clearly intended that indirect discrimination would be prohibited and that this should be underlined by the duty to make reasonable adjustments.[3] Whether that complies with the EC Framework Employment Directive remains to be seen.

3.2.44 There is nothing in Part 2 of the Act to prevent employers and others voluntarily affording disabled persons preferential treatment. The duty to make reasonable adjustments is an essential part of the prohibition on disability-related discrimination. Without employers and others in the employment field being required to adjust practices or policies and to modify physical features of premises, disabled persons would face potentially indirect discrimination in the employment field. For example, employers' requirements and conditions will frequently represent barriers to equal opportunity and might have a disproportionate adverse impact upon disabled persons. Unless respondents are required to re-examine norms and standards established by reference to the predominant society, culture or environment, historic discrimination and inequality of opportunity are merely perpetuated.

---

1   2000/78/EC, Art 5. This burden shall not be disproportionate when it is sufficiently remedied by measures existing within the framework of the disability policy of the Member State concerned.

2   HC Deb Standing Committee E, col 142.

3   Ibid, col 143.

Discrimination and the duty to make reasonable adjustments

3.2.45 For the purposes of Part 2 of the DDA 1995, a person also discriminates against a disabled person if that person fails to comply with a duty to make reasonable adjustments imposed on that person in relation to the disabled person.[1] In a case of disability-related discrimination,[2] if the respondent is under a duty to make reasonable adjustments in relation to a disabled person, but fails to comply with that duty, the respondent's treatment of that disabled person cannot be justified unless it would have been justified even if the respondent had complied with that duty.[3] A breach of the statutory duty is not otherwise an actionable breach of duty in itself but is merely an ingredient of the meaning of discrimination.[4]

3.2.46 An action for disability discrimination by way of a complaint that the respondent has failed to discharge a duty to make reasonable adjustments does not depend upon the claimant also bringing or succeeding in a claim of direct discrimination or disability-related discrimination.[5] It is possible that a breach of the duty to make reasonable adjustments could also amount to less favourable treatment for a reason related to disability.[6] Nevertheless, they are separate claims and should be dealt with explicitly as such by an employment tribunal.[7]

Justification

3.2.47 Prior to 1 October 2004, a failure *without justification* to comply with the statutory duty imposed on a person to make reasonable adjustments in relation to a disabled person amounted to an act of discrimination.[8] Prior to that date, a failure to comply with the duty could be justified if, but only if, the reason for the failure was both

---

1   DDA 1995, s 3A(2). *Code of Practice: Employment and Occupation* (2004), paras 4.24–4.26; *Code of Practice: Trade Organisations and Qualifications Bodies* (2004), paras 4.23–4.25.

2   Ibid, s 3A(1).

3   Ibid, s 3A(6). In *Nottinghamshire County Council v Meikle* [2004] IRLR 704, CA, the claimant's sick pay was reduced to half pay after 100 days' sickness in accordance with the respondent's policy. The question was whether the respondent had shown that if reasonable adjustments had been made, the claimant would not have been absent for over 100 days and thereby liable to half pay.

4   Ibid, s 18B(6).

5   *Clark v TDG Ltd t/a Novacold* [1999] IRLR 318, CA.

6   *Rowden v Dutton Gregory (a firm)* [2002] ICR 971, EAT (a disciplinary process conducted in breach of the duty to make reasonable adjustments, in that the employee's absence through illness made the process inadequate, could amount to less favourable treatment for a disability-related reason).

7   *Butterfield v Rapidmark Ltd t/a 3 MV* (1998) EAT 131/98.

8   DDA 1995, ss 5(2)(b), (4) and 6 (now repealed).

material to the circumstances of the particular case and substantial.[1] From 1 October 2004, however, a failure to comply with that duty can no longer be justified.[2] The sole test is one of reasonableness.[3]

3.2.48 Where a respondent has treated a disabled person less favourably for a reason which relates to disability,[4] but has failed to comply with a statutory duty to make reasonable adjustments, then the less favourable treatment cannot be justified[5] unless the respondent can show that it would have been justified even if the respondent had complied with the duty to make a reasonable adjustment.[6] The matter should not be tackled *de novo* by the tribunal and without reference to the steps actually taken by the respondent.[7] Before a respondent can seek to justify the less favourable treatment of a disabled person for a reason related to disability, it must first address its duty to make reasonable adjustments. The respondent cannot rely upon a material and substantial reason for less favourable treatment if that reason could have been rendered immaterial or insubstantial by carrying out a reasonable adjustment.

Victimisation

3.2.49 A person (A) discriminates against another person (B) if A treats B less favourably than A treats or would treat other persons whose circumstances are the same as B's, and A does so for one of a number of specified reasons.[8] The specified reasons are as follows.

---

1 The case-law is now of historic interest only. See: *HM Prison Service v Beart* [2003] IRLR 238, CA; *Collins v Royal National Theatre Board Ltd* [2004] EWCA Civ 144, [2004] IRLR 395 CA.

2 See the previous case-law, now no longer relevant: *Greater Manchester Fire & Civil Defence Authority v Bradley* (EAT, 27 April 2001, unreported); *British Gas Services v McCaull* [2001] IRLR 60, EAT; *Cosgrove v Caesar & Howie* [2001] IRLR 653, EAT; *Fu v London Borough of Camden* [2001] IRLR 186, EAT; *Callagan v Glasgow City Council* [2001] IRLR 724, EAT; *Quinn v Schwarzkopf Ltd* [2002] IRLR 602, Ct of Sess; *Johnson & Johnson Medical Ltd v Filmer* [2002] ICR 292, EAT; *Wright v Governors of Bilton High School and Warwickshire County Council* (2002) EAT/113/01, IDS Brief 711.

3 *Code of Practice: Employment and Occupation* (2004), paras 5.43–5.44; *Code of Practice: Trade Organisations and Qualifications Bodies* (2004), paras 5.26–5.27 (and examples).

4 DDA 1995, s 3A(1).

5 Ibid, s 3A(3).

6 Ibid, s 3A(6). See *Baynton v Saurus General Engineers Ltd* [1999] IRLR 604, EAT; *HJ Heinz Co Ltd v Kenrick* [2000] IRLR 144, EAT.

7 *Post Office v Jones* [2000] ICR 388, EAT (tribunal should not carry out the exercise based solely on the evidence tendered at the hearing). See now *Jones v Post Office* [2001] IRLR 384, CA.

8 DDA 1995, s 55(1); *Code of Practice: Employment and Occupation* (2004), paras 4.33–4.36 (and example); *Code of Practice: Trade Organisations and Qualifications Bodies* (2004), paras 4.32– 4.35 (and example). Victimisation is not a free-standing legal wrong and can only succeed

3.2.50   First, that B has brought proceedings against A or any other person under the Act.[1] Secondly, that B has given evidence or information in connection with such proceedings brought by any person.[2] Thirdly, that B has otherwise done anything under (or by reference to) the Act in relation to A or any other person.[3] Fourthly, that B has alleged that A or any other person has (whether or not the allegation so states) contravened the Act.[4] Where B is a disabled person (or a person who has had a disability), the disability in question shall be disregarded in comparing his or her circumstances with those of any other person for any of the above purposes.[5] Fifthly, that A believes or suspects that B has done or intends to do any of the above things.[6] The provisions on victimisation do not apply to the treatment of a person because of an allegation made by him or her if the allegation was false and not made in good faith.[7] In the case of an act which constitutes discrimination by virtue of victimisation, the relevant causes of action also apply to discrimination against a person who is not disabled.[8]

Discrimination by association or perception

3.2.51   The Act, as originally drafted and as subsequently amended, does not address the problem of discrimination against non-disabled persons because of their association with (or relationship to) a disabled person.[9] That is because it is only unlawful where a person discriminates against a disabled person on the ground of the disabled person's disability, or for a reason which relates to the disabled person's disability, or fails to comply with a duty to make reasonable adjustments imposed in relation to the disabled person, or subjects a disabled person to harassment for a reason which relates to the disabled person's disability. By the same reasoning, perceived discrimination – where a person is discriminated against because he or she is wrongly perceived to be a disabled person – falls outside the drafting of the Act. This is an obvious gap in the disability discrimination legislation, not found in

---

if the claimant can show that the victimisation has resulted in an act made unlawful by DDA 1995, s 4: *Bruce v Addleshaw Booth & Co* EAT 0404/03.

1   DDA 1995, s 55(2)(a)(i).

2   Ibid, s 55(2)(a)(ii).

3   Ibid, s 55(2)(a)(iii) and (6).

4   Ibid, s 55(2)(a)(iv).

5   Ibid, s 55(3).

6   Ibid, s 55(2)(b).

7   Ibid, s 55(4).

8   Ibid, s 55(5), modifying ss 4, 4B, 4D, 4G, 6A, 7A, 7C, 13, 14A, 14C and 16A for this purpose.

9   HC Deb Standing Committee E, cols 168 and 172.

other discrimination legislation, and may amount to a failure properly to implement the provisions of the EC Framework Employment Directive.

3.3 HARASSMENT

3.3.1 The EC Framework Employment Directive treats harassment as a deemed form of discrimination. It arises when unwanted conduct related to disability takes place, with the purpose or effect of violating the dignity of a person and of creating an intimidating, hostile, degrading, humiliating or offensive environment.[1] In this context, the concept of harassment may be defined in accordance with the national laws and practice of the Member States.

3.3.2 From 1 October 2004, for the purposes of Part 2 of the DDA 1995, a person subjects a disabled person to harassment where, for a reason which relates to the disabled person's disability, the person engages in unwanted conduct which has the purpose or effect of (a) violating the disabled person's dignity or (b) creating an intimidating, hostile, degrading, humiliating or offensive environment for him or her.[2] Conduct shall be regarded as having either of those effects only if, having regard to all the circumstances, including in particular the perception of the disabled person, it should reasonably be considered as having that effect.[3] However, if the conduct is engaged in with the purpose of having either of those effects, then harassment is established, regardless of its actual effect on the disabled person.[4]

3.4 DUTY TO MAKE REASONABLE ADJUSTMENTS

3.4.1 The duty to make reasonable adjustments pervades Part 2 of the DDA 1995. The House of Lords has stressed the positive nature of the duty to make reasonable adjustments and indicated that a respondent may be obliged to discriminate positively in favour of disabled persons.[5] As has been seen above, a person discriminates against a disabled

---

1   2000/78/EC, Art 2(3).

2   DDA 1995, s 3B(1).

3   Ibid, s 3B(2).

4   *Code of Practice: Employment and Occupation* (2004), paras 4.38–4.39 (and examples); *Code of Practice: Trade Organisations and Qualifications Bodies* (2004), paras 4.37–4.38 (and examples).

5   *Archibald v Fife Council* [2004] UKHL 32, [2004] IRLR 651, HL. Where an employer recruits a disabled employee to do a specific job, knowing of that employee's disability and that adjustments would have to be made, that is a material feature in relation to direct

person if that person fails to comply with a duty to make reasonable adjustments imposed on that person in relation to the disabled person.[1] In a case of disability-related discrimination,[2] if the respondent is under a duty to make reasonable adjustments in relation to a disabled person, but fails to comply with that duty, the respondent's treatment of that disabled person cannot be justified unless it would have been justified even if the respondent had complied with that duty.[3] The circumstances in which the duty to make reasonable adjustments is triggered will be examined in specific detail in the next chapter. Those circumstances differ according to whether the duty arises in the context of employment or in relation to the other occupational settings. However, there are some concepts of reasonable adjustment which are common to the employment field generally and these are examined here.

The duty illustrated

3.4.2   Unusually, the statute itself (rather than a Code of Practice) exemplifies the kinds of steps which a respondent might have to take in relation to a disabled person in order to comply with the duty to make reasonable adjustments.[4] The illustrations are as follows:

- making adjustments to premises;
- allocating some of the disabled person's duties to another person;
- transferring the disabled person to fill an existing vacancy;
- altering the disabled person's hours of working or training;
- assigning the disabled person to a different place of work or training;
- allowing the disabled person to be absent during working or training hours for rehabilitation, assessment or treatment;
- giving or arranging for training or mentoring (whether for the disabled person or any other person);
- acquiring or modifying equipment;
- modifying instructions or reference manuals;
- modifying procedures for testing or assessment;
- providing a reader or interpreter;

---

discrimination, to the duty to make reasonable adjustments and to the justification defence (if available): *Williams v J Walter Thompson Group Ltd* [2005] EWCA Civ 133, CA.

1   DDA 1995, s 3A(2). *Code of Practice: Employment and Occupation (2004)*, paras 4.24–4.26; *Code of Practice: Trade Organisations and Qualifications Bodies (2004)*, paras 4.23–4.25.

2   Ibid, s 3A(1).

3   Ibid, s 3A(6).

4   Ibid, s 18B(2); *Code of Practice: Employment and Occupation* (2004), para 5.18 (and examples); *Code of Practice: Trade Organisations and Qualifications Bodies* (2004), para 5.12 (and examples).

- providing supervision or other support.

In addition, the making of alterations to occupational pension scheme rules is an example of a step which trustees or managers of such a scheme may have to take in order to comply with their duty to make reasonable adjustments.[1]

3.4.3 This list is illustrative only of the types of adjustments that might be made and the Codes of Practice suggest further examples.[2] The list is not intended to be exhaustive or to be treated as a checklist.[3] More than one adjustment or a combination of adjustments might be required.[4] However, once the respondent has made reasonable adjustments, the duty to make reasonable adjustments does not require the respondent to accept reduced performance from the disabled person.[5]

3.4.4 So far as transferring a disabled person to fill an existing vacancy is concerned, it is not suggested that a respondent must create a vacancy.[6] However, if there is an existing vacancy, it might be reasonable to make adjustments to that vacancy so as to allow the disabled person to fill it. The duty to make reasonable adjustments might include transferring a disabled person to another position for which he or she was suited, without the need for competitive interview and selection.[7] It is not for the employment tribunal to identify a particular vacancy that the disabled person could have been offered. Provided it addresses itself to the statutory provision, the extent to which the tribunal needs to spell out what steps it would have been reasonable for a respondent to take will depend upon how controversial those matters are.[8] It is for the respondent to show that it addressed its mind to this question.[9] If suitable   alternative   work   is   offered,   even   at   a

---

1   DDA 1995, s 4H(2) (ie in addition to the examples set out in s 18B(2)). See **4.5**.

2   *Code of Practice: Employment and Occupation* (2004), para 5.20 (and examples); *Code of Practice: Trade Organisations and Qualifications Bodies* (2004), para 5.13.

3   *Humphreys v Environment Agency* (1999) EAT/24/95.

4   *Code of Practice: Employment and Occupation* (2004), para 5.19 (and example); *Code of Practice: Trade Organisations and Qualifications Bodies* (2004), para 5.12.

5   *Mulligan v Commissioner for Inland Revenue* (1999) EAT/691/99 (eg by lowering the quantity or volume of work being demanded).

6   *Electronic Data Systems Ltd v Travis* [2004] EWCA Civ 1256, CA (it is for the employer to bring evidence to show that there was no available alternative employment).

7   *Archibald v Fife Council* [2004] UKHL 32, [2004] IRLR 651, HL.

8   *Electronic Data Systems Ltd v Travis* [2004] EWCA Civ 1256, CA (it was enough for a tribunal to have found that a reasonable step would have been the provision of training to bring the skills of a disabled employee up to date following periods of disability-related absence and where that employee was at risk of redundancy).

9   *London Borough of Hillingdon v Morgan* (1999) EAT/1493/98, IDS Brief 649 (if the matter had been approached correctly by the employer, would adjustments have enabled the employee to return to work?).

reduced wage, the respondent may have satisfied the duty to make reasonable adjustments.[1]

3.4.5 A reasonable adjustment might involve altering the disabled person's hours of working or training. An offer of part-time work might be a reasonable adjustment, but not in circumstances where the disabled person has not sought it, has a serious absence and sickness record, and was not fit for any form of work at the relevant time.[2] Assigning the disabled person to a different place of work or training might include allowing a disabled person to work from home during a period of rehabilitation or as part of a phased return to work.[3] In one case, disability discrimination occurred where an employer failed to transfer an employee to a different workplace in circumstances where the employee was off work with depression as a result of a difficult working relationship with a line manager.[4] The payment of sick pay during disability-related absences can be a reasonable adjustment, all other things being equal.[5]

3.4.6 During the parliamentary debates, the Minister confirmed that the examples of reasonable adjustments that might be undertaken could include the provision of a sign-language interpreter, Minicom facilities or alterations to working hours. Furthermore, a reasonable adjustment 'could be a modification to a working environment, to a term or condition of employment or to any similar matter relating to the employment'.[6] Where a respondent has existing car-parking facilities for employees and others, it might be a reasonable adjustment to allocate a dedicated car-parking space to a person with a mobility disability.[7] Support for such initiatives might be sought from funds available under the Government's Access to Work scheme. However, the Minister also indicated that the taxpayer could not be expected to meet all the costs of reasonable adjustments. Respondents are expected to take some financial responsibility, especially in respect of adjustments and costs relating to working hours and retraining.[8]

---

1   *Arboshe v East London Bus & Coach Co Ltd* (1999) EAT/877/98 (unless an employee's wages would be protected in analogous circumstances?).

2   *Callagan v Glasgow City Council* [2001] IRLR 724, EAT.

3   *London Borough of Hillingdon v Morgan* (1999) EAT/1493/98, IDS Brief 649.

4   *HM Prison Service v Beart* (2002) EAT 650/01, IDS Brief 713 and [2003] IRLR 238, CA.

5   *London Clubs Management Ltd v Hood* [2001] IRLR 719, EAT; *Nottinghamshire County Council v Meikle* [2004] IRLR 703, CA.

6   HC Deb Standing Committee E, col 208.

7   HL Deb, vol 566, col 209.

8   HC Deb Standing Committee E, col 209.

What are reasonable steps to take?

3.4.7   The duty upon the respondent is only to take such steps as it is reasonable, in all the circumstances of the case, to take in order to prevent the provision, criterion or practice or physical feature having an adverse effect on the disabled person. The test is an objective one.[1] The fact that a tribunal does not mention every type of adjustment which might theoretically have been made will not necessarily vitiate a conclusion that a reasonable adjustment could not have been made.[2]

3.4.8   The respondent is entitled to take account of all the circumstances when deciding what steps it would be reasonable to take. For example, it might be reasonable to weigh 'whether the benefit to the disabled person would be proportionate to the cost and the difficulty of the measures in question'.[3] On the other hand, in deciding whether to make a reasonable adjustment, there is no compulsion upon a respondent to take advice. However, a failure to take advice or to seek assistance (eg from an occupational medical adviser or disability employment adviser) before determining whether or not to make a reasonable adjustment could be taken into account by an employment tribunal in considering whether the respondent had acted reasonably in the circumstances.[4] Equally, the test of reasonableness might need to take account of the extent to which the disabled person has co-operated with the respondent who attempts to make a reasonable adjustment.

3.4.9   In determining whether it is reasonable for a person to have to take a particular step in order to comply with the duty to make adjustments, regard is to be had, in particular, to the following matters:[5]

- the extent to which taking the step would prevent the effect in relation to which the duty is imposed;
- the extent to which it is practicable for the person to take the step;
- the financial and other costs that would be incurred by the person in taking the step;[6]

---

1   *Morse v Wiltshire CC* [1998] IRLR 352, EAT.

2   *Quinn v Schwarzkopf Ltd* [2002] IRLR 602, Ct of Sess.

3   HC Deb Standing Committee E, col 196.

4   Ibid, col 222.

5   DDA 1995, s 18B(1); *Code of Practice: Employment and Occupation* (2004), paras 5.28–5.41 (and examples); *Code of Practice: Trade Organisations and Qualifications Bodies* (2004), paras 5.14–5.25 (and examples).

6   *Code of Practice: Employment and Occupation* (2004), paras 5.25 and 5.32–5.35; *Code of Practice: Trade Organisations and Qualifications Bodies* (2004), para 5.21.

- the extent to which taking it would disrupt any of the person's activities;[1]
- the extent of the person's financial and other resources;
- the availability to the person of financial or other assistance with respect to taking the step;
- the nature of the person's activities and the size of the person's undertaking;
- where the step would be taken in relation to a private household, the extent to which taking it would disrupt that household or disturb any person residing there.

3.4.10 The Codes of Practice suggest that these factors make a useful checklist. The effectiveness and practicability of the adjustment might be considered first, before looking at the cost of the adjustment and the resources available to fund it.[2] The Codes of Practice also suggest that other factors might be relevant, such as the effect on other employees, adjustments made for other disabled employees and the extent to which the disabled person is willing to co-operate.[3]

3.4.11 In one case,[4] an employment tribunal erred by failing to consider the extent to which, if at all, adjustments proposed by the claimant could have overcome her medical symptoms which otherwise prevented her return to work. In another case,[5] the EAT held that these provisions do not require that the particular step should prevent the effect in question, but merely that the respondent is entitled to have regard to the extent to which taking that step would prevent the effect when considering whether it was under a duty to take that step. In that case, there was a substantial possibility that the step in question would have worked and the fact that it might not have succeeded totally did not assist the respondent. The significance of the cost of a step may depend in part on the value of the disabled person's experience and expertise to the respondent, including factors such as resources (such as training) already invested in the person and his or her length of service, level of skill and knowledge, quality of relationships with clients and level of pay. It is more likely to be reasonable for a respondent with substantial

---

1   The need to consider whether the adjustment would increase risks to health and safety arises and a risk assessment may be necessary: *Code of Practice: Employment and Occupation* (2004), para 5.26; *Code of Practice: Trade Organisations and Qualifications Bodies* (2004), para 5.17.

2   *Code of Practice: Employment and Occupation* (2004), para 5.27; *Code of Practice: Trade Organisations and Qualifications Bodies* (2004), para 5.18.

3   *Code of Practice: Employment and Occupation* (2004), para 5.42 (and examples); *Code of Practice: Trade Organisations and Qualifications Bodies* (2004), para 5.18.

4   *Fu v London Borough of Camden* [2001] IRLR 186, EAT. See also, on the same point: *Johnson & Johnson Medical Ltd v Filmer* [2002] ICR 292, EAT.

5   *HM Prison Service v Beart* EAT 650/01, (2002) IDS Brief 713 and [2003] IRLR 238, CA.

resources to have to make a significantly costly adjustment than it would be for a respondent with fewer resources.

3.4.12   Other factors might be relevant, depending upon the circumstances, including (in an employment context) the effect that an adjustment has upon other employees, any adjustments already made for other disabled employees, and the extent to which the disabled person is willing to co-operate with the employer's attempts to make an adjustment. It may also be reasonable for a respondent to have to make more than one adjustment. The above listed matters are the 'key criteria ... in no particular order of priority' by which the reasonableness of an adjustment will be judged.[1] For example, if the only possible adjustments that could be made to aid the output of a disabled person could result in no more than a small improvement in productivity, but at a price of cost or disruption, the adjustments might not be reasonable.[2] Similarly, if – after reasonable adjustments have been made – a disabled person's productivity is below normal, and where the person is paid according to performance, a respondent would not be expected to make further adjustments by compensating the disabled person for the loss of performance-related pay.

3.4.13   During the parliamentary debates, the Minister gave further illustrations.[3] It might not be reasonable for an employer (especially a small employer) needing an employee urgently to have to wait for an adjustment to be made to allow a disabled person to be employed. An adjustment that would involve a breach of safety laws or fire regulations could not be reasonable. However, health and safety law does not require the avoidance of all risks, but simply ensuring that risk is properly assessed, understood and managed.[4] The cost of the adjustment might also render it an unreasonable one to make. Cost will include use of staff and other resources, as well as direct monetary costs. The respondent's resources must be taken into account. It might be more reasonable for a respondent with considerable resources to make a significantly costly adjustment than for a respondent with fewer resources. Moreover, a step is not unreasonable if there is available compensatory help from an outside organisation or from the disabled person. For example, the respondent might not be expected to purchase specialist computer equipment adapted for use by a person with a sight disability. Such equipment might be available under the

---

1   HL Deb, vol 566, col 184.

2   Ibid, vol 566, cols 184–185.

3   Ibid, vol 566, col 185.

4   *Code of Practice: Employment and Occupation* (2004), paras 6.8–6.13 (and examples); *Code of Practice: Trade Organisations and Qualifications Bodies* (2004), paras 6.8–6.17 (and examples).

Access to Work scheme or from a disability charity. It would also be a reasonable adjustment to allow a disabled worker to use his or her own auxiliary aids or equipment at work.

3.5 RELATIONSHIPS WHICH HAVE COME TO AN END

3.5.1 Prior to 1 October 2004, post-employment acts of disability discrimination might also have been unlawful if there was a sufficient connection with the erstwhile employment relationship.[1] From 1 October 2004, explicit provision is made in Part 2 of the amended Act in respect of relationships which have come to an end.[2]

3.5.2 This arises where there has been a relevant relationship between a disabled person and another person (the relevant person) and the relationship has come to an end.[3] A relevant relationship is a relationship during the course of which an act of discrimination against (or harassment of) one party to the relationship by the other party to it is unlawful under the provisions of Part 2.[4] It also includes a relationship between a person providing employment services (within the meaning of Part 3 of the Act) and a person receiving such services.[5] Reference to an act of discrimination or harassment which is unlawful includes, in the case of a relationship which has come to an end before 1 October 2004, reference to such an act which would, after 1 October 2004, be unlawful.[6] It is unlawful for the relevant person to discriminate against the disabled person by subjecting him or her to a detriment, or to subject the disabled person to harassment, where the discrimination or harassment arises out of and is closely connected to the relevant relationship.[7]

3.5.3 A duty to make reasonable adjustments also arises in this context. It arises where a provision, criterion or practice applied by the relevant person to the disabled person in relation to any matter arising out of the relevant relationship places the disabled person at a substantial disadvantage in comparison with persons who are not

---

1   *Rhys-Harper v Relaxion Group plc; D'Souza v Lambeth London Borough Council; Jones v 3M Healthcare Ltd* [2003] UKHL 33, [2003] ICR 867, HL.

2   DDA 1995, s 16A; *Code of Practice: Employment and Occupation (2004)*, paras 8.28–8.32 (and examples); *Code of Practice: Trade Organisations and Qualifications Bodies* (2004), paras 7.23, 7.28–7.29, 8.13 and 8.18–8.19.

3   DDA 1995, s 16A(1).

4   Ibid, s 16A(2)(a).

5   Ibid, s 16A(2)(b).

6   Ibid, s 16A(7).

7   Ibid, s 16A(3).

disabled, but are in the same position as the disabled person in relation to the relevant person.[1] It also arises where a physical feature of premises which are occupied by the relevant person places the disabled person at a substantial disadvantage in comparison with persons who are not disabled, but are in the same position as the disabled person in relation to the relevant person.[2] In either case, it is the duty of the relevant person to take such steps as it is reasonable, in all the circumstances of the case, for that person to have to take in order to prevent the provision, practice or criterion, or feature, having that effect.[3] However, no duty is imposed on the relevant person if that person does not know (and could not reasonably be expected to know) that the disabled person has a disability and is likely to be affected in the way required.[4]

3.6   DISCRIMINATORY ADVERTISEMENTS

3.6.1   Prior to 1 October 2004, employment tribunals were enabled to make assumptions about an employer's reason for refusing employment to a disabled person where the employer had published an advertisement suggesting that it would discriminate against disabled persons.[5] Where the employer had published a discriminatory advertisement, there was a rebuttable presumption that any subsequent less favourable treatment of the disabled person was for a reason related to the claimant's disability. This was a difficult and convoluted provision. It has now been repealed.

3.6.2   From 1 October 2004, it is unlawful for a person to publish (or cause to be published) a discriminatory advertisement in certain circumstances.[6] The advertisement must be in relation to a relevant appointment or benefit which the person intends to make or confer. A relevant appointment or benefit means: (a) any employment, promotion or transfer of employment; (b) membership of (or a benefit under) an occupational pension scheme; (c) an appointment to any office or post; (d) any partnership in a firm; (e) any tenancy or pupillage; (f) any membership of a trade organisation; (g) any professional or trade qualification; (h) any work placement; and (i) any

---

1   DDA 1995, s 16A(4)(a).

2   Ibid, s 16A(4)(b).

3   Ibid, s 16A(5).

4   Ibid, s 16A(6).

5   Ibid, s 11 (now repealed).

6   Ibid, s 16B(1); *Code of Practice: Employment and Occupation* (2004), paras 7.11–7.15 (and examples); *Code of Practice: Trade Organisations and Qualifications Bodies* (2004),

employment services.[1] The advertisement must be an advertisement which invites applications for that appointment or benefit.[2] It must be an advertisement which indicates (or might reasonably be understood to indicate) that an application will (or may) be determined to any extent by reference to the applicant not having any disability or any particular disability.[3] Alternatively, it must be an advertisement which indicates (or might reasonably be understood to indicate) that an application will (or may) be determined to any extent by reference to any reluctance of the person determining the application to comply with a duty to make reasonable adjustments.[4] However, it is not unlawful for a person to publish (or cause to be published) a discriminatory advertisement in these circumstances where it would not in fact be unlawful under Part 2[5] for an application to be determined in the manner indicated (or understood to be indicated) in the advertisement.[6]

3.6.3   Only the Disability Rights Commission may bring proceedings in respect of discriminatory advertisements.[7] The Commission may present a complaint to an employment tribunal.[8] If the tribunal finds that the complaint is well founded, it shall make a declaration to that effect.[9] If it appears to the Commission that, unless restrained, a person is likely to repeat the unlawful act, the Commission may apply to a county court for an injunction (or, in Scotland, to a sheriff court for an interdict) restraining that person from doing such an act.[10] That application may be made only where a tribunal has made a finding that a

---

paras 3.22–3.25 (and examples). An advertisement includes every form of advertisement or notice, whether to the public or not: s 16B(4).

1   DDA 1995, s 16B(3), by reference to ss 4D, 6A, 7A, 7C, 13, 14A, 14C and Part 3.

2   Ibid, s 16B(1)(a).

3   Ibid, s 16B(1)(b)(i).

4   Ibid, s 16B(1)(b)(ii). In relation to employment services, that means the duty imposed by s 21(1), as modified by s 21A(6).

5   Or Part 3, to the extent that the advertisement relates to the provision of employment services.

6   DDA 1995, s 16B(2).

7   Ibid, s 17B(1) and (2).

8   An employment tribunal shall not consider a complaint under this provision unless it is presented before the end of the period of six months, beginning when the act to which it relates was done: DDA 1995, s 17B(7). The provisions of Sch 3, para 3(3) and (4) apply for this purpose as they apply for the purposes of Sch 3, para 3(1): s 17B(9). However, the tribunal may consider any such complaint which is out of time if, in all the circumstances of the case, it considers that it is just and equitable to do so: s 17B(8).

9   DDA 1995, s 17B(3).

10 Ibid, s 17B(4). A county court or sheriff court shall not consider an application under s 17B(4) unless it is made before the end of the period of five years, beginning when the act to which it relates was done: DDA 1995, s 17B(7). The provisions of

person has done such an unlawful act and that finding has become final. Upon that application, if the court is satisfied that the application is well founded, it may grant the injunction (or interdict) in the terms applied for or in more limited terms. A finding of a tribunal in respect of any act shall, if it has become final, be treated as conclusive by a county court or sheriff court upon such an application.[1] A finding of a tribunal becomes final for these purposes when an appeal against it is dismissed, withdrawn or abandoned, or when the time for appealing expires without an appeal having been brought.[2]

3.7 INSTRUCTIONS AND PRESSURE TO DISCRIMINATE

3.7.1 From 1 October 2004, it is unlawful for a person who has authority over another person (or in accordance with whose wishes that other person is accustomed to act) to instruct him or her to do any act which is unlawful under Part 2[3] or to procure (or attempt to procure) the doing by him of any such act.[4] It is also unlawful to induce (or attempt to induce) a person to do any act which contravenes Part 2[5] by providing (or offering to provide) him or her with any benefit[6] or subjecting (or threatening to subject) him or her to any detriment.[7]

3.7.2 Only the DRC may bring proceedings in respect of instructions and pressure to discriminate.[8] The procedural provisions discussed immediately above in respect of discriminatory advertisements apply here also.

Sch 3, para 3(3) and (4) apply for this purpose as they apply for the purposes of Sch 3, para 3(1): s 17B(9). However, the court may consider any such application which is out of time if, in all the circumstances of the case, it considers that it is just and equitable to do so: s 17B(8).

1 DDA 1995, s 17B(5).

2 Ibid, s 17B(6).

3 Or, to the extent that it relates to the provision of employment services, Part 3.

4 DDA 1995, s 16C(1), implementing 2000/78/EC, Art 2(4). See *Code of Practice: Employment and Occupation* (2004), para 3.22; *Code of Practice: Trade Organisations and Qualifications Bodies* (2004), para 3.21 (and example).

5 Or, to the extent that it relates to the provision of employment services, Part 3.

6 DDA 1995, s 16C(2)(a). An attempted inducement is not prevented from falling within s 16C(2) because it is not made directly to the person in question, if it is made in such a way that he or she is likely to hear of it: s 16C(3).

7 Ibid, s 16C(2)(b). The term 'detriment' (except in s 16C(2)(b)) does not include conduct of the nature referred to in s 3B (harassment): s 18D(2).

8 Ibid, s 17B(1) and (2).

3.8   DISABILITY DISCRIMINATION BILL

Discriminatory advertisements

3.8.1   The present law on discriminatory advertisements does not prohibit third parties (such as newspapers) from publishing discriminatory advertisements on behalf of the person placing the advertisement. The Disability Discrimination Bill will extend the scope of the prohibition on discriminatory advertisements to cover third-party publishers who publish a discriminatory advertisement on behalf of another. It also makes it clear that the prohibition applies so that it covers advertisements which indicate an intention to discriminate against a person who has had a disability, as well as a person who has a disability. A third-party publisher will be exempted from liability if it can prove that, in publishing the advertisement, it relied on a statement made by the person who placed the advertisement (such as an employer) to the effect that publication of the advertisement would not be unlawful, and that it was reasonable for the third party to rely on that statement. It will be an offence for a person knowingly or recklessly to make a false or misleading statement about the lawfulness of an advertisement. The offence will carry a fine not exceeding level 5 on the standard scale (currently £5,000) on summary conviction.

Chapter 4

THE EMPLOYMENT FIELD: UNLAWFUL ACTS

4.1 INTRODUCTION

4.1.1 The EC Framework Employment Directive applies to all persons in both the public and private sectors (including public bodies) in relation to:

- conditions for access to employment, to self-employment or to occupation (including selection criteria and recruitment conditions), whatever the branch of activity and at all levels of the professional hierarchy (including promotion);
- access to all types and to all levels of vocational guidance, vocational training, advanced vocational training and retraining (including practical work experience);
- employment and working conditions (including dismissals and pay); and
- membership of (and involvement in) an organisation of workers or employers, or any organisation whose members carry on a particular profession, including the benefits provided for by such organisations.[1]

Member States may provide that legislation addressing discrimination on the ground of disability shall not apply to the armed forces.[2]

4.1.2 As a result, from 1 October 2004, Part 2 of the DDA 1995 (as amended by the Disability Discrimination Act 1995 (Amendment) Regulations 2003) is concerned with prohibiting disability discrimination in the employment field at large.[3] This chapter deals with the causes of action created by Part 2 in complying with the Directive. This analysis will begin with discrimination and harassment by employers.

---

1   2000/78/EC, Art 3(1).

2   Ibid, Art 3(4).

3   In Northern Ireland, see the Disability Discrimination Act 1995 (Amendment) (Northern Ireland) Regulations 2004, SR 2004/55.

Separate consideration will be given later in this chapter to discrimination and harassment in relation to contract workers, office-holders, occupational pension schemes, insurance benefits, partnerships, barristers and advocates, trade organisations, qualifications bodies and practical work experience.

4.2 EMPLOYERS

Unlawful acts

4.2.1 What does the Act make unlawful in relation to employers? Disability discrimination does not take place in a vacuum. A claimant must show that the alleged act of disability discrimination falls within one of the unlawful acts of employment discrimination set out in s 4 of the Act.[1] Section 4 makes it unlawful for an employer to discriminate against a disabled person in specified circumstances. The meaning of 'discriminate' has been considered in Chapter 3. An employment tribunal may only deal with a complaint of unlawful discrimination as defined by the claimant.[2] It is thus important to state the scope of the complaint with sufficient particularity and detail in the claim. The Act begins by dealing with discrimination in recruitment and selection and in respect of employment applicants.

Recruitment and selection

4.2.2 First, it is unlawful for an employer to discriminate against a disabled person in the arrangements which the employer makes for the purpose of determining to whom the employer should offer employment.[3] The concept of 'arrangements' has a wide meaning.[4] It covers the recruitment and selection process, including job advertisements, application forms and information.[5] It includes job specifications, qualifications, the location and timing of interviews, the use of assessment techniques, the interview itself, selection criteria and

---

1   As amended by the Disability Discrimination Act 1995 (Amendment) Regulations 2003. See also *Code of Practice: Employment and Occupation* (2004), paras 3.15–3.21 and Chapters 7 and 8.

2   *British Gas Services Ltd v McCaull* [2001] IRLR 60, EAT.

3   DDA 1995, s 4(1)(a). The term 'employer' includes a person who has no employees but is seeking to employ another person: s 18D(2).

4   *Code of Practice: Employment and Occupation* (2004), para 7.6.

5   So far as job advertisements are concerned, see DDA 1995, s 16B, discussed at **3.6**, and *Code of Practice: Employment and Occupation* (2004), paras 7.11–7.14 (and examples). In respect of application forms and information, see *Code of Practice: Employment and Occupation* (2004), paras 7.16–7.18 (and examples).

pre-employment training.[1] For example, the inclusion of unnecessary or marginal requirements in a job specification (or blanket exclusions which do not take account of individual circumstances) can be discriminatory.[2] This does not prevent the employer from choosing the best person for the job.[3] However, if a disabled person is rejected for a job because he or she lacks a qualification specified by the employer, the rejection might be discriminatory if the lack of the particular qualification is related to that person's disability (eg because of the effect of dyslexia). The employer would need to justify the stipulation of that qualification (eg by reference to relevance and significance) or demonstrate that no reasonable adjustment in favour of the disabled applicant (eg re-allocating some duties to another employee or devising an alternative test of competence) could have been made.[4]

4.2.3 Secondly, it is unlawful for an employer to discriminate against a disabled person in the terms on which the employer offers that person employment.[5] Thirdly, it is unlawful for an employer to discriminate against a disabled person by refusing to offer (or deliberately not offering) him or her employment.[6] Discrimination by these means includes a deliberate failure or omission to offer employment to a disabled person. There does not have to be an express refusal to offer employment in order for potentially unlawful discrimination to have occurred. Next, the Act addresses discrimination in employment and against disabled employees.

Terms of employment

4.2.4 Fourthly, it is unlawful for an employer to discriminate against a disabled person whom the employer employs in the terms of employment which the employer affords the disabled employee.[7] Terms and conditions of service should not discriminate against disabled persons. That does not mean that an employer can never offer a disabled person a less favourable contract. However, subject to any duty to make reasonable adjustments, the employer must be prepared to justify the

---

1   In respect of selection, assessment and interview arrangements, see *Code of Practice: Employment and Occupation* (2004), paras 7.19–7.31 (and examples).

2   *Code of Practice: Employment and Occupation* (2004), paras 7.7–7.8 (and examples).

3   Ibid, para 7.4.

4   Ibid, para 7.10 (and examples).

5   DDA 1995, s 4(1)(b); *Code of Practice: Employment and Occupation* (2004), para 7.32 (and example).

6   Ibid, s 4(1)(c).

7   Ibid, s 4(2)(a); *Code of Practice: Employment and Occupation* (2004), paras 8.4–8.6 (and examples).

differential. Equally, employers must not discriminate in their induction procedures.[1] If necessary, a newly recruited disabled employee may need an individually tailored induction programme.

Employment opportunities and benefits

4.2.5 Fifthly, it is unlawful for an employer to discriminate against a disabled person whom the employer employs in the opportunities which the employer affords the disabled employee for promotion, a transfer, training or receiving any other benefit.[2] Sixthly, it is unlawful for an employer to discriminate against a disabled person whom the employer employs by refusing to afford the disabled employee (or deliberately not affording him or her) any such opportunity.[3] Benefits might include canteens, meal vouchers, social clubs and other recreational activities, dedicated car-parking spaces, discounts on products, bonuses, share options, hairdressing, clothes allowances, financial services, healthcare, private health insurance, medical assistance or insurance, transport to work, company cars, education assistance, workplace nurseries, rights to special leave and occupational pensions.[4] They will include facilities and services.[5]

4.2.6 The prohibitions on unlawful discrimination in relation to benefits do not apply to benefits of any description if the employer is concerned with the provision of benefits of that description to the public or to a section of the public which includes the employee in question.[6] It does not matter whether the benefits are being provided for payment or not. For example, the employer might be a bank providing loans to the public and loans to its employees (perhaps at favourable rates of interest) or a local authority providing welfare-related benefits to disabled persons in the community, including its own disabled employees. However, the prohibitions will apply where the provision differs in a material respect from the provision of the benefits

---

1   *Code of Practice: Employment and Occupation* (2004), para 8.7 (and examples).

2   DDA 1995, s 4(2)(b); *Code of Practice: Employment and Occupation* (2004), paras 8.8 and 8.13–8.14 (and examples).

3   Ibid, s 4(2)(c).

4   HL Deb, vol 566, col 169; *Code of Practice: Employment and Occupation* (2004), paras 8.9–8.11 (and examples).

5   DDA 1995, s 18D(2).

6   Ibid, s 4(4); *Code of Practice: Employment and Occupation* (2004), para 8.12 (and example).

by the employer to its employees.[1] They will also apply where the provision of the benefits to the employee in question is regulated by his or her contract of employment.[2] They will also apply where the benefits relate to training.[3]

4.2.7 These exceptions are designed to prevent unnecessary overlap with the provisions in Part 3 of the Act outlawing discrimination in the provision of goods, facilities and services. The intention is that if an employer offers goods, facilities or services to its employees in the same way as it offers them to members of the public, but disabled employees receive discriminatory treatment in that provision, then their right of action falls under Part 3 of the Act, if at all. Nevertheless, Part 2 of the Act will continue to apply to such discriminatory treatment if the provision of goods, facilities and services to the employer's employees is not identical to such provision to the public, or is an incident of the employment contract, or relates to training.

Dismissal

4.2.8 Seventhly, it is unlawful for an employer to discriminate against a disabled person whom the employer employs by dismissing him or her.[4] A potentially unlawful dismissal of a disabled employee might arise in the context of capability or absence,[5] but might equally arise from an unfair redundancy selection exercise.[6] A dismissal for this purpose includes the non-renewal of a fixed-term contract.[7] That arises where there is a termination of a person's employment by the expiration of any period. That includes a period expiring by reference to an event or circumstance. However, it does not include a termination immediately after which the employment is renewed on the same terms.

4.2.9 A dismissal also includes a constructive dismissal.[8] That is where a person's employment is terminated by any act of that person, including the giving of notice. The termination must have occurred in circumstances such that he or she is entitled to terminate it without notice by reason of the conduct of the employer. This overcomes the

---

1   DDA 1995, s 4(4)(a).

2   Ibid, s 4(4)(b).

3   Ibid, s 4(4)(c).

4   Ibid, s 4(2)(d); *Code of Practice: Employment and Occupation* (2004), paras 8.15–8.27 (and examples).

5   *Clark v TDG Ltd t/a Novacold* [1999] IRLR 318, CA.

6   *British Sugar plc v Kirker* [1998] IRLR 624, EAT.

7   DDA 1995, s 4(5)(a), as amended from 1 October 2004.

8   Ibid, s 4(5)(b), as amended from 1 October 2004.

earlier difficulties in the case-law as to whether a constructive dismissal was within the scope of Part 2.[1] A constructive dismissal is where the employee resigns in response to the employer's conduct amounting to a serious or fundamental or repudiatory breach of contract. In one case, the respondent was in fundamental breach of the contract of employment by its continuing failure to deal with disability discrimination against the claimant. The claimant had resigned in response to that breach. The breach comprised the respondent's persistent failure to agree to adjustments requested by the claimant in order to enable her to return to work after sickness absence.[2]

Any other detriment

4.2.10 Finally, it is unlawful for an employer to discriminate against a disabled person whom the employer employs by subjecting him or her to any other detriment.[3] The concept of 'any other detriment' is a potentially broad one.[4] It provides a catch-all for any other forms of employment discrimination against disabled persons, if not already caught by the specific categories above. Prior to 1 October 2004, harassment of a disabled person fell within this provision. Harassment is now dealt with separately,[5] although acts that fail to satisfy the statutory definition of harassment might still fall to be treated as a detriment.

Post-employment discrimination

4.2.11 Prior to 1 October 2004, there was some doubt, although largely assuaged by late developments in the case-law,[6] as to whether these provisions were wholly apt to address post-employment discrimination (eg a refusal to provide a reference or discrimination occurring

---

1   *Commissioner of Police of the Metropolis v Harley* [2001] IRLR 263, EAT; *Catherall v Michelin Tyre plc* [2003] IRLR 61, EAT.

2   *Nottinghamshire County Council v Meikle* [2004] EWCA Civ 859, [2004] IRLR 703, CA (the limitation period runs from the date of termination rather than from the date of the breach). See also: *Williams v J Walter Thompson Group Ltd* [2005] EWCA Civ 133, [2005] All ER(D) 261, CA.

3   DDA 1995, s 4(2)(d).

4   *Garry v London Borough of Ealing* [2001] IRLR 681, CA (a case decided under the comparable provision of the RRA 1976).

5   DDA 1995, s 3B and 4(3). The term 'detriment' (except in s 16C(2)(b)) does not include conduct of the nature referred to in s 3B (harassment): s 18D(2).

6   *Rhys-Harper v Relaxion Group plc; D'Souza v Lambeth London Borough Council; Jones v 3M Healthcare Ltd* [2003] UKHL 33, [2003] ICR 867, HL.

during post-termination appeal proceedings). Now, particular provision is made where there has been a relevant relationship between a disabled person and another person (the 'relevant person') and that relationship has come to an end.[1] This is considered in greater detail in Chapter 3.[2]

Harassment

4.2.12   It is also unlawful for an employer, in relation to employment by that employer, to subject to harassment a disabled person whom the employer employs or a disabled person who has applied to the employer for employment.[3] The meaning of 'harassment' has been considered in Chapter 3.[4]

Pre-employment health screening

4.2.13   The Act does not expressly address the question of pre-employment medical examinations and screening. Many employers utilise health-related questions in application forms or medical examinations as a pre-condition of employment. By screening employment applicants for disability or medical conditions, many employers effectively exclude a proportion of applicants from further competition in the selection process. An applicant with a disability might be prematurely excluded from further consideration and may lose the opportunity to demonstrate ability and merit.

4.2.14   An attempt was made during the original legislative process to prohibit pre-employment medical examinations or screening, but the amendments were rejected. The Government's view was that 'in general, employers should be free to use whatever recruitment procedures best meet their needs and to conduct medical examinations of employees where that seems appropriate'.[5] It was unwilling to forbid medical examinations or to limit enquiries about disability. Indeed, employers might find it necessary to question disabled applicants about a disability where such questions are designed to assist the disabled person in competing for employment opportunities.[6]

4.2.15   Nevertheless, that does not mean that health screens and examinations might not fall foul of the Act. Occupational health

---

1   DDA 1995, s 16A(1); *Code of Practice: Employment and Occupation* (2004), paras 8.28–8.32 (and examples).

2   At **3.5**.

3   DDA 1995, s 4(3).

4   At **3.3**.

5   HC Deb Standing Committee E, col 151.

6   HL Deb, vol 564, cols 1935–1936.

practitioners are likely to be treated as acting as the agent of the employer for this purpose.[1] Medical examinations, enquiries, questions or screening would undoubtedly constitute 'arrangements' made for the purpose of determining who should be offered employment.[2] If the effect of such arrangements was to amount to less favourable treatment of a disabled person for a reason related to disability, the employer would have to show that that treatment was justifiable. Even if all applicants and employees were medically examined, the effect might be to discriminate indirectly against disabled persons if the employer uses the evidence gleaned from the examination without further individualised enquiry as to the ability to do the job (including reasonable adjustments). The relevant Code of Practice provides some useful guidance in this area.[3]

Scope of the employment provisions

4.2.16   Section 4 of the Act applies only in relation to employment at an establishment in Great Britain (or in Northern Ireland).[4] It is concerned with acts of discrimination by an employer against a disabled person. The task of identifying the employer is not usually problematic.[5] The liability of an employer may be vicarious liability for the actions of employees in the course of employment.[6] The employer's liability may be shared with another person who knowingly aids in the commission of an unlawful act of discrimination.[7] These concepts are discussed in more detail in Chapter 10.

---

1   *London Borough of Hammersmith and Fulham v Farnsworth* [2000] IRLR 691, EAT (an occupational health report is unlikely to be treated as a confidential medical record where the examinee has consented to medical information being provided to the employer so as to enable it to reach an employment decision).

2   DDA 1995, s 4(1)(a).

3   *Code of Practice: Employment and Occupation* (2004), paras 6.14–6.16 (and examples), 7.9 (and example) and 7.27–7.31 (and examples).

4   DDA 1995, s 4(6), as modified by s 70(6) and Sch 8, para 3.

5   But see *Lancashire County Council v Mason* [1998] ICR 907, EAT, in which neither the school governors nor the local education authority were held to be liable for an alleged act of disability discrimination in employment selection arrangements in the context of a state maintained county school with a delegated budget. See now *Murphy v Slough Borough Council* [2004] ICR 1163, EAT, and [2005] EWCA Civ 122, CA (school governing body rather than local education authority liable for employment-related decision in breach of DDA 1995, and Education (Modification of Enactments Relating to Employment) Order 2003, SI 2003/1964 and Education (Modification of Enactments Relating to Employment) (England) (Amendment) Order 2004, SI 2004/2325.

6   DDA 1995, s 58.

7   Ibid, s 57.

Employment

4.2.17 The term 'employment' has the same extended definition as used in other discrimination statutes. The DDA 1995 embraces discrimination in employment under a contract of service or a contract of apprenticeship, but it also includes employment under a contract personally to do any work.[1] The dominant purpose of the contract must be the execution of personal work or labour.[2] Because disability discrimination is a statutory tort, the fact that the contract of employment (or its performance) may be tainted with illegality (such as receiving wages without deduction of tax) assumes less significance than it would do in employment law generally.[3]

Employment at an establishment in Great Britain

4.2.18 The phrase 'employment at an establishment in Great Britain' (and, by extension, Northern Ireland) has a particular meaning.[4] Great Britain includes such territorial waters of the United Kingdom as are adjacent to Great Britain.[5] Employment (including employment on board a ship or on an aircraft or hovercraft) is regarded as being employment at an establishment in Great Britain if the employee does his or her work wholly or partly in Great Britain.[6] However, if the employee does his or her work wholly outside Great Britain, the employment is still regarded as being employment at an establishment in Great Britain in certain circumstances.[7] Those circumstances are that: (a) the employer has a place of business at an establishment in Great Britain; (b) the work is for the purposes of the business carried on at the establishment; and (c) the employee is ordinarily resident in

---

1   DDA 1995, s 68(1) and Sch 8, para 47; *Code of Practice: Employment and Occupation* (2004), para 3.8.

2   *Sheehan v Post Office Counters Ltd* [1999] ICR 734, EAT; *Burton v Higham (t/a Ace Appointments)* [2003] IRLR 257, EAT; *South East Sheffield Citizens Advice Bureau v Grayson* [2004] IRLR 354, EAT; *Hawkins v Nigel Darken t/a Sawbridgeworth Motorcycles* [2004] EWCA Civ 1755, CA. See generally: *Quinnen v Hovells* [1984] IRLR 227, EAT; *Mirror Group Newspapers Ltd v Gunning* [1986] ICR 145, CA; *BP Chemicals Ltd v Gillick* [1995] IRLR 128, EAT; *Mingeley v Pennock and Ivory t/a Amber Cars* [2004] IRLR 373, CA.

3   *Hall v Woolston Hall Leisure Ltd* [2000] IRLR 578, CA (the question is whether the claim is so inextricably bound up with the illegal conduct that a tribunal could not award compensation without appearing to condone the illegality).

4   DDA 1995, s 68(1), applying s 68(2)–(4A), as substituted or inserted by the Disability Discrimination Act 1995 (Amendment) Regulations 2003, with effect from 1 October 2004. In Northern Ireland, see DDA 1998, s 68(2) and Sch 8, para 47(2).

5   Ibid, s 68(1).

6   Ibid, s 68(2)(a).

7   Ibid, s 68(2)(b).

Great Britain at the time at which he or she applies for or is offered the employment or at any time during the course of the employment.[1]

4.2.19 Employment on board a ship is also included if the ship is registered at a port of registry in Great Britain or it belongs to or is possessed by Her Majesty in right of the Government of the United Kingdom.[2] Employment on board an aircraft or hovercraft is also covered if it is registered in the United Kingdom and operated by a person who has his or her principal place of business (or is ordinarily resident) in Great Britain.[3] Alternatively, it is covered if it belongs to or is possessed by Her Majesty in right of the Government of the United Kingdom.[4] Otherwise, employment on board a ship or an aircraft or a hovercraft is not to be regarded as being employment at an establishment in Great Britain.[5] Special provision is made for employment of a prescribed kind or in prescribed circumstances to be regarded as not being employment at an establishment in Great Britain,[6] but no prescription has been made. A particular provision is also made for determining if employment concerned with the exploration of the seabed or sub-soil or the exploitation of their natural resources is outside Great Britain.[7]

Exclusion of small businesses

4.2.20 As originally enacted, the employment provisions of the DDA 1995 did not apply to small businesses. The threshold was first set in relation to employers with fewer than 20 employees.[8] From 1 December 1998, the threshold applied to employers with fewer than 15 employees.[9] From 1 October 2004, this exclusion is repealed by the Disability Discrimination Act 1995 (Amendment) Regulations 2003. Part 2 of the 1995 Act now applies to all employers (except the armed forces), regardless of size or the number of employees.

---

1   DDA 1995, s 68(2A).

2   Ibid, s 68(2), (2B).

3   Ibid, s 68(2), (2C)(a).

4   Ibid, s 68(2), (2C)(b).

5   Ibid, s 68(2D).

6   Ibid, s 68(4).

7   Ibid, s 68(4A), applying Sex Discrimination Act 1975, s 10(1) and (5) and Sex Discrimination and Equal Pay (Offshore Employment) Order 1987, SI 1987/930.

8   Ibid, s 7(1). The case-law on this provision is now of academic interest only: *Taylor v Lifesign Ltd* (2000) EAT/1437/98; *Hardie v CD Northern Ltd* [2000] IRLR 87, EAT; *Colt Group Ltd v Couchman* [2000] ICR 327, EAT; *Burton v Higham (t/a Ace Appointments)* [2003] IRLR 257, EAT; *South East Sheffield Citizens Advice Bureau v Grayson* [2004] IRLR 354, EAT; *Hawkins v Nigel Darken t/a Sawbridgeworth Motorcycles* [2004] EWCA Civ 1755, CA.

9   Disability Discrimination (Exemption for Small Employers) Order 1998, SI 1998/2618.

Other exemptions

4.2.21   As originally enacted, although the Act applied to employment by the Crown, government departments, statutory bodies and statutory office-holders,[1] its employment provisions did not apply to employment as a statutory office-holder (such as a police officer);[2] a member of certain statutory police forces; a prison officer (except custody officers); a fire-fighting member of a fire brigade; and a member of the naval, military or air forces of the Crown.[3] From 1 October 2004, these exemptions have been largely repealed by the Disability Discrimination Act 1995 (Amendment) Regulations 2003. The only exemption remaining relates to service in any of the naval, military or air forces of the Crown.[4] The wider question of the application of the Act to the Crown and to Parliament is considered in more detail in Chapter 9.

Police

4.2.22   From 1 October 2004, for the purposes of Part 2, the holding of the office of constable is to be treated as employment by the chief officer of police[5] as respects any act done by him or her in relation to a constable or that office.[6] For the same purposes, the holding of the office of constable is to be treated as employment by the police authority[7] as respects any act done by them in relation to a constable or that office.[8] This means that police officers now have the same rights as other employees under Part 2 of the DDA 1995.[9] So far as establishing vicarious liability for the acts of a police officer,[10] the holding of the office of constable shall be treated as employment by the chief officer of police (and as not being employment by any other person).[11] Anything done by a person holding such an office in the performance (or purported performance) of his or her functions shall be treated as done in the course of that employment.[12] The whole of this analysis

---

1   DDA 1995, s 64(1)–(2A) and (8).

2   *Photis and Bruce v KMC International Search and Selection, Heyes v Lord Chancellor's Department* (EAT/732/00, EAT/766/00 and EAT/960/00).

3   DDA 1995, s 64(5)–(8).

4   Ibid, s 64(7); *Code of Practice: Employment and Occupation* (2004), para 3.9.

5   Ibid, s 68A(4) and (7)–(8).

6   Ibid, s 68A(1)(a).

7   Ibid, s 68A(7)–(8).

8   Ibid, s 68A(1)(b).

9   *Code of Practice: Employment and Occupation* (2004), paras 3.11 and 9.23–9.24. See also Police (Appointments) Regulations (Northern Ireland) 2004, SR 2004/379.

10   DDA 1995, s 58.

11   Ibid, s 68A(2)(a).

12   Ibid, s 68A(2)(b).

immediately above applies equally to a police cadet[1] and appointment as a police cadet as it applies to a constable and the office of constable.[2]

4.2.23 Any compensation, costs or expenses awarded against a chief officer of police in any proceedings brought against him or her under Part 2 shall be paid out of the police fund.[3] That includes any costs or expenses incurred by a chief officer of police in any such proceedings so far as not recovered in the proceedings. Any sum required by a chief officer of police for the settlement of any claim made against him or her under Part 2 if the settlement is approved by the police authority shall also be paid out of the police fund if the settlement is approved by the police authority.[4] In such cases and to such extent as appears to a police authority to be appropriate, a police authority may pay out of the police fund any compensation, costs or expenses awarded in proceedings under Part 2 against a person under the direction and control of the chief officer of police; any costs or expenses incurred and not recovered by such a person in such proceedings; and any sum required in connection with the settlement of a claim that has or might have given rise to such proceedings.[5]

Charities

4.2.24 Exceptional treatment under Part 2 of the Act is given to charities.[6] Nothing in Part 2 of the Act affects any charitable instrument which provides for conferring benefits on one or more categories of person determined by reference to any physical or mental capacity.[7] Moreover, nothing in the employment provisions of the 1995 Act makes unlawful any act done by a registered or non-registered charity[8] in pursuance of any of its charitable purposes, so far as those purposes are connected with persons determined by reference to any physical or mental capacity.[9] The term 'charity' has the same meaning as in the Charities Act 1993.[10] A 'charitable instrument' is an enactment or other

---

1   DDA 1995, s 68A(7).

2   Ibid, s 68A(6).

3   Ibid, s 68A(3)(a) and (7).

4   Ibid, s 68A(3)(b).

5   Ibid, s 68A(5).

6   Ibid, s 18C(1), originally enacted as s 10(1).

7   Ibid, s 18C(1)(a).

8   Ibid, s 18C(3) provides that a recognised body is one for the purposes of Part I of the Law Reform (Miscellaneous Provisions) (Scotland) Act 1990.

9   Ibid, s 18C(1)(b).

10   Ibid, s 18C(3). In Northern Ireland, see the Charities Act (Northern Ireland) 1964 (by virtue of DDA 1995, Sch 8, para 7(3)).

instrument (whenever taking effect) so far as it relates to charitable purposes.[1]

Supported employment

4.2.25 Special provision is also made for persons providing supported employment under the Disabled Persons (Employment) Act 1944 or the Disabled Persons (Employment) Act (Northern Ireland) 1945. Nothing in Part 2 of the Act prevents a person who provides supported employment from treating members of a particular group of disabled persons (or persons who have had a disability in the past) more favourably than other persons in providing supported employment.[2] In this context, 'supported employment' means facilities provided or paid for under s 15 of the 1944 or 1945 Act.[3] Furthermore, nothing in Part 2 of the Act prevents the Secretary of State (or, in Northern Ireland, the Department of Higher and Further Education, Training and Employment) from agreeing to arrangements for the provision of supported employment which will (or may) have the effect of treating members of a particular group of disabled persons (or persons who have had a disability in the past) more favourably than other persons.[4]

4.2.26 The effect of these provisions is not to exclude persons employed under supported employment arrangements from the prohibition on disability discrimination *per se*. Rather, the intention is to allow employers providing supported employment to distinguish between different groups of disabled persons when extending supported employment opportunities. Providing supported employment opportunities for some disabled persons while excluding other persons with a disability would otherwise amount to disability-related discrimination or direct discrimination, contrary to the Act. For example, an employer is allowed to create a supported employment environment for workers with sight impairments and to do so without needing to provide similar facilities for other disabled workers. However, the supported employment in question must be within the framework provided by the 1944–1945 legislation. Moreover, this does not excuse acts of disability discrimination elsewhere in the employer's workplace.

---

1   DDA 1995, s 18C(3). In England and Wales (and Northern Ireland), charitable purposes are purposes which are exclusively charitable according to the law of England and Wales (and Northern Ireland) (s 18C(4) and Sch 8, para 7(4)). In Scotland only, charitable purposes are to be construed as if contained in the Income Tax Acts: s 18C(5).

2   Ibid, s 18C(2)(a).

3   Ibid, s 18C(3) and Sch 8, para 7.

4   Ibid, s 18C(2)(b) and Sch 8, para 7(2).

Employer's duty to make reasonable adjustments

4.2.27 Section 4 of the DDA 1995 defines the circumstances in which an employer acts unlawfully by discriminating against a disabled person in relation to employment.[1] The definition of 'discrimination' for this purpose includes a failure to comply with a duty to make reasonable adjustments imposed on the employer in relation to the disabled person.[2] In the case of disability-related discrimination,[3] if an employer is under a duty to make reasonable adjustments in relation to a disabled person but fails to comply with that duty, the employer's treatment of that person cannot be justified,[4] unless it would have been justified even if the employer had complied with that duty.[5]

When does the duty to make reasonable adjustments arise?

4.2.28 The employer's duty to make reasonable adjustments arises in one of two circumstances.[6] The first arises where a provision, criterion or practice is applied by (or on behalf of) the employer. The effect might be to place the disabled person concerned at a substantial disadvantage in comparison with persons who are not disabled. If so, it is the duty of the employer to take such steps as it is reasonable (in all the circumstances of the case) for it to have to take in order to prevent the provision, criterion or practice having that effect.[7] The second arises where any physical feature of premises occupied by the employer places the disabled person concerned at a substantial disadvantage in comparison with persons who are not disabled. It is then the duty of the employer to take such steps as it is reasonable (in all the circumstances of the case) for it to have to take in order to prevent the feature having that effect.[8]

To whom is the duty owed?

4.2.29 Who is the 'disabled person concerned' in these contexts?[9] In the case of a provision, criterion or practice for determining to whom employment should be offered, it means any disabled person who is (or who has notified the employer that he or she may be) an applicant for

---

1   DDA 1995, s 4(1) and (2).

2   Ibid, s 3A(2).

3   Ibid, s 3A(1).

4   Ibid, s 3A(3).

5   Ibid, s 3A(6). See generally the discussion at **3.2**.

6   *Code of Practice: Employment and Occupation* (2004), para 5.3 (and example).

7   DDA 1995, s 4A(1)(a).

8   Ibid, s 4A(1)(b).

9   *Code of Practice: Employment and Occupation* (2004), paras 5.5–5.7.

that employment.[1] The length of notice given by the disabled applicant to the employer might play a part in determining whether the employer has satisfied the duty to make reasonable adjustments. In any other case, it means a disabled person who is an applicant for the employment concerned or an employee of the employer concerned.[2]

4.2.30 In the case of an applicant or potential applicant for employment, the duty to make reasonable adjustments is not imposed on an employer in relation to a disabled person if the employer does not know (and could not reasonably be expected to know) that the disabled person concerned is (or may be) an applicant for the employment.[3] Moreover, in any case, the duty to make reasonable adjustments is not imposed on an employer in relation to a disabled person if the employer does not know (and could not reasonably be expected to know) that that person has a disability and is likely to be placed at a substantial disadvantage in comparison with persons who are not disabled.[4] The question of what the employer knew or could reasonably be expected to know is a question of fact for the tribunal.[5] What will be reasonable for an employer to know or expect will vary from case to case.

4.2.31 An employer may need to do all that it could reasonably be expected to do to find out whether a person has a disability which is likely to place him or her at a substantial disadvantage.[6] Of course, if a disabled person chooses to conceal a disability, that will lessen the possibility that the employer should be expected to carry out a reasonable adjustment, unless the circumstances are such that it would be reasonable for the employer to be expected to know of the disability without the necessity for revelation. Thus, employers need to be pro-active. They will not necessarily escape liability by simply not asking whether a person has a disability and whether the effects of any disability call for an adjustment to be made. The fact that the employer might not know of a person's disability will make no difference if, for example, a personnel officer, line manager or occupational health officer employed by the employer has that information.[7] The knowledge of an employee or agent of the employer is the vicarious knowledge of the employer itself.

---

1   DDA 1995, s 4A(2)(a).

2   Ibid, s 4A(2)(b).

3   Ibid, s 4A(3)(a).

4   Ibid, s 4A(3)(b).

5   *Hanlon v University of Huddersfield* (1998) EAT/166/98.

6   *Code of Practice: Employment and Occupation* (2004), paras 5.12–5.14 (and examples).

7   *London Borough of Hammersmith and Fulham v Farnsworth* [2000] IRLR 691, EAT; *Code of Practice: Employment and Occupation* (2004), paras 5.15–5.16 (and examples).

4.2.32   It is recommended that employers should only ask disability-related questions if disability is (or may be) relevant to the ability to do the job. Equally, employers should be positive in welcoming applications from disabled persons. Asking about the effects of a disability is seen as a necessary part of the process of considering what reasonable adjustments might be made for a disabled person. In any event, if a person asks for an adjustment to be made, the employer will be entitled to ask for evidence that the person has a disability such as to trigger the statutory duty. Moreover, because a reasonable adjustment might not work in practice without the co-operation of other employees,[1] it may be necessary to reveal the fact of a person's disability (where otherwise not obvious) to some of that person's work colleagues (particularly a supervisor or manager) *in confidence* (eg where special assistance may be needed). This should be done on a selective and 'need-to-know' basis. Employers should be careful not to commit a separate act of discrimination by revealing such information without consulting the disabled person first or without a legitimate management purpose in doing so.

4.2.33   There does appear to be some onus on the applicant or employee to make known to the employer their need for a reasonable adjustment. Disabled people should not have a duty imposed upon them to give to an employer a detailed account of their disability and its effects upon them, especially where this would only lead to an employer making adjustments that it would have been reasonable to make in any event.[2] However, it is equally undesirable to expect employers to ask intrusive questions of disabled people that would not have been asked of a non-disabled person. A tribunal has to measure the extent of the duty to make a reasonable adjustment, if any, against the actual or assumed knowledge of the employer, both as to the disability and its likelihood of causing the individual a substantial disadvantage in comparison with persons who are not disabled.

Provision, criterion or practice

4.2.34   The terms 'provision, criterion or practice' are not defined in the Act, except that they include any arrangements.[3] The Part 2 Code of Practice explains that they include arrangements for determining to whom employment should be offered, and terms, conditions or arrangements on which employment, promotion, transfer, training or

---

1   *Code of Practice: Employment and Occupation* (2004), para 5.22 (and example).

2   *Ridout v TC Group* [1998] IRLR 628, EAT.

3   DDA 1995, s 18D(2). The pre-1 October 2004 term was 'arrangement': DDA 1995, s 6(1)(a) and (2) (prior to the 2004 amendments).

any other benefit is offered or afforded.[1] Examples of such arrangements would include procedures for recruitment and selection or
promotion (such as application forms, interviews or employment tests),
and terms upon which employment opportunities are granted (such as
insistence upon mobility or flexibility clauses or satisfaction of medical
standards). It will be important for the claimant to identify the
provision, criterion, practice or arrangement that is said to have the
required comparative substantial disadvantage.[2]

4.2.35 In one case,[3] a need for occupational health clearance was held
to be not in itself an arrangement that created a substantial disadvantage. However, the occupational health adviser's assessment as to the
challenging and stressful nature of the post (and the claimant's
unfitness for it) was part of the arrangements for determining to whom
employment should be offered. That placed the claimant at a comparative substantial disadvantage and triggered the employer's duty to make
reasonable adjustments. That duty would include obtaining specialist
advice from the claimant's consultant, consulting the claimant, referring the matter back the occupational health adviser and adjusting the
job.

4.2.36 The use of the terms 'provision, criterion or practice' is
deliberately wider that the sole term 'arrangements' that was used
before 1 October 2004. Prior to that date, the duty to make adjustments
was held not to apply to a dismissal itself, although it did apply to the
process leading to dismissal.[4] That distinction is not doubtful. A
decision to dismiss is capable of amounting to an arrangement on which
employment is afforded. The list of examples of reasonable adjustments
contains many illustrations of adjustments that are relevant to the
retention of a disabled employee in lieu of dismissal.[5] However, not all
arrangements that might be necessary to enable a disabled person to
work fall within the duty to make adjustments.[6] The duty is not intended
to cover everything an employer *could* do (eg arranging transport to and
from work or providing a personal carer to assist with the disabled
person's personal needs while at work). Only job-related arrangements
(such as the way a job is structured or organised) are covered.

---

1   *Code of Practice: Employment and Occupation (2004)*, para 5.8 (and examples) effectively
    adopting the previous statutory definition.
2   *Paul v National Probation Service* [2004] IRLR 190, EAT.
3   Ibid.
4   *Clark v TDG Ltd t/a Novacold* [1999] IRLR 318, CA.
5   DDA 1995, s 18B(2).
6   *Kenny v Hampshire Constabulary* [1999] IRLR 76, EAT.

Physical features of premises

4.2.37   The Act defines the phrase 'physical feature of premises'.[1] The following are treated as physical features (whether permanent or temporary) of premises:

- any feature arising from the design or construction of a building on the premises;
- any feature on the premises of any approach to, exit from or access to such a building;
- any fixtures, fittings, furnishings, furniture, equipment or materials in or on the premises;
- any other physical element or quality of any land comprised in the premises.

The physical features of a building do not only include the physical fabric and structure of a building. Features such as lighting, air conditioning, building materials, fixtures and fittings, furniture and equipment are also included.[2] However, it is only the physical features of premises occupied by the employer which are in scope. The duty to make reasonable adjustments in respect of the physical features of premises does not extend to a disabled person's private house (eg in the case of a home-worker) or to the premises of another employer which a disabled employee might have to visit in the course of employment (eg a travelling sales executive visiting a customer's premises).[3]

Substantial disadvantage

4.2.38   The duty to make reasonable adjustments arises only if the provision, criterion or practice or the physical feature in question places the disabled person concerned at a *substantial* disadvantage in comparison with persons who are not disabled.[4] The duty to make reasonable adjustments is an individualised duty.[5] It arises only where the disabled person in question suffers an actual or hypothetical comparative disadvantage. It does not necessarily arise generally or in respect of a class or group of disabled persons. The duty is only imposed following a comparative assessment of the adverse effect upon the disabled person. The comparators are persons who are not disabled (and, in the case of a

---

1   DDA 1995, s 18D(2); *Code of Practice: Employment and Occupation* (2004), para 5.9 (and examples). The definition was previously in the Disability Discrimination (Employment) Regulations 1996, reg 9, now revoked (and the Disability Discrimination (Employment) Regulations (Northern Ireland) 1996).

2   A non-exhaustive list is provided in *Code of Practice: Employment and Occupation* (2004), para 5.10.

3   HL Deb, vol 566, col 184.

4   DDA 1995, s 4A(1), with emphasis added.

5   *Code of Practice: Employment and Occupation* (2004), para 5.4.

person with a past disability, persons who have not had a disability).[1] The tribunal must address the comparison and make findings of fact to enable it to determine whether the disabled person has been placed at a substantial disadvantage.[2]

4.2.39 The use of the word 'substantial' appears to create quite a high threshold for the operation of the duty to make reasonable adjustments. Substantial disadvantages are those which are not minor or trivial.[3] The intention is that minor and trivial disadvantages do not cause the duty to be imposed on respondents. Only disadvantages of substance will call for accommodations.[4] Prior to 1 October 2004, a term or practice under which the amount of a person's pay was wholly or partly dependent on that person's performance was not to be taken to place disabled persons at a substantial disadvantage.[5] That will now be a question of fact and subject to the duty to make reasonable adjustments.[6]

Judicial guidance

4.2.40 The appellate courts have provided important guidance to employment tribunals on the practical approach to the issues raised by the duty to make reasonable adjustments.[7] It is not an error of law for a tribunal to fail to follow these steps sequentially.[8] The judicial guidance has been modified in this discussion to reflect the October 2004 amendments to the statutory provisions.

4.2.41 The first question is whether, in the particular circumstances of the case, there is a duty to make reasonable adjustments imposed upon the employer.[9] If so, the next step is to enquire whether the employer has taken reasonable steps to prevent the 'provision, criterion or practice' or 'physical features of premises' having the effect of placing the disabled person at a comparative substantial disadvantage. That necessitates asking whether the employer reasonably could have taken

---

1   DDA 1995, s 2(2) and Sch 2, para 3, as amended.

2   *London Clubs Management Ltd v Hood* [2001] IRLR 719, EAT; *Cave v Goodwin* [2001] All ER (D) 163 (Mar), IDS Brief 687, CA.

3   *Code of Practice: Employment and Occupation* (2004), para 5.11.

4   HC Deb Standing Committee E, col 196.

5   Disability Discrimination (Employment) Regulations 1996, reg 3(2), now revoked (and Disability Discrimination (Employment) Regulations (Northern Ireland) 1996).

6   *Code of Practice: Employment and Occupation* (2004), paras 8.5–8.6.

7   *Morse v Wiltshire CC* [1998] IRLR 352, EAT; *British Gas Services Ltd v McCaull* [2001] IRLR 60, EAT; *Cosgrove v Caesar & Howie* [2001] IRLR 653, EAT; *Johnson & Johnson Medical Ltd v Filmer* [2002] ICR 292, EAT.

8   *Beart v HM Prison Service* [2003] IRLR 238, CA.

9   DDA 1995, s 4A(1).

any of the steps set out in the statutory provisions as illustrating the kinds of adjustments that might be made.[1] However, this does not mean that the employer is in breach of the duty to make reasonable adjustments if it was not aware of the statutory duty. The employer does not have to show that it consciously considered what steps it ought to take in the context of its statutory duty. The question is what steps the employer took and did not take. An employer may have taken all reasonable steps, despite being ignorant of its statutory duty or the statutory provisions. It may have taken no steps, but it will have a defence if it could not reasonably have taken any.[2] The duty is one placed upon the employer. If an employer has not turned its mind to what adjustments might be made, the fact that the claimant cannot suggest any reasonable adjustments does not mean that the duty has been discharged.[3]

4.2.42 In judging the reasonableness question, consideration will need to be given as to whether any of the factors set out in the Act apply.[4] A respondent is not prevented from arguing after the event or with the benefit of hindsight that a particular step was not a reasonable one to have to take simply because the respondent did not consider taking it at the time.[5] The test is an objective one of whether the respondent took such steps as it was reasonable in all the circumstances of the case for that respondent to have to take in order to prevent the application of a provision, criterion or practice or the physical features of premises placing the disabled person at a comparative substantial disadvantage.[6] The employment tribunal is not simply concerned with the reasonableness of the respondent's explanation. The tribunal can substitute its own judgment for that of the employer (or other person). It may not be sufficient for a respondent simply to assert that adjustments were considered and thought to be unreasonable. The tribunal might find that there were other reasonable adjustments which could have been made by that person.

4.2.43 Somewhat controversially, the Court of Session in *Archibald v Fife Council* held that the duty of reasonable adjustment only arises in

---

1   DDA 1995, s 18B(2).

2   Under the pre-1 October 2004 law, it would have been very difficult for an employer to justify a failure to take reasonable steps if it had not considered what steps should be taken: *British Gas Services Ltd v McCaull* [2001] IRLR 60, EAT. However, the justification defence has now been repealed and the emphasis is upon the reasonableness of the steps taken or not taken.

3   *Cosgrove v Caesar & Howie* [2001] IRLR 653, EAT; *Code of Practice: Employment and Occupation* (2004), para 5.24.

4   DDA 1995, s 18B(1).

5   *British Gas Services Ltd v McCaull* [2001] IRLR 60, EAT.

6   *Morse v Wiltshire County Council* [1998] IRLR 352, EAT; *British Gas Services Ltd v McCaull* [2001] IRLR 60, EAT; *Johnson & Johnson Medical Ltd v Filmer* [2002] ICR 292, EAT.

respect of an existing employee where he or she is placed at a substantial disadvantage in the performance of his or her particular employment in comparison with persons who are not disabled.[1] The duty would then be triggered only if it was open to the employer to make adjustments to the arrangements of that particular post. On further appeal, however, the House of Lords has stressed the positive nature of the duty to make reasonable adjustments.[2] It indicated that an employer may be obliged to discriminate positively in favour of disabled persons. On the facts, the liability of a disabled employee to be dismissed because her disability meant that she was no longer able to carry out the duties that she was employed to do amounted to an 'arrangement' which placed her at a substantial disadvantage compared to other employees. That triggered the duty to make reasonable adjustments, which might include transferring her to another position for which she was suited, without the need for competitive interview and selection.

Unfair dismissal and disability discrimination

4.2.44 Nothing in the Act creates an obligation to provide disability leave, although one of the Codes of Practice suggests otherwise.[3] Nor does it place a requirement upon employers to retain newly disabled employees.[4] However, an employee absent from work on account of disability or long-term chronic ill health will be entitled to the benefit of the duty upon employers to make reasonable adjustments, as well as the specific protection of unfair dismissal law. The combined effect of disability discrimination law and unfair dismissal standards produces an obligation upon employers to hesitate before dismissing an employee on the grounds of disability or incapacity. At the very least, such an employer will need to consider what reasonable adjustments might be made for the employee. This might have the effect of prolonging his or her employment tenure or of leading to redeployment. Nevertheless, many employers' existing redeployment policies (which tend to give preference to redundant workers) will be unable to deal sufficiently with the specific duty to make reasonable adjustments which arises in the context of disability. Treating a disabled worker as just another candidate for redeployment is likely to be insufficient.[5]

---

1 [2004] IRLR 197, Ct of Sess.
2 [2004] UKHL 32, [2004] IRLR 651, HL.
3 *Code of Practice: Employment and Occupation* (2004), para 5.20 (and example).
4 HC Deb Standing Committee E, col 220.
5 *London Borough of Hillingdon v Morgan* (1999) EAT/1493/98, IDS Brief 649; *Kent County Council v Mingo* [2000] IRLR 90, EAT; *Archibald v Fife Council* [2004] UKHL 32, [2004] IRLR 651, HL.

4.2.45   To enjoy statutory protection from unfair dismissal, a disabled employee must have one year's continuous employment with the dismissing employer.[1] There is no minimum service qualification required to bring a complaint in relation to dismissal under the DDA 1995. Disabled employees dismissed with less than one year's service must rely upon the DDA 1995 alone, but, for a longer-serving employee with a disability, a dual claim under the disability discrimination and unfair dismissal legislation will prove attractive. A tribunal must approach both claims separately and distinctly.[2] It does not inevitably follow that a discriminatory dismissal is an unfair dismissal.[3] An unfair dismissal is not necessarily a discriminatory dismissal. The tribunal should carefully address the statutory test of an unfair dismissal.[4] The rather subjective 'band of reasonable responses' test in unfair dismissal is not the same as the more objective questions that have to be asked in disability discrimination cases.

Performance-related pay

4.2.46   Prior to 1 October 2004, special provision was made by regulations for a justification defence in relation to performance-related pay.[5] These regulations have now been revoked and not replaced.[6] Instead, provision is now made in the Code of Practice.[7] Employers must ensure that the way in which performance-related pay arrangements operate does not discriminate against disabled employees. If an employee is denied the opportunity to receive performance-related pay on the ground of disability or for a disability-related reason, that is likely to be discrimination (and, in the case of direct discrimination, will not be capable of being justified). An employee whose disability adversely affects his or her performance might receive less performance-related pay as a result. In that case, the employer must consider whether there are reasonable adjustments which would overcome this substantial disadvantage, such as modifying performance-related pay arrangements.

---

1   Employment Rights Act 1996, ss 94 and 108 (with some exceptions).

2   *British Sugar plc v Kirker* [1998] IRLR 624, EAT.

3   *H J Heinz Co Ltd v Kenrick* [2000] IRLR 144, EAT.

4   Employment Rights Act 1996, s 98; *Kent County Council v Mingo* [2000] IRLR 90, EAT.

5   Disability Discrimination (Employment) Regulations 1996, SI 1996/1456, and Disability Discrimination (Employment) Regulations (Northern Ireland) 1996, SR 1996/419.

6   Disability Discrimination (Employment Field) (Leasehold Premises) Regulations 2004, SI 2004/153; Disability Discrimination (Employment Field) (Leasehold Premises) Regulations (Northern Ireland) 2004, SR 2004/374.

7   *Code of Practice: Employment and Occupation* (2004), paras 5.20 and 8.5–8.6 (and examples).

Agricultural wages

4.2.47 Prior to 1 October 2004, so far as agricultural wages were concerned, the Agricultural Wages Board was allowed to issue a permit to a disabled person incapable of earning the minimum wage set by the Board.[1] The permit allowed for the setting of a lower minimum wage for that person and/or the variation of other minimum terms and conditions (other than holidays) applicable to that worker. Because the payment of a lower rate of pay to a disabled worker might not be capable of justification under the 1995 Act simply by reason of the permit, special provision was made by regulations. Less favourable treatment of a disabled person was to be taken to be justified to the extent that it related to (and accorded with) a matter within the terms and conditions of a permit granted to incapacitated persons under the agricultural wages legislation.[2] A failure to take a step otherwise required to comply with a duty to make reasonable adjustments was also to be taken to be justified if that step would relate to a matter within the terms and conditions of the permit but would exceed the requirements of those terms and conditions.[3] These provisions did not allow employers in the agricultural sector to discriminate against disabled persons in employment matters other than pay and terms and conditions covered by a permit. However, the provisions in the Agricultural Wages Act 1948 relating to permits for incapacitated workers have been repealed with effect from 1 October 2004 and so these special provisions are no longer in place.[4]

4.3 CONTRACT WORKERS

4.3.1 In what is now s 4B, the Act deals with discrimination by principals against contract workers in respect of the provision of contract work.[5] As originally enacted, the intention is to protect

1   Agricultural Wages Act 1948, s 5 and Agricultural Wages (Scotland) Act 1949, s 5. A new order came into effect on 1 October 2004: Agricultural Wages Order 2004 (No 1).

2   Disability Discrimination (Employment) Regulations 1996, SI 1996/1456, reg 6(a) (and Disability Discrimination (Employment) Regulations (Northern Ireland) 1996).

3   Ibid, reg 6(b).

4   Department for Environment, Food and Rural Affairs, *Agricultural Wages: Repeal of the Permits for Incapacitated Persons Provisions* (March 2004); Agricultural Wages (Abolition of Permits to Incapacitated Persons) Regulations 2004, SI 2004/2178; Agricultural Wages (Permits to Infirm and Incapacitated Persons) (Repeals) (Scotland) Regulations 2004, SSI 2004/384. The provisions of the Disability Discrimination (Employment) Regulations 1996 were revoked by the Disability Discrimination (Employment Field) (Leasehold Premises) Regulations 2004, SI 2004/153, and Disability Discrimination (Employment Field) (Leasehold Premises) Regulations (Northern Ireland) 2004, SR 2004/374.

5   DDA 1995, s 4B replaces s 12 with amendments. See generally: *Code of Practice: Employment and Occupation* (2004), paras 9.3–9.13.

disabled persons 'working under employment business arrangements if a hirer either refuses to hire the disabled person or discriminates against the disabled person once he has begun working for the hirer'.[1] Such persons will be generally protected by Part 2 of the Act in respect of their relationship with their employer (perhaps an employment agency or labour supplier). That protection is extended as against a third party during the period when their services have been hired or contracted to the third party.[2] These provisions also apply to severely disabled workers supplied by a local authority or voluntary organisation to a host employer under the Workstep scheme (formerly known as the Supported Placement Scheme).[3]

Definitions

4.3.2 A 'principal' is a person who makes work available ('contract work') to be done by individuals who are employed by another person who supplies them under a contract made with the principal.[4] The existence of a contract between the principal and the contractor–employer for the supply of the employee's labour is crucial.[5] A 'contract worker' is any individual who is supplied to the principal under a contract made between the principal and the contractor–employer for contract work to be done.[6] Because of the expanded definition of 'employment' in the 1995 Act,[7] these provisions should be capable of applying to contract workers, whether or not they are employees of the contractor–employer or are self-employed but providing personal services under a contract with the contractor–employer.[8] The section applies only in relation to contract work done at an establishment in Great Britain (or Northern Ireland, as the case may be).[9]

---

1   HL Deb, vol 566, col 221.

2   *Code of Practice: Employment and Occupation* (2004), para 9.6.

3   Ibid, para 9.13.

4   DDA 1995, s 4B(9); *Code of Practice: Employment and Occupation* (2004), para 9.5 (and example).

5   *Rice v Fon-A-Car* [1980] ICR 133, EAT (a taxi driver was not a contract worker simply because his services were supplied to customers through a central agency, because the agency had no contractual relationship with the customers); *Harrods Ltd v Remick* [1997] IRLR 583, CA (employees of concessionaires in a department store were treated as contract workers, as they worked for the concessionaires but for the benefit of the store). See also: *CJ O'Shea Construction Ltd v Bassi* [1998] ICR 1130, EAT.

6   DDA 1995, s 4B(9).

7   Ibid, s 68(1).

8   See *Construction Industry Training Board v Labour Force Ltd* [1970] 3 All ER 220; *Tanna v Post Office* [1981] ICR 374; *Daley v Allied Suppliers Ltd* [1983] ICR 90, EAT; *Mirror Group Newspapers v Gunning* [1986] ICR 145.

9   DDA 1995, s 4B(8), applying s 68 with appropriate modifications. See **4.2.18**.

4.3.3   The breadth of the contractual relationships envisaged by these provisions is illustrated by *MHC Consulting Services Ltd v Tansell*.[1] Mr Tansell (T) was a disabled person. He had formed a company (I) as a vehicle for offering his computer skills and services to third parties. T had placed his name with MHC Consulting Services Ltd (MHC), an employment agency specialising in placing computer personnel with third parties. Abbey Life Assurance Co Ltd (AL) entered into a contract with MHC whereby MHC contracted to provide computer personnel to AL. In pursuance of that relationship, MHC placed T's services with AL. It did so by entering into a contract with I for the supply of T's services to AL. However, it was alleged by T that AL rejected his services because of his disability. In the legal proceedings that followed, T was found not to be an employee of AL or MHC. If he was an employee at all, then he was employed by I. The EAT gave a purposive construction to the statutory provisions. It ruled that T could proceed with his action against AL. T was employed by I, which supplied T's services through MHC to AL. This amounted to an unbroken chain of contracts between the individual (T) and the end-user (AL). In these circumstances, the end-user was a principal within the meaning of the section.

Unlawful discrimination

4.3.4   First, it is unlawful for a principal, in relation to contract work, to discriminate against a disabled person who is a contract worker (a 'disabled contract worker') in the terms on which the principal allows him or her to do that work.[2] Secondly, it is unlawful for a principal, in relation to contract work, to discriminate against a disabled contract worker by not allowing him or her to do or continue to do the contract work.[3] Thirdly, it is unlawful for a principal, in relation to contract work, to discriminate against a disabled contract worker in the way the principal affords him or her access to any benefits or by refusing or deliberately omitting to afford him or her access to any benefits.[4] Fourthly, it is unlawful for a principal, in relation to contract work, to discriminate against a disabled contract worker by subjecting him or her to any other detriment.[5] Fifthly, it is also unlawful for a principal, in relation to contract work, to subject a disabled contract worker to

---

1   [1999] IRLR 677, EAT, subsequently upheld *sub nom Abbey Life Assurance Co Ltd v Tansell* [2000] IRLR 387, CA.

2   DDA 1995, ss 3A and 4B(1)(a).

3   Ibid, ss 3A and 4B(1)(b); *BP Chemicals Ltd v Gillick* [1995] IRLR 128, EAT (the principal may have unlawfully discriminated by refusing to take on the contract worker).

4   Ibid, ss 3A and 4B(1)(c).

5   Ibid, ss 3A and 4B(1)(d).

harassment.[1] The meanings of 'discriminate' and 'harassment' have been considered in Chapter 3.

4.3.5 These categories of unlawful acts are very similar to those that apply in relation to discrimination against employment applicants and employees.[2] However, they do not include discrimination in recruitment, selection, engagement and dismissal. Any disability discrimination in those areas will have been perpetrated by the contractor–employer rather than the principal for whom the contract work is to be done. A claimant would have a potential cause of action against the contractor–employer.

4.3.6 As is the case in the parallel employment provisions,[3] the contract worker provisions do not apply to benefits of any description if the principal is concerned with the provision (whether for payment or not) of benefits of that description to the public (or a section of the public, including the contract worker) unless that provision differs in a material respect from the provision of the benefits by the principal to contract workers.[4] The term 'benefits' includes facilities and services.[5] However, in such a case, a contract worker might have a cause of action under Part 3 of the Act.

Contract work and reasonable adjustments

4.3.7 The principal is subject to a duty to make reasonable adjustments in relation to disabled contract workers.[6] The broader issues raised by this duty have been considered in Chapter 3. First, the duty is addressed where a provision, criterion or practice is applied by or on behalf of all or most of the principals to whom the disabled contract worker is or might be supplied. If, as a result, the disabled contract worker is likely (on each occasion on which he or she is supplied to a principal to do contract work) to be placed at a substantial disadvantage in comparison with persons who are not disabled which is the same or similar in each case, the duty arises.[7] Secondly, the duty is also addressed where there is a physical feature of premises occupied by all or most of the principals to whom the disabled contract worker is or

---

1   DDA 1995, ss 3B and 4B(2).

2   Ibid, s 4.

3   Ibid, s 4(4).

4   Ibid, s 4B(3).

5   Ibid, s 18B(2).

6   *Code of Practice: Employment and Discrimination* (2004), paras 9.7–9.13. The complex provisions on contract workers in the Disability Discrimination (Employment) Regulations 1996, SI 1996/1456, reg 7 (and Disability Discrimination (Employment) Regulations (Northern Ireland) 1996, SR 1996/419) are revoked from 1 October 2004.

7   DDA 1995, s 4B(4)(a).

might be supplied. If, as a result, the disabled contract worker is likely (on each occasion on which he or she is supplied to a principal to do contract work) to be placed at a substantial disadvantage in comparison with persons who are not disabled which is the same or similar in each case, the duty also arises.[1]

4.3.8 Where the duty arises in either case, the disabled contract worker's employer must take such steps as that employer would have to take if the provision, criterion or practice were applied by the employer (or on its behalf) or if the premises were occupied by the employer.[2] Furthermore, the employer's duty to make reasonable adjustments is also applied to the principal in relation to contract work as if the principal were (or would be) the employer of the disabled contract worker and as if any contract worker supplied to do work for the principal was an employee of the principal.[3] However, a principal is not required to take a step in relation to a disabled contract worker if the disabled contract worker's employer is required to take the step in relation to him or her.[4]

4.3.9 Thus, both the principal and the contractor–employer might be under separate (and sometimes overlapping) duties to make reasonable adjustments in relation to the disabled contract worker.[5] That imports an obligation on the principal and the contractor–employer to co-operate as far as is reasonable with adjustments already made for the contract worker by the employment business.[6] However, what will be a reasonable adjustment for a hirer to make will depend upon its individual circumstances and the rather limited, short-term nature of the labour-hiring relationship. For example, it might be unreasonable for a principal to have to make adjustments if the disabled contract worker is to be seconded to the principal for only a short time.[7] Also, in practice, it might be reasonable for the principal to allow an adjustment to be made in respect of the disabled contract worker, but for the employer to provide or pay for the necessary adjustment.

4.3.10 This might be best explained by adopting and modifying an example provided in the original Employment Code of Practice.[8] A

---

1   DDA 1995, s 4B(4)(b).

2   Ibid, s 4B(5), cross-referring to s 4A (and, by implication, s 18B).

3   Ibid, s 4B(6), cross-referring to s 4A (and, by implication, s 18B).

4   Ibid, s 4B(7), cross-referring to s 4A (and, by implication, s 18B).

5   *Code of Practice: Employment and Occupation* (2004), paras 9.9–9.12 (and examples).

6   HL Deb, vol 566, col 222; *Code of Practice: Employment and Occupation* (2004), para 9.12.

7   *Code of Practice: Employment and Occupation* (2004), para 9.8. No indication is given of what would amount to a short period of time, although the example accompanying para 9.8 suggests that two weeks would certainly be such a period.

8   *Employment Code of Practice* (1996), para 7.6.

disabled word-processor operator employed as a contract worker by a clerical agency requires a special keyboard as an adjustment for his or her disability. It can be anticipated that the contract worker will require such a keyboard wherever he or she is sent to work by the agency. It would be a reasonable step for the agency to supply the word-processor operator with the special keyboard. It would not be reasonable to expect any firm to whom that contract worker's services are supplied to have to acquire a special keyboard for him or her. However, those firms would be under a separate duty to co-operate with the adjustment made by the agency, eg by allowing the worker to carry and use the special keyboard at their premises. They might also have a residual duty to make a reasonable adjustment, eg by ensuring that the keyboard can be made compatible with their computer systems, such as might be achieved by installing the appropriate driver software.

4.4   OFFICE-HOLDERS

4.4.1   As a result of the EC Framework Employment Directive, office-holders are now explicitly covered by the DDA 1995, as amended by the Disability Discrimination Act 1995 (Amendment) Regulations 2003.[1] Unfortunately, the relevant provisions are amongst the most complex of the new amendments.[2]

Offices or posts

4.4.2   The new provisions apply to an 'office' or a 'post'. These terms are not defined. They will include company directors, judges and chairmen or members of non-departmental public bodies.[3] However, not all offices or posts are included. The provisions on discrimination and harassment,[4] and the duty to make reasonable adjustments,[5] apply to an office or post only if no 'relevant provision' of Part 2 applies in relation to an appointment to the office or post *and* one or more specified conditions is satisfied.[6] The relevant provisions of Part 2 for this purpose are those dealing with discrimination and harassment by employers, in relation to contract workers, by partnerships, by barristers

---

1   See **4.2.21–4.2.23**.

2   DDA 1995, ss 4C–4F.

3   *Code of Practice: Employment and Occupation (2004)*, para 9.14. Tribunal appointments such as those considered in *Photis and Bruce v KMC International Search and Selection, Heyes v Lord Chancellor's Department* (EAT/732/00, EAT/766/00 and EAT/960/00) prior to 1 October 2004 will now be covered.

4   DDA 1995, s 4D.

5   Ibid, s 4E.

6   Ibid, s 4C(1), subject to s 4C(5).

and advocates and in relation to practical work experience.[1] In other words, if a claimant's case falls within one of the other identified areas of the employment field, the case cannot be brought under the office-holder provisions.

4.4.3 What are the specified conditions one or more of which must also be satisfied? There are three possibilities. First, the office or post is one to which persons are appointed to discharge functions personally under the direction of another person and in respect of which they are entitled to remuneration.[2] For this purpose only, the holder of an office or post is to be regarded as discharging his or her functions under the direction of another person if that other person is entitled to direct him or her as to when and where he or she discharges those functions.[3] The holder of an office or post is not to be regarded as entitled to remuneration merely because he or she is entitled to payments in respect of expenses incurred by him or her in carrying out the functions of the office or post.[4] The holder of an office or post is also not to be regarded as entitled to remuneration merely because he or she is entitled to payments by way of compensation for the loss of income or benefits he or she would (or might) have received from any person had he or she not been carrying out the functions of the office or post.[5] Secondly, the office or post is one to which appointments are made by a Minister of the Crown, a government department, the National Assembly for Wales or any part of the Scottish Administration.[6] Thirdly, the office or post is one to which appointments are made on the recommendation of (or subject to the approval of) a Minister of the Crown, a government department, the National Assembly for Wales or any part of the Scottish Administration.[7] In Northern Ireland, the appropriate references are to appointments made by a Minister of the Crown, a Northern Ireland Minister or a government department, or to an office or post to which appointments are made on the recommendation of (or subject to the approval of) those persons or the Assembly.

---

1   DDA 1995, s 4C(2), referring to ss 4, 4B, 6A, 7A, 7C and 14C, respectively.

2   Ibid, s 4C(3)(a).

3   Ibid, s 4C(4)(a).

4   Ibid, s 4C(4)(b)(i).

5   Ibid, s 4C(4)(b)(ii).

6   Ibid, s 4C(3)(b).

7   Ibid, s 4C(3)(c).

Exclusions

4.4.4   The prohibitions on discrimination against (and the duty to make reasonable adjustments in relation to) office-holders do not apply to a raft of offices or posts.[1] The exclusions are as follows:

- any office of the House of Commons held by a member of it;
- a life peerage;[2]
- any office of the House of Lords held by a member of it;
- certain ministerial offices;[3]
- the offices of Leader of the Opposition, Chief Opposition Whip or Assistant Opposition Whip;[4]
- any office of the Scottish Parliament held by a member of it;
- a member of the Scottish Executive;[5]
- a junior Scottish Minister;[6]
- any office of the National Assembly for Wales held by a member of it;
- any office of a county council, a London borough council, a district council or a parish council held by a member of it (in England);
- any office of a county council, a county borough council or a community council held by a member of it (in Wales);
- any office of a council or community council held by a member of it (in Scotland);[7]
- any office of the Greater London Authority held by a member of it;
- any office of the Common Council of the City of London held by a member of it;
- any office of the Council of the Isles of Scilly held by a member of it;
- any office of a political party;
- any office of the Assembly held by a member of it (in Northern Ireland);
- any office of a district council held by a member of it (in Northern Ireland).

---

1   DDA 1995, s 4C(5).

2   Life Peerages Act 1958.

3   House of Commons Disqualification Act 1975, Sch 2.

4   Ministerial and other Salaries Act 1975.

5   Scotland Act 1998, s 44.

6   Ibid, s 49.

7   Local Government etc (Scotland) Act 1994, s 2; Local Government (Scotland) Act 1973, s 51.

Unlawful acts

4.4.5   A number of unlawful acts of discrimination and harassment are created in relation to office-holders from 1 October 2004.[1] The unlawful acts are capable of being committed by 'a relevant person'. Who that relevant person is in relation to any particular unlawful act will become apparent as the unlawful acts are described.[2] Appointment to an office or post does not include election to such office or post.[3] The meanings of 'discrimination' and 'harassment' have been considered in Chapter 3.

Offer of appointment

4.4.6   First, it is unlawful for a relevant person in relation to an appointment to an office or post to discriminate against a disabled person in the arrangements which the relevant person makes for the purpose of determining who should be offered the appointment.[4] Secondly, it is unlawful for a relevant person in relation to an appointment to an office or post to discriminate against a disabled person in the terms on which the relevant person offers him or her an appointment.[5] Thirdly, it is unlawful for a relevant person in relation to an appointment to an office or post to discriminate against a disabled person by refusing to offer him or her an appointment.[6] A refusal includes a deliberate omission.[7] In a case relating to an appointment to an office or post, the relevant person is the person with power to make that appointment.[8]

Recommendation or approval of appointment

4.4.7   Fourthly, it is unlawful for a relevant person in relation to an appointment to an office or post to discriminate against a disabled person in the arrangements which the relevant person makes for the purpose of determining who should be recommended or approved in relation to the appointment.[9] Fifthly, it is unlawful for a relevant person in relation to an appointment to an office or post to discriminate against

---

1   DDA 1995, s 4D; *Code of Practice: Employment and Occupation* (2004), paras 9.15–9.20.

2   *Code of Practice: Employment and Occupation* (2004), para 9.22.

3   DDA 1995, s 4F(1).

4   Ibid, s 4D(1)(a).

5   Ibid, s 4D(1)(b).

6   Ibid, s 4D(1)(c).

7   Ibid, s 4D(7)(b).

8   Ibid, s 4F(2)(a).

9   Ibid, s 4D(2)(a).

a disabled person in making or refusing to make a recommendation in relation to the appointment.[1] In both these cases, a recommendation includes the making of a negative recommendation.[2] Sixthly, it is unlawful for a relevant person in relation to an appointment to an office or post to discriminate against a disabled person in giving or refusing to give an approval in relation to the appointment.[3] In each of these three cases, the office or post must satisfy the particular condition that it is one to which appointments are made on the recommendation of (or subject to the approval of) a Minister of the Crown, a government department, the National Assembly for Wales or any part of the Scottish Administration.[4] In these three cases, the relevant person is the person or body with power to make that recommendation or (as the case may be) to give that approval.[5] A refusal includes a deliberate omission.[6]

Appointment terms and opportunities

4.4.8 Seventhly, it is unlawful for a relevant person, in relation to a disabled person who has been appointed to an office or post, to discriminate against him or her in the terms of the appointment.[7] In this case, the relevant person is the person with the power to determine those terms.[8] Eighthly, it is unlawful for a relevant person, in relation to a disabled person who has been appointed to an office or post, to discriminate against him or her in the opportunities which the relevant person affords him or her for promotion, a transfer, training or receiving any other benefit (or by refusing to afford him or her any such opportunity) – the so-called 'working conditions'.[9] In this case, the relevant person is the person with the power to determine those matters or, where there is no such person, the person with the power to make the appointment.[10] However, this provision does not apply to benefits of any description if the relevant person is concerned with the provision (for payment or not) of benefits of that description to the public (or a section of the public to which the disabled person belongs), except in three circumstances.[11] Those circumstances are that: (a) that provision

---

1   DDA 1995, s 4D(2)(b).

2   Ibid, s 4D(7)(a).

3   Ibid, s 4D(2)(b).

4   Ibid, s 4D(2), by reference to s 4C(3)(c).

5   Ibid, s 4F(2)(b), by reference to s 4C(3)(c).

6   Ibid, s 4D(7)(b).

7   Ibid, s 4D(3)(a).

8   Ibid, s 4F(2)(c).

9   Ibid, ss 4D(3)(b) and 4F(3)(a).

10   Ibid, s 4F(2)(d) and (3)(a).

11   Ibid, s 4D(5).

differs in a material respect from the provision of the benefits to persons appointed to offices or posts which are the same as (or not materially different from) that to which the disabled person has been appointed; (b) the provision of the benefits to the person appointed is regulated by the terms and conditions of his or her appointment; or (c) the benefits relate to training.

Termination of appointment and any other detriment

4.4.9   Ninthly, it is unlawful for a relevant person, in relation to a disabled person who has been appointed to an office or post, to discriminate against him or her by terminating the appointment.[1] The reference to the termination of the appointment includes a reference to the expiry of a fixed term without non-renewal and a constructive termination.[2] The relevant person is the person with power to terminate the appointment.[3] Tenthly, it is unlawful for a relevant person, in relation to a disabled person who has been appointed to an office or post, to discriminate against him or her by subjecting him or her to any other detriment in relation to the appointment.[4] The relevant person is any person or body with power to make the appointment, to recommend or approve the appointment, to determine the terms of appointment or its working conditions, or to terminate the employment, as the case may be.[5]

Harassment

4.4.10   Eleventhly, it is also unlawful for a relevant person, in relation to an office or post, to subject to harassment a disabled person: (a) who has been appointed to the office or post; (b) who is seeking or being considered for appointment to the office or post; or (c) who is seeking or being considered for a recommendation or approval in relation to an appointment to an office or post.[6] In respect of (c), the office or post must satisfy the particular condition that it is one to which appointments are made on the recommendation of (or subject to the approval of) a Minister of the Crown, a government department, the National Assembly for Wales or any part of the Scottish Administration.[7] The relevant person is any person or body with power to make the

---

1   DDA 1995, s 4D(3)(c).

2   Ibid, s 4D(6).

3   Ibid, s 4F(2)(e).

4   Ibid, s 4D(3)(d).

5   Ibid, s 4F(2)(f).

6   Ibid, s 4D(4).

7   Ibid, s 4D(4)(c), by reference to s 4C(3)(c).

appointment, to recommend or approve the appointment, to determine the terms of appointment or its working conditions, or to terminate the employment, as the case may be.[1]

Duty to make adjustments

4.4.11   Where a provision, criterion or practice applied by or on behalf of a relevant person places the disabled person concerned at a substantial disadvantage in comparison with persons who are not disabled, it is the duty of the relevant person to take such steps as it is reasonable, in all the circumstances of the case, for the relevant person to have to take in order to prevent the provision, criterion or practice having that effect.[2] Furthermore, where any physical feature of premises under the control of a relevant person, and at or from which the functions of an office or post are performed, places the disabled person concerned at a substantial disadvantage in comparison with persons who are not disabled, it is the duty of the relevant person to take such steps as it is reasonable, in all the circumstances of the case, for the relevant person to have to take in order to prevent the feature having that effect.[3] This provision is very similar to that which applies in relation to employers and which has been discussed above. The broader issues raised by the duty to make reasonable adjustments have been discussed in Chapter 3.[4]

Relevant person

4.4.12   The relevant person for these purposes has already been identified above.[5] In particular, in respect of adjustments to physical features of premises, the relevant person will be the person with the power to determine the feature in question or the person with the power to make the appointment.[6]

Disabled person concerned

4.4.13   Who is 'the disabled person concerned' in the case of a provision, criterion or practice for determining who should be appointed to (or recommended or approved in relation to) an office or post? It is any disabled person who is (or who has notified the relevant person that he or she may be) seeking appointment to (or seeking a

---

1   DDA 1995, s 4F(2)(f).

2   Ibid, s 4E(1)(a).

3   Ibid, s 4E(1)(b).

4   See also *Code of Practice: Employment and Occupation* (2004), para 9.21.

5   DDA 1995, s 4F(2) and (3)(b).

6   Ibid, s 4F(2)(d) and (3)(b).

recommendation or approval in relation to) that office or post.[1] It also includes any disabled person who is being considered for appointment to (or for a recommendation or approval in relation to) that office or post.[2] In any other case, 'the disabled person concerned' is a disabled person who is seeking or being considered for appointment to (or a recommendation or approval in relation to) the office or post concerned,[3] or who has been appointed to the office or post concerned.[4]

4.4.14 What does the relevant person need to know of the disabled person in the case of a person who is being considered for, or is or may be seeking, appointment to, or a recommendation or approval in relation to, an office or post? No duty is imposed on the relevant person in relation to the disabled person if the relevant person does not know (and could not reasonably be expected to know) that the disabled person concerned is, or may be, seeking appointment to, or seeking a recommendation or approval in relation to, that office or post.[5] No duty is imposed on the relevant person in relation to the disabled person if the relevant person does not know (and could not reasonably be expected to know) that the disabled person concerned is being considered for appointment to, or (as the case may be) for a recommendation or approval in relation to, that office or post.[6] In any case, no duty is imposed on the relevant person in relation to the disabled person if the relevant person does not know (and could not reasonably be expected to know) that the disabled person concerned has a disability and is likely to be placed at a substantial disadvantage in comparison with persons who are not disabled.[7]

4.5 OCCUPATIONAL PENSION SCHEMES

Employers' obligations

4.5.1 Part 2 of the 1995 Act is capable of covering the actions of an employer who provides opportunities to employees for occupational pensions. Discrimination against disabled persons in the terms of employment and in the opportunities afforded for receiving any other

---

1   DDA 1995, s 4E(2)(a)(i).

2   Ibid, s 4E(2)(a)(ii).

3   Ibid, s 4E(2)(b)(i).

4   Ibid, s 4E(2)(b)(ii).

5   Ibid, s 4E(3)(a)(i).

6   Ibid, s 4E(3)(a)(ii).

7   Ibid, s 4E(3)(b).

benefit is unlawful, all other things being equal.[1] If an employer discriminates against a disabled person in respect of access to or benefits from an occupational pension scheme (including the terms of membership), that might amount to an unlawful act of discrimination, unless otherwise capable of justification. The pre-1 October 2004 special provision made for benefits provided under an occupational pension scheme in respect of termination of service, retirement, old age, death, accident, injury, sickness or invalidity has now been revoked.[2]

Trustees and managers of occupational pension schemes

4.5.2   Occupational pension schemes are run and managed by trustees and managers, rather than by the employer. At the time of enacting the DDA 1995, the then Government was concerned that disabled persons might be unfairly denied access to an employer's pension scheme arrangements by the decisions of the scheme trustees or managers (and not simply by the actions of employers). As originally enacted, the Act stated that every occupational pension scheme shall be taken to include a provision to be referred to as 'a non-discrimination rule'.[3] The effect of this implied non-discrimination rule related to the terms on which persons become members of the scheme and the terms on which members of the scheme were treated. The non-discrimination rule also required the trustees or managers of the occupational pension scheme to refrain from any act or omission which, if done in relation to a person by an employer, would amount to unlawful discrimination under Part 2 of the Act. Moreover, the 'other provisions of the scheme' were to have effect subject to the implied non-discrimination rule. The effect of this provision meant that any discriminatory decision taken by trustees or managers would be contrary to the rules of the scheme. Any disabled person affected by such a discriminatory decision had to seek redress through the appropriate dispute resolution machinery for pension schemes, rather than in the employment tribunal.

4.5.3   The position is now changed as a result of the amendments made to the Act from 1 October 2004 by the Disability Discrimination Act 1995 (Pensions) Regulations 2003.[4]

---

1   DDA 1995, s 4(2); *Code of Practice: Employment and Occupation* (2004), paras 10.2–10.5 (and example).

2   Disability Discrimination (Employment) Regulations 1996, SI 1996/1456, reg 4(3). See also Disability Discrimination (Employment) Regulations (Northern Ireland) 1996, SR 1996/419.

3   DDA 1995, s 17(1), now repealed; HL Deb, vol 566, cols 994–995.

4   SI 2003/2770, inserting DDA 1995, ss 4G–4K and repealing s 17. See also: *Code of Practice: Employment and Occupation* (2004), paras 10.6–10.15 (and examples).

Non-discrimination rule

4.5.4 Every occupational pension scheme shall be taken to include a provision called 'the non-discrimination rule'.[1] The rule does not apply in relation to rights accrued (or benefits payable) in respect of periods of service prior to 1 October 2004. It does apply to communications[2] with members[3] or prospective members[4] of the scheme in relation to such rights or benefits.[5] The rule contains two requirements. The first is that the trustees or managers[6] of the scheme refrain from discriminating against a relevant disabled person in carrying out any of their functions in relation to the scheme.[7] That includes, in particular, their functions relating to the admission of members to the scheme and the treatment of members of the scheme. The second requirement is that the trustees or managers of the scheme do not subject a relevant disabled person to harassment in relation to the scheme. The other provisions of the scheme are to have effect subject to the non-discrimination rule.[8] That means that if there is a conflict between the non-discrimination rule and a rule of the scheme, the former prevails.[9] A relevant disabled person is a disabled person who is a member or prospective member of the scheme.[10]

---

1   DDA 1995, s 4G(1).

2   *Code of Practice: Employment and Occupation* (2004), para 10.10 (and example). In their application to communications, ss 4G–4J apply in relation to a disabled person who is entitled to the present payment of dependants' or survivors' benefits under an occupational pension scheme, or who is a pension credit member of such a scheme, as they apply in relation to a disabled person who is a pensioner member of the scheme: s 4K(1). Communications includes the provision of information and the operation of a dispute-resolution procedure: s 4K(2). A pension credit member and a pensioner member are defined by Pensions Act 1995, s 124(1), as at 1 October 2004: s 4K(2) (in Northern Ireland, Pensions (Northern Ireland) Order 1995, art 121(1)).

3   A member in relation to an occupational pension scheme means any active, deferred or pensioner member, as defined in Pensions Act 1995, s 124(1) as at 1 October 2004: DDA 1995, s 4K(2) (in Northern Ireland, Pensions (Northern Ireland) Order 1995, art 121(1)).

4   A prospective member is any person who, under the terms of his or her contract of employment or the scheme rules or both, is able (at his or her own option) to become a member of the scheme, or will become so able if he or she continues in the same employment for a sufficiently long period, or will be admitted to it automatically unless he or she makes an election not to become a member, or may be admitted to it subject to the consent of his or her employer: DDA 1995, s 4K(2).

5   DDA 1995, s 4G(4). 'Benefits' does not include facilities or services for this purpose: s 18D(2).

6   The terms 'managers' and 'trustees or managers' have the meanings given by Pensions Act 1995, s 124(1) as at 1 October 2004: DDA 1995, s 4K(2) (in Northern Ireland, Pensions (Northern Ireland) Order 1995, art 121(1)).

7   DDA 1995, s 4G(1)(a).

8   Ibid, s 4G(2).

9   *Code of Practice: Employment and Occupation* (2004), para 10.8.

10   DDA 1995, s 4K(2).

Unlawful acts

4.5.5 It is unlawful for the trustees or managers of an occupational pension scheme to discriminate against a relevant disabled person contrary to the first requirement of the non-discrimination rule or to subject a relevant disabled person to harassment contrary to the second requirement of the non-discrimination rule.[1] The meanings of 'discrimination' and 'harassment' have been discussed in Chapter 3.

Alterations to a scheme

4.5.6 The trustees or managers of an occupational pension scheme may, by resolution, make such alterations to the scheme as may be required to secure conformity with the non-discrimination rule,[2] if they do not otherwise have power to make such alterations.[3] They may also make such alterations if they have such power, but where the procedure for doing so is liable to be unduly complex or protracted, or involves the obtaining of consents which cannot be obtained (or can only be obtained with undue delay or difficulty).[4] The alterations may have effect in relation to a period before the alterations are made (but may not have effect in relation to a period before 1 October 2004).[5]

Duty to make reasonable adjustments

4.5.7 The trustees or managers of an occupational pension scheme have a duty to make reasonable adjustments in two situations. First, where a provision, criterion or practice (including a scheme rule) applied by or on behalf of the trustees or managers of an occupational pension scheme places a relevant disabled person at a substantial disadvantage in comparison with persons who are not disabled, it is the duty of the trustees or managers to take such steps as it is reasonable, in all the circumstances of the case, for them to have to take in order to prevent the provision, criterion or practice having that effect.[6] Secondly, where any physical feature of premises occupied by the trustees or managers places a relevant disabled person at a substantial disadvantage in comparison with persons who are not disabled, it is the duty of the trustees or managers to take such steps as it is reasonable, in all the circumstances of the case, for them to have to take in order to prevent

---

1   DDA 1995, s 4G(3).

2   *Code of Practice: Employment and Occupation* (2004), para 10.8 (and example).

3   DDA 1995, s 4G(5)(a).

4   Ibid, s 4G(5)(b).

5   Ibid, s 4G(6).

6   Ibid, s 4H(1)(a).

the feature having that effect.[1] The making of alterations to scheme rules is an example of a step which trustees or managers may have to take in order to comply with the duty.[2] The duty is not imposed on trustees or managers in relation to a disabled person if they do not know (and could not reasonably be expected to know) that the disabled person is a relevant disabled person or that that person has a disability and is likely to be placed at a substantial disadvantage in comparison with persons who are not disabled.[3] The broader issues raised by the duty to make reasonable adjustment are addressed in Chapter 3.

Procedure and remedies

4.5.8 Particular provision is made where a relevant disabled person presents a complaint to an employment tribunal that the trustees or managers of an occupational pension scheme have acted in relation to him or her in a way which is unlawful under Part 2.[4] In such a case, the employer in relation to that scheme shall be treated as a party and be entitled to appear and be heard in the proceedings.[5] This is because the employer may be required to fund any award made against the scheme.[6]

4.5.9 Particular provision is also made in respect of remedies where a relevant disabled person presents to an employment tribunal a complaint that the trustees or managers of an occupational pension scheme have acted in relation to him or her in a way which is unlawful under Part 2 or an employer has so acted in relation to him or her.[7] The complaint must relate to the terms on which persons become members of an occupational pension scheme or the terms on which members of the scheme are treated.[8] It assumes that the disabled person is not a pensioner member of the scheme[9] and that the tribunal finds that the

---

1   DDA 1995, s 4H(1)(b).

2   Ibid, s 4H(2) (ie in addition to the examples set out in s 18B(2)).

3   Ibid, s 4H(3).

4   Complaint may also be made via the dispute resolution mechanism of the scheme itself or to the Pensions Ombudsman or through the advice and conciliation service of the Pensions Advisory Service. See *Code of Practice: Employment and Occupation* (2004), para 10.15 and Appendix C.

5   DDA 1995, s 4I(1) (ie in proceedings brought under s 17A and for the purposes of the Employment Tribunals Rules of Procedure 2004). The employer in relation to an occupational pension scheme has the meaning given by Pensions Act 1995, s 124(1), as at 1 October 2004 (in Northern Ireland, Pensions (Northern Ireland) Order 1995, art 121(1)).

6   *Code of Practice: Employment and Occupation* (2004), para 10.12.

7   DDA 1995, s 4J(1)(a).

8   Ibid, s 4J(1)(b).

9   Ibid, s 4J(1)(c).

complaint is well founded.[1] If so, the tribunal may make a declaration that the claimant has a right to be admitted to the scheme in question or to membership of the scheme without discrimination (as the case may be).[2] The declaration may be made in respect of such period as the declaration may specify (but may not be made in respect of any period before 1 October 2004).[3] It may make such provision as the tribunal considers appropriate as to the terms upon which (or the capacity in which) the disabled person is to enjoy such admission or membership.[4] The tribunal may not award the disabled person any compensation (whether in relation to arrears of benefits or otherwise) other than compensation for injury to feelings or initial or increased compensation pursuant to a failure to comply with the tribunal's recommendation.[5]

4.6   INSURANCE BENEFITS

4.6.1   Insurance benefits (such as private health insurance) offered to employees by an employer are within the scope of the prohibition on employment discrimination.[6] Special provision is made where an employer makes arrangements with an insurer for insurance-related benefits to be received by the employer's employees.[7] This is designed to address discrimination by the insurance company rather than by the employer itself. It will be relevant where the insurer treats disabled persons differently from others for non-actuarial reasons.

4.6.2   The provision applies where a provider of insurance services enters into arrangements with an employer under which the employer's employees receive 'insurance services' provided by the insurer.[8] It also applies where the insurer enters into an arrangement with an employer under which the employer's employees are given an opportunity to receive insurance services provided by the insurer.[9] In both cases, it does not matter whether the employer–insurer arrangements cover all the employer's employees or only a class thereof.

---

1   DDA 1995, s 4J(1)(d).

2   Ibid, s 4J(2) (by reference to s 4J(1)(b)(i) or (ii), as the case may be). This is without prejudice to the generality of the tribunal's power under s 17A(2)(a).

3   Ibid, s 4J(3)(a).

4   Ibid, s 4J(3)(b).

5   Ibid, s 4J(4), by reference to ss 17A(5) and 17A(2)(b).

6   Ibid, s 4(2)(a)–(c) are particularly apposite.

7   Ibid, s 18.

8   Ibid, s 18(1)(a).

9   Ibid, s 18(1)(b).

4.6.3   Disability-related discrimination in respect of the provision of insurance benefits to employees under an employer–insurer arrangement is made unlawful by an awkward cross-reference to the provisions of Part 3 of the Act.[1] Part 3 establishes that it is unlawful to discriminate against a disabled person for a reason related to disability in respect of the provision of goods, facilities or services to members of the public unless the discrimination is capable of justification, eg by reference to actuarial evidence. For the purposes of Part 2 of the Act, in the context of employment benefits, an insurer is treated as having discriminated unlawfully against a disabled person who is a relevant employee if the insurer acts in relation to the disabled employee in a way which would be unlawful discrimination under Part 3.[2] Would the insurer have committed an act of discrimination if it was providing the service in question *to members of the public* and as if the insurance services in issue were being provided to the disabled person as a member of the public? A relevant employee is determined by whether the employer–insurer arrangement is designed to benefit the employer's employees generally or only a class of employee.[3] It includes a person who has applied (or is contemplating applying) for employment by the employer.[4]

4.6.4   This is an unhappy piece of statutory drafting. Its intended effect was explained as follows:

> 'The insurance company will act unlawfully against a disabled person . . . if it treats him in a way which would be an act of discrimination under [Part 3] if done by the company with regard to a member of the public. That means that refusal to insure a disabled employee, or levying a higher premium, will be unlawful unless it is justified; for example, where there are reasonable grounds for supposing that the disabled person represents a higher risk than normal.'[5]

The circumstances in which a service provider might justify less favourable treatment of a disabled person are more subjective and flexible than the (now limited) test for justification in the employment context. Disabled persons who suspect that they have been discriminated against in the provision of occupational insurance benefits would be entitled to take both the employer and the insurer to an employment tribunal.

---

1   DDA 1995, ss 19–21 (provision of goods, facilities or services), discussed in Chapter 5. See *Code of Practice: Employment and Occupation* (2004), paras 10.17–10.21.

2   Ibid, s 18(2).

3   Ibid, s 18(3).

4   Ibid, s 18(4).

5   HL Deb, vol 566, col 995.

4.6.5 What 'insurances services' are covered?[1] The prohibition on discrimination in relation to occupational insurance benefits encompasses the provision of benefits in respect of termination of service, retirement, old age, death, accident, injury, sickness or invalidity. It applies to insurance services provided under a group scheme (such as permanent health insurance benefits).[2]

4.6.6 It might not be the insurer that has discriminated against the disabled employee. The employer might have refused admission to the insurance scheme, anticipating possible higher costs to itself if the benefits are to be bought for a disabled person. This might amount to discrimination unless capable of being justifiable. The employer cannot justify disability-related discrimination without first addressing the duty to make reasonable adjustments.[3]

4.7   PARTNERSHIPS

4.7.1 From 1 October 2004, partnerships were brought within the scope of Part 2 of the DDA 1995 as a result of the amendments made by the Disability Discrimination Act 1995 (Amendment) Regulations 2003.[4] These provisions apply in relation to persons proposing to form themselves into a partnership as they apply in relation to a firm.[5] They also apply to a limited liability partnership as they apply to a firm. References to a partner in a firm are references to a member of the limited liability partnership.[6] In the case of a limited partnership, references to a partner shall be construed as references to a general partner.[7] The effect of the new provisions is to give partners and applicants for partnership similar rights against a firm as those enjoyed by an employee or employment applicant against an employer.[8]

---

1   DDA 1995, s 18(3) provides for regulations to prescribe the description of insurance services covered.

2   HL Deb, vol 566, col 1020; Disability Discrimination (Description of Insurance Services) Regulations 1999, SI 1999/2114 (group insurance is an insurance service for this purpose).

3   *Code of Practice: Employment and Occupation* (2004), para 10.16.

4   DDA 1995, ss 6A–6C; *Code of Practice: Employment and Occupation* (2004), paras 9.25–9.31.

5   Ibid, s 6C(1).

6   Ibid, s 6C(2).

7   Ibid, s 6C(3); Limited Partnerships Act 1907, s 3. A 'firm' has the meaning given by Partnership Act 1890, s 4.

8   *Code of Practice: Employment and Occupation* (2004), para 9.27 (and example).

Unlawful acts

4.7.2 It is unlawful for a firm, in relation to a position as a partner in the firm, to discriminate against a disabled person in the arrangements which the firm makes for determining who should be offered a partnership or in the terms on which the firm offers him or her partnership or by refusing (or deliberately omitting) to offer him or her partnership.[1] In a case where the disabled person already is a partner in the firm, it is also unlawful for the firm to discriminate against him or her in the way the firm affords him or her access to any benefits (or by refusing or deliberately omitting to afford him or her access to them).[2] This does not apply to benefits of any description if the firm is concerned with the provision (whether or not for payment) of benefits of that description to the public (or to a section of the public which includes the partner in question), unless that provision differs in a material respect from the provision of the benefits to the other partners.[3]

4.7.3 It is further unlawful for the firm to discriminate against the disabled person by expelling him or her as a partner or subjecting him or her to any other detriment.[4] Expulsion includes termination of a fixed-period partnership without renewal and constructive termination (where the disabled person is entitled to terminate the partnership without notice by reason of the conduct of the other partners).[5] Moreover, it is unlawful for the firm to subject to harassment a disabled person who is a partner or who has applied to be a partner.[6] Discrimination and harassment have been discussed in Chapter 3.

Duty to make reasonable adjustments

4.7.4 A duty to make reasonable adjustments applies to partnerships in much the same way as it applies elsewhere in the employment field.[7] The broader aspects of the duty have been discussed in Chapter 3. Where a provision, criterion or practice applied by or on behalf of a firm, or any physical feature of premises occupied by the firm, places the

---

1   DDA 1995, s 6A(1)(a)–(c).This applies in relation to persons proposing to form themselves into a partnership as it applies in relation to a firm: s 6C(1).

2   Ibid, s 6A(1)(d)(i).

3   Ibid, s 6A(3).

4   Ibid, s 6A(1)(d)(ii).

5   Ibid, s 6A(4).

6   Ibid, s 6A(2). This applies in relation to persons proposing to form themselves into a partnership as it applies in relation to a firm: s 6C(1).

7   Ibid, s 6B; *Code of Practice: Employment and Occupation* (2004), paras 9.30–9.31 (and example). This applies in relation to persons proposing to form themselves into a partnership as it applies in relation to a firm: s 6C(1).

disabled person concerned at a substantial disadvantage in comparison with persons who are not disabled, it is the duty of the firm to take such steps as it is reasonable, in all the circumstances of the case, for it to have to take in order to prevent the provision, criterion or practice, or feature, having that effect.[1]

4.7.5   In the case of a provision, criterion or practice for determining to whom the position of partner should be offered, the disabled person concerned is any disabled person who is (or who has notified the firm that he or she may be) a candidate for that position.[2] In any other case, it is a disabled person who is a partner or a candidate for the position of partner.[3] In the case of a candidate or potential candidate for partnership, no duty is imposed on a firm in relation to a disabled person if the firm does not know (and could not reasonably be expected to know) that the disabled person concerned is (or may be) a candidate for the position of partner.[4] In any case, no duty is imposed if the firm does not know (and could not reasonably be expected to know) that the disabled person has a disability and is likely to be placed at a substantial disadvantage in comparison with persons who are not disabled.[5]

4.7.6   Where a firm is required to take any steps in relation to the disabled person concerned, the cost of taking those steps shall be treated as an expense of the firm.[6] The extent to which such cost should be borne by the disabled person, where he or she is (or becomes) a partner in the firm, shall not exceed such amount as is reasonable, having regard in particular to the proportion in which he or she is entitled to share in the firm's profits.[7]

4.8   BARRISTERS AND ADVOCATES

England and Wales

4.8.1   Barristers (and, in Scotland, advocates) are already subject to Part 3 of the Act in relation to the provision of services to the public. They are also subject to Part 2 to the extent that they employ staff. From 1 October 2004, barristers and their clerks in England and Wales are more fully within the scope of Part 2 of the DDA 1995 as a result of the

---

1   DDA 1995, s 6B(1).

2   Ibid, s 6B(2)(a).

3   Ibid, s 6B(2)(b).

4   Ibid, s 6B(3)(a).

5   Ibid, s 6B(3)(b).

6   Ibid, s 6B(4).

7   *Code of Practice: Employment and Occupation* (2004), para 9.31 (and example).

amendments made by the Disability Discrimination Act 1995 (Amendment) Regulations 2003.[1]

4.8.2 Prior to that date, an unsuccessful attempt had been made in legal proceedings to bring barristers and their pupils within the trade organisation provisions of the Act.[2] A barrister's chambers accepted an application for pupillage from a disabled person, but refused to defer the pupillage due to the prospective pupil's ill health. A claim was brought under the DDA 1995, contending that the chambers were a trade organisation and that the application for a pupillage was an application for membership of that trade organisation. At the Court of Appeal, it was not in dispute that the chambers were a trade organisation, but the Court held that the application for pupillage could not be construed as an application for membership of the chambers.[3]

4.8.3 The new provisions overcome the difficulties created by the need to attempt a forced construction of the trade organisation provisions. Throughout the new provisions, a barrister's clerk includes any person carrying out any of the functions of a barrister's clerk. The terms 'pupil', 'pupillage' and 'set of chambers' have the meanings commonly associated with their use in the context of barristers practising in independent practice. The terms 'tenancy' and 'tenant' have the meanings commonly associated with their use in the context of barristers practising in independent practice. However, they also include reference to any barrister permitted to practise from a set of chambers (ie a 'squatter' or non-tenant).[4]

Unlawful acts

4.8.4 It is unlawful for a barrister or a barrister's clerk, in relation to any offer of a pupillage or tenancy, to discriminate against a disabled person in the arrangements which are made for the purpose of determining to whom it should be offered; in respect of any terms on which it is offered; or by refusing, or deliberately omitting, to offer it to

---

1   DDA 1995, ss 7A–7D; *Code of Practice: Employment and Occupation* (2004), paras 9.32–9.41 (and examples). The General Council of the Bar in England and Wales established its Equality and Diversity (Disability) Committee in 1991. The Bar's *Code of Conduct* (see paras 305 and 403) requires all barristers to have regard to the Bar's *Equality and Diversity Code* (revised 2004). It sets out the law and professional rules which prohibit discrimination. It also recommends good practice to chambers in relation to access to pupillages and tenancies, the conduct of work in chambers, complaints and grievances. See also The Law Society's *Solicitors Anti-Discrimination Rules 2004*.

2   DDA 1995, ss 13–15 (prior to their recent repeal and replacement).

3   *Paul Higham of 1 Pump Court Chambers v Horton* [2004] EWCA Civ 941. The legal or contractual position of a pupil and his or her chambers had been explored in *Edmonds v Lawson* [2000] ICR 567, CA.

4   DDA 1995, s 7A(5); *Code of Practice: Employment and Occupation* (2004), para 9.35.

him or her.[1] The meaning of 'discrimination' has been considered in Chapter 3.

4.8.5   It is also unlawful for a barrister or a barrister's clerk, in relation to a disabled pupil or tenant in the set of chambers in question, to discriminate against him or her in respect of any terms applicable to him or her as a pupil or tenant; in the opportunities for training or gaining experience which are afforded or denied to him or her; in the benefits which are afforded or denied to him or her; by terminating his or her pupillage or by subjecting him or her to any pressure to leave the chambers; or by subjecting him or her to any other detriment.[2]

4.8.6   It is further unlawful for a barrister or barrister's clerk, in relation to a pupillage or tenancy, to subject to harassment a disabled person who is (or who has applied to be) a pupil or tenant in the set of chambers in question.[3] The meaning of 'harassment' has been considered in Chapter 3. Moreover, it is also unlawful for any person, in relation to the giving, withholding or acceptance of instructions to a barrister, to discriminate against a disabled person or to subject him or her to harassment.[4] Thus, it is unlawful for a solicitor (or other professional with direct access to the Bar) to refuse to instruct a barrister on the ground of the barrister's disability or for a reason related to his or her disability.[5] However, the solicitor is not under a duty to make reasonable adjustments in relation to a barrister being instructed.[6]

Duty to make reasonable adjustments

4.8.7   A barrister or a barrister's clerk is subject to a duty to make reasonable adjustments. The broader concepts raised by this general duty have been discussed in Chapter 3. In the present context, it arises where a provision, criterion or practice applied by or on behalf of a barrister or barrister's clerk, or any physical feature of premises occupied by a barrister or a barrister's clerk, places the disabled person concerned at a substantial disadvantage in comparison with persons who are not disabled, it is the duty of the barrister or barrister's clerk to take such steps as it is reasonable, in all the circumstances of the case, for him or her to have to take in order to prevent the provision, criterion or practice, or feature, having that effect.[7] Where the duty arises in

---

1   DDA 1995, s 7A(1).

2   Ibid, s 7A(2); *Code of Practice: Employment and Occupation* (2004), para 9.33 (and example).

3   Ibid, s 7A(3).

4   Ibid, s 7A(4).

5   *Code of Practice: Employment and Occupation* (2004), para 9.37.

6   Ibid, para 9.39.

7   DDA 1995, s 7B(1).

relation to two or more barristers in a set of chambers, the duty is on each of them to take such steps as it is reasonable, in all of the circumstances of the case, for him or her to have to take.[1]

4.8.8 In the case of a provision, criterion or practice for determining to whom a pupillage or tenancy should be offered, the disabled person concerned is any disabled person who is (or who has notified the barrister or the barrister's clerk concerned that he or she may be) an applicant for a pupillage or tenancy.[2] In any other case, it is a disabled person who is a tenant, a pupil, or an applicant for a pupillage or tenancy.[3] In the case of an applicant or potential applicant for pupillage or tenancy, no duty is imposed on a barrister or a barrister's clerk in relation to a disabled person if he or she does not know (and could not reasonably be expected to know) that the disabled person concerned is (or may be) such an applicant.[4] In any case, no duty is imposed on a barrister or a barrister's clerk in relation to a disabled person if he or she does not know (and could not reasonably be expected to know) that that person has a disability and is likely to be placed at a substantial disadvantage in comparison with persons who are not disabled.[5]

Scotland

4.8.9 The provisions on barristers and barristers' clerks apply only in England and Wales.[6] Comparable provisions apply in Scotland in relation to advocates in relation to taking any person as a pupil or in relation to a disabled person who is a pupil or in relation to the giving, withholding or acceptance of instructions to an advocate.[7] These provisions are modified from those applying to barristers in recognition that in Scotland, advocates do not practise in sets of chambers.[8] That may affect the reasonableness of any adjustment that an advocate might otherwise be under a duty to make in relation to a disabled pupil. An advocate is a member of the Faculty of Advocates, practising as such. The term 'pupil' has the meaning commonly associated with its use in the context of a person training to be an advocate.[9]

---

1   DDA 1995, s 7B(2); *Code of Practice: Employment and Occupation* (2004), para 9.40.

2   Ibid, s 7B(3)(a).

3   Ibid, s 7B(3)(b).

4   Ibid, s 7B(4)(a).

5   Ibid, s 7B(4)(b).

6   Ibid, s 70(5A).

7   Ibid, ss 7C, 7D and 70(5B).

8   *Code of Practice: Employment and Occupation* (2004), paras 9.36 and 9.41.

9   DDA 1995, s 7C(5); *Code of Practice: Employment and Occupation* (2004), para 9.36.

Northern Ireland

4.8.10   Similar modifications are made in respect of barristers in Northern Ireland as are made in Scotland in respect of advocates.

4.9   TRADE ORGANISATIONS

4.9.1   As originally enacted, Part 2 of the DDA 1995 ensured that discrimination against disabled persons by trade organisations would be unlawful.[1] From 1 October 2004, the original provisions on trade organisations have been substituted.[2] Nevertheless, the effect of these provisions remains that:

> '... trade unions, employers' associations and analogous bodies would be covered by this [Act] in their relationship with their members or prospective members who are disabled or who have had a disability. Such organisations are already covered in the [Act] to the extent that they are employers. However, they are not covered by the access to services right because they are not providing services to members of the general public – just to their members.'[3]

A trade organisation will be covered by the employment provisions in Part 2 of the Act in so far as it employs persons. For example, a full-time officer of a trade union or a clerical worker employed by a trade association will be an employee (or would-be employee) of a trade organisation and will be protected from disability discrimination under Part 2.

4.9.2   However, there is nothing, in principle, to prevent trade organisations also being caught by Part 3 of the Act (the provisions on goods and services) where they also provide services to the public (as well as to their members).[4] For example, a trade union which allows its premises to be used as a meeting place by external groups (such as a local political party or community action group) will be subject to the duties and non-discrimination requirements contained in Part 3. Similarly, if a trade organisation allows its facilities to be used for social purposes (such as wedding receptions), open to individuals unconnected with that organisation, it will need to consider its Part 3 obligations.

---

1   DDA 1995, ss 13–15; *Code of Practice: Duties of Trade Organisations to their Disabled Members and Applicants* (1999) (a separate, but essentially identical, Code covered Northern Ireland).

2   Ibid, ss 13–14. The relevant Code of Practice is now *Code of Practice: Trade Organisations and Qualifications Bodies (2004)* (a separate, but essentially identical, Code covers Northern Ireland).

3   HL Deb, vol 566, cols 224–225.

4   See Chapter 5.

Nevertheless, the separate provisions of Part 2 in respect of discrimination by trade organisations against disabled members or disabled applicants for membership are largely self-contained measures and so warrant separate treatment.

Trade organisation

4.9.3 A 'trade organisation' is defined as 'an organisation of workers, an organisation of employers or any other organisation whose members carry on a particular profession or trade for the purposes of which the organisation exists'.[1] These terms are not further defined. There is no threshold of size or number of members. Part 2 thus applies to organisations of workers, organisations of employers and other organisations, but not qualifications bodies. However, some trade organisations (such as The Law Society) also confer qualifications and will also be subject to the Part 2 provisions on qualifications bodies, depending upon in which capacity the trade organisation is acting at the relevant time.[2]

Organisation of workers

4.9.4 This will obviously include trade unions.[3] A trade union is a temporary or permanent organisation of workers whose principal purposes include the regulation of relations between workers and employers or employers' associations.[4] A worker is a person who works (or seeks to work) under a contract of employment or under any other contract for the personal performance of any work or services (other than a professional and client relationship) or in Crown employment.[5] However, police officers are not 'workers', but office-holders, so that the Police Federation would not be an organisation of workers.[6] The position of the Prison Officers' Association is ambiguous.[7] The term does not exclude an organisation the majority of whose members practise a profession (such as medical or dental practitioners).[8]

---

1   DDA 1995, ss 13(4) and 68(1).

2   Ibid, ss 14A–14B; *Code of Practice: Trade Organisations and Qualifications Bodies (2004)*, paras 3.11 and 7.3–7.4.

3   HL Deb, vol 566, cols 224–229.

4   Trade Union and Labour Relations (Consolidation) Act 1992 (TULR(C)A 1992), s 1.

5   TULR(C)A 1992, s 296; *Writers' Guild of Great Britain v BBC* [1974] ICR 234; *Broadbent v Crisp* [1974] ICR 248; *Wiltshire Police Authority v Wynn* [1980] ICR 649.

6   *Home Office v Evans* (Divisional Court, 18 November 1993, unreported).

7   *Boddington v Lawton* [1994] ICR 478; but *cf* Criminal Justice and Public Order Act 1994, s 126.

8   *Medical Protection Society v Sadek* [2004] EWCA Civ 865, [2004] ICR 1263, [2005] IRLR 57, CA.

4.9.5   The term 'organisation' imports form, structure and stability, so that a mere loose association of workers would be insufficient.[1] The 1995 Act does not appear to make a distinction between permanent or temporary organisations of workers. As a result, any branch or other division of a trade union might constitute an organisation of workers, including unofficial workplace co-ordinating committees. It was feared that the DDA 1995:

> '... might render unions liable for any failure to make adjustments by an informal group of union members of whose existence the union's officers are unaware ... [including] groups of union members not recognising union rule books and with whom the national union does not communicate and who are given no powers or resources.'[2]

This concern is a real one, given the wording of the Act and the lack of a definition of 'organisation of workers' in the statute.

Organisation of employers

4.9.6   An 'organisation of employers' will include an employers' association. That is an organisation (whether temporary or permanent) which consists wholly or mainly of employers or individual owners of undertakings and whose principal purposes include the regulation of relations between employers and workers or trade unions.[3] It also includes an organisation which consists wholly or mainly of constituent or affiliated organisations (of the first kind or which themselves consist wholly or mainly of constituent or affiliated organisations of the first kind), or representatives of such constituent or affiliated organisations, and whose principal purposes include the regulation of relations between employers and workers or between employers and trade unions, or the regulation of relations between its constituent or affiliated organisations.[4]

Other organisations

4.9.7   Part 2 applies equally to 'any other organisation whose members carry on a particular profession or trade for the purposes of which the organisation exists'. The term 'profession' includes any vocation or occupation, while the term 'trade' encompasses any business.[5] This

---

1   *Conservative and Unionist Central Office v Burrell* [1982] 1 WLR 522; *cf Midland Cold Storage Ltd v Turner* [1972] ICR 230.

2   HL Deb, vol 566, cols 226–227.

3   TULR(C)A 1992, s 122(1)(a).

4   Ibid, s 122(1)(b).

5   DDA 1995, s 68(1).

category of trade organisations will include chartered professional institutions, other professional bodies and trade associations.[1]

Unlawful acts

4.9.8 First, it is unlawful for a trade organisation to discriminate against a disabled person: (a) in the arrangements which it makes for the purpose of determining who should be offered membership of the organisation; (b) in the terms on which it is prepared to admit him or her to membership of the organisation; or (c) by refusing to accept, or deliberately not accepting, his or her application for membership.[2] For example, a trade union which made it a condition of membership that a disabled person should pay a higher membership fee or joining fee than other applicants for membership would transgress this provision. Similarly, a professional body that would only admit disabled persons to membership after a longer period of apprenticeship or practice in the profession than in the normal case would also be in breach. A trade association which selectively or consistently refused membership of the association to disabled persons engaged in the relevant trade would commit a *prima facie* unlawful act. Similarly, a trade union which has received an application for membership from a disabled person, and deliberately fails to process that application, has committed a potential act of unlawful discrimination, even though it has not positively taken a step to reject the application. Its deliberate default in respect of the application might be tantamount to a non-acceptance.

4.9.9 Secondly, it is unlawful for a trade organisation, in the case of a disabled person who is a member of the organisation,[3] to discriminate against him or her: (a) in the way it affords him or her access to any benefits (or by refusing or deliberately omitting to afford him or her access to them); (b) by depriving him or her of membership, or varying the terms on which he or she is a member; or (c) by subjecting him or her to any other detriment.[4] In general, a trade organisation may not treat its disabled members as second-class members in respect of the rights and benefits of membership. This would include expulsion from

---

1   *Code of Practice: Trade Organisations and Qualifications Bodies* (2004), para 3.8 (giving as examples: The Law Society, the Royal College of Nursing, the Swimming Teachers' Association, the Society of Floristry, the British Computer Society and the Institute of Carpenters).

2   DDA 1995, s 13(1); *Code of Practice: Trade Organisations and Qualifications Bodies* (2004), paras 7.5–7.14 (and examples).

3   The Act does not protect corporate members of trade organisations, even where a disabled person is representing a corporate member: *Code of Practice: Trade Organisations and Qualifications Bodies* (2004), para 3.18 (and example).

4   DDA 1995, s 13(2); *Code of Practice: Trade Organisations and Qualifications Bodies* (2004), paras 7.15–7.29 (and examples).

membership where a non-disabled member would not be deprived of membership. Benefits include facilities and services.[1] That will include training facilities, welfare or insurance services, information about the organisation's activities, and assistance to members in an employer's disciplinary or dismissal procedure. Whether something is a benefit will depend upon the circumstances, including an organisation's rules and practice.[2]

4.9.10   Thirdly, it is also unlawful for a trade organisation, in relation to membership of that organisation, to subject to harassment a disabled person who is a member of the organisation or who has applied for membership of the organisation.[3] The meanings of 'discrimination' and 'harassment' have been considered in Chapter 3.

Duty to make reasonable adjustments

4.9.11   A trade organisation's duty to make reasonable adjustments arises where a provision, criterion or practice applied by or on behalf of a trade organisation, or any physical feature of premises occupied by the organisation, places the disabled person concerned at a substantial disadvantage in comparison with persons who are not disabled. It is then the duty of the organisation to take such steps as it is reasonable, in all the circumstances of the case, for it to have to take in order to prevent the provision, criterion or practice, or feature, having that effect.[4] The wider aspects of the duty to make reasonable adjustments have been considered in Chapter 3.

4.9.12   In the case of a provision, criterion or practice for determining to whom membership should be offered, the disabled person concerned is any disabled person who is (or who has notified the organisation that he or she may be) an applicant for membership.[5] In any other case, the disabled person concerned is a disabled person who is a member of the organisation or who is an applicant for membership of the organisation.[6] In the case of an applicant or potential applicant,

---

1   DDA 1995, s 18D(2); *Code of Practice: Trade Organisations and Qualifications Bodies* (2004), para 7.16 (and examples).

2   There is no equivalent of DDA 1995, s 4(4) (which applies to employers providing benefits to their employees and to the public) to prevent any overlap between Part 2 and Part 3. It does not seem necessary.

3   DDA 1995, s 13(3); *Code of Practice: Trade Organisations and Qualifications Bodies* (2004), paras 4.37–4.38 (and examples).

4   Ibid, s 14(1); *Code of Practice: Trade Organisations and Qualifications Bodies* (2004), paras 5.2–5.3, 5.6–5.10, 7.10–7.14, 7.19–7.21 and 7.27–7.29 (and examples).

5   Ibid, s 14(2)(a); *Code of Practice: Trade Organisations and Qualifications Bodies* (2004), paras 5.4–5.5.

6   Ibid, s 14(2)(b).

no duty is imposed on a trade organisation in relation to a disabled person if the organisation does not know (and could not reasonably be expected to know) that the disabled person concerned is (or may be) an applicant for membership of the organisation.[1] In any case, no duty is imposed on a trade organisation in relation to a disabled person if the organisation does not know (and could not reasonably be expected to know) that that person has a disability and is likely to be placed at a substantial disadvantage in comparison with persons who are not disabled.[2]

4.9.13 An interesting question concerns the overlap between the duty to make adjustments and the democratisation provisions in trade union law.[3] In particular, trade unions need to consider how to meet the stringent requirements upon unions in respect of ballots and elections while also complying with the duty to make reasonable adjustments for their disabled members. For example, elections to certain positions in a union are required to be conducted by secret postal ballot.[4] Union members must not be unreasonably excluded from candidature.[5] Union members with a disability may be able to use the 1995 Act to reinforce that right. The union is obliged to circulate election addresses for every candidate.[6] The DDA 1995 might require a union to ensure that Braille or large-print versions of such addresses are made available. The same is true of the scrutineer's report and the publication of the results of the ballot at the conclusion of the election process.

4.9.14 Voting in the election is to be by means of a fully postal secret ballot and no other form of voting is acceptable.[7] The system of fully postal voting works to the benefit of disabled members, some of whom might otherwise have been at a substantial disadvantage under a non-postal or partly postal voting system. However, a trade union might consider that the 1995 Act requires it to redesign the ballot paper so as to accommodate the needs of disabled members (especially those with visual or learning disabilities), while remaining within the form and content required by trade union law. Similar considerations in respect of the rights of trade union members with disabilities might also arise in respect of other aspects of trade union law relating to administration,

---

1   DDA 1995, s 14(3)(a); *Code of Practice: Trade Organisations and Qualifications Bodies* (2004), paras 5.11 and 7.30–7.36 (and examples).

2   Ibid, s 14(3)(b).

3   TULR(C)A 1992. Examples are given in *Code of Practice: Trade Organisations and Qualifications Bodies* (2004), paras 5.12–5.25 (and examples).

4   TULR(C)A 1992, Part I, Chapter IV.

5   Ibid, s 47.

6   Ibid, s 48.

7   Ibid, s 51.

elections, ballots before industrial action, union discipline, political fund resolutions and ballots, and so on.

4.10 QUALIFICATIONS BODIES

4.10.1 Prior to 1 October 2004, one area of doubt concerned the position of bodies which issue qualifications or authorisations required for (or facilitating engagement in) a trade or profession.[1] Examples might include The Law Society (in its regulatory capacity), the Council of Legal Education, or the General Medical Council (GMC).[2] Prior to the amendments to the DDA 1995 wrought by the Special Educational Needs and Disability Act 2001 (SENDA 2001), such bodies might have been excluded from DDA 1995 Part 3 (the provisions relating to goods and services) if they fell within the originally enacted exclusions in respect of education.[3] However, if they were not so excluded, they might have been caught by Part 3 in so far as they provide services to the public. Further or alternatively, they might be caught by the trade organisations provisions of the legislation in so far as they might be a professional or trade organisation.

4.10.2 Nevertheless, it was doubtful that qualifications bodies were covered by the DDA 1995 prior to 1 October 2004. There were no equivalent provisions in the DDA 1995 to those in the other discrimination statutes which explicitly dealt with discrimination by qualifications (or qualifying) bodies.[4] The Disability Rights Task Force recognised that there were no specific provisions in the DDA 1995 for qualifying bodies and recommended that this should be remedied.[5] In response,[6] the Government indicated that it wished to give further consideration to this recommendation about qualifying bodies in the light of the EC Framework Employment Directive.[7] In that context, the

---

1   See HL Deb, vol 566, col 226.

2   In *General Medical Council v Cox* (2002) EAT/76/01, the EAT ruled that the GMC is not a trade organisation for the purposes of DDA 1995, s 13 (as it then was) because its statutory purpose under Medical Act 1983, s 1(1) is the protection of members of the public consulting a medical practitioner. Otherwise, the GMC is undoubtedly a qualifications body: *General Medical Council v Goba* [1988] IRLR 425, EAT.

3   DDA 1995, s 19(5)–(6). See Chapters 5 and 7.

4   SDA 1975, s 13; RRA 1976, s 12.

5   Disability Rights Task Force, *From Exclusion to Inclusion: A Report of the Disability Rights Task Force for Disabled People* (1999, London: DfEE), recommendation 5.13.

6   *Towards Inclusion – Civil Rights for Disabled People: Government Response to the Disability Rights Task Force* (March 2001: DfEE), para 3.68. See also *Interim Government Response to the Report of the Disability Rights Task Force* (March 2000: DfEE).

7   2000/78/EC.

Government made it clear that it would ensure that all qualifying bodies are covered by the employment provisions of the DDA 1995, except to the extent that they are already covered by the provisions of the Act applying to further and higher education institutions.[1] Those changes have now been effected from 1 October 2004 as a result of the Disability Discrimination Act 1995 (Amendment) Regulations 2003.[2]

Qualifications bodies

4.10.3 A qualifications body is any authority or body which can confer (or renew or extend) a professional or trade qualification.[3] Examples of such bodies include the General Medical Council, the Nursing and Midwifery Council, the Driving Standards Agency, City and Guilds, the Institute of the Motor Industry, the Hospitality Awarding Body, and the Guild of Cleaners and Launders.[4] A professional or trade qualification is an authorisation, qualification, recognition, registration, enrolment, approval or certification which is needed for (or facilitates engagement in) a particular profession or trade.[5] However, to avoid overlap with the education provisions of Part 4 of the Act, a qualifications body does not include a responsible body in relation to a school or college or a local education authority in England or Wales, or an education authority in Scotland.[6]

Unlawful acts

4.10.4 It is unlawful for a qualifications body to discriminate against a disabled person: (a) in the arrangements which it makes for the purpose of determining upon whom to confer (or renew or extend) a professional or trade qualification; (b) in the terms on which it is prepared to confer (or renew or extend) a professional or trade qualification on him or her; (c) by refusing or deliberately omitting to grant any application by him or her for such a qualification; or (d) by withdrawing such a qualification from him or her or varying the terms

---

1 See *Towards Equality and Diversity: Implementing the Employment and Race Directives: Consultation Document* (December 2001: Cabinet Office), paras 14.23–14.25. See also *Legislative Review: First Review of the Disability Discrimination Act 1995: Consultation* (May 2002: Disability Rights Commission), p 7.

2 DDA 1995, ss 14A–14B; *Code of Practice: Trade Organisations and Qualifications Bodies* (2004), chapters 3 and 8.

3 Ibid, s 14A(5).

4 *Code of Practice: Trade Organisations and Qualifications Bodies* (2004), paras 3.9–3.11. Some qualifications bodies will also be trade associations and *vice versa*. They will be subject to ss 13–14 and 14A–14B, as the circumstances require.

5 DDA 1995, s 14A(5); *Code of Practice: Trade Organisations and Qualifications Bodies* (2004), paras 8.5–8.8.

6 Ibid, s 14A(5). See Chapter 7.

on which he or she holds it.[1] It is also unlawful for a qualifications body, in relation to a professional or trade qualification conferred (or renewed or extended) by it, to subject to harassment a disabled person who holds or applies for such a qualification.[2] The meanings of 'discrimination' and 'harassment' have been addressed in Chapter 3.

Competence standards and justification

4.10.5 A competence standard is an academic, medical or other standard applied by or on behalf of a qualifications body for the purpose of determining whether or not a person has a particular level of competence or ability.[3] In determining whether the application by a qualifications body of a competence standard to a disabled person constitutes disability-related discrimination, the application of the standard is justified if, but only if, the qualifications body can show that the standard is (or would be) applied equally to persons who do not have his or her particular disability, and its application is a proportionate means of achieving a legitimate aim.[4] In this context, disability-related less favourable treatment of a disabled person cannot be justified in this way if it amounts to direct discrimination.[5] The justification defence is considered generally in Chapter 3.

Duty to make reasonable adjustments

4.10.6 Where a provision, criterion or practice (other than a competence standard) applied by or on behalf of a qualifications body, or any physical feature of premises occupied by a qualifications body, places the disabled person concerned at a substantial disadvantage in comparison with persons who are not disabled, it is the duty of the qualifications body to take such steps as it is reasonable, in all the circumstances of the case, for it to have to take in order to prevent the provision, criterion or practice, or feature, having that effect.[6] The broader issues raised by the duty to make reasonable adjustments were considered in Chapter 3.

---

1   DDA 1995, s 14A(1).

2   Ibid, s 14A(2).

3   Ibid, s 14A(5). For example, eyesight standards for airline pilots, but not length of service or experience: *Code of Practice: Trade Organisations and Qualifications Bodies* (2004), paras 8.27–8.31 (and examples).

4   Ibid, s 14A(3), by reference to ss 3A and 3A(1)(b); *Code of Practice: Trade Organisations and Qualifications Bodies* (2004), paras 8.32–8.41 (and examples).

5   Ibid, s 14A(4)(b), modifying s 3A(3).

6   Ibid, s 14B(1); *Code of Practice: Trade Organisations and Qualifications Bodies (2004)*, chapter 5 and paras 8.15–8.26 (and examples).

4.10.7 In the case of a provision, criterion or practice for determining on whom a professional or trade qualification is to be conferred (or renewed or extended), the disabled person concerned is any disabled person who is (or who has notified the qualifications body that he or she may be) an applicant for the conferment (or renewal or extension) of that qualification.[1] In any other case, the disabled person concerned is a disabled person who holds a professional or trade qualification conferred (or renewed or extended) by the qualifications body or who applies for a professional or trade qualification which it confers (or renews or extends).[2]

4.10.8 In the case of an applicant or potential applicant for a professional or trade qualification, no duty is imposed on the qualifications body in relation to a disabled person if the body does not know (and could not reasonably be expected to know) that the disabled person concerned is (or may be) an applicant for the conferment (or renewal or extension) of a professional or trade qualification.[3] In any case, no duty is imposed on the qualifications body in relation to a disabled person if the body does not know (and could not reasonably be expected to know) that that person has a disability and is likely to be placed at a substantial disadvantage in comparison with persons who are not disabled.[4]

4.10.9 There is no duty to make reasonable adjustments in relation to competence standards and no discrimination by way of a failure to make reasonable adjustments in that limited respect.[5]

4.11 PRACTICAL WORK EXPERIENCE

4.11.1 From 1 October 2004, providers of practical work experience are also covered by Part 2 of the DDA 1995.[6] These provisions are concerned with work placements and placement providers. A work placement is practical work experience undertaken for a limited period for the purposes of a person's vocational training. A placement provider is any person who provides a work placement to a person whom the

---

1   DDA 1995, s 14B(2)(a).

2   Ibid, s 14B(2)(b).

3   Ibid, s 14B(3)(a).

4   Ibid, s 14B(3)(b).

5   Ibid, s 14A(4)(a), disapplying s 3A(2) and (6); *Code of Practice: Trade Organisations and Qualifications Bodies* (2004), paras 8.32–8.41 (and examples).

6   Ibid, ss 14C–14D.

placement provider does not employ.[1] The new law does not apply to anything made unlawful in relation to employers, or in respect of the provision of goods, facilities or services, or in the education field.[2] It also does not apply to a work placement undertaken in any of the naval, military and air forces of the Crown.[3]

Unlawful acts

4.11.2   In the case of a disabled person seeking or undertaking a work placement, it is unlawful for a placement provider to discriminate against him or her: (a) in the arrangements which it makes for the purpose of determining who should be offered a work placement; (b) in the terms on which it affords him or her access to any work placement or any facilities concerned with such a placement; (c) by refusing or deliberately omitting to afford him or her such access; (d) by terminating the placement; or (e) by subjecting him or her to any other detriment in relation to the placement.[4] In relation to a work placement, it is also unlawful for a placement provider to subject to harassment a disabled person to whom it is providing a placement or a disabled person who has applied to it for a placement.[5] The concepts of discrimination and harassment were explained in Chapter 3.

Duty to make reasonable adjustments

4.11.3   Where a provision, criterion or practice applied by or on behalf of a placement provider, or any physical feature of premises occupied by the placement provider, places the disabled person concerned at a substantial disadvantage in comparison with persons who are not disabled, it is the duty of the placement provider to take such steps as it is reasonable, in all the circumstances of the case, for it to have to take in order to prevent the provision, criterion or practice, or feature, having that effect.[6] The larger questions raised by the duty to make reasonable adjustments were posed in Chapter 3. The organisation sending the

---

1   DDA 1995, s 14C(4); *Code of Practice: Trade Organisations and Qualifications Bodies* (2004), para 9.44.

2   Ibid, s 14C(3), cross-referring to s 4 and Parts 3 and 4. The exclusion extends to anything which would be unlawful under s 4 or Parts 3 or 4 but for the operation of any other provision of the Act. See also *Code of Practice: Trade Organisations and Qualifications Bodies* (2004), para 9.45 (and examples).

3   Ibid, s 14C(5).

4   Ibid, s 14C(1); *Code of Practice: Trade Organisations and Qualifications Bodies* (2004), para 9.42 (and examples).

5   Ibid, s 14C(2); *Code of Practice: Trade Organisations and Qualifications Bodies* (2004), para 9.43 (and example).

6   Ibid, s 14D(1); *Code of Practice: Trade Organisations and Qualifications Bodies* (2004), paras 9.47–9.50.

disabled person on the work placement may also have its own duty to make reasonable adjustments in relation to the disabled person. This is likely to mean that that organisation and the placement provider will need to co-operate with one another in respect of any adjustments required.[1]

4.11.4   In the case of a provision, criterion or practice for determining to whom a work placement should be offered, the disabled person concerned is any disabled person who is (or who has notified the placement provider that he or she may be) an applicant for that work placement.[2] In any other case, it is a disabled person who is an applicant for the work placement concerned or who is undertaking a work placement with the placement provider.[3]

4.11.5   In the case of an applicant or potential applicant for a work placement, no duty is imposed on a placement provider in relation to the disabled person concerned if it does not know (and could not reasonably be expected to know) that the disabled person concerned is (or may be) an applicant for the work placement.[4] In any case, no duty is imposed on a placement provider in relation to the disabled person concerned if it does not know (and could not reasonably be expected to know) that that person has a disability and is likely to be placed at a substantial disadvantage in comparison with persons who are not disabled.[5]

4.12   ENFORCEMENT, REMEDIES AND PROCEDURES

The question of enforcement, remedies and procedures in the employment field at large is considered in Chapter 10.

4.13   DISABILITY DISCRIMINATION BILL

4.13.1   The Disability Discrimination Bill proposes to amend Part 2 of the DDA 1995 so as to make it unlawful for locally electable authorities to discriminate against their members in relation to the carrying-out of official business (as defined). This will include all local authorities in England, Wales and Scotland, as well as the Greater London Authority. The Bill will also make it unlawful for an authority to discriminate

---

1   DDA 1995, paras 9.49–9.50.

2   Ibid, s 14D(2)(a).

3   Ibid, s 14D(2)(b).

4   Ibid, s 14D(3)(a).

5   Ibid, s 14D(3)(b).

against a disabled member in relation to opportunities which it affords its members to receive training or any other facility it makes available to its members for the carrying-out of official business or by subjecting the disabled member to any other detriment in relation to the carrying-out of official business. It will also be unlawful for an authority to subject a disabled member to harassment in relation to the carrying-out of official business. A number of matters are to be excluded from the scope of these new duties, including election or appointment to an office of an authority (such as a cabinet post) or to a committee or sub-committee of an authority.

4.13.2 The Bill also contains a duty of an authority to make reasonable adjustments in relation to its disabled members. An authority will be under a duty to make an adjustment where a provision, criterion or practice it applies (or which is applied on its behalf), or a physical feature of premises which it occupies or controls, places a disabled member at a substantial disadvantage in comparison with non-disabled members in relation to the carrying-out of official business. In these circumstances, an authority will be under a duty to take reasonable steps to prevent the provision, criterion, practice or physical feature from having that effect. This provision works in a similar way to the duty elsewhere in Part 2.

4.13.3 The provisions contain extensive regulation-making powers. The new rights and duties will be enforced in an employment tribunal.

Group insurance

4.13.4 The Disability Discrimination Bill proposes to repeal the provisions concerning group insurance schemes contained in s 18 of the DDA 1995. The Government considers that s 18 is unnecessary and confusing. Its intention is that, following the repeal of s 18, it will be clear that a person who provides group insurance services to employees of particular employers would be regarded as a provider of services. That person would then be liable for an act of discrimination contrary to Part 3 which he or she may commit against disabled persons employed by those employers. An act of discrimination by an employer in relation to a group insurance scheme will fall within Part 2 of the Act. However, claims of discrimination against an insurer concerning the provision of group insurance services will not be subject to the Part 3 procedures and remedies in the county court or sheriff court. Instead, employment tribunals will have jurisdiction to consider such claims. The definition of 'group insurance arrangements' will be amended so that it covers all types of group insurance schemes – not just those relating to termin-ation of service; retirement, old age or death; or accident, injury, sickness or invalidity.

Chapter 5

GOODS, FACILITIES AND SERVICES

5.1 INTRODUCTION

5.1.1 The 1994 Green Paper[1] promised that consultation would take place on extending building regulations to ensure that physical barriers to access by disabled persons to public and domestic buildings would be removed or reduced. However, as the 1994 Green Paper acknowledged:

> '... removing physical impediments does nothing to banish the mental barriers of ignorance and prejudice. Making buildings easier to get into is of no avail if disabled people are kept outside because their appearance or behaviour is deemed too upsetting for other patrons or through mis-guided concern for their safety.'[2]

Instead, the 1994 Green Paper mooted a new right of access that would make it unlawful for providers of goods or services to treat an individual unfavourably because of that person's disability, except where there were physical barriers or genuine safety issues. In turn, the 1995 White Paper[3] proposed the introduction of a right of access to goods and services for disabled persons,[4] prohibiting discriminatory behaviour, while requiring reasonable and readily achievable positive action to overcome physical and communication barriers impeding access by disabled persons. Exceptionally, the new right would not apply to transport vehicles or to educational establishments. It would also not apply where the supply of the goods or services in question would pose a risk to the health and safety of the disabled person or others.[5]

---

1   A Consultation on Government Measures to Tackle Discrimination Against Disabled People (July 1994).

2   Ibid, para 4.2

3   *Ending Discrimination Against Disabled People*, Cm 2729 (January 1995).

4   Ibid, para 4.4.

5   Ibid, para 4.6.

Timetable

5.1.2   These novel rights of access are set out in Part 3 of the DDA 1995.[1] The Major administration intended that there would be a long lead-in time for businesses to adapt to these new provisions, with these measures being brought into force in stages over a period as long as ten years.[2] The Blair Government then agreed to accelerate the timetable for implementation. The simple duties on service providers not to refuse service to a disabled person, and not to discriminate in the manner, standard or terms of service, came into force on 2 December 1996.[3] The next rights of access – requiring service providers to make reasonable adjustments to service delivery, short of physical alterations to premises – came into force on 1 October 1999.[4] The remaining duties to remove physical barriers came into force on 1 October 2004.[5]

Code and regulations

5.1.3   The provisions of Part 3 of the DDA 1995 are supported by a statutory Code of Practice.[6] The Code gives practical advice on how to comply with the legal duties in Part 3 and is designed to help both disabled persons and service providers to understand the law. However, it does not impose legal obligations and is not an authoritative statement of the law. It may be used in evidence in legal proceedings and an adjudicating body (primarily, in this context, a court) must take

---

1   DDA 1995, ss 19–21. Enforcement of the DDA 1995 rights and related questions are dealt with in ss 25–28. Part 3 of the DDA 1995 is broadly modelled after comparable provisions in SDA 1975, ss 29–36 and RRA 1976, ss 20–27. However, there are important and subtle differences between Part 3 of the DDA 1995 and the provisions of the earlier Acts: *Clark v TDG Ltd t/a Novacold* [1999] IRLR 318, CA.

2   HL Deb, vol 566, col 1031.

3   DDA 1995, s 19(1) (except ss 19(1)(b) and 20(1)): SI 1996/1474.

4   Ibid, ss 19(1)(b), 20(2) and 21 (except s 21(2)(a)–(c)): SI 1999/1190.

5   Ibid, s 21(2)(a)–(c): SI 2001/2030 (England, Wales and Scotland) and SR 2001/439 (Northern Ireland).

6   *Code of Practice: Rights of Access: Goods, Facilities, Services and Premises* (2002, London: HMSO) referred to hereafter as the 'Rights of Access Code of Practice 2002'. The Code is prepared and issued by the DRC under DDA 1995, s 53A and came into effect on 27 May 2002: SI 2002/720 and SI 2002/721. It is based on proposals initially made by the NDC (in respect of which the present author acted as consultant) and then subsequently adopted by the DRC (following publication of a consultative draft in May 2000). It revises and replaces earlier versions of the Code of Practice published in 1996 and 1999. A separate,

account of it where relevant.[1] Regulations under Part 3 have also been issued and will be considered at appropriate points in the text below.[2]

Part 3 of the DDA 1995 outlined

5.1.4 The DDA 1995 applies to providers of goods, facilities or services.[3] It is unlawful for a service provider to discriminate against a disabled person by refusing to provide (or deliberately not providing) any service which it provides (or is prepared to provide) to members of the public;[4] or in the standard of service which it provides to the disabled person or the manner in which it provides it;[5] or in the terms on which it provides a service to the disabled person.[6] It is also unlawful for a service provider to discriminate by failing to comply with any statutory duty imposed on it to make reasonable adjustments in circumstances in which the effect of that failure is to make it impossible or unreasonably difficult for the disabled person to make use of goods, facilities or services.[7]

5.2 PROVISION OF SERVICES

Services

5.2.1 For the purposes of the present analysis, the provision of services includes the provision of any goods or facilities.[8] The terms are not defined in the statute or the extra-statutory sources, but the DDA 1995

---

but largely identical, Code of Practice has been issued in Northern Ireland (where the Equality Commission is the responsible body).

1   DDA 1995, s 53A(8) and (8A), as amended. See **9.3**. See generally Rights of Access Code of Practice 2002, Chapter 1.

2   Disability Discrimination (Services and Premises) Regulations 1996, SI 1996/1836 (in force from 2 December 1996); Disability Discrimination (Services and Premises) Regulations 1999, SI 1999/1191 (in force from 1 October 1999); and Disability Discrimination (Providers of Services) (Adjustment of Premises) Regulations 2001, SI 2001/3253, as amended by Disability Discrimination (Providers of Services) (Adjustment of Premises) (Amendment) Regulations 2004, SI 2004/1429 (in force from 1 October 2004, but not extending to Northern Ireland). These regulations derive their authority from DDA 1995, ss 19(5)(c), 20(7)–(8), 21(5)(a)–(b), (e), (h), 24(5), 27(3), 67(1)–(3) and 68(1), and Sch 4, paras 8–9.

3   Referred to throughout this chapter as 'service providers'. References to providing a service include providing goods or facilities (s 19(2)(a)). See generally Rights of Access Code of Practice 2002, Chapter 2.

4   DDA 1995, s 19(1)(a).

5   Ibid, s 19(1)(c).

6   Ibid, s 19(1)(d).

7   Ibid, ss 19(1)(b) and 21.

8   Ibid, s 19(2)(a).

provides a non-exhaustive list of examples of services to which the legislation applies:[1]

- access to and use of any place which members of the public are permitted to enter;
- access to and use of means of communication;
- access to and use of information services;
- accommodation in a hotel, boarding house or other similar establishment;
- facilities by way of banking or insurance or for grants, loans, credit or finance;
- facilities for entertainment, recreation or refreshment;
- facilities provided by employment agencies;
- certain training facilities;[2]
- the services of any profession or trade, or any local or other public authority.

The Rights of Access Code of Practice 2002 adds considerably to this list by way of illustration.[3] A wide range of establishments and businesses are covered by the rights of access. What is also clear is that it is irrelevant whether the goods, facilities or services are provided on payment or without payment.[4]

5.2.2 The illustrative list of services does not explicitly include access to civic rights and duties, health services, broadcasting, the judicial system and legal proceedings, careers services, trade unions and employers' associations, trade and professional associations, or qualifying bodies,[5] but many of these examples are implicitly covered.[6] The apparent legislative intention was 'to provide a universal, all-embracing right of non-discrimination against disabled people that is applicable to all providers of goods, facilities and services to the general public'.[7] The list of services is thus not exhaustive.[8] It seems to have been intended that, for example, facilities for telecommunication, the judicial system

---

1   DDA 1995, s 19(3); Rights of Access Code of Practice 2002, paras 2.18–2.19.

2   Provided under Employment and Training Act 1973, s 2 or Employment and Training Act (Northern Ireland) 1950, ss 1–2 (see DDA 1995, Sch 8, para 9(1)).

3   Rights of Access Code of Practice 2002, para 2.14.

4   DDA 1995, s 19(2)(c).

5   Trade unions, employers' associations, trade associations and professional associations are the subject of ss 13–15 of Part 2 of the DDA 1995. See Chapter 4.

6   Rights of Access Code of Practice 2002, para 2.14.

7   HC Deb Standing Committee E, cols 290–291.

8   There is doubt about whether services provided by a company to its shareholders (eg information and meetings) are caught by Part 3 of the DDA 1995. The Disability Rights Task Force (DRTF) recommended that the Department of Trade and Industry should examine this issue as part of its fundamental review of company law: see *From Exclusion to*

and legal proceedings,[1] broadcasting services,[2] medical and health services, and the constituency services of parliamentarians are covered.[3] However, where central or local government is acting in discharge of a statutory power or duty, there is a very strong argument – supported by case-law under comparable provisions[4] – that this does not entail the provision of a service (unless otherwise closely analogous to the kinds of services provided by a private sector undertaking) and thus is not covered by Part 3 of the DDA 1995.[5]

Goods and facilities

5.2.3   An everyday meaning of 'goods' as chattels or moveable property is probably intended and there seems no reason to import a definition from other statutory sources.[6] A refusal to supply goods which are in the nature of personal or moveable property will be covered. The literal meaning of 'facilities' suggests that the law is concerned with the provision of equipment or the physical means for doing something. For example, the provision of a telephone involves the provision of 'goods'; the supply of a link to the telecommunications network is the provision of a 'service'; while the means by which the service provider then bills

---

Inclusion: A Report of the Disability Rights Task Force for Disabled People (1999, London: DfEE) (DRTF Report), recommendation 6.11. The Government's response was broadly supportive of this recommendation: *Towards Inclusion – Civil Rights for Disabled People: Government Response to the Disability Rights Task Force* (2001, London: DfEE) (Government Response to DRTF Report), para 6.11. See the Companies Act 1985 (Electronic Communications) Order 2000, SI 2000/3373 (modifying various provisions of the Companies Act 1985 for the purpose of authorising or facilitating the use of electronic communications between companies and their members).

1   Part 3 of the DDA 1995 probably does not apply to service as a juror or witness: HL Deb, vol 566, cols 259–262.

2   As to the requirements of television companies (other than the BBC) in respect of teletext and subtitling services, note the provisions of the Broadcasting Acts 1990 and 1996 (and the guidelines published by the Independent Television Commission). See also HL Deb, vol 566, cols 269–271.

3   HC Deb Standing Committee E, cols 292–293; HL Deb, vol 564, col 1952.

4   See *R v Entry Clearance Officer Bombay, ex parte Amin* [1983] 2 AC 818 where, under the similar provisions of the RRA 1976, the House of Lords held that an immigration officer exercising powers under immigration rules was not providing a service to the subject of an immigration decision. See also DDA 1995, s 59 (discussed in Chapter 10).

5   The DRTF recommended that all functions of public authorities should be covered, subject only to careful consideration of the practical effect on those functions of the duty to make reasonable adjustments. It also recommended that the public sector should be under a statutory duty to promote the equalisation of opportunities for disabled people in the provision of services: DRTF Report, recommendations 6.12–6.13. The Government accepted these recommendations, but has not yet implemented them: Government Response to DRTF Report, paras 14–15.

6   Sale of Goods Act 1979, s 61 defines goods as including 'all personal chattels other than things in action and money' excluding non-physical property (such as shares or intellectual property).

the customer for the provision of the goods and service (and the medium by which the customer may settle that bill) would amount to 'facilities'. It may be that the distinction is merely artificial. The term 'facilities' simply embraces any matter not obviously amounting to goods or services.[1]

Service providers

5.2.4 Part 3 of the DDA 1995 applies to 'a provider of services'. A person is a provider of services only if that person is concerned with the provision of services 'to the public or to a section of the public'.[2] The use of the word 'person' will include legal entities (such as companies or local authorities) as well as individuals or associations of individuals (such as trade unions or partnerships).[3] It is clear, for example, that in many circumstances Part 3 embraces the provision of services to the public or community by local and other public authorities.[4] In some cases, there might be more than one service provider – for example, where services are provided from multiple-occupancy premises (such as a department store or shopping centre) or appear to be provided by more than one service provider (as in the case of a conference held in an hotel) – and it is important to determine which service provider has liability or whether such liability is shared.[5]

5.2.5 The service provider must also be 'concerned with the provision, in the United Kingdom, of services to the public'. The meaning of this phrase is unclear and potentially ambiguous. It is capable of meaning that the services themselves must be provided within the UK (and thus, for example, an overseas holiday would not be covered). Equally, it might mean that it is sufficient that the service provider is based in the UK (even if the services themselves will be used outside the UK). Given the territorial nature of statutory jurisdiction, it seems likely that a British court would interpret this clause narrowly and in favour of the former interpretation rather than the latter. That does not mean that, for example, a British tour operator offering holidays abroad is entirely untouched by the DDA 1995. The brochure and booking services which it offers to the public in the UK are services within the Act, even if the

---

1   The illustrations in the DDA 1995 (s 19(3)) of what amounts to 'services' appear to encompass 'facilities'.

2   DDA 1995, s 19(2)(b).

3   All those involved in the provision of services are affected: Rights of Access Code of Practice 2002, para 2.15.

4   HL Deb, vol 565, col 672. This must be subject to what is said in **5.2.2**.

5   Rights of Access Code of Practice 2002, paras 2.17 and 2.20–2.30 (and examples) addressing the difficult questions of liability under the DDA 1995 in multi-occupancy premises with common areas and landlord–tenant relationships.

actual holidays themselves may not be. This is a matter which awaits testing in litigation.

Manufacturers and designers

5.2.6   Part 3 of the DDA 1995 does not apply to manufacturers and designers, unless they supply goods or services directly to members of the public.[1] While such persons might wish to consider how to comply with the spirit of the legislation, they are not directly subject to its letter. There is no obligation upon manufacturers or producers of goods or services (who are not also direct suppliers to the public) to consider the accessibility of the design, labelling or packaging of those goods or services to disabled consumers. For example, there is no legal obligation upon manufacturers under the Act to include any user instructions bundled with goods or products in accessible formats (such as Braille, large print or audio-visual medium) and there would appear to be no such duty placed upon the retail supplier either.[2]

Private members' clubs

5.2.7   Private members' clubs (and organisations such as trade unions) are not covered by Part 3 of the DDA 1995 because they do not provide services *to the public* or a section of the public.[3] Such clubs (and organisations) are free to discriminate against disabled persons seeking membership or access.[4] The Code of Practice defines a private club as one where membership is a condition of participation and where there is a genuine selection process (usually under the club's rules).[5] Nevertheless, even a private membership club will be subject to Part 3

---

1   HL Deb, vol 566, cols 241–242. See Rights of Access Code of Practice 2002, paras 2.40–2.41 (and examples).

2   HL Deb, vol 566, col 251.

3   DDA 1995, s 19(2)(b). See Rights of Access Code of Practice 2002, paras 2.38–2.39. Discrimination by trade organisations (and bodies such as trade unions) is subject to DDA 1995, ss 13–15. See Chapter 4.

4   See the case-law to like effect under the now repealed provisions of the Race Relations Act 1968: *Dockers Labour Club and Institute Ltd v Race Relations Board* [1976] AC 285; *Charter v Race Relations Board* [1973] AC 885. Cf RRA 1976, s 25 and *Applin v Race Relations Board* [1975] AC 259.

5   See Rights of Access Code of Practice 2002, para 2.39. The DRTF recommended that private clubs should be covered, but without extending coverage to private social arrangements: DRTF Report, recommendation 6.10. The Government asked the DRC to address the issue of whether to develop a voluntary approach instead of legislating to reduce any problems disabled people may face in joining private clubs (including the making of reasonable adjustments) once the provisions in Part 3 of the DDA 1995 were fully in force as part of its ongoing duty to review the DDA 1995: Government Response to DRTF Report, para 3.73. The DRC has now endorsed the DRTF view. See *Legislative Review: First Review of the Disability Discrimination Act 1995: Consultation* (May 2002, Disability Rights

obligations if it uses its premises to provide some services of a public nature. For example, a private golf club that provides facilities to non-members for wedding receptions may not lawfully discriminate against a disabled wedding guest.

To whom the service is provided

5.2.8 It is clear that Part 3 of the DDA 1995 only addresses discrimination in the provision of services to disabled persons as consumers themselves. It does not directly address discrimination against a person because of that individual's relationship to or association with a disabled person (perhaps as a spouse, parent or friend). Members of a family who are refused service in a restaurant because they are accompanied by a disabled child have no remedy under the Act (although the child will also have been discriminated against and will have a cause of action which will have to be pursued on his or her behalf). However, the disabled person may be receiving services in his or her own right while acting on behalf of someone else or as a representative of a third party, and is likely to be covered by the DDA 1995 in those circumstances, all other things being equal.[1]

Excluded services

5.2.9 Part 3 of the DDA 1995 does not apply to education,[2] but it does apply to non-education services provided by educational institutions.[3] Part 3 also does not apply to transport.[4] The scope of these exclusions is clearly important and merits separate consideration in Chapters 7 and 8. The Act also provides that Part 3 will not apply to 'such other services'

Commission) (DRC Legislative Review), recommendation 23. The DRC has a statutory duty to keep under review the working of the DDA 1995. See DRCA 1999, s 2(1), and **9.1.7**.

1   Rights of Access Code of Practice 2002, para 2.16.

2   The exclusion of education was originally effected by DDA 1995, s 19(5)(a)–(ab) and (6) (as amended). This provision is now repealed by SENDA 2001, ss 38(1), (5)(a)–(b), 42(6) and Sch 9. The present position is that, by virtue of DDA 1995, s 19(5A) (inserted by SENDA 2001, s 38(1) and (6)), nothing in Part 3 of the DDA 1995 (the goods and services provisions) applies to the provision of a service which is made unlawful by DDA 1995, s 28A (discrimination against disabled pupils and prospective pupils), s 28F (duty of education authorities not to discriminate) or s 28R (discrimination against disabled students and prospective students), as inserted by SENDA 2001, ss 11, 16 and 26. See Rights of Access Code of Practice 2002, paras 2.31–2.35.

3   As is illustrated by *White v Clitheroe Royal Grammar School* (2002) Preston County Court (District Judge Ashton), reported in *Equal Opportunities Review No 106* (June 2002) 26–28 (student with diabetes discriminated against contrary to DDA 1995, Part 3 when excluded from a school holiday for a reason connected with his disability).

4   DDA 1995, s 19(5)(b) and Rights of Access Code of Practice 2002, paras 2.36–2.37. See *Ross v Ryanair Ltd and Stansted Airport Ltd* [2004] EWCA Civ 1751, discussed at **8.5.2**.

as may be prescribed by regulations.[1] No such regulations have been made to date.[2] It would appear that this was a precautionary piece of drafting and there has been no indication that this power will be used at any particular time or for any particular purpose.

5.3 UNLAWFUL DISCRIMINATION

5.3.1 Part 3 of the DDA 1995 provides that it is unlawful for a service provider to discriminate against a disabled person in a number of specified ways.[3]

Refusal to provide goods, facilities or services

5.3.2 First, it is an unlawful act for a service provider to discriminate against a disabled person in refusing to provide, or deliberately not providing, to a disabled person any service which the service provider provides, or is prepared to provide, to members of the public.[4] For example, a theatre which refuses to admit a person with cerebral palsy because of that individual's disability might be committing an unlawful act of discrimination.[5]

Standard or manner of service

5.3.3 Secondly, it is an unlawful act for a service provider to discriminate against a disabled person in the 'standard of service' which the service provider provides to the disabled person or by virtue of the 'manner in which' the service provider provides that service to the disabled person.[6] A restaurant that forces disabled customers to dine in a separate room unseen by other patrons might breach this provision.[7] A theatre which limits disabled patrons to matinee performances only might also fall foul of the Act, although there would be nothing to prevent a theatre arranging special matinee performances for disabled persons, provided they are also free to book seats for other times.[8]

---

1   DDA 1995, s 19(5)(c).

2   Although regulations clarifying the scope of the original exclusion of education were made: Disability Discrimination (Services and Premises) Regulations 1996, SI 1996/1836, reg 9. The present position of education in the context of disability discrimination is addressed in Chapter 7.

3   See generally Rights of Access Code of Practice 2002, Chapters 2–4.

4   DDA 1995, s 19(1)(a).

5   See the further examples in Rights of Access Code of Practice 2002, paras 3.17–3.19.

6   DDA 1995, s 19(1)(c).

7   1994 Green Paper, para 4.3.

8   See the further examples in Rights of Access Code of Practice 2002, paras 3.20–3.21.

Similarly, providing inferior goods or services to disabled persons would
be unlawful, although what would amount to *inferior* goods or services
might be difficult to measure. For example, requiring wheelchair users
to sit in a particular part of a theatre or restaurant when other customers
or patrons have a comparatively free choice as to where they sit could be
regarded as the provision of an inferior service.[1] Much will hinge upon
the application of the defence of justification for the differential
treatment in such cases,[2] but a service provider who adopts a deliberate
policy to discourage disabled customers (for example, by deliberately
surly, dilatory or inferior service) would have difficulty in justifying such
discrimination.[3]

Terms on which service is provided

5.3.4   Thirdly, it is an unlawful act for a service provider to discriminate
against a disabled person in the terms on which the service provider
provides a service (or goods or facilities) to the disabled person.[4] An
example of an act made unlawful by this provision would be a shop or
entertainment outlet which charged higher prices for purchases by or
admission to disabled persons in comparison with other customers.[5]

Failure to make reasonable adjustment

5.3.5   Finally, it is also an unlawful act for a service provider to
discriminate against a disabled person by failing to comply with a duty
imposed on it by the DDA 1995[6] to make reasonable adjustments in
circumstances in which the effect of the failure is to make it impossible
or unreasonably difficult for the disabled person to make use of any
goods, facilities or services provided to other members of the public.[7]
This is a pivotal duty under the Act and calls for separate and detailed
explication below.[8]

---

1   1994 Green Paper, para 4.4; Rights of Access Code of Practice 2002, para 3.20.

2   See **5.6**.

3   HL Deb, vol 566, col 267.

4   DDA 1995, s 19(1)(d).

5   1994 Green Paper, para 4.3. See the further examples in Rights of Access Code of Practice
2002, para 3.22.

6   DDA 1995, s 21.

7   Ibid, s 19(1)(b). This provision came into force on 1 October 1999 (the remaining
provisions of s 19(1) having been in force since 2 December 1996).

8   See **5.5**.

5.4 MEANING OF DISCRIMINATION

5.4.1 As has just been described, it is unlawful for a provider of services to 'discriminate' against a disabled person in a number of respects in relation to goods, facilities and services.[1] However, it is not sufficient to show that a disabled person has been badly or unreasonably treated in the outcomes set out above. It is also necessary to show that this is the result of discrimination by the service provider. What does 'discrimination' mean for this purpose and in this context? The definition of 'discrimination' in the context of Part 3 of the DDA 1995 is broadly similar to that used in Part 2 (discrimination in employment and contract work and by trade organisations).[2] It contains two alternative bases for establishing discrimination: broadly, less favourable treatment and a failure to make a reasonable adjustment.[3] The Act also treats 'victimisation' as unlawful discrimination for present purposes (this is dealt with further in Chapter 10).[4]

Less favourable treatment

5.4.2 A provider of services discriminates against a disabled person if, for a reason which relates to the disabled person's disability, the service provider treats the disabled person less favourably than the service provider treats (or would treat) others to whom the reason which relates to the disabled person's disability does not or would not apply, and the service provider cannot show that the less favourable treatment in question is justified.[5] Although this definition allows less favourable treatment to be 'justified', it is closely related to the concept of 'direct discrimination' used in other discrimination legislation. However, the use of the phrase 'for a reason which relates to the disabled person's

---

1   DDA 1995, s 19(1), and see **5.3**.

2   Ibid, s 20. Cf ss 5 and 14 (see Chapters 3 and 4). Decisions and judicial interpretation under ss 5 and 14 will be of assistance in applying the parallel definition in s 20, but care must be taken to ensure that in Part 3 cases direct reference is made to the wording of s 20 itself.

3   The DRTF recommended that the existing categories of discrimination should continue: DRTF Report, recommendation 6.1. The DRC suggests that an EU Directive is required with respect to discrimination on the grounds of disability in relation to a broad range of goods and services: DRC Legislative Review, recommendation 13.

4   DDA 1995, s 55. An act of victimisation will constitute an act of discrimination for the purposes of discrimination in relation to goods, facilities and services and will provide a cause of action, whether or not the person victimised is a disabled person. This is achieved on the face of ss 19–21 by virtue of s 19(4).

5   Ibid, s 20(1). See Rights of Access Code of Practice 2002, paras 2.4–2.8 and 3.3–3.13 (and the examples provided there). Part 3 of the Act does not prohibit positive action in favour of disabled people. Service providers may provide services to disabled people on more favourable terms: Rights of Access Code of Practice 2002, para 3.23.

disability' suggests a more flexible test of discrimination.[1] This phraseology makes 'it clear that if a disabled person is refused service – for example, in a café – for a reason connected with his disability, where non-disabled people are happily served', that will be a prima facie case of discrimination, subject to any 'defence' of justification.[2]

5.4.3   This concept of discrimination requires proof that the disabled person has been treated less favourably than other persons to whom the reason related to disability does not apply. This calls for a comparison of how the disabled person was treated relative to such other persons.[3] The question is not merely whether the disabled person has experienced poor, inadequate or sub-standard provision in respect of goods, facilities or services. Rather the issue is whether there has been differential and unfavourable treatment of the disabled person in circumstances where other persons (to whom the reason related to disability does not apply) have not been so treated. The comparator is another member of the public (or a hypothetical member of the public). This might include a person with a disability of a different kind from the complainant because the wording of the DDA 1995 does not rule out the unlawfulness of differential treatment by service providers among disabled persons themselves.

5.4.4   The less favourable treatment must be related to the disabled person's disability. While the intention, purpose or motive with which the service provider acted is irrelevant, there must be a causal connection between the discriminatory action and the complainant's disability. A disabled person who is refused admission to a cinema because he or she does not have the means to pay for entry, or who is refused service in a public house because he or she is drunk and disorderly, has not been discriminated against contrary to the DDA 1995.[4] The reason for the apparently less favourable treatment is not that person's disability, but rather a reason which is unrelated to disability. Indeed, in any event, in these illustrations it might be claimed that there has been no less favourable treatment at all, because the service provider might be able to show that any member of the public in like circumstances would have been treated in the same way.

5.4.5   However, following the logic of the Court of Appeal's decision in the DDA 1995, Part 2 case of *Clark v TDG Ltd t/a Novacold*,[5] it is essential

---

1   DDA 1995, s 20(1)(a).

2   HL Deb, vol 566, col 120. Strictly, justification is not a defence, but rather is one of the component parts of the definition of discrimination.

3   Rights of Access Code of Practice 2002, paras 3.3–3.10.

4   Ibid, paras 3.8–3.10.

5   [1999] IRLR 318, CA.

when approaching less favourable treatment discrimination under Part 3 to identify the reason why the disabled person is being treated less favourably than others. For example, suppose that a disabled person has cerebral palsy which causes her difficulty with physical co-ordination when eating. She is refused further service in a restaurant because the service provider objects to the messy way in which she eats. That is a refusal of service; the refusal is because of the way in which the customer eats; that is a reason which is related to the customer's disability (because her eating habits are affected by her disability); no other customers have been refused service in the restaurant; and so this amounts to less favourable treatment for a reason related to disability. It would not be sufficient for the restaurant to claim that it would have refused service to anyone who was a messy eater. The DDA 1995 does not require the comparison to be based upon a consideration of comparators in relevant circumstances which are the same or not materially different. This would be unlawful discrimination unless the restaurant can justify the treatment of the disabled customer.[1]

5.4.6 Nevertheless, in *R v Powys County Council, ex parte Hambidge (No 2)*,[2] the Court of Appeal has taken a narrower approach to the concept of less favourable treatment for a reason related to disability under Part 3 of the DDA 1995 than was taken in *Clark* under Part 2. The applicant was in receipt of disability living allowance and received home care services from the local authority.[3] The local authority introduced charges for home care services.[4] It did so by reference to three categories of service user: (A) those in receipt of income support only; (B) those in receipt of income support and either attendance allowance or disability living allowance; and (C) those not in receipt of income support (regardless of whether they were receiving any other benefits). Those in category (A) were not charged for home care services at all, while those in categories (B) and (C) were charged at differential rates. The applicant fell into category (B). She challenged the home care services charge by arguing that it amounted to less favourable treatment for a reason related to her disability.[5] Her argument was that the charges levied on category (B) were because those in category (B) had more income than those in category (A) and that the only reason for this was that those in category (B) received disability benefits by virtue of having a disability. The High Court and the Court of Appeal rejected the

---

1   The question of justification is addressed at **5.6**.

2   [2000] 2 FCR 69, CA.

3   Under National Health Service Community Care Act 1990, s 47 and Chronically Sick and Disabled Persons Act 1970, s 2(1).

4   Under Health and Social Services and Social Security Adjudications Act 1983, s 17(2).

5   Relying upon DDA 1995, ss 19(1)(d), (2)(c), (3)(h) and 20(1)(a).

applicant's contention that this amounted to disability discrimination unless justified. The appellate court thought that it could not have been intended that such a case was to be covered by s 20(1)(a). The charges were based upon means or income rather than disability status or disability benefits as such. The case is probably best explained as being one based upon its particular facts.

5.4.7   Is it an essential ingredient of this limb of discrimination to be able to show that the service provider knew that the service user was a disabled person or that it was aware of the disability to which the reason for the alleged unlawful treatment was related? The question of whether the service provider knew that the service user (being treated in a way which is allegedly unlawful) was disabled is likely to be an especially keen one under Part 3 of the DDA 1995. For example, a disability might affect the appearance or behaviour of the disabled person, leading the service provider to believe honestly, but wrongly, that the service user was drunk or was engaging in threatening or unacceptable behaviour. Can a service provider be said to have treated a person less favourably for a reason which relates to that person's disability if the service provider did not know that the person was disabled?

5.4.8   The issue of knowledge has been raised in the context of the employment provisions of Part 2 of the DDA 1995.[1] The wording of s 20(1) is for all intents and purposes virtually identical to that of the parallel provisions in s 3A(1). Under the employment provisions, the correct approach to the question of the knowledge of disability has divided opinion in the first tier appellate courts. One view is that an employer's knowledge of the disability is relevant.[2] An employer cannot be said to have treated a person less favourably *for a reason which relates to* that person's disability if the employer did not know that the person was disabled. Knowledge of the material features of the disability will be enough, but not simply knowledge of one or other equivocal symptom.[3] However, other judicial opinion has doubted the correctness of that view.[4] According to the later opinion, as the wording of the relevant statutory provision is silent on the question of knowledge, the test is an objective one of whether the disabled person has been treated less favourably for a reason which is related to disability *as a matter of fact*. The subjective question of the employer's knowledge or ignorance of the complainant's disability might then go to the issue of justification.

---

1   See **3.2.16–3.2.22**.

2   See eg *O'Neill v Symm & Co Ltd* [1998] IRLR 233, EAT.

3   Whether this view is compatible with the Court of Appeal's construction of s 3A(1) in *Clark v TDG Ltd t/a Novacold* [1999] IRLR 318, CA, is arguably questionable.

4   See eg *HJ Heinz Co Ltd v Kenrick* [2000] IRLR 144, EAT.

5.4.9 In the employment context, the latter view that knowledge of disability is not a requirement of establishing less favourable treatment discrimination is defensible both on policy grounds and in the framework of an employer's recourse to a broadly defined concept of justification. However, in relation to provision of goods and services, a service provider will not usually be possessed of the same degree of actual or potential knowledge of an individual's disability as an employer might be. Unless the service user immediately informs the service provider that he or she is disabled and explains the effects of the disability, a service provider might make a snap decision (for example, to refuse service) for a reason (for example, the appearance of being drunk) which later turns out to be a disability-related reason. Unlike the potential knowledge-based justification open to an employer, the service provider's justification 'defence' is narrowly defined and limited to the circumstances set out in Part 3 of the DDA 1995.[1] A literal interpretation of s 20(1) would suggest that knowledge of the disability is not relevant, but whether a court in a Part 3 case will interpret this provision in a services environment in the same way as it might be construed in an employment setting remains to be seen.[2] In *Council of the City of Manchester v Romano and Samari*[3] the Court of Appeal thought that if knowledge of the disability was not relevant, that could lead to absurd and unfair consequences. It suggested that Parliament should review the legislation at an early date.

Indirect discrimination

5.4.10 A service provider providing services subject to a requirement or condition which a smaller proportion of disabled persons than non-disabled persons can meet could be said to have indirectly discriminated against disabled persons if they suffer a detriment as a result and if the service provider cannot justify the imposition of the requirement or condition. The DDA 1995 does not contain an explicit

1   DDA 1995, s 20(1)(b), (3) and (4). See **5.6**. It would then be for the service provider to argue that it is enough that it reasonably believed that, for example, the disabled person's appearance or behaviour created a danger to health or safety (s 20(4)(a)) or would prevent other service users from being served (s 20(4)(c) or (d)).

2   The Rights of Access Code of Practice 2002 (at paras 3.11–3.13) prefers the test of whether, as a matter of fact, the treatment of the disabled person is for a reason related to disability. It counsels service providers that some disabilities are not visible and that staff should not attempt to make fine judgments as to whether an individual is disabled or not, but rather should focus on meeting the needs of each customer. It sets out helpful (non-statutory) guidance to service providers as to the steps they should consider taking so as to comply with the DDA 1995 and to prevent their employees from discriminating against disabled customers: para 3.16. See also paras 4.15–4.16 (in the context of the duty to make reasonable adjustments).

3   [2004] EWCA Civ 834.

prohibition on indirect discrimination in relation to services, unlike the comparable provisions of the SDA 1975 and the RRA 1976. This is because the 1994 Green Paper took the view that indirect discrimination would be 'more difficult to tackle effectively where disabled people are involved because disability occurs in many forms' and should not be the subject of legislation.[1] That view was reiterated in the 1995 White Paper which stated that 'a general prohibition of indirect discrimination ... could have unforeseen consequences which were unfairly burdensome for businesses'.[2] However, it was accepted that certain practices – which had an indirect effect upon the right of disabled persons to access to services – should be prevented. The White Paper gave the specific example of a service provider banning animals from its premises and the disproportionate adverse effect this would have on persons with visual impairments who rely upon guide dogs. This would be a case that would clearly call for reasonable practical adjustments or modifications to be made by the service provider. That leads us to a consideration of the duty to make reasonable adjustments.

5.5   DUTY TO MAKE REASONABLE ADJUSTMENTS

Introduction

5.5.1   While many incidents of indirect discrimination in relation to goods, facilities or services will be caught by the 'less favourable treatment' formula,[3] the duty to make reasonable adjustments assumes even greater importance as a means to prevent (or to require the adjustment of) unjustified practices, rules, policies, requirements or conditions which have a harsh or adverse impact upon access by disabled persons. The 1995 White Paper proposed that it would not be enough simply to prohibit discriminatory behaviour. Legislation would also require 'positive action which is reasonable and readily achievable to overcome the physical and communication barriers that impede disabled people's access'.[4] This would mean that policies, practices and procedures which discriminated against disabled persons would have to be prohibited, unless fundamental to the nature of the business. Auxiliary aids and services (such as information on tape for blind customers or induction loops in places of entertainment for individuals with hearing disabilities) would have to be provided, if this was

---

1   1994 Green Paper, para 4.11.

2   1995 White Paper, para 4.5.

3   DDA 1995, s 20(1). See **5.4.2**.

4   1995 White Paper, para 4.4.

reasonable and readily achievable. Physical barriers might also have to be removed or alternative means of access be provided.

5.5.2 Accordingly, the DDA 1995 places a duty on service providers to amend policies, procedures and practices which prevent disabled persons using a service; to remove or alter physical barriers; and to provide auxiliary aids or services.[1] The statutory duty placed upon service providers to make reasonable adjustments to allow disabled persons meaningful access to the provision of services provided to the public is the keystone to the rights of access contained in Part 3 of the Act. A breach of the duty to make reasonable adjustments is not actionable in itself and a failure to observe the duty on the part of a service provider does not give an aggrieved disabled person a common law right in tort to sue for breach of a statutory duty. Nevertheless, the duty to make reasonable adjustments is important for determining whether a service provider has discriminated against a disabled person.[2] An *unjustified* failure to comply with a s 21 duty imposed upon a service provider in relation to a disabled person is treated as amounting to discrimination against the disabled person.[3] Such a failure is potentially an *unlawful* act of discrimination if the failure has the effect of making it 'impossible or unreasonably difficult' for the disabled person to make use of a service which the service provider provides (or is prepared to provide) to the public.[4]

5.5.3 The Rights of Access Code of Practice 2002 attempts to cast light upon the meaning of this complex provision.[5] For example, the DDA 1995 does not define what is meant by 'impossible or unreasonably difficult' in the context of the effect upon the accessibility of a service to a disabled person as a result of a failure to make a reasonable adjustment.[6] Instead the Code offers some factors (such as time, inconvenience, effort, discomfort or loss of dignity entailed in using a

---

1   DDA 1995, s 21.

2   Ibid, s 21(10).

3   Ibid, s 20(2); Rights of Access Code of Practice 2002, paras 4.1–4.8 and 4.34.

4   Ibid, s 19(1)(b). The Act assumes that an action for a breach of the duty to make reasonable adjustments will be brought under the bespoke provision in s 19(1)(b). However, there seems to be no reason of statutory construction (reading ss 19(1), 20(2), (9) and 21 together) why such an action could not be brought within the other causes of action set out in s 19(1) (and where the threshold for action may not be so high). Similarly, it might be possible to pursue the breach via ss 19(1)(b) and 20(1) ('less favourable treatment' discrimination).

5   Rights of Access Code of Practice 2002, Chapters 4–5.

6   The DRC recommends that the DDA 1995 should be amended to require adjustments either where they would enable and/or facilitate the use of a service or where a disabled customer is at a substantial disadvantage in accessing a service: DRC Legislative Review, recommendation 25.

service) which go to the question of what would be unreasonably difficult for a disabled person to have to endure when attempting to use a service.[1] Again, the statute does not say what are 'reasonable steps' in relation to the duty of the service provider to make adjustments. Filling the gap, the Rights of Access Code 2002 borrows from the Employment Code of Practice.[2] What is a reasonable step for a service provider to have to take will vary according to the type of services being provided; the nature of the service provider and its size and resources; and the effect of the disability on the individual disabled person.[3] Other factors which may be relevant include the effectiveness of the steps; their practicability; financial and other costs;[4] disruption to the service provider's business; the extent of the service provider's financial and other resources (including any resources already expended on adjustments); and the availability of financial or other assistance.[5] A service provider with substantial financial resources may be expected to take greater steps than a service provider with fewer resources. On the other hand, steps need not be taken if they would fundamentally alter the nature of the service in question or which would alter the nature of the trade, profession or business that the service provider runs or owns.[6]

1　Rights of Access Code of Practice 2002, paras 4.32–4.33. The DRTF considers that the trigger point for making a reasonable adjustment should be monitored to see whether it has been set too high: DRTF Report, recommendation 6.5. That was a matter which the Government asked the DRC to keep under review: Government Response to DRTF Report, para 3.73. The DRC has recommended that, rather than requiring reasonable adjustments where it is impossible or unreasonably difficult to access a service, the DDA 1995 should be altered to require these either where they would enable and facilitate the use of a service or where a disabled customer is at a substantial disadvantage in accessing a service: DRC Legislative Review, recommendation 25.

2　Employment Code of Practice, paras 4.21–4.32. There is a noticeable and important difference here, however, in that the Employment Code builds upon the factors identified in s 6(4) in Part 2 of the DDA 1995 as being within the scope of the reasonable steps inquiry for the purposes of the employment-related duty to make adjustments. Part 3 contains no such statutory factors and so the Rights of Access Code 2002 strictly speaking is filling a vacuum.

3　Rights of Access Code of Practice 2002, paras 4.21–4.22.

4　The DDA 1995 allows for a future possibility that a service provider would not be required to take any steps incurring expenditure exceeding a prescribed maximum sum: s 21(7). Any prescribed maximum might be calculated by reference to criteria set out in s 21(8) and the regulations may provide for expenditure incurred by one service provider to be treated as incurred by another: s 21(9). There is no present intention to use this power.

5　Rights of Access Code of Practice 2002, para 4.22 (and example) and paras 4.23–4.24. The DRTF approved of these factors but recommended that they should be set out in legislation: DRTF Report, recommendation 6.2. The Government referred this question to the DRC: Government Response to DRTF Report, para 3.73. The DRC agrees with the DRTF: DRC Legislative Review, recommendation 32.

6　DDA 1995, s 21(6); Rights of Access Code of Practice 2002, paras 4.28–4.29.

5.5.4 Moreover, the Rights of Access Code of Practice 2002 describes the duty to make reasonable adjustments as one arising in relation to disabled people at large.[1] It counsels service providers to anticipate the requirements of disabled users of its services for reasonable adjustments to be made to the way in which its services are provided.[2] Section 21 of the DDA 1995 thus contains an anticipatory duty which is owed to disabled people at large, but the breach of which gives rise to a potential individual cause of action.[3] The duty is also a continuing and evolving one.[4] What may be a reasonable adjustment today may cease to be so in the future, especially as technological development gathers pace.

Practices, policies or procedures

5.5.5 The first aspect of the duty to make reasonable adjustments arises where a service provider has a 'practice, policy or procedure' which makes it 'impossible or unreasonably difficult' for disabled persons to make use of goods, facilities or services which the service provider provides or is prepared to provide to other members of the public.[5] In such a case, it is the duty of the service provider 'to take such steps as it is reasonable, in all the circumstances of the case',[6] for the service provider to have to take 'in order to change' the policy, practice or procedure in question so that 'it no longer has' the effect described (that is, making it impossible or unreasonably difficult for disabled persons to access the goods, facilities or services in point).[7] This may simply involve waiving a practice, or amending or abandoning a particular policy (such as a dress code in a restaurant or a requirement

---

1   Rights of Access Code of Practice 2002, para 4.13. See *Ross v Ryanair Ltd and Stansted Airport Ltd* [2004] EWCA Civ 1751, discussed at **8.5.2**.

2   Ibid, paras 4.14 and 4.17–4.18.

3   The description of the duty in s 21 speaks of its effect upon 'disabled persons' (in the plural), whereas ss 19(1)(b) and 20(2) – in defining what is unlawful discrimination – addresses 'the disabled person' (in the singular).

4   Rights of Access Code of Practice 2002, paras 4.19–4.20. The DRTF approved of these principles, but recommended that they should be expressed in legislation in clearer terms: DRTF Report, recommendation 6.4. The Government asked the DRC to look at this question: Government Response to DRTF Report, para 3.73. The DRC agrees with the DRTF approach: DRC Legislative Review, recommendation 32.

5   DDA 1995, s 21(1).

6   See Rights of Access Code of Practice 2002, paras 5.4–5.9.

7   Regulations may make provision as to the circumstances in which it is reasonable (or not reasonable) for a service provider to have to take steps of a prescribed description (s 21(5)(a)–(b)). Moreover, such regulations may prescribe what is to be included or not included within the meaning of a 'practice, policy or procedure' (s 21(5)(c)–(d)). No such regulations have been made at the time of writing.

of a driving licence as proof of identification) which creates difficulty for people with certain kinds of disabilities.[1]

5.5.6   The DDA 1995 provides no further guidance or interpretation as to the meaning of the s 21(1) duty or its component parts. Neither the 1994 Green Paper nor the 1995 White Paper cast further light on this duty. The parliamentary debates on the draft legislation are also unhelpful. The Code of Practice is a little bit more expansive.[2] However, the wording of the subsection is relatively unambiguous and the duty to make reasonable adjustments set out there is not likely to give rise to many disputes of legal interpretation. One obvious example that is caught by this duty is the policy or practice of shops or places of entertainment which exclude access to dogs accompanied by their owners. Such a policy or practice will need to be revisited and exception made (as was often the voluntary position previously) for service animals accompanied by a disabled person.[3] Similarly, cinemas or restaurants which refuse or limit access to wheelchair users have to rethink this practice.[4]

Physical features

5.5.7   The 1994 Green Paper referred to the fact that disabled persons cannot take access to non-domestic buildings for granted and pointed out that high steps, narrow doorways, and absence of lift access and aids to communication constituted typical physical barriers.[5] Accordingly, the second aspect of the duty to make reasonable adjustments applies where a physical feature makes it impossible or unreasonably difficult for disabled persons to make use of goods, facilities or services which a service provider provides or is prepared to provide to other members of the public.[6] Where a physical feature of this kind has the effect described, then there is a duty upon the service provider 'to take such steps as it is reasonable,[7] in all the circumstances of the case', for the service provider to have to take in order:

---

1   Rights of Access Code of Practice 2002, para 5.5 (and examples).

2   Ibid, paras 5.4–5.9.

3   Rights of Access Code of Practice 2002, para 5.6 (example).

4   Thus, there is an obvious overlap with the duty to provide auxiliary aids and services which arises under DDA 1995, s 21(4).

5   1994 Green Paper, para 3.3.

6   DDA 1995, s 21(2); Rights of Access Code of Practice (2002), para 5.31.

7   Regulations have been made under DDA 1995, s 21(5)(a)–(b) prescribing particular circumstances for the purposes of s 21 in which it is or is not reasonable for a service

- to remove the feature;[1]
- to alter it so that it no longer has that effect;[2]
- to provide a reasonable means of avoiding the feature;[3]
- to provide a reasonable alternative method of making the service in question available to disabled persons.[4]

While the last of these aspects of this particular duty was brought into force on 1 October 1999, the remaining aspects of the duties in respect of physical features came into force on 1 October 2004.[5]

5.5.8 The 2002 revision of the Code of Practice was designed to assist service providers to prepare for the 2004 duties during the transitional period.[6] What a service provider has done during the transitional period may be a relevant consideration for a court to take into account when judging whether a service provider has taken reasonable steps in relation to its duty after 1 October 2004.[7] The Code of Practice made the business cases for planning and implementing changes to physical features prior to 1 October 2004.[8] It also encourages service providers to carry out an access audit of their premises and to draw up an access plan or strategy.[9]

---

provider to have to take certain steps in relation to premises occupied under a lease or other binding obligation: Disability Discrimination (Providers of Services) (Adjustment of Premises) Regulations 2001, SI 2001/3253, as amended by SI 2004/1429 (in force from 1 October 2004). See also Rights of Access Code of Practice 2002, paras 6.27–6.49, and the extended discussion in Chapter 6.

1   DDA 1995, s 21(2)(a) (in force from 1 October 2004).

2   Ibid, s 21(2)(b) (in force from 1 October 2004).

3   Ibid, s 21(2)(c) (in force from 1 October 2004). Regulations yet to be enacted may prescribe matters which are to be taken into account in determining whether the providing of means to avoid a physical feature is 'reasonable' (s 21(3)(a)).

4   DDA 1995, s 21(2)(d), in force since 1 October 1999. Regulations may prescribe matters which are to be taken into account in determining whether the providing of an alternative method of making the service available to disabled persons is 'reasonable' (s 21(3)(a)). When this subsection was brought into force in 1999, no such prescriptive regulations were made in support.

5   SI 2001/2030 (England, Wales and Scotland) and SR 2001/439 (Northern Ireland); Rights of Access Code of Practice 2002, paras 5.3 and 5.32. See **5.1.2**.

6   Rights of Access Code of Practice 2002, para 5.33. Note that DDA 1995, s 27 and Sch 4, Part II and the Disability Discrimination (Providers of Services) (Adjustment of Premises) Regulations 2001, SI 2001/3253, as amended by SI 2004/1429 (in force from 1 October 2004), make special provision where a service provider occupies its premises under lease. Where the lease or the lessor prevents or hinders the occupier in making adjustments to the premises so as to comply with a s 21 duty, these provisions will modify the effect of the lease and place duties upon the lessor. See also Rights of Access Code of Practice 2002, paras 6.27–6.49 and the extended discussion in Chapter 6.

7   Rights of Access Code of Practice 2002, para 5.34 (and example).

8   Ibid, paras 5.33–5.35.

9   Ibid, paras 5.42–5.43.

5.5.9   By way of example in the statute itself, a 'physical feature' refers to a feature 'arising from the design or construction of a building or the approach or access to premises'.[1] However, regulations go further and for this purpose physical features include:[2]

- any feature arising from the design or construction of a building on the premises occupied by the service provider;
- any feature on those premises or any approach to, exit from or access to such a building;
- any fixtures, fittings, furnishings, furniture, equipment or materials in or on such premises;
- any fixtures, fittings, furnishings, furniture, equipment or materials brought onto premises (other than those occupied by the service provider) by or on behalf of the service provider in the course of (and for the purpose of) providing services to the public;
- any other physical element or quality of land comprised in the premises occupied by the service provider.

All these features which are within the boundaries of a service provider's premises are covered, whether temporary or permanent, inside or outside.[3] A building means an erection or structure of any kind.[4]

5.5.10   It is worth noting that s 21(2) of the DDA 1995 leaves to the service provider the choice of steps to be taken to overcome the adverse effects of a physical feature.[5] The duty itself might not be triggered at all if another reasonable adjustment has ensured that the physical feature does not make it impossible or unreasonably difficult for disabled persons to use the service.[6] The subsection does not require the service provider to remove or alter the physical feature as a priority and does not require a hierarchical approach to adjustments to physical features. Thus, somewhat controversially, the effect of this provision is not wholly

---

1   DDA 1995, s 21(2).

2   Disability Discrimination (Services and Premises) Regulations 1999, SI 1999/1191, regs 2–3, made under DDA 1995, s 21(5)(e)–(f); Rights of Access Code of Practice 2002, paras 5.44–5.47.

3   Rights of Access Code of Practice 2002, para 5.46. The Code of Practice illustrates physical features as including steps, stairways, kerbs, exterior surfaces and paving, parking areas, building entrances and exits (including emergency escape routes), internal and external doors, gates, toilet and washing facilities, public facilities (such as telephones), counters or service desks, lighting and ventilation, lifts and escalators, floor coverings, signs, furniture, and temporary or movable items (such as equipment and display racks): ibid, para 5.45. Physical features within the remit of a highway authority (such as street furniture) are covered where the highway authority is a service provider: ibid, para 5.47 (and example).

4   Disability Discrimination (Services and Premises) Regulations 1999, SI 1999/1191, reg 3; Rights of Access Code of Practice 2002, para 5.44.

5   Rights of Access Code of Practice 2002, paras 5.36–5.37 (and example).

6   Ibid, paras 5.36–5.37.

integrationist or inclusive. Although the Code of Practice encourages service providers to adopt an inclusive approach,[1] the Act appears to permit (but does not require) a 'separate but equal' or segregated approach to the provision of services to disabled persons. For example, if access to a museum is by a front entrance which could not be made accessible to wheelchair users without rebuilding or physical alteration, it might be reasonable for the museum trustees to provide a wheelchair-accessible entrance at the side or back of the building. However, such alternative means of access to the building might not be reasonable where the disabled visitor has to negotiate rubbish bins or other detritus in the process.[2] In such a case, physical alterations to the main entrance might be the only reasonable solution.

5.5.11 Regulations may exempt categories of service providers from the duty to make reasonable adjustments in respect of physical features only.[3] This power of exemption has not been used to date. If it was to be used in the future, then it is likely that it would be used to safeguard limited groups of service providers – such as occupiers of listed buildings[4] – who might otherwise be faced with a disproportionately heavy burden under s 21(2) of the DDA 1995 or for whom it would not be possible or sensible to make physical alterations.[5] Regulations make provision for the interplay between the building regulations, disability access standards for buildings and any duty to make an adjustment to the physical features of premises occupied by a service provider.[6]

5.5.12 This aspect of the duty to make reasonable adjustments calls for some imagination from service providers.[7] For example, a supermarket might reasonably consider whether the aisles between shelves or

---

1   Rights of Access Code of Practice 2002, paras 5.38–5.41. The DRC recommends that the DDA 1995 should require that when service providers make reasonable adjustments to their premises they must first consider removing or altering physical barriers, and only if this is not possible consider providing the service by an alternative means: DRC Legislative Review, recommendation 24.

2   HL Deb, vol 564, cols 2022–2023. Rights of Access Code of Practice 2002, paras 5.40 and 5.51–5.52 stress the dignity of disabled persons as a relevant consideration.

3   DDA 1995, s 21(3)(b).

4   Who might be generally protected, in any event, by DDA 1995, s 59 (acts done in compliance with existing enactments, such as listed buildings regulations). That said, there is no general exemption for listed buildings from the application of the s 21 duties: HL Deb, vol 564, cols 2021–2024.

5   HC Deb Standing Committee E, cols 358–359.

6   Disability Discrimination (Providers of Services) (Adjustment of Premises) Regulations 2001, SI 2001/3253, as amended by SI 2004/1429 (in force from 1 October 2004). See also Rights of Access Code of Practice 2002, paras 6.1–6.25, and the extended discussion in Chapter 6.

7   See the guidance and examples given in Rights of Access Code of Practice 2002, paras 5.48–5.52.

between the check-out tills are sufficiently wide to accommodate wheelchair users. A restaurant might consider how its seating arrangements are designed, while an art gallery might reconsider the height at which exhibits are hung, in both cases so as to accommodate diners or art lovers who are wheelchair users. Signage in public buildings is also counted as a physical feature and is often poorly designed or sited, without the needs of disabled persons in mind. The height and design of points of sale or service in stores, banks or post offices also frequently cause physical barriers between disabled customers and sales assistants. Lighting and ventilation in buildings is also regarded as a 'physical feature', so that the needs of persons with vision or respiratory impairments might call for reasonable adjustments to be made in these areas. Often very little effort or modification is required to remove or ameliorate the ill effects of physical barriers. Installing simple ramps or repositioning fixtures and fittings can often make a lot of difference for little or no expense. Other alterations might involve some cost, but with attendant benefits for all, as well as increased custom for the service provider. These might include widening entrance doors or installing two-way door hinges to assist wheelchair users, creating designated parking spaces for disabled customers or removing high pile, low density carpeting to aid the mobility of customers using a prosthesis or walking aid.

Auxiliary aids and services

5.5.13 Where an 'auxiliary aid or service' would enable disabled persons to make use of a service which a service provider provides (or is prepared to provide) to members of the public, it is the duty of the service provider to take such steps as it is reasonable, in all the circumstances of the case, for the service provider to have to take in order to provide the auxiliary aid or service in question.[1] Where an 'auxiliary aid or service' would facilitate the use by disabled persons of such a service, the duty also arises.[2] In either case, a failure to comply with the duty is an act of unlawful discrimination if its effect is to make it impossible or unreasonably difficult for the disabled person to make use of any goods, facilities or services.[3]

5.5.14 The term 'auxiliary aid or service' is exemplified by reference to the provision of information on audio tape or the provision of a sign

---

1   DDA 1995, s 21(4)(a). Note how the trigger for this duty differs from the duties in s 21(1) and (2).

2   Ibid, s 21(4)(b). See *Ross v Ryanair Ltd and Stansted Airport Ltd* [2004] EWCA Civ 1751, discussed at **8.5.2**.

3   Ibid, s 19(1)(b). In principle, the duty to provide auxiliary aids or services could be the subject of an expenditure cap formulated by regulations: s 21(7)–(9). No such cap has been introduced.

language interpreter.[1] Further illustrations include the provision of induction loops in theatres or cinemas, large print point of sale literature in shops or audio-visual telephones in hotel rooms for individuals with sensory impairments. However, in many cases, an auxiliary aid or service might amount to no more than the allocating of a particular member of staff to provide requested assistance to a disabled customer. For example, a blind customer in a self-service store might reasonably request that a store assistant should locate a particular item for purchase or should read out loud the description of goods from any product packaging. A training company organising a seminar for the legal profession would have to take reasonable steps to accommodate the known needs of disabled delegates attending the seminar (such as by providing a sign interpreter or a temporary induction loop system). It would need to choose the seminar location in a hotel or conference centre that was reasonably physically accessible for delegates with mobility disabilities.[2]

5.5.15 Until the balance of the duties in relation to reasonable adjustments and physical features came into force on 1 October 2004,[3] regulations provided that devices, structures or equipment – the installation, operation or maintenance of which would necessitate making a permanent alteration to (or which would have a permanent effect on) the physical fabric of premises, fixtures, fittings, furnishings, furniture, equipment or materials – were not to be treated as auxiliary aids or services.[4] The effect was that until 1 October 2004 service providers were not required to do (but were not prevented from doing) anything that would involve a permanent alteration to the physical fabric of premises (as broadly defined in the regulations) when providing an auxiliary aid.[5]

5.6 JUSTIFICATION

5.6.1 A provider of services discriminates against a disabled person in a case of disability-related less favourable treatment discrimination if it

---

1   DDA 1995, s 21(4). Future regulations may provide as to things which are to be treated, or which are not to be treated, as auxiliary aids or services: s 21(5)(g)–(h).

2   See the general advice and the further illustrations given in Rights of Access Code of Practice 2002, paras 5.10–5.30.

3   DDA 1995, s 21(2)(a)–(c).

4   Disability Discrimination (Services and Premises) Regulations 1999, SI 1999/1191, reg 4.

5   But see the positive advice on good practice given by Rights of Access Code of Practice 2002, para 5.15.

cannot show that the 'treatment in question is justified'.[1] Similarly, a
service provider also discriminates against a disabled person in a case
where it fails to comply with a duty to make reasonable adjustments in
relation to the disabled person if it cannot show that the 'failure to
comply with that duty is justified'.[2] The discriminatory treatment of a
disabled person (or a failure to comply with a duty to make reasonable
adjustments[3]) will be justified only if, in the service provider's opinion,
one or more statutory conditions are satisfied[4] and it is reasonable in all
the circumstances of the case for the service provider to hold that
opinion.[5]

5.6.2 This justification defence is a novel one.[6] First, discrimination
law in the fields of sex, race and equal pay (and fair employment in
Northern Ireland) does not contain an explicit justification defence to
direct discrimination (as opposed to indirect discrimination). Secondly, it might be argued that a justification defence is implicit in the
principle of direct discrimination, in the sense that a defendant can
always seek to show that the less favourable treatment complained of was
not based upon the protected characteristic of the claimant. However,
the justification defence is truly relevant only when the protected
characteristic of the claimant has played a part in the resultant
discrimination, but there are factors or criteria present which nevertheless excuse what would be otherwise discriminatory treatment, impacts
or effects. Under the DDA 1995, justification is relevant where a
disabled person has been treated less favourably 'for a reason which
relates to the disabled person's disability'.[7] In other words, a service
provider may be allowed to justify discrimination in circumstances
where the less favourable treatment has been informed by the complainant's disability. Thirdly, in existing discrimination legislation, the
justification defence in indirect discrimination is the subject of an

---

1   DDA 1995, s 20(1)(b); Rights of Access Code of Practice 2002, para 7.4.

2   Ibid, s 20(2)(b); Rights of Access Code of Practice 2002, paras 7.5–7.7.

3   Ibid, s 20(9) states that in s 20(3), (4) and (8) 'treatment' includes a failure to comply with
     a s 21 duty.

4   Ibid, s 20(3)(a).

5   Ibid, s 20(3)(b).

6   The DRTF recommends that the justification defence should be removed in the case of
     discrimination based upon a failure to comply with a duty to make reasonable adjustments
     and that the service provider should be able to rely only upon a set of expanded factors in
     the assessment of what is a 'reasonable' adjustment: DRTF Report, recommendation 6.7.
     The Government referred this question to the DRC: Government Response to DRTF
     Report, para 3.73. The DRC agrees with the DRTF: DRC Legislative Review,
     recommendation 31.

7   DDA 1995, s 20(1)(a).

objective test (albeit one of variable quality in the decided cases). Part 3 of the DDA 1995 bucks that trend.

5.6.3 The justification defence also differs significantly from the parallel defence in Part 2 of the DDA 1995 (the employment provisions). The Government's view was that 'service providers often have to take very quick and perhaps less informed decisions when serving someone [so that] an opinion-based approach remains appropriate'.[1] Unlike the employment provisions in Part 2 of the Act,[2] there is no suggestion that, in cases of less favourable treatment discrimination, a service provider cannot justify the treatment if a reasonable adjustment would have made a difference.[3] The Part 3 defence also exhaustively identifies the key reasons that might justify less favourable treatment of a disabled person by a service provider, whereas the defence is at large under Part 2.

Subjective opinion and objective reasonableness

5.6.4 The justification defence in Part 3 of the DDA 1995 is based upon a mixture of a subjective test and an objective test. While an opinion-based approach has been seen as appropriate, 'the proper degree of objectivity is imposed because the opinion must be shown to be reasonably held'.[4] The dual subjective–objective nature of the defence has also been recognised judicially.[5] The Rights of Access Code of Practice 2002 also emphasises this point, acknowledging that a service provider does not have to be an expert on disability, but is expected to take account of all the circumstances.[6]

5.6.5 The burden of proof is on the service provider. The service provider must be able to show that, *at the time of* the act of alleged discrimination, it actually held the opinion that one of the statutory

---

1   HL Deb, vol 566, col 119.

2   DDA 1995, s 5(5).

3   In an earlier edition of this book, the author attempted to suggest otherwise, but recanted that view in the last edition. The Rights of Access Code of Practice 2002 is largely silent on this point (but see paras 4.29, 7.13, 7.17, 7.20 and 7.23 on good practice).

4   HL Deb, vol 566, col 119.

5   *Rose v Bouchet* [1999] IRLR 463 (Sheriff Principal Nicholson QC), a case under the similar provisions in DDA 1995, s 24 (the justification defence for discrimination in the disposal or management of premises). The court did not think that assistance could be summoned from cases under Part 2 (the employment provisions).

6   Rights of Access Code of Practice 2002, para 7.8. The circumstances will include the available information, whether it was possible to seek advice, and whether the disabled person's input was sought and taken account of. However, the need to seek further information or make further inquiry will vary with the circumstances, and it might be reasonable to expect the disabled person to volunteer further information: *Rose v Bouchet* (above).

conditions for the operation of the defence was satisfied (a subjective test). The language and tense used in the statutory provision[1] make it clear that it is the service provider's opinion at the time of the discriminatory treatment that matters. An ex post facto rationalisation of events will not be sufficient or permissible.[2] In practice, the subjective test of opinion will not be difficult to pass. However, it must also be shown that it is reasonable, in all the circumstances of the case, for the service provider to hold that opinion (an objective test).[3] Again, the test of the reasonableness of the service provider's subjectively held opinion should be judged in the light of the circumstances known at the time of the discriminatory act.[4] The concept of reasonableness is one that tribunals and courts are very experienced in applying. However, it will not be the reasonableness of the opinion itself that matters. Rather the question is whether it was reasonable of the particular service provider to hold that opinion in the particular circumstances of the case and in respect of the particular disabled person who is the subject of the less favourable treatment (or failure to comply with a s 21 duty).[5]

Conditions for justification defence

5.6.6   The conditions, one or more of which (in the service provider's reasonably held opinion) must be satisfied for the operation of the statutory defence of justification, are set out exhaustively in the statute.[6] Some of these conditions apply generally, but some apply only in the context of particular forms of discrimination in relation to goods, facilities or services. The DDA 1995 contemplates five conditions or circumstances in which the justification defence might be operable.[7]

---

1   DDA 1995, s 20(3)(a).

2   This is confirmed in *Rose v Bouchet* (above). See also Rights of Access Code of Practice 2002, paras 7.8–7.10.

3   In *White v Clitheroe Royal Grammar School* (2002) Preston County Court (District Judge Ashton) reported in *Equal Opportunities Review No 106* (June 2002) 26–28, the court found that a student with diabetes was discriminated against contrary to DDA 1995, Part 3 when excluded from a school holiday for a reason connected with his disability and in circumstances where the school had failed to check the assumptions upon which the exclusion had been made, did not consult with the pupil or his parents, and carried out no risk assessment involving the holiday provider and the pupil's medical advisers.

4   DDA 1995, s 20(3)(b).

5   The wording of DDA 1995, s 20(3)(b) does not appear to admit a test of reasonableness based upon what a reasonable service provider faced with similar circumstances might have opined, although undoubtedly that will be a useful starting point.

6   DDA 1995, s 20(4).

7   The DRTF was generally content with the limited categories of justification available in Part 3 of the DDA 1995. It recommended that there should be better guidance to service providers on the appropriate use of the 'health and safety' and 'greater cost' justifications, and that the operation of the justification defence should be monitored: DRTF Report,

Health and safety

5.6.7 First, in any case, disability discrimination might be justified where the less favourable treatment (or failure to comply with a duty to make reasonable adjustments) is 'necessary' (not merely reasonably necessary) in order not to endanger the health or safety of any person.[1] This may include endangerment to the health or safety of the disabled person who is alleging discriminatory treatment. For example, a local authority recreation centre could be justified in refusing the use of its indoor climbing wall to a person with orthopaedic impairment, or in excluding a wheelchair user from its basketball league, on the ground of a risk to the health and safety of the individual or other participants. A swimming instructor might be justified in excluding a disabled person from a beginners' swimming class if, by having to focus most attention on the disabled learner, the safety of other members of the class would be put at risk.[2] It remains to be seen how narrowly this defence of justification will be interpreted and applied in practice. Health or safety risk is often relied upon by service providers as a blanket reason for excluding disabled persons from places of refreshment or entertainment (such as cinemas, theatres and restaurants). Inappropriate or unsupported reference is also frequently made to the requirements of fire regulations.[3] The use of the word 'necessary' calls for individual justification on the facts where a service provider seeks to rely upon health and safety as the grounds for compromising the civil rights of disabled persons.

---

recommendation 6.6. In its response, the Government recognised that in producing the 2002 version of the Code of Practice the DRC had already provided fuller guidance on the justifications (including those relating to health and safety and greater expense), but asked the DRC to review other guidance in the light of its monitoring of the justifications and developing case-law: Government Response to DRTF Report, para 3.75. The DRC has invited comments upon this issue: DRC Legislative Review, recommendation 26.

1   DDA 1995, s 20(4)(a). See *White v Clitheroe Royal Grammar School* (2002) Preston County Court (District Judge Ashton) reported in *Equal Opportunities Review No 106* (June 2002) 26–28 and referred to above.

2   HL Deb, vol 566, col 1025. See the further examples in Rights of Access Code of Practice 2002, paras 7.10–7.13. The revised Code of Practice stresses that health or safety reasons which are based on stereotypes or generalisations will provide no defence. Any action taken in relation to health and safety must be proportionate to the risk. Disabled persons are entitled to take risks within the same limits as other people.

3   Rights of Access Code of Practice 2002, para 7.12. Restrictions produced by genuine requirements of local fire regulations will excuse otherwise discriminatory treatment by virtue of s 59 (actions done in pursuance of a statutory authority).

Incapacity to contract

5.6.8 Secondly, in any case, the less favourable treatment of a disabled person (or failure to comply with a duty to make reasonable adjustments) can be justified if the disabled person is incapable of entering into an enforceable agreement, or of giving an informed consent, and for that reason the treatment (or failure) is reasonable in that case.[1] This provision generated some concern on behalf of persons with mental disabilities who, it was feared, might suffer discrimination in the provision of services on the basis of a service provider's perception that they lacked full legal capacity to make a contract. The Government's view was that:

> 'If a service provider has a reasonably held belief that a contract with a disabled customer might be invalid, he must be allowed, under this measure, to refuse to enter into an agreement until it is reasonably clear that it would be enforceable, without the fear of being accused of discrimination.'[2]

That would allow a service provider to refuse to sell goods to, or to enter into a consumer credit agreement with, a disabled person if it holds a reasonably held opinion that the customer lacks or might lack legal capacity (whether by virtue of age or mental incapacity). The test here is whether it is reasonable to discriminate within the particular circumstances of the case.[3] The Government believed that this justification would only apply when the purchase of a product or service would normally be the subject of a written agreement or contract formality. It would thus apply in only a few cases (such as motor car hire purchase or consumer credit agreements).[4]

5.6.9 Regulations have been made to disapply this provision where another person is acting for the disabled person under an enduring power of attorney[5] or where, in Scotland, a curator bonis, tutor or judicial factor has been appointed in relation to the disabled person's property or affairs.[6]

---

1   DDA 1995, s 20(4)(b); Rights of Access Code of Practice 2002, paras 7.14–7.17.

2   HC Deb Standing Committee E, col 349.

3   HC Deb, vol 257, col 893.

4   Ibid, col 350. It remains to be seen whether such cases are few (but what of contracts for holidays, which are typically made on written standard form conditions, for example, or car rental agreements?). It was doubted whether it would be reasonable for a shopkeeper to rely upon this exception when someone is buying a newspaper or confectionery (as opposed to a luxury car).

5   Or functions conferred by or under Mental Health Act 1983, Part VII.

6   DDA 1995, s 20(7); Disability Discrimination (Services and Premises) Regulations 1996, reg 8; Rights of Access Code of Practice, para 6.15. By virtue of Adults with Incapacity (Scotland) Act 2000, s 88(2) and Sch 5, para 1, the references in DDA 1995, s 20(7) to a

Providing the service

5.6.10 Thirdly, where disability discrimination takes the form of a refusal (or deliberate omission) to provide to a disabled person any goods, facilities or services provided to members of the public,[1] such less favourable treatment (or failure to comply with a duty to make reasonable adjustments) might be justified if it is 'necessary' (not merely reasonably necessary) because the service provider would otherwise be unable to provide the goods, facilities or services to members of the public.[2] The 1995 White Paper gave as an example that it would no longer be possible to bar disabled persons from places of entertainment, but a coach training champion athletes would still be able to exclude the majority of the population from coaching classes.[3] The Government believed that it had introduced a strict test for the application of this defence and that it would apply 'only in circumstances in which, if a service provider were to serve a particular disabled person, he would not be able to continue to provide his service at all'.[4] However, the preferences of other customers are not a justification for discrimination.[5]

Standard of service

5.6.11 Fourthly, in a case where the discriminatory treatment (or failure to comply with a duty to make reasonable adjustments) arises in the standard of service provided to disabled persons, or the manner in which or terms on which the service provider provides goods, facilities or services to disabled persons,[6] that treatment may be justified if it is 'necessary' (not merely reasonably necessary) in order for the service provider to be able to provide the service to the disabled person or to other members of the public.[7] This is clearly linked to the third condition above and is likely to apply in exactly the same way, if at all. By way of illustration, a cinema which reserves seats at the end of rows for persons with mobility disabilities might rely upon this provision to justify

---

'curator bonis' or 'tutor' are to be construed as references to a 'guardian' with similar powers appointed under the 2000 Act.

1   Under DDA 1995, s 19(1)(a).

2   DDA 1995, s 20(4)(c); Rights of Access Code of Practice 2002, paras 7.18–7.20.

3   1995 White Paper, para 4.4, and see the examples in Rights of Access Code of Practice 2002, paras 7.18–7.19.

4   HC Deb Standing Committee E, col 354. The Minister could not think of a meaningful example of when this provision would be applicable and his opinion was that it would only apply in extreme and rare circumstances.

5   Rights of Access Code of Practice 2002, para 7.19.

6   Under DDA 1995, s 19(1)(c)–(d).

7   Ibid, s 20(4)(d); Rights of Access Code of Practice 2002, paras 7.21–7.23.

what might amount to a differential standard or manner or service. Without making such arrangements, the cinema might argue that it could not admit such a disabled person at all without infringing fire regulations or otherwise causing greater inconvenience to other customers. Similarly, a museum which provides a daily guided tour of its exhibits might be justified in rostering a guide with sign language skills to assist deaf visitors on specified days of the week only.[1]

Greater cost

5.6.12 Fifthly, if the service provider has discriminated in the terms on which goods, facilities or services are provided to a disabled person,[2] that discrimination is capable of being justified where the difference in such terms as between that disabled person and other members of the public 'reflects the greater cost' to the service provider in providing the goods, facilities or services to the disabled person.[3] The Government indicated that this measure is aimed at small businesses, in particular, and gave as an example a shoe maker asked to make a shoe for a disabled person to an unusual design or in an unusual fabric.[4] If that task would involve greater labour or special equipment and materials, it might be reasonable for the shoe maker to charge the disabled customer a premium to reflect that.

5.6.13 Taken literally, however, this last condition might be thought to justify a hotelier charging a disabled person a room supplement for providing him or her with a room adapted to take a wheelchair or with an audio-visual fire alarm. It might also be taken to justify a service provider charging blind customers for the additional cost of providing Braille or tape formats of sales literature and so on. Nevertheless, a service provider who attempts to pass on the costs of compliance with the DDA 1995 to disabled persons (as opposed to spreading those costs across all customers or clients) would not be facilitated in doing so by this provision.[5] The DDA 1995 does not permit surcharges upon disabled persons for extra expenses or opportunity costs incurred by service providers in complying with the legislation. Moreover, the Act explicitly provides that any increase in the cost of providing services to a disabled person, resulting from the service provider's compliance with the statutory duty to make reasonable adjustments, is to be disregarded

---

1   See the further examples in Rights of Access Code of Practice 2002, paras 7.21–7.22.

2   Under DDA 1995, s 19(1)(d).

3   Ibid, s 20(4)(e); Rights of Access Code of Practice 2002, paras 7.24–7.25.

4   HC Deb Standing Committee E, col 357; HL Deb, vol 564, col 2009.

5   HC Deb Standing Committee E, col 357.

for the purposes of the 'greater cost' justification.[1] A service provider is not able to pass the costs of complying with its duties under the DDA 1995 directly to a disabled customer.[2]

Insurance services

5.6.14 The DDA 1995 contemplates that regulations might be made so as to provide for other circumstances in which less favourable treatment of a disabled person for a reason relating to disability could be deemed to be justified.[3] Regulations address the circumstances where, for a reason which relates to a disabled person's disability, a provider of insurance services (in connection with an insurance business[4] carried on by it) has treated a disabled person less favourably than it treats or would treat others to whom that reason does not or would not apply.[5] That treatment is to be taken as justified if it is based upon information which is relevant to the assessment of the risk to be insured and if it is reasonable having regard to the information relied upon and any other relevant factors.[6] The information, which might include actuarial or statistical data or a medical report, must be from a source upon which it is reasonable to rely.[7] This recognises that insurers may need to distinguish between individuals on the basis of the risks against which they seek to insure. The burden of proof will be upon the insurer to show that there was an additional risk associated with the disabled person which arises from his or her disability.[8]

---

1   DDA 1995, s 20(5); Rights of Access Code of Practice 2002, paras 4.30–4.31 and 7.25.

2   HL Deb, vol 564, cols 2009–2010; ibid, vol 566, col 119.

3   DDA 1995, s 20(8).

4   Within the meaning of the Insurance Companies Act 1982.

5   Disability Discrimination (Services and Premises) Regulations 1996, SI 1996/1836, regs 1(2), 2(1) and (2)(a). See generally Rights of Access Code of Practice 2002, paras 8.2–8.8. The DRTF recommended that the special treatment of insurance services should continue: DRTF Report, recommendation 6.19.

6   Disability Discrimination (Services and Premises) Regulations 1996, SI 1996/1836, reg 2(1) and (2)(b)–(c).

7   Ibid, reg 2(2)(b).

8   Transitional provision is made for insurance policies incepted before 2 December 1996: ibid, regs 1(2) and 3(4). Any treatment in relation to an insurance policy which existed before that date is taken to be justified until that policy falls for renewal or review (except as part of a general reassessment of the pricing structure for a group of policies) on or after that date: reg 3(2) and (3). Then it falls to be treated under s 20 and reg 2. Transitional provisions are also made in respect of cover documents and master policies: reg 4.

Guarantees

5.6.15 Regulations also deal with guarantees where, for a reason which relates to a disabled person's disability, a service provider treats that person less favourably in respect of a guarantee than it treats or would treat others to whom that reason does not or would not apply.[1] The guarantee, whether legally enforceable or not, must have been provided by the service provider. It must guarantee that the purchase price of services provided will be refunded if not of satisfactory quality or that services in the form of goods provided will be replaced or repaired if not of satisfactory quality.[2] The service provider must have refused to provide a replacement, repair or refund under the guarantee because damage (above the level at which the guarantee would normally be honoured) has occurred for a reason which relates to the disabled person's disability.[3] It must be reasonable in all the circumstances of the case for the service provider to refuse to provide a replacement, repair or refund under the guarantee.[4] If all these conditions are satisfied, the less favourable treatment is deemed to be automatically justified.[5] Accordingly, this provision deals with situations where a disabled person's disability results in higher than average wear or tear to goods or services supplied and where it would not be reasonable to expect service providers to honour a guarantee.[6]

Deposits

5.6.16 Regulations also deal with the question of deposits in respect of goods and facilities.[7] The circumstances in which this special provision operates are as follows. Goods or facilities have been provided to a disabled person for which that person is required to provide a deposit which is refundable if the goods or facilities are returned undamaged.[8] The service provider has refused to refund some or all of the deposit because damage has occurred to the goods or facilities for a reason which relates to the disabled person's disability.[9] That damage is above

---

1   Disability Discrimination (Services and Premises) Regulations 1996, SI 1996/1836, reg 5(1).

2   Ibid, reg 5(2)(a). A guarantee includes any document which has the effect referred to in reg 5(2)(a), whether or not so described: reg 5(3).

3   Ibid, reg 5(2)(b).

4   Ibid, reg 5(2)(c).

5   Ibid, reg 5(1).

6   See generally Rights of Access Code of Practice 2002, paras 8.9–8.13.

7   Disability Discrimination (Services and Premises) Regulations 1996, SI 1996/1836, reg 6.

8   Ibid, reg 6(2)(a).

9   Ibid, reg 6(2)(b).

the level at which the provider would normally refund the deposit in full.[1] If it is reasonable in all the circumstances of the case for the service provider to refuse to repay the deposit in full,[2] then that less favourable treatment (for a reason related to disability) is deemed to be justified.[3]

5.7 EMPLOYMENT SERVICES

5.7.1 The Disability Discrimination Act 1995 (Amendment) Regulations 2003 insert a new s 21A as part of Part 3 of the DDA 1995 in order to address disability discrimination in relation to employment services.[4] For this purpose, 'employment services' means vocational guidance or training. It also refers to services to assist a person to obtain or retain employment or to establish that person as self-employed.[5] It will include services provided by employment agencies, employment businesses and Jobcentre Plus.[6]

5.7.2 In relation to employment services, it is unlawful for a provider of employment services to subject to harassment a disabled person to whom the provider is providing such services or who has requested the provider to provide such services.[7] Otherwise, the provisions on discrimination in relation to goods, facilities and services in ss 19–21, already discussed above, apply to employment services.[8] However, there are some adjustments to those provisions as they apply to employment services only.

5.7.3 A bespoke s 19(1)(aa) provides that it is unlawful for a provider of employment services to discriminate against a disabled person in failing to comply with a s 21(1) duty to make reasonable adjustments (ie to practices, policies or procedures) in circumstances in which the effect of that failure is to place the disabled person at a substantial disadvantage in comparison with persons who are not disabled in

---

1 Disability Discrimination (Services and Premises) Regulations 1996, SI 1996/1836, reg 6(2)(b).

2 Ibid, reg 6(2)(c).

3 Ibid, reg 6(1). See generally Rights of Access Code of Practice 2002, paras 8.14–8.19.

4 SI 2003/1673, regs 3(1), 19(1) and in force from 1 October 2004. See generally Code of Practice: Employment and Occupation (2004), chapter 11.

5 DDA 1995, s 21A(1).

6 Code of Practice: Employment and Occupation (2004), para 11.4.

7 DDA 1995, s 21A(2). Section 3B (which defines 'harassment' in the context of the employment provisions in Part 2 of the Act) applies for this purpose. See Chapter 3. See generally Code of Practice: Employment and Occupation (2004), para 11.8 (and example).

8 DDA 1995, s 21A(3).

relation to the provision of the service.[1] An amended s 19(1)(b) also applies (only for this purpose and not generally), making it unlawful for a provider of employment services to discriminate against a disabled person in failing to comply with s 21(2) or (4) duty to make reasonable adjustments (ie in relation to physical features or an auxiliary aid or service) in circumstances in which the effect of that failure is to make it impossible or unreasonably difficult for the disabled person to make use of any such service.[2]

5.7.4 In defining discrimination in this contest,[3] a bespoke s 20(1A) then provides that, for the purposes of s 19, a provider of services also discriminates against a disabled person if the provider fails to comply with a s 21(1) duty to make reasonable adjustments (ie to practices, policies or procedures) in relation to the disabled person.[4] Section 20(2)(a) is to be read as referring to the s 21(2) and (4) duties (ie in relation to physical features or an auxiliary aid or service).[5] A new s 20(3A) is then read down to provide that the treatment of a disabled person cannot be justified under s 20(3) if it amounts to direct discrimination.[6]

5.7.5 The duty to make reasonable adjustments in s 21(1) is then modified in relation to employment services only.[7] Where a provider of employment services has a practice, policy or procedure which places disabled persons at a substantial disadvantage in comparison with persons who are not disabled in relation to the provision of the service which the provider provides (or is prepared to provide) to other members of the public, it is the provider's duty to take such steps as it is reasonable, in all the circumstances of the case, for the provider to have to take in order to change that practice, policy or procedure so that it no

---

1 DDA 1995, s 21A(4)(a). Section 19(2) is read as including a reference to s 21A: s 21A(4)(c). See generally Code of Practice: Employment and Occupation (2004), paras 11.5–11.7 (and examples).

2 DDA 1995, s 21A(4)(b). Section 19(2) is read as including a reference to s 21A: s 21A(4)(c).

3 See Code of Practice: Employment and Occupation (2004), paras 11.11–11.14. Note that the provisions of the DDA 1995 on relationships that have come to an end (s 16A), discriminatory advertisements (s 16B), unlawful instructions and pressure to discriminate (s 16C) and victimisation (s 55) will apply equally to employment services. See Code of Practice: Employment and Occupation (2004), para 11.10.

4 DDA 1995, s 21A(5)(a).

5 Ibid, s 21A(5)(b).

6 Ibid, s 21A(5)(c). Direct discrimination is defined in the DDA 1995, falling within s 3A(5). See Chapter 3. See Code of Practice: Employment and Occupation (2004), paras 11.20–11.22.

7 See Code of Practice: Employment and Occupation (2004), paras 11.15–11.19 (and examples).

longer has that effect.[1] A bespoke s 21(1A) then provides that a 'practice, policy or procedure' includes a provision or criterion for this purpose.[2]

5.7.6 Normally, any term in a contract for the provision of goods, facilities or services (or in any other agreement) is void in so far as it purports to require a person to do anything which would contravene Part 3 or which would exclude or limit the operation of Part 3 or prevent any person from making a claim under Part 3.[3] However, that is not the case in relation to any term in a contract (or other agreement) for the provision of employment services.[4]

5.8 ENFORCEMENT, REMEDIES AND PROCEDURES

5.8.1 A claim of unlawful discrimination in relation to the provision of goods, facilities or services under Part 3 of the DDA 1995 is the subject of civil proceedings for tort in the county court (in England and Wales or Northern Ireland) or in reparation for breach of a statutory duty in the sheriff court (in Scotland).[5] The usual remedy will be damages (including injury to feelings),[6] but a claimant (or pursuer) might also seek a declaration or an injunction.[7] The question of enforcement procedures and remedies is considered in more detail in Chapter 10.

5.8.2 However, the usual enforcement provisions applying to Part 3 cases do not apply to employment services claims falling under s 21A.[8] These claims may be presented as a complaint to an employment tribunal.[9]

---

1   DDA 1995, s 21A(6)(a).

2   Ibid, s 21A(6)(b).

3   Ibid, s 26(1).

4   Ibid, s 26(1A), inserted by the Disability Discrimination Act 1995 (Amendment) Regulations 2003, SI 2003/1673, regs 3(1) and 19(3) (in force from 1 October 2004).

5   Ibid, s 25(1), (3) and (4). The modification of s 25 for Northern Ireland is achieved in Sch 8, para 12.

6   Ibid, s 25(2). An upper limit to compensation may be prescribed under Sch 3, para 7. No such cap on compensation has been set to date.

7   Ibid, s 25(5).

8   Ibid, s 25(7) as amended by the Disability Discrimination Act 1995 (Amendment) Regulations 2003, SI 2003/1673, regs 3(1) and 19(2) (in force from 1 October 2004).

9   Ibid, s 25(8). Section 17A(1A)–(7) and Sch 3, paras 3–4 apply in relation to such a complaint as if it were a complaint under s 17A(1) (and Sch 3, paras 6–8 do not apply in relation to such a complaint): s 25(9). See Code of Practice: Employment and Occupation (2004), para 11.23.

5.9 DISABILITY DISCRIMINATION BILL

Public authorities and police

5.9.1 If enacted, the Disability Discrimination Bill will ensure that (with some exceptions) functions of public authorities not already covered by the DDA 1995 will be brought within the scope of Part 3.[1] It would be unlawful for a public authority, without justification, to discriminate against a disabled person when exercising its functions. The Bill also introduces a new duty on public authorities, requiring them, when exercising their functions, to have due regard to the need to eliminate unlawful discrimination against and harassment of disabled persons, and to promote equality of opportunity between disabled persons and other persons.[2] The Bill also clarifies who the correct defendant is in the case of a claim of discrimination being made against a police officer under Part 3 and authorises payment of compensation from the police fund in relation to such a claim. These provisions are dealt with further in Chapter 9 below.

Transport services

5.9.2 The Bill prospectively removes the existing exclusion of transport services from Part 3 of the DDA 1995 and replaces it with a more precise exclusion relating only to transport services consisting of the provision and use of a vehicle. A regulation-making power will enable such services to be brought within the scope of Part 3 in the future, in whole or in part to different transport vehicles at different times. Transport services which involve the provision or use of a vehicle will also be excluded from the duty to provide adjustments. It will not be reasonable for the service provider to have to take steps which would involve altering or removing a physical feature of a transport vehicle. It also specifies that it will not be reasonable to require a transport operator to have to take steps affecting whether vehicles are provided or what type of vehicle is provided, or to have to take steps affecting the services provided within a vehicle. However, future regulations may disapply these exclusions so as to enable them to be lifted in respect of different types of vehicle at different times. Regulations will enable the exclusion to be lifted for particular types of service within generic modes of transport at different times.

---

1   See Department for Work and Pensions, *Delivering Equality for Disabled People: A Consultation on the Extension of the Disability Discrimination Act to Functions of Public Authorities and the Introduction of a Duty to Promote Equality for Disabled People*, Cm 6255 (July 2004).

2   See the Disability Rights Commission's draft Code of Practice, *The Duty of Promote Disability Equality: Statutory Code of Practice*, which has been published for consultation in support of this provision. Separate versions are proposed for England and Wales and for Scotland.

Private clubs

5.9.3 If enacted, the Disability Discrimination Bill will make it unlawful for associations with 25 or more members to discriminate against disabled members, applicants for membership, associates and guests in certain circumstances. This will apply to any incorporated or unincorporated association with 25 or more members where admission to membership is regulated by its constitution (which may be written or oral) and is so conducted that its members do not constitute a section of the general public. This means that an association must operate a genuine policy of membership selection based on personal criteria so as to distinguish between members of the association and members of the public. A club which does not operate such a policy of membership selection is already covered by Part 3 of the DDA 1995 where it provides services to the public or a section of the public (whether for profit or not). The Bill sets out the circumstances in which an act of discrimination by an association will be unlawful against: an applicant for membership; a member or associate of the association; a guest of the association; and an intended guest of the association.

5.9.4 A disabled applicant for membership will be protected from discrimination in relation to a refusal by a club to admit him or her as a member or the terms on which membership is granted. Discrimination against a disabled member or a disabled associate will be prohibited in relation to the way in which he or she is granted access to a benefit, facility or service provided by the club; where he or she is refused access to a benefit, facility or service; where he or she is deprived of membership or his or her rights as an associate; where his or her terms of membership or rights as an associate are varied; or where he or she is subjected to any other detriment. A further provision would prohibit discrimination by an association against a disabled guest in the way in which the guest is afforded access to a benefit, facility or service provided by the club; where he or she is refused access to a benefit, facility or service; or where the guest is subjected to any other detriment. An association will also be prevented from discriminating against a disabled person where the association (or one of its members or associates) intends to invite him or her to be a guest of the association. It will be unlawful for an association to discriminate against a disabled person in the terms on which it is prepared to invite the person (or permit him or her to be invited by a member or associate) to be a guest of the association; by refusing or deliberately omitting to invite him to be a guest; or by refusing to grant a member or associate permission to invite him or her as a guest. An association cannot avoid liability for discriminating against a disabled person by omitting to invite him or her, or by refusing or withdrawing an invitation by one of its members or associates, to an event to which he or she would have been invited but for his or her disability.

5.9.5   The Bill will also make it unlawful for an association to discriminate against a disabled person by failing to comply with any duty to make reasonable adjustments imposed on the association by regulations to be made. Discrimination (and the defences to it) is broadly defined in a manner similar to that found elsewhere in Part 3. An association also discriminates against a disabled person if it fails to comply with a duty to make adjustments imposed on it and it cannot show that such a failure is justified. The Secretary of State will be empowered to make regulations prescribing the circumstances in which associations will be under a duty to make reasonable adjustments (which could include the alteration of physical features or the provision of an auxiliary aid).[1]

---

1   See Department of Work and Pensions, *Disability Discrimination Bill: Consultation on private clubs; premises; the definition of disability; and the questions procedure,* Cm 6402 (December 2004).

Chapter 6

PROPERTY, PREMISES AND LEASES

6.1 INTRODUCTION

6.1.1   Part 3 of the DDA 1995 also makes it unlawful for landlords and other persons who are disposing of or selling property to discriminate against a disabled person.[1] While it is not thought that discrimination against disabled persons is as widespread as racial discrimination once was in the property market, the Government felt sufficiently moved by at least one case of landlord discrimination against a disabled person to introduce an amendment to the DDA 1995 during its progress as a Bill.[2] As the provisions on discrimination in relation to premises are a free-standing part of Part 3 of the Act, they warrant separate treatment in this chapter. However, much of the terminology used in relation to property discrimination echoes many of the concepts used elsewhere in the DDA 1995. Accordingly, decisions reached and precedents made in respect of other sections will be influential and of assistance in the interpretation of the law on discrimination in respect of premises.

6.1.2   The DDA 1995 also makes provision for the position where employers, trade organisations and service providers occupy premises under the terms of a lease. It was recognised that such parties might find it difficult to discharge a duty to make reasonable adjustments for disabled persons, especially in respect of the physical features of premises, where the lease or the landlord prevented or hindered such adjustments. Accordingly, both Part 2 and Part 3 adjust the respective rights of the landlord and tenant to a commercial lease so as to accommodate the duties to make adjustments to premises. However, there is no duty to make reasonable adjustments in relation to the letting, disposal or management of premises. As these provisions affect property interests, they are logically dealt with in this chapter.

---

1   DDA 1995, ss 22–24 (in force since 2 December 1996). These provisions mirror similar measures in the sex and race discrimination statutes, although they are not in identical terms: SDA 1975, ss 30–32; RRA 1976, ss 21–24. See generally Rights of Access Code of Practice 2002, Chapter 9.

2   HC Deb Standing Committee E, col 453.

6.2   DISCRIMINATION IN RELATION TO PREMISES

6.2.1   The DDA 1995 makes it unlawful for 'a person with power to dispose of any premises' to discriminate against a disabled person in one of a number of ways.[1] It is also unlawful for 'a person managing any premises' to discriminate against a disabled person 'occupying those premises' in a similar fashion.[2] Furthermore, the legislation deals with discrimination which arises by the withholding of a licence or consent required for the disposal of premises to a disabled person.[3]

Unlawful acts of discrimination

6.2.2   First, it is unlawful to discriminate 'in the terms' on which a person with power to dispose of premises offers to dispose of those premises to a disabled person.[4] For example, a landlord cannot seek to charge a higher rent for premises to a disabled tenant than the landlord would otherwise charge to a non-disabled lessee.

6.2.3   Secondly, it is unlawful to discriminate where a person with power to dispose of premises refuses to dispose of those premises to a disabled person.[5] This is a self-evident measure designed to prevent a disabled person from being denied the right to own a legal interest in property solely because of a disability. It is analogous with the illegitimacy of a property owner's action in refusing to sell or lease property to a member of an ethnic minority. It does not prevent the property owner from refusing to dispose of the property to a disabled person for reasons unconnected with that person's disability (for example, their inability to meet the purchase price or evidence that as a tenant they would be a bad credit risk).

6.2.4   Thirdly, it is unlawful for a person with power to dispose of any premises to discriminate against a disabled person in his or her 'treatment' of that disabled person 'in relation to any list of persons in need of premises of that description'.[6] This prohibition most obviously addresses discrimination against disabled persons in relation to housing association or local authority housing lists or those of private letting

---

1   DDA 1995, s 22(1). See Rights of Access Code of Practice 2002, paras 9.1–9.4. The meaning of discrimination in this context is set out in s 24. See Rights of Access Code of Practice 2002, para 9.5.

2   Ibid, s 22(3).

3   Ibid, s 22(4).

4   Ibid, s 22(1)(a); Rights of Access Code of Practice 2002, paras 9.12–9.13.

5   Ibid, s 22(1)(b); Rights of Access Code of Practice 2002, para 9.14.

6   Ibid, s 22(1)(c); Rights of Access Code of Practice 2002, para 9.15.

agencies. For example, a refusal to include a disabled person on a housing list, or the removal of that person from such a list, or a failure to accord that person proper priority in accordance with their ranking on the list might all be acts of unlawful discrimination. Similarly, allocating less desirable property to a disabled person on a housing list where a non-disabled person is more favourably treated would constitute a likely act of discrimination.[1]

6.2.5 Fourthly, it is unlawful for a person managing any premises to discriminate against a disabled person occupying those premises 'in the way' the person managing the premises 'permits the disabled person to make use of any benefits or facilities' or by 'refusing or deliberately omitting' to permit the disabled person to make use of any benefits or facilities.[2] Inclusion of a person managing any premises clearly broadens the scope of this provision which is not solely concerned with discrimination by property owners. A property management agency, accommodation agency, housekeeper, estate agent or rent collection service could all constitute parties who might be liable under this provision (and those that follow below).[3] The terms 'benefits or facilities' are not defined and there is no express intention to include 'services' within these terms. However, the Code of Practice indicates that benefits or facilities include, for example, laundry facilities, access to a garden and parking facilities.[4]

6.2.6 Fifthly, it is unlawful for a person managing any premises to discriminate against a disabled person occupying those premises by 'evicting' the disabled person or by 'subjecting him [or her] to any other detriment'.[5] This does not prohibit the eviction of a disabled tenant in accordance with a lawful process where, for example, the disabled person has failed to pay rent or has breached the terms of the tenancy. Instead, it provides a disabled tenant, who has been evicted by a manager of premises because of a reason related to disability, an additional cause of action apart from any available under the law of

---

1   The DDA 1995 does not prohibit more favourable treatment or positive action in respect of disabled persons and housing lists.

2   DDA 1995, s 22(3)(a) and (b); Rights of Access Code of Practice 2002, para 9.25.

3   Rights of Access Code of Practice 2002, paras 9.23–9.24.

4   Ibid, para 9.25. For example, a property management agency, managing a residential block of flats on behalf of a landlord, may not discriminate by refusing a disabled tenant access to benefits or facilities, such as common garden or recreational areas.

5   DDA 1995, s 22(3)(c); Rights of Access Code of Practice 2002, paras 9.26–9.27. The Court of Appeal in *Council of the City of Manchester v Romano and Samari* [2004] EWCA Civ 834 considered the example at para 9.26 as inept in the context of the law relating to residential tenancies, but agreed that, if a landlord wished to obtain possession for a breach of tenancy agreement that has been committed for reasons relating to a disabled tenant's disability, the landlord will have to show that the action is justified under s 24.

landlord and tenant. The provision also obviously addresses harassment of a disabled tenant by the person managing the premises.

6.2.7 Finally, it is unlawful for any person 'whose licence or consent is required' for the disposal of any premises 'comprised in . . . a tenancy' to discriminate against a disabled person by withholding that licence or consent for the disposal of the premises to the disabled person.[1] In Scotland, this prohibition applies in respect of the disposal of any premises 'the subject of' a tenancy. This subsection applies to tenancies created before or after the passing of the DDA 1995.[2]

Person with power to dispose of any premises

6.2.8 The phrase 'a person with power to dispose of any premises'[3] is not defined in the DDA 1995. However, the word 'dispose' is defined,[4] and by this circuitous route some light can be cast upon the class of person whose potentially unlawful actions constitute the mischief at which this part of the Act is aimed. A person with the power to dispose of premises includes a person who has the power to grant a right to occupy the premises.[5] Where the premises are comprised in or the subject of a tenancy, the relevant party will be the person with the power to assign the tenancy or to sub-let or part with possession of the premises or any part of them. The Act thus covers both the sale and lease of premises and, by implication, any other form of legal disposal (for example, by licence).[6]

6.2.9 The DDA 1995 does not automatically apply to private occupiers disposing of premises by private agreement or transaction.[7] This is because the statutory provisions preventing discrimination against

---

1   DDA 1995, s 22(4); Rights of Access Code of Practice 2002, para 9.29.

2   DDA 1995, s 22(5).

3   As used in ibid, s 22(1).

4   In ibid, s 22(6), and see Rights of Access Code of Practice 2002, para 9.7.

5   This does not include the hire of premises or the booking of rooms in hotels or guest houses (which would be covered by the services provisions of DDA 1995, ss 19–21): Rights of Access Code of Practice 2002, para 9.7. The boundary between ss 22–24 and ss 19–21 will not always be clear.

6   *Quaere* whether the statute is also concerned with the disposal of premises by the operation of the law of succession or insolvency law.

7   See generally, Rights of Access Code of Practice 2002, paras 9.10–9.11. The DRTF saw no reason to interfere with this exemption. See *From Exclusion to Inclusion: A Report of the Disability Rights Task Force for Disabled People* (1999, London: DfEE) (DRTF Report), recommendation 6.23. The Government asked the DRC to keep this question under review: *Towards Inclusion – Civil Rights for Disabled People: Government Response to the Disability Rights Task Force* (2001, London: DfEE) (Government Response to DRTF Report), para 3.73.

disabled persons by a person with a power to dispose of premises do not apply to 'a person who owns an estate or interest in premises *and wholly occupies them*', unless further conditions are satisfied.[1] So the statute does not make any discrimination against a disabled person unlawful where a person with the power to dispose of premises is the owner (or owns a legal interest in the premises), wholly occupies the premises, and disposes of the premises by private agreement. However, the statutory prohibitions will still apply if such a person uses the services of an estate agent[2] or publishes an advertisement (or causes an advertisement to be published)[3] for the purpose of disposing of the premises.[4] That would cease to be a disposal by a purely private agreement.

Premises and tenancy

6.2.10 The term 'premises' is not statutorily defined.[5] Nevertheless, the ordinary or literal meaning of the word 'premises' suggests that the DDA 1995 is concerned with legal and equitable interests in houses, lands, tenements and buildings, while the Act makes no apparent distinction between commercial and non-commercial (or domestic) property. Thus the DDA 1995 would appear to cover, for example, dwelling-houses, office blocks, flats, bed-sits, factory premises, industrial or commercial sites, agricultural land and so on – in other words, real property of any description.[6] The Act also clearly impinges upon the law of landlord and tenant.[7] A 'tenancy' means a tenancy created by a lease or sub-lease, by an agreement for a lease or sub-lease, by a tenancy agreement, or in pursuance of any 'enactment' (for example, a statutory tenancy).[8]

---

1   DDA 1995, s 22(2) (emphasis added) for the purposes of s 22(1).

2   An 'estate agent' for this purpose is a person carrying on the trade or profession of providing services 'for the purpose of finding premises for persons seeking to acquire them or assisting in the disposal of premises': DDA 1995, s 22(6). That definition would appear to be wide enough to include not only an estate agent per se, but also an accommodation bureau or agency.

3   An 'advertisement' includes every form of advertisement or notice, whether to the public or not: DDA 1995, s 22(6). So the circulation to a small or select number of persons of the details of premises for disposal would constitute an advertisement of the premises and would trigger the provisions prohibiting discrimination against disabled persons in the subsequent disposal.

4   DDA 1995, s 22(2) (these are the further conditions referred to above).

5   Except to the extent that s 68(1) of the DDA 1995 indicates that premises include land of any description and s 22(8) makes it clear that the Act is only concerned with premises in the UK.

6   Rights of Access Code of Practice 2002, para 9.8.

7   DDA 1995, s 22 obviously and expressly applies to the granting of tenancies, their assignment and the right to sub-let.

8   Ibid, ss 22(6) and 68(1); Rights of Access Code of Practice 2002, para 9.9.

Exemption for small dwellings

6.2.11 Where certain cumulative conditions are satisfied, there is a statutory exemption[1] for small dwellings in respect of the provisions prohibiting discrimination against disabled persons in the disposal or management of premises[2] or by the withholding of a licence or consent for the disposal of premises.[3] The exemption is likely to apply to a multi-occupancy residential building with shared accommodation.[4] A necessary but not sufficient condition for the operation of this exemption is that the premises must be 'small premises'.[5] Premises are 'small premises' if there is not normally residential accommodation on the premises for more than six persons in addition to the relevant occupier and any members of the relevant occupier's household.[6] Alternatively, premises are 'small premises' if the premises satisfy four conditions:[7]

- only the relevant occupier and members of his or her household reside in the accommodation occupied by him or her;
- in addition to the accommodation occupied by the relevant occupier, the premises must comprise residential accommodation for at least one other household;
- the residential accommodation for each other household must be let (or available for letting) on a separate tenancy or similar agreement; and
- there must be not normally more than two such other households.

For example, a large house where the basement and an annex have been converted into self-contained residential dwellings or flats would satisfy these conditions if the owner also resides on the premises and there is an element of shared accommodation (other than for storage or access purposes).

---

1   DDA 1995, s 23(1). See generally Rights of Access Code of Practice 2002, paras 9.16–9.22, 9.28 and 9.30. The DRTF saw no reason to interfere with this exemption, except possibly to allow the threshold for its operation to be lowered: DRTF Report, recommendation 6.24. The Government replied that, when legislative time allowed, it would create a power to reduce to below six persons the exemption figure for small dwellings in the private disposal of premises provisions, and would use that power if it was shown to be necessary: Government Response to DRTF Report, para 3.72.

2   DDA 1995, s 22(1) and (3).

3   Ibid, s 22(4).

4   Rights of Access Code of Practice 2002, para 9.22.

5   DDA 1995, s 23(2)(d); Rights of Access Code of Practice 2002, paras 9.20–9.21.

6   Ibid, s 23(3) and (5). A householder who has converted part of his or her dwelling-house into bed-sit accommodation would fall outside this exemption if such accommodation embraced more than six tenants.

7   Ibid, s 23(4).

6.2.12 The fact that the premises are a small dwelling is not enough. Three further conditions must also be satisfied. First, the relevant occupier must reside, and must intend to continue to reside, on the premises.[1] The use of the word 'reside' indicates that this exemption is only enjoyed in respect of dwelling-houses or other residential property and does not apply to commercial or industrial premises. A 'relevant occupier' means a person with the power to dispose of the premises[2] or the person whose licence or consent is required for the disposal of the premises.[3] In both cases, the relevant occupier will include 'a near relative'.[4] Secondly, the relevant occupier must be sharing accommodation on the premises with persons who reside on the premises and who are not members of the occupier's household.[5] This condition contemplates a multi-occupancy residential building with shared accommodation. This might include a large house, sub-divided into individually let bed-sits, with a resident landlord and shared accommodation, such as communal kitchens or bathrooms. Thirdly, the shared accommodation must not be storage accommodation or a means of access.[6] This underlines the last observation illustrating the notion of shared accommodation. It indicates that it is not enough that there is a common entrance door or passageway. Equally, the premises would not include shared accommodation only by virtue of there being a garage or cellar in which the tenants or occupiers may store their personal effects.

Meaning of discrimination

6.2.13 The provisions of Part 3 of the DDA 1995 dealing with discrimination in relation to premises include a self-contained definition of discrimination.[7] This does not create a free-standing right to complain of discrimination and it will be necessary to show that

---

1   DDA 1995, s 23(2)(a) and (6).

2   In a case where DDA 1995, s 22(1) would otherwise apply (discrimination in relation to the disposal of premises).

3   In any case where DDA 1995, s 22(4) would otherwise apply (discrimination by withholding a licence or consent for the disposal of tenancy premises).

4   This term is exhaustively defined by DDA 1995, s 23(7) to mean a person's spouse, partner, child, grandparent, grandchild, or brother or sister (whether of full or half blood or by affinity). The term 'partner' means the other member of a couple consisting of a man and a woman who are not married to each other but are living together as husband and wife. It only becomes necessary to identify whether someone is a partner if the relevant occupier is not actually present on the premises when discrimination is alleged (eg while temporarily away on business): HL Deb, vol 564, col 2029.

5   DDA 1995, s 23(2)(b).

6   Ibid, s 23(2)(c).

7   Ibid, s 24.

discrimination has occurred in a way which is made unlawful.[1] While case-law on the meaning of discrimination as used elsewhere in the statute will be instructive, care must be taken to ensure that an action for alleged discrimination in the disposal or management of premises satisfies the definition of discrimination for present purposes.[2] In particular, there is no explicit duty to make reasonable adjustments for disabled persons in the context of the disposal or management of premises. It remains to be seen whether judicial interpretation of the meaning of discrimination will give rise to an implicit duty of this nature.[3] The Code of Practice suggests not, although it stresses that there is nothing in the DDA 1995 to prevent positive action.[4] It also notes that persons managing or disposing of premises (such as estate agents, accommodation bureaux or management companies) may have parallel duties as service providers and might be subject to a duty to make reasonable adjustments to the way in which they provide their services in relation to premises.[5]

6.2.14   A person discriminates against a disabled person if, for a reason which relates to the disabled person's disability, that person treats the disabled person less favourably than that person treats (or would treat) others to whom that reason does not or would not apply.[6] Such less favourable treatment for a reason related to disability will amount to potentially *unlawful* discrimination[7] if the alleged discriminator cannot

---

1   That is, under DDA 1995, s 22. That is the effect of the opening words of s 24(1): 'For the purposes of section 22 …'.

2   See the detailed discussion of the meaning of discrimination in Chapter 3 and Chapter 5.

3   The DRTF felt that the lack of a duty to make reasonable adjustments within ss 22–24 should be remedied. In particular, it recommended that there should be a duty on those covered by the disposal and management of premises provisions to make reasonable adjustments to policies, practices and procedures, and to provide auxiliary aids and services in the selling and letting process. It also recommended that covered persons should not be allowed to withhold consent unreasonably for a disabled person to make changes to the physical features of premises: DRTF Report, recommendations 6.25–6.27. The Government agreed in principle to extending to those who let or manage premises duties relating to reasonable adjustments to policies, practices and procedures, and the provision of auxiliary aids and services, and undertook to consult on the factors which might determine reasonableness when a landlord is asked by a disabled tenant to consent to changes to physical features: Government Response to DRTF Report, para 3.83.

4   Rights of Access Code of Practice 2002, para 9.6.

5   The boundary between DDA 1995, ss 19–21 and ss 22–24 will not always be easily drawn, especially where the question of reasonable adjustments is being raised.

6   DDA 1995, s 24(1)(a). See the discussion of the concept of disability-related less favourable treatment in Chapters 3 and 5. See also the examples given in Rights of Access Code of Practice 2002, para 9.5.

7   For the purposes of DDA 1995, s 22.

show that the treatment in question is justified.[1] The justification 'defence'[2] can only be made out if certain statutory criteria are met.[3] First, the alleged discriminator must hold the opinion that one or more statutory conditions are satisfied.[4] This is to be tested subjectively.[5] It must be shown that, at the time the treatment took place, *in the opinion* of the defendant, the treatment was necessary. It must be shown that this was an opinion held at that time and not an ex post facto rationalisation in the face of litigation. Secondly, it must be reasonable, in all the circumstances of the case, for that person to hold that opinion.[6] This calls for an objective assessment of all the relevant circumstances.[7] The objective reasonableness of the opinion may depend upon what information was available at the time, what further reasonable inquiries might have been made and what, if any, information has been proffered by the disabled person.[8]

6.2.15 There are four possible statutory (and exhaustive) conditions about the satisfaction of which the alleged discriminator must hold a reasonably held opinion.[9] These conditions are very similar to the parallel conditions for the operation of the justification defence in respect of discrimination arising in the context of goods, facilities or

---

1 DDA 1995, s 24(1)(b).

2 Strictly, the justification requirement is part of the definition of discrimination rather than an explicit defence.

3 DDA 1995, s 24(2). See generally Rights of Access Code of Practice 2002, paras 9.31–9.34.

4 Ibid, s 24(2)(a).

5 *Rose v Bouchet* [1999] IRLR 463 (Sheriff Principal Nicholson QC). This case concerned the refusal to let a flat to a blind person accompanied by a guide dog. The refusal was said by the landlord to be motivated by a concern for the disabled person's safety because of a missing handrail on the steps leading to the flat's entrance. The Sheriff Principal did not think it helpful to engage the assistance of cases decided under the employment provisions of the Act when construing s 24. See now *Council of the City of Manchester v Romano and Samari* [2004] EWCA Civ 834 (discussed at **6.2.19**).

6 DDA 1995, s 24(2)(b). Future regulations may amplify the circumstances in which it is reasonable (or not reasonable) for a person to hold the opinion that one or more of the statutory conditions are satisfied: s 24(4). No such regulations have been made at the time of writing.

7 *Rose v Bouchet* (above). On the facts, the landlord's opinion as to the safety issues arising from letting the flat to a blind person in the particular circumstances of the case was held to be objectively reasonable. See now *Council of the City of Manchester v Romano and Samari* [2004] EWCA Civ 834 (discussed at **6.2.19**).

8 *Rose v Bouchet* (above). See Rights of Access Code of Practice 2002, paras 7.8–7.10. See now *Council of the City of Manchester v Romano and Samari* [2004] EWCA Civ 834 (discussed at **6.2.19**).

9 DDA 1995, s 24(3). Future regulations may also provide for additional circumstances in which less favourable treatment of a disabled person is to be taken to be justified: s 24(5). No such regulations have been made at the time of writing.

services.[1] First, in any case, the person alleged to have discriminated may be able to justify less favourable treatment by showing that that person reasonably believed that the treatment was necessary in order not to endanger the health or safety of any person, including the disabled person.[2] Secondly, in any case, less favourable treatment might be justified by reference to a reasonably held opinion that the disabled person was incapable of entering into an enforceable agreement or of giving an informed consent, and for that reason the treatment was reasonable in the particular case.[3] Thirdly, in a case where a person managing premises has treated a disabled occupier less favourably in the way in which that occupier is allowed to make use of any benefits or facilities,[4] the alleged discriminator might be able to show a reasonably held opinion that the discriminatory treatment was necessary in order for the disabled person (or occupiers of other premises forming part of the building) to make use of a benefit or facility.[5] Finally, in a case where a person managing premises has treated a disabled occupier less favourably by refusing (or deliberately omitting) to permit that occupier to make use of any benefits or facilities,[6] less favourable treatment might be justified by demonstrating a reasonably held opinion that the treatment was necessary in order for the occupiers of other premises forming part of the building to make use of the benefit or facility.[7]

6.2.16 Regulations may provide for additional circumstances in which less favourable treatment of a disabled person is to be taken to be justified.[8] The only such provision to date affects deposits. It arises where a person with power to dispose of any premises ('the provider') grants a disabled person a right to occupy the premises, whether by a

---

1   DDA 1995, s 20(4). The justification defence in relation to the disposal or management of premises raises similar issues to those in respect of discrimination in the provision of goods, facilities or services. See Chapter 5 for a more considered analysis of these issues.

2   Ibid, s 24(3)(a); Rights of Access Code of Practice 2002, para 9.35 (and examples). It is sufficient to show that a person's health or safety is endangered or threatened. It is not necessary to prove actual damage. Health is a state of complete physical, mental and social well-being and not merely the absence of disease and infirmity, but trivial risks are to be disregarded: *Council of the City of Manchester v Romano and Samari* [2004] EWCA Civ 834 (construing DDA 1995, s 24(3)(a) in the light of Human Rights Act 1998, s 3).

3   DDA 1995, s 24(3)(b); Rights of Access Code of Practice 2002, para 9.36 (and examples). Note that the provisions on powers of attorney etc contained in Disability Discrimination (Services and Premises) Regulations 1996, SI 1996/1836, reg 8 do not apply to s 24 as they do to s 20 in the context of goods, facilities and services.

4   DDA 1995, s 22(3)(a).

5   Ibid, s 24(3)(c); Rights of Access Code of Practice 2002, para 9.37 (examples).

6   Ibid, s 22(3)(b).

7   Ibid, s 24(3)(d); Rights of Access Code of Practice 2002, para 9.37 (and examples).

8   Ibid, s 24(5).

formal tenancy agreement or otherwise.[1] The provider may have required the disabled person to provide a deposit in respect of his or her occupation of the premises. The deposit is intended to be refundable at the end of the occupation provided that the premises and contents are not damaged.[2] Suppose that the provider refuses to refund some or all of the deposit because the premises or contents have been damaged for a reason which relates to the disabled person's disability.[3] If the damage is above the level at which the provider would normally refund the deposit in full,[4] and if it is reasonable in all the circumstances of the case for the provider to refuse to refund the deposit in full,[5] then that apparently less favourable treatment of the disabled person for a reason relating to his or her disability is deemed to be justified.[6]

Victimisation

6.2.17 For present purposes,[7] a person (X) also discriminates against another person (Y) if X treats Y less favourably than X treats (or would treat) other persons whose circumstances are the same as Y's, and X does so for one of a number of statutory reasons.[8] Those statutory reasons relate to the fact that Y has exercised (or is believed or suspected by X as having exercised or as intending to exercise) rights under the DDA 1995.[9] For example, Y may have brought proceedings against X or given evidence in respect of such proceedings. This is victimisation.[10] An act of victimisation amounts to discrimination.[11] A person (whether disabled or not) who is victimised in this way has a cause of action for an unlawful act in relation to the disposal or management of premises.[12] By way of illustration, if Y was employed by local authority X and brought a complaint of disability-related employment discrimination against X, it would be an act of discrimination if X then victimised Y by removing Y from the local authority's housing waiting list. In these particular

---

1   Disability Discrimination (Services and Premises) Regulations 1996, SI 1996/1836, reg 7(2)(a). See generally Rights of Access Code of Practice 2002, paras 9.38–9.43.

2   Disability Discrimination (Services and Premises) Regulations 1996, SI 1996/1836, reg 7(2)(b).

3   Ibid, reg 7(2)(c).

4   Ibid, reg 7(2)(c).

5   Ibid, reg 7(2)(d).

6   Ibid, reg 7(1), for the purposes of s 24.

7   DDA 1995, ss 22–24 (as for Part 3 as a whole).

8   Ibid, s 55(1).

9   Ibid, s 55(2).

10   The concept of victimisation is explained in more detail in Chapter 10.

11   DDA 1995, s 22(7), for the purposes of ss 22–24.

12   As outlined in DDA 1995, s 22. See Rights of Access Code of Practice 2002, paras 10.2–10.5.

circumstances, it is not strictly necessary that Y should be a disabled person. It is sufficient that he or she has been victimised for doing something in relation to the DDA 1995 and has suffered a discriminatory act.

Enforcement and remedies

6.2.18   The provisions in respect of disability-informed discrimination in the disposal or management of premises are enforced (and remedies are sought) in exactly the same way as complaints of discrimination in respect of the provision of goods, facilities and services.[1] Further discussion is pursued in Chapter 10.

Judicial consideration of sections 22–24

6.2.19   In *Council of the City of Manchester v Romano and Samari*, the Court of Appeal has considered for the first time the interface of housing legislation, possession orders and ss 22–24 of the 1995 Act. The appeals concerned two secured tenants of the local authority. In each case, the local authority had obtained possession orders against the tenants under the Housing Act 1985 on the grounds of their anti-social behaviour. However, there was some evidence that their anti-social behaviour might be a product of a mental illness. The question was whether it was reasonable to make a possession order against a tenant with a mental impairment. That in turn raised the relevance of disability discrimination law to that question.[2]

6.2.20   The court considered that, in applying the definition of discrimination in s 24, it was bound by the approach that had been taken to the identical definition in the employment field.[3] It agreed that the eviction of the tenants would only be justified if, in the local authority's opinion, possession proceedings were necessary in order not to endanger the health or safety of neighbouring tenants *and* it was reasonable in all the circumstances of the case for it to hold that opinion. The case confirms that the test in s 24(2) is both subjective and objective. Did the landlord hold the opinion *and* was it reasonable for it

---

1   The relevant provisions are contained in DDA 1995, ss 25–28 and Sch 3, Part II.

2   DDA 1995, s 6(1)(b). The detail of this duty has been considered in Chapters 5, 3 and 4.

3   See generally: *Croydon London Borough Council v Moody* (1998) 31 HLR 738, CA. In *North Devon Homes Ltd v Brazier* [2003] EWHC 574, [2003] HLR 59, QBD, the court held that it was inappropriate to make an order for possession where an eviction was unlawful in the terms of the DDA 1995. The judge considered that the 1995 Act furnished its own code for justified eviction which required a higher threshold than merely to say that the degree of misbehaviour was significant and there was not much prospect of it abating. In addition, the limitations on interference with the defendant's right to respect for her home were set out in the 1995 Act, and the court's powers accorded by the Housing Act 1988 had to be read in a manner that was compatible with her rights under the Human Rights Act 1998.

to hold that opinion in all the circumstances of the case?[1] The reasonableness of that opinion has to be tested by reference to the facts known to the landlord at the time of the alleged discriminatory treatment (rather than after the event).[2] The court anticipated that there might be features that the landlord did not appreciate at the time, but that a court could be satisfied that the landlord had made sufficient inquiry. The landlord's opinion might be objectively justified, but the court might subsequently consider that it was not reasonable to make a possession order. That might be because circumstances had changed or because there were other relevant features of the situation that could not reasonably have been known by the landlord at the relevant time which fell to be weighed in the balance at the time of the hearing.

6.2.21 The court rejected a submission that the passage of ss 22–24 of the 1995 Act had been intended to leave the law on possession proceedings unaffected. However, it remarked that there were evident difficulties in ss 22–24 which needed to be remedied at an early date. It noted that the sections were not limited to residential tenancies and would apply equally to a business tenant. The court thought that a further difficulty arose from the fact that a tenant could assert that the landlord could not recover possession for non-payment of rent because the reason why the tenant could not manage his or her financial affairs related to a mental disability. Another difficulty was said to lie in the fact that a private landlord who does not have to establish a 'reasonableness' ground for possession may nevertheless be confronted by an assertion that he or she has caused detriment to a disabled tenant by selecting that tenant for eviction. The court suggested that unless Parliament took rapid remedial action, the courts may be confronted with a deluge of cases in which disabled tenants resisted possession proceedings by use of ss 22–24 of the Act.[3]

6.3   ALTERATIONS TO PREMISES

The duty to make reasonable adjustments to premises

6.3.1 In respect of Part 2 of the DDA 1995, where any physical features of premises occupied by a respondent place a disabled person at a substantial disadvantage in comparison with non-disabled persons, it is the duty of the respondent to take such steps as it is reasonable in all the circumstances of the case to take in order to prevent the physical feature

---

1   DDA 1995, s 5 (prior to the October 2004 amendments) and *Clark v TDG Ltd t/a Novacold* [1999] IRLR 318, CA.

2   See Rights of Access Code of Practice 2002, paras 7.8–7.9.

3   Approving *Rose v Bouchet* [1999] IRLR 463 (Sheriff Principal Nicholson QC).

in question having that effect.[1] That duty might require the respondent to make adjustments to the premises, subject to considerations such as practicability, cost and resources. A failure to consider or discharge that duty can amount to an act of unlawful discrimination.

6.3.2   In respect of Part 3 of the DDA 1995, a detailed duty to make reasonable adjustments is also placed upon service providers.[2] Where a physical feature of a building makes it impossible or unreasonably difficult for disabled persons to make use of a service provided to the public by a service provider, it is the duty of the service provider to make reasonable adjustments. A service provider's unjustified failure to discharge a duty to make reasonable adjustments to its premises in these ways is a potential act of discrimination.[3] There is no comparable duty to make reasonable adjustments to premises in respect of the disposal or management of premises.[4]

Building regulations: employment field

6.3.3   For the purposes of the statutory duty to make adjustments to premises occupied by a Part 2 respondent in the employment field, the fact that the design or construction of a building meets the requirements of Part M of the Building Regulations[5] does not diminish a respondent's duty to make reasonable adjustments in respect of its physical features.[6] It is unlikely to be reasonable for a respondent to have to make an adjustment to a physical feature of a building that it occupies if the design and construction of that physical feature are in accordance with the relevant British Standard.[7] It is also unlikely to be

---

1   The possibility of regulations made under DDA 1995, s 24(5) was canvassed by the court.

2   DDA 1995, s 21. See Chapter 5.

3   Ibid, s 20; Rights of Access Code of Practice 2002, chapter 6. See also the Disability Discrimination (Providers of Services) (Adjustment of Premises) Regulations 2001, SI 2001/3253 (as amended by SI 2004/1429), in force from 1 October 2004, but not extending to Northern Ireland.

4   DDA 1995, ss 22–24 (discussed at **6.2**).

5   Building Act 1984, s 122; Building Regulations 2000, SI 2000/2531, Sch 1; (in Scotland) Part T of the Technical Standards for compliance with the Building Standards (Scotland) Regulations 1990, SI 1990/2179 (amended by SI 1993/1457, SI 1994/1266, SI 1996/2251 and SI 1997/2157). In April 2000, in Scotland, Part T was discontinued and its general requirements were integrated into the general Technical Standards (SSI 1999/173 and SSI 2001/320).

6   Code of Practice: Employment and Occupation (2004), paras 12.6–12.11; Code of Practice: Trade Organisations and Qualifications Bodies (2004), paras 9.6–9.10. See previously: Disability Discrimination (Employment) Regualtions 1996, SI 1996/1456, regs 2 and 8 (now revoked).

7   British Standard 8300:2001, *Design of Buildings and their Approaches to Meet the Needs of Disabled People – Code of Practice.*

reasonable for a respondent to have to make an adjustment to a physical feature that accords with the relevant provisions of the most up-to-date version of Approved Document M (the guidance accompanying the Building Regulations).[1] It might also be necessary to obtain statutory consents to an alteration (planning permission, listed building consent, fire regulations approval, etc) and an adjustment would not be a reasonable one to make if the occupier has applied for such consent and it has been refused. In such a case, the duty to make adjustments should take account of alternative ways of achieving a viable adjustment.[2]

Building regulations: service providers

6.3.4 In relation to service providers and Part 3 of the DDA 1995, the revised Rights of Access Code of Practice 2002 gives helpful guidance on the interaction of the building regulations with the service provider's prospective duty to make adjustments to premises.[3] In general terms, if the physical features of a building in England and Wales accord with Approved Document M,[4] then it will comply with Part M (access and facilities for disabled people) of the building regulations by making reasonable provision for disabled people to gain access to and use the building with reasonable safety and convenience.[5] Part M applies to new buildings and some extensions to buildings since 1985.[6] Provided the relevant physical feature of a building meets the requirements of Part M by according with the guidance in Approved Document M, the service provider will enjoy an exemption from having to make adjustments to that feature if 10 years or less have passed since it was installed.[7]

---

1   The most recent version is the 2004 edition.

2   Code of Practice: Employment and Occupation (2004), paras 12.3–12.5 (and example); Code of Practice: Trade Organisations and Qualifications Bodies (2004), paras 9.3–9.5 (and example).

3   Rights of Access Code of Practice 2002, paras 6.2–6.25. This account draws from that source. The Code's explanation of what are complex provisions is difficult to improve upon.

4   This is the guidance issued to accompany the Building Regulations 1991 or 2000. See Rights of Access Code of Practice 2002, paras 6.2–6.8 and examples therein. Approved Document M for these purposes means the 1992 or 1999 or 2004 edition of that document: Disability Discrimination (Providers of Services) (Adjustment of Premises) Regulations 2001, SI 2001/3253 (as amended by SI 2004/1429), Schedule, para 2(1)(a). The 2004 edition came into force on 1 May 2004. It is more detailed than the earlier editions and might achieve greater accessibility for disabled persons.

5   The latest version of Part M of the Building Regulations is now found in Sch 1 to the Building Regulations 2000, SI 2000/2531.

6   Rights of Access Code of Practice 2002, paras 6.4–6.5.

7   Disability Discrimination (Providers of Services) (Adjustment of Premises) Regulations 2001, SI 2001/3253 (as amended by SI 2004/1429), reg 3(3) (in force from 1 October 2004).

Even if the feature in question does not accord with Approved Document M, it may have been accepted by the relevant authority (such as a building control officer) as meeting the requirements of Part M. If the feature in question enables disabled persons to access and use the building with comparable ease, it is unlikely to be reasonable for the service provider to have to make an adjustment to it within 10 years of its installation or construction.[1]

6.3.5   The position in Scotland is similar but not identical.[2] In Scotland, between April 1991 and April 2000, the appropriate reference was to Part T of the Technical Standards for compliance with the Building Standards (Scotland) Regulations 1990.[3] In April 2000, Part T was discontinued and its general requirements were integrated into the general Technical Standards.[4]

6.3.6   This general analysis flows from the provision in regulations that it is not reasonable for a service provider to have to remove or alter a physical feature where it was provided in (or in connection with) a building for the purpose of assisting people to have access to the building (or to use its facilities) and it satisfies the 'relevant design standard'.[5] The 'relevant design standard' is a reference in England and Wales to the relevant objectives, design considerations and provisions in the relevant editions of Approved Document M.[6] In Scotland it is a reference to the relevant Technical Standards in force between 30 June 1994 and 31 March 2002.[7] However, in Great Britain generally, a physical feature does not satisfy the relevant design standard where more than 10 years have elapsed since (a) the day on which the construction or installation was completed or (b) where the physical feature is provided as part of a larger building project, the day on which the works in relation to that project were completed.[8]

---

1   Rights of Access Code of Practice 2002, para 6.8 (and example). If the feature is not covered by Approved Document M, then the service provider may have to make an adjustment to it.

2   Ibid, para 6.11.

3   SI 1990/2179, issued by the Scottish Office in 1990 and subsequently amended (see SI 1993/1457, SI 1994/1266, SI 1996/2251 and SI 1997/2157).

4   See SSI 1999/173 and SSI 2001/320; Rights of Access Code of Practice, paras 6.9–6.11.

5   Disability Discrimination (Providers of Services) (Adjustment of Premises) Regulations 2001, SI 2001/3253 (as amended by SI 2004/1429), reg 3(3) (in force from 1 October 2004).

6   Ibid, reg 3(4) and Schedule, paras 1(1) and 2 (in force from 1 October 2004). See Rights of Access Code of Practice 2002, paras 6.12–6.16 and 6.22–6.25 (and examples).

7   Ibid, reg 3(4) and Schedule, paras 1(2) and 3 (in force from 1 October 2004). See Rights of Access Code of Practice 2002, paras 6.17–6.25 (and examples).

8   Ibid, reg 3(4) and Schedule, para 1(3) (in force from 1 October 2004).

The problem of leases

6.3.7 The duty to make reasonable adjustments to premises is primarily imposed upon the person who occupies those premises. Where that person owns the premises there can be no question that the person has a right to make alterations to the premises, subject only to planning, building and environmental regulation. In such a case, if there is a duty to make an adjustment, and if an alteration to the fabric or a physical feature of the premises would otherwise be a reasonable adjustment to make, then the occupier will be expected to take such steps, all other things being equal.

6.3.8 Nevertheless, many persons occupy premises as tenants under a commercial lease. A term or covenant in that lease might forbid or restrict alterations to the property or might only permit such alterations with the prior consent of the landlord. In that latter case, consent under the lease might not be forthcoming if the landlord reasonably or unreasonably withholds permission. In these circumstances, the occupier might be unable to discharge its duty to a disabled person to make reasonable adjustments.[1] This could amount to an unlawful act of disability discrimination, although the restriction in the lease or the landlord's refusal to countenance an alteration to the occupied premises might bring a justification defence into play, where available.

The effect of the DDA 1995 upon premises occupied under leases

6.3.9 The DDA 1995 clarifies the relation between the potentially conflicting legal obligations of disability discrimination law and the law of landlord and tenant. Separate provision is made for Part 2 (the employment field)[2] and Part 3 (service providers).[3] The effect may be to prevent landlords of commercial or industrial premises thwarting or undermining the objectives of the legislation. The relevant statutory provisions apply where the occupier occupies premises under a 'lease'.[4]

---

1   It is arguable (but uncertain) that a restrictive clause or covenant in a commercial lease, which prevents a tenant carrying out an alteration in pursuit of a duty to make a reasonable adjustment under the DDA 1995, is invalid as being a term of an agreement which limits the operation of the statute. See also HL Deb, vol 566, col 1016.

2   DDA 1995, s 18A (previously s 16) and Sch 4, Part I, in force since various dates in 1996. See also Code of Practice: Employment and Occupation (2004), paras 12.13–12.31 and Code of Practice: Trade Organisations and Qualifications Bodies (2004), paras 9.12–9.30.

3   DDA 1995, s 27 and Sch 4, Part II. Section 27(3) and (5) and Sch 4, paras 8–9 came into force on 9 May 2001 (in England, Wales and Scotland) and on 31 December 2001 (in Northern Ireland). Section 27(1), (2), (4) and (5) and Sch 4, paras 5–7 came into force in all jurisdictions on 1 October 2004. See SI 2001/2030 and SR 2001/439. See Rights of Access Code of Practice (2002), paras 6.26–6.49.

4   DDA 1995, ss 18A(1)(a) and 27(1)(a).

A 'lease' for this purpose includes a tenancy, sub-lease or sub-tenancy, and an agreement for a lease, tenancy, sub-lease or sub-tenancy.[1] The term 'sub-lease' means any sub-term created out of or deriving from a (superior) leasehold interest and 'sub-tenancy' means any tenancy created out of or deriving from a superior tenancy.[2] Where there are references in the statute[3] to a 'lessor', that reference is to be taken as referring to the lessor who is the occupier's immediate landlord in the case of an occupier occupying premises under a sub-lease or sub-tenancy.[4]

6.3.10   The statutory provisions apply if the effect of the lease would otherwise be that the occupier would not be entitled to make a particular alteration to the premises,[5] and if the alteration is one which the occupier proposes to make in order to comply with a statutory duty to make reasonable adjustments.[6] If the terms and conditions of a lease impose conditions which are to apply if the occupier alters the premises, then the occupier is treated[7] as not being entitled to make the alteration.[8] Similarly, if the terms and conditions of the lease entitle the lessor to impose conditions when giving any consent to the occupier to alter the premises, the occupier is treated[9] as not being entitled to make the alteration.[10] If the above conditions are satisfied,[11] the DDA 1995 provides that the lease shall have effect as if it provided for the occupier to be entitled to make the alteration with the written consent of the lessor.[12] In other words, a statutory term is implied into the lease or

---

1   DDA 1995, ss 18A(3) and 27(3). The Act provides that regulations may further define the meaning of these terms.

2   Disability Discrimination (Employment Field) (Leasehold Premises) Regulations 2004, SI 2004/153, reg 8 (for the purposes of DDA 1995, s 18A); Disability Discrimination (Providers of Services) (Adjustments of Premises) Regulations 2001, SI 2001/3253 (as amended by SI 2004/1429), reg 4 (for the purposes of DDA 1995, s 27).

3   DDA 1995, s 18A and Sch 4, para 1.

4   Disability Discrimination (Employment Field) (Leasehold Premises) Regulations 2004, SI 2004/153, reg 9 (for the purposes of DDA 1995, s 18A); Disability Discrimination (Providers of Services) (Adjustment of Premises) Regulations 2001, SI 2001/3253 (as amended by SI 2004/1429), reg 9(1), (2), (4) and (6) (for the purposes of s 27(2) and Sch 4, paras 5 and 6(1), (3) and (4), and in force from 1 October 2004).

5   DDA 1995, ss 18A(1)(b) and 27(1)(b).

6   Ibid, ss 18A(1)(c) and 27(1)(c).

7   For the purposes of ibid, ss 18A(1)(b) and 27(1)(b).

8   Ibid, ss 18A(4)(a) and 27(4)(a).

9   For the purposes of ibid, ss 18A(1)(b) and 27(1)(b).

10   Ibid, ss 18A(4)(b) and 27(4)(b).

11   Ibid, s 18A(1) or s 27(1).

12   Ibid, ss 18A(2)(a) and 27(2)(a). See Code of Practice: Employment and Occupation (2004), para 12.13; Code of Practice: Trade Organisations and Qualifications Bodies (2004), para 9.12; Rights of Access Code of Practice (2002), para 6.32.

agreement at issue. The statutory term requires that, if the occupier wishes to make an alteration to the premises, the occupier must first make a written application to the lessor for consent.[1] Furthermore, the Act implies into the terms of the lease a requirement that, if a written application for consent is made by the occupier, the lessor will not withhold consent unreasonably.[2] In turn, the lessor is deemed to be entitled to make any consent the subject of reasonable conditions.[3]

6.3.11 Where the occupier occupies premises under a sub-lease or sub-tenancy, any superior lease under which the premises are held has effect (except to the extent to which it expressly so provides) in relation to the lessor and lessee who are parties to the superior lease as if it provided for the lessee to have to make a written application to the lessor for consent to the alteration.[4] If such an application is made, the superior lease has effect as if it provided for the lessor not to withhold its consent unreasonably and for the lessor to be entitled to make its consent subject to reasonable conditions.

6.3.12 Rather puzzlingly, the statutory wording appears to restrict the vigour of this otherwise quite far-reaching adjustment of the rights of commercial landlord and tenant. It is apparent that a lease is to have effect as modified by the statutory implied terms 'except to the extent to which it expressly so provides'.[5] The reference to 'it' must be taken to be a reference to the lease.[6] This suggests that the landlord might impose express terms in the lease that have the intent and effect of thwarting the statutory implications made in the lease. If that is right – and the author does not believe that this is what was intended – then it may be that such express terms would have to surmount the test of an invalid agreement.

---

1   DDA 1995, ss 18A(2)(b) and 27(2)(b).

2   Ibid, ss 18A(2)(c) and 27(2)(c).

3   Ibid, ss 18A(2)(d) and 27(2)(d).

4   Ibid, s 18A(2A), inserted by Disability Discrimination (Employment Field) (Leasehold Premises) Regulations 2004, SI 2004/153, reg 9(b) and modifying s 18A (from 1 October 2004); DDA 1995, s 27(2A) inserted by Disability Discrimination (Providers of Services) (Adjustments of Premises) Regulations 2001, SI 2001/3253 (as amended by SI 2004/ 1429), reg 9(1) and (3) and modifying s 27 (in force from 1 October 2004). See Code of Practice: Employment and Occupation (2004), paras 12.15–12.16; Code of Practice: Trade Organisations and Qualifications Bodies (2004), paras 9.14–9.15; Rights of Access Code of Practice (2002), paras 6.34–6.35. The former provisions made by the Disability Discrimination (Employment) Regulations 1996 and the Disability Discrimination (Sub-leases and Sub-tenancies) Regulations 1996 have been revoked from 1 October 2004.

5   DDA 1995, ss 18A(2) and 27(2).

6   It is possible that it is a drafting error and that the reference was intended to be to the subsection rather than to the lease (the phrase 'except to the extent to which [the sub-section] expressly so provides' makes better sense). But see **7.5.21**.

Employment field cases

6.3.13 Prior to 1 October 2004, in cases in the employment field, it was not reasonable for a person (in relation to premises occupied by it) to have to take a step to comply with a statutory duty to make reasonable adjustments, if this would be contrary to the terms of any lease under which the person occupied the premises, in the following circumstances. The occupier had applied to the lessor in writing to take the step; the occupier had indicated in writing that it proposed to take the step (subject to the lessor's consent) in order to comply with its statutory duty; the lessor had withheld that consent; and the occupier had informed the disabled person that it had applied for the consent of the lessor and that the lessor had withheld that consent.[1] This provision has now been revoked and not replaced. It is nevertheless clear that the occupier must write to the lessor to seek consent to the proposed step under the lease.

6.3.14 Where, under any binding obligation, a person is required to obtain the consent of any person to any alteration of the premises occupied by it, it is always reasonable for the occupier to have to take steps (not including an application to a court or tribunal) to obtain that consent. It is never reasonable for the occupier to have to make that alteration before that consent is obtained.[2] In this context, a binding obligation means a legally binding obligation (not contained in a lease) in relation to the premises (whether arising from an agreement or otherwise).[3] An example of such an obligation would include a mortgage or a charge or, in Scotland, a feu disposition.[4]

6.3.15 It is implied that the lessor will not withhold consent unreasonably.[5] The landlord is entitled to make any consent the subject of reasonable conditions.[6] If so, the occupier must carry out the alteration, subject to those conditions. A lessor is to be taken to have withheld consent to an alteration where the lessor has received a written application by or on behalf of the occupier for consent to make the alteration and the lessor has failed within a period of 21 days (or such longer period as is reasonable) either:

---

1   Disability Discrimination (Employment) Regulations 1996, SI 1996/1456, reg 15 (now revoked).

2   DDA 1995, s 18B(3) and (4), replacing Disability Discrimination (Employment) Regulations 1996, reg 10 (from 1 October 2004).

3   DDA 1995, s 18B(5), replacing Disability Discrimination (Employment) Regulations 1996, reg 2 (from 1 October 2004).

4   Code of Practice: Employment and Occupation (2004) para 12.12 (and example); Code of Practice: Trade Organisations and Qualifications Bodies (2004), para 9.11.

5   DDA 1995, s 18A(2)(c).

6   Ibid, s 18A(2)(d).

- to reply consenting to or refusing the application; or
- to reply consenting to the application, subject to obtaining the consent of another person required under a superior lease or binding obligation (such as a mortgage or charge or, in Scotland, a feu disposition) *and* seek that consent.[1]

If the lessor belatedly meets the above requirements, it shall be taken to have withheld its consent from the date of the failure to meet the requirements on time, but then shall be treated as having not withheld its consent from the time when it belatedly met the requirements.[2] A lessor is treated as not having sought the consent of another person (if so required) unless the lessor has applied in writing to that person indicating that the lessor's consent to the alteration has been applied for in order to comply with a statutory duty to make a reasonable adjustment and that the lessor has given its consent conditionally upon obtaining the other person's consent.[3]

6.3.16   A lessor withholds consent unreasonably where the lease provides that consent shall or will be given to an alteration of the kind in question.[4] Consent is also withheld unreasonably where the lease provides that consent shall or will be given to an alteration of the kind in question if the consent is sought in a particular way and that has been complied with.[5] Moreover, a lessor withholds consent unreasonably where the lessor is treated as withholding consent.[6] On the other hand, a lessor is regarded as acting reasonably in withholding consent where there is a binding obligation (for example, a mortgage or charge) requiring the consent of a third party to an alteration; the lessor has taken steps to seek that consent; and that consent has not been given or has been given subject to a condition making it reasonable for the lessor

---

1   Disability Discrimination (Employment Field) (Leasehold Premises) Regulations 2004, SI 2004/153, reg 4(1) and (2) for the purposes of DDA 1995, s 18A and Sch 4, Part I. In this context, a binding obligation is a legally binding obligation (not contained in a lease) in relation to the premises, whether arising from an agreement or otherwise: reg 2. The period of 21 days begins with the day on which the application is received. See further Code of Practice: Employment and Occupation (2004), paras 12.16–12.21; Code of Practice: Trade Organisations and Qualifications Bodies (2004), paras 9.16–9.20.

2   Disability Discrimination (Employment Field) (Leasehold Premises) Regulations 2004, SI 2004/153, reg 4(3).

3   Ibid, reg 4(4).

4   Ibid, reg 5(1) and (2).

5   Ibid, reg 5(1) and (3).

6   Ibid, reg 5(1) and (4) by reference to reg 4 (see **6.3.15**). See further Code of Practice: Employment and Occupation (2004), paras 12.22–12.24 (and examples); Code of Practice: Trade Organisations and Qualifications Bodies (2004), paras 9.21–9.23 (and examples).

to withhold consent.[1] Alternatively, a lessor acts reasonably in withholding consent where the lessor is bound by an agreement allowing the lessor to consent to the alteration subject to a condition that the lessor makes a payment and that condition does not permit the lessor to make its consent subject to a condition that the occupier reimburse that payment.[2] If it would be reasonable for the lessor to withhold consent, but consent has nevertheless been given, it would be reasonable to impose a condition on that consent that upon expiry of the lease the occupier (or any assignee or successor) must reinstate any relevant part of the premises to its prior state.[3]

6.3.17   Where the lessor gives consent to an alteration, but subject to a condition, such a condition is regarded as *reasonable* if it is any of the following conditions (or a condition to a similar effect):

- the occupier must obtain any necessary planning permission (and any other consent or permission) required by or under any enactment;[4]
- the occupier must submit any plans or specifications for the alteration to the lessor for approval (provided the condition binds the lessor not to withhold approval unreasonably) and that the work is carried out in accordance with such plans or specifications;[5]
- the lessor must be permitted a reasonable opportunity to inspect the work when complete;[6] or
- the occupier must repay to the lessor the costs reasonably incurred in connection with the giving of the consent.[7]

6.3.18   Special provisions deal with a failure by an occupier to obtain consent to the alteration.[8] These apply where any question arises as to

---

1   Disability Discrimination (Employment Field) (Leasehold Premises) Regulations 2004, SI 2004/153, reg 6(1). In this context, a binding oblgiation is a legally binding obligation (not contained in a lease) in relation to the premises whether arising from an agreement or otherwise: reg 2. See further Code of Practice: Employment and Occupation (2004), para 12.25; Code of Practice: Trade Organisations and Qualifications Bodies (2004), para 9.24.

2   Disability Discrimination (Employment Field) (Leasehold Premises) Regulations 2004, SI 2004/153, reg 6(2).

3   Ibid, reg 7(2).

4   Ibid, reg 7(1)(a).

5   Ibid, reg 7(1)(b).

6   Ibid, reg 7(1)(c).

7   Ibid, reg 7(1)(d). See generally Code of Practice: Employment and Occupation (2004), paras 12.26–12.27; Code of Practice: Trade Organisations and Qualifications Bodies (2004), paras 9.25–9.26.

8   DDA 1995, Sch 4, Part I, supplementing s 18A.

whether an occupier occupying premises under a lease has failed to comply with its statutory duty to make a reasonable adjustment by failing to make a particular alteration to premises. In answering that question, the employment tribunal must ignore any constraint attributable to the fact that the occupier occupies the premises under a lease, unless the occupier has applied to the lessor in writing for consent to make the alteration. The occupier is denied recourse to a justification defence based upon the restrictive terms or covenants of a lease unless and until it has sought to obtain the landlord's consent to the making of the alteration despite that restriction.[1] In other words, the occupier of the premises cannot plead justification by pointing to the negative terms of a lease alone.[2] The occupier is expected to rely upon the statutory provisions and to seek the landlord's consent to the alteration by means of written application.

6.3.19 The sting in the tail of this provision is as follows.[3] In employment tribunal proceedings, where a question arises about a duty to make a reasonable adjustment by an alteration to premises occupied under a lease, either the claimant or the occupier may request the tribunal to join (in Scotland, sist) the lessor as a party to the proceedings.[4] The tribunal must grant such a request if it is made before the hearing commences,[5] otherwise the granting of such a request is at the tribunal's discretion.[6] Such a request to join the lessor to proceedings cannot be made once the tribunal has determined the complaint.[7] If the lessor has been thus joined (or sisted) as a party to the tribunal proceedings, the tribunal has certain powers in relation to the lessor if certain conditions are satisfied. It may determine whether the lessor has refused consent to the alteration or consented subject to one or more conditions.[8] If so, the tribunal may then determine whether the refusal or any of the conditions were unreasonable.[9] Where the tribunal has so determined, it may take one or more steps.[10] The tribunal may

---

1   DDA 1995, Sch 4, para 1.

2   Code of Practice: Employment and Occupation (2004), para 12.14; Code of Practice: Trade Organisations and Qualifications Bodies (2004), para 9.13.

3   See generally Code of Practice: Employment and Occupation (2004), paras 12.28–12.30; Code of Practice: Trade Organisations and Qualifications Bodies (2004), paras 9.27–9.29.

4   DDA 1995, Sch 4, para 2(1).

5   Ibid, Sch 4, para 2(2).

6   Ibid, Sch 4, para 2(3).

7   Ibid, Sch 4, para 2(4).

8   Ibid, Sch 4, para 2(5)(a).

9   Ibid, Sch 4, para 2(5)(b).

10 Ibid, Sch 4, para 2(6).

make such a declaration as it considers appropriate or make an order authorising the occupier to make an alteration specified in the order.[1] This latter power is quite novel and is likely to prove important in practice. An order made under this power may require the occupier to comply with any conditions specified in the order.[2] Alternatively or additionally, the tribunal may order the lessor to pay compensation to the claimant.[3] Any step taken by the tribunal above may be in substitution for or in addition to the usual statutory remedies available against the respondent.[4] However, if the tribunal decides to order the lessor to pay compensation to the claimant, it may not make a compensation order against the occupier (respondent).[5]

Goods and services cases

6.3.20   For the purposes of the service provider's duty to make reasonable adjustments, where under any 'binding obligation' a service provider is required to obtain the consent of any person to any alteration of the premises occupied by the service provider, it is reasonable for the service provider to have to request that consent.[6] This is subject to the proviso that the alteration must otherwise be a reasonable one to make in order to comply with the duty to make a reasonable adjustment. However, it is not reasonable for the service provider to have to make that alteration before that consent is obtained. In this context, a binding obligation means a legally binding obligation (not contained in a lease) in relation to the premises (whether arising from an agreement or otherwise).[7] An example of such an obligation would include a mortgage, a charge, a restrictive covenant or, in Scotland, a feu disposition.[8]

---

1   DDA 1995, Sch 4, para 2(6)(a) and (b).

2   Ibid, Sch 4, para 2(7).

3   Ibid, Sch 4, para 2(6)(c).

4   Ibid, Sch 4, para 2(8).

5   Ibid, Sch 4, para 2(9).

6   Disability Discrimination (Providers of Services) (Adjustment of Premises) Regulations 2001, SI 2001/3253 (as amended by SI 2004/1429), reg 3(2); Rights of Access Code of Practice 2002, para 6.31. Even where consent is not given, the service provider still has a duty to consider providing a reasonable means of avoiding the feature or providing the service by a reasonable alternative means: Rights of Access Code of Practice 2002, para 6.27.

7   Disability Discrimination (Providers of Services) (Adjustment of Premises) Regulations 2001, SI 2001/3253 (as amended by SI 2004/1429), reg 2.

8   Rights of Access Code of Practice 2002, para 6.31 (and example). It might also be necessary to obtain statutory consents to an alteration (planning permission, listed building consent, fire regulations approval, etc). An adjustment would not be a reasonable one to make if the occupier has applied for such consent and it has been refused (and see

6.3.21 As has been explained above,[1] where a service provider occupies premises under a lease, a statutory term is implied that, if the service provider wishes to make an alteration to the premises, the occupier must first make a written application to the lessor for consent.[2] If a written application for consent is made by the service provider, the lessor will not withhold consent unreasonably.[3] In turn, the lessor is deemed to be entitled to make any consent the subject of reasonable conditions.[4] Regulations deal with the further consequences of these provisions as follows.[5]

6.3.22 The lessor is treated as having withheld its consent where it fails to reply in writing (consenting to or refusing the alteration) within 42 days of receipt of the application for consent.[6] The same result arises where within the same timescale the lessor replies in writing consenting to the alteration subject to the consent of another person required under a superior lease (or pursuant to a binding obligation), but the lessor fails to seek that consent.[7] However, in either case, the lessor is not treated as having withheld consent where the service provider fails to submit with the application such plans and specifications as it is reasonable for the lessor to require before consenting to the alteration, provided the lessor has requested such a submission within 21 days of receiving the application.[8] However, where such plans and specifications are submitted to the lessor in response to a timely request, the lessor is treated as withholding consent to the alteration where it fails to reply in writing (consenting to or refusing the alteration) within 42 days of receiving those plans and specifications.[9] The same result accrues where within that timescale the lessor replies in writing consenting to the alteration subject to the consent of another person required under a

---

DDA 1995, s 59). In such a case, subject to any right of appeal, the duty to make adjustments should take account of alternative ways of achieving a viable adjustment: Rights of Access Code of Practice 2002, paras 6.28–6.30.

1   At **6.3.10–6.3.11**.

2   DDA 1995, s 27(2)(b).

3   Ibid, s 27(2)(c).

4   Ibid, s 27(2)(d).

5   Disability Discrimination (Providers of Services) (Adjustment of Premises) Regulations 2001, SI 2001/3253 (as amended by SI 2004/1429), reg 5 (in force from 1 October 2004); Rights of Access Code of Practice 2002, paras 6.36–6.40.

6   Ibid, SI 2001/3253, (as amended by SI 2004/1429), regs 5 (2)(a) and (7)(b). A lessor who complies outside the statutory time period is treated as having withheld its consent until such time as it did comply: ibid, reg 5(6).

7   Ibid, reg 5(2)(b) and (7)(b). A lessor who complies outside the statutory time period is treated as having withheld its consent until such time as it did comply: ibid, reg 5(6).

8   Ibid, reg 5(3).

9   Ibid, reg 5(4)(a) and (7)(b). A lessor who complies outside the statutory time period is treated as having withheld its consent until such time as it did comply: ibid, reg 5(6).

superior lease (or pursuant to a binding obligation), but the lessor fails to seek that consent.[1]

6.3.23 As can be seen immediately above, the regulations envisage circumstances where the lessor might reply in writing to the service provider consenting to the alteration subject to the consent of another person required under a superior lease (or pursuant to a binding obligation). Assuming the lessor has sought that consent, and has received it, the lessor is nevertheless treated as having withheld consent to the alteration where it fails to inform the service provider in writing of that fact within 14 days of the receipt of that consent.[2] The lessor is treated as not having sought the other person's consent unless it has applied in writing to that person indicating that the occupier (service provider) has applied for consent to the alteration of the premises in order to comply with a DDA 1995, s 21 duty. In addition, the lessor must indicate to that other person that it has given its consent conditionally upon obtaining that other person's consent. The lessor must also submit to that other person any plans and specifications which have been submitted by the occupier (service provider) to the lessor.[3]

6.3.24 When can a lessor be said to have withheld its consent to an alteration reasonably or unreasonably?[4] A lessor is treated as acting unreasonably in withholding its consent for an alteration to premises where the lease provides that it shall give its consent to an alteration of the kind in question and it has withheld its consent to that alteration.[5] In contrast, the lessor will be taken to have acted reasonably in withholding consent where there is a binding obligation requiring the consent of any person to the alteration, it has taken steps to seek that consent, and that consent has not been given or has been given subject to a condition making it reasonable to withhold the consent.[6] The lessor will also be taken to have acted reasonably in withholding consent where the lessor does not know, and could not be reasonably expected to know, that the alteration is one which the occupier (service provider) proposes to make in order to comply with a DDA 1995, s 21 duty.[7] Circumstances

---

1   Disability Discrimination (Providers of Services) (Adjustment of Premises) Regulations
     2001, SI 2001/3253 (as amended by SI 2004/1429), reg 5(4)(b) and (7)(b). A lessor who
     complies outside the statutory time period is treated as having withheld its consent until
     such time as it did comply: ibid, reg 5(6).

2   Ibid, reg 5(5). A lessor who complies outside the statutory time period is treated as having
     withheld its consent until such time as it did comply: ibid, reg 5(6).

3   Ibid, reg 5(7).

4   Ibid, regs 6–7; Rights of Access Code of Practice 2002, paras 6.41–6.44.

5   Ibid, reg 6.

6   Ibid, reg 7(2)(a).

7   Ibid, reg 7(2)(b).

are also prescribed where the giving of the lessor's consent subject to a condition is to be treated as reasonable.[1] If a condition is to the effect that:

- the occupier (service provider) must obtain any necessary planning permission (and any other consent or permission) required by or under any enactment;[2]
- the work must be carried out in accordance with any plans or specifications approved by the lessor;[3]
- the lessor must be permitted a reasonable opportunity to inspect the work (whether before or after it is completed);[4]
- the consent of another person required under a superior lease or a binding agreement must be obtained;[5] or
- the occupier must repay to the lessor the costs reasonably incurred in connection with the giving of the consent,[6]

it is regarded as reasonable.

6.3.25   Enforcement provisions in respect of a duty to make alterations to premises by providers of services under DDA 1995, Part 3 are similar, but slightly different, to those applicable to employers under Part 2.[7] Where any question arises as to whether a service provider occupying premises under a lease has failed to comply with a duty to make reasonable adjustments by failing to make a particular alteration to premises, any constraint attributable to the fact that the service provider occupies the premises under a lease must be ignored, unless the occupier has applied to the lessor in writing for consent to make the alteration.[8] A novelty is the provision for a reference to be made to the court where the lessor has refused consent for such an alteration to be made by the occupier.[9] A reference may also be made where the lessor has given consent to the alteration but has made the consent subject to

---

1   Discrimination (Providers of Services) (Adjustment of Premises) Regulations 2001, SI 2001/3253 (as amended by SI 2004/1429), reg 8(1); Rights of Access Code of Practice 2002, paras 6.45–6.46.

2   Ibid, reg 8(2)(a).

3   Ibid, reg 8(2)(b).

4   Ibid, reg 8(2)(c).

5   Ibid, reg 8(2)(d).

6   Ibid, reg 8(2)(e).

7   DDA 1995, s 27 and Sch 4, Part II. The differences are explained in Code of Practice: Employment and Occupation (2004), para 12.31, and Code of Practice: Trade Organisations and Qualifications Bodies (2004), para 9.30.

8   Ibid, Sch 4, para 5; Rights of Access Code of Practice 2002, paras 6.32–6.33.

9   Ibid, Sch 4, para 6(1); Rights of Access Code of Practice 2002, para 6.47. There is no equivalent in employment cases.

one or more conditions. In both cases, the occupier must have applied in writing to the lessor for the necessary consent. In these circumstances, the occupier or a disabled person (who has an interest in the proposed alteration to the premises being made) may refer the matter to the county court.[1] It does not seem to be contemplated that such a reference can be made only where legal proceedings have been commenced.[2] These provisions would appear to provide for a preliminary clarification of the rights of the parties concerned by the court, even where litigation based upon a complaint of unlawful disability discrimination has not been initiated or contemplated.

6.3.26 Regulations provide for the modification of these provisions where the occupier (service provider) occupies the premises under a sub-lease or sub-tenancy.[3] In those circumstances, references to a 'lessor' are treated as a reference to the 'immediate landlord'.[4] The regulations then provide that, except to the extent which it expressly so provides, any superior lease in respect of the premises shall have effect in relation to the lessor and the lessee who are parties to the superior lease as if it provided:

- for the lessee to be entitled to give its consent to the alteration with the written consent of the lessor;
- for the lessee to have to make a written application to the lessor for consent if it wishes to give its consent to the alteration;
- for the lessor not to withhold its consent unreasonably if such an application is made; and
- for the lessor to be entitled to make its consent subject to reasonable conditions.[5]

Where the lessee of any superior lease in relation to the premises has applied in writing to its lessor for consent to the alteration, and that consent has been refused or the lessor has made its consent subject to one or more conditions, then the occupier (service provider), lessee or a disabled person who has an interest in the proposed alteration to the premises being made may refer the matter to a county court (or, in Scotland, to the sheriff).[6]

---

1   In Scotland, the sheriff court. See DDA 1995, Sch 4, para 6(2).

2   Under DDA 1995, s 25.

3   Disability Discrimination (Providers of Services) (Adjustment of Premises) Regulations 2001, SI 2001/3253 (as amended by SI 2004/1429), reg 9(1), modifying DDA 1995, s 27 and Sch 5, paras 5–7; Rights of Access Code of Practice 2002, paras 6.34–6.35.

4   Ibid, reg 9(2), modifying DDA 1995, s 27(2).

5   Ibid, reg 9(3), inserting DDA 1995, s 27(2A).

6   Disability Discrimination (Providers of Services) (Adjustment of Premises) Regulations 2001, SI 2001/3253 (as amended by SI 2004/1429), reg 9(5), inserting DDA 1995, Sch 4, para 6(1A).

6.3.27   Where the matter has been referred to the court by these various means, the court shall determine whether the refusal of the lessor (or the immediate landlord, as the case might be) was unreasonable or whether any conditions imposed upon consent are unreasonable.[1] If the court decides that the refusal of consent to the alteration (or any conditions imposed upon the consent) by the lessor (or the immediate landlord, as the case might be) was unreasonable, then the court may make an appropriate declaration at its discretion. It may also make an order authorising the occupier to make an alteration specified in the order.[2] Such an order may require the occupier to comply with specified conditions.[3]

6.3.28   If litigation has been commenced, then in any court proceedings where a question arises about a duty to make a reasonable adjustment by an alteration to premises occupied under a lease, either the claimant (in Scotland, the pursuer) or the occupier may ask the court to join (in Scotland, sist) any lessor (including a superior landlord, as the case might be) as a party to the proceedings.[4] The court must grant such a request if it is made before the hearing commences,[5] otherwise the granting of such a request is at the court's discretion.[6] Such a request to join the lessor to proceedings cannot be made once the court has determined the claim.[7] If the lessor has been joined (or sisted) as a party to the proceedings, then the court has certain powers in relation to the lessor if certain conditions are satisfied.

6.3.29   The court may determine whether the lessor has refused consent to the alteration at issue or whether the lessor has consented to the alteration but subject to one or more conditions.[8] If so, in either case, the tribunal may then determine whether the refusal (or any of the

---

1   DDA 1995, Sch 4, para 6(3); Disability Discrimination (Providers of Services) (Adjustment of Premises) Regulations 2001, SI 2001/3253 (as amended by SI 2004/1429), reg 9(6).

2   DDA 1995, Sch 4, para 6(4); Disability Discrimination (Providers of Services) (Adjustment of Premises) Regulations 2001, SI 2001/3253 (as amended by SI 2004/1429), reg 9(6).

3   DDA 1995, Sch 4, para 6(5).

4   Ibid, Sch 4, para 7(1); Disability Discrimination (Providers of Services) (Adjustment of Premises) Regulations 2001, SI 2001/3253 (as amended by SI 2004/1429), reg 9(7)(a); Rights of Access Code of Practice 2002, paras 6.48–6.49.

5   DDA 1995, Sch 4, para 7(2). Where the premises are occupied under a sub-lease or sub-tenancy, the request shall be granted if it is made before the hearing of the claim begins, unless it appears to the court that another lessor should be joined or sisted as a party to the proceedings: Disability Discrimination (Providers of Services) (Adjustment of Premises) Regulations 2001, SI 2001/3253 (as amended by SI 2004/1429), reg 9(7)(b), substituting DDA 1995, Sch 4, para 7(2).

6   DDA 1995, Sch 4, para 7(3).

7   Ibid, Sch 4, para 7(4).

8   Ibid, Sch 4, para 7(5)(a).

conditions) was unreasonable.[1] Where such a finding has been made, the court may make such a declaration as it considers appropriate or order the lessor to pay compensation to the claimant or pursuer.[2] Although this is not made explicit, it seems logical that any such remedy against the lessor may be made in addition to or instead of any remedy that the court would be able to make against the occupier who is the defendant (or defender) to the proceedings. However, if the court decides to order the lessor to pay compensation to the claimant or pursuer, it may not make a parallel compensation order against the occupier.[3] Moreover, the court is also given an additional or alternative power which might prove quite radical in practice. If the court has determined that the lessor's refusal of consent to (or conditions imposed upon) an alteration was unreasonable, it may make an order authorising the occupier to make an alteration specified in the order.[4] Such an order may require the occupier to comply with any conditions specified in the order.[5]

Management and disposal of premises

6.3.30 The above provisions[6] do not apply to discrimination against disabled persons in relation to the disposal and management of premises.[7] This is because there is no parallel duty to make reasonable adjustments in that area as there is in respect of the employment field or the provision of services. There is no duty upon a private or domestic landlord to make or consent to changes or alterations to the property when a disabled person is seeking to become a tenant.[8] However, as previously noted, the provisions of DDA 1995, s 26 may act to invalidate any prejudicial term within a main tenancy agreement, such as one seeking to prevent the tenant sub-letting the rented property to disabled persons.

---

1   DDA 1995, Sch 4, para 7(5)(b). Any future regulations made under Sch 4, para 8 will be relevant to this exercise.

2   Ibid, Sch 4, para 7(6)(a) or (c).

3   Ibid, Sch 4, para 7(8).

4   Ibid, Sch 4, para 7(6)(b).

5   Ibid, Sch 4, para 7(7).

6   Ibid, s 27 and Sch 4, Part II.

7   Under ibid, ss 22–24.

8   HL Deb, vol 566, col 1016.

6.4 EDUCATIONAL INSTITUTIONS AND ALTERATION OF LEASEHOLD PREMISES

6.4.1 As will be discussed in Chapter 7, the SENDA 2001 has made extensive reforms to DDA 1995, Part IV (now known as Part 4) in the education field. This reform includes a new duty to make reasonable adjustments placed upon educational institutions in the further and higher education sectors. That duty is being introduced in stages. There will be no obligation to make adjustments to physical features of premises until 1 September 2005. Nevertheless, the amended DDA 1995 and regulations make provision for dealing with the problems that will arise when educational institutions address their new duty to make reasonable adjustments involving alterations to physical features of premises occupied under lease. That provision is very similar to the rules applying in employment and services cases discussed above, but it is best understood in the context of the wider reforms of disability discrimination law in education. This is discussed further in Chapter 7.

6.5 DISABILITY DISCRIMINATION BILL

6.5.1 If enacted, the Disability Discrimination Bill would impose a duty to provide reasonable adjustments on landlords and others who manage rented premises. It would also confer a power to modify or end the current small dwellings exemption.[1]

6.5.2 It would become unlawful for landlords and managers, in relation to premises that they wish to let or that are let, to discriminate against a disabled tenant or prospective tenant by failing, without justification, to comply with a duty to provide a reasonable adjustment for the disabled person. This would cover the letting of both commercial and residential premises. The duty would apply to require a landlord or manager to take reasonable steps to change a policy, practice or procedure having an adverse impact on disabled persons. The provisions would also require a landlord or manager to take reasonable steps to provide an auxiliary aid or service in those circumstances. The proposed duties would not require the making of any alteration to the physical features of premises by a landlord or manager. A landlord or manager would not have to take any steps under the new provisions unless requested to do so by the tenant or prospective tenant. The provisions will not apply to the principal or only home of the landlord or manager or where a small dwelling exception

---

1   See Department of Work and Pensions, *Disability Discrimination Bill: Consultation on private clubs; premises; the definition of disability; and the questions procedure*, Cm 6402 (December 2004).

arises. There will be a limited justification defence, protection from victimisation of a disabled tenant arising from the new duties and provisions dealing with the distribution of costs arising from them.

6.5.3 The Bill also envisages regulation-making powers to deal with the practical consequences of the extension of the duty to make reasonable adjustments in relation to the physical features of premises in relation to local councillors, public authorities, general qualifications bodies and private clubs.

Chapter 7

EDUCATION

7.1 INTRODUCTION

7.1.1 The 1994 Green Paper anticipated that the right of access to goods and services would not apply to educational facilities.[1] It was thought that provision for disabled pupils and students was already best served by being the subject of other legislation.[2] This disapplication of the new right of access was confirmed by the 1995 White Paper, which went on to promise fresh initiatives in respect of educational opportunities for disabled persons.[3] The exclusion of access to education from the new right not to be discriminated against as a disabled person in relation to the provision of goods, facilities and services was envisaged.

7.1.2 Thus, somewhat controversially, the DDA 1995 *as originally enacted* did not include access to education within the scope of its anti-discrimination provisions. Instead, in contrast to the position in discrimination law generally,[4] education was explicitly excluded from the scope of services for the purposes of Part 3 of the Act.[5] The controversial aspect of this exclusion was that education is recognised as being crucial to the aspirations of disabled persons to enjoy full and equal opportunities.[6] In many respects, the right to freedom from discrimination in employment[7] may be undermined if educational opportunities are not equally available to disabled persons to enable them to compete with a well-qualified labour force as they seek to enter the competitive labour market. Nevertheless, the Act did address the

---

1   *A Consultation on Government Measures to Tackle Discrimination Against Disabled People* (July 1994), para 4.9.

2   As this book is a text on disability discrimination law, it is not proposed to explore the relevant law of education in any detail.

3   *Ending Discrimination Against Disabled People*, Cm 2729 (1995), para 4.6, and Chapter 6.

4   See Part III of the SDA 1975 and Part III of the RRA 1976.

5   DDA 1995, s 19(5). As to the provisions on services generally, see ss 19–21, and Chapter 5.

6   See generally Disability Rights Task Force, *From Exclusion to Inclusion: A Report of the Disability Rights Task Force for Disabled People* (1999, London: DfEE) (DRTF Report), Chapter 4.

7   DDA 1995, Part 2. See Chapter 3.

question of access to education by means other than via the anti-discrimination framework contained in Part 3 of the Act. This was achieved in Part IV of the Act (now referred to as Part 4), provisions of which are now found in other statutes (but discussed below).

7.1.3   The DRTF regarded the lack of protection from unfair discrimination in education for disabled children as unacceptable, but rejected the simplistic solution of removing the education exclusion from the DDA 1995.[1] Instead, it recommended that providers of school education of all descriptions should be placed under a statutory duty not to discriminate unfairly against a disabled pupil, for a reason relating to his or her disability, in the provision of education. It also recommended that the pupil's parents should have a right of redress and that there should be a defence of *acceptable* less favourable treatment.[2] The DRTF went further by advocating a statutory duty on school education providers to review policies, practices and procedures and to make reasonable adjustments to any that discriminate against or have an adverse impact upon disabled pupils.[3] Moreover, a duty to make reasonable adjustments – by taking reasonable steps to provide education by an alternative method – was suggested to overcome physical barriers which place disabled pupils at a substantial disadvantage in comparison with non-disabled pupils.[4] Furthermore, a right to adjustments to achieve physical access and access to the curriculum was urged.[5] Similar proposals affecting further, higher and adult education (and the Youth Service provision of local authorities) were also made.[6]

7.1.4   The Government broadly (but not completely) accepted the DRTF recommendations on education and enacted the Special Educational Needs and Disability Act 2001 (SENDA 2001) in response. Accordingly, from 1 September 2002,[7] the position is somewhat

---

1   DRTF Report, p 48, para 14.

2   Ibid, recommendation 4.4.

3   Ibid, recommendations 4.5 and 4.6.

4   Ibid, recommendation 4.7.

5   Ibid, recommendation 4.10.

6   Ibid, recommendations 4.13 and 4.17.

7   See Special Educational Needs and Disability Act 2001 (Commencement No 5) Order 2002, SI 2002/2217, which brought into force in England and (where applicable) in Scotland on 1 September 2002 the provisions of DDA 1995, ss 28A–28S, 28U–28V, 28X, 31A–31C and Schs 3 (Part 3), 4 (Part 3) and 4A–4C. These provisions also came into force in Wales on 1 September 2002, with the exception of DDA 1995, ss 28D–28E, which came into force in Wales on 1 September 2003: Special Educational Needs and Disability Act 2001 (Commencement No 2) (Wales) Order 2003, SI 2003/2532 (W 247). DDA 1995, s 28T was also brought into force in England, Wales and Scotland on 1 September 2002 (but subject to the modification that DDA 1995, s 28T(1) shall not require a responsible body to provide auxiliary aids or services before 1 September 2003 or to remove or alter a physical feature before 1 September 2005).

changed. The exclusion of education was originally effected by DDA 1995, s 19(5).[1] This provision is now repealed.[2] The present position is that, by virtue of DDA 1995, s 19(5A),[3] nothing in Part 3 of the DDA 1995 (the goods and services provisions) applies to the provision of a service which is made unlawful by new provisions of the DDA 1995 designed to prohibit discrimination against disabled pupils or students and prospective pupils or students, and placing a duty upon education authorities not to discriminate.[4]

7.1.5 Before addressing the radical changes to the law effected by the SENDA 2001, it is necessary to rehearse the pre-September 2002 law. This is in recognition that readers may need to consider the position of alleged acts of discrimination in education occurring prior to 1 September 2002 but being litigated after that date and because aspects of the pre-September 2002 law remain in force alongside the new law. It will also assist an understanding of the significance of the new provisions.

7.2   THE LAW PRE-SEPTEMBER 2002

Education and Part 3 of the DDA 1995

7.2.1 Prior to 1 September 2002, the anti-discrimination provisions in Part 3 of the DDA 1995[5] did not apply to education which was funded or secured by a 'relevant body'.[6] A 'relevant body' was statutorily defined as meaning:[7]

- a local education authority in England and Wales;
- an education authority in Scotland;
- the Scottish Further Education Funding Council;[8]

---

1   DDA 1995, s 19(5)(a)–(ab) and (6) (as amended by Education Act 1996, s 582(1) and Sch 37, para 129; School Standards and Framework Act 1998, s 140(3) and Sch 31; Teaching and Higher Education Act 1998, s 38; and Learning and Skills Act 2000, ss 149 and 153, and Sch 9, paras 1 and 49, and Sch 11).

2   SENDA 2001, ss 38(1), 38(5)(a)–(b), 42(6) and Sch 9.

3   Inserted by ibid, s 38(1) and (6).

4   DDA 1995, s 28A (discrimination against disabled pupils and prospective pupils), s 28F (duty of education authorities not to discriminate) or s 28R (discrimination against disabled students and prospective students), as inserted by SENDA 2001, ss 11, 16 and 26. See Rights of Access Code of Practice 2002, paras 2.31–2.35.

5   DDA 1995, ss 19–21.

6   Ibid, s 19(5)(a), as amended by Education Act 1996, s 582(1) and Sch 37, para 129.

7   Ibid, s 19(6), as amended by School Standards and Framework Act 1998, s 140(3) and Sch 31; Teaching and Higher Education Act 1998, s 38; and Learning and Skills Act 2000, s 153 and Sch 11.

8   Established by an order under Further and Higher Education (Scotland) Act 1992, s 7(1).

- the Higher Education Funding Council for England (HEFCE);
- the Scottish Higher Education Funding Council (SHEFC);
- the Higher Education Funding Council for Wales (HEFCW);
- the Teacher Training Agency;
- a voluntary organisation;
- a body of a prescribed kind;[1]
- an education and library board in Northern Ireland.[2]

Part 3 also did not apply to education 'provided at an establishment which is funded by' one of the relevant bodies listed above or which is funded by a Minister of the Crown (including the Treasury) or by the Department of Education in Northern Ireland.[3] Those provisions of the Act further did not apply to education provided at 'any other establishment which is a school' as defined.[4] This exclusion ensured that private educational establishments were treated on an equal footing with those in the public and maintained sectors. Part 3 was not applicable to education provided within the further education sector as defined[5] or education which was provided by such establishments as may be specified by order by the Secretary of State.[6]

7.2.2 This was a comprehensive list of exclusions which applied to schools, colleges and universities in the public sector or which were in receipt of public funds or which were wholly in the private sector. The effect of these provisions was to exclude education in pre-school institutions, primary schools, secondary schools, colleges and universities from the rights of access provided in Part 3 of the DDA 1995. Education did not count as the provision of goods, facilities or services for the purposes of the anti-discrimination measures in Part 3 of the Act. While employment in educational establishments was within the prohibition on disability discrimination contained in Part 2 of the Act, the 1995 legislation did not touch upon educational opportunities or the rights of disabled pupils or students within such educational establishments. In particular, the aspirations of disabled children to mainstream education, rather than segregated education, were not addressed by the DDA 1995 as originally enacted, nor was the right of

---

1   Ie one prescribed by regulations under the DDA 1995.

2   By virtue of DDA 1995, Sch 8, para 9(3).

3   Ibid, s 19(5)(a)(i) and Sch 8, para 9(2).

4   Ibid, s 19(5)(a)(ii) (as amended by Education Act 1996, s 582(1) and Sch 37, para 129) and Sch 8, para 9(2). A 'school' is one defined in Education Act 1996, s 4(1)–(2); Education (Scotland) Act 1980, s 135(1); or Education and Libraries (Northern Ireland) Order 1986, SI 1986/594.

5   DDA 1995, s 19(5)(aa), as inserted by Learning and Skills Act 2000, s 149 and Sch 9, paras 1 and 49.

6   Ibid, s 19(5)(ab), as inserted by Learning and Skills Act 2000, s 149 and Sch 9, paras 1 and 49.

disabled children or adults to physical access to and reasonable accommodation within educational institutions.

7.2.3 There was one lacuna (which may or may not have been intentional) in the exclusion of education from the anti-discrimination framework. The exclusion clearly only applied to 'education' per se. Although the term 'education' was not defined in the DDA 1995, it clearly did not extend to non-educational facilities or services which an educational establishment happened to provide alongside its curricular activities, such as school trips or holidays.[1] For example, many schools and colleges allow the public to use their sporting facilities (such as swimming pools, playing fields and racquet sports arenas) with or without payment and outside the core scholastic timetable. Such arrangements necessarily involve the public provision of facilities or services which would have been caught by Part 3 rather than by the exclusion of education. Schools are also often used as polling stations during local and central government elections, and it is possible that access to such buildings for this purpose would involve the provision of a facility to the public.[2] Of course, in both examples, it would be necessary to identify who the provider of the facilities or services was – but it would not matter whether it was the school authority itself or whether it was some other legal person merely using the educational premises under a licence or other legal relationship.[3]

Exempted educational services

7.2.4 The Secretary of State exempted certain educational services from Part 3 (in its pre-September 2002 state).[4] In so doing, the

---

1　As is illustrated by *White v Clitheroe Royal Grammar School* (2002) Preston County Court (District Judge Ashton) reported in *Equal Opportunities Review No 106* (June 2002) 26–28 (student with diabetes discriminated against contrary to DDA 1995, Part 3 when excluded from a school holiday for a reason connected with his disability and in circumstances where the school had failed to check the assumptions upon which the exclusion had been made, did not consult with the pupil or his parents, and carried out no risk assessment involving the holiday provider and the pupil's medical advisers).

2　Local authorities are, in any event, under a duty to review arrangements for polling stations, including disabled access, by virtue of Representation of the People Act 1983, s 18. See also HL Deb, vol 564, cols 2005–2006.

3　Note DDA 1995, s 19(3)(h).

4　Insofar as they did not already fall within s 19(5)(a) as explained at **7.2.2**. See Disability Discrimination (Services and Premises) Regulations 1996, SI 1996/1836, reg 9 (exemption from DDA 1995, ss 19–21 for certain educational services) made under DDA 1995, s 19(5)(c). Regulation 9 came into force on 2 December 1996, but was revoked with effect from 1 September 2002 (except in Northern Ireland) to coincide with the coming into force of DDA 1995, ss 28A–28X, inserted by SENDA 2001, Part 2. See Disability Discrimination (Services and Premises) (Amendment) Regulations 2002, SI 2002/1980, regs 2 and 4.

regulations may have plugged some of the gaps in the original exclusion of education from the anti-discrimination framework of the DDA 1995. Regulations served to exclude from Part 3 coverage of certain youth and community services provided by education authorities or voluntary organisations (such as the scouts or guides), the provision of facilities for research in certain circumstances, and some examination and assessment services.[1]

7.2.5 First,[2] DDA 1995, Part 3 did not apply to services provided by a local education authority (in Scotland, an education authority) in carrying out its functions under certain education legislation.[3] This related to the statutory duty on an education authority to secure the provision for its area of adequate facilities for full-time or part-time further education suitable for the requirements of persons over compulsory school age. This included vocational, social, physical and recreational training. It also included organised leisure-time occupation – provided in connection with the provision of further education – in such organised cultural training and recreative activities as are suited to their requirements, for any persons over compulsory school age who are able and willing to profit by facilities provided for that purpose. Education authorities must give particular attention to persons with learning difficulties when exercising these functions. The regulations also covered the statutory duty placed on such authorities to secure that the facilities for further education included adequate facilities for recreation and social and physical training. An education authority may establish, maintain and manage camps, holiday classes, playing fields, play centres and other places (including playgrounds, gymnasiums and swimming baths) for this purpose, and may organise games, expeditions and other activities. The anti-discrimination provisions of Part 3 of the DDA 1995 did not apply to these facilities or services.

7.2.6 Secondly,[4] Part 3 did not apply to the provision by a voluntary organisation of social, cultural and recreational activities and facilities for physical education and training where such activities were designed to promote the personal or educational development of persons taking part in them. Thirdly,[5] the provision of facilities for research (including

---

1   Rights of Access Code of Practice 2002, paras 2.33–2.34.

2   Disability Discrimination (Services and Premises) Regulations 1996, SI 1996/1836, reg 9(1) (a) (now revoked as explained at **7.2.4**).

3   Education Act 1996, s 2 or s 508; Education (Scotland) Act 1980, s 1(3).

4   Disability Discrimination (Services and Premises) Regulations 1996, SI 1996/1836, reg 9(1) (b) (now revoked as explained at **7.2.4**). The DRTF recommended the abolition of this exemption: DRTF Report, recommendation 4.18.

5   Ibid, reg 9(1)(c).

the supervision of or guidance of research) at a relevant establishment was not covered by the provisions of Part 3 of the DDA 1995.[1] Fourthly,[2] those provisions did not embrace the assessment at a relevant establishment of pupils or students in connection with education provided to them by the establishment or by another relevant establishment. This also excluded the assessment at a relevant establishment of pupils or students to whom education has not been provided by the establishment where the assessment was undertaken.[3]

7.2.7 These were complex provisions and experience of them did not test how far the regulations operated wholly to exclude these services which are closely connected with the provision of education. However, these regulations were not wide enough to exclude from the scope of Part 3 a whole raft of services, facilities and activities which may be provided on school, college or university premises. In addition to the examples already given, student unions did not seem to be excluded,[4] while many colleges and universities allow their halls of residence to be used for conferences and self-catering holiday facilities open to the public during vacations and were thus subject to the Act.[5]

Education and policy-making

7.2.8 Although the provision of education was not generally subject to the anti-discrimination principles in the DDA 1995, the original Part 4 of the Act amended existing education legislation so as to encourage policy-making and action by educational institutions to promote the integration of disabled pupils and students.[6] These provisions applied to schools, colleges and universities.

Schools

7.2.9 The DDA 1995 approached the task of improving educational opportunities and access for disabled pupils by amending the provisions

1   A 'relevant establishment' meant an establishment funded by one of the bodies listed in **7.2.1** (except a body of a prescribed kind or, in Northern Ireland, an education and library board) or by a Minister of the Crown or any other establishment which is a school as defined: ibid, reg 9(2)(a) and (b) which cross-refer to DDA 1995, s 19(5)(a)(ii) and (6).

2   Disability Discrimination (Services and Premises) Regulations 1996, SI 1996/1836, reg 9(1)(d)(i) and see reg 9(2) (now revoked as explained at **7.2.4**).

3   Ibid, reg 9(1)(d)(ii).

4   Unless they are caught by the Disability Discrimination (Services and Premises) Regulations 1996, SI 1996/1836, reg 9(1)(b) (now revoked as explained at **7.2.4**). See **7.2.6**.

5   See the further examples given in Rights of Access Code of Practice 2002, para 2.34.

6   See originally DDA 1995, ss 29–31.

of the Education Acts setting out the duties of governing bodies (in the case of county, voluntary or grant-maintained schools) and local education authorities (in the case of maintained nursery schools) in relation to pupils with special educational needs (SEN).[1] Information relating to pupils with SEN was required to be included in annual reporting mechanisms.[2] As the Government at that time explained:

> 'One of the major themes in the Education Act 1993 was that mainstream schools should play their full part in providing for pupils with special needs at every stage; and that a school's duties should be clarified through the code of practice for the identification and assessment of such children... Local accountability is ensured through the requirement on schools to formulate and publish information about their policy for children with special needs, keeping parents and prospective parents informed. The publication of SEN policies will help to prevent the possibility that parents could feel inclined to send their child to a special school on the basis that they did not know enough about the SEN provision in local mainstream schools.'[3]

The 1995 reforms were intended to build upon that foundation.

7.2.10   Since 1 January 1997, the 'annual report' for each county, voluntary or grant-maintained school was required to include a report containing information as to the:

- arrangements for admission of disabled pupils;
- steps taken to prevent disabled pupils from being treated less favourably than other pupils; and
- facilities provided to assist access to school by disabled pupils.[4]

From 1 September 2002, this requirement is affected by the changes contained in the SENDA 2001.[5] The 'annual report' in question is a reference to the report to parents required to be prepared under the articles of government for the school.[6] This gloss upon the existing obligations of schools' governing bodies applies only in respect of pupils

---

1   See Education Act 1993, s 161(5); now Education Act 1996, s 317(5), as amended by SENDA 2001, Sch 8, para 5.

2   See originally DDA 1995, s 29(1), now repealed by Education Act 1996, s 582(2) and Sch 38, Part I.

3   HL Deb, vol 564, cols 1993–1994.

4   Education Act 1993, s 161(6), as inserted by DDA 1995, s 29(2) (which was repealed by Education Act 1996, s 582(2) and Sch 38, Part I); see now Education Act 1996, s 317(6)–(7), as amended by SENDA 2001, s 14(2). See *School Prospectuses and Governors' Annual Reports* (DfEE Circulars 11/96 (primary schools) and 12/96 (secondary schools)).

5   SENDA 2001, s 14(2). See **7.4.15**.

6   In accordance with Education Act (No 2) Act 1986, s 30 or Education Act 1993, Sch 6, para 8. The cross-reference is made in Education Act 1993, s 161(7), as inserted by DDA 1995, s 29(2) (which was repealed by Education Act 1996, s 582(2) and Sch 38, Part I). See now Education Act 1996, s 317(6)–(7), as amended by SENDA 2001, s 14(2).

who are disabled persons within the meaning of the DDA 1995,[1] whether or not they have a statutory SEN statement. It was intended that by these means schools that are inaccessible to disabled children would be required to admit it and to consider how they might be made accessible in a cost-effective way.[2] Parental rights might also be strengthened by giving dissatisfied parents a means to voice concerns about a school's non-compliance with its own stated policies through the existing local admissions appeals arrangements. The measures were hoped to encourage genuine and full integration of disabled pupils in mainstream education 'as far as possible'.[3]

Teacher Training Agency

7.2.11 The Teacher Training Agency is the body which has responsibility for funding institutions providing teacher training. In exercising its functions, the Teacher Training Agency must have regard to the requirements of disabled persons.[4] Although this is not made clear, it is arguable that this covers the needs of disabled persons entering the teaching profession as well as the training of teachers in respect of the needs of disabled pupils.

Further education colleges and institutions

7.2.12 In justifying the exclusion of further and higher education from the services provisions of Part 3 of the DDA 1995, the Government at that time was said to be placing a high priority on widening access to colleges and universities.[5] However, it wished to consider the practical effects of inclusion and sought to avoid undermining the strategic role which the further and higher education funding councils play.[6] The Government elected for what it regarded as a coherent programme for encouraging access, enforceable through the existing complaints procedures rather than by litigation.[7] Nevertheless, it recognised that there was a genuine problem in guaranteeing access for disabled persons to educational opportunities in colleges and universities.

---

1 Education Act 1993, s 161(7), as inserted by DDA 1995, s 29(2) (which was repealed by Education Act 1996, s 582(2) and Sch 38, Part I). See now Education Act 1996, s 317(6)–(7), as amended by SENDA 2001, s 14(2).

2 HL Deb, vol 564, col 1994.

3 Ibid, cols 1994–1995.

4 Education Act 1994, s 1(4), as inserted originally by DDA 1995, s 29(3) and re-enacted by SENDA 2001, s 40(2) when SENDA 2001, s 40(1) repealed DDA 1995, s 29.

5 HL Deb, vol 564, col 1989.

6 Ibid, col 1989.

7 Ibid, col 1990.

7.2.13 The DDA 1995 amended the provisions of the Further and Higher Education Act 1992 which set out the framework for further and higher education for disabled students (including those with learning disabilities) in England and Wales. The amendments contained in the DDA 1995 applied only to England and Wales and not to Scotland. Legislation already required Scottish colleges to submit development plans including information on provisions made for disabled students.[1] The Further and Higher Education Act 1992 required 'the further education funding councils to act in a strategic manner to secure sufficient and adequate provision of further education'.[2] The further education funding councils (FEFCs) had to take particular account of the needs of the population in terms of location, equipment, aptitudes and abilities, and they had particular responsibilities in respect of disabled students. To those ends, the Further Education Funding Council for England (FEFCE) required colleges to submit strategic plans, including analysis of local needs, and its funding methodology took into account the needs of disabled students. Part 4 of the DDA 1995 sought to build upon the existing strategy by amending the Further and Higher Education Act 1992.[3]

7.2.14 The FEFCs were required to place conditions upon the financial support they gave to such educational establishments.[4] In particular, the administration of funds by FEFCs was subject to a new set of conditions for financial support given to further education colleges.[5] The new conditions were expressly without prejudice to the funding councils' existing powers to impose conditions on the granting of such financial support.[6] Those additional specific conditions required the governing body to publish annual 'disability statements' containing information about the provision of facilities for education made by the institution in respect of 'disabled persons' and may have included conditions relating to the provision made (or to be made) by the institution with respect to disabled persons.[7]

7.2.15 The information to be contained in an annual disability statement about the provision of facilities made by further education

---

1   Further and Higher Education (Scotland) Act 1992, s 22.

2   HL Deb, vol 564, col 1990.

3   DDA 1995, s 30(1).

4   Further and Higher Education Act 1992, s 5.

5   Ibid, s 5(6)(b) and (7A), as amended by DDA 1995, s 30(2).

6   Ibid, s 5(6)(b).

7   Ibid, s 5(7A), as inserted by DDA 1995, s 30(3). The phrase 'disabled persons' means only such persons as satisfy the definition of 'disabled person' in DDA 1995, ss 1–2 and Schs 1–2 (see Chapter 2): Further and Higher Education Act 1992, s 5(7B), as inserted by DDA 1995, s 30(3).

institutions in England and Wales in respect of disabled persons was prescribed by regulations.[1] An annual disability statement had to cover the following matters:[2]

- policies of the institution relating to the provision of facilities for education;
- names of a member or members of staff with special responsibility for disabled persons;
- admission arrangements;
- educational facilities and support, including academic and curriculum support, relevant staff expertise, and technology and equipment available;
- additional support or special arrangements during examinations and assessments;
- facilities and support associated with educational facilities and support, including counselling and welfare arrangements;
- physical access to educational and other facilities.

The statement should also have contained information about arrangements for handling complaints and (where applicable) appeals in respect of admission arrangements; educational facilities and support; additional support or special arrangements during examinations and assessments; facilities and support associated with educational facilities and support (including counselling and welfare arrangements); and physical access to educational and other facilities.

7.2.16 These provisions are not affected by the changes made in SENDA 2001. They did not give disabled students directly enforceable rights as such, but they would have been 'able to seek redress from the councils on the rare occasions when provision fails to meet expectations raised by the information' contained in a statutory disability statement.[3] It would seem that ultimately an FEFC could demand repayment of a grant paid to a college which failed to meet the new legislative requirements.

Further education funding councils

7.2.17 Further amendments to the Further and Higher Education Act 1992 built upon the strategic role of the FEFCs. The funding councils were required to make an annual written report to the Secretary of State

---

1 Education (Disability Statements for Further Education Institutions) Regulations 1996, SI 1996/1664, made under Further and Higher Education Act 1992, ss 5(7A)–(7B) and 89(4), as amended by DDA 1995, s 30. The regulations came into force on 31 July 1996.

2 Education (Disability Statements for Further Education Institutions) Regulations 1996, SI 1996/1664, reg 2.

3 HL Deb, vol 564, col 1991.

on the progress made during the previous year in the provision of further education for disabled students in their area and their plans for future provision of further education for disabled students.[1] It was envisaged that the FEFCs would draw on existing review and planning mechanisms, as well as new information generated from the disability statements produced by colleges and the evidence gathered by the FEFCE's committee on education and disability (the Tomlinson Committee).[2] The functions performed by the FEFCs have been taken over by the Learning and Skills Council for England and the National Council for Education and Training for Wales.[3] They are responsible for post-16 learning (other than higher education) and will have general oversight of the provision of adult education by local education authorities (LEAs). The SENDA 2001 removes the power of these two bodies to require providers of learning to publish disability statements by imposing a condition of grant.[4]

Local education authorities

7.2.18   The DDA 1995 amended the functions of LEAs in respect of further education in order to underpin the duties of colleges and funding councils.[5] Prior to 1 September 2002, LEAs were placed under a duty to publish disability statements at prescribed intervals.[6] Such statements had to contain information (prescribed by regulations) about the provision of facilities for further education made by the LEA in respect of disabled persons within the meaning of the DDA 1995.[7] The intention was to ensure that courses provided by LEAs enjoyed 'parity of esteem' with FEFC-funded courses and that disabled students should be better informed about such locally provided courses.[8] That duty is now removed by the SENDA 2001.[9]

---

1   Further and Higher Education Act 1992, s 8(6), as inserted by DDA 1995, s 30(4). The term 'disabled students' refers only to students who are disabled persons under the DDA 1995: Further and Higher Education Act 1992, s 8(7), as inserted by DDA 1995, s 30(4).

2   HL Deb, vol 564, col 1991.

3   Learning and Skills Act 2000, ss 1 and 30.

4   SENDA 2001, s 34(7)–(8), repealing Learning and Skills Act 2000, ss 6(4), (6), 35(4) and (6).

5   Education Act 1944, s 41, as amended by DDA 1995, s 30(7) then repealed by Education Act 1996, s 582(2) and Sch 38, Part I and overtaken by Education Act 1996, ss 2, 15 and 528.

6   Ibid, s 41(2A), as inserted by DDA 1995, s 30(8) then repealed by Education Act 1996, s 582(2) and Sch 38, Part I and overtaken by Education Act 1996, s 528.

7   Education Act 1944, s 41(2B), as inserted by DDA 1995, s 30(8) then repealed by Education Act 1996, s 582(2) and Sch 38, Part I and overtaken by Education Act 1996, s 528.

8   HL Deb, vol 566, cols 1032–1033.

9   SENDA 2001, s 34(3), providing that Education Act 1996, s 528 ceases to have effect.

Universities and higher education institutions

7.2.19 Prior to the DDA 1995, the Secretary of State provided mere guidance to the higher education funding councils that they should have regard to the needs of disabled students in universities and institutions of higher education. In a much debated change,[1] since 31 July 1996, the higher education funding councils for England, Wales and Scotland have been required to have regard to the requirements of disabled persons when exercising their statutory functions.[2] In both cases, that statutory duty applied only in respect of disabled persons within the meaning of the DDA 1995.[3] These provisions are unaffected by the SENDA 2001.

7.2.20 Prior to the changes wrought by the SENDA 2001, the higher education funding councils were also empowered to make grants, loans or other payments to the governing body of a university or higher education institution conditional upon a requirement that the governing body should publish 'disability statements'.[4] This was without prejudice to the existing powers of the funding councils to impose conditions on governing bodies, except that the requirement to publish periodic disability statements was mandatory. Disability statements had to be published at intervals specified in the conditions subject to which grants, loans or other payments were made by a council.[5] A 'disability statement' was a statement containing information (specified in the conditions subject to which grants, loans or other payments were made by a council) about the provision of facilities for education and research made by the university or institution in respect of disabled persons (as defined in the DDA 1995).[6] The Higher Education Funding Council for England (HEFCE) and its Welsh and Scottish counterparts (the HEFCW and the SHEFC) each issued a specification for disability

---

1   See eg HL Deb, vol 564, cols 874–876 and 1983–1986.

2   Further and Higher Education Act 1992, s 62(7A), as inserted by DDA 1995, s 30(5); Further and Higher Education (Scotland) Act 1992, s 37(4A), as inserted by DDA 1995, s 31(1)–(2).

3   Further and Higher Education Act 1992, s 62(7B), as inserted by DDA 1995, s 30(5); Further and Higher Education (Scotland) Act 1992, s 37(4B), as inserted by DDA 1995, s 31(2).

4   Further and Higher Education Act 1992, s 65(4A), as inserted by DDA 1995, s 30(6); Further and Higher Education (Scotland) Act 1992, s 40(5), as inserted by DDA 1995, s 31(3). These provisions are repealed by SENDA 2001, s 34(1)–(2).

5   Further and Higher Education Act 1992, s 65(4B), as inserted by DDA 1995, s 30(6); Further and Higher Education (Scotland) Act 1992, s 40(6), as inserted by DDA 1995, s 31(3). These provisions are repealed by SENDA 2001, s 34(1)–(2).

6   Further and Higher Education Act 1992, s 65(4B), as inserted by DDA 1995, s 30(6); Further and Higher Education (Scotland) Act 1992, s 40(6), as inserted by DDA 1995, s 31(3). It is clear that the 'facilities' referred to did not merely include *physical* facilities:

statements required from institutions funded by each council.[1] It was anticipated that a disability statement would be produced every three years, but should be updated and resubmitted where there had been significant changes.[2] Statements had to be published and could be referred to in other publications (such as prospectuses).[3]

7.2.21 While a disability statement should have described facilities for education and research offered by a higher education institution to disabled persons, it was also designed to inform the funding council about such provision and to highlight good practice.[4] Although institutions were free to decide what facilities should be offered, they were encouraged to consider provision for disabled students and 'to plan strategically for future developments'.[5] Statements should have been 'concise, informative and developmental'; if necessary could have made reference to accessible secondary sources; and may have needed to be produced in alternative formats or media.[6] Statements were to be structured so as to provide information under the headings of current policy, current provision, and future activity and policy development.

7.2.22 As far as current policy was concerned, the statement was to contain general information on policies and procedures relating to disabled students for:[7]

- equal opportunities;
- access and admissions;
- examinations and assessments;
- quality assessment, and monitoring and evaluation of support services;
- staff development and training programmes;
- provision of financial assistance to disabled students;
- charging students for certain facilities.

If an institution did not have policies for the above areas, it should have given an overview of its policies affecting disabled students.

HL Deb, vol 566, cols 278–279. These provisions are repealed by SENDA 2001, s 34(1)–(2).

1   See HEFCE Circular 8/96 (May 1996); HEFCW Circular W96/43HE (June 1996); SHEFC Circular 47/96 (October 1996). See also SHEFC, *Disability Discrimination and the Changing Legislative Context: Implications for the Scottish Higher Education Sector* (SHEFC Circular 9/99).

2   See eg HEFCE Circular 8/96, para 18.

3   Ibid, paras 20–21.

4   See eg ibid, para 8.

5   Ibid, para 9.

6   See eg ibid, para 10.

7   Ibid, paras 12–13. The date on which the policy or procedure became effective should also have been stated. The HEFCW also included complaints and appeals procedures in the list of existing policy: HEFCW Circular W96/43HE, para 8.

7.2.23 In connection with current provision, the statement should have described the nature and range of provision for disabled students, including:[1]

- names and titles (and contact details) of the co-ordinator and member of senior management responsible for disabled students;
- examples of the types of information, advice, services and materials available, and a broad picture of how the institution provided support;[2]
- academic services and support arrangements (for example, special provision for examinations and marking);
- information technology provision;
- a general description of the physical environment;
- specific information on medical facilities, transport, religious and spiritual worship, external services, and award ceremonies.

The statement should have indicated any restrictions on services and facilities, and an indication of the number of disabled students at the institution.[3] Finally, the statement should have outlined plans for policy development and improvements to provision in the short to long term, covering at least the next three years.[4]

7.2.24 The amendments to the powers of the higher education funding councils in respect of the administration of funds were designed to achieve the:

> '... intention that the [disability] statements would assist disabled students and funding councils generally in understanding the provision available for education and research in the particular institution ... The statements would thus go wider than simply including information about physical facilities. It will be a matter for the funding councils, in consultation, to determine how to specify the information needed in the statements to achieve that in a viable and cost-effective way ... [T]he provision of information will not *ipso facto* require any changes in the nature of the facilities offered by the institution.'[5]

This was apparently achieved without compromising the guarantees of academic freedom inherent in the 1992 legislation. There was nothing in the DDA 1995 as originally enacted that might require a university to change admissions arrangements, modify course structures or alter assessment programmes in order to meet the needs of disabled students. Moreover, nothing in a disability statement was intended to be

1 See eg HEFCE Circular 8/96, para 14.

2 The HEFCE Circular posed some questions that might be addressed: ibid, para 14.b.

3 Ibid, paras 15–16.

4 Ibid, para 17.

5 HL Deb, vol 564, col 1993.

used to pressurise universities or funding councils to change curriculum and admissions policies.[1] However, it was hoped that disability statements would concentrate the minds of universities and would encourage them to be receptive to the needs of disabled students.

7.2.25 This is all now rather academic (no pun intended). The SENDA 2001 removes the duty from the Higher Education Funding Councils in England, Scotland and Wales to require providers of learning to publish disability statements by imposing a condition of grant. This is because these duties are superseded by the new anti-discrimination duties discussed below. The change is effected by repealing key provisions of the statutory framework erected by the DDA 1995.[2]

7.3   THE LAW POST-SEPTEMBER 2002

Special Educational Needs and Disability Act 2001

7.3.1 The SENDA 2001 received the Royal Assent on 11 May 2001.[3] Part 2 of the SENDA 2001 is the result of the Government's response to the Final Report of the DRTF.[4] It addresses the key recommendations in the DRTF Final Report on education. It amends Part IV of the DDA 1995 (now to be known as Part 4) to introduce rights for disabled persons in education. It applies in England, Wales and Scotland, but not Northern Ireland.[5] As has been noted above, the exemption of publicly

---

1   HL Deb, vol 566, col 1036.

2   SENDA 2001, s 34(1)–(2), repealing Further and Higher Education Act 1992, s 65(4A)–(4B) and Further and Higher Education (Scotland) Act 1992, s 40(5)–(6). SENDA 2001, s 34(5)–(6) also repeals DDA 1995, ss 30(6) and 31(3).

3   The complete legislative history of the Act is as follows:

   House of Lords: Introduction (7 December 2000) HL Deb, vol 620, col 31; 2nd Reading (19 December 2000) HL Deb, vol 620, cols 634–710; Committee (23 and 29–30 January 2001 and 6 February 2001) HL Deb, vol 621, cols CWH1–284); Report (20–21 February 2001) HL Deb, vol 622, cols 598–667, 683–808; 3rd Reading (1 March 2001) HL Deb, vol 622, cols 1283–1354.

   House of Commons: Introduction (5 March 2001) Votes & Proceedings (5 March 2001); 2nd Reading (20 March 2001) HC Deb, vol 365, cols 215–305; Committee (27 March to 5 April 2001) Standing Committee B; Report and 3rd Reading (26 April 2001) HC Deb, vol 367, cols 477–541.

4   Disability Rights Task Force, *From Exclusion to Inclusion: A Report of the Disability Rights Task Force for Disabled People* (1999, London: DfEE); *Interim Government Response to the Report of the Disability Rights Task Force* (2000, London: DfEE); *Towards Inclusion – Civil Rights for Disabled People: Government Response to the Disability Rights Task Force* (2001, London: DfEE).

5   In November 2002, the Departments of Education and of Employment and Learning in Northern Ireland proposed the introduction of a Special Educational Needs and Disability Bill in Northern Ireland. This would introduce equivalent legislation to that existing in Great Britain. A draft order was published in April 2004 and was the subject of

funded providers of education services and private schools from Part 3
of the DDA 1995 is removed. As a result, any provider of education
previously exempted from Part 3 and not covered by the new Part 4
duties becomes subject to the duties in Part 3 of the DDA 1995.[1] SENDA
2001, Part 2 contains the provisions on disability discrimination in
education which amend Part 4 of the DDA 1995.[2] Chapter 1 of DDA
1995, Part 4 deals with schools and education authorities and Chapter 2
of Part 4 deals with further and higher education.[3] Each Part is dealt
with in turn below.

7.4 SCHOOLS AND EDUCATION AUTHORITIES

7.4.1 As a result of the changes brought about by the SENDA 2001
there are now three sources of support available to disabled pupils in
school. These are:

(1) the new disability discrimination duties;
(2) the new planning duties; and
(3) the existing and amended SEN framework.

A discussion of the SEN framework is beyond the scope of this book, but
it is important to note that the new duties in DDA 1995, Part 4, Chapter 1
are designed to dovetail with it. The statutory provisions containing the
new duties are supported by the *Disability Discrimination Act 1995 Part 4
Code of Practice for Schools* (Schools Code of Practice) (2002) issued by the
DRC under DDA 1995, s 53A at the request of the Secretary of State for
Education and Skills.[4] The Schools Code of Practice applies to all

---

consultation until 28 June 2004. Once enacted, it is intended that the new law will be
effective from 1 September 2005.

1   *Explanatory Notes to Special Educational Needs and Disability Act 2001.* See the discussion of
DDA 1995, Part 3 in Chapter 5. Notably, this will include local authority day nurseries and
family centres, private and voluntary playgroups and pre-schools, and accredited
childminders which would not otherwise be covered by the new provisions of DDA 1995,
Part 4. See *Disability Discrimination Act 1995 Part 4 Code of Practice for Schools*, paras 10.7–10.9.

2   SENDA 2001, Part 1 amends the law relating to special educational needs and is beyond
the scope of this book.

3   Chapter 3 of SENDA 2001, Part 2 deals with miscellaneous matters, including extending
the role of the DRC, providing for codes of practices and making provision for
conciliation of disputes. Various schedules deal with the consequential effects of the
changes to the DDA 1995. These provisions are addressed in appropriate chapters of this
book.

4   See the overview of the legislation provided in the Schools Code of Practice, Chapters 2
(Scotland) and 3 (England and Wales). As well as describing the interaction of the DDA
1995 with the SEN framework, the Schools Code of Practice (Chapter 10) usefully explains
the relationship of the DDA 1995 with other legislation and responsibilities (such as data
protection legislation, health and safety law and regulations, fire safety legislation,
occupiers' liability, defective premises law, the Human Rights Act 1998, sex and race
discrimination legislation, etc).

schools and LEAs (known as education authorities in Scotland) in England, Wales and Scotland, and to young people over the age of 16 when in school.[1] Further guidance is also available from various other sources.[2]

Disability discrimination duties

7.4.2 By virtue of the new s 28A(1) of the DDA 1995,[3] it is unlawful for 'the body responsible for a school' to discriminate against a 'disabled person':[4]

- in the arrangements it makes for determining admission to the school as a pupil;[5]
- in the terms on which it offers to admit him or her to the school as a pupil; or
- by refusing or deliberately omitting to accept an application for his or her admission to the school as a pupil.

It is also unlawful for 'the body responsible for a school' to discriminate against a disabled pupil[6] in the education or associated services provided for (or offered to) pupils at the school by that body.[7] It is

---

1 Schools Code of Practice, paras 1.2–1.3. Its purpose and status is set out in paras 1.4–1.7 (and see further the discussion in **9.3**). It does not apply in Northern Ireland, but takes account of devolved government and the differences between the education systems in the different parts of Great Britain: paras 1.8–1.10.

2 See the guidance issued to local authorities, LEAs and schools in England by the Department for Education and Skills: *Accessible Schools: Planning to Increase Access to Schools for Disabled Pupils* (LEA/0168/2002: July 2002). See also Disability Rights Commission, *A Guide for Schools in England*; Disability Rights Commission, *A Guide for Schools in Scotland*; Disability Rights Commission, *Information for School Governors in England*.

3 See Schools Code of Practice, para 4.22. For early examples of appellate courts considering these provisions, see: *McAuley Catholic High School v (1) CC; (2) PC; and (3) Special Educational Needs and Disability Tribunal* [2003] EWHC 3045 (Admin), [2004] ICR 1543, QBD, and *R (on the application of D) v Governing Body of Plymouth High School for Girls* [2004] EWHC 1923 (Admin), Collins J.

4 A 'disabled person' is a person falling within DDA 1995, ss 1–2 and Schs 1–2 (discussed in Chapter 2). This section also applies to discrimination against a person who is not disabled in the case of an act which constitutes discrimination by virtue of DDA 1995, s 55 (victimisation): DDA 1995, s 28A(6). See Schools Code of Practice, Chapter 4 and paras 10.10–10.14 (and examples).

5 This includes any criteria for deciding who will be admitted to the school when it is over-subscribed and includes the operation of those criteria: Schools Code of Practice, para 4.22. By virtue of DDA 1995, s 28Q(3), the term 'pupil' (as used throughout this analysis) has the meaning assigned to it by Education Act 1996, s 3(1) and Education (Scotland) Act 1980, s 135(1). See Schools Code of Practice, Chapter 4.

6 By virtue of DDA 1995, s 28Q(2), the term 'disabled pupil' (as used throughout this analysis) means a pupil who is a disabled person. See Schools Code of Practice, Chapter 4.

7 DDA 1995, s 28A(2). The Secretary of State may by regulations prescribe services which are or are not to be regarded for this purpose as being 'education' or 'an associated service': DDA 1995, s 28A(3). See Schools Code of Practice, paras 4.23–4.26 which define

further unlawful for 'the body responsible for a school' to discriminate against a disabled pupil by excluding him or her from the school, whether permanently or temporarily.[1] A school's failure to provide a pupil with autistic spectrum disorder with such personal guidance and support within the school's pastoral care system as he required has been hold to amount to an unlawful act of disability discrimination.[2]

7.4.3 The meaning of the term 'the body responsible for a school' (referred to as the 'responsible body') depends upon the kind of school involved.[3] In England and Wales, in the case of a maintained school or maintained nursery school, it is the LEA[4] or governing body,[5] according to which has the function in question; in the case of a pupil referral unit, it is the LEA; and in the case of an independent school or a special school not maintained by the LEA, it is the proprietor of the school.[6] In Scotland,[7] in the case of a school managed by an education authority, it is the education authority; in the case of an independent school, it is the proprietor of the school; in the case of a self-governing school, it is

---

education and associated services (without intending to be exhaustive) as including: preparation for entry to the school; the curriculum; teaching and learning; classroom organisation; timetabling; grouping of pupils; homework; access to school facilities; activities to supplement the curriculum (eg a drama group visiting the school); school sports; school policies; breaks and lunchtimes; the serving of school meals; interaction with peers; assessment and exam arrangements; school discipline and sanctions; exclusion procedures; school clubs and activities; school trips; the school's arrangements for working with other agencies; preparation of pupils for the next phase of education.

1   DDA 1995, s 28A(4). It does not matter whether the exclusion takes the form (in Scotland) of a temporary exclusion or an exclusion/removal from the register or (in England and Wales) a permanent or fixed-term exclusion: Schools Code of Practice, para 4.27.

2   *McAuley Catholic High School v (1) CC; (2) PC; and (3) Special Educational Needs and Disability Tribunal* [2003] EWHC 3045 (Admin), [2004] ICR 1563, QBD

3   DDA 1995, ss 28A(5) and 28Q(6), and Sch 4A, as amended by Education Act 2002. In Scotland, the term 'school' (used throughout this analysis) has the meaning assigned by Education (Scotland) Act 1980, s 135(1). In England and Wales, the term 'school' (used throughout this analysis) means a maintained school (within the meaning of School Standards and Framework Act 1998, s 20(7)); a maintained nursery school (within the meaning of School Standards and Framework Act 1998, s 22(9)); an independent school (within the meaning of Education Act 1996, s 463); a special school which is not a maintained special school but which is approved by the Secretary of State (in England) or by the National Assembly (in Wales) under Education Act 1996, s 342; or a pupil referral unit (within the meaning of Education Act 1996, s 19(2)). See DDA 1995, s 28Q(4)–(5). See Schools Code of Practice, Chapter 4.

4   As defined in School Standards and Framework Act 1998, s 22(8).

5   The 'governing body' in relation to a maintained school means the body corporate which the school has as a result of Education Act 2002, s 19; DDA 1995, s 28Q(7).

6   As defined in Education Act 1996, s 579.

7   In this account, the terms 'board of management', 'education authority', 'managers' and 'proprietor' are defined in Education (Scotland) Act, s 135(1).

the board of management of the school; and in the case of a school in respect of which the managers are for the time being receiving grants,[1] it is the managers of the school.

Discrimination

7.4.4   The meaning of discrimination for this purpose is set out in DDA 1995, s 28B. There are two kinds of discrimination contemplated by the section. They might be referred to in shorthand as (1) less favourable treatment, and (2) failure to make reasonable adjustments.

Less favourable treatment

7.4.5   A responsible body discriminates against a disabled person if, for a reason which relates to his or her disability,[2] it treats him or her less favourably than it treats or would treat others to whom that reason does not (or would not apply)[3] and it cannot show that the treatment in question is justified.[4] Less favourable treatment of a person is justified if it is the result of a permitted form of selection.[5] Otherwise, less

---

1   Under Education (Scotland) Act 1980, s 73(c) or (d).

2   There has to be a link between the reason and the disability: Schools Code of Practice, paras 5.7–5.8 (and examples).

3   This calls for a real or hypothetical comparison: Schools Code of Practice, paras 5.9–5.10 (and examples). The comparison is between a disabled pupil and a pupil who is not disabled: *R (on the application of D) v Governing Body of Plymouth High School for Girls* [2004] EWHC 1923 (Admin).

4   DDA 1995, s 28B(1). See Schools Code of Practice, Chapter 5. See *R (on the application of D) v Governing Body of Plymouth High School for Girls* [2004] EWHC 1923 (Admin). A school discriminated against a disabled pupil without justification by failing to assist her properly in relation to a work placement. The pupil had filled in her work placement form incompletely by failing to answer a question about her disability, but the school failed to take steps to remedy the position. Her disability appeared to be a factor in her failure to obtain a placement. Her treatment was for a reason related to her disability.

5   DDA 1995, s 28B(6) by virtue of s 28B(5) and see Schools Code of Practice, paras 5.18–5.23 (and examples). In England and Wales, the term 'permitted form of selection' in relation to a maintained school which is not designated as a grammar school (under School Standards and Framework Act 1998, s 104) means any form of selection mentioned in School Standards and Framework Act 1998, s 99(2) or (4); in relation to a maintained school which is so designated as a grammar school it means any of its selective admission arrangements; and in relation to an independent school it means any arrangements which make provision for any or all of its pupils to be selected by reference to general or special ability or aptitude with a view to admitting only pupils of high ability or aptitude: DDA 1995, s 28Q(9). In Scotland, the term 'permitted form of selection' in relation to a school managed by an education authority (within the meaning of Education (Scotland) Act 1980, s 135(1)) means such arrangements as have been approved by the Scottish Ministers for the selection of pupils for admission; and in relation to an independent school or a self-governing school (within the meaning of Education (Scotland) Act 1980, s 135(1)) it means any arrangements which make provision for any or all of its pupils to be selected by reference to general or special ability or aptitude with a view to admitting only pupils of

favourable treatment is justified only if the reason for it is both material to the circumstances of the particular case and substantial (that is, more than minor or trivial).[1] If the responsible body is under a duty to make reasonable adjustments (imposed by DDA 1995, s 28C) in relation to the disabled person, but it fails without justification to comply with that duty, its treatment of that person cannot be justified by reference to a material and substantial reason[2] unless that treatment would have been justified even if it had complied with that duty.[3] The concept of unjustified less favourable treatment discrimination arising here is broadly similar to the parallel provision in Part 2 of the DDA 1995 (discrimination in employment) and the case-law there is likely to be instructive.[4]

Failure to make reasonable adjustments

7.4.6 A responsible body also discriminates against a disabled person if it fails, to his or her detriment, to comply with the duty to make reasonable adjustments contained in DDA 1995, s 28C and it cannot show that its failure to comply is justified.[5] Before this kind of discrimination can be explored further it is necessary to examine the duty to make reasonable adjustments in this context.[6]

7.4.7 There are two aspects to the duty to make reasonable adjustments upon schools.[7] First, the responsible body for a school must take such steps as it is reasonable for it to have to take to ensure that, in relation to the arrangements it makes for determining the admission of pupils to the school, disabled persons are not placed at a substantial

---

high ability or aptitude: DDA 1995, s 28Q(10)–(11). See further Department for Education and Skills, *Code of Practice on School Admissions* (1999); Welsh Office, *School Admissions Code of Practice* (1999).

1   DDA 1995, s 28B(7), by virtue of s 28B(5). See Schools Code of Practice, paras 5.11–5.15 (and examples).

2   DDA 1995, s 28B(7).

3   Ibid, s 28B(8). See Schools Code of Practice, para 5.16 (and example).

4   This has been confirmed in *McAuley Catholic High School v (1) CC; (2) PC; and (3) Special Educational Needs and Disability Tribunal* [2003] EWHC 3045 (Admin), [2004] ICR 1563, QBD, applying *Clark v TDG Ltd t/a Novacold* [1999] ICR 951, CA, and *Rowden v Dutton Gregory (a firm)* [2002] ICR 971, EAT, to the terms of s 28B(1). See Chapter 3 and see the further examples in Schools Code of Practice, para 5.17. See also: *VK v Norfolk County Council and the Special Educational Needs and Disability Tribunal* [2004] EWHC 2921 (Admin), Stanley Burnton J.

5   That is, the reason for failing to comply with the duty to make reasonable adjustments is both material to the circumstances of the particular case and substantial: DDA 1995, s 28B(7). See Schools Code of Practice, paras 6.35–6.36.

6   See Schools Code of Practice, Chapter 6.

7   DDA 1995, s 28C imposes duties only for the purpose of determining whether a responsible body has discriminated against a disabled person. A breach of any duty under s 28C is not actionable as such. See ibid, s 28C(8).

disadvantage in comparison with persons who are not disabled.[1] Secondly, it must also take such steps as it is reasonable for it to have to take to ensure that, in relation to education and associated services provided for (or offered to) pupils at the school by it, disabled pupils are not placed at a substantial disadvantage in comparison with pupils who are not disabled.[2] The duty is an anticipatory duty and a continuing one.[3] However, neither aspect of the duty requires the responsible body to remove or alter a physical feature (for example, one arising from the design or construction of the school premises or the location of resources) or to provide auxiliary aids or services.[4] What triggers the duty is the requirement for a comparative substantial (that is, more than minor or trivial) disadvantage. A number of factors may have to be taken into account in measuring that requirement, including the time and effort that might need to be expended by a disabled child; the inconvenience, indignity or discomfort a disabled child might suffer; the loss of opportunity or the diminished progress that a disabled child may make in comparison with his or her peers who are not disabled.[5]

7.4.8 Regulations may make provision for these purposes as to circumstances in which it is (or is not) reasonable for a responsible body to have to take steps of a prescribed description or as to steps which it is always or never reasonable for a responsible body to have to take.[6] A responsible body must have regard to any relevant provisions of a code of practice[7] in considering whether it is reasonable for it to have to take

---

1   DDA 1995, s 28C(1)(a).

2   Ibid, s 28C(1)(b). See *R (on the application of D) v Governing Body of Plymouth High School for Girls* [2004] EWHC 1923 (Admin), discussed at **7.4.5**, footnote 6. See also *McAuley Catholic High School v (1) CC; (2) PC; and (3) Special Educational Needs and Disability Tribunal* [2003] EWHC 3045 (Admin), [2004] ICR 1563, QBD, discussed at **7.4.2**.

3   Schools Code of Practice, paras 6.12–6.18 (and examples).

4   DDA 1995, s 28C(2). As the code of practice explains, the reasonable adjustments duty does not apply to auxiliary aids and services. It is anticipated that in schools in the maintained sector (in England and Wales) or the publicly funded sector (in Scotland) such provision will be made through the SEN framework. While physical alterations to schools are not required under the reasonable adjustments duty as it is anticipated that these will be achieved through a longer-term and more strategic approach to improving access for disabled pupils: Schools Code of Practice, paras 2.8, 3.8 and 6.19–6.27 (and examples).

5   Schools Code of Practice, paras 6.9–6.11 (and examples).

6   DDA 1995, s 28C(3). No regulations have been made at the time of writing, but Schools Code of Practice, paras 6.28–6.34 (and examples) suggest that the following factors may be relevant: the need to maintain academic, musical, sporting and other standards; the financial resources available to the responsible body; the cost of taking a particular step; the extent to which it is practicable to take a particular step; the extent to which aids and services will be provided to disabled pupils at the school (under Education Act 1996, Part IV or Education (Scotland) Act 1980, ss 60–65G); health and safety requirements; and the interests of other pupils and persons who may be admitted to the school as pupils.

7   Issued under DDA 1995, s 53A.

a particular step in order to comply with its duty to make reasonable adjustments.[1]

7.4.9 Particular provision is made where a 'confidentiality request' has been made in relation to a person and the responsible body is aware of it.[2] A 'confidentiality request' is a request which asks for the nature of (or the existence of) a disabled person's disability to be treated as confidential.[3] It must have been made by that person's parent[4] or by that person himself (in which case the responsible body must reasonably believe that he or she has sufficient understanding of the nature of the request and of its effect).[5] In determining whether it is reasonable for the responsible body to have to take a particular step in relation to that person in order to comply with its duty to make reasonable adjustments, regard shall be had to the extent to which taking the step in question is consistent with compliance with that request.[6]

Knowledge of disability

7.4.10 The question of the relevance of what an alleged discriminator knew or did not know about the fact of a disabled person's disability has bedevilled the interpretation of the employment and services provisions of the DDA 1995.[7] The new provisions in Part 4 of the Act attempt to address that question head on. In relation to a failure to take a particular step, a responsible body does not 'discriminate' against a person if it shows that, at the time in question, it did not know and could not reasonably have been expected to know, that he or she was disabled, and that its failure to take the step was attributable to that lack of knowledge.[8] Knowledge might be actual or constructive. Furthermore, the taking of a particular step by a responsible body in relation to a person does not amount to 'less favourable treatment' if it shows that at the time in question it did not know, and could not reasonably have been expected to know, that he or she was disabled.[9]

---

1   DDA 1995, s 28C(4).

2   Ibid, s 28C(5). See Schools Code of Practice, paras 7.13–7.17 (and examples).

3   Ibid, s 28C(7).

4   Ibid, s 28C(7)(a). The term 'parent' has the meaning assigned to it by Education Act 1996, s 576 and Education (Scotland) Act 1980, s 135(1): DDA 1995, s 28Q(8).

5   DDA 1995, s 28C(7)(b).

6   Ibid, s 28C(6).

7   Parts 2 and 3. See Chapters 3–5.

8   DDA 1995, s 28B(3). See Schools Code of Practice, paras 7.4–7.12. The use of the word 'discriminate' here clearly suggests that knowledge of the disability is a necessary ingredient of both less favourable treatment discrimination and failure to make reasonable adjustments discrimination arising from an act of omission.

9   DDA 1995, s 28B(4). See Schools Code of Practice, paras 7.4–7.12. Clearly, this provision is only concerned with an act of commission which would otherwise amount to less favourable treatment discrimination.

Justification

7.4.11 As has been noted, less favourable treatment of a person is justified if it is the result of a permitted form of selection.[1] Otherwise, less favourable treatment or a failure to comply with the duty to make reasonable adjustments is justified only if the reason for it is both material to the circumstances of the particular case and substantial.[2] However, in a case of less favourable treatment discrimination, if the responsible body is under a duty to make reasonable adjustments under DDA 1995, s 28C in relation to the disabled person, but it fails without justification to comply with that duty, its treatment of that person cannot be justified[3] unless that treatment would have been justified even if it had complied with that duty.[4] Again, the parallels with the comparable provisions of DDA 1995, Part 2 (discrimination in employment) will be apparent and instructive.[5]

Accessibility strategies and plans

7.4.12 Complementing the anti-discrimination provisions of the amended DDA 1995 as they affect schools are new provisions[6] placing a duty on LEAs[7] and schools in England and Wales to develop 'accessibility strategies' and 'accessibility plans'[8] for disabled pupils.[9] Broadly comparable (but not identical) duties have been introduced in Scotland by the Scottish Parliament as a result of the Education

---

1   DDA 1995, s 28B(6), by virtue of s 28B(5).

2   Ibid, s 28B(7), by virtue of s 28B(5).

3   Under ibid, s 28B(7).

4   Ibid, s 28B(8).

5   See Chapter 3. See: *VK v Norfolk County Council and the Special Educational Needs and Disability Tribunal* [2004] EWHC 2921 (Admin), Stanley Burnton J, applying *Post Office v Jones* [2001] EWCA Civ 558, [2001] IRLR 384, CA.

6   See generally DDA 1995, ss 28D–28E. These provisions came into force in England on 1 September 2002 by virtue of Special Educational Needs and Disability Act 2001 (Commencement No 5) Order 2002, SI 2002/2217, art 4 and Sch 1, Part 2. These provisions did not come into force in Wales on 1 September 2002 because SENDA 2001, s 43(6)(d) provides that the relevant provisions will be brought into force as respects Wales on such day as the National Assembly for Wales may appoint by order. The operative date in Wales was 8 October 2003: Special Educational Needs and Disability Act 2001 (Commencement No 2) (Wales) Order 2003, SI 2003/2532 (W 247).

7   A 'local education authority' (LEA) is defined in Education Act 1996, s 12: DDA 1995, s 28D(16). See the comparable provisions in Education (Disability Strategies and Pupils' Records) (Scotland) Act 2002, s 6(1).

8   By virtue of DDA 1995, s 28Q(13), these terms have the meaning assigned to them in DDA 1995, s 28D.

9   A 'disabled pupil' includes a disabled person who may be admitted to a school as a pupil: DDA 1995, s 28D(18). See the comparable provisions in Education (Disability Strategies and Pupils' Records) (Scotland) Act 2002, s 6(1).

(Disability Strategies and Pupils' Records) (Scotland) Act 2002.[1] The discussion below is based upon the legislation in England and Wales, with cross-references to the Scottish legislation in the footnotes.

7.4.13 Each LEA must prepare an 'accessibility strategy' in relation to schools for which it is responsible.[2] An accessibility strategy is a strategy for:

- increasing the extent to which disabled pupils can participate in the schools' curriculums;[3]
- improving the physical environment of the schools for the purpose of increasing the extent to which disabled pupils are able to take advantage of education and associated services provided or offered by the schools;[4] and
- improving the delivery to disabled pupils of information which is provided in writing for pupils who are not disabled, within a reasonable time and in ways which are determined after taking account of their disabilities and any preferences expressed by them or their parents.[5]

---

1   The relevant provisions of this Act (ss 1–3) came into force on 15 August 2002 by virtue of the Education (Disability Strategies and Pupils' Records) (Scotland) Act 2002 (Commencement) Order 2002, SSI 2002/367, the remainder of the Act having come into force with the Royal Assent on 30 April 2002. The Act is supported by the Education (Disability Strategies) (Scotland) Regulations 2002, SSI 2002/391, in force on 1 October 2002 and the *Guidance on Planning to Improve Access to Education for Pupils with Disabilities* issued by the Scottish Executive.

2   DDA 1995, s 28D(1)(a). Each LEA must also prepare 'further such strategies' at such times as may be prescribed: DDA 1995, s 28D(1)(b). In Scotland, the obligation of a school's responsible body to prepare an 'accessibility strategy' is found in Education (Disability Strategies and Pupils' Records) (Scotland) Act 2002, s 1. For this purpose, the responsible body will be the education authority, the proprietor of an independent school, the managers of a grant-receiving school, or the board of management of a self-governing school, as the case may be: Education (Disability Strategies and Pupils' Records) (Scotland) Act 2002, s 6(1). In Scotland, an education authority also has additional responsibilities for developing accessibility strategies in relation to the education of children under school age (or who are of school age and are travelling people) outwith schools: Education (Disability Strategies and Pupils' Records) (Scotland) Act 2002, s 2.

3   DDA 1995, s 28D(2)(a). See the comparable provisions in Education (Disability Strategies and Pupils' Records) (Scotland) Act 2002, s 1(2)(a).

4   DDA 1995, s 28D(2)(b). Regulations may prescribe services which are (or which are not) to be regarded for these purposes as being education or an associated service: DDA 1995, s 28D(15). See the comparable provisions in Education (Disability Strategies and Pupils' Records) (Scotland) Act 2002, s 1(2)(b) and (6).

5   DDA 1995, s 28D(2)(c). See the comparable provisions in the Education (Disability Strategies and Pupils' Records) (Scotland) Act 2002, s 1(2)(c).

The accessibility strategy must be in writing[1] and relate to a prescribed period.[2] In England, the prescribed period to which an accessibility strategy must relate is the period of three years from 1 April 2003 to 31 March 2006.[3] The LEA must keep the accessibility strategy under review during the period to which it relates and revise it if necessary.[4] In preparing the accessibility strategy, the LEA must have regard to:

- the need to allocate adequate resources for implementing it;[5]
- any guidance issued as to its content, the form in which it is to be produced and the persons to be consulted in its preparation;[6] and
- any guidance issued as to compliance with the requirement to keep the strategy under review.[7]

---

1   In Scotland, the law provides for the provision of accessibility strategies in alternative forms (ie orally, on audio tape, through sign language or lip speaking, on video tape (using signing and/or lip speaking), in Braille, in large print, on CD-ROM or other means of electronic communication, or in any other form which the responsible body regards as a reasonable form in which to provide information): Education (Disability Strategies and Pupils' Education Records) (Scotland) Act 2002, s 3(5)(b) and Education (Disability Strategies) (Scotland) Regulations 2002, SSI 2002/391, reg 3.

2   DDA 1995, s 28D(2) and (3). In relation to Wales, this means prescribed in regulations made by the National Assembly: DDA 1995, s 28D(17). See the comparable provisions in Education (Disability Strategies and Pupils' Records) (Scotland) Act 2002, s 1(2) and (3).

3   Disability Discrimination (Prescribed Periods for Accessibility Strategies and Plans for Schools) (England) Regulations 2002, SI 2002/1981, reg 2. These regulations came into force on 1 September 2002 and apply only in relation to England: reg 1. In Scotland, the responsible body shall prepare its first accessibility strategy by 1 April 2003 for a period of up to three years starting by 1 April 2003, and further accessibility strategies shall be prepared by a date not more than three years after the date of preparation of the previous strategy and shall be for a further period of three years commencing immediately on the expiry of the period to which the previous strategy related: Education (Disability Strategies) (Scotland) Regulations 2002, SSI 2002/391, reg 2. In Wales, see Disability Discrimination (Prescribed Periods for Accessibility Strategies and Plans for Schools) (Wales) Regulations 2003, SI 2003/2531 (W 246) (in force 8 October 2003) where the first accessibility strategies are to commence on 1 April 2004 for a three-year period.

4   DDA 1995, s 28D(4). See the comparable provisions in Education (Disability Strategies and Pupils' Records) (Scotland) Act 2002, s 1(4).

5   DDA 1995, s 28E(1)(a). See the comparable provisions in Education (Disability Strategies and Pupils' Records) (Scotland) Act 2002, s 3(1)(a).

6   DDA 1995, s 28E(1)(b). Such guidance may be issued by the Secretary of State (in relation to England) or by the National Assembly (in relation to Wales): DDA 1995, s 28E(3). See the comparable provisions in Education (Disability Strategies and Pupils' Records) (Scotland) Act 2002, s 3(1)(b)–(c) and (2).

7   DDA 1995, s 28E(2), cross-referencing to s 28D(4). Such guidance may be issued by the Secretary of State (in relation to England) or by the National Assembly (in relation to Wales): DDA 1995, s 28E(3). See the comparable provisions in Education (Disability Strategies and Pupils' Records) (Scotland) Act 2002, s 3(3).

It is the statutory duty of the LEA to implement its accessibility strategy.[1] A statutory inspection of an LEA[2] may extend to the performance by it of its functions in relation to the preparation, review, revision and implementation of its accessibility strategy.[3] The LEA must provide a copy of its accessibility strategy if the Secretary of State (in England) or the National Assembly (in Wales) asks for a copy.[4]

7.4.14 Maintained schools, independent schools and approved non-maintained special schools[5] are subject to parallel duties in relation to the development of an 'accessibility plan'.[6] The body responsible for such a school (the responsible body or, in the case of a maintained school or maintained nursery school, the governing body[7]) must prepare an 'accessibility plan' in relation to the school.[8] An accessibility plan is a plan for:

1   DDA 1995, s 28D(5). See the comparable provisions in Education (Disability Strategies and Pupils' Records) (Scotland) Act 2002, s 1(5).

2   Under Education Act 1997, s 38.

3   DDA 1995, s 28D(6). Note that in relation to schools and accessibility plans (s 28D(13)) there is an additional function of 'publication' which is not found in the comparable provision relating to LEAs and accessibility strategies. However, if asked to do so, an LEA must make a copy of its accessibility strategy available for inspection at such reasonable times as it may determine: DDA 1995, s 28E(7). See the comparable provisions in Education (Disability Strategies and Pupils' Records) (Scotland) Act 2002, s 3(4)–(6).

4   DDA 1995, ss 28E(5)–(6) and 28Q(14). See the comparable provisions in Education (Disability Strategies and Pupils' Records) (Scotland) Act 2002, s 3(4)–(6).

5   The terms 'maintained school' and 'independent school' are defined in School Standards and Framework Act 1998, s 20(7) and Education Act 1996, s 463 respectively: DDA 1995, ss 28D(19) and 28Q(5). The term 'approved non-maintained special school' is coined by the author to describe special schools which are not maintained schools but which are approved by the Secretary of State (or by the National Assembly of Wales) under Education Act 1996, s 342: see DDA 1995, s 28D(7)(c).

6   DDA 1995, s 28D(7)–(13). In Scotland, the obligation of a school's responsible body to prepare an 'accessibility strategy' (as opposed to a 'plan') is found in Education (Disability Strategies and Pupils' Records) (Scotland) Act 2002, s 1. For this purpose, the responsible body will be the education authority, the proprietor of an independent school, the managers of a grant-receiving school, or the board of management of a self-governing school, as the case may be: Education (Disability Strategies and Pupils' Records) (Scotland) Act 2002, s 6(1).

7   DDA 1995, s 28D(14), as amended by Education Act 2002, s 215(1) and Sch 21, para 26 (from 1 September 2003 in England only, at the time of writing). As has been seen, the meaning of the term 'the body responsible for a school' (referred to as the 'responsible body') depends upon the kind of school involved: DDA 1995, s 28A(5) and Sch 4A, as amended by Education Act 2002. See **7.4.3**.

8   DDA 1995, s 28D(8)(a). The responsible body must also prepare 'further such plans' at such times as may be prescribed: DDA 1995, s 28D(8)(b). See the comparable provisions in Education (Disability Strategies and Pupils' Records) (Scotland) Act 2002, s 1(1).

- increasing the extent to which disabled pupils can participate in the school's curriculum;[1]
- improving the physical environment of the school for the purpose of increasing the extent to which disabled pupils are able to take advantage of education and associated services provided or offered by the school;[2] and
- improving the delivery to disabled pupils of information which is provided in writing for pupils who are not disabled, within a reasonable time and in ways which are determined after taking account of their disabilities and any preferences expressed by them or their parents.[3]

It must be in writing and relates to a prescribed period.[4] In England only, the prescribed period to which an accessibility plan must relate is the period of three years from 1 April 2003 to 31 March 2006.[5] The responsible body must keep the accessibility plan under review during the period to which it relates and revise it if necessary.[6] In preparing the accessibility strategy, the responsible body must have regard to the need to allocate adequate resources for implementing it.[7] It is the statutory duty of the responsible body to implement its accessibility plan.[8] A statutory inspection of a school[9] may extend to the performance by the responsible body of its functions in relation to the preparation, publication, review, revision and implementation of its accessibility

---

1   DDA 1995, s 28D(9)(a). See the comparable provisions in Education (Disability Strategies and Pupils' Records) (Scotland) Act 2002, s 1(2)(a).

2   DDA 1995, s 28D(9)(b). Regulations may prescribe services which are (or which are not) to be regarded for these purposes as being education or an associated service: DDA 1995, s 28D(15). See the comparable provisions in Education (Disability Strategies and Pupils' Records) (Scotland) Act 2002, s 1(2)(b) and (6).

3   DDA 1995, s 28D(9)(c). See the comparable provisions in Education (Disability Strategies and Pupils' Records) (Scotland) Act 2002, s 1(2)(c).

4   DDA 1995, s 28D(9) and (10). In relation to Wales, this means prescribed in regulations made by the National Assembly: DDA 1995, s 28D(17). See the comparable provisions in Education (Disability Strategies and Pupils' Records) (Scotland) Act 2002, s 1(2) and (3).

5   Disability Discrimination (Prescribed Periods for Accessibility Strategies and Plans for Schools) (England) Regulations 2002, SI 2002/1981, reg 2. These regulations came into force on 1 September 2002 and apply only in relation to England: reg 1. In respect of a school established after 1 April 2003, the prescribed period begins with the date on which the school is established and ends on 31 March 2006: reg 3. In Wales, see the Disability Discrimination (Prescribed Periods for Accessibility Strategies and Plans for Schools) (Wales) Regulations 2003, SI 2003/2531 (W 246).

6   DDA 1995, s 28D(11). See the comparable provisions in Education (Disability Strategies and Pupils' Records) (Scotland) Act 2002, s 1(4).

7   DDA 1995, s 28E(4).

8   DDA 1995, s 28D(12). See the comparable provisions in Education (Disability Strategies and Pupils' Records) (Scotland) Act 2002, s 1(5).

9   Under the Schools Inspection Act 1996.

plan.[1] The proprietor of an independent school (other than a city academy[2]) must provide a copy of its accessibility plan if the Secretary of State (in England) or the National Assembly (in Wales) asks for a copy.[3] If asked to do so, such a proprietor must also make a copy of its accessibility plan available for inspection at such reasonable times as it may determine.[4]

7.4.15   As has been seen,[5] since 1 January 1997, the 'annual report' for a relevant school has been required to include a report containing certain information relating to disabled pupils.[6] From 1 September 2002, the governors' report[7] shall include information as to:

- the arrangements for the admission of disabled persons[8] as pupils at the school;
- the steps taken to prevent disabled pupils from being treated less favourably than other pupils;
- the facilities provided to assist access to the school by disabled pupils; and
- the accessibility plan prepared by the governing body.[9]

This is as a result of the amendments made by the SENDA 2001.[10]

---

1   DDA 1995, s 28D(13). Note the additional function of 'publication' which is not found in the comparable provision (s 28D(6)) relating to LEAs and accessibility strategies.

2   The term 'city academy' means a school which is known as a city academy as a result of Education Act 1996, s 482(3) or (3A): DDA 1995, s 28Q(12).

3   DDA 1995, s 28E(5)–(6).

4   Ibid, s 28E(8).

5   See **7.2.10**.

6   Education Act 1993, s 161(6), as inserted by DDA 1995, s 29(2) (which was repealed by Education Act 1996, s 582(2) and Sch 38, Part I); see now Education Act 1996, s 317(6)–(7). See *School Prospectuses and Governors' Annual Reports* (DfEE Circulars 11/96 (primary schools) and 12/96 (secondary schools)).

7   The report prepared under School Standards and Framework Act 1998, s 42(1): Education Act 1996, s 317(7), as amended by SENDA 2001, s 14(2).

8   As defined in the DDA 1995: Education Act 1996, s 317(7A), as amended by SENDA 2001, s 14(2).

9   That is, the accessibility plan prepared under DDA 1995, s 28D.

10   Education Act 1996, s 317(6)–(7), as amended by SENDA 2001, s 14(2).

Residual duty of education authorities

7.4.16 Education authorities have residual duties under DDA 1995, ss 28F–28G.[1] These duties arise in relation to the functions – other than functions that may be prescribed[2] – of LEAs in England and Wales[3] and education authorities in Scotland.[4] In discharging the relevant functions, it is unlawful for the authority to discriminate against a disabled pupil or a disabled person who may be admitted to a school as a pupil,[5] but only if no other provision of DDA 1995, Part 4, Chapter 1 (that is, ss 28A–28Q) applies.[6] The meaning of discrimination for this purpose is set out in DDA 1995, s 28B. This is achieved by applying s 28B for the purposes of s 28F with modifications.[7]

7.4.17 Thus, an authority[8] discriminates against a disabled person if, for a reason which relates to his or her disability, it treats him or her less favourably than it treats or would treat others to whom that reason does not (or would not) apply and it cannot show that the treatment in question is justified.[9] Less favourable treatment of a person is justified if it is the result of a permitted form of selection.[10] Otherwise, less favourable treatment is justified only if the reason for it is both material to the circumstances of the particular case and substantial.[11] If the authority is under a duty to make reasonable adjustments[12] in relation to

---

1   See Schools Code of Practice, paras 10.1–10.6 (and examples).

2   DDA 1995, s 28F(2). No such functions have been prescribed at the time of writing. Schools Code of Practice, para 10.3 suggests that the functions which are covered include policies such as the authority's policies on SEN, capital building programmes, sports, cultural activities, transport and early years provision; the education authority's policy and arrangements on school admissions and exclusions, and (in England and Wales) the school's admissions policy and arrangements; the deployment of the authority's non-delegated budget and any other arrangements which might directly affect disabled pupils; and services to pupils (such as weekend or after-school leisure and sporting activities, school trips, and cultural activities).

3   Under the Education Acts as defined in Education Act 1996, s 578: DDA 1995, s 28F(1)(a) and (7). See Education Act 1996, s 12: DDA 1995, s 28F(6).

4   Under the Education (Scotland) Act 1980; the Education (Scotland) Act 1996; and the Standards in Scotland's Schools etc Act 2000: DDA 1995, s 28F(1)(b). See Education (Scotland) Act 1980, s 135(1) and DDA 1995, s 28F(8).

5   DDA 1995, s 28F(3). In the case of an act which constitutes discrimination by virtue of ibid, s 55 (ie victimisation), these provisions also apply to discrimination against a person who is not disabled: ibid, s 28F(5).

6   Ibid, s 28F(4).

7   Ibid, s 28G(1).

8   An LEA in England and Wales or an education authority in Scotland: DDA 1995, s 28G(7).

9   Ibid, s 28B(1).

10   Ibid, s 28B(6), as modified by virtue of s 28B(5).

11   Ibid, s 28B(7), as modified by virtue of s 28B(5).

12   Imposed by ibid, s 28G(2)–(4), by virtue of the modifications in s 28G(1)(b).

the disabled person, but it fails without justification to comply with that duty, its treatment of that person cannot be justified by reference to a material and substantial reason[1] unless that treatment would have been justified even if it had complied with that duty.[2]

7.4.18   An authority also discriminates against a disabled person if it fails, to his or her detriment, to comply with the duty to make reasonable adjustments contained in DDA 1995, s 28G(2)–(4), and it cannot show that its failure to comply is justified. An authority must take such steps as it is reasonable for it to have to take to ensure that, in discharging any function to which s 28F above applies, disabled persons who may be admitted to a school as pupils are not placed at a substantial disadvantage in comparison with persons who are not disabled.[3] It must also take such steps as it is reasonable for it to have to take to ensure that, in discharging any function to which s 28F above applies, disabled pupils are not placed at a substantial disadvantage in comparison with pupils who are not disabled.[4] However, neither aspect of the duty requires the authority to remove or alter a physical feature or to provide auxiliary aids or services.[5] In relation to a failure to take a particular step, an authority does not discriminate against a person if it shows that, at the time in question, it did not know and could not reasonably have been expected to know that he or she was disabled, and that its failure to take the step was attributable to that lack of knowledge.[6] Furthermore, the taking of a particular step by an authority in relation to a person does not amount to less favourable treatment if it shows that at the time in question it did not know, and could not reasonably have been expected to know, that he or she was disabled.[7]

Enforcement

7.4.19   In England and Wales, the new anti-discrimination provisions in the field of education and applying to schools and education authorities, as described above,[8] are enforced by the Special Educational Needs and Disability Tribunal (SENDIST).[9] The Secretary of State (in England) and the National Assembly (in Wales) also have a

---

1   DDA 1995, s 28B(7), as modified.

2   Ibid, s 28B(8), as modified.

3   Ibid, s 28G(2)(a).

4   Ibid, s 28G(2)(b).

5   Ibid, s 28G(3).

6   Ibid, s 28B(3), as modified.

7   Ibid, s 28B(4), as modified.

8   Ibid, Part 4, Chapter 1 (ie particularly ss 28A–28G), as described in **7.4.2–7.4.11** and **7.4.16–7.4.18**.

9   Ibid, ss 28H–28L. See Schools Code of Practice, Chapter 9.

role to play in this context.[1] In Scotland, enforcement is by way of civil proceedings in a sheriff court.[2] These provisions are examined in more detail in Chapter 10.

7.5   FURTHER AND HIGHER EDUCATION

7.5.1   The new DDA 1995, Part 4, Chapter 2 addressed the rights of disabled students in relation to further and higher education – broadly post-16 education and related services.[3] The Government is implementing the new duties in three stages.[4] The main provisions came into force on 1 September 2002 and make it unlawful to discriminate against disabled people or students by treating them less favourably than others. In addition, they require responsible bodies to provide certain types of reasonable adjustments to provision where disabled students or other disabled people might otherwise be substantially disadvantaged. The duty on responsible bodies to make adjustments involving the provision of auxiliary aids and services came into effect on 1 September 2003. The duty on responsible bodies to make adjustments to physical features of premises where these put disabled people or students at a substantial disadvantage will be in force from 1 September 2005.

7.5.2   The statutory provisions containing the new duties placed upon the providers of post-16 education services are supported by the *Disability Discrimination Act 1995 Part 4 Code of Practice for Providers of Post-16 Education and Related Services* (Post-16 Code of Practice) (2002) issued by the DRC under DDA 1995, s 53A at the request of the Secretary of State for Education and Skills.[5] The new law and the Code of Practice apply throughout Great Britain (but not Northern Ireland) to a variety of further and higher education institutions; LEAs (known as education authorities in Scotland) in relation to the provision by them of further education, adult and community education, and youth and community

---

1   DDA 1995, s 28M.

2   Ibid, s 28N. See Schools Code of Practice, Chapter 8.

3   SENDA 2001, Part 2, Chapter 2, inserting new ss 28R–28X and 31A into the DDA 1995.

4   See Special Educational Needs and Disability Act 2001 (Commencement No 5) Order 2002, SI 2002/2217, arts 3 and 5–6, and Schs 1 (Part 1) and 2.

5   Post-16 Code of Practice, Chapter 1. Its purpose and status is set out in paras 1.1–1.7 (and see further the discussion in **9.3**). The Code of Practice (Chapter 10) usefully explains the relationship of the DDA 1995 with other legislation and responsibilities (such as data protection legislation, health and safety law and regulations, fire safety legislation, occupiers' liability, defective premises law, the Human Rights Act 1998, sex and race discrimination legislation, etc).

services; and schools providing further education for adults.[1] Further guidance is also available from various other sources.[2] Wholly privately funded post-16 providers and providers of work-based training are not covered by these provisions but will be within the scope of Part 3 of the DDA 1995.[3]

Disability discrimination duties

7.5.3 By virtue of s 28R(1) of the DDA 1995,[4] it is unlawful for 'the body responsible for an educational institution' to discriminate against a 'disabled person':[5]

- in the arrangements it makes for determining admissions to the institution;
- in the terms on which it offers to admit him or her to the institution; or
- by refusing or deliberately omitting to accept an application for his or her admission to the institution.

It is further unlawful for 'the body responsible for an educational institution' to discriminate against a disabled student[6] by excluding him or her from the institution, whether permanently or temporarily.[7]

---

1   Post-16 Code of Practice, paras 2.7 and 3.1. Where a school makes provision for pupils post-16 that provision is covered by DDA 1995, Part 4, Chapter 1 and the Schools Code of Practice.

2   Association of Colleges, *Rights to Access: A Toolkit to Help Colleges Meet or Exceed the Requirements of the Disability Discrimination Act*; Learning and Skills Council, *The Special Educational Needs and Disability Act 2001* (Equality and Diversity Guidance 02/2002); Education and Learning Wales, *Disability Access Planning* (NC/C/01/11LL); Department for Education and Skills, *Guidance for LEAs and Adult Education Providers on the Implementation of the Disability Discrimination Act Part 4*.

3   Post-16 Code of Practice, paras 2.8 and 3.2–3.4. See Chapter 5. In particular, non-statutory youth services (eg clubs and activities run by voluntary organisations, the scouts or youth clubs) will be covered by DDA 1995, Part 3 rather than the new Part 4.

4   See Post-16 Code of Practice, paras 3.9 and 4.11–4.13 (and examples).

5   A 'disabled person' is a person falling within DDA 1995, ss 1–2 and Schs 1–2 (discussed in Chapter 2). This section also applies to discrimination against a person who is not disabled in the case of an act which constitutes discrimination by virtue of DDA 1995, s 55 (victimisation): DDA 1995, s 28R(4). See Post-16 Code of Practice, paras 2.1–2.6 and 8.1–8.4 (and examples).

6   By virtue of DDA 1995, s 31A(2), the term 'disabled student' (as used throughout this analysis) means a student who is a disabled person. A 'student' means a person who is attending or undertaking a course of study at an educational institution: DDA 1995, s 31A(3). It does not matter whether that person is completing an entire course. Someone enquiring about, applying to, attending or undertaking a course of study (however short or long) at an educational institution is covered. See Post-16 Code of Practice, paras 2.6 and 3.17.

7   DDA 1995, s 28R(3); Post-16 Code of Practice, paras 3.10 and 4.14 (and examples).

It is also unlawful for 'the body responsible for an educational institution' to discriminate against a disabled student in the student services[1] it provides (or offers to provide).[2] The Post-16 Code of Practice suggests that such services might include: teaching (including classes, lectures, seminars, practical sessions); curriculum design; examinations and assessments; field trips and outdoor education; arranging study abroad or work placements; outings and trips; research degrees and research facilities; informal/optional study skills sessions; short courses; day or evening adult education courses; training courses; distance learning; independent learning opportunities (such as e-learning); learning facilities (such as classrooms, lecture theatres, laboratories, studios, darkrooms, etc); learning equipment and materials (such as laboratory equipment, computer facilities, class handouts, etc); libraries, learning centres, and information centres and their resources; information and communication technology and resources; placement finding services; careers advice and training; careers libraries; job references; job shops and employment-finding services; graduation and certificate ceremonies; leisure, recreation, entertainment and sports facilities; the physical environment; chaplaincies and prayer areas; health services; counselling services; catering facilities; childcare facilities; campus or college shops; car parking; residential accommodation; accommodation-finding services; financial advice; and welfare services.[3] Many (but not all) of these services would have been caught by DDA 1995, Part 3 prior to 1 September 2002,[4] but now will be within the exclusive scope of DDA 1995, Part 4.

7.5.4 In England and Wales, an 'educational institution' is an institution within the further education or higher education sector or designated as such by an Order (where the Secretary of State is satisfied that the institution is wholly or partly funded from public funds).[5] In Scotland, it is an institution within the higher education sector;[6] a

---

1   The term 'student services' means services of any description which are provided wholly or mainly for students: DDA 1995, s 28R(11). Regulations may prescribe services which are (or are not) to be regarded for this purpose as being 'student services': ibid, s 28R(3).

2   Ibid, s 28R(2). See generally Post-16 Code of Practice, paras 3.11–3.16 and 4.15 (and examples).

3   Post-16 Code of Practice, para 3.14.

4   They will continue to be caught where they are being provided to persons other than students (such as the provision by an educational institution of commercial conference facilities or commercial research and consultancy services): Post-16 Code of Practice, paras 3.15 and 3.20.

5   DDA 1995, s 28R(6) (to be read with Further and Higher Education Act 1992, s 91) and (9). See the Disability Discrimination (Designation of Educational Institutions) Order 2002, SI 2002/1459.

6   Within the meaning of Further and Higher Education (Scotland) Act 1992, s 56(2).

college of further education with a board of management;[1] a central institution;[2] a college of further education maintained by an education authority;[3] or an institution designated as such by an order (where the Secretary of State is satisfied that the institution is wholly or partly funded from public funds).[4] The 'body responsible for an educational institution' (referred to as the 'responsible body') is to be determined in accordance with DDA 1995, Sch 4B.[5] In England and Wales, the responsible body will be the governing body of the institution[6] or, in the case of an institution designated by order, the body specified in the order. In Scotland, as the case might be, the responsible body will usually be the governing body, the board of management, an education authority, the managers of a school or, in the case of an institution designated by order, the body specified in the order.

Discrimination

7.5.5 The meaning of discrimination for this purpose is set out in DDA 1995, s 28S. There are two kinds of discrimination contemplated by the section. They might be referred to in shorthand as (1) less favourable treatment, and (2) failure to make reasonable adjustments.[7]

Less favourable treatment

7.5.6 A responsible body discriminates against a disabled person if, for a reason which relates to his disability,[8] it treats him less favourably than it treats or would treat others to whom that reason does not (or would not) apply[9] and it cannot show that the treatment in question is justified.[10] Less favourable treatment of a person is justified if it is necessary in order to maintain academic standards (or standards of any

---

1   Within the meaning of Further and Higher Education (Scotland) Act 1992, s 36.

2   Within the meaning of Education (Scotland) Act 1980, s 135.

3   In the exercise of its further education functions in providing courses of further education within the meaning of ibid, s 1(5)(b)(ii).

4   DDA 1995, s 28R(7), (9)–(10). See the Disability Discrimination (Designation of Educational Institutions) Order 2002, SI 2002/1459.

5   Ibid, ss 28R(5) and 31A(4), and Sch 4B. See Post-16 Code of Practice, para 2.9 and Appendix 2.

6   As defined in Further and Higher Education Act 1992, s 90.

7   Post-16 Code of Practice, para 2.17. DDA 1995, Part 4 does not prohibit more favourable treatment of disabled persons: Post-16 Code of Practice, para 4.16.

8   There has to be a link between the reason and the disability: Post-16 Code of Practice, paras 4.3–4.10 (and examples).

9   This calls for a real or hypothetical comparison: Post-16 Code of Practice, paras 4.4–4.9 (and examples).

10   DDA 1995, s 28S(1). See Post-16 Code of Practice, Chapter 4.

other prescribed kind).[1] It is also justified where it is of a prescribed kind, or it occurs in prescribed circumstances, or where it is both of a prescribed kind *and* occurs in prescribed circumstances.[2] Otherwise, less favourable treatment is justified only if the reason for it is both material to the circumstances of the particular case and substantial (that is, more than minor or trivial).[3] If the responsible body is under a duty to make reasonable adjustments (imposed by DDA 1995, s 28T) in relation to the disabled person, but it fails without justification to comply with that duty, its treatment of that person cannot be justified by reference to a material and substantial reason[4] unless that treatment would have been justified even if it had complied with that duty.[5] The concept of unjustified less favourable treatment discrimination arising here is broadly similar to the parallel provision in Part 2 of the DDA 1995 (discrimination in employment) and the case-law there is likely to be instructive.[6]

Failure to make reasonable adjustments

7.5.7 By virtue of DDA 1995, s 28S(2) a responsible body also discriminates against a disabled person if it fails, to his or her detriment, to comply with the duty to make reasonable adjustments contained in DDA 1995, s 28T and it cannot show that its failure to comply is justified.[7] Before this kind of discrimination can be explored further, it is necessary to examine the duty to make reasonable adjustments in this context.[8]

7.5.8 There are two aspects to the duty to make reasonable adjustments upon educational institutions.[9] First, the responsible body must take such steps as it is reasonable for it to have to take to ensure that, in

---

1   DDA 1995, s 28S(6), by virtue of s 28S(5). Post-16 Code of Practice, paras 4.22–4.27 (and examples).

2   Ibid, s 28S(7), by virtue of s 28S(5). Post-16 Code of Practice, paras 4.22–4.25 and 4.28 (and examples).

3   Ibid, s 28S(8), by virtue of s 28S(5). Post-16 Code of Practice, paras 4.22–4.25 and 4.29–4.31 (and examples).

4   Ibid, s 28S(8).

5   Ibid, s 28S(9). Post-16 Code of Practice, para 4.25 (and example).

6   See Chapter 3.

7   That is, the reason for failing to comply with the duty to make reasonable adjustments is both material to the circumstances of the particular case and substantial: DDA 1995, s 28S(8), by virtue of s 28S(5). See Post-16 Code of Practice, para 5.16 (and example).

8   See Post-16 Code of Practice, Chapter 5.

9   DDA 1995, s 28T imposes duties only for the purpose of determining whether a responsible body has discriminated against a disabled person. A breach of any duty under s 28T is not actionable as such. See ibid, s 28T(6).

relation to the arrangements it makes for determining the admissions to the institution, disabled persons are not placed at a substantial disadvantage in comparison with persons who are not disabled.[1] Secondly, it must also take such steps as it is reasonable for it to have to take to ensure that, in relation to student services provided for (or offered to) students by it, disabled students are not placed at a substantial disadvantage in comparison with students who are not disabled.[2] The duty is an anticipatory duty and a continuing one, and is owed to disabled students at large.[3] However, what triggers the duty is the requirement for a comparative substantial (that is, more than minor or trivial) disadvantage.[4] A number of factors may have to be taken into account in measuring that requirement, including the time, inconvenience, effort or discomfort entailed in comparison with other people or students.[5]

7.5.9 What reasonable steps might the responsible body of an educational institution have to take to discharge its DDA 1995, s 28T duty? The responsible body must have regard to any relevant provisions of a code of practice[6] in considering whether it is reasonable for it to have to take a particular step in order to comply with its duty to make reasonable adjustments.[7] Obviously, the Post-16 Code of Practice is relevant here, especially as the Act does not define what are reasonable steps. The Code anticipates that responsible bodies will have to consider a wide range of adjustments.[8] However, the duty to make reasonable adjustments is being introduced in stages. While the main duty came into force on 1 September 2002, there was no obligation to provide auxiliary aids or services until 1 September 2003, and there will be no obligation to make adjustments to physical features of premises until 1 September 2005.[9]

7.5.10 Nevertheless, those temporal limits aside, the Code of Practice does suggest some criteria that might be taken into account when determining what is reasonable.[10] In particular, the Code of Practice speculates that what is reasonable will depend on all the circumstances

---

1   DDA 1995, s 28T(1)(a).

2   Ibid, s 28T(1)(b).

3   Post-16 Code of Practice, paras 5.5–5.7 and 5.9 (and examples).

4   Ibid, para 5.2 (and examples).

5   Ibid, para 5.2 (and examples).

6   Issued under DDA 1995, s 53A, as amended by SENDA 2001, s 36.

7   DDA 1995, s 28T(2).

8   Post-16 Code of Practice, para 5.8 (and examples).

9   Ibid, paras 5.3–5.4.

10 Ibid, Chapter 6.

of the case and will vary according to the type of services being offered; the nature of the institution or service and its size and resources; and the effect of the disability on the individual disabled person or student.[1] Some of the factors that might be taken into account are suggested as including:[2]

- the need to maintain academic and other prescribed standards;[3]
- the financial resources available to the responsible body;[4]
- grants or loans likely to be available to disabled students (and only disabled students) for the purpose of enabling them to receive student services, such as Disabled Students' Allowances;[5]
- the cost of taking a particular step;[6]
- the extent to which it is practicable to take a particular step;[7]
- the extent to which aids or services will otherwise be provided to disabled people or students;[8]
- health and safety requirements;[9]
- the relevant interests of other people including other students.[10]

7.5.11   Particular provision is made where a 'confidentiality request' has been made in relation to a person and the responsible body is aware of it.[11] A 'confidentiality request' is a request made by a disabled person which asks for the nature of (or the existence of) his or her disability to be treated as confidential.[12] In determining whether it is reasonable for the responsible body to have to take a particular step in relation to that person in order to comply with its duty to make reasonable adjustments, regard shall be had to the extent to which taking the step in question is consistent with compliance with that request.[13]

Knowledge of disability

7.5.12   The question of the relevance of what an alleged discriminator knew or did not know about the fact of a disabled person's disability has

---

1   Post-16 Code of Practice, para 6.1.

2   Ibid, para 6.2.

3   Ibid, paras 6.3–6.6 (and examples).

4   Ibid, para 6.7 (and example).

5   Ibid, paras 6.8–6.9 (and examples).

6   Ibid, para 6.10 (and example).

7   Ibid, para 6.11 (and examples).

8   Ibid, paras 6.12 (and example).

9   Ibid, paras 6.13–6.15 (and examples).

10   Ibid, paras 6.16–6.17 (and examples).

11   DDA 1995, s 28T(3). See Post-16 Code of Practice, paras 6.18–6.20 (and examples).

12   Ibid, s 28T(5).

13   Ibid, s 28T(4).

bedevilled the interpretation of the employment and services provisions of the DDA 1995.[1] The new provisions in Part 4 of the Act attempt to address that question head on. In relation to a failure to take a particular step, a responsible body does not 'discriminate' against a person if it shows that, at the time in question, it did not know and could not reasonably have been expected to know, that he or she was disabled, and that its failure to take the step was attributable to that lack of knowledge.[2] Knowledge might be actual or constructive.[3] Furthermore, the taking of a particular step by a responsible body in relation to a person does not amount to 'less favourable treatment' if it shows that at the time in question it did not know, and could not reasonably have been expected to know, that he or she was disabled.[4]

Justification

7.5.13 As has been noted, less favourable treatment of a person or a failure to make reasonable adjustments may be justified in specified circumstances.[5] Those circumstances include the maintenance of academic or other prescribed standards, or other prescribed kinds or circumstances of treatment. Otherwise, less favourable treatment or a failure to comply with the duty to make reasonable adjustments is justified only if the reason for it is both material to the circumstances of the particular case and substantial.[6] However, in a case of less favourable treatment discrimination, if the responsible body is under a duty to make reasonable adjustments under DDA 1995, s 28T in relation to the disabled person, but it fails without justification to comply with that duty, its treatment of that person cannot be justified[7] unless that treatment would have been justified even if it had complied with that duty.[8] Again, the parallels with the comparable provisions of DDA 1995,

---

1   Parts 2 and 3. See Chapters 3–5.

2   DDA 1995, s 28S(3). See Post-16 Code of Practice, paras 4.17–4.21 and 5.10–5.15. The use of the word 'discriminate' here clearly suggests that knowledge of the disability is a necessary ingredient of both less favourable treatment discrimination and failure to make reasonable adjustments discrimination arising from an act of omission.

3   Post-16 Code of Practice, paras 5.14–5.15 (and example). See also Department for Education and Skills, *Finding Out About People's Disability: A Good Practice Guide for Further and Higher Education Institutions* (DfES/0024/2002).

4   DDA 1995, s 28S(4). See Post-16 Code of Practice, paras 4.17–4.21. Clearly, this provision is only concerned with an act of commission which would otherwise amount to less favourable treatment discrimination.

5   DDA 1995, s 28S(5)–(9).

6   Ibid, s 28S(8), by virtue of s 28S(5). Post-16 Code of Practice, para 5.16 (and example) suggests that there may be rare occasions where a reasonable step might be taken, but there is a justification for not taking it.

7   Under DDA 1995, s 28S(8).

8   Ibid, s 28S(9).

Part 2 (discrimination in employment) will be apparent and instructive.[1]

Other providers of further education or training facilities

7.5.14 The provisions of DDA 1995, ss 28R and 28T are modified for the purpose of their application in England and Wales in relation to higher education secured by an LEA; further education secured by the LEA or provided by the governing body of a maintained school; or recreational or training facilities secured by an LEA.[2] Similar modifications are made in respect of the comparable provision of further education or training facilities in Scotland.[3] These modifications are rehearsed here only to show the differences which arise in the relevant statutory provisions. Otherwise, reference should be made to the discussion above.

7.5.15 The modified s 28R of the DDA 1995[4] applies to any course[5] of further education[6] or higher education[7] secured by an LEA[8] and any course of further education provided by the governing body of a maintained school in England and Wales;[9] and any course of further education secured by an education authority in Scotland.[10] It is unlawful for the LEA (an education authority in Scotland) or governing body to discriminate against a disabled person:

- in the arrangements they make for determining who should be enrolled on the course;

---

1   See Chapter 3.

2   DDA 1995, s 28U(1) and Sch 4C, Part 1.

3   Ibid, s 28U(2) and Sch 4C, Part 2.

4   Modified by DDA 1995, s 28U and Sch 4C.

5   The term 'course' in relation to further education secured by an LEA includes each of the component parts of a course of further education if there is no requirement imposed on persons registered for any component part of the course to register for any other component part of that course. The term 'enrolment' in relation to such a course includes registration for any one of those parts. See DDA 1995, s 28R(8), as modified.

6   As defined in Education Act 1996, s 2(3) or School Standards and Framework Act 1998, s 80(1): DDA 1995, s 28R(7), as modified.

7   The term 'higher education' is defined in Education Act 1996, s 579(1): DDA 1995, s 28R (9), as modified.

8   'Local education authority' is defined in Education Act 1996, s 12: DDA 1995, s 28R(10), as modified.

9   DDA 1995, s 28R(1) and (11), as modified. Note the references in this modified section to Education Reform Act 1988, s 120 and School Standards and Framework Act 1998, s 80.

10   Ibid, s 28R(1), as modified in Scotland. The terms 'further education' and 'education authority' in the Scottish context have the meanings given in Education (Scotland) Act 1980, ss 1(5) and 135(1): DDA 1995, s 28R(7)–(8), as modified in Scotland.

- in the terms on which they offer to enrol him or her on the course; or
- by refusing or deliberately omitting to accept an application for his or her enrolment on the course.

It is also unlawful for the LEA (an education authority in Scotland) or governing body to discriminate against a disabled person who has enrolled on the course in the services[1] which they provide (or offer to provide).[2] It is further unlawful for the LEA (an education authority in Scotland) to discriminate against a disabled person in the terms on which it provides (or offers to provide) recreational or training facilities.[3]

7.5.16 The meaning of discrimination for this purpose is set out in DDA 1995, s 28S without modification. As already discussed, there are two kinds of discrimination contemplated by the section: less favourable treatment and failure to make reasonable adjustments. The duty to make reasonable adjustments is that which arises under s 28T, with the following modification to s 28T(1) only. The responsible body[4] must take such steps as it is reasonable for it to have to take to ensure that, in relation to its arrangements for enrolling persons on a course of further or higher education (further education in Scotland) provided by it, and in relation to services provided (or offered) by it, disabled persons are not placed at a substantial disadvantage in comparison with persons who are not disabled.[5]

Enforcement

7.5.17 The new anti-discrimination provisions in the field of further and higher education, as described above,[6] are enforced by way of civil proceedings in the same way as any other claim in tort or (in Scotland) in reparation for breach of statutory duty.[7] Proceedings will be in the county court (in Scotland, the sheriff court). These provisions are examined in more detail in Chapter 10.

---

1 The term 'services' means services of any description which are provided wholly or mainly for persons enrolled on the course: DDA 1995, s 28R(4), as modified.

2 Ibid, s 28R(3). See Post-16 Code of Practice, para 3.14.

3 Ibid, s 28R(5), as modified. The term 'recreational or training facilities' means any facilities secured or provided by the LEA under Education Act 1996, s 508(1) or (1A).

4 That is, the LEA (an education authority in Scotland) or the governing body of a maintained school, as the case may be: DDA 1995, s 28R(6), as modified.

5 Ibid, s 28T(1) as modified.

6 Ibid, Part 4, Chapter 2 (ie particularly ss 28R–28U), as described in **7.5**.

7 Ibid, s 28V.

Reasonable adjustments and the problem of leases

7.5.18   As is already the case in the employment and services field,[1] the new education provisions of the DDA 1995 deal with the potentially conflicting legal obligations of disability discrimination law and the law of landlord and tenant which will arise when the duty to make reasonable adjustments embraces potential alterations to physical features of premises from 1 September 2005.[2] The relevant statutory provisions apply where an educational institution occupies premises under a 'lease'.[3] A 'lease' for this purpose includes a tenancy, sub-lease or sub-tenancy, and an agreement for a lease, tenancy, sub-lease or sub-tenancy.[4] Where the premises are occupied under a sub-lease or sub-tenancy, the references in the statute[5] to a 'lessor' are to be taken as referring to the lessor who is the educational institution's immediate landlord.[6]

7.5.19   The statutory provisions apply if the effect of the lease would otherwise be that the responsible body would not be entitled to make a particular alteration to the premises,[7] and if the alteration is one which the responsible body proposes to make in order to comply with its statutory duty[8] to make reasonable adjustments.[9] If the terms and

---

1   See **6.3**.

2   DDA 1995, s 28W and Sch 4, Part 3.

3   DDA 1995, s 28W(1)(a). This provision is slightly modified when being applied in the context of the modified provisions of ss 28R and 28T as they apply to further and higher education provided by local education authorities or the governing body of a maintained school: ibid, Sch 4C, para 3.

4   Ibid, s 28W(3). The DDA 1995 provides that future regulations may further define the meaning of these terms: ibid, Sch 4, para 14.

5   Ibid, s 28W and Sch 4, Part 3, paras 10–12. See Post-16 Code of Practice, paras 7.1–7.3.

6   Disability Discrimination (Educational Institutions) (Alteration of Leasehold Premises) Regulations 2002, SI 2002/1458, reg 7(1), (3)–(4) and (6) (in force 28 June 2002). See generally Post-16 Code of Practice, paras 7.4–7.5 (and example). The regulations purport to be made only under DDA 1995, Sch 6, para 13, when clearly para 14 is also a relevant power. It also appears that reg 7 refers in error to Sch 6 rather than Sch 4 to the DDA 1995. The confusion probably arises from the fact that it is Sch 6 to the SENDA 2001 which amends Sch 4 to the DDA 1995. These errors have been acknowledged by the Department for Education and Skills and led to the Regulations being reported to both Houses of Parliament by the Joint Committee on Statutory Instruments (in its 35th Report of 2001–2002) as being defectively drafted and as failing to comply with proper drafting practice. As a result the Department has undertaken to remake the Regulations, but that does not appear to have been done.

7   DDA 1995, s 28W(1)(b).

8   Under ibid, s 28T.

9   Ibid, s 28W(1)(c).

conditions of a lease impose conditions which are to apply if the responsible body alters the premises, then the responsible body is treated[1] as not being entitled to make the alteration.[2] Similarly, if the terms and conditions of the lease entitle the lessor to impose conditions when giving any consent to the responsible body to alter the premises, the responsible body is treated[3] as not being entitled to make the alteration.[4] If the above conditions are satisfied,[5] the DDA 1995 provides that the lease shall have effect as if it provided for the responsible body to be entitled to make the alteration with the written consent of the lessor.[6] In other words, a statutory term is implied into the lease or agreement at issue. The statutory term requires that, if the responsible body wishes to make an alteration to the premises, it must first make a written application to the lessor for consent.[7] Furthermore, the Act implies into the terms of the lease a requirement that, if a written application for consent is made by the responsible body, the lessor will not withhold consent unreasonably.[8] In turn, the lessor is deemed to be entitled to make any consent the subject of reasonable conditions.[9]

7.5.20 Where the educational institution occupies premises under a sub-lease or sub-tenancy, any superior lease under which the premises are held has effect (except to the extent to which it expressly so provides) in relation to the lessor and lessee who are parties to the superior lease as if it provided for the lessee to have to make a written application to the lessor for consent to the alteration.[10] If such an application is made, the superior lease has effect as if it provided for the lessor not to withhold its consent unreasonably and for the lessor to be entitled to make its consent subject to reasonable conditions.

7.5.21 As has been noted in respect of the comparable provisions in the employment and services field,[11] the statutory wording appears to restrict the vigour of this otherwise quite far-reaching adjustment of the rights of commercial landlord and tenant. It is apparent that a lease is to have effect as modified by the statutory implied terms 'except to the

---

1   For the purposes of ibid, s 28W(1).

2   Ibid, s 28W(4)(a).

3   For the purposes of ibid, s 28W(1).

4   Ibid, s 28W(4)(b).

5   Ibid, s 28W(1) and (4).

6   Ibid, s 28W(2)(a).

7   Ibid, s 28W(2)(b).

8   Ibid, s 28W(2)(c).

9   Ibid, s 28W(2)(d).

10   Ibid, s 28W(2A), inserted by Disability Discrimination (Educational Institutions) (Alteration of Leasehold Premises) Regulations 2002, SI 2002/1458, reg 7(2).

11   See **6.3.12**.

extent to which it expressly so provides'.[1] The reference to 'it' might be taken to be a reference to the lease.[2] This suggests that the landlord might impose express terms in the lease that have the intent and effect of thwarting the statutory implications made in the lease. If that is right, then it may be that such express terms would have to surmount the test of an invalid agreement.[3] However, upon further reflection, the fact that the draftsman has continued with the use of the suspect phrase indicates strongly that the words have been chosen carefully. The phrase 'except to the extent to which it [that is, the lease] expressly so provides' may be a benign one and may be meant to do no more than anticipate that the lease may already contain terms which favour the making of reasonable adjustments to the premises in particular circumstances.

7.5.22 As has been explained above, where an educational institution occupies premises under a lease, a statutory term is implied that, if the responsible body wishes to make an alteration to the premises, it must first make a written application to the lessor for consent.[4] If such a written application for consent is made, the lessor will not withhold consent unreasonably.[5] In turn, the lessor is deemed to be entitled to make any consent the subject of reasonable conditions.[6] Regulations deal with the further consequences of these provisions as follows.[7]

7.5.23 Where the lessor has received the required written application from the responsible body,[8] the lessor is treated as having withheld its consent where it fails to reply in writing (consenting to or refusing the alteration) within 42 days of receipt of the application for consent.[9] The same result arises where within the same timescale the lessor replies in writing consenting to the alteration subject to the consent of another person required under a superior lease (or pursuant to a 'binding

---

1   DDA 1995, s 28W(2).

2   It is possible that it is a drafting error and that the reference was intended to be to the subsection rather than to the lease (the phrase 'except to the extent to which [the sub-section] expressly so provides' makes better sense).

3   DDA 1995, ss 28P and 28X.

4   Ibid, s 28W(2)(b).

5   Ibid, s 28W(2)(c) and 27(2)(c).

6   Ibid, s 28W(2)(d).

7   Disability Discrimination (Educational Institutions) (Alteration of Leasehold Premises) Regulations 2002, SI 2002/1458 (in force 28 June 2002). See also Post-16 Code of Practice 2002, Chapter 7.

8   Ibid, reg 2.

9   Disability Discrimination (Educational Institutions) (Alteration of Leasehold Premises) Regulations 2002, SI 2002/1458, regs 3(1), (2)(a) and (7)(b). A lessor who complies outside the statutory time period is treated as having withheld its consent until such time

obligation'[1]), but the lessor fails to seek that consent.[2] However, in either case, the lessor is not treated as having withheld consent where the responsible body fails to submit with the application such plans and specifications as it is reasonable for the lessor to require before consenting to the alteration, provided the lessor has requested such a submission within 21 days of receiving the application.[3] However, where such plans and specifications are submitted to the lessor in response to a timely request, the lessor is treated as withholding consent to the alteration where it fails to reply in writing (consenting to or refusing the alteration) within 42 days of receiving those plans and specifications.[4] The same result accrues where within that timescale the lessor replies in writing consenting to the alteration subject to the consent of another person required under a superior lease (or pursuant to a binding obligation), but the lessor fails to seek that consent.[5]

7.5.24   As can be seen immediately above, the regulations envisage circumstances where the lessor might reply in writing to the educational institution consenting to the alteration subject to the consent of another person required under a superior lease (or pursuant to a binding obligation). Assuming the lessor has sought that consent, and has received it, the lessor is nevertheless treated as having withheld consent to the alteration where it fails to inform the educational institution in writing of that fact within 14 days of the receipt of that consent.[6] The lessor is treated as not having sought the other person's consent unless it has applied in writing to that person indicating that the occupier (the educational institution) has applied for consent to the alteration of the premises in order to comply with a s 28T duty. In addition, the lessor must indicate to that other person that it has given its consent conditionally upon obtaining that other person's consent.

---

as it did comply: ibid, reg 3(6). See generally Post-16 Code of Practice, paras 7.6–7.11 (and example).

1   A 'binding obligation' means a legally binding obligation (not contained in a lease) in relation to premises whether arising from an agreement or otherwise: Disability Discrimination (Educational Institutions) (Alteration of Leasehold Premises) Regulations 2002, SI 2002/1458, reg 2.

2   Disability Discrimination (Educational Institutions) (Alteration of Leasehold Premises) Regulations 2002, SI 2002/1458, reg 3(1), (2)(b) and (7)(b). A lessor who complies outside the statutory time period is treated as having withheld its consent until such time as it did comply: ibid, reg 3(6).

3   Ibid, reg 3(3).

4   Ibid, reg 3(4)(a) and (7)(b). A lessor who complies outside the statutory time period is treated as having withheld its consent until such time as it did comply: ibid, reg 3(6).

5   Ibid, reg 3(4)(b) and (7)(b). A lessor who complies outside the statutory time period is treated as having withheld its consent until such time as it did comply: ibid, reg 3(6).

6   Ibid, reg 3(5). A lessor who complies outside the statutory time period is treated as having withheld its consent until such time as it did comply: ibid, reg 3(6).

The lessor must also submit to that other person any plans and specifications which have been submitted by the occupier (service provider) to the lessor.[1]

7.5.25 When can a lessor be said to have withheld its consent to an alteration reasonably or unreasonably?[2] A lessor is treated as acting unreasonably in withholding its consent for an alteration to premises where the lease provides that it shall give its consent to an alteration of the kind in question and it has withheld its consent to that alteration.[3] In contrast, the lessor will be taken to have acted reasonably in withholding consent where there is a binding obligation requiring the consent of any person to the alteration; it has taken steps to seek that consent; and that consent has not been given or has been given subject to a condition making it reasonable to withhold the consent.[4] The lessor will also be taken to have acted reasonably in withholding consent where the lessor does not know, and could not be reasonably expected to know, that the alteration is one which the occupier (the educational institution) proposes to make in order to comply with a s 28T duty.[5] Circumstances are also prescribed where the giving of the lessor's consent subject to a condition is to be treated as reasonable.[6] If a condition is to the effect that:

- the occupier (the educational institution) must obtain any necessary planning permission (and any other consent or permission) required by or under any enactment;[7]
- the work must be carried out in accordance with any plans or specifications approved by the lessor (such approval not to be unreasonably withheld);[8]
- the lessor must be permitted a reasonable opportunity to inspect the work (whether before or after it is completed);[9]
- the consent of another person required under a superior lease or a binding agreement must be obtained;[10] or

---

1   Disability Discrimination (Educational Institutions) (Alteration of Leasehold Premises) Regulations 2002, SI 2002/1458, reg 3(7).

2   Ibid, regs 4–5. See generally Post-16 Code of Practice, paras 7.12–7.16.

3   Ibid, reg 4.

4   Ibid, reg 5(1) and (2)(a).

5   Ibid, reg 5(1) and (2)(b).

6   Ibid, reg 6(1). See generally Post-16 Code of Practice, paras 7.17–7.18.

7   Ibid, reg 6(2)(a).

8   Ibid, reg 6(2)(b).

9   Ibid, reg 6(2)(c).

10   Ibid, reg 6(2)(d).

- the occupier (the educational institution) must repay to the lessor the costs reasonably incurred in connection with the giving of the consent,[1]

it is regarded as reasonable.

7.5.26 Enforcement provisions in respect of a duty to make alterations to premises by an educational institution under DDA 1995, Part 4 are similar but slightly different to those applicable to service providers under Part 3.[2] Where any question arises as to whether a responsible body occupying premises under a lease has failed to comply with a duty to make reasonable adjustments by failing to make a particular alteration to premises, any constraint attributable to the fact that the premises are occupied under a lease must be ignored, unless the responsible body has applied to the lessor in writing for consent to make the alteration.[3] A reference may be made to the court where the lessor has refused consent for such an alteration to be made by the responsible body.[4] A reference may also be made where the lessor has given consent to the alteration but has made the consent subject to one or more conditions.[5] In both cases, the responsible body must have applied in writing to the lessor for the necessary consent. In these circumstances, the responsible body or a disabled person (who has an interest in the proposed alteration to the premises being made) may refer the matter to the county court (or, in Scotland, the sheriff court).[6] It does not seem to be contemplated that such a reference can be made only where legal proceedings have been commenced. These provisions would appear to provide for a preliminary clarification of the rights of the parties concerned by the court, even where litigation based upon a complaint of unlawful disability discrimination has not been initiated or contemplated.

7.5.27 Regulations provide for the modification of these provisions where the occupier (the educational institution) occupies the premises under a sub-lease or sub-tenancy.[7] In those circumstances, references to a 'lessor' are treated as a reference to the 'immediate landlord'.[8] The

---

1 Disability Discrimination (Educational Institutions) (Alteration of Leasehold Premises) Regulations 2002, SI 2002/1458, reg 6(2)(e).

2 DDA 1995, s 27 and Sch 4, Part 2. See **6.3**. See generally Post-16 Code of Practice, paras 7.19–7.25 (and examples).

3 Ibid, Sch 4, para 10.

4 Ibid, Sch 4, para 11(1)(a).

5 Ibid, Sch 4, para 11(1)(b).

6 Ibid, Sch 4, para 11(1).

7 Disability Discrimination (Educational Institutions) (Alteration of Leasehold Premises) Regulations 2002, SI 2002/1458, reg 7(4)–(5), modifying DDA 1995, Sch 4, paras 10–11 and inserting Sch 4, para 11(1A).

8 Ibid, reg 7(4).

regulations then provide that, except to the extent which it expressly so provides, any superior lease in respect of the premises shall have effect in relation to the lessor and the lessee who are parties to the superior lease as if it provided:

- for the lessee to be entitled to give its consent to the alteration with the written consent of the lessor;
- for the lessee to have to make a written application to the lessor for consent if it wishes to give its consent to the alteration;
- for the lessor not to withhold its consent unreasonably if such an application is made; and
- for the lessor to be entitled to make its consent subject to reasonable conditions.[1]

Where the lessee of any superior lease in relation to the premises has applied in writing to its lessor for consent to the alteration, and that consent has been refused or the lessor has made its consent subject to one or more conditions, then the occupier (the educational institution), lessee or a disabled person who has an interest in the proposed alteration to the premises being made may refer the matter to a county court (or, in Scotland, to the sheriff court).[2]

7.5.28   Where the matter has been referred to the court by these various means, the court shall determine whether the refusal of the lessor (or the immediate landlord, as the case might be) was unreasonable or whether any conditions imposed upon consent are unreasonable.[3] If the court decides that the refusal of consent to the alteration (or any conditions imposed upon the consent) by the lessor (or the immediate landlord, as the case might be) was unreasonable, then the court may make an appropriate declaration at its discretion. It may also make an order authorising the responsible body to make an alteration specified in the order.[4] Such an order may require the responsible body to comply with specified conditions.[5]

7.5.29   If litigation has been commenced,[6] then in any court proceedings where a question arises about a duty to make a reasonable adjustment by an alteration to premises occupied under a lease, either the claimant (in Scotland, the pursuer) or the responsible body may ask the court to join (in Scotland, sist) any lessor (including a superior

---

1   Disability Discrimination (Educational Institutions) (Alteration of Leasehold Premises) Regulations 2002, SI 2002/1458, reg 7(2), inserting DDA 1995, s 28W(2A).

2   Ibid, reg 7(5), inserting DDA 1995, Sch 4, para 11(1A).

3   DDA 1995, Sch 4, para 11(2); Disability Discrimination (Educational Institutions) (Alteration of Leasehold Premises) Regulations 2002, SI 2002/1458, reg 7(4).

4   Ibid.

5   Ibid, para 11(4).

6   Under DDA 1995, s 28V.

landlord, as the case might be) as a party to the proceedings.[1] The court must grant such a request if it is made before the hearing commences,[2] otherwise the granting of such a request is at the court's discretion.[3] Such a request to join the lessor to proceedings cannot be made once the court has determined the claim.[4]

7.5.30 If the lessor has been joined (or sisted) as a party to the proceedings, then the court has certain powers in relation to the lessor if certain conditions are satisfied. The court may determine whether the lessor has refused consent to the alteration at issue or whether the lessor has consented to the alteration but subject to one or more conditions.[5] If so, in either case, the court may then determine whether the refusal (or any of the conditions) was unreasonable.[6] Where such a finding has been made, the court may make such a declaration as it considers appropriate or authorise the responsible body to make a specified alteration (subject to compliance with specified conditions) or order the lessor to pay compensation to the claimant or pursuer.[7] Although this is not made explicit, it seems logical that any such remedy against the lessor may be made in addition to or instead of any remedy that the court would be able to make against the occupier (the educational institution) who is the defendant (or defender) to the proceedings. However, if the court decides to order the lessor to pay compensation to the claimant or pursuer, it may not make a parallel compensation order against the responsible body.[8]

7.6 DISABILITY DISCRIMINATION BILL

General qualifications bodies

7.6.1 If enacted, the Disability Discrimination Bill will amend Part 4 of the DDA 1995 so as to prohibit unlawful discrimination against disabled

---

1 DDA 1995, Sch 4, para 12(1); Disability Discrimination (Educational Institutions) (Alteration of Leasehold Premises) Regulations 2002, SI 2002/1458, reg 7(6)(a).

2 DDA 1995, Sch 4, para 12(2). Where the premises are occupied under a sub-lease or sub-tenancy, the request shall be granted if it is made before the hearing of the claim begins, unless it appears to the court that another lessor should be joined (or sisted) as a party to the proceedings: Disability Discrimination (Educational Institutions) (Alteration of Leasehold Premises) Regulations 2002, SI 2002/1458, reg 7(6)(b), substituting DDA 1995, Sch 4, para 12(2).

3 DDA 1995, Sch 4, para 12(3).

4 Ibid, Sch 4, para 12(4).

5 Ibid, Sch 4, para 12(5)(a).

6 Ibid, Sch 4, para 12(5)(b).

7 Ibid, Sch 4, para 12(6)–(7).

8 Ibid, Sch 4, para 12(8).

persons by general qualifications bodies in relation to the award of relevant qualifications. The proposed prohibitions to a large extent reflect those imposed under Part 2 in relation to qualifications bodies which award trade or professional qualifications (see Chapter 4). A 'relevant qualification' will be prescribed in regulations and it is intended that this power will be used to prescribe qualifications such as A-levels, GCSEs and other non-vocational qualifications. Something that is a 'trade or professional qualification' cannot become a relevant qualification for this purpose. A 'general qualifications body' is any authority or body which can confer a relevant qualification, but this does not include responsible bodies (eg schools), local education authorities, Scottish education authorities, or other prescribed authorities or bodies.

7.6.2 The definitions of 'unlawful discrimination' and 'unlawful harassment' reflect the definitions used in Part 2 of the Act in relation to qualifications bodies which confer trade or professional qualifications. If the application of a competence standard by a general qualifications body amounts to less favourable treatment, it may only be justified if the standard is applied equally to all persons and its application is a proportionate means of achieving a legitimate aim. A competence standard is any academic, medical or other standard applied by a qualifications body in order to determine whether a person has a particular level of competence or ability.

7.6.3 The Bill will require general qualifications bodies in certain circumstances to make reasonable adjustments where disabled persons suffer substantial disadvantage in comparison with others. There is no duty to make reasonable adjustments in relation to competence standards, but the duty is imposed where a general qualifications body applies provisions, criteria or practices to disabled persons. It also applies in relation to the physical features of premises occupied by general qualifications bodies. The extent of the duty will be addressed through regulations. Regulations will also make provision with respect to enforcement matters and about cases where leasehold premises are occupied by qualifications bodies and how the reasonable adjustment duty impacts in this context.

Chapter 8

PUBLIC TRANSPORT

8.1 INTRODUCTION

8.1.1 The 1994 Green Paper considered whether the proposed general right of access should be extended to facilities for transport or travel.[1] It anticipated that the new right would not require modifications to transport systems where existing physical barriers prevented access. The 1995 White Paper confirmed that the new right would not apply to transport vehicles but would apply to stations.[2] It suggested that further initiatives would take place outside the framework of the proposed disability discrimination legislation. In the event, the initiatives were taken in Part 5 of the DDA 1995. Part 5 is not fully in force at the time of writing.

Transport services and Part 3 of the DDA 1995

8.1.2 The goods, facilities and services provisions in Part 3[3] do not apply to any service 'so far as it consists of the use of any means of transport'.[4] This means that the Part 3 rights of access to services may require transport providers to make some (but not all) of their facilities or services accessible without discrimination to disabled people.[5] For example, facilities and services such as timetables, ticketing arrangements, booking facilities, waiting areas, toilet facilities, platforms and other public areas are subject to the anti-discrimination provisions of the DDA 1995. Transport providers must consider what reasonable

---

1   *A Consultation on Government Measures to Tackle Discrimination Against Disabled People* (July 1994), para 4.5.

2   *Ending Discrimination Against Disabled People*, Cm 2729 (1995), para 4.6.

3   DDA 1995, ss 19–21.

4   Ibid, s 19(5)(b), subject to any provision to the contrary in future regulations (no such regulations have been proposed to date).

5   See Rights of Access Code of Practice 2002, paras 2.36–2.37.

adjustments might be made in order to ensure that disabled passengers enjoy effective access to such facilities or services.[1]

8.1.3   However, Part 3 does not require buses, coaches, taxis, trains, aeroplanes, ferries, ships or other forms of public transport (including heritage vehicles) to be accessible without discrimination or to be accommodating of the needs of disabled passengers.[2] There may be other legal or extra-legal sources which assist disabled persons to achieve a right of access in respect of transport vehicles. For example, some local authorities already make the accessibility of taxis the subject of licensing conditions. Nevertheless, the DDA 1995 does not create a general right of transport accessibility. For example, hire car and breakdown recovery services are not fully subject to the Part 3 duty to make reasonable adjustments (so far as they consist of the use of a means of transport, such as the hire car itself or a breakdown relay vehicle). Furthermore, discriminatory behaviour on board a transport vehicle (such as refusal to serve a disabled person in a restaurant car of a train) is not unlawful. The Disability Rights Task Force (DRTF) has recommended that the exemption for transport operators from the pre-2004 rights of access[3] should be removed, and that car hire and breakdown recovery services should be brought within the fold.[4] The Government intends to act on these recommendations and has already consulted on the proposal to do so.[5] Measures to effect the change have been included in the Disability Discrimination Bill and are expected to be implemented from December 2006.[6]

Transport employers and Part 2 of the DDA 1995

8.1.4   The exclusion of transport services from Part 3 of the DDA 1995 does not prevent disabled persons from enjoying a right to equal

---

1   See the rather artificial example in *Roads v Central Trains Ltd* [2004] EWCA Civ 1541, CA. A train operator was required to make an adjustment for a wheelchair-user passenger where a station's platforms were not otherwise easily accessible. That involved the provision of an accessible taxi from another town to ferry the passenger from one side of the station to the other. The artificiality of the agreed facts of the case (including a concession that cost was not a factor) reduces its value as a precedent.

2   HL Deb, vol 566, col 463. See Rights of Access Code of Practice 2002, paras 2.36–2.37.

3   That is, the provisions of ss 19–21 with the exception of s 21(2)(a)–(c). See Chapter 5.

4   Disability Rights Task Force, *From Exclusion to Inclusion: A Report of the Disability Rights Task Force for Disabled People* (1999, London: DfEE) (DRTF Report). See, ibid, recommendations 7.2 and 7.5.

5   See **5.9**. See Department for Transport, *Consultation on the Government's Proposals to Lift the Exemption for Transport Services from Some of the Civil Rights Duties in Part III of the Disability Discrimination Act 1995* (November 2002). See generally: Department for Transport, *Inclusive Mobility* (undated).

6   Department for Work and Pensions, *Draft Disability Discrimination Bill*, Cm 6058 (December 2003); *Explanatory Notes*, Cm 6058-ii; *Draft Regulatory Impact Assessment*, Cm 6058-iii. See, in

employment opportunity under Part 2 of the Act in respect of transport employers. By way of illustration, a disabled bus driver would be entitled not to be discriminated against by the transport provider in its guise as employer. Ironically, that might call for modifications to be made to a vehicle if that would be a reasonable adjustment called for under the provisions of Part 2 of the DDA 1995.[1] For example, a driver with impaired hearing might be entitled to the installation of a simple audio-visual signalling system that indicated when a passenger wished to alight.

Public transport and Part 5 of the DDA 1995

8.1.5   Although transport systems are not fully covered by the anti-discrimination measures in the DDA 1995, the Act does empower the Government to enact new accessibility standards for public transport. These accessibility standards will apply to taxis, public service vehicles and rail vehicles. They apply only to land-based transport services and do not apply to aircraft or ferries. These are the measures set out in Part 5 of the Act which provides a statutory framework for accessibility regulations. Each of the methods of transport covered by Part 5 is now examined in turn. Not all aspects of Part 5 are in force at the time of this edition.[2]

8.2   TAXIS

8.2.1   While many local authorities have attempted to improve the accessibility of taxis to disabled passengers through licensing conditions, the Government took the view during the passage of the DDA 1995 that such a piecemeal approach had been tried and failed. The sponsors of the Act expressed their 'clear intention' to introduce 'provisions to require that, from days to be determined, taxis newly licensed must, as a condition of licence, be accessible to all disabled people, including those who use wheelchairs'.[3] Whilst accepting that

---

particular: Joint Committee on the Draft Disability Discrimination Bill, *First Report* (April 2004); Department for Work and Pensions, *The Government's Response to the Report of the Joint Committee on the Draft Disability Discrimination Bill*, Cm 6276 (July 2004).

1   DDA 1995, s 6. See Chapter 3.

2   See generally: Department for Transport, *Inclusive Mobility* (undated). Note also that when the Government announced its 10-year Transport Plan in July 2000, it indicated that access for disabled persons would be a condition of all new investment in public transport. See further: House of Commons Transport Select Committee, *6th Report: Disabled People's Access to Transport* (March 2004, HC 439); Department for Transport, *The Government's Response to the Transport Select Committee 6th Report: Disabled People's Access to Transport*, Cm 6184 (June 2004).

3   HL Deb, vol 564, col 2034. A date for the implementation of the taxi accessibility standards was not indicated at the time: ibid, vol 566, cols 453–454.

there had been criticism of the current models of wheelchair-accessible taxis, it was also made 'absolutely clear that we are not talking about a universal requirement for the current purpose-built taxi design'.[1]

Taxi accessibility regulations

8.2.2   The Secretary of State is given power by the DDA 1995 to make 'taxi accessibility regulations'.[2] This power has not yet been brought into force and no regulations have been made to date. The purpose of the regulations when made will be to secure that it is possible for disabled persons:

- to get into and out of taxis in safety;
- to be carried in taxis in safety and in reasonable comfort;
- to be conveyed in safety into and out of taxis while remaining in their wheelchairs (where a wheelchair user);
- to be carried in taxis in safety and in reasonable comfort while remaining in their wheelchairs (where a wheelchair user).

The regulations are intended to 'focus clearly on the needs of all disabled people and will be drawn up in close consultation with the Disabled Persons' Transport Advisory Committee' (DPTAC). Design parameters will be defined based on research and experience to provide 'optimum levels of accessibility' and manufacturers will be expected to meet the new market demand so created.[3]

8.2.3   Such taxi accessibility regulations may in particular require 'regulated taxis' to conform with regulations as to:

- the size of door openings for passenger use;
- the floor area of 'passenger compartments';[4]
- the amount of headroom in passenger compartments; and
- the fitting of restraining devices designed to ensure the stability of a wheelchair while the taxi is moving.[5]

Moreover, the regulations may require drivers of regulated taxis plying for hire (or under hire) to comply with regulations as to the carrying of ramps or other devices designed to facilitate the loading and unloading of wheelchairs.[6] The regulations might also require the driver of a

---

1   HL Deb, vol 564, cols 2034–2035.

2   DDA 1995, s 32(1). A commencement date has not been appointed. In Scotland, the powers to introduce the regulations are contained in s 20 of the Civic Government (Scotland) Act 1982, as amended by the DDA 1995.

3   HL Deb, vol 564, col 2035.

4   The meaning of this term is to be prescribed in future regulations: DDA 1995, s 32(5).

5   Ibid, s 32(2)(a).

6   Ibid, s 32(2)(b).

regulated taxi, in which a disabled person in a wheelchair is being carried (while remaining in the wheelchair), to comply with regulations as to the position in which the wheelchair is to be secured.[1] The effect of these provisions is that taxi drivers must recognise their duty to carry disabled customers. It would not be lawful for drivers to refuse to pick up a disabled passenger in a wheelchair 'on the pretext . . . that they are not carrying the ramps'.[2] A failure to comply with such accessibility regulations by a driver plying for hire (or under hire) will be a criminal offence.[3]

Taxis to be covered by the regulations

8.2.4 To what taxis will these new regulations and duties apply? The regulations will define which taxis are to be regulated for these purposes. However, the regulations can only apply to a 'taxi' as narrowly defined.[4] A 'taxi' for this purpose means only a licensed vehicle.[5] It does not include a taxi which is drawn by a horse or other animal. The effect is that any new accessibility standards for taxis will apply only to hackney cabs or so-called 'black cabs' and will not apply to private hire cars or 'minicabs'.[6] At the same time, it is not intended that the taxi trade will in future be expected to make universal use of the London-style black cab or that the legislation (when in force) will produce a universal purpose-built taxi design.[7]

8.2.5 In order 'to ensure an orderly transition to the new require-ments without damaging the viability of the taxi trade',[8] taxi licensing authorities[9] shall not grant a taxi licence unless the taxi conforms with the relevant taxi accessibility regulations.[10] However, the licensing requirements by reference to any taxi accessibility regulations apply

---

1   DDA 1995, s 32(2)(c).

2   HL Deb, vol 564, col 2035.

3   DDA 1995, s 32(3). On summary conviction, a person guilty of such an offence will be liable to a fine not exceeding level 3 on the standard scale: ibid, s 32(4).

4   Ibid, s 32(5).

5   That is, one licensed under Town Police Clauses Act 1847, s 37 or Metropolitan Public Carriage Act 1869, s 6. In Northern Ireland, a taxi is a vehicle licensed to stand or ply for hire under Road Traffic (Northern Ireland) Order 1981, art 61 and which seats not more than eight passengers in addition to the driver: DDA 1995, Sch 8, para 16(2).

6   HL Deb, vol 566, col 451. The DRTF recommends that the DRC should consider mechanisms for increasing the availability of accessible private hire vehicles (including the carrying of registered assistance dogs): DRTF Report, recommendation 7.3.

7   Ibid, col 453.

8   Ibid, vol 564, col 2035.

9   See DDA 1995, s 68(1) as to the meaning of this term.

10   Ibid, s 34(1). Like s 32, s 34 is not yet in force and no date for its commencement has been appointed.

only to newly licensed taxis, as opposed to taxis with existing licences and seeking renewal.[1] The intention is to regulate only new entrants to the taxi trade (or newly acquired taxis). It does not prevent the relicensing of non-accessible taxis provided that, subject to 28 days' grace, the new licence comes into force immediately on the expiry of the previous licence.[2] As the relevant Minister put it, this:

> '... provides that a licensing authority may, after a certain date, only license taxis which comply with the construction requirements that will be set out in the regulations ... We are also mindful of the need to protect the interests of the cab trade, much of which comprises small businesses. While it is reasonable to expect new taxis to be fully accessible, it would ... be unreasonable to require someone who had recently purchased and licensed a new non-accessible vehicle to dispose of it prematurely.'[3]

However, it is not intended that this exceptional treatment should continue indefinitely. The Secretary of State may provide by order that this exemption shall cease to have effect on a specified date.[4] The effect of such an order may be varied for different areas or localities.[5] Thus it is contemplated that there will be a future date beyond which no non-accessible vehicle can be relicensed as a taxi. That date is to be the subject of consultation with the trade.

Exemption regulations

8.2.6   It is hoped that these provisions will open up new markets for the taxi trade. However, it is acknowledged that compliance with the new standards could create difficulties. The Government recognised 'the enormously wide variations in types of area and of taxi use in this country'.[6] The 'strong presumption must be that, whatever the area, there will be now, or may be in the future, disabled people whose mobility would be enhanced by the availability of accessible vehicles'.[7] However, at the same time, the possibility that Part 5 of the DDA 1995 'could jeopardise the viability of the trade in a particular area to the point at which there ceased to be taxi provision for anyone' was recognised.[8] The legislature wished to avoid that result.

---

1   DDA 1995, s 34(2). The provisions of s 34 are applied to Northern Ireland with appropriate substitutions: Sch 8, para 18.

2   HL Deb, vol 566, cols 440–441.

3   Ibid, vol 564, col 2035.

4   DDA 1995, s 34(3).

5   Ibid, s 34(4). By virtue of s 67(7), this is without prejudice to the generality of the powers to make regulations or orders by statutory instrument conferred by s 67(2)–(3).

6   HL Deb, vol 564, col 2036.

7   Ibid, col 2036.

8   Ibid, col 2036.

8.2.7 Accordingly, the Secretary of State may make 'exemption regulations' to enable taxi licensing authorities[1] to apply for an order to be exempt from the new licensing provisions.[2] This is so if the licensing authority believes that, having regard to 'circumstances prevailing in its area', the application of the licensing conditions would be 'inappropriate' and if their application would result in 'an unacceptable reduction in the number of taxis' in that area.[3] The exemption regulations may make particular provision and prescriptions requiring a licensing authority proposing to apply for an exemption order to carry out consultations,[4] to publish its proposal, to consider any representations made about the proposal (before it applies for an order), and to make its application in a prescribed form.[5] The Secretary of State must consider any application for an exemption order and consult DPTAC (and any other persons the Secretary of State considers appropriate). Then the Secretary of State may make an exemption order (in the terms applied for or in such other terms as the Secretary of State considers appropriate) or refuse to make such an order.[6]

Swivel seat regulations

8.2.8 Even if a taxi is exempted from the taxi accessibility regulations, there is still power to require an 'exempt taxi' to comply with 'swivel seat regulations' as to the fitting and use of swivel seats in the taxi. The Secretary of State is given a power to make 'swivel seat regulations' requiring any 'exempt taxi' plying for hire in an area in respect of which an exemption order[7] is in force to conform with provisions as to the fitting and use of swivel seats.[8] The term 'swivel seats' will be defined in regulations.[9] No further light on these proposed regulations is cast by the parliamentary debates on the legislation.[10] The power to make such

1   That is, a licensing authority responsible for licensing taxis in any area of England and Wales other than the area to which the Metropolitan Public Carriage Act 1869 applies: DDA 1995, s 35(7).

2   DDA 1995, s 35(1). Section 35 does not apply in Northern Ireland: DDA 1995, Sch 8, para 19. Like ss 32 and 34, s 35 is not yet in force and no date for its commencement has been appointed.

3   Ibid, s 35(3).

4   Including 'as a matter of course, disabled people and the taxi trade': HL Deb, vol 564, col 2036.

5   DDA 1995, s 35(2).

6   Ibid, s 35(4).

7   That is, an order made under DDA 1995, s 35.

8   Ibid, s 35(5). An 'exempt taxi' is a taxi in relation to which s 34(1) would apply if there was not a s 35 exemption order in force: ibid, s 35(7). Note s 35(6) which cross-refers to s 34.

9   Ibid, s 35(7).

10 Although see HL Deb, vol 566, cols 1042–1043.

regulations is not yet in force, and no such regulations have been proposed or made.

Duties of taxi drivers towards disabled passengers

8.2.9 Drivers of regulated taxis will be placed under new duties in respect of a taxi which has been hired by or for a disabled person in a wheelchair; or by a person who wishes to be accompanied by a disabled person in a wheelchair.[1] These duties (which are not yet in force) will be:

- to carry in the taxi the passenger while he or she remains in the wheelchair;
- to make no additional charge for doing so;
- to carry the wheelchair in the taxi if the passenger chooses to sit in a passenger seat; and
- to take such steps as are necessary to ensure that the passenger is carried in the taxi in safety and in reasonable comfort.[2]

In addition, it will be the driver's statutory duty to give such assistance as may be reasonably required:

- to enable the passenger to get into or out of the taxi;
- to enable the passenger to be conveyed into and out of the taxi while in the wheelchair if the passenger wishes to remain in the wheelchair;
- to load the passenger's luggage into or out of the taxi; and
- to load the wheelchair into or out of the taxi if the passenger does not wish to remain in the wheelchair.[3]

A failure to comply with any of these duties without lawful excuse will be a criminal offence punishable upon summary conviction by a fine not exceeding level 3 on the standard scale.[4] However, there are certain defences and exemptions as follows.

8.2.10 The driver of a taxi is not required to carry more than one person in a wheelchair, or more than one wheelchair, on any one journey.[5] A taxi driver is not required to carry any person in circumstances in which it would otherwise be lawful for the driver to

---

1   DDA 1995, s 36(1). Like ss 32 and 34–35, s 36 is not yet in force and no date for its commencement has been appointed.

2   Ibid, s 36(3)(a)–(d). The term 'the passenger' means the disabled person concerned and 'carry' means carry in the taxi concerned: s 36(2).

3   Ibid, s 36(3)(e).

4   Ibid, s 36(5).

5   Ibid, s 36(4)(a) which also contemplates an exception in the case of a taxi of a prescribed description. No such prescription has been made at the time of writing.

refuse to carry that person.[1] For example, a taxi driver could not be required to carry a disabled passenger where the taxi is already exceeding the number of passengers who may be carried in accordance with its licence. It will also be a defence to show that, even though the taxi conformed with any taxi accessibility regulations,[2] it would not have been possible for the wheelchair of the disabled passenger concerned to be carried in safety in the taxi.[3]

8.2.11 Provision is also made for the exemption of taxi drivers from these new statutory duties on medical grounds. A taxi licensing authority shall issue a driver with a certificate of exemption from the duties above if it is satisfied that it is appropriate to exempt the driver on medical grounds.[4] An exemption certificate may also be issued on the ground that the driver's physical condition makes it impossible or unreasonably difficult for him or her to comply with a taxi driver's duties imposed under the DDA 1995.[5] The Government felt that this exception was important, especially for taxi drivers who themselves had a disability.[6] Provision is made for an appeal against a refusal to grant an exemption certificate.[7] The currency of the certificate of exemption shall be for such period as the licensing authority specifies in the certificate when issued.[8] Once an exemption certificate has been issued to a taxi driver, and so long as it remains in force, the driver is exempt from the statutory duties imposed,[9] provided an exemption notice (in a prescribed form and in a prescribed manner) is exhibited on the taxi.[10]

---

1   DDA 1995, s 36(4)(b).

2   That is, under ibid, s 32.

3   Ibid, s 36(6).

4   Ibid, s 36(7)(a). In Northern Ireland, this power lies with the Department of the Environment: ibid, Sch 8, para 20. Provision is made in s 49 for criminal offences committed in connection with exemption certificates (eg forgery or the making of false statements).

5   Ibid, s 36(7)(b).

6   HL Deb, vol 564, col 2036.

7   DDA 1995, s 38(1), as amended by the Private Hire Vehicles (Carriage of Guide Dogs etc) Act 2002 and the Courts Act 2003. Any person who is aggrieved by a refusal of a licensing authority to issue an exemption certificate under s 36 (or ss 37 and 37A, discussed at **8.2.12** to **8.2.21**) may appeal to a magistrates' court (or, in Northern Ireland, a court of summary jurisdiction): s 38(3). An appeal must be made within 28 days of the refusal: s 38(1). If the court allows such an appeal, it may direct the licensing authority to issue an exemption certificate and may specify the period of the currency of the exemption: s 38(2).

8   Ibid, s 36(8).

9   Under ibid, s 36(3).

10   Ibid, s 36(9). The necessary prescriptions have yet to be made.

Carrying of guide dogs and hearing dogs in taxis

8.2.12   In order to address the problem of persons with sensory impairments (who use guide or hearing dogs) being refused access to taxis because they wish to be accompanied by their animal, the DDA 1995 imposes additional duties on taxi drivers.[1] This aspect of the provisions of Part 5 affecting taxis has been fully in force from 31 March 2001 in England and Wales, and from 1 August 2001 in Northern Ireland.[2] Comparable provisions came into force in Scotland on 2 December 2002 and have since been updated. The statutory provisions are amplified by regulations.[3]

8.2.13   These duties arise where the taxi has been hired by or for a disabled person ('the passenger') accompanied by a guide dog or hearing dog.[4] The duties also apply where the taxi has been hired by a person who wishes to be accompanied in the taxi by a disabled person ('the passenger') accompanied by a guide or hearing dog.[5] A guide dog is a dog trained to guide a blind person, while a hearing dog is a dog trained to assist a deaf person.[6] The statute provides for this section (DDA 1995, s 37) to be applied by regulations to any other category of dog trained to assist a disabled person with a prescribed disability.[7] The regulations provide that an 'assistance dog' is prescribed as a category of dog for this purpose.[8] An 'assistance dog' is a dog which is trained by a 'specified charity' to assist a disabled person with a physical impairment[9] which consists of epilepsy or otherwise affects his or her mobility, manual dexterity, physical coordination or ability to lift, carry or

---

1   DDA 1995, s 37.

2   Disability Discrimination Act 1995 (Commencement No 8) Order 2000, SI 2000/2989; Disability Discrimination Act 1995 (Commencement No 7) Order (Northern Ireland) 2001, SR 2001/163.

3   Disability Discrimination Act 1995 (Taxis) (Carrying of Guide Dogs etc) (England and Wales) Regulations 2000, SI 2000/2990; Disability Discrimination Act 1995 (Taxis) (Carrying of Guide Dogs etc) (Northern Ireland) Regulations 2001, SR 2001/169. See also Department for Transport, Carriage of Guide, Hearing and Other Assistance Dogs in Taxis (advice leaflet for taxi drivers) and Travelling with Assistance Dogs in Taxis (advice leaflet for disabled people).

4   DDA 1995, s 37(1)(a) and (2).

5   Ibid, s 37(1)(b) and (2).

6   Ibid, s 37(11).

7   Ibid, s 37(9)–(10) and Sch 8, para 21(3).

8   Disability Discrimination Act 1995 (Taxis) (Carrying of Guide Dogs etc) (England and Wales) Regulations 2000, SI 2000/2990, reg 3(1); Disability Discrimination Act 1995 (Taxis) (Carrying of Guide Dogs etc) (Northern Ireland) Regulations 2001, SR 2001/169, reg 3(1).

9   That is, for the purpose of DDA 1995, s 1.

otherwise move everyday objects.[1] At the time that the disabled person whom the assistance dog is assisting hires a taxi, the dog must be wearing a jacket on which is prominently inscribed the name of a 'specified charity'.[2] A 'specified charity' for this purpose means one of three charities registered with the Charity Commission, namely: Dogs for the Disabled; Support Dogs; or Canine Partners for Independence.[3]

8.2.14 The duties of a taxi driver in the above situations are to carry the disabled passenger's dog, allowing it to remain with the passenger in the taxi, and not to make any additional charge for so doing.[4] A breach of these duties is a criminal offence punishable on summary conviction by a fine not exceeding level 3 on the standard scale.[5] It is noteworthy that these duties apply to all taxis and not just to regulated taxis.

8.2.15 However, in like manner to the excusal from the duties relating to the carrying of passengers in wheelchairs,[6] a licensing authority may exempt a driver from the duties in respect of a disabled passenger accompanied by a guide dog, hearing dog or prescribed assistance dog.[7] This is achieved by means of an exemption certificate if the licensing authority is satisfied that such exemption is appropriate on medical grounds.[8] In deciding that question, the authority must have

---

1   Disability Discrimination Act 1995 (Taxis) (Carrying of Guide Dogs etc) (England and Wales) Regulations 2000, SI 2000/2990, reg 3(2)(a); Disability Discrimination Act 1995 (Taxis) (Carrying of Guide Dogs etc) (Northern Ireland) Regulations 2001, SR 2001/169, reg 3(2)(a).

2   Disability Discrimination Act 1995 (Taxis) (Carrying of Guide Dogs etc) (England and Wales) Regulations 2000, SI 2000/2990, reg 3(2)(b); Disability Discrimination Act 1995 (Taxis) (Carrying of Guide Dogs etc) (Northern Ireland) Regulations 2001, SR 2001/169, reg 3(2)(b).

3   Disability Discrimination Act 1995 (Taxis) (Carrying of Guide Dogs etc) (England and Wales) Regulations 2000, SI 2000/2990, reg 3(3); Disability Discrimination Act 1995 (Taxis) (Carrying of Guide Dogs etc) (Northern Ireland) Regulations 2001, SR 2001/169, reg 3(3).

4   DDA 1995, s 37(3).

5   Ibid, s 37(4).

6   Ibid, s 36.

7   Ibid, s 37. Provisions are made as to the issue and currency of a s 37 exemption certificate and the display of such certificate in the taxi: s 37(7)–(8). See Disability Discrimination Act 1995 (Taxis) (Carrying of Guide Dogs etc) (England and Wales) Regulations 2000, SI 2000/2990, reg 2 and Schs 1–2; Disability Discrimination Act 1995 (Taxis) (Carrying of Guide Dogs etc) (Northern Ireland) Regulations 2001, SR 2001/169, reg 2 and Schedule. See also Department for Transport, 'Carriage of Guide, Hearing and Other Assistance Dogs in Taxis' (guidance leaflet for licensing authorities).

8   DDA 1995, s 37(5). In Northern Ireland, this power lies with the Department of the Environment: Sch 8, para 21. Provision is made in s 49 for criminal offences committed in connection with exemption certificates (eg forgery or the making of false statements). See further: Department for Transport, *Carriage of Assistance Dogs in Taxis: Medical Exemption for Drivers: Regulatory Impact Assessment* (November 2000; modified January 2004).

particular regard to the physical characteristics of the taxi in question.[1] For example, this exemption might cover a driver who has a medical condition that is aggravated by dogs, such as an asthmatic condition or an allergy.[2] Provision is made for an appeal against a refusal to grant an exemption certificate.[3]

Carrying of assistance dogs in private hire vehicles

8.2.16   The DDA 1995 has recently been amended by the Private Hire Vehicles (Carriage of Guide Dogs etc) Act 2002. As a result, a new s 37A now deals with the carrying of an 'assistance dog' in private hire vehicles in England and Wales.[4] For this purpose, an 'assistance dog' is a dog which has been trained to guide a blind person or to assist a deaf person, or which has been trained by a prescribed charity to assist a disabled person who has a disability which consists of epilepsy or otherwise affects his or her mobility, manual dexterity, physical co-ordination or ability to lift, carry or otherwise move everyday objects.[5] A 'private hire vehicle' means a vehicle licensed under specified statutory provisions.[6] Section 37A is fully in force from 31 March 2004.[7] The new section creates a number of criminal offences. A person who is guilty of an offence under s 37A is liable on summary conviction to a fine not exceeding level 3 on the standard scale.[8]

8.2.17   First, it is an offence for the operator of a private hire vehicle to fail (or refuse) to accept a booking for a private hire vehicle if the booking is requested by (or on behalf of) a disabled person (or a person who wishes a disabled person to accompany him or her) and the reason for the failure (or refusal) is that the disabled person will be

---

1   DDA 1995, s 37(6).

2   HL Deb, vol 564, col 2037.

3   See footnote 5 at **8.2.11**.

4   Inserted by the Private Hire Vehicles (Carriage of Guide Dogs etc) Act 2002, s 1(1). See generally: Department for Transport, *Carriage of Assistance Dogs in Private Hire Vehicles: Consultation Paper* (November 2003); Department for Transport, *Carriage of Assistance Dogs in Private Hire Vehicles: Regulatory Impact Assessment* (December 2003); DPTAC, *Making Private Hire Services More Accessible to Disabled People: A Good Practice Guide for Private Hire Vehicle Operators and Drivers* (December 2003).

5   DDA 1995, s 37A(9). The prescribed charities for this purpose are Dogs for the Disabled, Support Dogs, and Canine Partners for Independence: Disability Discrimination Act 1995 (Private Hire Vehicles) (Carriage of Guide Dogs etc) (England and Wales) Regulations 2003, SI 2003/3122, reg 3.

6   DDA 1995, s 37A(9). The statutory provisions are Private Hire Vehicles (London) Act 1998, s 6; Local Government (Miscellaneous Provisions) Act 1976, s 48; or an equivalent provision of a local enactment.

7   Private Hire Vehicles (Carriage of Guide Dogs etc) Act 2002 (Commencement No 1) Order 2003, SI 2003/3123.

8   DDA 1995, s 37A(4).

accompanied by his or her assistance dog.[1] Secondly, it is an offence for the operator of a private hire vehicle to make an additional charge for carrying an assistance dog which is accompanying a disabled person.[2] In both cases, the term 'operator' means a person who holds a licence granted under specified statutory provisions.[3] Thirdly, it is an offence for the driver of a private hire vehicle to fail (or refuse) to carry out a booking accepted by the operator of the vehicle if the booking was made by (or on behalf of) a disabled person (or a person who wishes a disabled person to accompany him or her) and the reason for the failure (or refusal) is that the disabled person is accompanied by his or her assistance dog.[4] For this purpose, a 'driver' means a person who holds a licence granted under specific statutory provisions.[5]

8.2.18 However, in this third case only, if the licensing authority[6] is satisfied that it is appropriate on medical grounds to issue a certificate of exemption to a driver in respect of this provision, it must do so.[7] In determining whether to issue a certificate of exemption, the licensing authority shall have particular regard to the physical characteristics of the private hire vehicle which the applicant drives or those of any kind of private hire vehicle in relation to which he or she requires the certificate.[8] A certificate of exemption shall be issued with respect to a specified private hire vehicle (or a specified kind of private hire vehicle) and for such period as may be specified in the certificate.[9] No offence is committed by a driver[10] if a certificate of exemption issued to him or her is in force with respect to the private hire vehicle and the prescribed notice is exhibited on the private hire vehicle in the prescribed

---

1   DDA 1995, s 37A(1).

2   Ibid, s 37A(2).

3   Ibid, s 37A(9). The statutory provisions are Private Hire Vehicles (London) Act 1998, s 3; Local Government (Miscellaneous Provisions) Act 1976, s 55; or an equivalent provision of a local enactment.

4   Ibid, s 37A(3).

5   Ibid, s 37A(9). The statutory provisions are Private Hire Vehicles (London) Act 1998, s 13; Local Government (Miscellaneous Provisions) Act 1976, s 51; or an equivalent provision of a local enactment.

6   Ibid, s 37A(9): licensing authority, in relation to any area of England and Wales, means the authority responsible for licensing private hire vehicles in that area.

7   Ibid, s 37A(5).

8   Ibid, s 37A(6).

9   Ibid, s 37A(7).

10   That is, under s 37A(3).

manner.[1] Provision is made for an appeal against a refusal to grant an exemption certificate.[2]

Taxi accessibility at designated transport facilities

8.2.19   The Secretary of State may by regulations provide for the application of any provision of the DDA 1995 relating to taxis or taxi drivers (that is, those described above) to be extended to vehicles (or their drivers) used for the provision of services under 'a franchise agreement'.[3] These regulations may apply any such taxi provisions with such modifications as the Secretary of State considers appropriate.[4] A 'franchise agreement' is a contract entered into by the 'operator' of a 'designated transport facility' for the provision by the other party to the contract of 'hire car' services for members of the public using any part of the transport facility and which involves vehicles entering any part of that facility.[5] A 'designated transport facility' means any premises which form part of any port, airport, railway station or bus station which has been designated for the present purpose by an order made by the Secretary of State.[6] The 'operator' of such a facility means any person who is concerned with the management or operation of the facility.[7] The definition of 'hire car' will be prescribed by regulations.[8]

8.2.20   The intention behind this provision, when brought into force, is to ensure that 'taxis' (using that term here in the popular, loose sense) that ply for hire at airports, railway stations and other transport termini could be brought within the accessibility regime for taxis.[9] It is not designed to capture those taxis that already fall within the definition of a taxi regulated for any of the purposes of the taxi provisions of Part 5 of the DDA 1995. They will be already subject to the new duties and standards. Instead, it is intended to embrace those taxis that are private

---

1   DDA 1995, s 37A(8). See Disability Discrimination Act 1995 (Private Hire Vehicles) (Carriage of Guide Dogs etc) (England and Wales) Regulations 2003, SI 2003/3122, reg 2.

2   See footnote 5 at **8.2.11**. Provision is also made by s 49 (as amended) for criminal offences committed in connection with exemption certificates (eg forgery or the making of false statements).

3   DDA 1995, s 33(2), as read with s 33(4). This power also applies to the potential extension of regulations made in pursuance of the Civic Government (Scotland) Act 1982, s 20(2A). Under the Scotland Act 1998, functions under this section are transferred to the Scottish Ministers (insofar as they are exercisable in or as regards Scotland) by Transfer of Functions to the Scottish Ministers etc Order 1999, SI 1999/1750, art 2, Sch 1.

4   Ibid, s 33(3).

5   Ibid, s 33(1).

6   Ibid, s 33(4).

7   Ibid.

8   Ibid.

9   Created by ibid, ss 32–39.

hire cars or mini-cabs and which are entitled to provide car hire services to passengers under a monopoly contract or franchise with the operator of the transport terminus in question (such as, for example, the British Airports Authority at London Gatwick Airport).[1]

Application to Scotland and Northern Ireland

8.2.21 On the face of the DDA 1995, the new duties and statutory framework affecting taxis apply only in England and Wales. However, these provisions also apply to Northern Ireland.[2] From 5 February 2003, the Civic Government (Scotland) Act 1982 has been amended so as to enable these provisions to be extended to Scotland by means of regulatory powers.[3]

Implementation

8.2.22 With the exception of the provisions relating to the carrying of guide dogs, hearing dogs and prescribed assistance dogs in taxis, the remaining provisions of DDA 1995, Part 5 (ss 32–39) affecting taxis are not yet in force. In July 1997, various government departments jointly issued an informal consultation document covering the features which could be included in regulations and suggesting dates for implementation of the proposed regulations.[4] The Government was expected to commence formal consultation on the implementation of these proposals during the course of 2000 or 2001, but that did not occur. Draft regulations have not been published. The informal consultation document proposed that taxi accessibility regulations would come into force for newly licensed vehicles in January 2002. At the same time, interim regulations would come into force for previously licensed wheelchair-accessible taxis. By January 2012, all taxis would be required to comply with the main taxi accessibility regulations. It is clear that this timetable has not been adhered to.

8.2.23 The latest position is recorded in a Government policy document issued in October 2003.[5] The Government intends to vary

---

1   HC Deb, vol 265, cols 159–160.

2   With the appropriate modifications contained in DDA 1995, Sch 8, paras 16–23.

3   DDA 1995, s 39 and Disability Discrimination Act 1995 (Commencement No 10) (Scotland) Order 2003, SI 2003/215. See: Taxi Drivers' Licences (Carrying of Guide Dogs and Hearing Dogs) (Scotland) Regulations 2003, SSI 2003/73 (revoking earlier regulations and in force 3 March 2003); Private Hire Car Drivers' Licences (Carrying of Guide Dogs and Hearing Dogs) (Scotland) Regulations 2004, SSI 2004/88 (in force 31 March 2004). The duties in Scotland are imposed through a condition in the taxi or private hire car driver's licence.

4   'The Government's Proposals for Taxis' (1997, London: DETR).

5   *Taxi Accessibility Regulations – Policy Proposals* (2003, London: Department for Transport). See also: House of Commons Transport Committee, *6th Report: Disabled People's Access to*

the application of the proposed regulations to target areas in which it is thought that accessible taxis will best meet the needs of disabled people without causing a disparate impact from additional costs. These areas are being referred to as 'first phase' authorities. It is proposed to introduce taxi accessibility regulations in these areas between 2010 and 2020. Those authorities meet one or more of the following criteria: a licensing authority population of at least 120,000 people; a major transport interchange; a major tourist attraction; or an existing mandatory policy resulting in 100 per cent accessible vehicles. Licensing authorities outside the first phase would not be subject to the regulations in the first instance, but would be subject to voluntary guidance on establishing an appropriate mix of vehicles and on the design parameters. The Government will monitor the introduction of accessible vehicles in these areas to determine whether the guidance is effective, so that a view would then be taken on the necessity of extending the regulations to these areas. The proposals will be the subject of a public consultation process in due course. Separate consultation exercises will be held in Scotland and Northern Ireland.

8.3   PUBLIC SERVICE VEHICLES

8.3.1   Introducing the provisions of the DDA 1995 dealing with access to buses, coaches and rail services,[1] the relevant Minister stated that they 'add up to a very significant change in the field of transport' and acknowledged that the transport industry had worked closely with the Department of Transport for many years 'to promote and encourage the introduction of better designs and operating practices to meet the needs of disabled people'.[2] Nevertheless, the then Government believed that legislation was necessary to continue progress towards an accessible transport system. At the same time, however, these new statutory measures are not retrospective and are designed to apply only to new vehicles.[3] It is intended to provide a legal framework compatible with existing transport requirements, but flexible enough to allow the introduction of new requirements that are workable and viable in a technical, operational and economic sense.

Transport HC 439 (March 2004); Department for Transport, *The Government's Response to Transport Select Committee 6th Report: Disabled People's Access to Transport*, Cm 6184 (June 2004). See further: Department for Transport, *Determination of Accessible Taxi Requirements: Phase 1* (November 2003) and *Phase 2* (June 2004).

1   DDA 1995, ss 40–48.
2   HL Deb, vol 565, cols 714–715.
3   Ibid, vol 566, col 463. Heritage and replica vehicles are thus implicitly outside the new regime.

8.3.2 From 30 August 2000, these provisions apply to 'public service vehicles' (PSVs).[1] A PSV is a vehicle adapted to carry more than eight passengers (in addition to the driver) and which is in public service.[2] These provisions thus apply to buses and coaches of the required capacity offering a public transport service.

PSV accessibility regulations

8.3.3 The Secretary of State is empowered to make 'PSV accessibility regulations'.[3] In England and Wales, regulations have been enacted in the form of the Public Service Vehicles Accessibility Regulations 2000.[4] The regulations came into force on 30 August 2000. Much of the content of the Public Service Vehicles Accessibility Regulations 2000 is technical in nature and it is not proposed to reproduce it here. Appropriate cross-references to the regulations are made below.

8.3.4 The purpose of the regulations is to secure that it is possible for disabled persons to get on to and off 'regulated public service vehicles' in safety and without unreasonable difficulty. In the case of disabled persons in wheelchairs, the regulations seek to achieve this purpose while a disabled person remains in his or her wheelchair.[5] Furthermore, the regulations attempt to secure that it is possible for disabled persons to be carried in 'regulated public service vehicles' in safety and reasonable comfort.[6] As used in this context, a 'regulated public service vehicle' means a PSV to which the PSV accessibility regulations are expressed to apply.[7] This implies that the Secretary of State has discretion in defining which vehicles or kinds of public service are covered by the accessibility regulations. Moreover, the regulations may make different provision as respects different classes or descriptions of vehicle and as respects the same class or description of vehicle in

---

1   DDA 1995, ss 40–45, which came into force on 30 August 2000: SI 2000/1969.

2   Ibid, s 40(5) and Sch 8, para 24(2). See also the provisions of the Public Passenger Vehicles Act 1981 and the Road Traffic (Northern Ireland) Order 1981.

3   Ibid, s 40(1), after due consultation with the DPTAC and other representative organisations: DDA 1995, s 40(7) and Sch 8, para 24(3). The power to make such regulations in Northern Ireland is vested with the Department of the Environment: Sch 8, para 24(1).

4   SI 2000/1970, as amended by the Public Service Vehicles Accessibility (Amendment) Regulations 2000, SI 2000/3318, the Public Service Vehicles Accessibility (Amendment) Regulations 2002, SI 2002/2981, and the Public Service Vehicles Accessibility (Amendment) Regulations 2004, SI 2004/1881. See further Department for Transport, 'The Public Service Vehicles Accessibility Regulations 2000 Guidance'. See further: Department for Transport, *Proposed PSV accessibility regulations: regulatory impact assessment* (February 2001, modified May 2003).

5   DDA 1995, s 40(1)(a).

6   Ibid, s 40(1)(b).

7   Ibid, s 40(5).

different circumstances.[1] For example, in the case of full-size single-deck buses, an access solution might be low floors, whereas, in the case of coaches, a lift might be appropriate.[2] It was anticipated that local and regional variations might also be necessary, as might flexibility of timescales for implementation.

8.3.5 In fact, the Public Service Vehicles Accessibility Regulations 2000 apply to single-deck and double-deck buses and to single-deck and double-deck coaches with a capacity of more than 22 passengers which are used to provide local and scheduled services (so-called 'regulated public service vehicles').[3] The Regulations recognise the impact their provisions will have on the bus manufacturing and operating industry by providing for a phased implementation of their requirements. The detailed technical requirements to be met by regulated public service vehicles are contained in three Schedules dealing with wheelchair accessibility requirements (Sch 1) and with the general accessibility requirements for buses (Sch 2) and coaches (Sch 3) respectively. These requirements are then applied to the various types of PSV according to the date when they are first used.[4] New buses weighing more than 7.5 tonnes and new double-deck buses must comply with both Sch 1 and Sch 2 from 31 December 2000 and all such buses which are in use must meet these requirements after 2016 and 2017. New buses weighing 7.5 tonnes or less and new coaches must comply with Sch 2 or Sch 3 respectively from 31 December 2000 until 1 January 2005, after which new vehicles of these kinds must also comply with Sch 1. All these regulated PSVs must meet the wheelchair accessibility requirements and those of the appropriate general accessibility requirements if in use after 1 January 2015 (for buses weighing 7.5 tonnes or less) or 2020 (for coaches). There is an exception in the case of regulated PSVs that are manufactured before 1 October 2000 and 1 October 2004. They are not required to comply with the requirements of the relevant Schedules unless and until they are in use on or after 1 January in either 2015 or 2016 or 2017 or 2020 as appropriate.

8.3.6 The PSV accessibility regulations may, in particular, make provision as to the construction, use and maintenance of regulated PSVs.[5] Such provision may include:

---

1   DDA 1995, s 40(6). By virtue of s 67(7), this is without prejudice to the generality of the powers to make regulations or orders by statutory instrument conferred by s 67(2)–(3).

2   HL Deb, vol 565, col 716.

3   It is clear that the regulations do not apply to small buses carrying less than 22 passengers, but see the non-statutory initiative of DPTAC, 'Accessibility Specification for Small Buses'.

4   Public Service Vehicles Accessibility Regulations 2000, SI 2000/1970 (as amended), reg 3, subject to certain exemptions or delayed implementation set out in reg 4. Regulation 5 provides for the recognition of EEA (European Economic Area) equivalent requirements.

5   DDA 1995, s 40(2).

- provision as to the fitting of equipment to vehicles;
- equipment to be carried by vehicles;
- the design of such equipment;
- the fitting and use of restraining devices designed to ensure the stability of wheelchairs while vehicles are moving;
- the position in which wheelchairs are to be secured while vehicles are moving.

It is not intended that this list should be exhaustive.[1]

8.3.7 In the event, the Public Service Vehicle Accessibility Regulations 2000 address the following matters in relation to relevant PSVs and disabled passengers in respect of wheelchair accessibility requirements:

- wheelchair spaces and provisions;[2]
- boarding lifts and ramps;[3]
- entrances and exits;[4]
- gangways;[5]
- signs and markings;[6]
- communication devices;[7]
- lighting.[8]

They also lay down general accessibility requirements for single-deck and double-deck buses and coaches covering the following areas:

- floors and gangways;[9]
- seats or priority seats;[10]
- steps;[11]
- handrails and handholds;[12]
- communication devices;[13]

---

1   HL Deb, vol 565, col 716.

2   Public Service Vehicles Accessibility Regulations 2000, SI 2000/1970 (as amended), reg 3 and Sch 1, paras 2–4. Schedule 1, para 1 supplies definitions for the purposes of Sch 1, paras 2–10.

3   Ibid, Sch 1, para 5.

4   Ibid, Sch 1, para 6.

5   Ibid, Sch 1, para 7.

6   Ibid, Sch 1, para 8.

7   Ibid, Sch 1, para 9.

8   Ibid, Sch 1, para 10 (as amended).

9   Ibid, reg 3, Sch 2, para 2 and Sch 3, para 2. Schedule 2, para 1 (as amended) and Sch 3, para 1 (as amended) supply definitions for the purposes of Sch 2, paras 2–8 and Sch 3, paras 2–7.

10 Ibid, reg 3, Sch 2, para 3 and Sch 3, para 3.

11 Ibid, reg 3, Sch 2, para 4 (as amended) and Sch 3, para 4.

12 Ibid, Sch 2, para 5 (as amended) and Sch 3, para 5.

13 Ibid, Sch 2, para 6 (buses only).

- kneeling systems;[1]
- route and destination displays.[2]

8.3.8 Although frequent reference is made here to the needs of wheelchair users, the accessibility regulations are intended to make provision for the needs of other disabled travellers, including those with sensory impairments (for example, by the use of colour contrast on handrails and seating and improved lighting levels).[3] The general power to make codes of practice under the DDA 1995 might also be used to give guidance to transport staff on assistance to disabled persons (for example, in respect of audible announcements).[4] As a further consequence of the Public Service Vehicles Accessibility Regulations 2000, amendments have been made to the Public Service Vehicles (Conditions of Fitness, Equipment, Use and Certification) Regulations 1981 so as to ensure greater consistency between the two sets of regulations as they affect the use of PSVs by disabled persons.[5]

8.3.9 A regulated PSV shall not be used on the road unless it conforms with the provisions of any PSV accessibility regulations.[6] To do otherwise is a criminal offence punishable on summary conviction by a fine not exceeding level 4 on the standard scale.[7] It is also a criminal offence of like weight to contravene or fail to comply with any provision of the PSV accessibility regulations or to cause or permit a regulated PSV to be used on a road in non-conformity with such regulations.[8]

8.3.10 Provision is made for offences committed by a body corporate.[9] If such an offence is committed with the consent or connivance of

---

1   Public Service Vehicles Accessibility Regulations 2000, SI 2000/1970, Sch 2, para 7 and Sch 3, para 6. A kneeling system is one which enables a PSV to be raised and/or lowered relative to its normal height of travel.

2   Ibid, Sch 2, para 8 and Sch 3, para 7.

3   HL Deb, vol 566, cols 459–460.

4   See Department for Transport, *Guidance on the Public Service Vehicles (Conduct of Drivers, Inspectors, Conductors and Passengers) (Amendment) Regulations 2002* (December 2002) and Department for Transport, *Conduct of Drivers, Inspectors and Conductors – A Guide for Bus and Coach Staff* (October 2003), published to support new duties introduced on 1 October 2002 as a result of the Public Service Vehicles (Conduct of Drivers, Inspectors, Conductors and Passengers) (Amendment) Regulations 2002, SI 2002/1724, that amend the Public Service Vehicles (Conduct of Drivers, Inspectors, Conductors and Passengers) Regulations 1990, SI 1990/1020.

5   Public Service Vehicles (Conditions of Fitness, Equipment, Use and Certification) Regulations 1981, SI 1981/257, as amended by the Public Service Vehicles (Conditions of Fitness, Equipment, Use and Certification) (Amendment) Regulations 2002, SI 2002/335.

6   DDA 1995, s 40(3)(b).

7   Ibid, s 40(4).

8   Ibid, s 40(3)(a),(c).

9   Ibid, ss 40 and 48.

a director,[1] manager, secretary or other similar officer, then there is joint liability for the offence.[2] Joint liability may also arise where the offence is attributable to any neglect on the part of any such officers. The position is also the same where the offence is committed with the consent or connivance (or is attributable to any neglect on the part) of a person purporting to act in such a capacity. In addition, in Scotland only, an offence committed by a partnership or other unincorporated association in the above circumstances can lead to a partner or a person concerned in the management or control of the association incurring joint criminal liability.[3]

Accessibility certificates

8.3.11 Without prejudice to the generality of the restraints and offences created above,[4] a regulated PSV shall not be used on a road unless a vehicle examiner[5] has issued an 'accessibility certificate'.[6] An 'accessibility certificate' is a certificate which certifies that the prescribed provisions of the PSV accessibility regulations have been satisfied in respect of the vehicle in question.[7] This will parallel the existing initial roadworthiness certification procedure for PSVs and it is envisaged that accessibility certificates will be issued at the same time as certificates of initial fitness.[8] A fee may be payable on application or issue.[9] If a regulated PSV is used on a road without an accessibility certificate, the operator of the vehicle is guilty of an offence and is liable on summary conviction to a fine not exceeding level 4 on the standard scale.[10]

---

1 Where the affairs of a body corporate are managed by its members, a director will include any such member: ibid, s 48(2).

2 Ibid, s 48(1).

3 Ibid, s 48(3).

4 By ibid, s 40.

5 Appointed under Road Traffic Act 1988, s 66A.

6 DDA 1995, s 41(1)(a). Provision is made for appeal to the Secretary of State against the refusal of a vehicle examiner to issue an accessibility certificate: s 44(3)–(6). A fee may be charged for such an appeal: s 45.

7 Provision is made in DDA 1995, s 49 for criminal offences committed in connection with accessibility certificates (eg forgery or the making of false statements).

8 HL Deb, vol 565, col 716 and vol 566, col 463.

9 DDA 1995, s 45(1)(b).

10 Ibid, s 41(3). This is subject to s 41(1)(b) and the provisions of s 42. See **8.2.13**. By virtue of s 41(4), the term 'operator' has the same meaning as in the Public Passenger Vehicles

8.3.12 After due consultation,[1] the Secretary of State has made regulations with respect to applications for accessibility certificates and their issue.[2] Their technical detail is not explored further here.

8.3.13 Where the Secretary of State[3] is satisfied that prescribed provisions of the PSV accessibility regulations for the purposes of accessibility certificates have been satisfied in respect of a particular vehicle, that vehicle may be given approval on application and payment of a fee.[4] A vehicle approved in this manner is referred to as a 'type vehicle'.[5] This provision will clearly apply to vehicles produced in large numbers. The Secretary of State may at any time withdraw approval of a type vehicle.[6]

8.3.14 If the Secretary of State refuses an application for the approval of a vehicle,[7] provision is made for a review of that decision.[8] A request for review must be made within 28 days.[9] In reviewing the original decision, the Secretary of State must consider any written representations made by the applicant before the end of the prescribed period.[10]

Type approval certificates

8.3.15 If a person authorised by the Secretary of State has made a declaration in the prescribed form that a particular vehicle conforms in design, construction and equipment with a type vehicle (a 'declaration of conformity'), then a vehicle examiner may issue 'an approval certificate' to the effect that subsequent individual vehicles conform to

---

    Act 1981. The appropriate modification of s 41(3)–(4) for Northern Ireland is made by Sch 8, para 25(2).

1   DDA 1995, s 40(7).

2   Ibid, s 41(2) (in Northern Ireland, the Department of the Environment: Sch 8, para 25(1)). See Public Service Vehicles Accessibility Regulations 2000, SI 2000/1970 (as amended), regs 6–8 and Sch 4.

3   In Northern Ireland, the Department of the Environment.

4   DDA 1995, ss 42(1) and 45(1)(a). The Northern Ireland modifications to s 42 are contained in Sch 8, para 26. In accordance with s 42(5)(a), the Secretary of State may make regulations with respect to applications for (and grants of) approval under s 42(1): see Public Service Vehicles Accessibility Regulations 2000, SI 2000/1970 (as amended), regs 9–12.

5   DDA 1995, s 42(2).

6   Ibid, s 42(6).

7   Ibid, s 42(1).

8   Ibid, s 44; Public Service Vehicles Accessibility Regulations 2000, SI 2000/1970 (as amended), reg 19.

9   Ibid, s 44(1); Public Service Vehicles Accessibility Regulations 2000, SI 2000/1970 (as amended), reg 19(3). The applicant for review must pay any fee fixed under s 45.

10   Ibid, s 44(2). The provisions appertaining to reviews, appeals and fees generally under ss 44–45 are modified for the purposes of Northern Ireland by Sch 8, paras 28–29.

the type vehicle.[1] The vehicle examiner may issue such an approval certificate after examining the vehicle to which the statutory declaration applies, if he or she thinks fit.[2] However, these provisions are clearly designed to avoid the need for each vehicle of the same type to be individually inspected.[3]

8.3.16 If the Secretary of State withdraws approval of a type vehicle,[4] then a vehicle examiner may not issue any further approval certificates by reference to the type vehicle.[5] However, any approval certificate issued by reference to the type vehicle before such withdrawal of approval shall continue to have effect.[6]

Offences and exemptions

8.3.17 A regulated PSV shall not be used on a road unless it has an accessibility certificate[7] or unless, alternatively, an approval certificate[8] has been issued in respect of the vehicle.[9] Use of a regulated PSV in contravention of these alternative conditions is a criminal offence punishable on summary conviction by a fine not exceeding level 4 on the standard scale.[10]

8.3.18 These provisions[11] do not prevent the use of a regulated PSV on the road if the Secretary of State has by order authorised its use by reference to the class or description of the vehicle or by explicit specification.[12] This allows special operating authorisation for vehicles which do not comply with the PSV accessibility regulations and for which an accessibility or approval certificate is not in force. The Government recognised that there might be circumstances in which an

---

1   DDA 1995, s 42(3), (4) and (8). Regulations may make general provision in respect of approval certificates: s 42(5) and see Public Service Vehicles Accessibility Regulations 2000, SI 2000/1970 (as amended), regs 13–17, 19(3) and Schs 5–6. Note the consultation requirements of s 40(7). Provision is made in s 49 for criminal offences committed in connection with approval certificates (eg forgery or the making of false statements).

2   Ibid, s 42(4). Provision is made for appeal to the Secretary of State against the refusal of a vehicle examiner to issue an approval certificate: s 44(3)–(6). A fee may be charged for such an appeal: s 45.

3   HL Deb, vol 565, col 717.

4   Under DDA 1995, s 42(6).

5   DDA 1995, s 42(7)(a).

6   For s 41 purposes: DDA 1995, s 42(7)(b).

7   Under ibid, s 41.

8   Under ibid, s 42.

9   Ibid, s 41(1).

10   Ibid, s 41(3).

11   Ibid, ss 40–42.

12   Ibid, s 43(1). In Northern Ireland, the s 43 powers are vested in the Department of the Environment: Sch 8, para 27.

individual vehicle or class of vehicles could not reasonably be expected to meet the full requirements of the new vehicle accessibility standards.[1] Such circumstances might be used to recognise the difficulty or undesirability of attempting to make vintage or heritage vehicles fully accessible.[2] Special authorisation may be given subject to specified restrictions or conditions[3] and even an order authorising the use of a vehicle in these circumstances may require it to conform with certain aspects of the PSV accessibility regulations, with specified modifications or exceptions.[4]

8.3.19 Ordinarily, where the Secretary of State is given a power under the DDA 1995 to make an order, that power is exercisable by statutory instrument.[5] An exception is provided for[6] in respect of an order[7] by which the Secretary of State has authorised the use on roads of a regulated PSV which does not comply with the PSV accessibility regulations or which does not possess an accessibility or approval certificate.[8] Such an authorisation order need not be made by statutory instrument if it applies only to a specified vehicle or to vehicles of a specified person. Nevertheless, such an order is capable of being amended or revoked as if it was an order made by statutory instrument.[9]

8.4 RAIL VEHICLES

8.4.1 Although provision has already been made in railways legislation to ensure that rail transport operators have a duty to have regard to the needs of disabled passengers, the last Conservative Government regarded the provision of accessible rail services as 'a key link in the transport chain'.[10] Relevant provisions of the DDA 1995 are intended to strengthen the existing legislative framework by addressing access to rail services, including light rapid transit and tram systems.[11]

---

1   HL Deb, vol 565, col 717.

2   Ibid, vol 566, col 463.

3   DDA 1995, s 43(2).

4   Ibid, s 43(3).

5   Ibid, s 67(1).

6   Under ibid, s 67(6).

7   Under ibid, s 43.

8   Under ibid, ss 40–42.

9   Ibid, s 67(6).

10   HL Deb, vol 565, col 717.

11   DDA 1995, ss 46–47. See also Strategic Rail Authority, *Train and Station Services for Disabled Passengers: A Code of Practice* (February 2002) and *Guidance on Disabled Persons' Protection Policies* (April 2002) (the latter made under the powers in the Railways Act 1993 (as

Rail vehicle accessibility regulations

8.4.2 The Secretary of State is empowered[1] to make 'rail vehicle accessibility regulations' after appropriate consultations.[2] The Rail Vehicle Accessibility Regulations 1998 came into force on 1 November 1998.[3] They are supported by non-statutory guidance for the railway industry indicating the scope of coverage of the regulations, detailed guidance on the regulatory requirements, best practice, how the exemption procedure works, and how the regulations will be enforced.[4] The purpose of the regulations is to secure that it is possible for disabled persons to get on to and off 'regulated rail vehicles' in safety and without unreasonable difficulty, and to be carried in such vehicles in safety and in reasonable comfort.[5] Moreover, the regulations make provision for securing that it is possible for disabled persons in wheelchairs to get on to and off 'regulated rail vehicles' in safety and without unreasonable difficulty while remaining in their wheelchairs, as well as to be carried in such vehicles in safety and reasonable comfort while remaining in their wheelchairs.[6]

8.4.3 The DDA 1995 anticipated that particular provision would be made in the rail vehicle accessibility regulations as to the construction, use and maintenance of 'regulated rail vehicles'.[7] Special provision might also be made in the regulations as to the fitting of equipment to rail vehicles; equipment to be carried by rail vehicles; the design of equipment to be fitted to or carried by rail vehicles; the use of equipment fitted to or carried by rail vehicles; the toilet facilities to be provided in rail vehicles; the location and floor area of the wheelchair

---

amended), s 71B). See further National Rail, *Rail Travel for Disabled Passengers* (regularly updated).

1 DDA 1995, s 46(1).

2 Ibid, s 46(11) and Sch 8, para 30(4). In Northern Ireland, the s 46 powers are vested in the Department for Regional Development: Sch 8, para 30(1). Consultation upon the relevant regulations (discussed below) took place in May and June 1998. It took the form of the issue by the Mobility Unit of the DETR of draft regulations, together with a compliance cost assessment.

3 SI 1998/2456 (made under DDA 1995, s 46(1), (2) and (5)), as amended by the Rail Vehicle Accessibility (Amendment) Regulations 2000, SI 2000/3215 (applying the 1998 Regulations to an additional form of guided transport, namely systems which are track-based with side guidance, and making some other amendments to access requirements). In Northern Ireland, see the Rail Vehicle Accessibility Regulations (Northern Ireland) 2001, SR 2001/264 (in force 19 October 2001).

4 Department for Transport, 'Rail Vehicle Accessibility Regulations 1998 (RVAR) Guidance'.

5 DDA 1995, s 46(1)(a).

6 Ibid, s 46(1)(b).

7 Ibid, s 46(2).

accommodation to be provided in rail vehicles;[1] and assistance to be given to disabled persons.[2] While the statutory provisions make frequent reference to the needs of wheelchair users, the accessibility regulations are intended to make provision for the needs of other disabled travellers, including those with sensory impairments (for example, by the use of colour contrast on handrails and seating, and improved lighting levels).[3]

8.4.4 It is not proposed to reproduce the content of the 1998 Regulations (as amended) here. Much of their provision is technical and detailed. However, in summary, the rail vehicle accessibility regulations cover the following requirements:

- for the marking of doors, their warning devices and their controls;[4]
- relating to steps on the exterior and in the interior of vehicles;[5]
- relating to floors;[6]
- for priority seating for the use of disabled persons;[7]
- for request-stop controls in a tramcar, if the tramcar is fitted with such controls;[8]
- relating to interior transparent surfaces;[9]
- for handrails and for handholds fitted to the backs of seats;[10]
- for the minimum force needed to operate a door handle;[11]
- for audible and visual announcements inside and outside the vehicle including their use and contents;[12]
- for any toilets which are fitted to a vehicle;[13]
- the provision of wheelchair spaces, their dimensions and other requirements;[14]
- the provision of wheelchair-compatible sleeping compartments;[15]

---

1   The meaning of the term 'wheelchair accommodation' is defined by regulations: ibid, s 46(6).
2   DDA 1995, s 46(2)(a)–(g).
3   HL Deb, vol 566, cols 459–460.
4   Rail Vehicle Accessibility Regulations 1998, SI 1998/2456, regs 4 and 5 (as amended).
5   Ibid, reg 6.
6   Ibid, reg 7.
7   Ibid, reg 8.
8   Ibid, reg 9 (as amended).
9   Ibid, reg 10.
10   Ibid, reg 11.
11   Ibid, reg 12.
12   Ibid, reg 13.
13   Ibid, regs 14 and 20 (as amended).
14   Ibid, regs 15–16 (as amended).
15   Ibid, reg 17.

- the provision of tables in wheelchair spaces, if other passengers have them;[1]
- the provision of wheelchair-compatible doorways and passageways to wheelchair spaces and wheelchair-compatible sleeping compartments;[2]
- requirements relating to telephones for passengers' use;[3]
- minimum internal door width;[4]
- the provision of boarding devices, which may be lifts or ramps, and requirements relating to them;[5]
- catering services, if such services are available for other passengers;[6] and
- wheelchair access to on-board facilities,[7]

in each case, for the benefit of disabled persons.

8.4.5   The statute anticipates that different provisions may be made in the regulations so as to differentiate between different classes or descriptions of rail vehicles and as respects different 'networks'.[8] Similarly, different provision may be made in the rail vehicle accessibility regulations as respects the same class or description of rail vehicle in different circumstances.[9] This apparently recognises that 'the design and use of rail vehicles will vary according to a range of factors' including locality, systems and uses. For example, the 1998 Regulations do make differing provisions for tramcars as opposed to trains.[10] It seems also to be intended that there should be future flexibility so that the 'accessibility regulations do not undermine the historic character of heritage railways'.[11] In addition, different provision might be made to reflect the different operating conditions and vehicle design on different parts of the London Underground railway (for example, those lines that use tubes rather than orthodox tunnels to carry rail vehicles).

---

1   Public Vehicle Accessibility Regulations 1998, SI 1998/2456, reg 18.

2   Rail Vehicle Accessibility Regulations 1998, SI 1998/2456, reg 19.

3   Ibid, reg 21.

4   Ibid, reg 22.

5   Ibid, reg 23.

6   Ibid, reg 24.

7   Ibid, reg 20A (as amended).

8   DDA 1995, s 46(5)(a), (c). The term 'network' means any permanent way or other means of guiding or supporting rail vehicles or any section of such a network: s 46(6).

9   Ibid, s 46(5)(b). By virtue of s 67(7), these powers are without prejudice to the generality of the powers to make regulations or orders by statutory instrument conferred by s 67(2)–(3).

10   See eg Rail Vehicle Accessibility Regulations 1998, SI 1998/2456, regs 9, 11 and 15 (as amended).

11   HL Deb, vol 565, col 718.

Offences

8.4.6 If a 'regulated rail vehicle' is used for carriage while not conforming with any appropriate provisions of the rail vehicle accessibility regulations, the 'operator'[1] commits a criminal offence punishable on summary conviction by a fine not exceeding level 4 on the standard scale.[2] A person uses a rail vehicle for carriage if that person uses it for the carriage of members of the public for hire or reward at separate fares.[3] Provision is made for offences committed by a body corporate.[4] If such an offence is committed with the consent or connivance of a director,[5] manager, secretary or other similar officer, then there is joint liability for the offence.[6] Joint liability may also arise where the offence is attributable to any neglect on the part of any such officers. The position is also the same where the offence is committed with the consent or connivance (or is attributable to any neglect on the part) of a person purporting to act in such a capacity. In addition, in Scotland only, an offence committed by a partnership or other unincorporated association in the above circumstances can lead to a partner or a person concerned in the management or control of the association incurring joint criminal liability.[7]

Regulated rail vehicles

8.4.7 The key to an understanding of these access provisions is an appreciation of which rail vehicles are covered by the regulations. The rail vehicle accessibility regulations apply only to 'regulated rail vehicles'.[8] Thus, the scope of the regulations is determined in the accessibility regulations themselves as the term 'regulated rail vehicle' is said to be 'any rail vehicle to which the rail vehicle accessibility regulations are expressed to apply'.[9] It is clear that the Secretary of State has maximum flexibility to determine which rail vehicles are to be included or excluded from the access requirements. The 1998 Regulations apply to passenger-carrying vehicles used on railways, tramways, monorail systems, magnetic levitation systems or track-based with side

---

1   The person having the management of that vehicle: DDA 1995, s 46(6).

2   Ibid, s 46(3)–(4).

3   Ibid, s 46(10).

4   Ibid, ss 46 and 48.

5   Where the affairs of a body corporate are managed by its members, a director will include any such member: DDA 1995, s 48(2).

6   Ibid, s 48(1).

7   Ibid, s 48(3).

8   Ibid, s 46(6).

9   Ibid.

guidance ('regulated rail vehicles'),[1] which are first brought into use, or belong to a class of vehicle first brought into use, on or after 1 January 1999.[2]

8.4.8 However, it is equally plain that the regulations can only apply to modes of passenger transport that satisfy the root definition of a 'rail vehicle': namely, a vehicle constructed or adapted to carry passengers on any railways, tramway or 'prescribed system'.[3] Except in Northern Ireland,[4] the terms 'railway' and 'tramway' have the same meaning as in the Transport and Works Act 1992. The use of the term 'prescribed system' means a transport system using a prescribed mode of guided transport within the meaning of the 1992 Act.[5]

8.4.9 Yet, however the term 'rail vehicle' is defined, it is also clear that the accessibility standards do not apply to any rail vehicle (or class of rail vehicle) first brought into use on or before 31 December 1998.[6] At the time of the passage of these provisions, the Government at that time made it clear in debate that it intended to use the regulation-making powers only in respect of new railway rolling stock and that there was no intention to require modifications to any existing rolling stock.[7] However, the DRTF recommends that an end date by which all passenger rail vehicles should comply with the 1998 Regulations should be introduced following consultation. It also recommends that the accessibility standards should be applied to the refurbishment of existing rolling stock.[8] This is likely to be the subject of future consultation.

---

1 Rail Vehicle Accessibility Regulations 1998, SI 1998/2456, reg 3(1) (as amended). In accordance with reg 2(1), 'railway' and 'tramway' have the same meaning as in the Transport and Works Act 1992; 'magnetic levitation' and 'monorail' have the meaning provided for in the Transport and Works (Guided Transport Modes) Order 1992, SI 1992/3231.

2 DDA 1995, s 46(1).

3 Ibid, s 46(6). In Northern Ireland, the term 'rail vehicle' means a vehicle constructed or adapted to carry passengers by rail: Sch 8, para 30(2).

4 Ibid, Sch 8, para 30(3).

5 Ibid, s 46(7).

6 Ibid, s 46(6). The time at which a rail vehicle or class of rail vehicle is to be treated for s 46 purposes as first brought into use is determined by regulations made under s 46(8). Such regulations may provide for the disregarding of periods of testing or other prescribed periods of use: s 46(9).

7 HL Deb, vol 565, col 717.

8 DRTF Report, recommendation 7.1.

Exemptions

8.4.10   General provision is made for exemptions from the rail vehicle accessibility regulations.[1] After due consideration and consultation,[2] the Secretary of State (in Northern Ireland, the Department for Regional Development) may make exemption orders[3] to authorise the use for carriage of any regulated rail vehicle of a specified description (or in specified circumstances) even though that vehicle does not conform with the appropriate provisions of the rail vehicle accessibility regulations. An exemption order may be made subject to specified restrictions or conditions.[4] The regulations may provide for procedural issues in respect of the application for, granting of, currency of or revocation of exemption orders.[5]

8.4.11   The Secretary of State has made the Rail Vehicle (Exemption Applications) Regulations 1998.[6] These regulations specify the manner in which applications for exemption from the Rail Vehicle Accessibility Regulations 1998 are to be made, including the information which is to be supplied with an application. An application must be in writing.[7] It must provide the following particulars with the application:[8]

- name and address of applicant;
- description of rail vehicle;
- applicable circumstances of the exemption;
- relevant requirements from which exemption is sought;
- the technical, economic and operational reasons why exemption is sought;
- the effect which the exemption would have on a disabled person's ability to use the rail vehicle so described;[9]

---

1   DDA 1995, s 47.

2   Ibid, s 47(3).

3   Ibid, s 47(1).

4   Ibid, s 47(4)–(5).

5   Ibid, s 47(2). It was not envisaged that the s 47 powers of exemption would be widely used: HL Deb, vol 565, col 718.

6   SI 1998/2457, made under DDA 1995, s 47 and in force from 1 November 1998. In Northern Ireland, see the Rail Vehicle (Exemption Applications) Regulations (Northern Ireland) 2001, SR 2001/265 (in force 19 October 2001).

7   Rail Vehicle (Exemption Applications) Regulations 1998, SI 1998/2457, reg 3.

8   Ibid, reg 3 and Schedule.

9   The meaning of 'use' is set out in Rail Vehicle (Exemption Applications) Regulations 1998, SI 1998/2457, Schedule, para 11.

- any measures which could be taken to enable disabled persons to use such rail vehicles if exemption is granted;[1]
- any proposals for the later modification of such rail vehicles to secure compliance with the rail vehicle accessibility regulations within a stated period;
- the period of exemption (unless permanent exemption is sought).

These regulations also make provision for the period and revocation of exemptions.[2] Numerous and various exemptions for particular descriptions of rail vehicles on particular rail systems have been sought and granted.[3]

8.5   AVIATION AND SHIPPING

8.5.1   The DDA 1995 does not directly address the rights of disabled people in respect of aviation or shipping services. Airports and passenger terminals are subject to Part 3 (on access to goods, facilities and services) insofar as they are providing facilities or services. However, aeroplanes, helicopters, airships, ferries, hovercraft, boats and ships are excluded from Part 3, being 'the use of any means of transport'.[4] They are also not the subject of the framework for vehicle accessibility standards in Part 5 of the Act. The DRTF welcomed steps taken to develop a non-statutory code of practice on access for disabled people to air travel and suggests that the code might be given statutory backing.[5] It also recommends a formal review, including the need for legislative provisions, for accelerating progress in compliance with the International Maritime Organization and the DPTAC guidance on access for disabled people in the shipping industry.[6] Both recommendations have been endorsed by the DRC.

---

1   The meaning of 'use' is set out in Rail Vehicle (Exemption Applications) Regulations 1998, SI 1998/2457, Schedule, para 11.

2   Ibid, reg 4.

3   The details of these exemption orders are not reproduced here.

4   DDA 1995, s 19(5)(b). However, the proposals in the Disability Discrimination Bill will extend Part 3 to a vehicle for transporting people by land, air or water. See: Department for Work and Pensions, *Draft Disability Discrimination Bill*, Cm 6058 (December 2003); *Explanatory Notes* Cm 6058-ii; *Draft Regulatory Impact Assessment*, Cm 6058-iii. See, in particular: Joint Committee on the Draft Disability Discrimination Bill, *First Report* (April 2004); Department for Work and Pensions, *The Government's Response to the Report of the Joint Committee on the Draft Disability Discrimination Bill*, Cm 6276 (July 2004).

5   DRTF Report, recommendation 7.8. See Department for Transport, 'Code of Practice: Access to Air Travel for Disabled People'. See also DPTAC, 'Design of Large Passenger Ships and Passenger Infrastructure: Guidance on Meeting the Needs of Disabled People'. The Government Response to the DRTF Report suggested that it might be prepared to give the code statutory backing.

6   DRTF Report, recommendation 7.9.

8.5.2   In *Ross v Ryanair Ltd and Stansted Airport Ltd* the Court of Appeal held that an airline and an airport operator were jointly liable under Part 3 of the Act for a failure to provide wheelchair access through the airport to the airplane for a mobility-impaired passenger.[1] In addition, the airline was liable for seeking to charge the disabled passenger for providing the auxiliary aid of a wheelchair. Because the duty to make reasonable adjustments is owed to disabled persons as a class, and not to any particular individual, it was irrelevant that the claimant might have the financial means to meet the charge. Nor did it matter that the service provider might be said to have treated other disabled persons (such as disabled passengers with their own wheelchair) more favourably. The service in question was not excluded by the use of any means of transport exemption in s 19(5)(b).

8.6   DISABILITY DISCRIMINATION BILL

Rail vehicles

8.6.1   In response to the DRTF Report, the Government consulted on a recommendation that called for the introduction of an end date by which all rail vehicles must comply with the Rail Vehicle Accessibility Regulations 1998 (and regulations covering the refurbishment of rail vehicles) and some associated questions (including changes to the enforcement regime and the removal of the requirement for exemptions to be granted by statutory instrument).[2] The consultation ended on 26 January 2004. It is intended that the Disability Discrimination Bill will be used as the vehicle for change.[3]

8.6.2   The Disability Discrimination Bill, if enacted, will enable the Secretary of State to achieve the policy objective of applying the rail vehicle accessibility regulations to rail vehicles first brought into use before 1 January 1999 and also to newer vehicles which are of the same type as ones first used before the regulations came into force on 1 January 1999. This change of definition will enable the Secretary of

---

1   [2004] EWCA Civ 1751. DDA 1995, ss 19(1)(b), 19(2)(a), 21(2)(d) and 21(4)(b) applied. See also Department of Transport, *Code of Practice: Access to Air Travel for Disabled People* (2003), para 2.14; Rights of Access Code of Practice (2002), para 2.36.

2   Department for Transport, *Consultation on Government's Proposals to Amend Rail Provisions in Part V of DDA* (November 2003).

3   See: Department for Work and Pensions, *Draft Disability Discrimination Bill*, Cm 6058 (December 2003); *Explanatory Notes*, Cm 6058-ii, *Draft Regulatory Impact Assessment*, Cm 6058-iii. See, in particular: Joint Committee on the Draft Disability Discrimination Bill, *First Report* (April 2004); Department for Work and Pensions, *The Government's Response to the Report of the Joint Committee on the Draft Disability Discrimination Bill*, Cm 6276 (July 2004).

State to set a date in the regulations by which time all rail vehicles must comply with their requirements. A new provision in the Bill continues to allow the Secretary of State to make exemption orders in respect of regulated rail vehicles but clarifies the law by specifically allowing exemptions from the operational requirements of the rail vehicle accessibility regulations as well as construction requirements. It expressly confers power to exempt the use of vehicles of a specified description in specified circumstances (eg a heritage railway).

8.6.3 The Bill proposes new provisions, the effect of which will be to require prescribed rail vehicles to have a rail vehicle accessibility compliance certificate. It is intended that the requirement to have a certificate will apply to all new rail vehicles and vehicles that are refurbished. The effect of this is to set up a rail vehicle accessibility regulations certification scheme. The provisions include power for the Secretary of State to make regulations providing for the appointment of independent assessors who will be responsible for checking regulated rail vehicles for compliance against each regulatory requirement to which that vehicle is required to conform. They also empower the Secretary of State to make regulations setting out the procedure for obtaining certificates, including provisions for assessors to charge fees, and a mechanism for disputes between assessors and applicants for certificates to be referred to the Secretary of State. A regulated rail vehicle would be prohibited from being used for carriage unless a valid compliance certificate has been issued for that vehicle. The provisions with which vehicles are required to conform will be prescribed in the regulations, including different requirements in the case of refurbished vehicles.

8.6.4 Much of this new law will be contained in regulations to be made under proposed new powers. The Bill will also replace the existing criminal sanctions for non-compliance with the rail vehicle accessibility regulations with a civil enforcement regime which enables penalties to be levied. The Secretary of State will be enabled to issue an operator with an improvement notice, which sets a deadline for a non-compliance to be rectified. If the non-compliance continues after the improvement deadline, a final notice can be issued. If the final deadline is missed the Secretary of State can impose a penalty. An operator can lodge an objection with the Secretary of State against either the imposition or level of a penalty. The provisions also provide a right of appeal to the court.

Disabled persons' parking badges

8.6.5 The Disability Discrimination Bill will amend the Chronically Sick and Disabled Persons Act 1970, which established the disabled persons' parking badge ('blue badge') scheme. This scheme provides for certain parking concessions to operate in favour of disabled people whose vehicles display blue badges. New provisions will provide that the holders of foreign disabled persons' badges shall be afforded the same concessions as holders of domestic blue badges in respect of parking concessions. The clause makes provision to formalise existing (non-statutory) recognition of parking badges issued in the EU or in certain other European countries (for which there is reciprocal recognition) and to extend this recognition to badges issued in other countries.

Chapter 9

INSTITUTIONAL FRAMEWORK

9.1 DISABILITY RIGHTS COMMISSION

Introduction

9.1.1 When the DDA 1995 was first enacted, the then Government rejected arguments for the creation of a Disability Rights Commission.[1] However, the Disability Rights Task Force (DRTF) was charged with the job of developing proposals to create a Commission.[2] This led to the Disability Rights Commission Act 1999 (DRCA 1999), which established the Disability Rights Commission (DRC).[3] The Act applies to England, Wales and Scotland.[4] In Northern Ireland, similar powers in respect of disability rights are exercised by the Equality Commission for Northern Ireland.[5] The DRC supersedes the former National Disability Council (and its Northern Ireland equivalent).[6] It has functions similar to those of the Equal Opportunities Commission (EOC) and the Commission for Racial Equality (CRE). The DRC opened for business on 25 April 2000. It has established offices in London, Manchester, Edinburgh and Cardiff. It also has an internet presence.[7]

---

1   HL Deb, vol 565, cols 639–642 and vol 566, cols 408–410.

2   Disability Rights Task Force, *Recommendations to Government on the Proposed Role and Functions of a Disability Rights Commission* (March 1998); Disability Rights Task Force, *Moving Towards the Establishment of a Disability Rights Commission* (DRTF/1/98); *Promoting Disabled People's Rights: Creating a Disability Rights Commission Fit for the 21st Century*, Cm 3977 (1998, London, HMSO).

3   DRCA 1999, ss 1(1), (3) and 16(1) and Sch 1. Subsequent amendments to the Act have been made by the Special Educational Needs and Disability Act 2001 (SENDA 2001) and the Disability Discrimination Act 1995 (Amendment) Regulations 2003, SI 2003/1673. The Northern Ireland institutional framework has been subject to amendments made by the Disability Discrimination Act 1995 (Amendment) Regulations 2004, SR 2004/55.

4   Ibid, s 16(4), (5).

5   Northern Ireland Act 1998, ss 73–78 and Sch 8; Equality (Disability, etc) (Northern Ireland) Order 2000, SI 2000/1110 (NI 2).

6   DRCA 1999, s 1(4); Northern Ireland Act 1998, s 74. The National Disability Council (and Northern Ireland Disability Council) had been established under DDA 1995, Part 6 (ss 50–52) and Sch 5 (and Sch 8, paras 33–35) now largely or prospectively repealed.

7   www.drc-gb.org.

Status

9.1.2   The DRC is a body corporate and is not the servant or agent of the Crown.[1] It does not enjoy any status, immunity or privilege of the Crown. Its property is not to be regarded as property of or as held on behalf of the Crown.[2] The DRCA 1999 binds the Crown (but does not affect Her Majesty in her private capacity or in right of Her Duchy of Lancaster or the Duke of Cornwall).[3]

Staffing of the Commission

9.1.3   The DRCA 1999 makes provision for the staffing of the DRC.[4] The DRC has a chief executive appointed by it, subject to the approval of the Secretary of State.[5] The DRC may also employ such other employees as it may appoint, subject to the approval of the Secretary of State as to numbers and terms and conditions of service.[6] It employs about 180 staff, of which approximately one-third have a declared disability.[7]

Commissioners

9.1.4   The DRC must consist of not less than 10 and not more than 15 commissioners appointed by the Secretary of State.[8] In order to ensure the proper representation of disabled persons on the DRC, the Secretary of State may appoint as a commissioner a person who is not disabled (and has not had a disability) only if satisfied that after the appointment more than half of the commissioners will be disabled

---

1   See the comparable provisions as to the Equality Commission for Northern Ireland: Northern Ireland Act 1998, s 73.

2   DRCA 1999, Sch 1, para 1.

3   Ibid, s 15. In Northern Ireland, the comparable provision is found in the Equality (Disability, etc) (Northern Ireland) Order 2000, SI 2000/1110 (NI 2), art 17.

4   Ibid, Sch 1, para 10. See the comparable provisions as to the Equality Commission for Northern Ireland: Northern Ireland Act 1998, Sch 8. Financial provision for the expenses of the DRC is made in s 1(2) and there is a requirement on the DRC to keep proper accounts: Sch 1, para 15.

5   In fact, the first appointment of a chief executive is made by the Secretary of State: DRCA 1999, Sch 1, para 10(2).

6   Employment with the DRC is subject to pension provision made under Superannuation Act 1972, s 1 and Sch 1: DRCA 1999, Sch 1, para 11.

7   Disability Rights Commission, *Annual Report and Annual Accounts 2003–04* (HC 880, July 2004).

8   DRCA 1999, Sch 1, para 2(1). The DRC may pay to any commissioner such remuneration or expenses as the Secretary of State may determine: Sch 1, para 8. In like fashion, it may pay (or make provision for the payment of) pensions, allowances or gratuities to or in respect of any commissioner. See the comparable provisions as to the Equality Commission for Northern Ireland: Northern Ireland Act 1998, Sch 8.

persons (or persons who have had a disability).[1] Thus, it is intended that the majority of commissioners shall be disabled persons within the meaning of the DDA 1995. At the time of writing, there are 15 commissioners, 10 of whom are disabled persons. One of the commissioners shall be a person who appears to the Secretary of State to have special knowledge of Scotland.[2] In practice, there are at least two commissioners drawn from Wales and Scotland respectively.[3]

9.1.5 Commissioners hold and vacate office in accordance with the terms of their appointment.[4] A commissioner shall not be appointed for less than two or more than five years, although such a person may be reappointed.[5] A commissioner may resign by written notice to the Secretary of State.[6] The Secretary of State may also terminate the appointment of a commissioner if satisfied that, without the consent of the chairman of the DRC, the commissioner has failed to attend meetings of the DRC during a continuous period of six months beginning not earlier than nine months before the termination.[7] The office of commissioner may also be ended if he or she has become bankrupt, has had his or her estate sequestrated, has made a composition or arrangement with (or granted a trust deed for) his or her creditors, or is otherwise unable or unfit to carry out the functions as a commissioner.[8] In special circumstances, a person who has ceased to be a commissioner might receive compensation on the direction of the Secretary of State.[9]

9.1.6 One commissioner is to be appointed as chairman of the DRC by the Secretary of State.[10] Provision is also made for either one or two

---

1   DRCA 1999, Sch 1, para 2(2); but this provision does not apply in respect of the first three appointments to the office of commissioner: Sch 1, para 2(3).

2   Ibid, Sch 1, para 2(1A) inserted by Scotland Act (Modification of Functions) Order 2000, SI 2000/1458, art 2 and in force from 1 June 2000.

3   As part of the devolution of government, the functions of the Secretary of State under DRCA 1999, Sch 1, para 2 shall be exercisable with the agreement of the National Assembly for Wales, so far as necessary to ensure there is at all times one commissioner who has been appointed with such agreement. See National Assembly for Wales (Transfer of Functions) Order 2000, SI 2000/253, art 3, Sch 2. In addition, those functions, so far as they are exercisable in or as regards Scotland, shall be exercisable only with the agreement of the Scottish Ministers. See Scotland Act 1998 (Transfer of Functions to the Scottish Ministers etc) Order 2000, SI 2000/1563, art 5(1).

4   DRCA 1999, Sch 1, para 3(1).

5   Ibid, Sch 1, para 3(2).

6   Ibid, Sch 1, para 4.

7   Ibid, Sch 1, para 5(a).

8   Ibid, Sch 1, para 5(b)–(c).

9   Ibid, Sch 1, para 9.

10   Ibid, Sch 1, para 6(1). The first chairman is Mr Bert Massie.

other commissioners as deputy chairmen. At least one of the persons holding office as chairman or deputy chairman should be a disabled person (or a person who has had a disability).[1] The chairman and deputy chairmen hold and vacate that office in accordance with the terms of their appointment, may resign by written notice to the Secretary of State, and shall cease to hold that office if they cease to be commissioners.[2]

Functions and powers

9.1.7 The DRC has a number of general functions,[3] including the following duties:[4]

- to work towards the elimination of discrimination against and harassment of disabled persons;[5]
- to promote the equalisation of opportunities for disabled persons;
- to take such steps as it considers appropriate with a view to encouraging good practice in the treatment of disabled persons; and
- to keep under review the working of the DDA 1995 and the DRCA 1999.[6]

9.1.8 The DRC has *locus standi* to bring judicial review proceedings.[7] However, its functions and duties do not entitle the DRC to make representations to a tribunal or court in cases to which it is not a party. It will be only in exceptional circumstances that a tribunal or court will consider it appropriate to receive representations from the DRC.[8] However, an employment tribunal now has the power to order that any person whom it considers has an interest in the outcome of the

---

1   DRCA 1999, Sch 1, para 6(2).

2   Ibid, Sch 1, para 7.

3   In Northern Ireland, the general functions of the Equality Commission are set out in Equality (Disability, etc) (Northern Ireland) Order 2000, SI 2000/1110 (NI 2), art 4.

4   DRCA 1999, s 2(1) (as amended).

5   The term 'disabled persons' includes persons who have had a disability; the term 'discrimination' means anything which is discrimination for the purposes of any provision of Part 2 or Part 3 or (the amended) Part 4 of the DDA 1995: DRCA 1999, s 2(5), as amended by SENDA 2001, s 35 and Sch 7, paras 1–2. In any event, expressions used in the DRCA 1999 have the same meaning as defined for the purposes of the DDA 1995: DRCA 1999, s 13(2).

6   See Disability Rights Commission, *Legislative Review: First Review of the Disability Discrimination Act 1995: Consultation* (May 2002).

7   *R v Secretary of State for Employment, ex parte Equal Opportunities Commission* [1994] ICR 317, HL.

8   *McNicol v Balfour Beatty Rail Maintenance Ltd* [2002] EWCA Civ 1074, [2002] IRLR 711, CA. See also *R (A and B, X and Y) v East Sussex County Council and Disability Rights Commission* [2003] EWHC 167 (Admin), (2003) 6 CCLR 194 ('There will be, if only occasionally, cases

proceedings may be joined as a party to the proceedings.[1] This might apply to the DRC, among others. Without limiting its powers, and for any purpose connected with the performance of its functions, the DRC may:[2]

- make proposals or give other advice[3] to any Minister of the Crown as to any aspect of the law or a proposed change to the law;[4]
- make proposals or give other advice to any Government agency or other public authority as to the practical application of any law;
- undertake, or arrange for or support (whether financially or otherwise), the carrying out of research or the provision of advice or information.

It may also make charges for facilities or services made available by it for any purpose.[5] The DRC may regulate its own procedure (including its quorum).[6] The validity of any proceedings of the DRC is not affected by a vacancy among the commissioners or by a defect in the appointment of a commissioner.[7] The DRC may delegate its powers. It may authorise any committee of the DRC or any commissioner to exercise such of its functions (other than functions relating to the conduct of a formal investigation) as it may determine.[8]

---

in which a body like the DRC can assist the Administrative Court. In the final analysis it must be for the court itself to decide whether in the particular case such assistance should be accepted').

1   Employment Tribunals Rules of Procedure 2004, r 10(2)(r).

2   DRCA 1999, s 2(2). The Explanatory Notes to the DRCA 1999 state that s 2(1)–(2) enables the DRC to undertake a wide range of activities (including running conferences, seminars and workshops, providing advice and assistance on reasonable adjustments, and devising guidance for employers and service providers in particular sectors).

3   At the request of a relevant Minister, the DRC may be required to make proposals or give other advice on any specified matter. The Explanatory Notes to the DRCA 1999 state that s 2(2)–(3) enables the DRC to give advice on amendments to the DDA 1995, the implementation of any relevant EU Directive or the Human Rights Act 1998, or on other legislation where the needs of disabled persons are in issue (such as housing legislation).

4   DRCA 1999, s 2(3). The term 'the law' includes EC law and the international obligations of the UK: DRCA 1999, s 2(5).

5   Ibid, s 2(4).

6   Ibid, Sch 1, para 12(1). The quorum for meetings of the DRC shall in the first instance be determined by a meeting of the DRC attended by at least five commissioners: Sch 1, para 12(2). The quorum has been set at six: Minutes of the First Meeting of the Disability Rights Commission (4 February 2000), minute 1/6.2. The minutes of meetings of the DRC may be found at www.drc-gb.org.

7   Ibid, Sch 1, para 13.

8   Ibid, Sch 1, para 14(1). This does not affect any power of the DRC to authorise its employees to do anything on its behalf: Sch 1, para 14(2). See generally the DRC's *Corporate Governance Arrangements* and *Management Statement Between the Disability Rights Commission and the Department for Work and Pensions* (available at www.drc-gb.org).

9.1.9   The DRC must submit to the Secretary of State an annual report on its activities during the previous accounting year.[1] The annual report must include (among other things):

- a report on anything done by the Commission, in the performance of its primary statutory functions,[2] jointly or otherwise in co-operation with any other organisation;
- a general survey of developments in matters within the scope of the Commission's functions; and
- proposals for the Commission's activities in the current year.

The Secretary of State shall lay a copy of the report before Parliament and arrange for such further publication as is considered appropriate.

Assistance in relation to proceedings

9.1.10   Provision is made in the DRCA 1999[3] for the DRC to provide assistance to individuals in relation to the bringing of actual or potential legal proceedings.[4] The power to provide such assistance applies to proceedings which an individual has brought (or proposes to bring) in an employment tribunal or county court (or, in Scotland, a sheriff court) or the Special Educational Needs and Disability Tribunal (SENDIST)[5] in respect of a complaint or claim about unlawful discrimination under Parts 2, 3 and 4 of the DDA 1995 (discrimination in the employment field, in respect of goods, facilities, services or premises, and in relation to education).[6] Such assistance may also be provided in respect of proceedings of a prescribed description (being proceedings in which an individual who has or has had a disability relies or proposes to rely on a matter relating to that disability).[7]

9.1.11   Where the individual concerned applies to the DRC for assistance in relation to any relevant proceedings, the DRC may grant the application on any of the following grounds:[8]

- that the case raises a question of principle;

---

1   DRCA 1999, Sch 1, para 16 (ie the year to 31 March: Sch 1, para 15). In Northern Ireland, there are comparable provisions in Equality (Disability, etc) (Northern Ireland) Order 2000, SI 2000/1110 (NI 2), art 19 amending the Northern Ireland Act 1998, Sch 8.

2   That is, under DRCA 1999, s 2(1)(a)–(c).

3   In Northern Ireland, the comparable powers of the Equality Commission are set out in Equality (Disability, etc) (Northern Ireland) Order 2000, SI 2000/1110 (NI 2), art 9.

4   DRCA 1999, s 7, as amended. This would include assistance to non-disabled persons using the victimisation provisions in DDA 1995, s 55.

5   That is, under DDA 1995, ss 17A, 25, 28I, 28K, 28L, 28N or 28V, as amended.

6   DRCA 1999, s 7(1)(a), as amended.

7   Ibid, s 7(1)(b). At the time of writing, no such prescription has been made.

8   Ibid, s 7(2).

- that it is unreasonable to expect the applicant to deal with the case unaided (because of its complexity, because of the applicant's position in relation to another party or for some other reason);
- that there is some other special consideration which makes it appropriate for the DRC to provide assistance.

If the DRC grants an application, it may:[1]

- provide or arrange for the provision of legal advice;
- arrange for legal or other representation (which may include any assistance usually given by a solicitor or counsel);[2]
- seek to procure the settlement of any dispute;
- provide or arrange for the provision of any other assistance which it thinks appropriate.

The DRC may authorise any employee of the DRC to exercise such of these functions as it may determine.[3]

9.1.12 Provision is made for the recovery of expenses incurred by the DRC[4] in providing assistance.[5] This may arise where the DRC has given an individual assistance under the provisions above in relation to any proceedings and, in respect of the matter in connection with which the assistance is given, any costs or expenses (however described) have become payable to that individual by another person.[6] A sum equal to any expenses incurred by the DRC in providing the assistance shall be a first charge for the benefit of the DRC on the costs or expenses concerned.[7] It does not matter whether the costs or expenses concerned are payable by virtue of a decision of a court or tribunal, an

---

1   DRCA 1999, s 7(3).

2   This does not affect the law and practice as to who may represent a person in relation to any proceedings: ibid, s 7(4).

3   Ibid, s 7(5).

4   In Northern Ireland, the comparable powers of the Equality Commission are set out in Equality (Disability, etc) (Northern Ireland) Order 2000, SI 2000/1110 (NI 2), art 10.

5   DRCA 1999, s 8. Provision may be made by regulations made by the Secretary of State for the determination of the expenses of the Commission in cases where this section applies: s 8(5). See the Disability Rights Commission (Expenses) (Scotland) Regulations 2000, SI 2000/1888.

6   Ibid, s 8(1).

7   Ibid, s 8(2). By virtue of s 8(4) (as amended from 1 April 2000 by Access to Justice Act 1999, s 24 and Sch 4, para 56), the charge thus created is subject to any charge imposed by s 10(7) of the Access to Justice Act 1999 and any provision in, or made under, Part I of that Act for the payment of any sum to the Legal Services Commission. It is also subject to any charge or obligation for payment in priority to other debts under the Legal Aid (Scotland) Act 1986 and any provision in that Act for payment of any sum into the Scottish legal aid fund.

agreement arrived at to avoid proceedings or to bring them to an end, or otherwise.[1]

Formal investigations

9.1.13　The DRC[2] may conduct a formal investigation in two circumstances.[3] First, it may decide to conduct a formal investigation for any purpose connected with the performance of its statutory duties.[4] Secondly, it must conduct a formal investigation if directed to do so by the Secretary of State.[5] At any time the DRC may decide to stop or to suspend the conduct of a formal investigation.[6] The Explanatory Notes to the DRCA 1999 suggest that the DRC's powers to conduct a formal investigation embrace three different kinds of investigation. A general investigation may be undertaken to find out what is happening in a particular sector of society or in relation to a particular kind of activity. In contrast, a named party investigation may confine the investigation to the activities of one or more named persons, who may be individuals or organisations.[7] In addition, a formal investigation might be used to monitor compliance with the requirements of a non-discrimination notice or a statutory agreement in lieu of enforcement proceedings.[8]

9.1.14　When conducting a formal investigation (of whatever kind), the DRC may nominate one or more commissioners (with or without one or more additional commissioners appointed for the purposes of the investigation) to conduct the investigation on its behalf.[9] It may also authorise those persons to exercise such of its functions in relation to the investigation (which may include drawing up or revising terms of reference) as it may determine.[10] With the approval of the Secretary of

---

1　DRCA 1999, s 8(3).

2　In Northern Ireland, the formal investigation powers of the Equality Commission are set out in Equality (Disability, etc) (Northern Ireland) Order 2000, SI 2000/1110 (NI 2), art 5 and Sch 1, Part 1.

3　DRCA 1999, Sch 3, Part I (as amended) has effect in respect of the conduct of formal investigations. See s 3(5) and Sch 3, para 1(1). The Secretary of State may make regulations making provision supplementing Part I in connection with any matter concerned with the conduct of formal investigations: DRCA 1995, Sch 3, para 26. See the Disability Rights Commission (Time Limits) Regulations 2000, SI 2000/879, and the Equality Commission (Time Limits) Regulations (Northern Ireland) 2001, SR 2001/6.

4　Ibid, s 3(1) for the purposes of its duties under s 2(1).

5　Ibid, s 3(2) for the purposes of its duties under s 2(1).

6　Ibid, s 3(3). Such a decision requires the approval of the Secretary of State if the investigation is being conducted under a direction by the Secretary of State under s 3(2).

7　See ibid, Sch 3, para 3.

8　That is, under ibid, ss 4–5, as amended.

9　Ibid, s 3(4)(a).

10　Ibid, s 3(4)(b).

State, the DRC may appoint one or more individuals as additional commissioners for the purposes of a formal investigation.[1] The DRCA 1999 makes provision for the appointment and tenure of office of such additional commissioners.[2] An additional commissioner holds office (and will vacate office or may be reappointed) in accordance with the terms of his or her appointment.[3] The DRC may not alter the terms of appointment of an additional commissioner except with his or her consent and with the approval of the Secretary of State.[4] It may pay such remuneration or expenses to any additional commissioner – and pay (or make provision for the payment of) pensions, allowances or gratuities in respect of any additional commissioner – as the Secretary of State may determine.[5] Subject to the approval of the Secretary of State, the DRC may terminate the appointment of an additional commissioner if satisfied that, without reasonable excuse, the commissioner has failed to carry out his or her duties during a continuous period of three months beginning not earlier than six months before the termination.[6] A commissioner's appointment may also be terminated if he or she has become bankrupt, has had his or her estate sequestrated or has made a composition or arrangement with (or granted a trust deed for) his or her creditors.[7] Moreover, an appointment is terminable if an additional commissioner is otherwise unable or unfit to carry out his or her duties.[8] Otherwise, the appointment will terminate at the conclusion of the relevant formal investigation.[9] At the discretion of the Secretary of State, if there are special circumstances which make it right that an additional commissioner should receive compensation upon the termination or ending of the appointment, the DRC may be directed to pay such compensation, as determined by the Secretary of State.[10]

9.1.15 Before the DRC takes any steps in the conduct of a formal investigation it must draw up terms of reference for the investigation.[11]

---

1   DRCA 1999, Sch 2, para 1(1). In Northern Ireland, see the comparable provisions in Equality (Disability, etc) (Northern Ireland) Order 2000, SI 2000/1110 (NI 2), art 18.

2   Ibid, s 3(5) and Sch 2. An additional commissioner is not a servant or agent of the Crown: Sch 2, para 1(2).

3   Ibid, Sch 2, para 2(1). An additional commissioner may resign by notice in writing to the Commission: Sch 2, para 4(1).

4   Ibid, Sch 2, para 2(2).

5   Ibid, Sch 2, para 3.

6   Ibid, Sch 2, para 4(2)(a).

7   Ibid, Sch 2, para 4(2)(b).

8   Ibid, Sch 2, para 4(2)(c).

9   Ibid, Sch 2, para 4(3).

10   Ibid, Sch 2, para 5.

11   Ibid, Sch 3, para 2(1)(a).

Those terms of reference shall be drawn up (and may be revised[1]) either by the Secretary of State (after consulting the DRC) if the investigation is held at the direction of the Secretary of State or, in any other case, by the DRC.[2] The DRC must also serve or publish notice of the holding of the investigation and its terms of reference.[3] Where the terms of reference confine the investigation to activities of one or more named persons, that notice shall be served on each of those persons.[4] Where the terms of reference do not so confine the investigation, the notice shall be published in such manner as appears to the DRC appropriate to bring it to the attention of persons likely to be affected by it.[5]

9.1.16   In the course of a formal investigation (whether or not the investigation has already begun) the DRC might propose to investigate whether:

- a person has committed (or is committing) any unlawful act;[6]
- any requirement imposed by a non-discrimination notice[7] served on a person (including a requirement to take action specified in an action plan[8]) has been or is being complied with;[9]
- any undertaking given by a person in an agreement made with the DRC is being or has been complied with.[10]

In any of these instances, the DRC may not investigate any such matter unless the terms of reference of the investigation confine it to the activities of one or more named persons (and the person concerned is one of those persons).[11] In particular, the DRC may not investigate whether a person has committed (or is committing) any unlawful act unless it has reason to believe that the person concerned may have

---

1   If the terms of reference are revised, the provisions of DRCA 1999, Sch 3, para 2 apply again in relation to the revised investigation and its terms of reference: Sch 3, para 2(5).

2   Ibid, Sch 3, para 2(2).

3   Ibid, Sch 3, para 2(1)(b).

4   Ibid, Sch 3, para 2(3).

5   Ibid, Sch 3, para 2(4).

6   Ibid, Sch 3, para 3(1)(a). An 'unlawful act' is an act which is unlawful under DDA 1995, Parts 2, 3 or 4: DRCA 1999, Sch 3, para 3(10), as amended. It would also include any other unlawful act of a description prescribed in regulations for present purposes. No such prescriptive regulations have been made at the time of writing, but might include acts which breach Human Rights Act 1998, s 6 as it affects disabled persons.

7   DRCA 1999, s 4 and Sch 3, Part II.

8   Ibid, Sch 3, Part III.

9   Ibid, Sch 3, para 3(1)(b).

10   Ibid, Sch 3, para 3(1)(c).

11   Ibid, Sch 3, para 3(2).

committed (or may be committing) the act in question,[1] or that matter is to be investigated in the course of a formal investigation into that person's compliance with any requirement or undertaking mentioned immediately above.[2]

9.1.17   The DRC shall serve a notice on the person concerned offering that person the opportunity to make written and oral representations about the matters being investigated.[3] If the DRC is investigating whether the person concerned has committed (or is committing) any unlawful act – otherwise than in the course of a formal investigation into that person's compliance with any requirement or undertaking[4] – the DRC shall include in this notice a statement informing that person that the DRC has reason to believe that that person may have committed (or may be committing) any unlawful act.[5] The DRC shall not make any findings in relation to any matter[6] without giving the person concerned (or a representative) a reasonable opportunity to make written and oral representations.[7] However, the DRC may refuse to receive oral representations made on behalf of the person concerned by a person (not being counsel or a solicitor) to whom the DRC reasonably objects as being unsuitable.[8] In such a case, it must give written reasons for its objection.[9]

9.1.18   As part of a formal investigation, the DRC may serve a notice on any person requiring that person to give such written information as may be described in the notice or to attend and give oral information about any matter specified in the notice, and to produce all documents in that person's possession or control relating to any such matter.[10] Such a notice may only be served on the written authority of the Secretary of State unless the terms of reference confine the investigation to the activities of one or more named persons and the person being served is

---

1   DRCA 1999, Sch 3, para 3(3)(a). See the case-law under comparable provisions in the RRA 1976: *Hillingdon London Borough Council v Commission for Racial Equality* [1982] AC 779, HL; *Re Prestige Group plc; Commission for Racial Equality v Prestige Group plc* [1984] ICR 473, HL.

2   Ibid, Sch 3, para 3(3)(b) (ie in Sch 3, para 3(1)(b) or (c)).

3   Ibid, Sch 3, para 3(4). Such a notice may be included in a notice of the holding of an investigation and the terms of reference required (by Sch 3, para 2(3)) to be served on named persons where the investigation is confined to the activities of such named persons: Sch 3, para 3(9).

4   That is, under DRCA 1999, Sch 3, para 3(1)(b) or (c).

5   Ibid, Sch 3, para 3(5).

6   That is, a matter mentioned in ibid, Sch 3, para 3(1).

7   Ibid, Sch 3, para 3(6).

8   Ibid, Sch 3, para 3(7). The Act does not define unsuitability.

9   Ibid, Sch 3, para 3(8).

10 Ibid, Sch 3, para 4(1).

one of those persons.[1] However, a person may not be required by such a notice to give information, or produce a document, which that person could not be compelled to give in evidence, or produce, in civil proceedings before the High Court (in England and Wales) or the Court of Session (in Scotland).[2] Furthermore, a person may not be required by such a notice to attend at any place unless the necessary expenses of a journey to and from that place are paid or tendered.[3] What if a person has been served with such a notice and that person fails to comply with it or the DRC has reasonable cause to believe that that person intends not to comply with it?[4] In such circumstances, the DRC may apply to a county court (in England and Wales) or by summary application to the sheriff (in Scotland) for an order requiring the person concerned to comply with the notice or with such directions for the same purpose as may be contained in the order.[5]

9.1.19   The time limit for the completion of a formal investigation is specified by regulations.[6] The primary period for completion of a formal investigation is known as the 'reporting period'.[7] This is the period of 18 months beginning with the day on which notice of the holding of the investigation and the terms of reference[8] are first served or published,[9] as the case may be.[10] The reporting period may be extended by the Secretary of State for specified purposes and on more than one occasion.[11] Certain consequences flow from a failure by the DRC to publish the investigation report[12] (where it has decided to conduct a formal investigation) or to serve it on the Secretary of State

---

1   DRCA 1999, Sch 3, para 4(2).

2   Ibid, Sch 3, para 4(3)(a).

3   Ibid, Sch 3, para 4(3)(b).

4   Ibid, Sch 3, para 5(1).

5   Ibid, Sch 3, para 5(2).

6   Disability Rights Commission (Time Limits) Regulations 2000, SI 2000/879. In Northern Ireland, comparable provisions (which are not rehearsed here) are found in the Equality Commission (Time Limits) Regulations (Northern Ireland) 2001, SR 2001/6.

7   Ibid, reg 2(2)(a).

8   Under DRCA 1999, Sch 3, para 2: Disability Rights Commission (Time Limits) Regulations 2000, SI 2000/879, reg 1(2).

9   In accordance with DRCA 1999, Sch 3, para 2(3) or (4).

10 Disability Rights Commission (Time Limits) Regulations 2000, SI 2000/879, reg 1(2). The reporting period (or an extended reporting period) ceases to run during any period beginning with the day specified in an information notice for compliance with the notice and ending with the day on which the notice is fully complied with: reg 2(5). Note the DRC's annual reporting requirement in respect of this: reg 2(6).

11 Ibid, reg 2(2)(b), (4) and (7). Note the DRC's annual reporting requirement in respect of this: reg 2(6).

12 Under DRCA 1999, Sch 3, para 7: Disability Rights Commission (Time Limits) Regulations 2000, SI 2000/879, reg 1(2).

(where he or she has directed the DRC to conduct a formal investigation) before the expiration of the reporting period (or the extended period).[1] In either case, any requirement contained in a non-discrimination notice served by the DRC in relation to the formal investigation shall cease to have effect; any requirement contained in an information notice[2] served in relation to the formal investigation which has not yet been complied with shall cease to have effect; and no steps or further steps may be taken by the DRC in the conduct of the formal investigation.[3]

9.1.20 The DRCA 1999 entitles the DRC to make recommendations in the light of its findings in a formal investigation.[4] It may recommend that any person make changes in policies or procedures (or as to any other matter) with a view to promoting the equalisation of opportunities for disabled persons or persons who have had a disability.[5] It may also make recommendations to the Secretary of State for changes in the law or otherwise.[6] The DRC may make such recommendations before the conclusion of the formal investigation itself.[7] It must also prepare a report of its findings in any formal investigation.[8] That report must exclude any matter which relates to an individual's private affairs or any person's business interests if publication of that matter might, in the Commission's opinion, prejudicially affect that individual or person, and its exclusion is consistent with the Commission's duties and the object of the report.[9]

Formal investigation into website accessibility

9.1.21 In March 2003, the DRC announced its first formal investigation. This was into website accessibility for disabled people. The investigation was confined to publicly accessible sites to which Part 3 of the DDA 1995 applied. Intranets and private sites for which employers might have duties under Part 2 of the DDA 1995 were not within the

---

1   Disability Rights Commission (Time Limits) Regulations 2000, SI 2000/879, reg 2(1), subject to reg 2(5).

2   Under DRCA 1999, Sch 3, para 4(1): Disability Rights Commission (Time Limits) Regulations 2000, SI 2000/879, reg 1(2).

3   Disability Rights Commission (Time Limits) Regulations 2000, SI 2000/879, reg 2(3) and (7). Note the DRC's annual reporting requirement in respect of this: reg 2(6).

4   DRCA 1999, Sch 3, para 6(1).

5   Ibid, Sch 3, para 6(2)(a).

6   Ibid, Sch 3, para 6(2)(b).

7   Ibid, Sch 3, para 6(3).

8   Ibid, Sch 3, para 7(1). The report will be published: Sch 3, para 7(3), (4). The obligation to prepare and publish a report does not affect the Commission's power to issue a non-discrimination notice before a report is prepared or published: Sch 3, para 7(5).

9   Ibid, Sch 3, para 7(2).

scope of the investigation. The report of the formal investigation was published in April 2004.[1] It contains a number of findings and recommendations. The DRC is also conducting a formal investigation into health inequalities.

Non-discrimination notices

9.1.22 In the course of a formal investigation, if the DRC[2] is satisfied that a person has committed (or is committing) an unlawful act,[3] it may serve on that person a 'non-discrimination notice'.[4] Certain procedural requirements must be complied with.[5] The DRC must serve on the person concerned a notice informing that person that the DRC is considering issuing a non-discrimination notice (and of the grounds for doing so) and offering an opportunity to make written and oral representations.[6] It must also give the person concerned (or a representative) the opportunity to make oral and written representations within a period specified in the notice of not less than 28 days.[7] Moreover, the DRC may refuse to receive oral representations made on behalf of the person concerned by a person (not being counsel or a solicitor) to whom the DRC reasonably objects as being unsuitable.[8] In such a case, the DRC must give written reasons for its objection.[9]

9.1.23 A non-discrimination notice must give details of the unlawful act which the DRC has found that the person has committed (or is committing).[10] It must also require that person not to commit any

1   *The Web: Access and Inclusion for Disabled People: A Formal Investigation Conducted by the Disability Rights Commission* (2004, London: TSO).

2   In Northern Ireland, the comparable powers of the Equality Commission are set out in Equality (Disability, etc) (Northern Ireland) Order 2000, SI 2000/1110 (NI 2), art 6 and Sch 1, Part II.

3   An 'unlawful act' is an act which is unlawful under DDA 1995, Part 2, 3 or 4 (as amended). It would also include any other unlawful act of a description prescribed in regulations for present purposes. No such prescriptive regulations have been made at the time of writing, but might include acts which breach Human Rights Act 1998, s 6 as it affects disabled persons.

4   DRCA 1999, s 4(1). The provisions of Sch 3, Part II have effect in relation to non-discrimination notices: s 4(6). The Secretary of State may make regulations making provision supplementing Part II in connection with any matter concerned with the procedure for issuing non-discrimination notices: ibid, Sch 3, para 26. See the Disability Rights Commission (Time Limits) Regulations 2000, SI 2000/879.

5   By virtue of DRCA 1999, Sch 3, para 8(1), the DRC is prohibited from issuing a non-discrimination notice addressed to any person unless it has complied with the requirements of Sch 3, para 8.

6   Ibid, Sch 3, para 8(2).

7   Ibid, Sch 3, para 8(3).

8   Ibid, Sch 3, para 8(4). What amounts to unsuitability is not specified.

9   Ibid, Sch 3, para 8(5).

10   Ibid, s 4(1)(a).

further unlawful acts of the same kind.[1] The notice may also include recommendations to the person concerned as to action which the DRC considers that person could reasonably be expected to take with a view to complying with that requirement.[2] On issuing a non-discrimination notice, the DRC must serve a copy on the person to whom it is addressed.[3]

9.1.24 Provision is made for appealing against the issue of a non-discrimination notice. A person on whom a non-discrimination notice is served may appeal against any requirement imposed by the notice.[4] The appeal must be made within six weeks following the day on which the notice was served. In employment matters, the appeal lies to an employment tribunal; in non-employment matters, the appeal lies to a county court (in England and Wales) or a sheriff court (in Scotland).[5] If the tribunal or court considers a requirement in a non-discrimination to be unreasonable, it may quash (in Scotland, recall) any requirement appealed against.[6] In the case of a requirement not to commit (or to cease committing) any further unlawful acts of the same kind as the DRC found to be committed (or is being committed),[7] the tribunal or court may quash (in Scotland, recall) the requirement if it considers that the Commission's finding was based on an incorrect finding of fact.[8]

9.1.25 Where a court or tribunal quashes (or recalls) a requirement, it may direct that the non-discrimination notice shall have effect with such modifications as it considers appropriate.[9] Such modifications may include the substitution of a requirement in different terms.[10] In the case of a requirement not to commit (or to cease committing) any further unlawful acts of the same kind as the DRC found to be committed (or is being committed),[11] the modifications may include modifications to the details of the unlawful act which the DRC has found

---

1   DRCA 1999, s 4(1)(b). If the finding is that the person is committing an unlawful act, the notice will require that person to cease doing so.

2   Ibid, s 4(2).

3   Ibid, Sch 3, para 9.

4   Ibid, Sch 3, para 10(1) (ie a requirement under s 4(1)(b) or (3)).

5   Ibid, Sch 3, para 10(2).

6   Ibid, Sch 3, para 10(3)(a).

7   That is, a case falling under ibid, s 4(1)(b).

8   Ibid, Sch 3, para 10(3)(b).

9   Ibid, Sch 3, para 10(4). There is no right of appeal against a direction that a non-discrimination order shall have effect as modified by the tribunal or court: ibid, Sch 3, para 10(6).

10   Ibid, Sch 3, para 10(5)(a).

11   That is, a case falling under ibid, s 4(1)(b).

has been committed or is being committed,[1] so far as necessary to describe any unlawful act on which the requirement could properly have been based.[2] If a tribunal or court allows an appeal against the non-discrimination notice without quashing (or recalling) the whole of the notice, the DRC may give notice to the person concerned and vary the non-discrimination notice. This can be done by revoking or altering any recommendation[3] or by making new recommendations.[4]

9.1.26   A non-discrimination notice becomes final when any appeal against the notice is dismissed, withdrawn or abandoned or the time for appealing expires without an appeal having been brought.[5] It also becomes final when such an appeal is allowed without the whole notice being quashed (in Scotland, recalled).[6] The question of enforcement of a non-discrimination notice might then arise. A non-discrimination notice is enforceable during the period of five years beginning on the date on which the notice has become final.[7] During this period, the DRC may apply to a county court (in England and Wales) or by summary application to the sheriff (in Scotland) for an enforcement order. Such an application may be made if it appears to the DRC that the person concerned has failed to comply with any requirement imposed by the notice[8] or the DRC has reasonable cause to believe that the person concerned intends not to comply with any such requirement.[9] An enforcement order will require the person concerned to comply with the requirement or with such directions for the same purpose as are contained in the order.[10]

Action plans

9.1.27   A non-discrimination notice may require the person concerned to propose an 'adequate action plan',[11] with a view to securing compliance with a requirement in the notice not to commit further

---

1   That is, under the terms of DRCA 1999, s 4(1)(a).

2   Ibid, Sch 3, para 10(5)(b).

3   Included in the notice in pursuance of the Commission's power under DRCA 1999, s 4(2).

4   Ibid, Sch 3, para 10(7).

5   Ibid, Sch 3, para 11(a). Provision is made in Sch 3, para 13 for the DRC to maintain a register of non-discrimination notices which have become final.

6   Ibid, Sch 3, para 11(b).

7   Ibid, Sch 3, para 12(1).

8   That is, under ibid, s 4(1)(b).

9   Ibid, Sch 3, para 12(2).

10   Ibid, Sch 3, para 12(3).

11   An action plan is a plan subject to and in accordance with DRCA 1999, Sch 3, Part III. See s 4(3)(a) and (6). The Secretary of State may make regulations making provision

unlawful acts.[1] An 'action plan' is a document drawn up by the person concerned.[2] It specifies action (including action the person has already taken) intended to change anything in that person's practices, policies, procedures or other arrangements which caused or contributed to the commission of the unlawful act concerned (or is liable to cause or contribute to a failure to comply with a requirement in the non-discrimination notice).[3] The action specified in an action plan may include ceasing an activity or taking continuing action over a period. An action plan is 'adequate' if the action specified in it would be sufficient to ensure, within a reasonable time, that the person is not prevented from complying with that requirement by anything in that person's practices, policies, procedures or other arrangements.[4] Once such an action plan has been proposed by that person and has become final, a non-discrimination notice may further require the person concerned to take any action which is specified in the plan (and which has not already been taken) at the time or times specified in the plan.[5]

9.1.28   Where a person (referred to in the DRCA 1999 as 'P') has been served with a non-discrimination notice which has become final and includes a requirement for P to propose an action plan, further provision is made for a 'first action plan'.[6] P must serve the proposed action plan on the DRC within the period specified in the non-discrimination notice.[7] If P fails to do so, the DRC may apply to a county court (in England and Wales) or by way of summary application to the sheriff (in Scotland) for an order directing P to serve the proposed action plan within such period as the order may specify.[8] When P serves a proposed action plan on the DRC (either in response to the non-discrimination notice or to a court order), the action plan becomes

---

amending Part III in relation to the procedures for finalising action plans: ibid, Sch 3, para 26. See the Disability Rights Commission (Time Limits) Regulations 2000, SI 2000/879. In Northern Ireland, comparable provisions (which are not rehearsed here) are found in the Equality Commission (Time Limits) Regulations (Northern Ireland) 2001, SR 2001/6.

1   DRCA 1999, s 4(1)(b). An 'unlawful act' is an act which is unlawful under DDA 1995, Parts 2, 3 or 4: DRCA 1995, s 4(5) as amended. It would also include any other unlawful act of a description prescribed in regulations for present purposes. No such prescriptive regulations have been made at the time of writing.

2   In Northern Ireland, the comparable powers of the Equality Commission are set out in Equality (Disability, etc) (Northern Ireland) Order 2000, SI 2000/1110 (NI 2), art 6 and Sch 1, Part III.

3   DRCA 1999, s 4(4)(a).

4   Ibid, s 4(4)(b) and Sch 3, para 14(2).

5   Ibid, s 4(3)(b).

6   Ibid, Sch 3, para 14(1).

7   Ibid, Sch 3, para 15(1).

8   Ibid, Sch 3, para 15(2).

final at the end of the prescribed period.[1] The prescribed period by which a proposed action plan becomes final is 12 weeks beginning with the day on which the proposed action plan is served upon the DRC.[2] An action plan which has become final may be varied by written agreement between the DRC and P.[3]

9.1.29   The DRCA 1999 makes provision for the revision of a first proposed action plan at the invitation of the DRC where the DRC considers that a proposed action plan served on it is not an 'adequate' action plan. The DRC may give notice to P stating its view that the plan is not adequate. It may invite P to serve on the DRC a revised action plan which is adequate within a specified period.[4] In that notice the DRC may include recommendations as to action which it considers might be included in an adequate action plan.[5] If P serves a revised proposed action plan on the DRC in response, the revised action plan supersedes the previous action plan and becomes final at the end of the prescribed period.[6] The prescribed period by which a revised action plan becomes final is eight weeks beginning with the day on which the revised action plan is served upon the DRC.[7] If P does not serve a revised action plan in response, the action plan previously served on the DRC becomes final at the end of the prescribed period.[8] The prescribed period by which a

---

1   DRCA 1999, Sch 3, para 15(3) unless the DRC has given notice to P under Sch 3, para 16 (dealt with in **9.1.29**).

2   Disability Rights Commission (Time Limits) Regulations 2000, SI 2000/879, reg 3(1), subject to reg 3(9), for the purposes of DRCA 1999, Sch 3, para 15(3). If the prescribed period has started to run, it ceases to run during any period beginning with the day on which a notice is served by the DRC in respect of its power to obtain information for the purposes of determining whether a proposed action plan is adequate (DRCA 1999, Sch 3, para 21(1)(a)) and ending with the day on which the notice is fully complied with: Disability Rights Commission (Time Limits) Regulations 2000, SI 2000/879, reg 3(9). In Northern Ireland, comparable provisions (which are not rehearsed here) are found in the Equality Commission (Time Limits) Regulations (Northern Ireland) 2001, SR 2001/6.

3   DRCA 1999, Sch 3, para 19.

4   Ibid, Sch 3, para 16(1).

5   Ibid, Sch 3, para 16(2).

6   Ibid, Sch 3, para 16(3) unless the DRC applies for an order under Sch 3, para 17 (dealt with in **9.1.30**).

7   Disability Rights Commission (Time Limits) Regulations 2000, SI 2000/879, reg 3(2), subject to reg 3(9), for the purposes of DRCA 1999, Sch 3, para 16(3). If the prescribed period has started to run, it ceases to run during any period beginning with the day on which a notice is served by the DRC in respect of its power to obtain information for the purposes of determining whether a proposed action plan is adequate (DRCA 1999, Sch 3, para 21(1)(a)) and ending with the day on which the notice is fully complied with: Disability Rights Commission (Time Limits) Regulations 2000, SI 2000/879, reg 3(9). In Northern Ireland, comparable provisions (which are not rehearsed here) are found in the Equality Commission (Time Limits) Regulations (Northern Ireland) 2001, SR 2001/6.

8   DRCA 1999, Sch 3, para 16(4) unless the DRC applies for an order under Sch 3, para 17 (dealt with in **9.1.30**).

proposed action plan becomes final where no revised action plan is served is four weeks beginning with the expiration of the original period (specified in the relevant notice[1]) for service of the revised action plan or, where the DRC has extended the period for such service, that extended period.[2]

9.1.30 The DRC might decide to take court action in relation to an inadequate action plan. If it considers that a proposed action plan served on it is not an adequate action plan, the DRC may apply to the county court (in England and Wales) or by way of summary application to the sheriff (in Scotland) for an order.[3] Such an application may not be made[4] unless a notice requiring the revision of the first proposed action plan[5] has been served on P by the DRC and P has not served a revised action plan in response within the specified period in the notice.[6] Where these requirements have been met, the court may make an order declaring that the proposed action plan in question is not an adequate action plan. The order may require P to revise the proposals and to serve on the DRC an adequate action plan within such a period specified in the order. The order may also contain such directions (if any) as the court considers appropriate as to the action which should be specified in the adequate action plan required by the order.[7] If the court does not make such an order, the proposed action plan otherwise becomes final at the end of the prescribed period.[8] The prescribed period where the court does not make an order because it has decided not to do so is seven days beginning with the day on which the decision has become final.[9] Where the court does not make an order because

---

1   Under DRCA 1999, Sch 3, para 16(1).

2   Disability Rights Commission (Time Limits) Regulations 2000, SI 2000/879, reg 3(3) and (4), subject to reg 3(9), for the purposes of DRCA 1999, Sch 3, para 16(4). If the prescribed period has started to run, it ceases to run during any period beginning with the day on which a notice is served by the DRC in respect of its power to obtain information for the purposes of determining whether a proposed action plan is adequate (DRCA 1999, Sch 3, para 21(1)(a)) and ending with the day on which the notice is fully complied with: Disability Rights Commission (Time Limits) Regulations 2000, SI 2000/879, reg 3(9). In Northern Ireland, comparable provisions (which are not rehearsed here) are found in the Equality Commission (Time Limits) Regulations (Northern Ireland) 2001, SR 2001/6.

3   DRCA 1999, Sch 3, para 17(1).

4   Even where the action plan was served in compliance with a court order under ibid, Sch 3, para 15(2) (see **9.1.28**).

5   That is, under ibid, Sch 3, para 16 (see **9.1.29**).

6   Ibid, Sch 3, para 17(2). The reference to the specified period in the notice is a reference to the provision in Sch 3, para 16(1)(b).

7   Ibid, Sch 3, para 17(3).

8   Ibid, Sch 3, para 17(4).

9   Disability Rights Commission (Time Limits) Regulations 2000, SI 2000/879, reg 3(5)(a), for the purposes of DRCA 1999, Sch 3, para 17(4). A decision of the court becomes final when an appeal against it is dismissed, withdrawn or abandoned or when the time for

the DRC has withdrawn its application for an order, the prescribed period is seven days beginning with the day on which the withdrawal is notified to the person who served the action plan on the DRC.[1]

9.1.31   What is the position where a court order requires P to serve an adequate action plan on the Commission? In response to the order, P might then serve an action plan on the Commission.[2] That action plan becomes final at the end of the prescribed period, unless the DRC has applied to a county court (England and Wales) or to the sheriff (in Scotland) to enforce the order on the ground that the plan does not comply with the order and any directions of the court.[3] The prescribed period is eight weeks beginning with the day on which the action plan is served on the DRC.[4] If the DRC makes such an application to the court, the action plan becomes final at the end of the prescribed period if the DRC withdraws its application or if the court considers that the action plan complies with the order.[5] The prescribed period is seven days beginning with the day on which the withdrawal of the application of the DRC is notified to the person who served the action plan on the DRC or seven days beginning with the date on which the decision of the court on the application made has become final, as the case may be.[6]

9.1.32   If during the period of five years (beginning on the date on which an action plan drawn up by P becomes final) the DRC considers

appealing expires without an appeal having been brought: reg 3(10). In Northern Ireland, comparable provisions (which are not rehearsed here) are found in the Equality Commission (Time Limits) Regulations (Northern Ireland) 2001, SR 2001/6.

1   Disability Rights Commission (Time Limits) Regulations 2000, SI 2000/879, reg 3(5)(b), for the purposes of DRCA 1999, Sch 3, para 17(4). In Northern Ireland, comparable provisions (which are not rehearsed here) are found in the Equality Commission (Time Limits) Regulations (Northern Ireland) 2001, SR 2001/6.

2   DRCA 1999, Sch 3, para 18(1).

3   Ibid, Sch 3, para 18(2).

4   Disability Rights Commission (Time Limits) Regulations 2000, SI 2000/879, reg 3(6), subject to reg 3(9), for the purposes of DRCA 1999, Sch 3, para 18(2). If the prescribed period has started to run, it ceases to run during any period beginning with the day on which a notice is served by the DRC in respect of its power to obtain information for the purposes of determining whether a proposed action plan is adequate (DRCA 1999, Sch 3, para 21(1)(a)) and ending with the day on which the notice is fully complied with: Disability Rights Commission (Time Limits) Regulations 2000, SI 2000/879, reg 3(9). In Northern Ireland, comparable provisions (which are not rehearsed here) are found in the Equality Commission (Time Limits) Regulations (Northern Ireland) 2001, SR 2001/6.

5   DRCA 1999, Sch 3, para 18(3)(a) and (b).

6   Disability Rights Commission (Time Limits) Regulations 2000, SI 2000/879, reg 3(7) and (8), for the purposes of DRCA 1999, Sch 3, para 18(3)(a) and (b). A decision of the court becomes final when an appeal against it is dismissed, withdrawn or abandoned or when the time for appealing expires without an appeal having been brought: reg 3(10). In Northern Ireland, comparable provisions (which are not rehearsed here) are found in the Equality Commission (Time Limits) Regulations (Northern Ireland) 2001, SR 2001/6.

that P has failed to comply with a requirement[1] to carry out any action specified in the action plan, it may apply to a county court (in England and Wales) or by summary application to the sheriff (in Scotland) for an order requiring P to comply with that requirement or with such directions for the same purpose as are contained in the order.[2]

9.1.33 The DRCA 1999 gives the DRC powers to obtain information in connection with the assessment or enforcement of action plans. This may be done for the purposes of determining whether an action plan proposed by P is an adequate action plan. It may also be done for the purposes of determining whether P has complied (or is complying) with the requirement to take the action specified in an action plan which has become final. The DRC may serve a notice on *any* person requiring that person to give information in writing, or copies of documents in that person's possession or control, which relate to any matters described in the notice.[3] However, a person may not be required to give information or produce a document which that person could not be compelled to give in evidence or produce in civil proceedings before the High Court (in England and Wales) or the Court of Session (in Scotland).[4] If the person in question fails to comply with the Commission's notice (requiring information), the DRC may apply to a county court (in England and Wales) or by summary application to the sheriff (in Scotland) for an order requiring the person concerned to comply with the notice or with such directions for the same purpose as may be contained in the order.[5]

Agreements in lieu of enforcement action

9.1.34 The DRCA 1999[6] makes novel provision where the DRC has reason to believe that a person has committed (or is committing) an act made unlawful under the DDA 1995.[7] In such a case,[8] the DRC may enter into a written agreement with that person on the assumption that

---

1   Under DRCA 1999, s 4(3)(b).

2   Ibid, Sch 3, para 20.

3   Ibid, Sch 3, para 21(1).

4   Ibid, Sch 3, para 21(2).

5   Ibid, Sch 3, para 21(3)–(4).

6   In Northern Ireland, the comparable powers of the Equality Commission are set out in Equality (Disability, etc) (Northern Ireland) Order 2000, SI 2000/1110 (NI 2), art 7.

7   DRCA 1999, s 5(1), (12) and Sch 3. An 'unlawful act' is one which is unlawful under Part 2, 3 or 4 of the DDA 1995 or any other unlawful act of a description prescribed by regulations for the purposes of DRCA 1999, s 5: s 5(11), as amended. No such prescription has been made to date, but might in future include acts which breach Human Rights Act 1998, s 6 as it affects disabled persons.

8   DRCA 1999, s 5, subject to s 3(3).

that belief is well founded. This may be done whether or not the person admits that the act in question was committed or is being committed.[1]

9.1.35   The agreement contemplated by this provision is an agreement in lieu of enforcement action, but without affecting the Commission's powers to settle or compromise legal proceedings of any description.[2] The DRC must undertake not to take any 'relevant enforcement action' in relation to the unlawful act in question.[3] This means that the DRC must not begin a formal investigation into the commission by the person concerned of the unlawful act in question.[4] If such an investigation has begun – whether or not the investigation is confined to that matter – the DRC must not take any further steps in the investigation of that matter.[5] Moreover, the DRC must not take any steps (or further steps) with a view to the issue of a non-discrimination notice based on the commission of the unlawful act in question.[6] In turn, the person concerned must undertake not to commit any further unlawful acts of the same kind (and, where appropriate, to cease committing the unlawful act in question).[7] In addition, that person must undertake to take such action as may be specified in the agreement.[8] That action may include ceasing an activity or taking continuing action over any period. The action must be intended to change anything in the practices, policies, procedures or other arrangements of the person concerned which caused or contributed to the commission of the unlawful act in question[9] or which is liable to cause or contribute to a failure to comply with an undertaking not to commit any further unlawful acts of the same kind (and, where appropriate, to cease committing the unlawful act in question).[10]

9.1.36   The DRCA 1999 treats these undertakings as binding on the parties to the agreement.[11] Such an agreement may include terms providing for incidental or supplementary matters (including the

---

1   DRCA 1999, s 5(1). The DRC has entered into a s 5 agreement with Bradford University. The University has agreed to review all its practices, policies and procedures in relation to teaching materials and assessment of students. The DRC will work with the University for a period of five years to improve its practices, procedures and policies and to develop what is hoped will be exemplary accessibility for disabled students.

2   Ibid, s 5(10).

3   Ibid, s 5(2)(a).

4   Ibid, s 5(4)(a).

5   Ibid, s 5(4)(b).

6   Ibid, s 5(4)(c).

7   Ibid, s 5(2)(b)(i).

8   Ibid, s 5(2)(b)(ii).

9   Ibid, s 5(5)(a).

10   Ibid, s 5(5)(b).

11   Ibid, s 5(3). However, undertakings under s 5(2)(b) are only enforceable by the DRC as provided for in s 5(8).

termination of the agreement, or the right of either party to terminate it, in certain circumstances) and may be varied or revoked by agreement of the parties.[1] The agreement may not include any other terms or provisions, unless their inclusion is authorised by regulations made by the Secretary of State.[2] The agreement is designed to be enforceable at the initiative of the DRC. It may apply to a county court (in England and Wales) or by summary application to the sheriff (in Scotland) for an order if the other party to the agreement has failed to comply with any undertaking (mentioned above) or if the DRC has reasonable cause to believe that that party intends not to comply with any such undertaking.[3] The court's order may require the other party to comply with the undertaking or with such directions for the same purpose as are contained in the order.[4]

Persistent discrimination

9.1.37 The DRCA 1999 empowers the DRC to take court action if it believes that a person would commit further unlawful acts of disability discrimination.[5] This power arises at any time within five years of a non-discrimination notice served upon the person becoming final.[6] The power also arises within five years of a final finding in proceedings[7] that a person has committed an act which is unlawful for the purposes of any provision of Part 2, 3 or 4 of the DDA 1995.[8] Moreover, the DRC is similarly empowered (and within the same time period) where there is a final finding by a court or tribunal in any other proceedings that a person has committed an act of a prescribed description.[9] In any of these cases, if it appears to the DRC that, unless restrained, the person concerned is likely to do one or more unlawful acts, the DRC may apply to a county court for an injunction (in England and Wales) or to the sheriff for an interdict (in Scotland) restraining the person from doing

---

1   DRCA 1999, s 5(6).

2   Ibid, s 5(7). However, any provisions so authorised are not enforceable by the DRC in the manner contemplated by s 5(8) (see **9.1.39**).

3   Ibid, s 5(8).

4   Ibid, s 5(9).

5   In Northern Ireland, the comparable powers of the Equality Commission are set out in Equality (Disability, etc) (Northern Ireland) Order 2000, SI 2000/1110 (NI 2), art 8.

6   DRCA 1999, s 6(1)(a).

7   Under DDA 1995, ss 17A, 25, 28I, 28K, 28L, 28N or 28V (the provisions in respect of discrimination in the employment field; those relating to goods, facilities, services and premises; and education): DRCA 1999, s 6(1)(b), as amended.

8   DRCA 1999, s 6(1)(b), as amended. A finding becomes final when an appeal against it is dismissed, withdrawn or abandoned or when the time for appealing expires without an appeal having been brought: s 6(5), as amended.

9   Ibid, s 6(1)(c) and (4), as amended. No prescription has been made at the time of writing.

so.[1] If the court is satisfied that the application is well founded, it may grant the injunction or interdict in the terms applied for or in more limited terms.[2] The injunction or interdict is not confined to unlawful acts which have been the subject of the original non-discrimination notice or legal proceedings.

Disclosure of information

9.1.38 No information given to the DRC by any person (referred to in the DRCA 1999 as 'the informant') in connection with formal investigations, non-discrimination notices, action plans and agreements in lieu of enforcement action shall be disclosed by the DRC or its past and present commissioners, additional commissioners or employees.[3] The restriction on disclosure does not apply to any disclosure made:[4]

- on the order of a court;
- with the informant's consent;
- in the form of a summary or other general statement published by the DRC which does not identify the informant or any other person to whom the information relates;
- in a report of the investigation published by the DRC;
- to a commissioner, an additional commissioner or an employee of the DRC, or, so far as is necessary for the proper performance of the DRC's functions, to other persons; or
- for the purpose of any civil proceedings to which the DRC is a party, or of any criminal proceedings.[5]

A person who discloses information contrary to these provisions is guilty of an offence and liable on summary conviction to a fine not exceeding level 5 on the standard scale.[6]

Enforcement of court orders

9.1.39 The DRCA 1999 makes provision for the enforcement of any court orders made as part of the Commission's functions or powers discussed above.[7] In England and Wales, in relation to a failure to

---

1   DRCA 1999, s 6(2).

2   Ibid, s 6(3).

3   Ibid, Sch 3, para 22(1). In Northern Ireland, the comparable provisions are set out in Equality (Disability, etc) (Northern Ireland) Order 2000, SI 2000/1110 (NI 2), Sch 1, Part IV.

4   Ibid, Sch 3, para 22(2).

5   For the purpose of this particular provision (DRCA 1999, Sch 3, para 22(2)(f)) see Anti-terrorism, Crime and Security Act 2001, s 17 and Sch 4, Part 1, para 46.

6   DRCA 1999, Sch 3, para 22(3).

7   That is (by virtue of ibid, Sch 3, para 23(1)), any order made by a county court or the sheriff under DRCA 1999, s 5(8) or Sch 3. In Northern Ireland, the comparable provisions

comply with an order made by a county court, statutory provisions dealing with penalties for failure to give evidence will apply with modifications.[1] Any person who fails without reasonable excuse to comply with the order may be fined up to £1,000.[2] The county court, at its discretion, may direct that the whole or any part of that fine (after deducting costs) shall be applied to indemnify the DRC for expenses incurred or wasted in consequence of the failure to comply with the order.[3] In Scotland, where the sheriff finds a person to be in contempt of court in respect of a failure to comply with an order, the sheriff shall not commit the person to prison,[4] but may grant decree in favour of the DRC for such amount of any fine imposed for the contempt as appears to the sheriff to be appropriate in respect of the expense incurred or wasted by the DRC in consequence of the failure to comply with the order.[5] If the DRC applies to a county court (in England and Wales) or to the sheriff (in Scotland) to enforce a court order, the court may modify the order.[6]

Offences

9.1.40 The DRCA 1999 creates two offences in relation to the exercise by the DRC of its powers and functions.[7] First, a person who deliberately alters, suppresses, conceals or destroys a document required to be produced as part of a formal investigation[8] or as part of the DRC's powers to seek information[9] is guilty of an offence and liable on summary conviction to a fine not exceeding level 5 on the standard scale. Secondly, an identical offence is committed by a person who makes any statement which that person knows to be false or misleading in a material particular (or recklessly makes a statement which is false or misleading in a material particular) when complying with a notice in relation to a formal investigation or the DRC's powers to seek

---

are set out in Equality (Disability, etc) (Northern Ireland) Order 2000, SI 2000/1110 (NI 2), Sch 1, Part IV.

1 County Courts Act 1984, s 55.

2 Ibid, s 55(1) and (2), as substituted by DRCA 1999, Sch 3, para 23(2)(a). The provisions of s 55(3) of the County Courts Act 1984 are omitted for this purpose: DRCA 1999, Sch 3, para 23(2)(b).

3 County Courts Act 1984, s 55(4), as substituted by DRCA 1999, Sch 3, para 23(2)(c).

4 Notwithstanding Contempt of Court Act 1981, s 15.

5 DRCA 1999, Sch 3, para 23(3).

6 Ibid, Sch 3, para 23(4).

7 Ibid, Sch 3, para 24(1). In Northern Ireland, the comparable provisions are set out in the Equality (Disability, etc) (Northern Ireland) Order 2000, SI 2000/1110 (NI 2), Sch 1, Part IV.

8 Under DRCA 1999, Sch 3, para 4 (or an order under para 5).

9 Under ibid, Sch 3, para 21 (or an order under para 21(3)).

information,[1] a non-discrimination notice, an agreement in lieu of enforcement or an order of a court.[2] Proceedings for these offences may be instituted against any person at any place at which the person has an office or other place of business, and against an individual at any place where he or she resides (or at which he or she is for the time being).[3]

Service of notices

9.1.41 Any notice required or authorised to be served on a person under the DRCA 1999 may be served by delivering it to that person, by leaving it at that person's proper address or by sending it by post to that address.[4] In the case of a corporation, the notice may be served on the secretary or clerk of that body. In the case of a partnership, the notice may be served on any partner or a person having control or management of the partnership business. In the case of an unincorporated association (other than a partnership), the notice may be served on any member of its governing body.[5] For present purposes, in the case of a corporation, its secretary or clerk, the proper address of any person is the address of its registered or principal office in the UK. In the case of an unincorporated association (other than a partnership) or a member of its governing body, the proper address is its principal office in the UK. In any other case, the proper address is the person's usual or last-known address (whether of his or her residence or of a place where the person carries on business or is employed).[6]

9.2 COMMISSION FOR EQUALITY AND HUMAN RIGHTS

9.2.1 In December 2001, as part of its consultation on implementing the EC Employment and Race Directives, the Government mooted the possibility of a single equality commission (effectively combining the DRC, CRE and EOC and embracing the new areas of discrimination law introduced in recent years).[7] That led to further consultation in

---

1   Under DRCA 1999, Sch 3, paras 4 or 21.

2   Under ibid, s 5(8) or Sch 3.

3   Ibid, Sch 3, para 24(2).

4   Ibid, Sch 3, para 25(1). In Northern Ireland, the comparable provisions are set out in the Equality (Disability, etc) (Northern Ireland) Order 2000, SI 2000/1110 (NI 2), Sch 1, Part IV.

5   Ibid, Sch 3, para 25(2).

6   Ibid, Sch 3, para 25(3).

7   *Towards Equality and Diversity: Implementing the Employment and Race Directives: Consultation Document* (Cabinet Office, 2001), paras 7.1–7.5. See also the announcement on 15 May 2002 of a review of the equality framework (including a proposal of a single equality body) by Barbara Roche, Cabinet Office minister: Cabinet Office press release (CAB 053/02).

October 2002 on refined plans to that end.[1] As a result, in May 2004, the Government published a White Paper proposing the establishment of a Commission for Equality and Human Rights (CEHR).[2] The proposed establishment of the CEHR has been broadly welcomed by the DRC, although it would also like to see all discrimination legislation codified in a single equalities statute, so as best to protect the interests of disabled people in the new umbrella commission.[3] A Bill to establish the CEHR is expected during the 2004–2005 parliamentary session. If enacted, the Bill will incorporate the DRC and its powers within the new CEHR by 2006.

9.3 CODES OF PRACTICE

9.3.1 Under the DDA 1995, as originally enacted, there existed a rather labyrinthine process for producing codes of practice in support of the substantive legislation.[4] Under the original provisions, three codes of practice were produced (on employment; on trade organisations; and on goods, facilities, services and premises) in 1996 and a revised code of practice was issued in 1999 (on goods, facilities, services and premises). These provisions were swept away by the DRCA 1999.[5] A considerably simpler and unified process for issuing codes of practice is now in place.[6]

9.3.2 The DRC may prepare and issue codes of practice giving practical guidance on how to avoid acts which are unlawful under Parts 2, 3 and 4 of the DDA 1995 – or any matter relating to the operation of any provision of those Parts – to employers, service providers, responsible bodies in relation to schools or educational institutions, or other

---

1   *Equality and Diversity: The Way Ahead* (Department of Trade and Industry, 2002); *Equality and Diversity: Making It Happen* (Cabinet Office, 2002). See also: Parliamentary Joint Committee on Human Rights, *The Case for a Human Rights Commission: Interim Report* (22nd Report, 2001–02, HL 160 and HC 1142); Parliamentary Joint Committee on Human Rights, *The Case for a Human Rights Commission* (6th Report, 2002–03, HL 67 and HC 489).

2   *Fairness for All: A New Commission for Equality and Human Rights* (Cm 6185). See also: Parliamentary Joint Committee on Human Rights, *Commission for Equality and Human Rights: Structure, Functions and Powers* (11th Report, 2003–04, HL 78 and HC 536); *Government Response to Joint Committee on Human Rights: 11th Report of Session 2003–04*, Cm 6295 (2004); Parliamentary Joint Committee on Human Rights, *Commission for Equality and Human Rights: The Government's White Paper* (16th Report, 2003–04, HL 156 and HC 998).

3   DRC, *Government White Paper: Fairness for All – A New Commission for Equality and Human Rights: Response from the Disability Rights Commission* (DRC, August 2004); DRC, *Provisional Position on the CEHR White Paper* (DRC, May 2004).

4   DDA 1995, ss 51–54 (now either revoked or prospectively repealed).

5   DRCA 1999, s 14(2) and Sch 5; Equality (Disability, etc) (Northern Ireland) Order 2000, SI 2000/1110 (NI 2), art 16 and Sch 2.

6   Ibid, s 9, introducing DDA 1995, s 53A.

persons to whom the provisions of those Parts apply.[1] It may also prepare and issue codes of practice giving practical guidance to any persons on any other matter, with a view to promoting the equalisation of opportunities for disabled persons (and persons who have had a disability) or encouraging good practice in the way such persons are treated, in any field of activity regulated by Part 2, 3 or 4.[2] In neither case does this power extend to include accessibility strategies or plans in education.[3] The power to make codes of practice does not affect the Commission's general powers to give practical guidance on matters connected with its functions.[4] In addition, when requested to do so by the Secretary of State, the DRC shall prepare a code of practice dealing with the matters specified in the request.[5] In Northern Ireland, the Equality Commission enjoys comparable powers in respect of codes of practice.[6]

9.3.3   In preparing a code of practice, the DRC shall carry out such consultations as it considers appropriate (which shall include the publication for public consultation of proposals relating to the code).[7] The DRC must maintain a list of the organisations that it has consulted generally for the purposes of any of its functions.[8] The DRC shall make the list available to the public in whatever way it considers appropriate (subject to any charge it may impose).[9] An organisation may be removed from the list if it has not been consulted generally in the 12 months preceding its removal.[10]

9.3.4   The DRC may not issue a code of practice unless a draft of it has been submitted to and approved by the Secretary of State and laid before both Houses of Parliament, and unless a 40-day period has elapsed without either House resolving not to approve the draft.[11] If the Secretary of State does not approve a draft code of practice, the DRC must be provided with a written statement of reasons.[12] A code of practice issued by the DRC may be revised in whole or part, and

---

1   DDA 1995, s 53A(1) and (9).

2   Ibid, s 53A(1A).

3   Ibid, s 53A(1B), by reference to s 28D or 28E.

4   DRCA 1999, s 9(3).

5   DDA 1995, s 53A(2).

6   Ibid, s 54A, inserted by Equality (Disability, etc) (Northern Ireland) Order 2000, SI 2000/1110 (NI 2), art 11(1), and see art 11 generally.

7   Ibid, s 53A(3); DRCA 1999, s 9(2).

8   DRCA 1999, Sch 1, para 17(1), (3).

9   Ibid, Sch 1, para 17(4).

10   Ibid, Sch 1, para 17(2).

11   DDA 1995, s 53A(4).

12   Ibid, s 53A(5).

re-issued, by it.[1] A code may also be revoked by an order made by the Secretary of State at the request of the DRC.[2] Where the DRC proposes to revise a code of practice, it must follow the same procedures as for a new code.[3] A code of practice issued by the DRC comes into effect on such day as the Secretary of State may, by order, appoint.[4]

9.3.5 As at 1 October 2004, there are five current codes of practice applicable under the DDA 1995.[5] A failure to observe any provision of a code of practice does not of itself make a person liable to any proceedings.[6] However, if a provision of a code of practice appears to a court, tribunal or other body hearing any proceedings under Part 2, 3 or 4 of the DDA 1995 to be relevant, it must take that provision into account.[7] In *Archibald v Fife Council*, the Court of Session took the view that the terms of a code of practice may not be prayed in aid when interpreting the provisions of the DDA 1995. That view has now been resiled from by the House of Lords on appeal.[8]

9.4 GUIDANCE ON MEANING OF DISABILITY

9.4.1 The Secretary of State is empowered to issue statutory guidance about the matters to be taken into account in determining whether an impairment has a substantial adverse effect on a person's ability to carry out normal day-to-day activities or whether such an impairment has a long-term adverse effect.[9] An 'adjudicating body' addressing these questions, for any purpose of the legislation, is obliged to take account of any statutory guidance issued by the Secretary of State which appears to it to be relevant.[10] If any such statutory guidance has been issued, the

---

1 DDA 1995, s 53A(6)(b).

2 Ibid, s 53A(6)(c).

3 Ibid, s 53A(7).

4 Ibid, s 53A(6)(a).

5 Under Part 2, the Code of Practice: Employment and Occupation (2004) and the Code of Practice: Trade Organisations and Qualifications Bodies (2004); under Part 3, the Code of Practice: Rights of Access: Goods, Facilities, Services and Premises (2002); and under Part 4, the Code of Practice for Schools (2002) and the Code of Practice for Providers of Post-16 Education and Related Services (2002).

6 DDA 1995, s 53A(8), as amended.

7 Ibid, s 53A(8A). See generally: *Ridout v TC Group* [1998] IRLR 628, EAT; *Goodwin v The Patent Office* [1999] IRLR 4, EAT; *London Borough of Hillingdon v Morgan* (1999) IDS Brief 649/10, EAT; *Clark v TDG Ltd t/a Novacold* [1999] IRLR 318, CA; *HJ Heinz Co Ltd v Kenrick* [2000] IRLR 144, EAT; *Archibald v Fife Council* [2004] UKHL 32, [2004] IRLR 651, HL.

8 [2004] IRLR 197, Ct of Sess; [2004] UKHL 32, [2004] IRLR 651, HL.

9 DDA 1995, s 3(1). In Northern Ireland, see ibid, Sch 8, para 2.

10 Ibid, s 3(3) and (12), as amended. An 'adjudicating body' is a court or a tribunal, but also includes any other person who (or body which) may decide a claim under the new

Secretary of State may from time to time revise the whole or any part of such guidance and reissue it.[1] The Secretary of State also has authority to revoke any guidance by order.[2]

9.4.2 The power to issue such statutory guidance is at large, but such guidance may give examples in four particular circumstances and in relation to particular activities:[3]

- effects which it would be reasonable to regard as substantial adverse effects;
- effects which it would not be reasonable to regard as substantial adverse effects;
- substantial adverse effects which it would be reasonable to regard as long-term;
- substantial adverse effects which it would not be reasonable to regard as long-term.

The then Minister for Disabled People gave an assurance in Committee that the guidance powers would not be used to weaken the definition of disability or to exclude particular impairments.[4] The guidance is intended to illustrate and exemplify rather than to exclude or limit the statutory definitions.

9.4.3 In preparing a draft of any statutory guidance (or revised statutory guidance), the Secretary of State is required to consult such persons as he or she considers appropriate.[5] If the Secretary of State proposes to issue any statutory guidance (or to reissue any revised statutory guidance), he or she must first publish a draft of it, consider any representations that are made about the draft and, if the Secretary of State thinks it appropriate, may modify the proposals in the light of any of those representations.[6]

9.4.4 During the legislative process, concerns were expressed about parliamentary scrutiny of any statutory guidance to be issued or reissued by the Secretary of State. The then Government conceded that there was a strong case for making such guidance subject to the same parliamentary scrutiny as applied to codes of practice prepared under the DDA

education provisions of DDA 1995, Part 4: DDA 1995, s 3(3A). This would obviously include the SENDIST.

1   DDA 1995, s 3(11)(a).

2   Ibid, s 3(11)(b).

3   Ibid, s 3(2). Further interpretative assistance is to be found in Sch 1 to the DDA 1995 and in the discussion of the concept of 'disability' in Chapter 2.

4   HC Deb Standing Committee E, col 124.

5   DDA 1995, s 3(4).

6   Ibid, s 3(5).

1995, namely the negative resolution procedure.[1] Accordingly, if the Secretary of State decides to proceed with any proposed statutory guidance (or revised statutory guidance), he or she shall lay a draft of it before each House of Parliament.[2] If either House resolves not to approve the draft guidance within the next 40 days,[3] the Secretary of State shall take no further steps in relation to the proposed guidance,[4] although a new draft of the proposed guidance may be subsequently laid before Parliament.[5] If no such resolution is made within the 40-day period, the Secretary of State shall issue the guidance in the form of the draft proposal and the guidance shall come into force on a date to be appointed by order.[6]

9.4.5 The Secretary of State has issued statutory guidance on the meaning of disability which came into force on 31 July 1996.[7] The substance of this guidance has been considered in Chapter 2.

9.5 APPLICATION TO THE CROWN

9.5.1 The DDA 1995 applies to any act (or deliberate omission) done by (or for the purposes of) a Minister of the Crown or Government department in exactly the same way as it would apply to an act (or deliberate omission) done by a private person.[8] It also similarly applies to an act (or deliberate omission) done on behalf of the Crown by a statutory body or a person holding a statutory office.[9] The Crown Proceedings Act 1947 applies to proceedings against the Crown brought under the 1995 Act.[10]

9.5.2 Following the October 2004 amendments, Part 2 of the DDA 1995 (the employment field) applies to service for the purposes of a

---

1   HL Deb, vol 566, cols 122–123.

2   DDA 1995, s 3(6).

3   Calculated in accordance with ibid, s 3(12).

4   Ibid, s 3(7).

5   Ibid, s 3(10).

6   DDA 1995, s 3(8)–(9).

7   *Guidance on matters to be taken into account in determining questions relating to the definition of disability* (1996, London: HMSO). The Guidance came into force on 31 July 1996 by virtue of Disability Discrimination (Guidance and Code of Practice) (Appointed Day) Order 1996, SI 1996/1996, art 2. A separate edition of the Guidance has been issued in Northern Ireland.

8   DDA 1995, ss 64(1)(a) and 68(1) and Sch 8, para 44.

9   Ibid.

10 Ibid, s 64(3)–(4), (8) and Sch 8, para 44(1) and (4)(b); Crown Proceedings Act 1947, s 23 and Parts II to V, but not ss 20 and 44 (removal of proceedings from the county court to the High Court or from the sheriff court to the Court of Session).

Minister of the Crown or Government department (other than service of a person holding a statutory office) as it applies to employment by a private person.[1] Service for the purposes of a Minister of the Crown or Government department does not include service in certain ministerial offices or service as the head of a Northern Ireland department.[2] Part 2 also applies to service on behalf of the Crown for the purposes of a person holding a statutory office or for the purposes of a statutory body as it applies to employment by a private person.[3] A 'statutory body' is one set up by or under an enactment and a 'statutory office' is construed accordingly.[4] The effect is to provide that civil servants are to be regarded as employees, but not a person holding a statutory office (although a person employed by an office-holder is covered).[5] However, office-holders are now explicitly included within Part 2 of the Act from 1 October 2004.[6]

9.5.3   The explicit exclusion of service as a prison officer and as a fire-fighting member of a fire brigade has been revoked from 1 October 2004. However, the exclusion of service in the naval, military or air forces remains.[7] Originally, police officers were implicitly outside the scope of the Act, as they were neither employees nor Crown servants.[8] In addition, Part 2 of the Act did not apply to service in certain statutory police forces.[9] These exclusions have also been revoked from 1 October 2004 (and have been discussed in Chapter 4).

9.6   APPLICATION TO PARLIAMENT

9.6.1   The DDA 1995 applies to an act (or deliberate omission) done by (or for the purposes of) the House of Lords or the House of Commons.[10] In other words, the Act is equally applicable to Parliament as it would be to a private person. Nothing in any rule of law or the law or

1   DDA 1995, s 64(2)(a), as amended.

2   Ibid, s 64(8) and Sch 8, para 44; House of Commons Disqualification Act 1975, Sch 2.

3   Ibid, s 64(2)(b).

4   Ibid, s 64(8).

5   HC Deb Standing Committee E, cols 441–442. See *Photis and Bruce v (1) KMC International Search & Selection and (2) Department of Trade & Industry; Heyes v Lord Chancellor's Department* (EAT/732/00, 766/00 and 960/00).

6   DDA 1995, ss 4C–4F, as amended (discussed in Chapter 4). The previous provisions on statutory office-holders in s 66 are now repealed.

7   Ibid, s 64(7).

8   See now DDA 1995, s 64A (subject to which s 64(1) and (2) have effect).

9   Ibid, s 64(5) (now repealed); Ministry of Defence Police Act 1987, s 1; British Transport Commission Act 1949, s 53; Parks Regulation Act 1872; Special Constables Act 1923, s 3.

10 Ibid, s 65(1).

practice of Parliament prevents proceedings being instituted under the DDA 1995 against either of the Houses of Parliament in an employment tribunal or a court. Otherwise parliamentary privilege would dictate that the Act would not apply to the legislature itself.

9.6.2 As far as the employment discrimination provisions of Part 2 of the DDA 1995 are concerned, the Corporate Officer of the House of Commons is to be treated as the employer of any person who is (or would be) a relevant member of the House of Commons staff.[1] In respect of discrimination in relation to the provision of goods, facilities or services to members of the public under Part 3 of the Act, the relevant provider of any services in question would be the Corporate Officer of the House of Commons and the Corporate Officer of the House of Lords respectively.[2] The two Houses provide a number of obvious services to visitors, such as refreshment facilities and information services. However, where the service at issue is the access to and use of any place in the Palace of Westminster which members of the public are permitted to enter (such as the public galleries in the debating chambers), the Corporate Officers of both Houses are treated as joint providers of such a service.[3] This makes it plain that physical access to the political process of the legislature itself is a matter that can be addressed and redressed under the relevant provisions of the DDA 1995.

9.7 REGULATIONS AND ORDERS

9.7.1 The DDA 1995 makes provision in several places for the enactment of regulations and orders which amplify the substantive provisions of the legislation. Any power under the Act to make regulations or orders is to be exercised by statutory instrument.[4] The term 'regulations' means regulations made by the Secretary of State.[5] Any such power may be exercised to make different provision for different cases, including different provision for different areas.[6] The power to make regulations and orders under the Act includes the power

---

1   DDA 1995, s 65(2) for the purposes of Employment Rights Act 1996, s 195.

2   Ibid, s 65(3).

3   Ibid, s 65(4).

4   Ibid, s 67(1). An exception is provided for under s 67(6) in respect of an order under s 43 by which the Secretary of State may authorise the use on roads of a regulated public service vehicle (PSV) which does not comply with the PSV accessibility regulations or which does not possess an accessibility or approval certificate under ss 40–42 of the Act. See Chapter 8.

5   Ibid, s 68(1).

6   Ibid, s 67(2).

to make incidental, supplemental, consequential or transitional provisions.[1] That power is exercised by the Secretary of State as appears to
him or her as expedient. The power to make regulations and orders may
also provide for a person to exercise a discretion in dealing with any
matter.[2] A statutory instrument made under the DDA 1995 is subject to
annulment by a resolution of either House of Parliament.[3]

9.8   DISABILITY DISCRIMINATION BILL

Public authorities

9.8.1   The Disability Discrimination Bill proposes that (with some
exceptions) the functions of public authorities will be brought within
the scope of the DDA 1995. It would be unlawful for a public authority to
discriminate (without justification) against a disabled person when
exercising its functions. This will cover decisions by Ministers, local
authorities, the police and other governmental organisations. Exception would be made for public functions of legislation, prosecution,
judicial acts and state security. A duty to make reasonable adjustments is
proposed as part of the prohibition on discrimination.[4]

9.8.2   If enacted, the Bill will also introduce a new duty on public
authorities. They will be required, when exercising their functions, to
have due regard to the need to eliminate unlawful discrimination
against (and harassment of) disabled persons. They will also be required
to promote equality of opportunity between disabled persons and other
persons. This would bring the DDA 1995 into line with the Race
Relations Act 1976, as amended. The new duty is intended to ensure
that bodies which exercise public functions 'mainstream' disability
rights issues when exercising those functions. When making decisions
or when developing or implementing a new policy, public authorities
must consider the needs of disabled persons as an integral part of the
policy-making or decision-making process. They will be required to do

---

1   DDA 1995, s 67(3)(a).

2   Ibid, s 67(3)(b). Nothing in s 34(4) (licensing of taxis in compliance with taxi accessibility
    regulations) or s 40(6) (public service vehicle accessibility regulations) or s 46(5) (rail
    vehicle accessibility regulations) affects the powers conferred by s 67(2) or (3) above.

3   Ibid, s 67(5). However, that annulment procedure does not apply to a statutory instrument
    made under s 3(9) (an order appointing the date on which any s 3 guidance as to the
    meaning of disability is to come into force), s 53A(6)(a) (an order appointing the day on
    which a code of practice shall come into force) or s 70(3) (an order appointing the date
    when the provisions of the Act come into force).

4   See Department for Work and Pensions, *Delivering Equality for Disabled People: A Consultation
    on the Extension of the Disability Discrimination Act to Functions of Public Authorities and the
    Introduction of a Duty to Promote Equality for Disabled People*, Cm 6255 (July 2004).

so with a view to eliminating discrimination and harassment against disabled people and improving opportunities for disabled persons.

9.8.3   The new provisions applying to public authorities will apply to the Crown. Provision is also to be made for Crown liability in respect of the acts of Crown servants.

Police

9.8.4   The Bill will also amend the DDA 1995 so as to clarify who the correct defendant is in the case of a claim of discrimination being made against a police officer under Part 3 of the Act. It will authorise payment of compensation from the police fund in relation to such a claim. This new provision will be relevant, for example, where it is alleged that a police officer has discriminated against a disabled person when carrying out a function as such an officer.

Codes of practice

9.8.5   The Bill will enable the DRC to issue codes of practice relating to discrimination by public authorities, private clubs and general qualifications bodies, and in relation to the exercise by public authorities of the proposed new duties to be imposed upon them.

Chapter 10

LIABILITY AND REMEDIES

10.1 VICTIMISATION

10.1.1 For the purposes of Part 2 (the employment field) or Part 3 (goods, facilities and services, and premises) and Part 4 (education) of the DDA 1995, a person is discriminated against if he or she is victimised by another person in connection with the exercise of any rights contained within the Act.[1] The concept of liability arising from the victimisation of a person because he or she sought to exercise statutory rights is one which is established in discrimination law and in employment law generally.[2] The victimisation provisions in the DDA 1995 are drafted in a slightly different way from the other discrimination statutes, but the case-law under the comparable provisions of other discrimination statutes will be informative.[3]

10.1.2 A complaint of victimisation is separate and different from any earlier complaint of discrimination which is said to have informed the later act of victimisation.[4] However, it does not create any cause of action in or of itself. It is not a free-standing provision. It merely defines an additional form of discrimination for the purposes of acts which are made unlawful (if at all) by Part 2, 3 or 4 of the Act. It does not (without more) provide that discrimination by way of victimisation is unlawful *per se*.[5]

10.1.3 A person (A) discriminates against another person (B) if A treats B less favourably than A treats or would treat other persons whose

---

1   DDA 1995, s 55.

2   See, eg SDA 1975, s 4; RRA 1976, s 2; ERA 1996, s 104.

3   HC Deb Standing Committee E, cols 425–426. See, eg *Bradford Hospitals NHS Trust v Al-Shabib* [2003] IRLR 4, EAT; *Jiad v Byford* [2003] IRLR 232, CA; *Visa International Service Association v Paul* [2004] IRLR 42, EAT; *St Helens MBC v Derbyshire* [2004] IRLR 851, EAT.

4   *Air Canada and Alpha Catering Services v Basra* [2000] IRLR 683, EAT.

5   *Bruce v Addleshaw Booth & Co* (EAT/0404/03, 11 February 2004).

circumstances are the same as B's and A does so for one of a number of reasons.[1] Those alternative reasons are:[2]

- B has brought proceedings against A or any other person (C) under the Act;
- B has given evidence or information in connection with proceedings brought by a person (D) against A or C under the Act;
- B has otherwise done anything under the Act in relation to A or any other person (C);
- B has alleged (expressly or impliedly) that A or C has contravened the Act;
- A believes or suspects that B has done or intends to do any of the above things.

The effect is to treat the listed forms of victimisation as amounting to acts of discrimination for the purpose of establishing an ingredient of acts made unlawful under Part 2, 3 or 4 of the DDA 1995.

10.1.4   However, victimisation of B by A in any of these circumstances is not made unlawful solely by virtue of the victimisation provisions if the less favourable treatment of B by A is because of an allegation made by B which was false and not made in good faith.[3] Furthermore, if the person being victimised (B) is a disabled person or a person who has had a disability, the disability in question is to be disregarded when comparing B's circumstances with those of any other person who is the comparator for judging A's less favourable treatment of B.[4] It is also clear that a tribunal or court could determine how B has been treated in comparison with a hypothetical comparator.[5]

10.1.5   Where B brings an action alleging unlawful discrimination by dint of victimisation in the employment field,[6] or in the provision of goods, facilities and services,[7] or in respect of the disposal (or management) of premises,[8] or in respect of education,[9] it does not matter whether B is or is not a disabled person within the meaning of the

---

1   DDA 1995, s 55(1), as amended.

2   Ibid, s 55(2). For the purposes of DDA 1995, Part 4, Chapter 1 only (ie the provisions affecting schools), references in s 55(2) to B include references to a person who is (for the purposes of that Chapter) B's parent, and a sibling of B: DDA 1995, s 55(3A).

3   Ibid, s 55(4).

4   Ibid, s 55(3).

5   HC Deb Standing Committee E, col 426.

6   DDA 1995, ss 4, 4B, 4D, 4G, 6A, 7A, 7C, 13, 14A, 14C and 16A.

7   Ibid, s 19.

8   Ibid, s 22.

9   Ibid, ss 28A, 28F and 28R.

DDA 1995.[1] The victimisation provisions provide the only basis for a cause of action under the Act for a person who either does not satisfy the definition of a disabled person in Part 1 or who is not a disabled person at all.

10.1.6 The victimisation provisions of the DDA 1995 will or should catch the following illustrations:[2]

- B, a disabled person, is dismissed by A (his or her employer) because B took A to an employment tribunal under the Act for refusing him or her access to a training opportunity or a promotion;
- B, a non-disabled person, is demoted and receives a cut in pay because he or she gave evidence in court proceedings brought under the Act against A (B's employer) by C (a disabled person) who had been refused service in A's restaurant because C was a wheelchair-user;
- B, a disabled tenant of A (a local authority landlord), is evicted from his or her rented flat or removed from the housing list by A because B wrote to the local press complaining that A was failing to make provision under the Act to allow disabled persons physical access to the local community centre;
- B, a non-disabled activist on disability rights, is refused entry to A's cinema because B had picketed the cinema, alleging that it was physically inaccessible to disabled persons, contrary to the Act;
- B, a non-disabled pupil, is denied a part in a school play because he or she acted as a witness in support of a complaint against a school by a disabled pupil to the SENDIST.

10.1.7 However, judicial interpretation of the victimisation provisions in discrimination law at large demonstrates that not all forms of apparent victimisation will be caught. There must be a causal link between the victimisation and a protected act.[3] However, it is not necessary to show conscious or deliberate victimisation.[4] In *Chief*

---

1   DDA 1995, ss 19(4), 22(7), 28A(6), 28F(5), 28R(4) and 55(5), as amended.

2   See also Code of Practice: Employment and Occupation (2004), paras 4.33–4.36; Code of Practice: Trade Organisations and Qualifications Bodies (2004), paras 4.32–4.35; Rights of Access Code of Practice (2002), paras 10.2–10.5; Schools Code of Practice (2002), paras 10.10–10.14; Post-16 Code of Practice (2002), paras 8.1–8.4.

3   See, eg *British Airways Engine Overhaul Ltd v Francis* [1981] IRLR 9, EAT (there must be a connection between B's actions, A's actions and the provisions of the Act); *Aziz v Trinity Street Taxis Ltd* [1988] ICR 534, CA (there must be a causal link between the victimisation and a protected act).

4   *Nagarajan v London Regional Transport* [1999] ICR 877, HL (motive is irrelevant and victimisation might be inferred from subconscious acts). See also: *Cornelius v University College of Swansea* [1987] IRLR 141, CA; *Kirby v Manpower Services Commission* [1980] ICR 420, EAT; *Waters v Metropolitan Police Commissioner* [1997] ICR 1073, CA.

Constable of West Yorkshire v Khan, the House of Lords held that whether a claimant had been victimised by reason of having done a protected act was not to be determined simply by application of a 'but for' test.[1] In that case, a reference had been withheld by an employer. It was held that it had not been withheld by reason that the claimant had brought discrimination proceedings, but rather because the employer temporarily needed to preserve its position in the outstanding legal proceedings. Lord Nicholls suggested that the phrase 'by reason that' does not give rise to a test of causation in the usual way, but that the test is a subjective one (why did the alleged discriminator act as he or she did?). Lord Hoffmann considered that the test of causation was whether the fact that the proceedings had been brought was a reason why the person had been treated less favourably. Lord Scott suggested that it is necessary to look for the real reason or core reason or the motive for the treatment complained of.

10.2 LEGAL LIABILITY

10.2.1   The DDA 1995 established a number of ways upon which legal liability for acts of unlawful discrimination or harassment can be based. In particular, provision is made for the liability of employers and principals, and of those who aid unlawful acts. There are also cases where there is an exemption from liability which would otherwise arise (most notably in respect of the exceptions for statutory authority and national security).

Aiding unlawful acts

10.2.2   A person who knowingly aids another person to do an 'unlawful act' is treated for the purposes of the legislation as having done the same kind of unlawful act in his or her own right.[2] An 'unlawful act' means an act made unlawful by any provision of the DDA 1995 other than a provision contained in Part 4, Chapter 1 (the anti-discrimination provisions affecting education in schools).[3] The effect is that a person can become liable for a discriminatory act committed contrary to the DDA 1995 merely by aiding and abetting the person who is primarily

---

1   [2001] UKHL 48, [2001] IRLR 830, HL.

2   DDA 1995, s 57(1), as amended. See generally: Code of Practice: Employment and Occupation (2004), paras 3.24–3.25; Code of Practice: Trade Organisations and Qualifications Bodies (2004), paras 3.28–3.29; Rights of Access Code of Practice (2002), paras 10.6–10.7; Post-16 Code of Practice (2002), paras 8.8–8.10.

3   DDA 1995, s 57(6).

responsible for the discriminatory conduct.[1] For example, if a company's personnel officer knowingly or deliberately discriminates against disabled applicants for employment, the company will be primarily responsible under the principle of statutory vicarious liability,[2] but the personnel officer may also be liable,[3] having aided the company to commit the discrimination in question. The word 'aids' bears no technical or special meaning in this context, and it does not matter who instigates or initiates the relationship.[4] However, difficulty may arise in proving that a person 'knowingly' aided an unlawful act. The mental element of knowledge or intention is crucial. Furthermore, there may be little to be gained in terms of remedies.

10.2.3 A person faced with an allegation of aiding another person to commit an act made unlawful by the legislation has an explicit defence.[5] For present purposes, a person does not knowingly aid another to do an unlawful act if he or she acts in reliance on a statement made to him or her by that other person. The statement must be to the effect that the act would not be unlawful because of any provision of the DDA 1995 and it must be reasonable to rely upon that statement. That other person is guilty of a criminal offence if he or she knowingly or recklessly makes such a statement which is false or misleading in a material respect.[6]

---

1   By virtue of DDA 1995, s 57(2), the person aiding the unlawful act (such as an employee) might be solely and personally liable for the unlawful act if the person who would otherwise be primarily liable (such as an employer) escapes vicarious liability by showing that it took such steps as were reasonably practicable to prevent its employee from doing the act in question (ie under the statutory defence in DDA 1995, s 58(5)): *Yeboah v Crofton* [2002] EWCA Civ 794, [2002] IRLR 634, CA (a case decided under the comparable provisions of RRA 1976, ss 32(3) and 33(1)–(2)).

2   Under DDA 1995, s 58 (discussed below). In *London Borough of Hammersmith & Fulham v Farnsworth* [2000] IRLR 691, EAT, the vicarious liability of the local authority for the actions of an occupational health physician (as an agent of the authority) informing an employment decision by the authority (and the relevance of the provisions of DDA 1995, ss 57–58) would have been in issue but for a concession made during the appeal.

3   Under DDA 1995, s 57. See *AM v WC and SPV* [1999] IRLR 410, EAT.

4   *Anyanwu v South Bank Students' Union* [2001] UKHL 14, [2001] IRLR 305, HL (a person aids another person if he or she helps or assists, or co-operates or collaborates with that other person, and whether or not that help is substantial and productive, provided it is not so insignificant as to be negligible); *Hallam v Cheltenham Borough Council* [2001] UKHL 15, [2001] IRLR 312, HL (what is required is more than a general attitude of helpfulness and co-operation – what must be shown is aid to another to do the unlawful act).

5   DDA 1995, s 57(3).

6   Ibid, s 57(4). A person guilty of that offence is liable upon summary conviction to a fine not exceeding level 5 on the standard scale (s 57(5)). An employer or principal cannot be made vicariously liable for such an offence committed by an employee or agent (s 58(4)).

Liability of employers

10.2.4 Anything done by a person in the course of his or her employment is treated for the purposes of the DDA 1995 as also done by his or her employer, whether or not it was done with the employer's knowledge or approval.[1] This statutory principle of vicarious liability is an important inclusion because the DDA 1995 speaks of unlawful acts committed by 'an employer', 'a principal' (in relation to contract work), 'a relevant person' (in relation to an office-holder), 'the trustees or managers of an occupational pension scheme', 'a firm' (in relation to a partner), 'a barrister or a barrister's clerk', 'an advocate', 'a trade organisation', 'a qualifications body', 'a placement provider' (in relation to practical work experience), 'a relevant person' (in relation to relationships that have come to an end), 'a person' (in relation to discriminatory advertisements and instructions or pressure to discriminate), 'the insurer' (in relation to insurance services), 'a provider of services', 'a person with power to dispose' (of any premises), 'the body responsible for a school', a (local education) 'authority', or 'the body responsible for an educational institution'.[2] It reflects similar provisions in other discrimination statutes.[3] The effect is that while an employer will be liable in its own right for its own discriminatory acts,[4] the employer is also vicariously liable for the discriminatory acts of an employee during the course of employment. However, both the employer and the employee remain potentially liable, because the employee may have knowingly aided the employer in the commission of an unlawful act of discrimination.[5] The employee is not released from any individual liability that might arise.[6] So, even though the employee might not be capable of committing an act of discrimination made

---

1   DDA 1995, s 58(1). See generally: Code of Practice: Employment and Occupation (2004), para 3.23; Code of Practice: Trade Organisations and Qualifications Bodies (2004), paras 3.26–3.27; Rights of Access Code of Practice (2002), paras 10.8–10.10; Schools Code of Practice (2002), paras 10.15–10.19; Post-16 Code of Practice (2002), paras 8.5–8.7. By virtue of s 58(4), vicarious liability cannot extend to an offence committed under s 57(4).

2   DDA 1995, ss 4, 4B, 4D, 4G, 6A, 7A, 7C, 13, 14A, 14C, 16A, 16B, 16C, 18, 19, 22, 28A, 28F and 28R respectively.

3   SDA 1975, s 41; RRA 1976, s 32. See also DDA 1995, s 64A (liability of a chief officer of police for the actions of a police officer).

4   The employer will be liable under the DDA 1995, but may also have liability in negligence at common law for any breach of a duty of care: *Waters v Commissioner of Police of the Metropolis* [2000] IRLR 720, HL (employer alleged to have behaved negligently in failing to deal with an employee's complaint that she had been sexually assaulted by a male colleague).

5   DDA 1995, s 57 (discussed at **10.2.2**). See under the SDA 1975: *Enterprise Glass Co Ltd v Miles* [1990] ICR 787, EAT; *AM v WC and SPV* [1999] IRLR 410, EAT.

6   *Yeboah v Crofton* [2002] EWCA Civ 794, [2002] IRLR 634, CA (a case decided under the comparable provisions of RRA 1976, ss 32(3) and 33(1)–(2)).

unlawful by the Act, he or she may be deemed to have aided the employer's unlawful act.[1]

10.2.5 At common law, the meaning of 'in the course of employment' has been the subject of a long line of case-law[2] which establishes that it is insufficient that the act was done while on duty or that the occasion to commit the act was provided in the context of employment, but it is enough that the act that gave rise to the discriminatory conduct was authorised by the employer, although carried out in an unauthorised or prohibited fashion.[3] Most recently, the House of Lords has ruled that the correct approach is to concentrate on the relative closeness of the connection between the nature of the employment and the employee's wrongdoing.[4] The question is whether the employee's tort is so closely connected with his or her employment that it would be fair and just to hold the employer vicariously liable. However, the common law principles on the meaning of 'in the course of employment' are not applicable to the statutory concept of vicarious liability.[5] The test of what will amount to 'in the course of employment' for the purposes of establishing vicarious liability for acts of disability discrimination is more flexible and is ultimately a question of fact for the court or tribunal.[6]

10.2.6 In a case founded upon the vicarious liability provision, an employer has a possible defence. The employer might escape vicarious liability (but not any liability faced in its own right) by proving that it took such steps as were reasonably practicable to prevent the employee from doing the act complained of or doing acts of the same description in the course of employment.[7] It may be sufficient to avoid vicarious liability by showing, for example, that the employer was unaware of the discriminatory acts being perpetrated by the employee and that there

---

1   This is because DDA 1995, s 57(2) provides that an employee for whose act the employer is liable under s 58 shall be taken to have aided the employer to do the act. For an illustration of this under the SDA 1975, see *Read v Tiverton District Council* [1977] IRLR 202.

2   See most recently *Fennely v Connex South Eastern Ltd* [2001] IRLR 390, CA, and *Balfron Trustees Ltd v Peterson* [2001] IRLR 758, HC.

3   See eg *Irving and Irving v Post Office* [1987] IRLR 289, CA; *Aldred v Nacanco* [1987] IRLR 292, CA; *Heasmans v Clarity Cleaning Co Ltd* [1987] IRLR 286, CA.

4   *Lister v Hesley Hall Ltd* [2001] UKHL 22, [2001] IRLR 472, HL.

5   *Jones v Tower Boot Co Ltd* [1997] IRLR 168, CA; *Sidhu v Aerospace Composite Technology Ltd* [2000] IRLR 602, CA.

6   See eg *Chief Constable of Lincolnshire Police v Stubbs* [1999] IRLR 81, EAT (vicarious liability for sexual harassment during work-connected social activities).

7   DDA 1995, s 58(5).

was proper and adequate staff supervision, including appropriate training and the dissemination of an anti-discrimination or equal opportunities policy.[1] The burden of proof will be upon the employer. Case-law establishes that it is necessary to determine whether the employer took any steps at all to prevent the employee doing the act complained of in the course of employment and then to consider whether there were any further steps that could have been taken which were reasonably practicable. Whether taking any such steps would have prevented the discriminatory acts is not determinative of the question.[2]

Liability of principals

10.2.7　The statutory provision on vicarious liability also applies in part to the relationship of principal and agent. Anything done by a person as agent for a principal, and with the principal's express or implied authority,[3] is treated for the purposes of the DDA 1995 as also done by the principal, whether the authority was given before or after the act in question.[4] Once again, this means that the principal is vicariously liable for the discriminatory actions of the agent and is jointly liable with the agent. The agent will be treated as having aided the principal to commit

---

1　*Balgobin and Francis v London Borough of Tower Hamlets* [1987] IRLR 401, EAT (a sex discrimination case under comparable provisions).

2　*Canniffe v East Riding of Yorkshire Council* [2000] IRLR 555, EAT (a case decided under the comparable provisions of SDA 1975, s 41(3)). See also *Pearce v Governing Body of Mayfield Secondary School* [2000] IRLR 548, EAT.

3　The authority referred to must be the authority to do an act which is capable of being done in a discriminatory manner just as it is capable of being done in a lawful manner: *Lana v Positive Action Training in Housing (London) Ltd* [2001] IRLR 501, EAT (ruling that SDA 1975, s 41(2), the equivalent of DDA 1995, s 58(2), is not restricted to situations in which the contract gives the agent authority to discriminate).

4　DDA 1995, s 58(2)–(3). Whatever a person has power to do may be done by an agent. Without such a power vested in the principal, an agent has no power deriving from agency. See *Halsbury's Laws of England*, Vol 1(2) (4th edn, 1990), para 3. In a case brought under DDA 1995, s 4, the governing body of a state-maintained school with a delegated budget was held not to be the agent of an LEA when committing an alleged act of disability discrimination in recruitment and selection arrangements because the LEA had no statutory power to carry out the governors' functions: *Lancashire County Council v Mason* [1998] ICR 907, EAT. But see now *Murphy v Slough Borough Council* [2004] ICR 1163, EAT; [2005] EWCA Civ 122, CA; and Education (Modification of Enactments Relating to Employment) Order 1999, SI 1999/2256 (in relation to Wales) and Education (Modification of Enactments Relating to Employment) Order 2003, SI 2003/1964, art 3 and Schedule, as amended by the Education (Modification of Enactments Relating to Employment) (England) (Amendment) Order 2004, SI 2004/2325 (in relation to England).

the unlawful act.[1] There is no defence available to the principal as there would be to an employer in a case of vicarious liability.[2]

Statutory authority

10.2.8 The DDA 1995 contains an exception to liability in respect of statutory authority. Nothing in the 1995 legislation causes an act or deliberate omission to be made unlawful where that act or omission is done in any of the following circumstances:[3]

- in pursuance of any 'enactment';
- in pursuance of any 'instrument' made by a Minister of the Crown under any 'enactment';
- to comply with any condition or requirement imposed by a Minister of the Crown (whether before or after the passing of the Act) by virtue of any 'enactment'.

An 'enactment' for this purpose will include an Act of Parliament (including legislation of the Welsh Assembly and the Scottish Parliament), subordinate legislation (such as a statutory instrument) and any Order in Council,[4] whether passed or made before or after the date the DDA 1995 received the Royal Assent.[5] An 'instrument' clearly refers to subordinate legislation made by a Minister under statutory delegated authority, whether made before or after the passing of the DDA 1995.

10.2.9 The use of the phrase 'in pursuance of' any enactment or instrument is deliberate. In the comparable provisions of race discrimination law,[6] the draftsman also used this term rather than the phrasing 'under' any enactment or instrument. This has led to a narrow

---

1   By virtue of DDA 1995, s 57(2). In *London Borough of Hammersmith & Fulham v Farnsworth* [2000] IRLR 691, EAT, the vicarious liability of the local authority for the actions of an occupational health physician (as an agent of the authority) informing an employment decision by the authority (and the relevance of the provisions of DDA 1995, ss 57–58) would have been in issue but for a concession made during the appeal.

2   Under DDA 1995, s 58(5).

3   Ibid, s 59(1). See also: Code of Practice: Employment and Occupation (2004), para 4.40; Code of Practice: Trade Organisations and Qualifications Bodies (2004), para 4.39; Rights of Access Code of Practice (2002), para 10.12; Schools Code of Practice (2002), chapter 11; Post-16 Code of Practice (2002), chapter 10.

4   DDA 1995, s 68(1) (which cross-refers to Interpretation Act 1978, s 21), as amended by the Scotland Act 1998 (Consequential Modifications) Order 2000, SI 2000/2040. Also included (by virtue of Sch 8, para 47(1)) is any statutory provision within the meaning of Interpretation Act (Northern Ireland) 1954, s 1(f).

5   DDA 1995, s 59(2) (namely, 8 November 1995).

6   RRA 1976, s 41.

interpretation of the exception by the courts. The exemption applies only to actions reasonably necessary to comply with a statutory obligation and not to acts done in exercise of a power of discretion conferred by the enactment or instrument.[1] The use of the word 'under' (contained originally in the 1995 Bill) may well have had the effect of inviting a wider interpretation of the statutory authority exemption. The result may have been that the exception would have applied to anything done under statutory authority, whether of a discretionary nature or not, and that would have gone some way towards undermining the objectives of the 1995 legislation. That possibility has apparently been excluded.

10.2.10   An example of how this exception might operate was given by a Minister when the DDA 1995 was being enacted:

> 'Under s 12 of the Health and Safety at Work etc Act 1974, the Secretary of State is given the power to give the Health and Safety Commission directions about ways in which it carries out its functions. If one of those functions, in the Secretary of State's opinion, required the Commission to do something which adversely affected disabled people, it would not be unlawful and could not be challenged under the provisions of the [Act].'[2]

It was also made clear that it was important that the exception should apply to both existing and future enactments. This point was illustrated by reference to the hypothetical possibility that a future safety legislative provision might require employers to modify equipment for the protection of employee operators. As a result of that modification, a disabled person might find it no longer physically possible to operate the equipment. The exception ensures that, by refusing to remove or alter the modification, the employer would not be in breach of the duty to accommodate disabled persons under the DDA 1995. The new safety law would override the disability discrimination legislation to that extent alone, although other forms of reasonable adjustment might remain appropriate for the employee.[3]

---

1   *Hampson v Department of Education and Science* [1990] IRLR 302, HL. See also, under the DDA 1995, *Post Office v Jones* [2000] ICR 388, EAT; [2001] IRLR 324, CA.

2   HC Deb Standing Committee E, col 428. See also the examples in respect of alterations to the highway or to listed buildings given at HL Deb, vol 565, col 673. An example under the DDA 1996 arose in *Lane Group plc v Farmiloe* EAT 0352/03 and 0357/03 (IDS Brief 772) where an employee was dismissed in circumstances where a skin condition prevented him from wearing protective footwear. The employer had attempted to make alternative arrangements and to make reasonable adjustments, but could not overcome the absolute duty under health and safety legislation in relation to protective footwear: DDA 1995, s 59 applied.

3   There would be nothing to prevent a future enactment being made expressly subject to the DDA 1995. For example, the Local Government and Housing Act 1989, s 7 requires all local government staff to be appointed on merit. However, that has effect expressly subject to DDA 1995, ss 4, 4A, 4D and 4E (discrimination and duties to make reasonable

10.2.11 In any proceedings in respect of discrimination in the employment field,[1] a certificate signed by or on behalf of a Minister of the Crown (or a Northern Ireland Department) which certifies that any conditions or requirements specified in the certificate were imposed by a Minister (or that Department), and were in operation at or throughout a specified time, shall be conclusive evidence of the matters certified.[2] A document purporting to be such a certificate shall be received in evidence and, unless the contrary is proved, is deemed to be such a certificate.[3] Similar provision is made in respect of proceedings under Part 3 of the DDA 1995 in respect of goods, facilities, services and premises[4] or the new Part 4 in respect of education.[5]

National security

10.2.12 Nothing in Part 2 of the DDA 1995 makes unlawful any act done for the purpose of safeguarding national security if the doing of the act was justified by that purpose. Nothing in Part 3 of the Act (to the extent that it relates to the provision of employment services) makes unlawful any act done for the purpose of safeguarding national security if the doing of the act was justified by that purpose. Otherwise, nothing in the DDA 1995 makes unlawful any act done for the purpose of safeguarding national security.[6] The implications of national security in proceedings before an employment tribunal under Part 2 of the DDA 1995 are now dealt with in the Employment Tribunals Act 1996 (ETA 1996), as amended.[7] As far as proceedings in goods, facilities, services and premises cases before a court under Part 3 of the DDA 1995 are concerned, a certificate signed by or on behalf of a Minister of the Crown which certifies that an act specified in the certificate was done for the purpose of safeguarding national security is to be conclusive evidence of the matter certified.[8] A document purporting to be such a

---

adjustments in relation to employees and office-holders). Thus, while local government appointments must be made on merit, that is always subject to the duty to make reasonable adjustments for disabled persons. That may include transferring a disabled employee to a higher grade post (for which the employee is otherwise qualified) without a competitive interview: *Archibald v Fife Council* [2004] UKHL 32, [2004] IRLR 651, HL.

1   DDA 1995, s 17A.

2   Ibid, Sch 3, para 4(1)(a), as amended.

3   Ibid, Sch 3, paras 4(2).

4   Ibid, Sch 3, paras 8(1)(a) and (2) in respect of proceedings under s 25. The modification of this provision in the context of Northern Ireland is set out in Sch 8, para 50(4).

5   Ibid, Sch 3, paras 11 and 15, in respect of proceedings under ss 28I, 28K, 28L and 28V.

6   Ibid, s 59(2A) and (3).

7   ETA 1996, ss 10–10B, and see the Employment Tribunals (Normal Security) Rules of Procedure 2004.

8   DDA 1995, Sch 3, para 8(1)(b). In Northern Ireland, the relevant certificate must be signed by the Secretary of State (Sch 8, para 50(2)).

certificate shall be received in evidence and, unless the contrary is proved, is deemed to be such a certificate.[1] There are no comparable provisions affecting education cases under the new Part 4 of the DDA 1995.

10.3   EMPLOYMENT CASES

Statutory questionnaire

10.3.1   Provision is made for help for persons suffering disability discrimination in relation to employment.[2] This applies to a claimant who considers that he or she may have been discriminated against (or subjected to harassment) by a respondent in contravention of Part 2 (the employment field) or Part 3 (employment services) of the DDA 1995 and against whom the claimant may decide to make a complaint (or has already done so).[3] This provision is modelled after similar provisions for assisting aggrieved persons to obtain information in cases of potential sex or race discrimination.[4]

10.3.2   The Secretary of State is mandated to prescribe by order forms by which the complainant may question the respondent on the respondent's reasons for doing any relevant act or on any other matter which is or may be relevant.[5] These questionnaire forms may be used either before or after proceedings have been commenced. Forms may also be prescribed by which the respondent may (if the respondent so wishes) reply to any questions. The power to prescribe such forms is to be taken with a view to helping the claimant to decide whether, in the first place, to make a complaint against the respondent and, in the second place, to formulate and present the case in the most effective manner. The Secretary of State may also prescribe the period within which any questionnaire must be served on the respondent and the manner in which the questionnaire (and any reply) must be served.[6]

---

1   DDA 1995, Sch 3, para 8(2).

2   Ibid, s 56, as amended.

3   Ibid, s 56(1).

4   SDA 1975, s 74; RRA 1976, s 65. See generally: *Greater Glasgow Health Board v Carey* [1987] IRLR 484, EAT; *City of Bradford Metropolitan Council v Arora* [1989] IRLR 442, EAT; *Carrington v Helix Lighting Ltd* [1990] IRLR 6, EAT; *King v The Great Britain-China Centre* [1991] IRLR 513, CA.

5   DDA 1995, s 56(2). In Northern Ireland, these powers are exercised by the Office of the First Minister and Deputy First Minister: Sch 8, para 38.

6   Ibid, s 56(4).

10.3.3   The most recent exercise of these powers has resulted in the Disability Discrimination (Questions and Replies) Order 2004.[1] The Order prescribes forms by which the claimant may question the respondent on its reasons for doing any relevant act (or on any other relevant matter) and by which the respondent may, if it wishes, reply to any questions.[2] A statutory questionnaire may be served upon the respondent by delivering it to the respondent; or by sending it by post to the respondent's usual (or last known) residence or place of business; or where the respondent is acting by a solicitor, by delivering it at (or by sending it by post to) the solicitor's address for service.[3] Where the person to be served is a body corporate or is a trade union or employers' association, the questionnaire may be served by delivering it to the secretary or clerk of the body, union or association at its registered or principal office or by sending it by post to the secretary or clerk at that office.[4] The respondent may serve a reply on the claimant by delivering the reply, or sending it by post, to him or her at the address for reply as stated in the questionnaire or at his or her usual (or last known) address.[5]

10.3.4   A respondent served with a statutory questionnaire must consider very carefully how to reply to the questions. The questions and any reply by the respondent are admissible in evidence in any subsequent employment tribunal proceedings.[6] However, this is subject to any enactment or rule of law regulating the admissibility of evidence in tribunal proceedings.[7] While the rules of evidence are not strictly applied in employment tribunals, the credibility and compelling nature of evidence in such proceedings do depend upon the tribunal weighing and assessing such evidence in the light of those rules. Where a questionnaire is served before a complaint has been presented to a tribunal, a question is only admissible as evidence if it was served within three months of the alleged act of discrimination or the extended period allowed by the dispute resolution provisions.[8] Where it was served after a complaint has been presented to a tribunal, a question is

---

1   SI 2004/1168. On the significance of the questionnaire, and how to devise and respond to it, see: Casserley and Gor, *Disability Discrimination Claims: An Adviser's Handbook* (2001, Bristol: Jordans), chapter 4.

2   Disability Discrimination (Questions and Replies) Order 2004, SI 2004/1168, reg 3 and Schs 1 and 2.

3   Ibid, reg 5(a) and (d).

4   Ibid, reg 5(c).

5   Ibid, reg 5(b).

6   DDA 1995, s 56(3)(a).

7   Ibid, s 56(5).

8   Disability Discrimination (Questions and Replies) Order 2004, SI 2004/1168, reg 4(a) by reference to DDA 1995, Sch 3, para 3, and Employment Act 2002 (Dispute Resolution) Regulations 2004, SI 2004/752, reg 15.

admissible if it was served within 28 days of the presentation of the complaint (or, if it was served with the leave of a tribunal, within the period specified by that tribunal).[1]

10.3.5   In subsequent employment tribunal proceedings, if it appears to the tribunal that, without reasonable excuse, the respondent deliberately omitted to reply to the questionnaire within eight weeks of the questionnaire being served on it, the tribunal may draw any inference which it considers it just and equitable to draw.[2] This might include an inference that the respondent has contravened Part 2 (or Part 3, in respect of employment services) of the DDA 1995. A similar adverse inference may be drawn if it appears to the tribunal that the respondent's reply to a questionnaire is evasive or equivocal.[3] The questionnaire procedure is without prejudice to any other enactment or rule of law regulating interlocutory and preliminary matters in proceedings before an employment tribunal.[4]

Employment tribunal proceedings

10.3.6   A complaint by any person that another person has unlawfully discriminated against him or her (or subjected him or her to harassment) contrary to Part 2 (or, in respect of employment services, Part 3) of the DDA 1995 may be presented to an employment tribunal.[5] A complaint survives the death of the claimant.[6] A Part 2 claim can only be brought via employment tribunal proceedings (except in those cases where the DRC has statutory enforcement powers).[7] It does not give rise to any other civil or criminal proceedings, except by way of judicial review or through the Pensions Ombudsman.[8] The employment tribunal will also have jurisdiction to hear complaints where the claimant alleges that another person is to be treated as having acted unlawfully.[9] However, employment tribunal proceedings cannot be brought in respect of acts of qualifications bodies made unlawful under

---

1   Disability Discrimination (Questions and Replies) Order 2004, SI 2004/1168, reg 4(b).

2   DDA 1995, s 56(3)(b)(i).

3   Ibid, s 56(3)(b)(ii).

4   Ibid, s 56(5). See generally: Casserley and Gor, *Disability Discrimination Claims: An Adviser's Handbook* (2001, Bristol: Jordans), chapters 7–8.

5   Ibid, ss 17A(1) and 25(7)–(9), as amended. The term 'person' includes an individual, a body corporate and an unincorporated association: Interpretation Act 1978, Sch 1.

6   Law Reform (Miscellaneous Provisions) Act 1934, s 1(1); *Harris (representative of Andrews) v Lewisham and Guy's Mental Health NHS Trust* [2000] IRLR 320, CA; *Executors of Soutar v James Murray and Co (Cupar) Ltd and Scottish Provident Institution* [2002] IRLR 22, EAT.

7   See Chapter 3.

8   DDA 1995, Sch 3, para 2.

9   Ibid, ss 57 (aiding unlawful acts) and 58 (liability of employers and principals). See generally **10.2**.

Part 2 of the DDA 1995 where an appeal (or proceedings in the nature of an appeal) may be brought under any enactment.[1]

10.3.7 It is not intended to rehearse the constitution and procedures of the employment tribunal here.[2] Proceedings are commenced by presenting a claim within the statutory time limits and the respondent may then present a defence in the form of a response.[3] Judgments of an employment tribunal are made unanimously or by a majority. An appeal from a judgment of an employment tribunal may be made to the Employment Appeal Tribunal (EAT) on a point of law, and from there to the Court of Appeal and, with leave, to the House of Lords. Employment tribunals are themselves subject to the DDA 1995 and will be covered by the rights of access to goods, facilities and services contained in Part 3 of the Act.[4]

Time-limits

10.3.8 An employment tribunal shall not consider a complaint under the DDA 1995 unless it is presented before the end of the period of three months, beginning when the act (or deliberate omission) complained of was done.[5] The time limit goes to the jurisdiction of the employment tribunal to hear the claim. In the case of an isolated act, the presumption will be that time starts to run from the date of the act (or omission). For example, time does not start to run in respect of a dismissal until the notice of dismissal expires and the employment ceases.[6] In a constructive dismissal, time runs from the date of termination rather than from the date of the breach.[7] In employment selection cases, time will start to run from when the applicant for employment is rejected.[8] A deliberate omission is to be treated as done when the person in question decided upon it.[9] Subject to rebutting

---

1   DDA 1995, s 17A(1A) and (1B) by reference to s 14A(1) or (2).

2   Employment Tribunals (Constitution and Rules of Procedure) Regulations 2004, SI 2004/1861, as amended by SI 2004/2351; Industrial Tribunals (Constitution and Rules of Procedure) Regulations (Northern Ireland) 2004, SR 2004/165.

3   See generally: Casserley and Gor, *Disability Discrimination Claims: An Adviser's Handbook* (2001, Bristol: Jordans), chapters 5–6.

4   HC Deb Standing Committee E, col 279. See Chapter 5. Legal aid is not generally available in employment tribunal proceedings.

5   DDA 1995, s 68(1) and Sch 3, para 3(1).

6   *British Gas Services Ltd v McCaull* [2001] IRLR 60, EAT (time did not start to run until an employer's failure to supply an employee with information about a proposed alternative job resulted in his refusing the alternative employment and his refusal resulted in his dismissal).

7   *Nottinghamshire County Council v Meikle* [2004] EWCA Civ 859, [2004] IRLR 703, CA.

8   *Tyagi v BBC World Service* [2001] EWCA Civ 549, [2001] IRLR 465, CA.

9   DDA 1995, Sch 3, para 3(3)(c).

evidence, a person is treated as having decided upon an omission when he or she does an act inconsistent with doing the omitted act or, in the absence of such inconsistent behaviour, when the period expires within which he or she might reasonably have been expected to do the omitted act if it was to be done.[1] In the case of an act or omission which extends over a period of time, the three months' limitation provision will not start to run until the end of the period in question.[2] Where the alleged unlawful act is attributable to a term in a contract, time does not start to expire until the end of the contract. The unlawful act is said to extend throughout the duration of the contract.[3]

10.3.9 Even where a complaint has been presented out of time, an employment tribunal may nevertheless entertain it if, in all the circumstances of the case, it considers that it is just and equitable to do so.[4] This allows an employment tribunal considerable discretion to admit late claims.[5] Tribunal decisions to extend the time-limit in such cases are rarely challengeable on appeal.[6] For example, tribunals might allow a late claim to proceed where the claimant was unaware of a cause of action or the time-limits governing it.[7] However, the discretion to extend time is not without limitations. For example, the fact that the claimant has delayed presenting a claim to the tribunal because he or she was seeking to redress a grievance through an employer's internal grievance procedure before embarking on legal proceedings has not, as a general principle, made it just and equitable to extend time and to admit a late claim.[8] This was merely one factor to be taken into account. However, this is now subject to the new dispute resolution procedures.

---

1   DDA 1995, Sch 3, para 3(4). Eg *Swithland Motors plc v Clarke* [1994] ICR 231, EAT.

2   Ibid, Sch 3, para 3(3)(b). See *Amies v Inner London Education Authority* [1977] ICR 308, EAT; *Sougrin v Haringey Health Authority* [1991] ICR 791, EAT; *Calder v James Finlay Corporation Ltd* [1989] IRLR 55, EAT; *Littlewoods Organisation plc v Traynor* [1993] IRLR 154, EAT; *Hendricks v Commissioner of Police for the Metropolis* [2003] IRLR 96, CA. On continuing acts of discrimination generally, see *Barclays Bank plc v Kapur* [1991] ICR 208, HL; *Robertson v Bexley Community Centre* [2003] IRLR 434, CA.

3   DDA 1995, Sch 3, para 3(3)(a).

4   Ibid, Sch 3, para 3(2).

5   *Hawkins v Ball* [1996] IRLR 258, EAT; *DPP v Marshall* [1998] ICR 518, EAT; *London Borough of Southwark v Afolabi* [2003] IRLR 220, CA.

6   *Hutchinson v Westward Television Ltd* [1977] ICR 279, EAT.

7   *Foster v South Glamorgan Health Authority* [1988] ICR 526, EAT.

8   *Apelogun-Gabriels v London Borough of Lambeth* [2001] EWCA Civ 1853, [2002] IRLR 116, CA; *Robinson v Post Office* [2000] IRLR 804, EAT; *Aniagwu v London Borough of Hackney* [1999] IRLR 303, EAT.

Dispute resolution procedures

10.3.10 From 1 October 2004, disability discrimination claims are subject to the new statutory dispute resolution procedures.[1] These are complex provisions and any detailed analysis of them is beyond the scope of this book. Their effect on disability discrimination claims may be summarised as follows.

10.3.11 When presenting a claim to the employment tribunal, the claimant must provide certain required information. That includes the details of the claim; whether or not the claimant is or was an employee of the respondent; whether or not the claim includes a complaint that the respondent has dismissed the claimant or has contemplated doing so; whether or not the claimant has raised the subject-matter of the claim with the respondent in writing at least 28 days prior to presenting the claim; and, if not, why not.[2] If that information is not provided, the claim will be rejected.[3] Put simply, unless the claim is about a dismissal (other than a constructive dismissal), the claimant must first raise a statutory grievance with the respondent.[4] He or she must do so no later than one month after the statutory time-limit of three months. The claimant must then wait 28 days before presenting a claim to the tribunal. He or she may then do so within a further three months of the end of the initial three-month time-limit.[5] These provisions are subject to various exceptions and qualifications.[6]

ACAS conciliation and arbitration

10.3.12 The DDA 1995 anticipates that there will be an attempt to reach a conciliated settlement between the parties before a complaint proceeds to a hearing by an employment tribunal.[7] Provision is made for a copy of a complaint of disability discrimination to be sent to a conciliation officer of the Advisory, Conciliation and Arbitration Service (ACAS).[8] In such a case, the conciliation officer must try to promote a settlement of the complaint, without a tribunal hearing, if requested to do so by both parties or if the conciliation officer considers

---

1   Employment Act 2002, ss 29–40 and Schs 2–5; Employment Act 2002 (Dispute Resolution) Regulations 2004, SI 2004/752; Employment Tribunals Rules of Procedure 2004, as amended, rules 1–9.

2   Employment Tribunals Rules of Procedure 2004, rule 1.

3   Ibid, rules 2–3.

4   Employment Act 2002, Sch 2.

5   Ibid, s 32 and Sch 4.

6   Employment Act 2002 (Dispute Resolution) Regulations 2004, SI 2004/752.

7   Employment Tribunals Act 1996, s 18, as amended (replacing DDA 1995, Sch 3, para 1).

8   Ibid, ss 18(1)(c), (2) and 42(1). In Northern Ireland, the Labour Relations Agency so acts: DDA 1995, Sch 8, para 50(1).

that there is a reasonable prospect of a successful attempt to promote a settlement being made.[1] This latter provision allows the conciliation officer to be proactive, even if only one of the parties has requested a conciliatory intervention. Moreover, where a complaint has yet to be presented to an employment tribunal, but a person is contemplating presenting such a complaint, the conciliation officer shall try to promote a settlement if asked to do so by the potential claimant or potential respondent.[2] Disability discrimination proceedings are not subject to the new provisions on fixed periods of conciliation during which the case cannot be listed for a hearing.[3]

10.3.13 If a conciliated settlement has been agreed with the assistance of an ACAS conciliation officer, the agreement will usually be recorded in writing using form COT3. An oral agreement would be equally valid, although less certain.[4] A conciliated settlement will be a valid agreement and will not be void if it merely records an agreement not to institute proceedings or an agreement to discontinue proceedings before an employment tribunal.[5] Unless the conciliated settlement is otherwise challengeable or invalid, the employment tribunal will then have no jurisdiction to hear the complaint which is the subject of the conciliation. Even if a respondent reneges on an ACAS-brokered settlement, the claimant will usually be required to sue on the agreement rather than seek to reopen the complaint. An agreement to submit the dispute to ACAS arbitration is also covered.[6]

Compromise contracts

10.3.14 A compromise contract is also valid if certain conditions are satisfied.[7] The contract must be in writing. It must relate to the particular complaint. The claimant must have received advice from a relevant independent adviser as to the terms and effect of the proposed contract and, in particular, its effect on his or her ability to pursue a complaint before an employment tribunal. There must be in force, when the adviser gives the advice, a contract of insurance (or an indemnity provided for members of a profession or professional body) covering the risk of a claim by the claimant in respect of loss arising in consequence of the advice. The contract must identify the adviser. It

---

1   ETA 1996, s 18(2)

2   Ibid, s 18(3).

3   Employment Tribunals Rules of Procedure 2004, rules 22–24.

4   *Gilbert v Kembridge Fibres Ltd* [1984] ICR 188, EAT.

5   DDA 1995, s 17C and Sch 3A, paras 1 and 2(1)(a).

6   Ibid, Sch 3A, para 2(8).

7   Ibid, s 17C and Sch 3A, paras 1, 2(1)(b) and 2(2).

must state that the conditions regulating compromise contracts have been satisfied.

10.3.15 A person is a relevant independent adviser for these purposes if he or she is a qualified lawyer.[1] Also covered is an officer, official, employee or member of an independent trade union who has been certified in writing by the trade union as competent to give advice and as authorised to do so on behalf of the trade union. A person is also a relevant independent adviser if he or she works at an advice centre (whether as an employee or a volunteer) and has been certified in writing by the centre as competent to give advice and as authorised to do so on behalf of the centre.[2] However, a person is not a relevant independent adviser for these purposes if he or she is, is employed by or is acting in the matter for the other party or a person who is connected with the other party.[3] In respect of a trade union or advice centre, it is not a relevant independent adviser if it is the other party or a person who is connected with the other party. In respect of an advice centre, it is not a relevant independent adviser if the claimant makes a payment for the advice received from the adviser.[4]

Restriction on publicity

10.3.16 Where evidence of a personal nature is likely to be heard by the employment tribunal hearing a complaint of disability discrimination, special provision is made for the restriction of publicity.[5] Evidence of a personal nature means any evidence of a medical or other intimate nature which might reasonably be assumed to be likely to cause significant embarrassment to the complainant if reported.[6] The Secretary of State is empowered to make regulations with respect to the procedure of employment tribunals so as to achieve this objective.[7] This

---

1   DDA 1995, Sch 3A, para 2(5): a qualified lawyer is a barrister (whether in practice as such or employed to give legal advice), a solicitor who holds a practising certificate, or a person other than a barrister or solicitor who is an authorised advocate or authorised litigator (within the meaning of the Courts and Legal Services Act 1990). In Scotland, a qualified lawyer is an advocate (whether in practice as such or employed to give legal advice), or a solicitor who holds a practising certificate.

2   Ibid, Sch 3A, para 2(3).

3   Ibid, Sch 3A, para 2(7): any two persons are to be treated as connected (a) if one is a company of which the other (directly or indirectly) has control; or (b) if both are companies of which a third person (directly or indirectly) has control.

4   Ibid, Sch 3A, para 2(4).

5   ETA 1996, s 12(1) (formerly DDA 1995, s 62(1)). See also *X v Stevens* [2003] IRLR 411, EAT.

6   Ibid, s 12(7).

7   Ibid, s 12(2).

is achieved in the employment tribunal procedural rules on restricted reporting orders.[1]

10.3.17 A restricted reporting order has the effect of prohibiting the publication in Great Britain (or Northern Ireland) of 'identifying matter' in a 'written publication' available to the public.[2] A written publication would obviously include a newspaper or magazine, but it also includes a film, a soundtrack and any other record in a permanent form.[3] A restricted reporting order will also have the effect of prohibiting the inclusion of any 'identifying matter' in a relevant radio or television programme for reception in Great Britain, or Northern Ireland, as the case may be.[4] This will effectively prevent the press and broadcast media from reporting any 'identifying matter' about the case. In this context, 'identifying matter' means any matter which is likely to lead members of the public to identify the claimant or any other persons named in the restricted reporting order.[5]

10.3.18 A restricted reporting order has effect until the promulgation of the tribunal's decision in the case, unless the order is revoked earlier.[6] If the restricted reporting order is broken by a newspaper or periodical, the proprietor, editor or publisher of the newspaper or periodical is guilty of a summary offence, punishable by a fine not exceeding level 5 on the standard scale.[7] Where the order is breached in a publication in any other form, the publisher of the matter shall be so liable.[8] Where the identifying matter is published in breach of a restricted reporting order by a radio or television broadcast, the broadcast company and the programme editor face criminal liability.[9] In any case, it is a defence to prove that, at the time of the alleged offence, the person charged was not aware (and neither suspected nor had reason to suspect) that the publication or programme in question was of (or included) the matter in question.[10]

---

1   Employment Tribunals Rules of Procedure 2004, rules 18(7)(g) and 50.

2   ETA 1996, s 12(7), Sch 8, para 42(2).

3   Ibid, s 12(7).

4   Ibid, s 12(7), Sch 8, para 42(2).

5   Ibid, s 12(7).

6   Ibid, s 12(2)(a).

7   Ibid, s 12(3)(a).

8   Ibid, s 12(3)(b).

9   Ibid, s 12(3)(c).

10   Ibid, s 12(4). Note also s 12(5)–(6), which makes provision for offences of joint liability where the breach of a restricted reporting order is committed by a body corporate, with the consent or connivance of (or attributable neglect of) a director, manager, secretary or other similar officer.

10.3.19 Provision is also made for the restriction of publicity on certain appeals from an employment tribunal to the EAT under the DDA 1995.[1] This applies to proceedings on an appeal against an employment tribunal's decision to make (or not make) a restricted reporting order in disability discrimination cases. It also applies in such cases on an appeal against any interim decision of an employment tribunal in proceedings in which the employment tribunal has made a restricted reporting order which it has not revoked.

Burden of proof

10.3.20 Where the claimant proves facts from which the employment tribunal could conclude, in the absence of an adequate explanation, that the respondent has acted in a way which is unlawful under Part 2 of the DDA 1995, the tribunal shall uphold the complaint unless the respondent proves that it did not so act.[2] This is the reversal of the burden of proof required by the EC Employment Framework Directive.[3] The Court of Appeal has recently given authoritative guidance on the reversal of the burden of proof and has updated the guidance given in earlier cases, which may be paraphrased and applied to disability discrimination as follows.[4]

It is for the claimant to prove on the balance of probabilities facts from which the tribunal could conclude, in the absence of an adequate explanation, that the respondent has committed an act of unlawful discrimination. If the claimant does not prove such facts, he or she will fail. It is unusual to find direct evidence of disability discrimination. Few employers would be prepared to admit such discrimination. In some

---

1 ETA 1996, s 32 (previously DDA 1995, s 63); Employment Appeal Tribunal Rules 1993, rule 23A, as amended.

2 DDA 1995, s 17A(1C), as amended. On the general power of tribunals to draw inferences of discrimination before the statutory introduction of the reversal of the burden of proof, see *King v The Great Britain-China Centre* [1991] IRLR 513, CA; *Zafar v Glasgow City Council* [1998] ICR 125, HL; *Nagaragan v London Regional Transport* [1999] IRLR 572, HL; *Anya v University of Oxford* [2001] IRLR 364, CA; *Rowden v Dutton Gregory (a firm)* [2002] ICR 971, EAT; *Barton v Investec Henderson Crosthwaite Securities Ltd* [2003] IRLR 332, EAT; *University of Huddersfield v Wolff* [2004] IRLR 534, EAT; *Chamberlain Solicitors v Emokpae* [2004] IRLR 592, EAT; *Bahl v The Law Society* [2004] IRLR 799, CA; *Madden v Preferred Technical Group Cha Ltd* [2005] IRLR 46, CA.

3 2000/78/EC, Art 10. On the general power of tribunals to draw inferences of discrimination after the statutory introduction of the reversal of the burden of proof, see *Barton v Investec Henderson Crosthwaite Securities Ltd* [2003] IRLR 332, EAT; *University of Huddersfield v Wolff* [2004] IRLR 534, EAT; *Chamberlain Solicitors v Emokpae* [2004] IRLR 592, EAT; *Sinclair Roche and Temperly v Heard* [2004] IRLR 763, EAT; *Webster v Brunel University* EAT 0730/04.

4 *Igen Ltd v Wong; Chamberlin Solicitors v Emokpae; Brunel University v Webster (EOC, CRE and DRC intervening)* [2005] EWCA Civ 142, CA, overturning the decisions of the EAT in *Emokpae* (above) and in *Webster* (above), and revising the guidance given in *Barton* (above).

cases, the discrimination will merely be based on an assumption that the claimant would not have fitted in. In deciding whether the claimant has proved such facts, the outcome will usually depend on what inferences it is proper to draw from the primary facts. It is important to note the word 'could' in s 17A(1C). At this stage, the tribunal does not have to reach a definitive determination that such facts would lead it to the conclusion that there was an act of unlawful discrimination. A tribunal is looking at the primary facts to see what inferences of secondary fact could be drawn from them. In considering what inferences or conclusions can be drawn from the primary facts, the tribunal must assume that there is no adequate explanation for those facts. These inferences can include any inferences that it is just and equitable to draw from an evasive or equivocal reply to a statutory questionnaire. Inferences may also be drawn from any failure to comply with any relevant code of practice. Where the claimant has proved facts from which conclusions could be drawn that the respondent has treated the claimant less favourably on the ground of disability or for a disability-related reason, then the burden of proof moves to the respondent. It is then for the respondent to prove that it did not commit (or is not to be treated as having committed) that act. It is necessary for the respondent to prove, on the balance of probabilities, that the treatment was in no sense whatsoever on the ground of disability or for a disability-related reason. That requires a tribunal to assess not merely whether the respondent has proved an explanation for the facts from which such inferences can be drawn, but further that it is adequate to discharge the burden of proof on the balance of probabilities that disability was not a ground for the treatment in question. Since the facts necessary to prove an explanation would normally be in the possession of the respondent, a tribunal would normally expect cogent evidence to discharge that burden of proof. In particular, the tribunal will need to examine carefully explanations for failure to deal with the questionnaire procedure or a code of practice.

Remedies

10.3.21 Where an employment tribunal finds that a complaint of unlawful disability discrimination or harassment in the employment field contrary to Part 2 of the DDA 1995 is well founded, it shall take one or more of the following steps as it considers just and equitable.[1] First, it may make a declaration as to the rights of the claimant and the respondent in relation to the matters to which the complaint relates. Secondly, it may order the respondent to pay compensation to the claimant. Thirdly, it may recommend that the respondent take, within a specified period, action appearing to the tribunal to be reasonable, in

---

1   DDA 1995, s 17A(2).

all the circumstances of the case, for the purpose of obviating or reducing the adverse effect on the claimant of any matter to which the complaint relates.

Declaration of rights

10.3.22 Where a claimant has successfully brought a disability discrimination claim, the very least that the disabled person will be entitled to is a declaration that he or she has suffered unlawful discrimination or harassment in certain particulars or that his or her rights have been unlawfully transgressed.[1] A declaration of the claimant's rights alone is likely to be appropriate in those cases where he or she has suffered no measurable loss or where there is only a point of principle involved. A tribunal might occasionally use its declaratory powers to encourage the respondent to take some positive step towards the successful claimant (such as offer employment to or reinstate him or her), although the legal effect of such a declaration is of doubtful value.

Compensation and interest

10.3.23 The EAT has guided tribunals on the procedural approach to the assessment of compensation under the DDA 1995.[2] A separate remedies hearing will be appropriate. The parties' preparation for that hearing should be conducted under careful judicial case management, often involving the making of further case management orders and the exchange of statements of case and witness statements prior to the hearing. Where medical expert evidence is required (typically to assist the tribunal's findings as to the future employment prospects of the claimant for the purpose of assessing future loss of earnings), the listing of the case may need to take account of the availability of the expert witness.[3]

10.3.24 Where a tribunal orders compensation to be paid in an employment discrimination case,[4] the amount of the compensation is calculated according to the principles applicable to the calculation of damages in claims in tort (or, in Scotland, in reparation for breach of a statutory duty).[5] In other words, disability discrimination compensation will be assessed like any claim for damages in tort and according to

---

1   DDA 1995, s 17A(2)(a).

2   *Buxton v Equinox Design Ltd* [1999] IRLR 158, EAT.

3   See also generally the advice given in relation to expert witnesses and expert evidence in *De Keyser v Wilson* [2001] IRLR 324, EAT.

4   DDA 1995, s 17A(2)(b).

5   Ibid, s 17A(3).

common-law principles. Case-law under the other discrimination statutes will be instructive. There is no limit on the maximum amount of compensation that can be awarded for a breach of Part 2 of the DDA 1995.

10.3.25 A successful claimant will be entitled to be compensated for any actual financial or pecuniary loss up to the date of the tribunal decision, provided that it is caused by or attributable to the unlawful act or omission. The tribunal may also be invited to calculate future or continuing losses within the award. The main head of damages is likely to be present or future loss of earnings which has resulted as a consequence of the unlawful act. This will include loss of basic wages or salary, together with any fringe benefits (such as a bonus, commission, company car, private health insurance, pension entitlements, and so on) to which the individual would have been entitled but for the discriminatory action. The claimant will be subject to a duty to mitigate any loss.[1]

10.3.26 The amount of compensation may also include compensation for injury to feelings, whether or not the award includes compensation under any other head.[2] It is suggested that such an element of damages will be appropriate (and easily implied without pleading) in most cases unless exceptional.[3] It will also include compensation for physical or psychiatric injury *caused by* an act of disability discrimination.[4] Such awards may be particularly in point in DDA cases where the claimant's disability is a mental illness which has been exacerbated by the act of discrimination. The tribunal will be careful to avoid an overlap with injury to feelings damages so as not to encourage double recovery.

---

1   *Wilding v British Telecommunications plc* [2002] EWCA Civ 349, [2002] IRLR 524, CA (depending upon all the circumstances, a refusal to accept an offer of re-employment may amount to a failure to mitigate loss). This may require the compensation to take account of state benefits received: *Chief Constable of West Yorkshire Police v Vento (No. 2)* [2002] IRLR 177, EAT, and [2003] IRLR 102, CA. See also: *Atos Origin IT UK Ltd v Haddock* [2005] IRLR 20, EAT (allowance should also be made for payments which might be made under the employer's permanent health insurance scheme where the premiums have been paid by the employer without contribution from the employee).

2   DDA 1995, s 17A(4). See generally: *Armitage v Johnson* [1997] IRLR 162, EAT; *Heil v Rankin* [2000] IRLR 334, CA; *Chief Constable of West Yorkshire v Khan* [2000] IRLR 324, CA; [2001] UKHL 48, [2001] IRLR 830, HL; *ICTS (UK) Ltd v Tchoula* [2000] IRLR 643, EAT; *O'Donoghue v Redcar and Cleveland Borough Council* [2001] IRLR 615, EAT; *Chief Constable of West Yorkshire Police v Vento (No. 2)* [2002] IRLR 177, EAT and [2003] IRLR 102, CA; *Doshoki v Draeger Ltd* [2002] IRLR 340, EAT; *British Telecommunications plc v Reid* [2004] IRLR 327, CA; *Scott v Commissioners of Inland Revenue* [2004] IRLR 713, CA.

3   *Murray v Powertech (Scotland) Ltd* [1992] IRLR 257, EAT. The award is not, in principle, to be grossed-up for tax: *Orthet Ltd v Vince-Cain* [2004] IRLR 857, EAT.

4   *Sheriff v Klyne Tugs (Lowestoft) Ltd* [1999] IRLR 481, CA. As to the judicial approach to the assessment of compensation for psychiatric injury, see *HM Prison Service v Salmon* [2001] IRLR 425, EAT; *Essa Ltd v Laing* [2003] IRLR 346, EAT.

Aggravated damages may be awarded in exceptional cases where a respondent has acted in a high-handed, malicious, insulting or oppressive manner.[1] Exemplary damages were thought to be inappropriate in disability discrimination claims because of developments in the common law,[2] but now may be available in exceptional cases.[3]

10.3.27 The DDA 1995 also provided for regulations to be made to give tribunals the power to award interest on an award of compensation and to specify how that interest is to be determined.[4] The Employment Tribunals (Interest on Awards in Discrimination Cases) Regulations 1996 provide for the award of interest in proceedings for payment of compensation under the DDA 1995.[5]

10.3.28 In the case of an act which is *both* unfair dismissal *and* unlawful disability discrimination or harassment, recovery of the same loss under more than one provision is prohibited.[6] The employment tribunal shall not award compensation, for example, under the heading of disability discrimination in respect of any loss or matter which has already been accounted for in the award of compensation for unfair dismissal. The effect is to prevent double recovery of a loss already compensated for in the tribunal's award, whether the issue arises in the same proceedings before the tribunal in question or whether it arises in separate proceedings. For example, if the claimant has been dismissed and brought a successful unfair dismissal claim, it is likely that he or she will have been awarded compensation for loss of earnings to the date of the tribunal hearing and/or for future loss of earnings. A later tribunal considering a separate complaint of disability discrimination in respect of that dismissal must take account of the award for lost earnings when calculating any award under the DDA 1995.

---

1   *Armitage v Johnson* [1997] IRLR 162, EAT; *HM Prison Service v Salmon* [2001] IRLR 425, EAT; *Chief Constable of West Yorkshire Police v Vento (No. 2)* [2002] IRLR 177, EAT; [2003] IRLR 102, CA; *Zaiwalla & Co v Walia* [2002] IRLR 697, EAT; *Scott v Commissioners of Inland Revenue* [2004] IRLR 713, CA.

2   *Alexander v Home Office* [1988] IRLR 190, CA; *City of Bradford Metropolitan Borough Council v Arora* [1991] IRLR 165, CA; *AB v South Western Water Services Ltd* [1993] 1 All ER 609, CA; *Deane v Ealing London Borough Council* [1993] IRLR 209, EAT.

3   *Kuddus v Chief Constable of Leicestershire Constabulary* [2001] UKHL 29, [2001] 3 All ER 193, HL, overruling *AB v South Western Water Services Ltd* [1993] 1 All ER 609, CA.

4   DDA 1995, s 17A(6).

5   SI 1996/2803. For examples of the judicial approach to the award of interest, see *Derby Specialist Fabrication Ltd v Burton* [2001] IRLR 69, EAT, and *Bentwood Bros (Manchester) Ltd v Shepherd* [2003] IRLR 364, CA.

6   ERA 1996, s 126, as amended. Where a claimant has been dismissed unfairly, that does not terminate liability for an earlier wrong of disability discrimination, and all further losses do not fall to be assessed as compensation for unfair dismissal subject to the statutory cap on such compensation: *HM Prison Service v Beart (No 2)* [2005] IRLR 171, EAT.

10.3.29   However, problems are still likely to arise in respect of awards of loss of earnings. These will often be capped by the statutory maximum (from time to time) for an unfair dismissal compensatory award. As there is no statutory limit to awards under the DDA 1995, it is in the claimant's interest to ensure that the award of lost earnings is dealt with explicitly under the DDA 1995 rather than the 1996 Act. What is not clear is what should happen where such an award has already been made under the unfair dismissal compensation provisions of the 1996 Act and has then been capped by the statutory maximum. Is an employment tribunal considering making an award of loss of earnings under the DDA 1995 bound to decide that this is a loss which has already been taken into account in the earlier award (even though the amount of the loss has been artificially capped)? Alternatively, should the tribunal apportion the compensation awarded in the unfair dismissal claim and award the balance under the DDA 1995? The latter approach seems preferable, although it is not easily reconcilable with the statutory language.

10.3.30   Where an employment tribunal in an unfair dismissal case makes a reinstatement or re-engagement order,[1] but the employer disobeys the order by refusing to re-employ the unfairly dismissed employee, the tribunal shall make an award of compensation for unfair dismissal,[2] plus an additional award of compensation to be paid by the employer to the employee.[3] An additional award will not be made if the employer satisfies the tribunal that it was not practicable to comply with the reinstatement or re-engagement order.[4] The appropriate amount of the additional award is usually between 13 and 26 weeks' pay.[5] However, the tribunal will award a higher additional award where the unfair dismissal was also found to be an unlawful act under the DDA 1995.[6] The higher additional award in such cases is between 26 and 52 weeks' pay.[7]

10.3.31   An award of compensation in a DDA case may also have to be adjusted up or down to reflect the extent to which either the claimant or the respondent previously failed to complete the new statutory dispute resolution procedures.[8]

---

1   ERA 1996, s 113.

2   Ibid, ss 118–127, and see s 117(8).

3   Ibid, s 117(3); *Morganite Electrical Carbon Ltd v Donne* [1988] ICR 8, EAT; *Motherwell Railway Club v McQueen* [1989] ICR 418, EAT.

4   Ibid, s 117(4)(a), and see s 117(7).

5   Ibid, s 117(5)(b). A 'week's pay' is subject to the statutory maximum.

6   Ibid, s 117(6)(c), as amended.

7   Ibid, s 117(5)(a).

8   Employment Act 2002, s 31 and Sch 3.

Recommendations

10.3.32 Where the employment tribunal has upheld a complaint of disability discrimination or harassment, it may recommend that the respondent take, within a specified period, action appearing to the tribunal to be 'reasonable', in all the circumstances of the case, for the purpose of obviating or reducing the adverse effect on the claimant of any 'matter' to which the complaint relates.[1] It is clear that the power to make recommendations may only be used by the tribunal to attempt to obviate or reduce the adverse effects of the discrimination on the claimant. This does not give the tribunal broader powers to effect changes for the benefit of a wider class of persons who are not party to the proceedings. The recommendation must be directed towards an individualised remedy rather than a class-based remedy. So the respondent cannot be ordered to review the wider effect of the discriminatory act nor to cease committing such an act in the future.[2] The tribunal's attention must be entirely focused upon making a recommendation which will counteract or reduce the discriminatory effect upon the claimant.

10.3.33 This might include, for example, a recommendation that the respondent should consider the claimant for the next available suitable vacancy or reconsider the training opportunities or career development of a disabled claimant already in the respondent's employment. It might also include a recommendation that the employer take steps that would amount to the making of reasonable adjustments to arrangements or the physical features of premises if this would be within that employer's statutory duty and directed towards preventing a substantial disadvantage to the disabled claimant created by those unadjusted arrangements or physical features. Nevertheless, in one case, the EAT suggested that the tribunal should simply recommend that the respondent should take action to make reasonable adjustments within a specified time, rather than make a particular adjustment contended for.[3]

10.3.34 It is a moot point whether the employment tribunal's statutory powers allow it to recommend that the disabled claimant should actually be engaged for or promoted to the next available suitable vacancy. Such a power was clearly not within the letter or spirit of sex or race discrimination legislation because the respondent, in obeying such a recommendation, might then commit an act of unlawful positive or

---

1   DDA 1995, s 17A(2)(c). See generally: *Chief Constable of West Yorkshire Police v Vento (No 2)* [2002] IRLR 177, EAT; [2003] IRLR 102, CA.

2   But see the powers of the DRC discussed in Chapter 9.

3   *Post Office v Jones* [2000] ICR 388, EAT.

reverse discrimination.[1] That does not appear to be a problem under the DDA 1995 because the legislation is asymmetrical. The Act does not prohibit (but neither does it require) positive discrimination in favour of disabled persons, and a non-disabled person treated less favourably than a disabled person has no cause of action under the DDA 1995. In the other employment discrimination jurisdictions, compensation is frequently regarded as the primary remedy. Given the emphasis in the DDA 1995 upon the respondent's duties to make reasonable adjustments to accommodate disabled persons, it is perhaps surprising that there has not been a shift away in DDA cases from first reliance upon compensatory remedies and towards recommendations of positive action.

10.3.35	If the respondent fails 'without reasonable justification' to comply with a recommendation made by an employment tribunal, the tribunal may, if it thinks it just and equitable, order the payment of compensation or increase the amount of a compensation order already made.[2] What will amount to 'reasonable justification' is clearly a question of fact and will vary from case to case.[3] For example, if a recommendation has been made to the effect that the claimant should be considered for promotion, but, in the meanwhile, he or she has lost his or her employment due to a genuine redundancy exercise, that would probably amount to a reasonable justification for the failure to comply with the recommendation. It is unlikely that justification could be advanced by reference to factors which are themselves made unlawful under the DDA 1995. So, for example, if the claimant was only selected as a redundancy candidate because he or she was a disabled person, that would not be a justifying reason.

## 10.4	SERVICES AND PREMISES CASES

Proceedings in the county court or sheriff court

10.4.1	Claims of disability discrimination arising under Part 3 of the DDA 1995 in respect of goods, facilities, services and premises are the subject of civil proceedings in the same way as any other claim in tort (or, in Scotland, in reparation for breach of a statutory duty).[4] Proceedings in England and Wales, and in Northern Ireland, may be

---

1	*Noon v North West Thames Regional Health Authority (No 2)* [1988] IRLR 530, CA; *British Gas plc v Sharma* [1991] IRLR 101, EAT.

2	DDA 1995, s 17A(5).

3	*Nelson v Tyne and Wear Passenger Transport Executive* [1978] ICR 1183, EAT.

4	DDA 1995, s 25(1). However, Part 3 employment services cases are dealt with in the employment tribunal: s 25(7)–(8).

brought only in the county court.[1] In Scotland, proceedings may be brought only in a sheriff court.[2] No civil or criminal proceedings may be brought in respect of an act merely because the act is made unlawful under the provisions of Part 3 of the DDA 1995.[3] This does not prevent proceedings for judicial review arising in respect of any decision taken in relation to Part 3.[4] It is likely that, in many instances, Part 3 cases will brought under the small claims arbitration procedure.

Time-limits

10.4.2 The limitation period for Part 3 claims is six months. A county court or sheriff court shall not consider a Part 3 claim unless proceedings in respect of it have been instituted before the end of the period of six months beginning when the act complained of was done.[5] The court may consider a claim which is otherwise time-barred if, in all the circumstances of the case, the court considers that it is just and equitable to do so.[6]

10.4.3 Questions about the operation of this limitation period are likely to arise in a similar way to those which arise in respect of the comparable provisions affecting employment cases. In particular, in the case of an isolated act of disability discrimination, the presumption will be that time starts to run from the date of the act or the omission itself. A deliberate omission is to be treated as done when the person in question decided upon it.[7] Subject to rebutting evidence, a person is treated as having decided upon an omission when he or she does an act inconsistent with doing the omitted act or, in the absence of such inconsistent behaviour, when the period expires within which he or she might reasonably have been expected to do the omitted act if it was to be done.[8] However, in other cases, there is more flexibility in measuring the date upon which time starts to run. In the case of any act or omission which extends over a period of time, the six-months limitation provision will not start to run until the end of the period in question.[9] Moreover, where the alleged unlawful act of discrimination is attributable to a term in a contract, time does not start to expire until the end of the contract.

---

1   DDA 1995, s 25(3) and Sch 8, para 12.

2   Ibid, s 25(4).

3   Ibid, Sch 3, para 5(1).

4   Ibid, Sch 3, para 5(2).

5   Ibid, Sch 3, para 6(1) (but see **10.4.6**). An 'act' includes a deliberate omission (s 68(1)).

6   Ibid, Sch 3, para 6(3).

7   Ibid, Sch 3, para 6(4)(c).

8   Ibid, Sch 3, para 6(5).

9   Ibid, Sch 3, para 6(4)(b).

The unlawful act is said to extend throughout the duration of the contract.[1]

Conciliation

10.4.4　The DRC may make arrangements with any other person for the provision of 'conciliation services' by that person (or by persons appointed by that person) in relation to disputes arising under Part 3 of the DDA 1995.[2] In deciding what arrangements (if any) to make, the DRC shall have regard to the desirability of securing, so far as reasonably practicable, that conciliation services are available for all disputes arising under Part 3 which the parties may wish to refer to conciliation.[3] No member or employee of the DRC may provide conciliation services in relation to such disputes.[4] The DRC must ensure that any such arrangements include appropriate safeguards to prevent the disclosure to members or employees of the DRC of information obtained by a person in connection with the provision of such conciliation services.[5] However, that does not apply to information relating to a dispute which is disclosed with the consent of the parties to that dispute.[6] Equally, it does not apply to information which is not identifiable with a particular dispute or a particular person, and is reasonably required by the DRC for the purpose of monitoring the operation of the arrangements concerned.[7] Anything communicated to a person while providing such conciliation services is not admissible in evidence in any proceedings (except with the consent of the person who communicated it to that person).[8]

10.4.5　The services previously provided by the Disability Access Rights Advisory Service (DARAS) were transferred to the DRC on 25 April 2000. The information and advice services which were provided by DARAS and the DDA Helpline have been merged to form the DRC Helpline. An independent conciliation service (the Disability Conciliation Service) has been outsourced by the DRC to Mediation UK.

10.4.6　Normally, civil proceedings for an alleged breach of the provisions of Part 3 of the DDA 1995 must be commenced within six

---

1　DDA 1995, Sch 3, para 6(4)(a).

2　Ibid, s 28(1), as substituted. The term 'conciliation services' means advice and assistance provided by a conciliator to the parties to a dispute with a view to promoting its settlement otherwise than through the courts: DDA 1995, s 28(8), as substituted by DRCA 1999, s 10.

3　Ibid, s 28(2), as substituted.

4　Ibid, s 28(3), as substituted.

5　Ibid, s 28(4), as substituted.

6　Ibid, s 28(5), as substituted.

7　Ibid, s 28(6), as substituted.

8　Ibid, s 28(7), as substituted.

months of the act of discrimination.[1] However, if the dispute concerned is referred for conciliation in pursuance of statutory arrangements made by the DRC before the end of the six-months limitation period, then the limitation period within which civil proceedings must be commenced is extended by a further two months.[2]

Settlements

10.4.7 Any term in a contract for the provision of goods, facilities or services is void so far as it purports to require any person to do anything which would contravene any provision of (or made under) Part 3 of the DDA 1995.[3] This invalidating principle also applies to any term in any other agreement (which would presumably include a tenancy agreement or lease) which purports to have that effect. In like manner, a term in a contract or agreement which purports to exclude or limit the operation of any provision of Part 3, or which seeks to prevent any person from making a claim under this part of the statute, is void.

10.4.8 The effect of such terms being voided is to make them unenforceable, but this does not apparently render the contract or agreement itself null and void. Instead, a person interested in an agreement containing such a void term may apply to a county court (or a sheriff court in Scotland) for an order modifying the agreement to take account of the effect of the term being void.[4] The court may make such an order as it thinks just and this may include provision as respects any period before the order was made.[5] The court may not make any such order unless the affected parties have been given notice of the application (subject to any rules of court to the contrary) and have been afforded an opportunity to make representations to the court.[6]

10.4.9 This provision concerning the validity of contract terms does not prevent parties to a dispute under Part 3 of the DDA 1995 settling legal proceedings by an agreement on terms. A Part 3 claim by a person in civil proceedings may be settled by an agreement that has the effect of excluding or limiting the operation of any provision of Part 3 or prevents a person from pursuing or continuing a claim under the DDA 1995.[7] It cannot, of course, require any person to do anything that would contravene the statute.

---

1   DDA 1995, Sch 3, para 6(1).

2   Ibid, Sch 3, para 6(2), as amended.

3   Ibid, s 26(1). However, that is not the case in relation to any term in a contract (or other agreement) for the provision of employment services: s 26(1A), as amended.

4   Ibid, s 26(3).

5   Ibid, s 26(6).

6   Ibid, s 26(4)–(5).

7   Ibid, s 26(2).

Remedies

10.4.10 In any proceedings in respect of discrimination in non-employment cases under Part 3 of the DDA 1995, any damages awarded by the court in respect of discrimination found to be unlawful may include compensation for injury to feelings.[1] Such a head of damages may be awarded alone or in tandem with compensation for other heads of loss. However, the DDA 1995 provides for the possibility that the amount of any damages awarded for injury to feelings shall not exceed a figure to be prescribed by regulations.[2] No such figure has been prescribed to date. If such a figure were to be prescribed in the future (which does not appear likely), it would not be a general ceiling on compensation that may be awarded in non-employment cases. It would be a limit only upon that element of any award that reflects injury to feelings.[3] The effect might be that any such limitation would ensure that the majority of litigation brought under Part 3 of the DDA 1995 would be pursued through the county court small claims procedure for claims under £5,000 (as seems likely, in any event).[4] At the other end of the scale, it is likely that the civil courts will follow the authorities on awards for injury to feelings in employment discrimination cases. An award of less than £750 would be unusual.[5]

10.4.11 Otherwise, the remedies available in civil proceedings under DDA 1995, Part 3 are those which are available in the High Court or, in Scotland, the Court of Session.[6] In appropriate cases, therefore, a successful claimant (or pursuer) may be enabled to seek a declaration of his or her rights or an injunction to prevent further or continuing acts of discrimination.

---

1   DDA 1995, s 25(2). In one of the few reported Part 3 cases, a county court awarded £1,000 for injury to feelings and £2,000 aggravated damages to a school pupil discriminated against in relation to a school holiday: *White v Clitheroe Royal Grammar School*, a 2002 decision of District Judge Ashton in Preston County Court reported in *Equal Opportunities Review* No 106 (June 2002), 26–28. The damages awarded contained a reduction for contributory conduct, but reflected the fact that the school had persisted in its discriminatory actions despite the protests of the pupil's parents and others. Other examples of Part 3 awards are noted briefly on the DRC website: www.drg-gb.org.

2   Ibid, Sch 3, para 7.

3   HL Deb, vol 566, col 1065.

4   Ibid, vol 565, cols 734–735.

5   *Purves v Joydisk Ltd* [2003] Scot SC 16, [2003] IRLR 420 (Sheriff Principal Iain McPhail QC). The court increased an award for injury to feelings from £350 to £1,000 in a case where a disabled person with a guide dog was refused service at a restaurant. In so doing, the court expressly referred to the case authorities, such as those cited at **10.3.31**.

6   DDA 1995, s 25(5).

10.5 EDUCATION CASES: SCHOOLS

Special Educational Needs and Disability Tribunal

10.5.1 In England and Wales, the new anti-discrimination provisions[1] applying to schools and disabled pupils (with the exception of claims relating to admissions or exclusion decisions) are enforceable in the SENDIST.[2] This is the new title of the former Special Educational Needs Tribunal.[3] Regulations may make provision about the proceedings of SENDIST on a claim of unlawful discrimination under Part 4, Chapter 1 of the DDA 1995 and the making of a claim.[4] The regulations may include particular provision:[5]

- as to the manner in which a claim must be made;
- for determining by which tribunal any claim is to be heard and for the transfer of proceedings from one tribunal to another;[6]
- for enabling functions which relate to matters preliminary or incidental to a claim to be performed by the President of the SENDIST or by the chairman of the tribunal;[7]
- for enabling hearings to be conducted in the absence of any member other than the chairman;
- as to the persons who may appear on behalf of the parties;
- for granting any person such disclosure or inspection of documents or right to further particulars as might be granted by a county court;[8]

---

1 See **7.4**.

2 See generally, Schools Code of Practice, Chapter 9. According to SENDIST, *Annual Report 2002–2003* (November 2003) in the first year of the new Part 4 provisions, only 104 claims were received, of which 78 were registered. These resulted in decisions in 10 claims, with 7 claims struck out. It appears that 81 claims were registered in 2003/2004.

3 DDA 1995, s 28H, inserted by SENDA 2001, s 17(1), as amended by Education Act 2002, s 195 and Sch 18. The SENDIST will continue to perform the existing jurisdiction of the Special Educational Needs Tribunal under Part 4 of the Education Act 1996. That jurisdiction (concerned with the special educational needs of pupils) is outside the scope of this book. The provisions which follow came into force on 1 September 2002: Special Educational Needs and Disability Act 2001 (Commencement No 5) Order 2002, SI 2002/2217. In Wales, SENDIST is known as the Special Educational Needs and Disability Tribunal for Wales.

4 DDA 1995, s 28J(1). Section 28J has been inserted into the DDA 1995 by SENDA 2001, s 19(1), as amended by Education Act 2002, s 195 and Sch 18.

5 DDA 1995, s 28J(2).

6 That is, if the jurisdiction of the SENDIST is being exercised by more than one tribunal.

7 Including, in particular, decisions under DDA 1995, Sch 3, para 10(3) (see below).

8 A person who without reasonable excuse fails to comply with such a requirement imposed by the regulations is guilty of an offence and is liable on summary conviction to a fine not exceeding level 3 on the standard scale: DDA 1995, s 28J(9)–(10).

- requiring persons to attend to give evidence and produce documents;[1]
- for authorising the administration of oaths to witnesses;
- for the determination of claims without a hearing in prescribed circumstances;
- as to the withdrawal of claims;
- for enabling the tribunal to stay proceedings on a claim;
- for the award of costs or expenses;
- for taxing or otherwise settling costs or expenses (and, in particular, for enabling costs to be taxed in the county court);
- for the registration and proof of decisions and orders; and
- for enabling prescribed decisions to be reviewed, or prescribed orders to be varied or revoked, in such circumstances as may be determined in accordance with the regulations.

Regulations have been made in the form of the Special Educational Needs and Disability Tribunal (General Provisions and Disability Claims Procedure) Regulations 2002.[2] Schedule 3, Part 3 of the DDA 1995, makes further provision about enforcement of Part 4, Chapter 1 of the DDA 1995 and about procedure.[3]

10.5.2 Proceedings before the SENDIST are to be held in private, except in prescribed circumstances.[4] The Secretary of State may pay such allowances for the purpose of or in connection with the attendance of persons at the SENDIST as he or she may, with the consent of the Treasury, determine.[5] Part 1 of the Arbitration Act 1996 does not apply to proceedings before the SENDIST, but regulations may make provision (in relation to such proceedings) corresponding to any provision of that Part.[6] The regulations may make provision for a claim under Part 4, Chapter 1 of the DDA 1995, to be heard, in prescribed circumstances, with an appeal under Part 4 of the Education Act 1996.[7]

Claim and remedies

10.5.3 A claim that a responsible body has discriminated against a person (A) in a way which is made unlawful under Part 4, Chapter 1 of

---

1   A person who without reasonable excuse fails to comply with such a requirement imposed by the regulations is guilty of an offence and is liable on summary conviction to a fine not exceeding level 3 on the standard scale: DDA 1995, s 28J(9)–(10).

2   SI 2002/1985, made under DDA 1995, s 28J(1)–(3), (8). An account of the practice and procedure of the tribunal is beyond the scope of this book.

3   DDA 1995, s 28J(11).

4   Ibid, s 28J(3).

5   Ibid, s 28J(5). In relation to Wales, the power conferred by s 28J(5) may be exercised only with the agreement of the National Assembly: s 28J(6).

6   Ibid, s 28J(7).

7   That is, an appeal under the SEN framework: ibid, s 28J(8). See Schools Code of Practice, paras 9.9–9.10.

the DDA 1995, may be made to the SENDIST by A's parent under s 28I.[1] This will include a claim where the responsible body is to be treated as having discriminated against a person (A) in such a way by virtue of being an employer or principal.[2] If the SENDIST considers that the claim is well founded it may declare that A has been unlawfully discriminated against and, if it does so, it may make such order as it considers reasonable in all the circumstances of the case.[3] The power to make such an order in particular may be exercised with a view to obviating or reducing the adverse effect on the person concerned of any matter to which the claim relates, but does not include power to order the payment of any sum by way of compensation.[4]

10.5.4 Special provision is made by s 28K of the DDA 1995 as to claims relating to admissions.[5] The provisions of s 28I do not apply to such claims.[6] Section 28K will apply if statutory arrangements (appeal arrangements) have been made[7] or a statutory agreement has been entered into between the responsible body for an academy and the Secretary of State[8] enabling an appeal to be made against the decision by A's parent.[9] If that condition is satisfied, then s 28K applies to a claim in relation to an 'admissions decision'[10] that a responsible body has discriminated against a person (A) in a way which is made unlawful under Part 4, Chapter 1 of the DDA 1995.[11] In such a case, the claim must be made under the appeal arrangements.[12] The body hearing the claim has the same powers as it has in relation to an appeal under the appeal arrangements.[13]

---

1   DDA 1995, s 28I(1). Section 28I was inserted by SENDA 2001, s 18, as amended by Education Act 2002, s 195 and Sch 18. It does not apply to claims to which s 28K or s 28L apply (admissions or exclusions): DDA 1995, s 28I(2).

2   Ibid, s 58.

3   Ibid, s 28I(3). See Schools Code of Practice, para 9.11 for examples of the kinds of order the SENDIST might make.

4   Ibid, s 28I(4).

5   Ibid, s 28K was inserted by SENDA 2001, s 20, as amended by Education Act 2002, s 16 and Sch 7.

6   Ibid, s 28I(2).

7   Under School Standards and Framework Act 1998, s 94.

8   Under Education Act 1996, s 482.

9   DDA 1995, s 28K(2).

10   An 'admissions decision' means a decision of a kind mentioned in the School Standards and Framework Act 1998, s 94(1) or (2), or a decision as to the admission of a person to a city academy taken by the responsible body or on its behalf: DDA 1995, s 28K(5).

11   DDA 1995, s 28K(1). This will include a claim where the responsible body is to be treated under s 58 as having discriminated against a person (A) in such a way by virtue of being an employer or principal.

12   Ibid, s 28K(3). See Schools Code of Practice, paras 9.14–9.20.

13   Ibid, s 28K(4).

10.5.5   Special provision is made by s 28L of the DDA 1995 as to claims relating to exclusions.[1] The provisions of s 28I do not apply to such claims.[2] Section 28L will apply if statutory arrangements (appeal arrangements) have been made[3] or a statutory agreement has been entered into between the responsible body for a city academy and the Secretary of State[4] enabling an appeal to be made against the decision by A or A's parent.[5] If that condition is satisfied, then s 28L applies to a claim in relation to an 'exclusion decision'[6] that a responsible body has discriminated against a person (A) in a way which is made unlawful under Part 4, Chapter 1 of the DDA 1995.[7] In such a case, the claim must be made under the appeal arrangements.[8] The body hearing the claim has the powers it has in relation to an appeal under the appeal arrangements.[9]

10.5.6   Except as provided for by ss 28I, 28K and 28L of the DDA 1995 as described above, no civil or criminal proceedings may be brought against any person in respect of an act merely because the act is unlawful under Part 4, Chapter 1 of the DDA 1995.[10] This does not prevent the making of an application for judicial review.

Time-limits

10.5.7   SENDIST shall not consider a claim under s 28I of the DDA 1995 unless proceedings in respect of the claim are instituted before the

---

1   DDA 1995, s 28L was inserted by SENDA 2001, s 21, as amended by Education Act 2002, s 215 and Sch 21. The meaning of an exclusion for the purpose of s 28L has been considered in *McAuley Catholic High School v (1) CC; (2) PC; and (3) Special Educational Needs and Disability Tribunal* [2003] EWHC 3045 (Admin), (2003) 6 CCLR 194. A temporary exclusion for a short fixed period did not exclude the subsequent jurisdiction of SENDIST under s 28I.

2   Ibid, s 28I(2).

3   Under Education Act 2002, s 52(3)(c).

4   Under Education Act 1996, s 482.

5   DDA 1995, s 28L(2).

6   An 'exclusion decision' means a decision of a kind mentioned the Education Act 2002, s 52(3)(c), or a decision not to reinstate a pupil who has been permanently excluded from an academy by its head teacher, taken by the responsible body or on its behalf: DDA 1995, s 28L(5). A responsible body in relation to a maintained school (as defined in s 28Q(5)) includes the discipline committee of the governing body if that committee is required to be established as a result of regulations made under Education Act 2002, s 19: DDA 1995, s 28L(6)–(7).

7   DDA 1995, s 28L(1). This will include a claim where the responsible body is to be treated under s 58 as having discriminated against a person (A) in such a way by virtue of being an employer or principal.

8   Ibid, s 28L(3). See Schools Code of Practice, paras 9.21–9.27.

9   Ibid, s 28L(4).

10   Ibid, Sch 3, Part 3, para 9. This Part of Sch 3 was inserted by SENDA 2001, s 19(2) and Sch 3, para 1.

end of the period of six months beginning when the act complained of was done.[1] However, if in relation to proceedings (or prospective proceedings) under s 28I the dispute concerned is referred for conciliation[2] before the end of that period of six months, the period is extended by two months.[3] Nevertheless, the SENDIST may consider a claim which is out of time if, in all the circumstances of the case, it considers that it is just and equitable to do so.[4] If an unlawful act of discrimination is attributable to a term in a contract, that act is to be treated as extending throughout the duration of the contract.[5] Any act extending over a period shall be treated as done at the end of that period.[6] A deliberate omission shall be treated as done when the person in question decided upon it.[7] In the absence of evidence establishing the contrary, a person shall be taken to decide upon an omission when he or she does an act inconsistent with doing the omitted act or (if he or she has done no such inconsistent act) when the period expires within which he or she might reasonably have been expected to do the omitted act if it was to be done.[8]

Roles of the Secretary of State and the Welsh Assembly

10.5.8 If the Secretary of State in England or the National Assembly in Wales (in both cases referred to as the 'appropriate authority') is satisfied (whether on a complaint or otherwise) that a responsible body has acted (or is proposing to act) unreasonably in the discharge of a duty imposed by or under s 28D or s 28E of the DDA 1995 (or has failed to discharge a duty imposed by or under either of those sections) the appropriate authority may give that body such directions as to the

---

1   DDA 1995, Sch 3, Part 3, para 10(1).

2   In pursuance of arrangements under DDA 1995, s 31B.

3   Ibid, Sch 3, Part 3, para 10(2).

4   Ibid, Sch 3, Part 3, para 10(3)–(4). But this does not permit the SENDIST to decide to consider a claim if a decision not to consider that claim has previously been taken under para 10(3).

5   Ibid, Sch 3, Part 3, para 10(5)(a).

6   Ibid, Sch 3, Part 3, para 10(5)(b).

7   Ibid, Sch 3, Part 3, para 10(5)(c).

8   Ibid, Sch 3, Part 3, para 10(6).

discharge of the duty as appear to it to be expedient.[1] Particular provision is made in relation to special schools which are not maintained special schools (but which are approved by the Secretary of State or by the National Assembly[2]) and also for city academies.[3] In relation to such special schools and city academies, if the appropriate authority is satisfied (whether on a complaint or otherwise) that a responsible body has acted (or is proposing to act) unreasonably in the discharge of a duty which that body has in relation to the provision to the appropriate authority of copies of that body's accessibility plan or the inspection of that plan, or has failed to discharge that duty, the appropriate authority may give that body such directions as to the discharge of the duty as appear to it to be expedient.[4]

10.5.9   Where the SENDIST has made an order under s 28I(3) of the DDA 1995,[5] if the Secretary of State is satisfied (whether on a complaint or otherwise) that the responsible body concerned has acted (or is proposing to act) unreasonably in complying with the order or has failed to comply with the order, he or she may give that body such directions as to compliance with the order as appear to him or her to be expedient.[6]

Enforcement in Scotland

10.5.10   The position in Scotland regarding the enforcement of rights under DDA 1995, Part 4, Chapter 1 is somewhat different and simpler

---

1   DDA 1995, s 28M(1), (8). Section 28M was inserted by SENDA 2001, s 22. Directions may be given even if the performance of the duty is contingent upon the opinion of the responsible body: DDA 1995, s 28M(4). Directions may be varied or revoked by the directing authority and may be enforced (on the application of the directing authority) by a mandatory order obtained in accordance with Supreme Court Act 1981, s 31: DDA 1995, s 28M(7). The term 'directing authority' means the Secretary of State in relation to a direction given by him or her, and the National Assembly in relation to a direction given by it: ibid, s 28M(9).

2   Under Education Act 1996, s 342.

3   DDA 1995, s 28M(2).

4   Ibid, s 28M(3). Directions may be given even if the performance of the duty is contingent upon the opinion of the responsible body: ibid, s 28M(4). Directions may be varied or revoked by the directing authority and may be enforced (on the application of the directing authority) by a mandatory order obtained in accordance with Supreme Court Act 1981, s 31: DDA 1995, s 28M(7). The term 'directing authority' means the Secretary of State in relation to a direction given by him or her, and the National Assembly in relation to a direction given by it: ibid, s 28M(9).

5   If SENDIST considers that a claim is well founded, it may declare that A has been unlawfully discriminated against and, if it does so, it may make such order as it considers reasonable in all the circumstances of the case.

6   DDA 1995, s 28M(5)–(6). Directions may be varied or revoked by the directing authority and may be enforced (on the application of the directing authority) by a mandatory order obtained in accordance with Supreme Court Act 1981, s 31: DDA 1995, s 28M(7). The

than the position in England and Wales,[1] although not necessarily more accessible. Section 28N of the DDA 1995 applies exclusively to Scotland.[2] A claim that a responsible body in Scotland has discriminated against a person in a way which is unlawful under Part 4 of the DDA 1995 may be made the subject of civil proceedings in the same way as any other claim for the enforcement of a statutory duty.[3] Proceedings in Scotland may be brought only in a sheriff court.[4] The remedies available in such proceedings are those which are available in the Court of Session other than an award of damages.[5] Financial compensation is not available, but a declaration of rights, an interdict or an order requiring positive action will be.[6]

Validity and revision of agreements of responsible bodies

10.5.11 Section 28P of the DDA 1995 makes provision for the validity and revision of agreements of responsible bodies.[7] By virtue of s 28P(1), any term in a contract or other agreement made by or on behalf of a responsible body is void so far as it purports to:

- require a person to do anything which would contravene any provision of (or made under);
- exclude or limit the operation of any provision of (or made under); or
- prevent any person from making a claim under,

Part 4, Chapter 1 of the DDA 1995.[8]

This does not prevent an agreement settling a claim under s 28I or s 28N or to which s 28K or s 28L apply.[9] On the application of any person

---

term 'directing authority' means the Secretary of State in relation to a direction given by him or her, and the National Assembly in relation to a direction given by it: ibid, s 28M(9).

1   See generally, Schools Code of Practice, Chapter 8.

2   Inserted by SENDA 2001, s 23.

3   DDA 1995, s 28N(1). This will include a claim where the responsible body is to be treated under s 58 as having discriminated against a person in such a way by virtue of being an employer or principal.

4   Ibid, s 28N(2).

5   Ibid, s 28N(3). Ibid, Sch 3, Part 3 makes further provision about enforcement in Scotland and about procedure: s 28N(4). In relation to civil proceedings in Scotland, in Sch 3, Part 3, references to ss 28I, 28K and 28L (or any of them) are to be construed as a reference to s 28N, and references to the SENDIST are to be construed as references to the sheriff court: s 28N(5).

6   Schools Code of Practice, paras 8.7–8.9. In an exclusion case, the sheriff court has the power to reduce (ie to annul or overturn) the decision to exclude.

7   Inserted by SENDA 2001, s 24. See Schools Code of Practice, paras 10.20–10.21.

8   DDA 1995, s 28P(1).

9   Ibid, s 28P(2).

interested in an agreement to which s 28P(1) applies, a county court (or a sheriff court in Scotland) may make such order as it thinks just for modifying the agreement to take account of the effect of s 28P(1).[1] No such order may be made unless all persons affected have been given notice of the application and afforded an opportunity to make representations to the court.[2] Such an order may include provision as respects any period before the making of the order.[3]

Conciliation

10.5.12   Section 31B of the DDA 1995 makes provision for conciliation for disputes arising in education cases.[4] The DRC may make arrangements with any other person for the provision of conciliation services by that person in connection with disputes (or by persons appointed by that person).[5] In deciding what arrangements (if any) to make, the DRC must have regard to the desirability of securing, so far as reasonably practicable, that conciliation services are available for all disputes which the parties may wish to refer to conciliation.[6] The DRC's independent conciliation services have been extended to cover education.[7]

10.5.13   No member or employee of the DRC may provide conciliation services in connection with disputes.[8] The Commission must ensure that the statutory arrangements for conciliation include appropriate safeguards to prevent the disclosure to members or employees of the DRC of information obtained by any person in connection with the provision of conciliation services in accordance with the arrangements.[9] This does not apply to information which is disclosed with the consent of the parties to the dispute to which it relates.[10] It also does not apply to information which does not identify a particular dispute or a particular

---

1   DDA 1995, s 28P(3).

2   Ibid, s 28P(4), subject to any rules of court providing for notice to be dispensed with: s 28P(5).

3   Ibid, s 28P(6).

4   Inserted by SENDA 2001, s 37.

5   DDA 1995, s 31B(1). 'Conciliation services' means advice and assistance provided to the parties to a dispute, by a conciliator, with a view to promoting its settlement otherwise than through a court, tribunal or other body: ibid, s 31B(8). 'Dispute' means a dispute arising under DDA 1995, Part 4, Chapter 1 or 2 concerning an allegation of discrimination: s 31B(9). 'Discrimination' means anything which is made unlawful discrimination by a provision of DDA 1995, Part 4, Chapter 1 or 2: s 31B(10).

6   DDA 1995, s 31B(2).

7   Schools Code of Practice, paras 9.28–9.31 (England and Wales) and paras 8.10–8.12 (Scotland).

8   DDA 1995, s 31B(3).

9   Ibid, s 31B(4).

10   Ibid, s 31B(5).

person and is reasonably required by the DRC for the purpose of monitoring the operation of the arrangements concerned.[1] Anything communicated to a person providing conciliation services in accordance with arrangements under DDA 1995, s 31B is not admissible in evidence in any proceedings except with the consent of the person who communicated it.[2]

10.6   EDUCATION CASES: FURTHER AND HIGHER EDUCATION

10.6.1   Section 28V of the DDA 1995 makes provision for the enforcement of the new anti-discrimination rights in further and higher education.[3] A claim by a person that a responsible body has discriminated against him or her in a way which is unlawful under Part 4, Chapter 2 of the DDA 1995 may be made the subject of civil proceedings in the same way as any other claim in tort or (in Scotland) in reparation for breach of statutory duty.[4] Proceedings in England and Wales may be brought only in a county court, whereas proceedings in Scotland may be brought only in a sheriff court.[5] The fact that a person who brings proceedings under Part 4, Chapter 2 of the DDA 1995 (the education provisions) against a responsible body may also be entitled to bring proceedings against that body under Part 2 (the employment provisions) does not affect the proceedings under Part 4.[6] No civil or criminal proceedings may be brought against any person in respect of an act merely because the act is unlawful under Part 4, Chapter 2 of the DDA 1995, but this does not prevent the making of an application for judicial review.[7]

Time-limits

10.6.2   A county court (or a sheriff court in Scotland) shall not consider a claim under s 28V of the DDA 1995 unless proceedings in

---

1   DDA 1995, s 31B(6).

2   Ibid, s 31B(7).

3   Inserted by SENDA, 2001, s 30(1). DDA 1995, Sch 3, Part 4 (inserted by SENDA 2001, s 30(2) and Sch 3, para 2) makes further provision about the enforcement and about procedure: s 28V(7). See generally Post-16 Code of Practice, Chapter 9.

4   DDA 1995, s 28V(1). This includes a claim that a responsible body is by virtue of ibid, s 57 (aiding unlawful acts) or s 58 (liability of employers and principals) to be treated as having discriminated against him or her in such a way, or that a person is by virtue of s 57 (aiding unlawful acts) to be treated as having discriminated against him in such a way.

5   Ibid, s 28V(3)–(4).

6   Ibid, s 28V(6). See Post-16 Code of Practice, para 9.6.

7   Ibid, Sch 3, Part 4, para 12.

respect of the claim are instituted before the end of the period of six
months beginning when the act complained of was done.[1] If, in relation
to proceedings (or prospective proceedings) under s 28V, the dispute
concerned is referred for conciliation[2] before the end of that period of
six months, the period allowed shall be extended by two months.[3] A
court may consider any claim under s 28V which is out of time if, in all
the circumstances of the case, it considers that it is just and equitable to
do so.[4] If an unlawful act of discrimination is attributable to a term in a
contract, that act is to be treated as extending throughout the duration
of the contract.[5] Any act extending over a period shall be treated as done
at the end of that period.[6] A deliberate omission shall be treated as done
when the person in question decided upon it.[7] In the absence of
evidence establishing the contrary, a person shall be taken to decide
upon an omission when he or she does an act inconsistent with doing
the omitted act or, if he or she has done no such inconsistent act, when
the period expires within which he or she might reasonably have been
expected to do the omitted act if it was to be done.[8]

Remedies

10.6.3   The remedies available in proceedings brought under Part 4,
Chapter 2 of the DDA 1995 are those which are available in the High
Court or (in Scotland) the Court of Session.[9] These will include a
declaration of rights, an injunction (an interdict in Scotland) and
damages. Damages may include compensation for injury to feelings
(whether or not they include compensation under any other head).[10]

Validity and revision of agreements of responsible bodies

10.6.4   Section 28P of the DDA 1995 makes provision for the validity
and revision of agreements of responsible bodies.[11] This applies equally

---

1   DDA 1995, Sch 3, Part 4, para 13(1).

2   In pursuance of arrangements under ibid, s 31B.

3   Ibid, Sch 3, Part 4, para 13(2).

4   Ibid, Sch 3, Part 4, para 13(3).

5   Ibid, Sch 3, Part 4, para 13(3)(a).

6   Ibid, Sch 3, Part 4, para 13(3)(c).

7   Ibid, Sch 3, Part 4, para 13(3)(a).

8   Ibid, Sch 3, Part 4, para 13(4).

9   Ibid, s 27V(5). See Post-16 Code of Practice, para 9.5.

10 Ibid, s 28V(2). The amount of any damages awarded as compensation for injury to feelings
    shall not exceed a prescribed amount: ibid, Sch 3, Part 4, para 14. No maximum amount
    has been prescribed.

11 Inserted by SENDA 2001, s 24. See **10.5.11**.

to claims brought against responsible bodies in further and higher education as it does in relation to schools.[1]

Conciliation

10.6.5 Section 31B of the DDA 1995 makes provision for conciliation for disputes arising in education cases.[2] The DRC's independent conciliation services have been extended to cover education and apply equally in the present context.[3]

10.7 DISABILITY DISCRIMINATION BILL

10.7.1 In its final report, the DRTF made a number of recommendations for the future reform of employment tribunal powers and procedures in relation to the DDA 1995.[4] It suggested that employment tribunals should be able to order re-instatement or re-engagement in disability-related dismissal cases and be empowered to make enforceable recommendations regarding the future conduct of an employer found liable for discrimination. The DRTF recommended that the time-limits for completing the pre-proceedings statutory questionnaire should be fine-tuned and that, wherever possible, a tribunal hearing a DDA case should include at least one person with disability expertise. Those recommendations were taken up by the DRC.[5] The Government indicated its intention to act when the legislative timetable permitted.[6]

10.7.2 That opportunity has now come with the Disability Discrimination Bill, but many of the DRTF recommendations in this area have been largely ignored. If enacted, the Bill will extend s 56 of the DDA 1995 so as to provide a procedure for questions and replies for claims under Part 3 of the Act, similar to that already in place for Part 2 claims.[7]

---

1 DDA 1995, s 28X. See Post-16 Code of Practice, paras 8.11–8.12.

2 Inserted by SENDA 2001, s 37. See **10.5.12**.

3 Post-16 Code of Practice, paras 9.3–9.4.

4 Disability Rights Task Force, *From Exclusion to Inclusion: A Report of the Disability Rights Task Force for Disabled People* (1999, London: DfEE), Chapter 3.

5 *Legislative Review: First Review of the Disability Discrimination Act 1995: Consultation* (Disability Rights Commission, May 2002).

6 *Towards Inclusion – Civil Rights for Disabled People: Government Response to the Disability Rights Task Force* (DfEE, March 2001), para 3.51. See also: Department for Work and Pensions, *Draft Disability Discrimination Bill*, Cm 6058 (December 2003); Joint Committee on the Draft Disability Discrimination Bill, *First Report* (April 2004); Department for Work and Pensions, *The Government's Response to the Report of the Joint Committee on the Draft Disability Discrimination Bill*, Cm 6276 (July 2004).

7 See Department of Work and Pensions, *Disability Discrimination Bill: Consultation on private clubs; premises; the definition of disability; and the questions procedure*, Cm 6402 (December 2004).

Various procedural amendments are made in order to reflect the expansion of the scope of the DDA 1995 effected elsewhere.

Appendix I

DISABILITY DISCRIMINATION ACT 1995
(1995 c. 50)

(AS AMENDED)

ARRANGEMENT OF SECTIONS

PART I

DISABILITY

Section		Page
1	Meaning of 'disability' and 'disabled person'	377
2	Past disabilities	377
3	Guidance	377

PART II

THE EMPLOYMENT FIELD

Meaning of 'discrimination' and 'harassment'

3A	Meaning of 'discrimination'	379
3B	Meaning of 'harassment'	380
4	Employers: discrimination and harassment	380
4A	Employers: duty to make adjustments	381
4B	Contract workers	382
4C	Office-holders: introductory	383
4D	Office-holders: discrimination and harassment	384
4E	Office-holders: duty to make adjustments	385
4F	Office-holders: supplementary	386

Occupational pension schemes

4G	Occupational pension schemes: non-discrimination rule	387
4H	Occupational pension schemes: duty to make adjustments	388
4I	Occupational pension schemes: procedure	388
4J	Occupational pension schemes: remedies	388
4K	Occupational pension schemes: supplementary	389
5	(*repealed*)	
6	(*repealed*)	
6A	Partnerships: discrimination and harassment	390
6B	Partnerships: duty to make adjustments	391
6C	Partnerships: supplementary	391

7   (*repealed*)

Barristers and advocates

7A Barristers: discrimination and harassment   392
7B Barristers: duty to make adjustments   393
7C Advocates: discrimination and harassment   393
7D Advocates: duty to make adjustments   394
8   (*repealed*)
9   (*repealed*)
10   (*repealed*)
11   (*repealed*)
12   (*repealed*)

Trade and professional bodies

13   Trade organisations: discrimination and harassment   396
14   Trade organisations: duty to make adjustments   396
14A Qualifications bodies: discrimination and harassment   397
14B Qualifications bodies: duty to make adjustments   398

Practical work experience

14C Practical work experience: discrimination and harassment   399
14D Practical work experience: duty to make adjustments   399
15   (*repealed*)
16   (*repealed*)

Other unlawful acts

16A Relationships which have come to an end   401
16B Discriminatory advertisements   401
16C Instructions and pressure to discriminate   402
17   (*repealed*)

Enforcement etc

17A Enforcement, remedies and procedure   403
17B Enforcement of sections 16B and 16C   404
17C Validity of contracts, collective agreements and rules of undertakings   405
18   Insurance services   405

Supplementary and general

18A Alterations to premises occupied under leases   406
18B Reasonable adjustments: supplementary   407

18C Charities and support for particular groups of persons   408
18D Interpretation of Part 2   409

PART III

DISCRIMINATION IN OTHER AREAS

Goods, facilities and services

19   Discrimination in relation to goods, facilities and services   409
20   Meaning of 'discrimination'   410
21   Duty of providers of services to make adjustments   412
21A Employment services   413

Premises

22   Discrimination in relation to premises   414
23   Exemption for small dwellings   415
24   Meaning of 'discrimination'   416

Enforcement, etc

25   Enforcement, remedies and procedure   417
26   Validity and revision of certain agreements   418
27   Alterations to premises occupied under leases   418
28   Conciliation of disputes   419

PART 4

EDUCATION

Chapter 1
Schools

Duties of responsible bodies

28A Discrimination against disabled pupils and prospective pupils   420
28B Meaning of 'discrimination'   420
28C Disabled pupils not to be substantially disadvantaged   421
28D Accessibility strategies and plans   422
28E Accessibility strategies and plans: procedure   424

Residual duty of education authorities

28F Duty of education authorities not to discriminate   425
28G Residual duty: supplementary provisions   426

Enforcement: England and Wales

28H Tribunals   426
28I   Jurisdiction and powers of the Tribunal   427
28J   Procedure   427
28K Admissions   429
28L Exclusions   429
28M Roles of the Secretary of State and the National Assembly   430

Enforcement: Scotland

28N Civil proceedings   431

Agreements relating to enforcement

28P Validity and revision of agreements of responsible bodies   432

Interpretation of Chapter 1

28Q Interpretation   433

Chapter 2
Further and Higher Education

Duties of responsible bodies

28R Discrimination against disabled students and prospective students   434
28S Meaning of 'discrimination'   435
28T Disabled students not to be substantially disadvantaged   436

Other providers of further education or training facilities

28U Further education etc provided by local education authorities and schools 437

Enforcement, etc

28V Enforcement, remedies and procedure   438
28W Occupation of premises by educational institutions   438
28X Validity and revision of agreements   439
29   (*repealed*)

Duties of funding councils

30   Further and higher education of disabled persons   439
31   Further and higher education of disabled persons: Scotland   440

Interpretation of Chapter 2

31A Interpretation 440

Chapter 3
Supplementary

31B Conciliation for disputes 440
31C Application to Isles of Scilly 441

PART V

PUBLIC TRANSPORT

Taxis

32   Taxi accessibility regulations 442
33   Designated transport facilities 443
34   New licences conditional on compliance with taxi accessibility regulations 443
35   Exemption from taxi accessibility regulations 443
36   Carrying of passengers in wheelchairs 444
37   Carrying of guide dogs and hearing dogs 445
37A Carrying of assistance dogs in private hire vehicles 446
38   Appeal against refusal of exemption certificate 448
39   Requirements as to disabled passengers in Scotland 448

Public service vehicles

40   PSV accessibility regulations 449
41   Accessibility certificates 450
42   Approval certificates 450
43   Special authorisations 451
44   Reviews and appeals 451
45   Fees 451

Rail vehicles

46   Rail vehicle accessibility regulations 452
47   Exemption from rail vehicle accessibility regulations 453

Supplemental

48   Offences by bodies corporate etc 454
49   Forgery and false statements 454

PART VI

THE NATIONAL DISABILITY COUNCIL

50   (*repealed*)
51   *Codes of practice prepared by the Council*
52   *Further provision about codes issued under section 51*

PART VII

SUPPLEMENTAL

53A   Codes of practice   455
53   *Codes of practice prepared by the Secretary of State*
54   *Further provision about codes issued under section 53*
55   Victimisation   457
56   Help for persons suffering discrimination   458
57   Aiding unlawful acts   459
58   Liability of employers and principals   460
59   Statutory authority and national security etc   460

PART VIII

MISCELLANEOUS

60   Appointment by Secretary of State of advisers   461
61   Amendment of Disabled Persons (Employment) Act 1944   461
62,
63   (*repealed*)
64   Application to Crown etc   463
64A   Police   464
65   Application to Parliament   466
66   (*repealed*)
67   Regulations and orders   466
68   Interpretation   467
69   Financial provisions   469
70   Short title, commencement, extent etc   469

      SCHEDULES:
          Schedule 1—Provisions Supplementing Section 1   470
          Schedule 2—Past Disabilities   473
          Schedule 3—Enforcement and Procedure   474
              Part I—Employment   474
              Part II—Discrimination in Other Areas   475
              Part 3—Discrimination in Schools   476
              Part 4—Discrimination in Further and Higher Education
                  Institutions   478
          Schedule 3A—Validity of Contracts, Collective Agreements and Rules of
                  Undertakings   480
          Schedule 4—Premises Occupied Under Leases   484
              Part I—Occupation by Employer   484
              Part II—Occupation by Provider of Services   486
              Part 3—Occupation by Educational Institutions   488

Schedule 4A—Responsible Bodies for Schools 490
Schedule 4B—Responsible Bodies for Educational Institutions 491
Schedule 4C—Modifications of Chapter 2 of Part 4 492
      Part 1—Modifications for England and Wales 492
      Part 2—Modifications for Scotland 494
Schedule 5—(*repealed*)
Schedule 6—Consequential Amendments 495
Schedule 7—Repeals 496
Schedule 8—Modifications of this Act in its Application to Northern
      Ireland 497

An Act to make it unlawful to discriminate against disabled persons in connection with employment, the provision of goods, facilities and services or the disposal or management of premises; to make provision about the employment of disabled persons; and to establish a National Disability Council.
[8 November 1995]

PART I

DISABILITY

1 Meaning of 'disability' and 'disabled person'

(1) Subject to the provisions of Schedule 1, a person has a disability for the purposes of this Act if he has a physical or mental impairment which has a substantial and long-term adverse effect on his ability to carry out normal day-to-day activities.

(2) In this Act 'disabled person' means a person who has a disability.

2 Past disabilities

(1) The provisions of this Part and Parts II to 4 apply in relation to a person who has had a disability as they apply in relation to a person who has that disability.

(2) Those provisions are subject to the modifications made by Schedule 2.

(3) Any regulations or order made under this Act may include provision with respect to persons who have had a disability.

(4) In any proceedings under Part II, 3 or 4 of this Act, the question whether a person had a disability at a particular time ('the relevant time') shall be determined, for the purposes of this section, as if the provisions of, or made under, this Act in force when the act complained of was done had been in force at the relevant time.

(5) The relevant time may be a time before the passing of this Act.

Amendment – Amended by Special Educational Needs and Disability Act 2001, s 38(1), (2).

---

3 Guidance

(1) The Secretary of State may issue guidance about the matters to be taken into account in determining—

    (a)   whether an impairment has a substantial adverse effect on a person's ability to carry out normal day-to-day activities; or

    (b)   whether such an impairment has a long-term effect.

(2) The guidance may, among other things, give examples of—

    (a)   effects which it would be reasonable, in relation to particular activities, to regard for purposes of this Act as substantial adverse effects;

    (b)   effects which it would not be reasonable, in relation to particular activities, to regard for such purposes as substantial adverse effects;

    (c)   substantial adverse effects which it would be reasonable to regard, for such purposes, as long-term;

    (d)   substantial adverse effects which it would not be reasonable to regard, for such purposes, as long-term.

(3) An adjudicating body determining, for any purpose of this Act, whether an impairment has a substantial and long-term adverse effect on a person's ability to carry out normal day-to-day activities, shall take into account any guidance which appears to it to be relevant.

(3A) 'Adjudicating body' means—

    (a)   a court;

    (b)   a tribunal; and

    (c)   any other person who, or body which, may decide a claim under Part 4.

(4) In preparing a draft of any guidance, the Secretary of State shall consult such persons as he considers appropriate.

(5) Where the Secretary of State proposes to issue any guidance, he shall publish a draft of it, consider any representations that are made to him about the draft and, if he thinks it appropriate, modify his proposals in the light of any of those representations.

(6) If the Secretary of State decides to proceed with any proposed guidance, he shall lay a draft of it before each House of Parliament.

(7) If, within the 40-day period, either House resolves not to approve the draft, the Secretary of State shall take no further steps in relation to the proposed guidance.

(8) If no such resolution is made within the 40-day period, the Secretary of State shall issue the guidance in the form of his draft.

(9) The guidance shall come into force on such date as the Secretary of State may appoint by order.

(10) Subsection (7) does not prevent a new draft of the proposed guidance from being laid before Parliament.

(11) The Secretary of State may—

    (a)   from time to time revise the whole or part of any guidance and re-issue it;

    (b)   by order revoke any guidance.

(12) In this section—

    '40-day period', in relation to the draft of any proposed guidance, means—

        (a)   if the draft is laid before one House on a day later than the day on which it is laid before the other House, the period of 40 days beginning with the later of the two days, and

        (b)   in any other case, the period of 40 days beginning with the day on which the draft is laid before each House, no account being taken of any period during which Parliament is dissolved or prorogued or during which both Houses are adjourned for more than 4 days; and

'guidance' means guidance issued by the Secretary of State under this section and includes guidance which has been revised and re-issued.

Amendment – Amended by Special Educational Needs and Disability Act 2001, s 38(1), (3), (4).

PART II

THE EMPLOYMENT FIELD

Meaning of 'discrimination' and 'harassment'

Amendment – Amended by Disability Discrimination Act 1995 (Amendment) Regulations 2003, SI 2003/ 1673, regs 3(1), 4(1), (2).

3A Meaning of 'discrimination'

(1) For the purposes of this Part, a person discriminates against a disabled person if—

  (a)   for a reason which relates to the disabled person's disability, he treats him less favourably than he treats or would treat others to whom that reason does not or would not apply, and

  (b)   he cannot show that the treatment in question is justified.

(2) For the purposes of this Part, a person also discriminates against a disabled person if he fails to comply with a duty to make reasonable adjustments imposed on him in relation to the disabled person.

(3) Treatment is justified for the purposes of subsection (1)(b) if, but only if, the reason for it is both material to the circumstances of the particular case and substantial.

(4) But treatment of a disabled person cannot be justified under subsection (3) if it amounts to direct discrimination falling within subsection (5).

(5) A person directly discriminates against a disabled person if, on the ground of the disabled person's disability, he treats the disabled person less favourably than he treats or would treat a person not having that particular disability whose relevant circumstances, including his abilities, are the same as, or not materially different from, those of the disabled person.

(6) If, in a case falling within subsection (1), a person is under a duty to make reasonable adjustments in relation to a disabled person but fails to comply with that duty, his treatment of that person cannot be justified under subsection (3) unless it would have been justified even if he had complied with that duty.

Amendment – Inserted by Disability Discrimination Act 1995 (Amendment) Regulations 2003, SI 2003/1673, regs 3(1), 4(2).

3B Meaning of 'harassment'

(1) For the purposes of this Part, a person subjects a disabled person to harassment where, for a reason which relates to the disabled person's disability, he engages in unwanted conduct which has the purpose or effect of—

- (a) violating the disabled person's dignity, or
- (b) creating an intimidating, hostile, degrading, humiliating or offensive environment for him.

(2) Conduct shall be regarded as having the effect referred to in paragraph (a) or (b) of subsection (1) only if, having regard to all the circumstances, including in particular the perception of the disabled person, it should reasonably be considered as having that effect.

Amendment – Inserted by Disability Discrimination Act 1995 (Amendment) Regulations 2003, SI 2003/1673, regs 3(1), 4(2).

Employment

Amendment – Inserted by Disability Discrimination Act 1995 (Amendment) Regulations 2003, SI 2003/1673, regs 3(1), 5.

---

4 Employers: discrimination and harassment

(1) It is unlawful for an employer to discriminate against a disabled person—

- (a) in the arrangements which he makes for the purpose of determining to whom he should offer employment;
- (b) in the terms on which he offers that person employment; or
- (c) by refusing to offer, or deliberately not offering, him employment.

(2) It is unlawful for an employer to discriminate against a disabled person whom he employs—

- (a) in the terms of employment which he affords him;
- (b) in the opportunities which he affords him for promotion, a transfer, training or receiving any other benefit;
- (c) by refusing to afford him, or deliberately not affording him, any such opportunity; or
- (d) by dismissing him, or subjecting him to any other detriment.

(3) It is also unlawful for an employer, in relation to employment by him, to subject to harassment—

- (a) a disabled person whom he employs; or
- (b) a disabled person who has applied to him for employment.

(4) Subsection (2) does not apply to benefits of any description if the employer is concerned with the provision (whether or not for payment) of benefits of that

description to the public, or to a section of the public which includes the employee in question, unless—

(a)   that provision differs in a material respect from the provision of the benefits by the employer to his employees;

(b)   the provision of the benefits to the employee in question is regulated by his contract of employment; or

(c)   the benefits relate to training.

(5) The reference in subsection (2)(d) to the dismissal of a person includes a reference—

(a)   to the termination of that person's employment by the expiration of any period (including a period expiring by reference to an event or circumstance), not being a termination immediately after which the employment is renewed on the same terms; and

(b)   to the termination of that person's employment by any act of his (including the giving of notice) in circumstances such that he is entitled to terminate it without notice by reason of the conduct of the employer.

(6) This section applies only in relation to employment at an establishment in Great Britain.

Amendment – Amended by Disability Discrimination Act 1995 (Amendment) Regulations 2003, SI 2003/1673, regs 3(1), 5.

4A   Employers: duty to make adjustments

(1) Where—

(a)   a provision, criterion or practice applied by or on behalf of an employer, or

(b)   any physical feature of premises occupied by the employer,

places the disabled person concerned at a substantial disadvantage in comparison with persons who are not disabled, it is the duty of the employer to take such steps as it is reasonable, in all the circumstances of the case, for him to have to take in order to prevent the provision, criterion or practice, or feature, having that effect.

(2) In subsection (1), 'the disabled person concerned' means—

(a)   in the case of a provision, criterion or practice for determining to whom employment should be offered, any disabled person who is, or has notified the employer that he may be, an applicant for that employment;

(b)   in any other case, a disabled person who is—

(i)   an applicant for the employment concerned, or

(ii)   an employee of the employer concerned.

(3) Nothing in this section imposes any duty on an employer in relation to a disabled person if the employer does not know, and could not reasonably be expected to know—

(a)   in the case of an applicant or potential applicant, that the disabled person concerned is, or may be, an applicant for the employment; or

(b)   in any case, that that person has a disability and is likely to be affected in the way mentioned in subsection (1).

Amendment – Inserted by Disability Discrimination Act 1995 (Amendment) Regulations 2003, SI 2003/1673, regs 3(1), 5.

4B Contract workers

(1) It is unlawful for a principal, in relation to contract work, to discriminate against a disabled person who is a contract worker (a 'disabled contract worker')—

(a)   in the terms on which he allows him to do that work;

(b)   by not allowing him to do it or continue to do it;

(c)   in the way he affords him access to any benefits or by refusing or deliberately omitting to afford him access to them; or

(d)   by subjecting him to any other detriment.

(2) It is also unlawful for a principal, in relation to contract work, to subject a disabled contract worker to harassment.

(3) Subsection (1) does not apply to benefits of any description if the principal is concerned with the provision (whether or not for payment) of benefits of that description to the public, or to a section of the public which includes the contract worker in question, unless that provision differs in a material respect from the provision of the benefits by the principal to contract workers.

(4) This subsection applies to a disabled contract worker where, by virtue of—

(a)   a provision, criterion or practice applied by or on behalf of all or most of the principals to whom he is or might be supplied, or

(b)   a physical feature of premises occupied by such persons,

he is likely, on each occasion when he is supplied to a principal to do contract work, to be placed at a substantial disadvantage in comparison with persons who are not disabled which is the same or similar in each case.

(5) Where subsection (4) applies to a disabled contract worker, his employer must take such steps as he would have to take under section 4A if the provision, criterion or practice were applied by him or on his behalf or (as the case may be) if the premises were occupied by him.

(6) Section 4A applies to any principal, in relation to contract work, as if he were, or would be, the employer of the disabled contract worker and as if any contract worker supplied to do work for him were an employee of his.

(7) However, for the purposes of section 4A as applied by subsection (6), a principal is not required to take a step in relation to a disabled contract worker if under that section the disabled contract worker's employer is required to take the step in relation to him.

(8) This section applies only in relation to contract work done at an establishment in Great Britain (the provisions of section 68 about the meaning of 'employment at an establishment in Great Britain' applying for the purposes of this subsection with the appropriate modifications).

(9) In this section—

'principal' means a person ('A') who makes work available for doing by individuals who are employed by another person who supplies them under a contract made with A;

'contract work' means work so made available; and

'contract worker' means any individual who is supplied to the principal under such a contract.

Amendment – Inserted by Disability Discrimination Act 1995 (Amendment) Regulations 2003, SI 2003/1673, regs 3(1), 5.

4C   Office-holders: introductory

(1) Subject to subsection (5), sections 4D and 4E apply to an office or post if—

(a)   no relevant provision of this Part applies in relation to an appointment to the office or post; and

(b)   one or more of the conditions specified in subsection (3) is satisfied.

(2) The following are relevant provisions of this Part for the purposes of subsection (1)(a): section 4, section 4B, section 6A, section 7A, section 7C and section 14C.

(3) The conditions specified in this subsection are that—

(a)   the office or post is one to which persons are appointed to discharge functions personally under the direction of another person, and in respect of which they are entitled to remuneration;

(b)   the office or post is one to which appointments are made by a Minister of the Crown, a government department, the National Assembly for Wales or any part of the Scottish Administration;

(c)   the office or post is one to which appointments are made on the recommendation of, or subject to the approval of, a person referred to in paragraph (b).

(4) For the purposes of subsection (3)(a) the holder of an office or post—

(a)   is to be regarded as discharging his functions under the direction of another person if that other person is entitled to direct him as to when and where he discharges those functions;

(b)   is not to be regarded as entitled to remuneration merely because he is entitled to payments—

(i) in respect of expenses incurred by him in carrying out the functions of the office or post, or

(ii) by way of compensation for the loss of income or benefits he would or might have received from any person had he not been carrying out the functions of the office or post.

(5) Sections 4D and 4E do not apply to—

(a)   any office of the House of Commons held by a member of it,

(b)   a life peerage within the meaning of the Life Peerages Act 1958, or any office of the House of Lords held by a member of it,

(c)   any office mentioned in Schedule 2 (Ministerial offices) to the House of Commons Disqualification Act 1975,

(d)   the offices of Leader of the Opposition, Chief Opposition Whip or Assistant Opposition Whip within the meaning of the Ministerial and other Salaries Act 1975,

    (e)   any office of the Scottish Parliament held by a member of it,

    (f)   a member of the Scottish Executive within the meaning of section 44 of the Scotland Act 1998, or a junior Scottish Minister within the meaning of section 49 of that Act,

    (g)   any office of the National Assembly for Wales held by a member of it,

    (h)   in England, any office of a county council, a London borough council, a district council or a parish council held by a member of it,

    (i)   in Wales, any office of a county council, a county borough council or a community council held by a member of it,

    (j)   in relation to a council constituted under section 2 of the Local Government etc (Scotland) Act 1994 or a community council established under section 51 of the Local Government (Scotland) Act 1973, any office of such a council held by a member of it,

    (k)   any office of the Greater London Authority held by a member of it,

    (l)   any office of the Common Council of the City of London held by a member of it,

    (m)   any office of the Council of the Isles of Scilly held by a member of it, or

    (n)   any office of a political party.

Amendment – Inserted by Disability Discrimination Act 1995 (Amendment) Regulations 2003, SI 2003/1673, regs 3(1), 5.

4D   Office-holders: discrimination and harassment

(1) It is unlawful for a relevant person, in relation to an appointment to an office or post to which this section applies, to discriminate against a disabled person—

    (a)   in the arrangements which he makes for the purpose of determining who should be offered the appointment;

    (b)   in the terms on which he offers him the appointment; or

    (c)   by refusing to offer him the appointment.

(2) It is unlawful for a relevant person, in relation to an appointment to an office or post to which this section applies and which satisfies the condition set out in section 4C(3)(c), to discriminate against a disabled person—

    (a)   in the arrangements which he makes for the purpose of determining who should be recommended or approved in relation to the appointment; or

    (b)   in making or refusing to make a recommendation, or giving or refusing to give an approval, in relation to the appointment.

(3) It is unlawful for a relevant person, in relation to a disabled person who has been appointed to an office or post to which this section applies, to discriminate against him—

    (a)   in the terms of the appointment;

    (b)   in the opportunities which he affords him for promotion, a transfer, training or receiving any other benefit, or by refusing to afford him any such opportunity;

    (c)   by terminating the appointment; or

    (d)   by subjecting him to any other detriment in relation to the appointment.

(4) It is also unlawful for a relevant person, in relation to an office or post to which this section applies, to subject to harassment a disabled person—

    (a)   who has been appointed to the office or post;

(b)　who is seeking or being considered for appointment to the office or post; or

(c)　who is seeking or being considered for a recommendation or approval in relation to an appointment to an office or post satisfying the condition set out in section 4C(3)(c).

(5) Subsection (3) does not apply to benefits of any description if the relevant person is concerned with the provision (for payment or not) of benefits of that description to the public, or a section of the public to which the disabled person belongs, unless—

(a)　that provision differs in a material respect from the provision of the benefits to persons appointed to offices or posts which are the same as, or not materially different from, that to which the disabled person has been appointed;

(b)　the provision of the benefits to the person appointed is regulated by the terms and conditions of his appointment; or

(c)　the benefits relate to training.

(6) In subsection (3)(c) the reference to the termination of the appointment includes a reference—

(a)　to the termination of the appointment by the expiration of any period (including a period expiring by reference to an event or circumstance), not being a termination immediately after which the appointment is renewed on the same terms and conditions; and

(b)　to the termination of the appointment by any act of the person appointed (including the giving of notice) in circumstances such that he is entitled to terminate the appointment by reason of the conduct of the relevant person.

(7) In this section—

(a)　references to making a recommendation include references to making a negative recommendation; and

(b)　references to refusal include references to deliberate omission.

Amendment – Inserted by Disability Discrimination Act 1995 (Amendment) Regulations 2003, SI 2003/1673, regs 3(1), 5.

4E　Office-holders: duty to make adjustments

(1) Where—

(a)　a provision, criterion or practice applied by or on behalf of a relevant person, or

(b)　any physical feature of premises—
　　(i)　under the control of a relevant person, and
　　(ii)　at or from which the functions of an office or post to which this section applies are performed,

places the disabled person concerned at a substantial disadvantage in comparison with persons who are not disabled, it is the duty of the relevant person to take such steps as it is reasonable, in all the circumstances of the case, for him to have to take in order to prevent the provision, criterion or practice, or feature, having that effect.

(2) In this section, 'the disabled person concerned' means—

(a)　in the case of a provision, criterion or practice for determining who should be appointed to, or recommended or approved in relation to, an office or post to which this section applies, any disabled person who—

(i) is, or has notified the relevant person that he may be, seeking appointment to, or (as the case may be) seeking a recommendation or approval in relation to, that office or post, or

(ii) is being considered for appointment to, or (as the case may be) for a recommendation or approval in relation to, that office or post;

(b) in any other case, a disabled person—

(i) who is seeking or being considered for appointment to, or a recommendation or approval in relation to, the office or post concerned, or

(ii) who has been appointed to the office or post concerned.

(3) Nothing in this section imposes any duty on the relevant person in relation to a disabled person if the relevant person does not know, and could not reasonably be expected to know—

(a) in the case of a person who is being considered for, or is or may be seeking, appointment to, or a recommendation or approval in relation to, an office or post, that the disabled person concerned—

(i) is, or may be, seeking appointment to, or (as the case may be) seeking a recommendation or approval in relation to, that office or post, or

(ii) is being considered for appointment to, or (as the case may be) for a recommendation or approval in relation to, that office or post; or

(b) in any case, that that person has a disability and is likely to be affected in the way mentioned in subsection (1).

Amendment – Inserted by Disability Discrimination Act 1995 (Amendment) Regulations 2003, SI 2003/1673, regs 3(1), 5.

4F   Office-holders: supplementary

(1) In sections 4C to 4E, appointment to an office or post does not include election to an office or post.

(2) In sections 4D and 4E, 'relevant person' means—

(a) in a case relating to an appointment to an office or post, the person with power to make that appointment;

(b) in a case relating to the making of a recommendation or the giving of an approval in relation to an appointment, a person or body referred to in section 4C(3)(b) with power to make that recommendation or (as the case may be) to give that approval;

(c) in a case relating to a term of an appointment, the person with power to determine that term;

(d) in a case relating to a working condition afforded in relation to an appointment—

(i) the person with power to determine that working condition; or

(ii) where there is no such person, the person with power to make the appointment;

(e) in a case relating to the termination of an appointment, the person with power to terminate the appointment;

(f) in a case relating to the subjection of a disabled person to any other detriment or to harassment, any person or body falling within one or more of paragraphs (a) to (e) in relation to such cases as are there mentioned.

(3) In subsection (2)(d), 'working condition' includes—

(a)   any opportunity for promotion, a transfer, training or receiving any other benefit; and

(b)   any physical feature of premises at or from which the functions of an office or post are performed.

Amendment – Inserted by Disability Discrimination Act 1995 (Amendment) Regulations 2003, SI 2003/1673, regs 3(1), 5.

Occupational pension schemes

Amendment – Inserted by Disability Discrimination Act 1995 (Pensions) Regulations 2003, SI 2003/2770, regs 2, 3.

4G   Occupational pension schemes: non-discrimination rule

(1) Every occupational pension scheme shall be taken to include a provision ('the non-discrimination rule') containing the following requirements—

(a)   a requirement that the trustees or managers of the scheme refrain from discriminating against a relevant disabled person in carrying out any of their functions in relation to the scheme (including in particular their functions relating to the admission of members to the scheme and the treatment of members of the scheme);

(b)   a requirement that the trustees or managers of the scheme do not subject a relevant disabled person to harassment in relation to the scheme.

(2) The other provisions of the scheme are to have effect subject to the non-discrimination rule.

(3) It is unlawful for the trustees or managers of an occupational pension scheme—

(a)   to discriminate against a relevant disabled person contrary to requirement (a) of the non-discrimination rule; or

(b)   to subject a relevant disabled person to harassment contrary to requirement (b) of the non-discrimination rule.

(4) The non-discrimination rule does not apply in relation to rights accrued, or benefits payable, in respect of periods of service prior to the coming into force of this section (but it does apply to communications with members or prospective members of the scheme in relation to such rights or benefits).

(5) The trustees or managers of an occupational pension scheme may, if—

(a)   they do not (apart from this subsection) have power to make such alterations to the scheme as may be required to secure conformity with the non-discrimination rule, or

(b)   they have such power but the procedure for doing so—
        (i) is liable to be unduly complex or protracted, or
        (ii) involves the obtaining of consents which cannot be obtained, or can only be obtained with undue delay or difficulty,

by resolution make such alterations to the scheme.

(6) The alterations referred to in subsection (5) may have effect in relation to a period before the alterations are made (but may not have effect in relation to a period before the coming into force of this section).

Amendment – Inserted by Disability Discrimination Act 1995 (Pensions) Regulations 2003, SI 2003/2770, regs 2, 3.

4H   Occupational pension schemes: duty to make adjustments

(1) Where—

- (a)   a provision, criterion or practice (including a scheme rule) applied by or on behalf of the trustees or managers of an occupational pension scheme, or
- (b)   any physical feature of premises occupied by the trustees or managers,

places a relevant disabled person at a substantial disadvantage in comparison with persons who are not disabled, it is the duty of the trustees or managers to take such steps as it is reasonable, in all the circumstances of the case, for them to have to take in order to prevent the provision, criterion or practice, or feature, having that effect.

(2) The making of alterations to scheme rules is (in addition to the examples set out in section 18B(2)) an example of a step which trustees or managers may have to take in order to comply with the duty set out in subsection (1).

(3) Nothing in subsection (1) imposes any duty on trustees or managers in relation to a disabled person if they do not know, and could not reasonably be expected to know—

- (a)   that the disabled person is a relevant disabled person; or
- (b)   that that person has a disability and is likely to be affected in the way mentioned in subsection (1).

Amendment – Inserted by Disability Discrimination Act 1995 (Pensions) Regulations 2003, SI 2003/2770, regs 2, 3.

4I   Occupational pension schemes: procedure

(1) Where under section 17A a relevant disabled person presents a complaint to an employment tribunal that the trustees or managers of an occupational pension scheme have acted in relation to him in a way which is unlawful under this Part, the employer in relation to that scheme shall, for the purposes of the rules governing procedure, be treated as a party and be entitled to appear and be heard in accordance with those rules.

(2) In this section, 'employer', in relation to an occupational pension scheme, has the meaning given by section 124(1) of the Pensions Act 1995 as at the date of coming into force of this section.

Amendment – Inserted by Disability Discrimination Act 1995 (Pensions) Regulations 2003, SI 2003/2770, regs 2, 3.

4J   Occupational pension schemes: remedies

(1) This section applies where—

- (a)   under section 17A a relevant disabled person presents to an employment tribunal a complaint that—
  - (i)   the trustees or managers of an occupational pension scheme have acted in relation to him in a way which is unlawful under this Part; or

      (ii) an employer has so acted in relation to him;
(b)   the complaint relates to—
      (i)   the terms on which persons become members of an occupational pension scheme, or
      (ii) the terms on which members of the scheme are treated;
(c)   the disabled person is not a pensioner member of the scheme; and
(d)   the tribunal finds that the complaint is well-founded.

(2) The tribunal may, without prejudice to the generality of its power under section 17A(2)(a), make a declaration that the complainant has a right—

(a)   (where subsection (1)(b)(i) applies) to be admitted to the scheme in question; or
(b)   (where subsection (1)(b)(ii) applies) to membership of the scheme without discrimination.

(3) A declaration under subsection (2)—

(a)   may be made in respect of such period as the declaration may specify (but may not be made in respect of any period before the coming into force of this section);
(b)   may make such provision as the tribunal considers appropriate as to the terms upon which, or the capacity in which, the disabled person is to enjoy such admission or membership.

(4) The tribunal may not award the disabled person any compensation under section 17A(2)(b) (whether in relation to arrears of benefits or otherwise) other than—

(a)   compensation for injury to feelings;
(b)   compensation pursuant to section 17A(5).

Amendment – Inserted by Disability Discrimination Act 1995 (Pensions) Regulations 2003, SI 2003/2770, regs 2, 3.

4K   Occupational pension schemes: supplementary

(1) In their application to communications, sections 4G to 4J apply in relation to a disabled person who is—

(a)   entitled to the present payment of dependants' or survivors' benefits under an occupational pension scheme; or
(b)   a pension credit member of such a scheme,

as they apply in relation to a disabled person who is a pensioner member of the scheme.

(2) In sections 4G to 4J and in this section—

'active member', 'deferred member', 'managers', 'pension credit member', 'pensioner member' and 'trustees or managers' have the meanings given by section 124(1) of the Pensions Act 1995 as at the date of coming into force of this section;
'communications' includes—
    (i)   the provision of information, and
    (ii)   the operation of a dispute resolution procedure;
'member', in relation to an occupational pension scheme, means any active, deferred or pensioner member;

'non-discrimination rule' means the rule in section 4G(1);

'relevant disabled person', in relation to an occupational pension scheme, means a disabled person who is a member or prospective member of the scheme; and

'prospective member' means any person who, under the terms of his contract of employment or the scheme rules or both—

    (i)   is able, at his own option, to become a member of the scheme,

    (ii)   will become so able if he continues in the same employment for a sufficiently long period,

    (iii)   will be admitted to it automatically unless he makes an election not to become a member, or

    (iv)   may be admitted to it subject to the consent of his employer.

Amendment – Inserted by Disability Discrimination Act 1995 (Pensions) Regulations 2003, SI 2003/2770, regs 2, 3.

5   (*repealed*)

Amendment – Repealed by Disability Discrimination Act 1995 (Amendment) Regulations 2003, SI 2003/1673, regs 3(1), 5.

6   (*repealed*)

Amendment – Repealed by Disability Discrimination Act 1995 (Amendment) Regulations 2003, SI 2003/1673, regs 3(1), 5.

6A   Partnerships: discrimination and harassment

(1) It is unlawful for a firm, in relation to a position as partner in the firm, to discriminate against a disabled person—

    (a)   in the arrangements which they make for the purpose of determining who should be offered that position;

    (b)   in the terms on which they offer him that position;

    (c)   by refusing or deliberately omitting to offer him that position; or

    (d)   in a case where the person already holds that position—

        (i) in the way they afford him access to any benefits or by refusing or deliberately omitting to afford him access to them; or

        (ii) by expelling him from that position, or subjecting him to any other detriment.

(2) It is also unlawful for a firm, in relation to a position as partner in the firm, to subject to harassment a disabled person who holds or has applied for that position.

(3) Subsection (1) does not apply to benefits of any description if the firm are concerned with the provision (whether or not for payment) of benefits of that description to the public, or to a section of the public which includes the partner in question, unless that provision differs in a material respect from the provision of the benefits to other partners.

(4) The reference in subsection (1)(d)(ii) to the expulsion of a person from a position as partner includes a reference—

(a) to the termination of that person's partnership by the expiration of any period (including a period expiring by reference to an event or circumstance), not being a termination immediately after which the partnership is renewed on the same terms; and

(b) to the termination of that person's partnership by any act of his (including the giving of notice) in circumstances such that he is entitled to terminate it without notice by reason of the conduct of the other partners.

Amendment – Inserted by Disability Discrimination Act 1995 (Amendment) Regulations 2003, SI 2003/1673, regs 3(1), 6.

6B Partnerships: duty to make adjustments

(1) Where—

(a) a provision, criterion or practice applied by or on behalf of a firm, or

(b) any physical feature of premises occupied by the firm,

places the disabled person concerned at a substantial disadvantage in comparison with persons who are not disabled, it is the duty of the firm to take such steps as it is reasonable, in all the circumstances of the case, for them to have to take in order to prevent the provision, criterion or practice, or feature, having that effect.

(2) In this section, 'the disabled person concerned' means—

(a) in the case of a provision, criterion or practice for determining to whom the position of partner should be offered, any disabled person who is, or has notified the firm that he may be, a candidate for that position;

(b) in any other case, a disabled person who is—
    (i) a partner, or
    (ii) a candidate for the position of partner.

(3) Nothing in this section imposes any duty on a firm in relation to a disabled person if the firm do not know, and could not reasonably be expected to know—

(a) in the case of a candidate or potential candidate, that the disabled person concerned is, or may be, a candidate for the position of partner; or

(b) in any case, that that person has a disability and is likely to be affected in the way mentioned in subsection (1).

(4) Where a firm are required by this section to take any steps in relation to the disabled person concerned, the cost of taking those steps shall be treated as an expense of the firm; and the extent to which such cost should be borne by that person, where he is or becomes a partner in the firm, shall not exceed such amount as is reasonable, having regard in particular to the proportion in which he is entitled to share in the firm's profits.

Amendment – Inserted by Disability Discrimination Act 1995 (Amendment) Regulations 2003, SI 2003/1673, regs 3(1), 6.

6C Partnerships: supplementary

(1) Sections 6A(1)(a) to (c) and (2) and section 6B apply in relation to persons proposing to form themselves into a partnership as they apply in relation to a firm.

(2) Sections 6A and 6B apply to a limited liability partnership as they apply to a firm; and, in the application of those sections to a limited liability partnership, references to a partner in a firm are references to a member of the limited liability partnership.

(3) In the case of a limited partnership, references in sections 6A and 6B to a partner shall be construed as references to a general partner as defined in section 3 of the Limited Partnerships Act 1907.

(4) In sections 6A and 6B and in this section, 'firm' has the meaning given by section 4 of the Partnership Act 1890.

Amendment – Inserted by Disability Discrimination Act 1995 (Amendment) Regulations 2003, SI 2003/1673, regs 3(1), 6.

---

7   (*repealed*)

Amendment – Repealed by Disability Discrimination Act 1995 (Amendment) Regulations 2003, SI 2003/1673, regs 3(1), 7.

Barristers and advocates

Amendment – Inserted by Disability Discrimination Act 1995 (Amendment) Regulations 2003, SI 2003/1673, regs 3(1), 8.

7A   Barristers: discrimination and harassment

(1) It is unlawful for a barrister or a barrister's clerk, in relation to any offer of a pupillage or tenancy, to discriminate against a disabled person—

- (a)   in the arrangements which are made for the purpose of determining to whom it should be offered;
- (b)   in respect of any terms on which it is offered; or
- (c)   by refusing, or deliberately omitting, to offer it to him.

(2) It is unlawful for a barrister or a barrister's clerk, in relation to a disabled pupil or tenant in the set of chambers in question, to discriminate against him—

- (a)   in respect of any terms applicable to him as a pupil or tenant;
- (b)   in the opportunities for training, or gaining experience, which are afforded or denied to him;
- (c)   in the benefits which are afforded or denied to him;
- (d)   by terminating his pupillage or by subjecting him to any pressure to leave the chambers; or
- (e)   by subjecting him to any other detriment.

(3) It is unlawful for a barrister or barrister's clerk, in relation to a pupillage or tenancy, to subject to harassment a disabled person who is, or has applied to be, a pupil or tenant in the set of chambers in question.

(4) It is also unlawful for any person, in relation to the giving, withholding or acceptance of instructions to a barrister, to discriminate against a disabled person or to subject him to harassment.

(5) In this section and in section 7B—

'barrister's clerk' includes any person carrying out any of the functions of a barrister's clerk;

'pupil', 'pupillage' and 'set of chambers' have the meanings commonly associated with their use in the context of barristers practising in independent practice; and

'tenancy' and 'tenant' have the meanings commonly associated with their use in the context of barristers practising in independent practice, but they also include reference to any barrister permitted to practise from a set of chambers.

Amendment – Inserted by Disability Discrimination Act 1995 (Amendment) Regulations 2003, SI 2003/1673, regs 3(1), 8.

7B   Barristers: duty to make adjustments

(1) Where—

(a)   a provision, criterion or practice applied by or on behalf of a barrister or barrister's clerk, or

(b)   any physical feature of premises occupied by a barrister or a barrister's clerk,

places the disabled person concerned at a substantial disadvantage in comparison with persons who are not disabled, it is the duty of the barrister or barrister's clerk to take such steps as it is reasonable, in all the circumstances of the case, for him to have to take in order to prevent the provision, criterion or practice, or feature, having that effect.

(2) In a case where subsection (1) applies in relation to two or more barristers in a set of chambers, the duty in that subsection is a duty on each of them to take such steps as it is reasonable, in all of the circumstances of the case, for him to have to take.

(3) In this section, 'the disabled person concerned' means—

(a)   in the case of a provision, criterion or practice for determining to whom a pupillage or tenancy should be offered, any disabled person who is, or has notified the barrister or the barrister's clerk concerned that he may be, an applicant for a pupillage or tenancy;

(b)   in any other case, a disabled person who is— .
        (i)   a tenant;
        (ii) a pupil; or
        (iii) an applicant for a pupillage or tenancy.

(4) Nothing in this section imposes any duty on a barrister or a barrister's clerk in relation to a disabled person if he does not know, and could not reasonably be expected to know—

(a)   in the case of an applicant or potential applicant, that the disabled person concerned is, or may be, an applicant for a pupillage or tenancy; or

(b)   in any case, that that person has a disability and is likely to be affected in the way mentioned in subsection (1).

Amendment – Inserted by Disability Discrimination Act 1995 (Amendment) Regulations 2003, SI 2003/1673, regs 3(1), 8.

7C   Advocates: discrimination and harassment

(1) It is unlawful for an advocate, in relation to taking any person as his pupil, to discriminate against a disabled person—

(a)   in the arrangements which he makes for the purpose of determining whom he will take as his pupil;

(b)   in respect of any terms on which he offers to take the disabled person as his pupil; or

(c)   by refusing, or deliberately omitting, to take the disabled person as his pupil.

(2) It is unlawful for an advocate, in relation to a disabled person who is a pupil, to discriminate against him—

(a)   in respect of any terms applicable to him as a pupil;

(b)   in the opportunities for training, or gaining experience, which are afforded or denied to him;

(c)   in the benefits which are afforded or denied to him;

(d)   by terminating the relationship or by subjecting him to any pressure to leave; or

(e)   by subjecting him to any other detriment.

(3) It is unlawful for an advocate, in relation to taking any person as his pupil, to subject to harassment a disabled person who is, or has applied to be taken as, his pupil.

(4) It is also unlawful for any person, in relation to the giving, withholding or acceptance of instructions to an advocate, to discriminate against a disabled person or to subject him to harassment.

(5) In this section and section 7D—

'advocate' means a member of the Faculty of Advocates practising as such; and
'pupil' has the meaning commonly associated with its use in the context of a person training to be an advocate.

Amendment – Inserted by Disability Discrimination Act 1995 (Amendment) Regulations 2003, SI 2003/1673, regs 3(1), 8.

7D   Advocates: duty to make adjustments

(1) Where—

(a)   a provision, criterion or practice applied by or on behalf of an advocate, or

(b)   any physical feature of premises occupied by, and under the control of, an advocate,

places the disabled person concerned at a substantial disadvantage in comparison with persons who are not disabled, it is the duty of the advocate to take such steps as it is reasonable, in all the circumstances of the case, for him to have to take in order to prevent the provision, criterion or practice, or feature, having that effect.

(2) In this section, 'the disabled person concerned' means—

(a)   in the case of a provision, criterion or practice for determining whom he will take as his pupil, any disabled person who has applied, or has notified the advocate that he may apply, to be taken as a pupil;

(b)   in any other case, a disabled person who is—

(i) an applicant to be taken as the advocate's pupil, or

(ii) a pupil.

(3) Nothing in this section imposes any duty on an advocate in relation to a disabled person if he does not know, and could not reasonably be expected to know—

(a)   in the case of an applicant or potential applicant, that the disabled person concerned is, or may be, applying to be taken as his pupil; or

(b)   in any case, that that person has a disability and is likely to be affected in the way mentioned in subsection (1).

Amendment – Inserted by Disability Discrimination Act 1995 (Amendment) Regulations 2003, SI 2003/1673, regs 3(1), 8.

... (*repealed*)

Amendment – Repealed by Disability Discrimination Act 1995 (Amendment) Regulations 2003, SI 2003/1673, regs 3(1), 9(1).

---

8   (*repealed*)

Amendment – Repealed by Disability Discrimination Act 1995 (Amendment) Regulations 2003, SI 2003/1673, regs 3(1), 9(1).

---

9   (*repealed*)

Amendment – Repealed by Disability Discrimination Act 1995 (Amendment) Regulations 2003, SI 2003/1673, regs 3(1), 10

---

10   (*repealed*)

Amendment – Repealed by Disability Discrimination Act 1995 (Amendment) Regulations 2003, SI 2003/1673, regs 3(1), 11.

---

11   (*repealed*)

Amendment – Repealed by Disability Discrimination Act 1995 (Amendment) Regulations 2003, SI 2003/1673, regs 3(1), 12.

... (*repealed*)

Amendment – Repealed by Disability Discrimination Act 1995 (Amendment) Regulations 2003, SI 2003/1673, regs 3(1), 12.

---

12   (*repealed*)

Amendment – Repealed by Disability Discrimination Act 1995 (Amendment) Regulations 2003, SI 2003/1673, regs 3(1), 12.

Trade and professional bodies

Amendment – Inserted by Disability Discrimination Act 1995 (Amendment) Regulations 2003, SI 2003/1673, regs 3(1), 13.

13   Trade organisations: discrimination and harassment

(1) It is unlawful for a trade organisation to discriminate against a disabled person—

  (a)   in the arrangements which it makes for the purpose of determining who should be offered membership of the organisation;

  (b)   in the terms on which it is prepared to admit him to membership of the organisation; or

  (c)   by refusing to accept, or deliberately not accepting, his application for membership.

(2) It is unlawful for a trade organisation, in the case of a disabled person who is a member of the organisation, to discriminate against him—

  (a)   in the way it affords him access to any benefits or by refusing or deliberately omitting to afford him access to them;

  (b)   by depriving him of membership, or varying the terms on which he is a member; or

  (c)   by subjecting him to any other detriment.

(3) It is also unlawful for a trade organisation, in relation to membership of that organisation, to subject to harassment a disabled person who—

  (a)   is a member of the organisation; or

  (b)   has applied for membership of the organisation.

(4) In this section and section 14 'trade organisation' means—

  (a)   an organisation of workers;

  (b)   an organisation of employers; or

  (c)   any other organisation whose members carry on a particular profession or trade for the purposes of which the organisation exists.

Amendment – Amended by Disability Discrimination Act 1995 (Amendment) Regulations 2003, SI 2003/1673, regs 3(1), 13.

14   Trade organisations: duty to make adjustments

(1) Where—

  (a)   a provision, criterion or practice applied by or on behalf of a trade organisation, or

  (b)   any physical feature of premises occupied by the organisation,

places the disabled person concerned at a substantial disadvantage in comparison with persons who are not disabled, it is the duty of the organisation to take such steps as it is reasonable, in all the circumstances of the case, for it to have to take in order to prevent the provision, criterion or practice, or feature, having that effect.

(2) In this section 'the disabled person concerned' means—

(a)   in the case of a provision, criterion or practice for determining to whom membership should be offered, any disabled person who is, or has notified the organisation that he may be, an applicant for membership;

(b)   in any other case, a disabled person who is—

(i)   a member of the organisation, or

(ii)   an applicant for membership of the organisation.

(3) Nothing in this section imposes any duty on an organisation in relation to a disabled person if the organisation does not know, and could not reasonably be expected to know—

(a)   in the case of an applicant or potential applicant, that the disabled person concerned is, or may be, an applicant for membership of the organisation; or

(b)   in any case, that that person has a disability and is likely to be affected in the way mentioned in subsection (1).

Amendment – Amended by Disability Discrimination Act 1995 (Amendment) Regulations 2003, SI 2003/ 1673, regs 3(1), 13.

14A   Qualifications bodies: discrimination and harassment

(1) It is unlawful for a qualifications body to discriminate against a disabled person—

(a)   in the arrangements which it makes for the purpose of determining upon whom to confer a professional or trade qualification;

(b)   in the terms on which it is prepared to confer a professional or trade qualification on him;

(c)   by refusing or deliberately omitting to grant any application by him for such a qualification; or

(d)   by withdrawing such a qualification from him or varying the terms on which he holds it.

(2) It is also unlawful for a qualifications body, in relation to a professional or trade qualification conferred by it, to subject to harassment a disabled person who holds or applies for such a qualification.

(3) In determining for the purposes of subsection (1) whether the application by a qualifications body of a competence standard to a disabled person constitutes discrimination within the meaning of section 3A, the application of the standard is justified for the purposes of section 3A(1)(b) if, but only if, the qualifications body can show that—

(a)   the standard is, or would be, applied equally to persons who do not have his particular disability; and

(b)   its application is a proportionate means of achieving a legitimate aim.

(4) For the purposes of subsection (3)—

(a)   section 3A(2) (and (6)) does not apply; and

(b)   section 3A(4) has effect as if the reference to section 3A(3) were a reference to subsection (3) of this section.

(5) In this section and section 14B—

'qualifications body' means any authority or body which can confer a professional or
trade qualification, but it does not include—

(a)   a responsible body (within the meaning of Chapter 1 or 2 of Part 4),

(b)   a local education authority in England or Wales, or

(c)   an education authority (within the meaning of section 135(1) of the
Education (Scotland) Act 1980);

'confer' includes renew or extend;

'professional or trade qualification' means an authorisation, qualification, recognition, registration, enrolment, approval or certification which is needed for, or
facilitates engagement in, a particular profession or trade;

'competence standard' means an academic, medical or other standard applied by or
on behalf of a qualifications body for the purpose of determining whether or not
a person has a particular level of competence or ability.

Amendment – Inserted by Disability Discrimination Act 1995 (Amendment) Regulations 2003, SI 2003/1673,
regs 3(1), 13.

14B Qualifications bodies: duty to make adjustments

(1) Where—

(a)   a provision, criterion or practice, other than a competence standard, applied by
or on behalf of a qualifications body; or

(b)   any physical feature of premises occupied by a qualifications body,

places the disabled person concerned at a substantial disadvantage in comparison with
persons who are not disabled, it is the duty of the qualifications body to take such steps as
it is reasonable, in all the circumstances of the case, for it to have to take in order to
prevent the provision, criterion or practice, or feature, having that effect.

(2) In this section 'the disabled person concerned' means—

(a)   in the case of a provision, criterion or practice for determining on whom a
professional or trade qualification is to be conferred, any disabled person who
is, or has notified the qualifications body that he may be, an applicant for the
conferment of that qualification;

(b)   in any other case, a disabled person who—

(i)   holds a professional or trade qualification conferred by the qualifications
body, or

(ii) applies for a professional or trade qualification which it confers.

(3) Nothing in this section imposes a duty on a qualifications body in relation to a
disabled person if the body does not know, and could not reasonably be expected to
know—

(a)   in the case of an applicant or potential applicant, that the disabled person
concerned is, or may be, an applicant for the conferment of a professional or
trade qualification; or

(b)   in any case, that that person has a disability and is likely to be affected in the way
mentioned in subsection (1).

Amendment – Inserted by Disability Discrimination Act 1995 (Amendment) Regulations 2003, SI 2003/1673,
regs 3(1), 13.

Practical work experience

Amendment – Inserted by Disability Discrimination Act 1995 (Amendment) Regulations 2003, SI 2003/1673, regs 3(1), 13.

14C   Practical work experience: discrimination and harassment

(1) It is unlawful, in the case of a disabled person seeking or undertaking a work placement, for a placement provider to discriminate against him—

(a)   in the arrangements which he makes for the purpose of determining who should be offered a work placement;

(b)   in the terms on which he affords him access to any work placement or any facilities concerned with such a placement;

(c)   by refusing or deliberately omitting to afford him such access;

(d)   by terminating the placement; or

(e)   by subjecting him to any other detriment in relation to the placement.

(2) It is also unlawful for a placement provider, in relation to a work placement, to subject to harassment—

(a)   a disabled person to whom he is providing a placement; or

(b)   a disabled person who has applied to him for a placement.

(3) This section and section 14D do not apply to—

(a)   anything made unlawful by section 4 or any provision of Part 3 or 4; or

(b)   anything which would be unlawful under that section or any such provision but for the operation of any other provision of this Act.

(4) In this section and section 14D—

'work placement' means practical work experience undertaken for a limited period for the purposes of a person's vocational training;

'placement provider' means any person who provides a work placement to a person whom he does not employ.

(5) This section and section 14D do not apply to a work placement undertaken in any of the naval, military and air forces of the Crown.

Amendment – Inserted by Disability Discrimination Act 1995 (Amendment) Regulations 2003, SI 2003/1673, regs 3(1), 13.

14D   Practical work experience: duty to make adjustments

(1) Where—

(a)   a provision, criterion or practice applied by or on behalf of a placement provider, or

(b)   any physical feature of premises occupied by the placement provider, places the disabled person concerned at a substantial disadvantage in comparison with persons who are not disabled, it is the duty of the placement provider to take such steps as it is reasonable, in all the circumstances of the case, for him to have to take in order to prevent the provision, criterion or practice, or feature, having that effect.

(2) In this section, 'the disabled person concerned' means—

(a)   in the case of a provision, criterion or practice for determining to whom a work placement should be offered, any disabled person who is, or has notified the placement provider that he may be, an applicant for that work placement;

(b)   in any other case, a disabled person who is—

(i) an applicant for the work placement concerned, or

(ii) undertaking a work placement with the placement provider.

(3) Nothing in this section imposes any duty on a placement provider in relation to the disabled person concerned if he does not know, and could not reasonably be expected to know—

(a)   in the case of an applicant or potential applicant, that the disabled person concerned is, or may be, an applicant for the work placement; or

(b)   in any case, that that person has a disability and is likely to be affected in the way mentioned in subsection (1).

Amendment – Inserted by Disability Discrimination Act 1995 (Amendment) Regulations 2003, SI 2003/1673, regs 3(1), 13.

15   (*repealed*)

Amendment – Repealed by Disability Discrimination Act 1995 (Amendment) Regulations 2003, SI 2003/1673, regs 3(1), 13.

. . . (*repealed*)

Amendment – Repealed by Disability Discrimination Act 1995 (Amendment) Regulations 2003, SI 2003/1673, regs 3(1), 14(1).

16   (*repealed*)

Amendment – Repealed by Disability Discrimination Act 1995 (Amendment) Regulations 2003, SI 2003/1673, regs 3(1), 14(2).

Other unlawful acts

Amendment – Inserted by Disability Discrimination Act 1995 (Amendment) Regulations 2003, SI 2003/1673, regs 3(1), 15(1).

16A Relationships which have come to an end

(1) This section applies where—

    (a)   there has been a relevant relationship between a disabled person and another person ('the relevant person'), and

    (b)   the relationship has come to an end.

(2) In this section a 'relevant relationship' is—

    (a)   a relationship during the course of which an act of discrimination against, or harassment of, one party to the relationship by the other party to it is unlawful under any preceding provision of this Part; or

    (b)   a relationship between a person providing employment services (within the meaning of Part 3) and a person receiving such services.

(3) It is unlawful for the relevant person—

    (a)   to discriminate against the disabled person by subjecting him to a detriment, or

    (b)   to subject the disabled person to harassment,

where the discrimination or harassment arises out of and is closely connected to the relevant relationship.

(4) This subsection applies where—

    (a)   a provision, criterion or practice applied by the relevant person to the disabled person in relation to any matter arising out of the relevant relationship, or

    (b)   a physical feature of premises which are occupied by the relevant person,

places the disabled person at a substantial disadvantage in comparison with persons who are not disabled, but are in the same position as the disabled person in relation to the relevant person.

(5) Where subsection (4) applies, it is the duty of the relevant person to take such steps as it is reasonable, in all the circumstances of the case, for him to have to take in order to prevent the provision, practice or criterion, or feature, having that effect.

(6) Nothing in subsection (5) imposes any duty on the relevant person if he does not know, and could not reasonably be expected to know, that the disabled person has a disability and is likely to be affected in the way mentioned in that subsection.

(7) In subsection (2), reference to an act of discrimination or harassment which is unlawful includes, in the case of a relationship which has come to an end before the commencement of this section, reference to such an act which would, after the commencement of this section, be unlawful.

Amendment – Inserted by Disability Discrimination Act 1995 (Amendment) Regulations 2003, SI 2003/1673, regs 3(1), 15(1).

16B Discriminatory advertisements

(1) It is unlawful for a person, in relation to a relevant appointment or benefit which he intends to make or confer, to publish or cause to be published an advertisement which—

(a)   invites applications for that appointment or benefit; and
(b)   indicates, or might reasonably be understood to indicate, that an application will or may be determined to any extent by reference to—
  (i)   the applicant not having any disability, or any particular disability, or
  (ii) any reluctance of the person determining the application to comply with a duty to make reasonable adjustments or (in relation to employment services) with the duty imposed by section 21(1) as modified by section 21A(6).

(2) Subsection (1) does not apply where it would not in fact be unlawful under this Part or, to the extent that it relates to the provision of employment services, Part 3 for an application to be determined in the manner indicated (or understood to be indicated) in the advertisement.

(3) In subsection (1), 'relevant appointment or benefit' means—

(a)   any employment, promotion or transfer of employment;
(b)   membership of, or a benefit under, an occupational pension scheme;
(c)   an appointment to any office or post to which section 4D applies;
(d)   any partnership in a firm (within the meaning of section 6A);
(e)   any tenancy or pupillage (within the meaning of section 7A or 7C);
(f)   any membership of a trade organisation (within the meaning of section 13);
(g)   any professional or trade qualification (within the meaning of section 14A);
(h)   any work placement (within the meaning of section 14C);
(i)   any employment services (within the meaning of Part 3).

(4) In this section, 'advertisement' includes every form of advertisement or notice, whether to the public or not.

Amendment – Inserted by Disability Discrimination Act 1995 (Amendment) Regulations 2003, SI 2003/1673, regs 3(1), 15(1).

16C   Instructions and pressure to discriminate

(1) It is unlawful for a person—

(a)   who has authority over another person, or
(b)   in accordance with whose wishes that other person is accustomed to act,

to instruct him to do any act which is unlawful under this Part or, to the extent that it relates to the provision of employment services, Part 3, or to procure or attempt to procure the doing by him of any such act.

(2) It is also unlawful to induce, or attempt to induce, a person to do any act which contravenes this Part or, to the extent that it relates to the provision of employment services, Part 3 by—

(a)   providing or offering to provide him with any benefit, or
(b)   subjecting or threatening to subject him to any detriment.

(3) An attempted inducement is not prevented from falling within subsection (2) because it is not made directly to the person in question, if it is made in such a way that he is likely to hear of it.

Amendment – Inserted by Disability Discrimination Act 1995 (Amendment) Regulations 2003, SI 2003/1673, regs 3(1), 15(1).

... (*repealed*)

Amendment – Repealed by Disability Discrimination Act 1995 (Pensions) Regulations 2003, SI 2003/2770, regs 2, 4(1).

17 (*repealed*)

Amendment – Repealed by Disability Discrimination Act 1995 (Pensions) Regulations 2003, SI 2003/2770, regs 2, 4(1).

Enforcement etc

Amendment – Inserted by Disability Discrimination Act 1995 (Amendment) Regulations 2003, SI 2003/1673, regs 3(1), 9(1).

17A Enforcement, remedies and procedure

(1) A complaint by any person that another person—

(a) has discriminated against him, or subjected him to harassment, in a way which is unlawful under this Part, or

(b) is, by virtue of section 57 or 58, to be treated as having done so,

may be presented to an employment tribunal.

(1A) Subsection (1) does not apply to a complaint under section 14A(1) or (2) of an act in respect of which an appeal, or proceedings in the nature of an appeal, may be brought under any enactment.

(1B) In subsection (1A), 'enactment' includes an enactment comprised in, or in an instrument made under, an Act of the Scottish Parliament.

(1C) Where, on the hearing of a complaint under subsection (1), the complainant proves facts from which the tribunal could, apart from this subsection, conclude in the absence of an adequate explanation that the respondent has acted in a way which is unlawful under this Part, the tribunal shall uphold the complaint unless the respondent proves that he did not so act.

(2) Where an employment tribunal finds that a complaint presented to it under this section is well-founded, it shall take such of the following steps as it considers just and equitable—

(a) making a declaration as to the rights of the complainant and the respondent in relation to the matters to which the complaint relates;

(b) ordering the respondent to pay compensation to the complainant;

(c)   recommending that the respondent take, within a specified period, action appearing to the tribunal to be reasonable, in all the circumstances of the case, for the purpose of obviating or reducing the adverse effect on the complainant of any matter to which the complaint relates.

(3) Where a tribunal orders compensation under subsection (2)(b), the amount of the compensation shall be calculated by applying the principles applicable to the calculation of damages in claims in tort or (in Scotland) in reparation for breach of statutory duty.

(4) For the avoidance of doubt it is hereby declared that compensation in respect of discrimination in a way which is unlawful under this Part may include compensation for injury to feelings whether or not it includes compensation under any other head.

(5) If the respondent to a complaint fails, without reasonable justification, to comply with a recommendation made by an employment tribunal under subsection (2)(c) the tribunal may, if it thinks it just and equitable to do so—

(a)   increase the amount of compensation required to be paid to the complainant in respect of the complaint, where an order was made under subsection (2)(b); or

(b)   make an order under subsection (2)(b).

(6) Regulations may make provision—

(a)   for enabling a tribunal, where an amount of compensation falls to be awarded under subsection (2)(b), to include in the award interest on that amount; and

(b)   specifying, for cases where a tribunal decides that an award is to include an amount in respect of interest, the manner in which and the periods and rate by reference to which the interest is to be determined.

(7) Regulations may modify the operation of any order made under section 14 of the Employment Tribunals Act 1996 (power to make provision as to interest on sums payable in pursuance of employment tribunal decisions) to the extent that it relates to an award of compensation under subsection (2)(b).

(8) Part I of Schedule 3 makes further provision about the enforcement of this Part and about procedure.

Amendment – Inserted and amended by Disability Discrimination Act 1995 (Amendment) Regulations 2003, SI 2003/1673, regs 3(1), 9(1), (2)(a)–(c) and Employment Rights (Dispute Resolution) Act 1998, s 1(2)(a), (c).

17B   Enforcement of sections 16B and 16C

(1) Only the Disability Rights Commission may bring proceedings in respect of a contravention of section 16B (discriminatory advertisements) or section 16C (instructions and pressure to discriminate).

(2) The Commission shall bring any such proceedings in accordance with subsection (3) or (4).

(3) The Commission may present to an employment tribunal a complaint that a person has done an act which is unlawful under section 16B or 16C; and if the tribunal finds that the complaint is well-founded it shall make a declaration to that effect.

(4) Where—

(a)   a tribunal has made a finding pursuant to subsection (3) that a person has done an act which is unlawful under section 16B or 16C,

(b)   that finding has become final, and

(c)   it appears to the Commission that, unless restrained, he is likely to do a further act which is unlawful under that section,

the Commission may apply to a county court for an injunction, or (in Scotland) to a sheriff court for an interdict, restraining him from doing such an act; and the court, if satisfied that the application is well-founded, may grant the injunction or interdict in the terms applied for or in more limited terms.

(5) A finding of a tribunal under subsection (3) in respect of any act shall, if it has become final, be treated as conclusive by a county court or sheriff court upon an application under subsection (4).

(6) A finding of a tribunal becomes final for the purposes of this section when an appeal against it is dismissed, withdrawn or abandoned or when the time for appealing expires without an appeal having been brought.

(7) An employment tribunal shall not consider a complaint under subsection (3) unless it is presented before the end of the period of six months beginning when the act to which it relates was done; and a county court or sheriff court shall not consider an application under subsection (4) unless it is made before the end of the period of five years so beginning.

(8) A court or tribunal may consider any such complaint or application which is out of time if, in all the circumstances of the case, it considers that it is just and equitable to do so.

(9) The provisions of paragraph 3(3) and (4) of Schedule 3 apply for the purposes of subsection (7) as they apply for the purposes of paragraph 3(1) of that Schedule.

Amendment – Inserted by Disability Discrimination Act 1995 (Amendment) Regulations 2003, SI 2003/1673, regs 3(1), 16(1).

17C Validity of contracts, collective agreements and rules of undertakings

Schedule 3A shall have effect.

Amendment – Inserted by Disability Discrimination Act 1995 (Amendment) Regulations 2003, SI 2003/1673, regs 3(1), 16(1).

18 Insurance services

(1) This section applies where a provider of insurance services ('the insurer') enters into arrangements with an employer under which the employer's employees, or a class of his employees—

(a)   receive insurance services provided by the insurer; or

(b)   are given an opportunity to receive such services.

(2) The insurer is to be taken, for the purposes of this Part, to discriminate unlawfully against a disabled person who is a relevant employee if he acts in relation to that

employee in a way which would be unlawful discrimination for the purposes of Part III if—

(a)   he were providing the service in question to members of the public; and

(b)   the employee was provided with, or was trying to secure the provision of, that service as a member of the public.

(3) In this section—

'insurance services' means services of a prescribed description for the provision of benefits in respect of—

(a)   termination of service;

(b)   retirement, old age or death;

(c)   accident, injury, sickness or invalidity; or

(d)   any other prescribed matter; and

'relevant employee' means—

(a)   in the case of an arrangement which applies to employees of the employer in question, an employee of his;

(b)   in the case of an arrangement which applies to a class of employees of the employer, an employee who is in that class.

(4) For the purposes of the definition of 'relevant employee' in subsection (3), 'employee', in relation to an employer, includes a person who has applied for, or is contemplating applying for, employment by that employer or (as the case may be) employment by him in the class in question.

Supplementary and general

Amendment – Inserted by Disability Discrimination Act 1995 (Amendment) Regulations 2003, SI 2003/1673, regs 3(1), 17(1).

18A   Alterations to premises occupied under leases

(1) This section applies where—

(a)   a person to whom a duty to make reasonable adjustments applies ('the occupier') occupies premises under a lease;

(b)   but for this section, the occupier would not be entitled to make a particular alteration to the premises; and

(c)   the alteration is one which the occupier proposes to make in order to comply with that duty.

(2) Except to the extent to which it expressly so provides, the lease shall have effect by virtue of this subsection as if it provided—

(a)   for the occupier to be entitled to make the alteration with the written consent of the lessor;

(b)   for the occupier to have to make a written application to the lessor for consent if he wishes to make the alteration;

(c)   if such an application is made, for the lessor not to withhold his consent unreasonably; and

(d)   for the lessor to be entitled to make his consent subject to reasonable conditions.

(3) In this section—

'lease' includes a tenancy, sub-lease or sub-tenancy and an agreement for a lease, tenancy, sub-lease or sub-tenancy; and
'sub-lease' and 'sub-tenancy' have such meaning as may be prescribed.

(4) If the terms and conditions of a lease—

(a) impose conditions which are to apply if the occupier alters the premises, or
(b) entitle the lessor to impose conditions when consenting to the occupier's altering the premises,

the occupier is to be treated for the purposes of subsection (1) as not being entitled to make the alteration.

(5) Part I of Schedule 4 supplements the provisions of this section.

Amendment – Inserted by Disability Discrimination Act 1995 (Amendment) Regulations 2003, SI 2003/1673, regs 3(1), 14(2), (3)(a), (b).

18B Reasonable adjustments: supplementary

(1) In determining whether it is reasonable for a person to have to take a particular step in order to comply with a duty to make reasonable adjustments, regard shall be had, in particular, to—

(a) the extent to which taking the step would prevent the effect in relation to which the duty is imposed;
(b) the extent to which it is practicable for him to take the step;
(c) the financial and other costs which would be incurred by him in taking the step and the extent to which taking it would disrupt any of his activities;
(d) the extent of his financial and other resources;
(e) the availability to him of financial or other assistance with respect to taking the step;
(f) the nature of his activities and the size of his undertaking;
(g) where the step would be taken in relation to a private household, the extent to which taking it would—
     (i) disrupt that household, or
     (ii) disturb any person residing there.

(2) The following are examples of steps which a person may need to take in relation to a disabled person in order to comply with a duty to make reasonable adjustments—

(a) making adjustments to premises;
(b) allocating some of the disabled person's duties to another person;
(c) transferring him to fill an existing vacancy;
(d) altering his hours of working or training;
(e) assigning him to a different place of work or training;
(f) allowing him to be absent during working or training hours for rehabilitation, assessment or treatment;
(g) giving, or arranging for, training or mentoring (whether for the disabled person or any other person);
(h) acquiring or modifying equipment;
(i) modifying instructions or reference manuals;
(j) modifying procedures for testing or assessment;

(k)   providing a reader or interpreter;

(l)   providing supervision or other support.

(3) For the purposes of a duty to make reasonable adjustments, where under any binding obligation a person is required to obtain the consent of another person to any alteration of the premises occupied by him—

(a)   it is always reasonable for him to have to take steps to obtain that consent; and

(b)   it is never reasonable for him to have to make that alteration before that consent is obtained.

(4) The steps referred to in subsection (3)(a) shall not be taken to include an application to a court or tribunal.

(5) In subsection (3), 'binding obligation' means a legally binding obligation (not contained in a lease (within the meaning of section 18A(3)) in relation to the premises, whether arising from an agreement or otherwise.

(6) A provision of this Part imposing a duty to make reasonable adjustments applies only for the purpose of determining whether a person has discriminated against a disabled person; and accordingly a breach of any such duty is not actionable as such.

Amendment – Inserted by Disability Discrimination Act 1995 (Amendment) Regulations 2003, SI 2003/1673, regs 3(1), 17(2).

18C   Charities and support for particular groups of persons

(1) Nothing in this Part—

(a)   affects any charitable instrument which provides for conferring benefits on one or more categories of person determined by reference to any physical or mental capacity; or

(b)   makes unlawful any act done by a charity or recognised body in pursuance of any of its charitable purposes, so far as those purposes are connected with persons so determined.

(2) Nothing in this Part prevents—

(a)   a person who provides supported employment from treating members of a particular group of disabled persons more favourably than other persons in providing such employment; or

(b)   the Secretary of State from agreeing to arrangements for the provision of supported employment which will, or may, have that effect.

(3) In this section—

'charitable instrument' means an enactment or other instrument (whenever taking effect) so far as it relates to charitable purposes;

'charity' has the same meaning as in the Charities Act 1993;

'recognised body' means a body which is a recognised body for the purposes of Part I of the Law Reform (Miscellaneous Provisions) (Scotland) Act 1990; and

'supported employment' means facilities provided, or in respect of which payments are made, under section 15 of the Disabled Persons (Employment) Act 1944.

(4) In the application of this section to England and Wales, 'charitable purposes' means purposes which are exclusively charitable according to the law of England and Wales.

(5) In the application of this section to Scotland, 'charitable purposes' shall be construed in the same way as if it were contained in the Income Tax Acts.

Amendment – Inserted by Disability Discrimination Act 1995 (Amendment) Regulations 2003, SI 2003/1673, regs 3(1), 11.

18D   Interpretation of Part 2

(1) Subject to any duty to make reasonable adjustments, nothing in this Part is to be taken to require a person to treat a disabled person more favourably than he treats or would treat others.

(2) In this Part—

'benefits', except in sections 4G to 4K, includes facilities and services;

'detriment', except in section 16C(2)(b), does not include conduct of the nature referred to in section 3B (harassment);

'discriminate', 'discrimination' and other related expressions are to be construed in accordance with section 3A;

'duty to make reasonable adjustments' means a duty imposed by or under section 4A, 4B(5) or (6), 4E, 4H, 6B, 7B, 7D, 14, 14B, 14D or 16A(5);

'employer' includes a person who has no employees but is seeking to employ another person;

'harassment' is to be construed in accordance with section 3B;

'physical feature', in relation to any premises, includes any of the following (whether permanent or temporary)—

(a)   any feature arising from the design or construction of a building on the premises,

(b)   any feature on the premises of any approach to, exit from or access to such a building,

(c)   any fixtures, fittings, furnishings, furniture, equipment or material in or on the premises,

(d)   any other physical element or quality of any land comprised in the premises;

'provision, criterion or practice' includes any arrangements.

Amendment – Inserted by Disability Discrimination Act 1995 (Amendment) Regulations 2003, SI 2003/1673, regs 3(1), 18. Amended by Disability Discrimination Act 1995 (Pensions) Regulations 2003 SI 2003/2770, regs 2, 4(2)(a), (b).

PART III

DISCRIMINATION IN OTHER AREAS

Goods, facilities and services

19   Discrimination in relation to goods, facilities and services

(1) It is unlawful for a provider of services to discriminate against a disabled person—

(a)   in refusing to provide, or deliberately not providing, to the disabled person any service which he provides, or is prepared to provide, to members of the public;

(b)   in failing to comply with any duty imposed on him by section 21 in circumstances in which the effect of that failure is to make it impossible or unreasonably difficult for the disabled person to make use of any such service;

(c)   in the standard of service which he provides to the disabled person or the manner in which he provides it to him; or

(d)   in the terms on which he provides a service to the disabled person.

(2) For the purposes of this section and sections 20 and 21—

(a)   the provision of services includes the provision of any goods or facilities;

(b)   a person is 'a provider of services' if he is concerned with the provision, in the United Kingdom, of services to the public or to a section of the public; and

(c)   it is irrelevant whether a service is provided on payment or without payment.

(3) The following are examples of services to which this section and sections 20 and 21 apply—

(a)   access to and use of any place which members of the public are permitted to enter;

(b)   access to and use of means of communication;

(c)   access to and use of information services;

(d)   accommodation in a hotel, boarding house or other similar establishment;

(e)   facilities by way of banking or insurance or for grants, loans, credit or finance;

(f)   facilities for entertainment, recreation or refreshment;

(g)   facilities provided by employment agencies or under section 2 of the Employment and Training Act 1973;

(h)   the services of any profession or trade, or any local or other public authority.

(4) In the case of an act which constitutes discrimination by virtue of section 55, this section also applies to discrimination against a person who is not disabled.

(5) Except in such circumstances as may be prescribed, this section and sections 20 and 21 do not apply to—

(a)–(ab) (*repealed*)

(b)   any service so far as it consists of the use of any means of transport; or

(c)   such other services as may be prescribed.

(5A) Nothing in this Part applies to the provision of a service in relation to which discrimination is made unlawful by section 28A, 28F or 28R.

(6) (*repealed*)

Amendments – Amended by Education Act 1996, s 582(1), Sch 37, Pt I, para 129; School Standards and Framework Act 1998, s 140(3), Sch 31; Teaching and Higher Education Act 1998, s 38; Learning and Skills Act 2000, ss 149, 153, Sch 9, paras 1, 49, Sch 11; Special Educational Needs and Disability Act 2001, ss 38(1), (5), (6), 42(6), Sch 9.

---

20   Meaning of 'discrimination'

(1) For the purposes of section 19, a provider of services discriminates against a disabled person if—

(a)   for a reason which relates to the disabled person's disability, he treats him less favourably than he treats or would treat others to whom that reason does not or would not apply; and

(b)   he cannot show that the treatment in question is justified.

(2) For the purposes of section 19, a provider of services also discriminates against a disabled person if—

(a) he fails to comply with a section 21 duty imposed on him in relation to the disabled person; and

(b) he cannot show that his failure to comply with that duty is justified.

(3) For the purposes of this section, treatment is justified only if—

(a) in the opinion of the provider of services, one or more of the conditions mentioned in subsection (4) are satisfied; and

(b) it is reasonable, in all the circumstances of the case, for him to hold that opinion.

(4) The conditions are that—

(a) in any case, the treatment is necessary in order not to endanger the health or safety of any person (which may include that of the disabled person);

(b) in any case, the disabled person is incapable of entering into an enforceable agreement, or of giving an informed consent, and for that reason the treatment is reasonable in that case;

(c) in a case falling with section 19(1)(a), the treatment is necessary because the provider of services would otherwise be unable to provide the service to members of the public;

(d) in a case falling within section 19(1)(c) or (d), the treatment is necessary in order for the provider of services to be able to provide the service to the disabled person or to other members of the public;

(e) in a case falling within section 19(1)(d), the difference in the terms on which the service is provided to the disabled person and those on which it is provided to other members of the public reflects the greater cost to the provider of services in providing the service to the disabled person.

(5) Any increase in the cost of providing a service to a disabled person which results from compliance by a provider of services with a section 21 duty shall be disregarded for the purposes of subsection (4)(e).

(6) Regulations may make provision, for purposes of this section, as to circumstances in which—

(a) it is reasonable for a provider of services to hold the opinion mentioned in subsection (3)(a);

(b) it is not reasonable for a provider of services to hold that opinion.

(7) Regulations may make provision for subsection (4)(b) not to apply in prescribed circumstances where—

(a) a person is acting for a disabled person under a power of attorney;

(b) functions conferred by or under Part VII of the Mental Health Act 1983 are exercisable in relation to a disabled person's property or affairs; or

(c) powers are exercisable in Scotland in relation to a disabled person's property or affairs in consequence of the appointment of a curator bonis, tutor or judicial factor.

(8) Regulations may make provision, for purposes of this section, as to circumstances (other than those mentioned in subsection (4)) in which treatment is to be taken to be justified.

(9) In subsections (3), (4) and (8) 'treatment' includes failure to comply with a section 21 duty.

21   Duty of providers of services to make adjustments

(1) Where a provider of services has a practice, policy or procedure which makes it impossible or unreasonably difficult for disabled persons to make use of a service which he provides, or is prepared to provide, to other members of the public, it is his duty to take such steps as it is reasonable, in all the circumstances of the case, for him to have to take in order to change that practice, policy or procedure so that it no longer has that effect.

(2) Where a physical feature (for example, one arising from the design or construction of a building or the approach or access to premises) makes it impossible or unreasonably difficult for disabled persons to make use of such a service, it is the duty of the provider of that service to take such steps as it is reasonable, in all the circumstances of the case, for him to have to take in order to—

    (a)   remove the feature;
    (b)   alter it so that it no longer has that effect;
    (c)   provide a reasonable means of avoiding the feature; or
    (d)   provide a reasonable alternative method of making the service in question available to disabled persons.

(3) Regulations may prescribe—

    (a)   matters which are to be taken into account in determining whether any provision of a kind mentioned in subsection (2)(c) or (d) is reasonable; and
    (b)   categories of providers of services to whom subsection (2) does not apply.

(4) Where an auxiliary aid or service (for example, the provision of information on audio tape or of a sign language interpreter) would—

    (a)   enable disabled persons to make use of a service which a provider of services provides, or is prepared to provide, to members of the public, or
    (b)   facilitate the use by disabled persons of such a service,

it is the duty of the provider of that service to take such steps as it is reasonable, in all the circumstances of the case, for him to have to take in order to provide that auxiliary aid or service.

(5) Regulations may make provision, for the purposes of this section—

    (a)   as to circumstances in which it is reasonable for a provider of services to have to take steps of a prescribed description;
    (b)   as to circumstances in which it is not reasonable for a provider of services to have to take steps of a prescribed description;
    (c)   as to what is to be included within the meaning of 'practice, policy or procedure';
    (d)   as to what is not to be included within the meaning of that expression;
    (e)   as to things which are to be treated as physical features;
    (f)   as to things which are not to be treated as such features;
    (g)   as to things which are to be treated as auxiliary aids or services;
    (h)   as to things which are not to be treated as auxiliary aids or services.

(6) Nothing in this section requires a provider of services to take any steps which would fundamentally alter the nature of the service in question or the nature of his trade, profession or business.

(7) Nothing in this section requires a provider of services to take any steps which would cause him to incur expenditure exceeding the prescribed maximum.

(8) Regulations under subsection (7) may provide for the prescribed maximum to be calculated by reference to—

(a)   aggregate amounts of expenditure incurred in relation to different cases;
(b)   prescribed periods;
(c)   services of a prescribed description;
(d)   premises of a prescribed description; or
(e)   such other criteria as may be prescribed.

(9) Regulations may provide, for the purposes of subsection (7), for expenditure incurred by one provider of services to be treated as incurred by another.

(10) This section imposes duties only for the purpose of determining whether a provider of services has discriminated against a disabled person; and accordingly a breach of any such duty is not actionable as such.

21A   Employment services

(1) In this Part, 'employment services' means—

(a)   vocational guidance;
(b)   vocational training; or
(c)   services to assist a person to obtain or retain employment, or to establish himself as self-employed.

(2) It is unlawful for a provider of employment services, in relation to such services, to subject to harassment a disabled person—

(a)   to whom he is providing such services, or
(b)   who has requested him to provide such services;

and section 3B (meaning of 'harassment') applies for the purposes of this subsection as it applies for the purposes of Part 2.

(3) In their application to employment services, the preceding provisions of this Part have effect as follows.

(4) Section 19 has effect as if—

(a)   after subsection (1)(a), there were inserted the following paragraph—

'(aa) in failing to comply with a duty imposed on him by subsection (1) of section 21 in circumstances in which the effect of that failure is to place the disabled person at a substantial disadvantage in comparison with persons who are not disabled in relation to the provision of the service;';
(b)   in subsection (1)(b), for 'section 21' there were substituted 'subsection (2) or (4) of section 21';
(c)   in subsection (2), for 'sections 20 and 21' there were substituted 'sections 20, 21 and 21A'.

(5) Section 20 has effect as if—

    (a)   after subsection (1), there were inserted the following subsection—

        '(1A) For the purposes of section 19, a provider of services also discriminates against a disabled person if he fails to comply with a duty imposed on him by subsection (1) of section 21 in relation to the disabled person.';

    (b)   in subsection (2)(a), for 'a section 21 duty imposed' there were substituted 'a duty imposed by subsection (2) or (4) of section 21';

    (c)   after subsection (3), there were inserted the following subsection—

        '(3A) But treatment of a disabled person cannot be justified under subsection (3) if it amounts to direct discrimination falling within section 3A(5).'.

(6) Section 21 has effect as if—

    (a)   in subsection (1), for 'makes it impossible or unreasonably difficult for disabled persons to make use of' there were substituted 'places disabled persons at a substantial disadvantage in comparison with persons who are not disabled in relation to the provision of';

    (b)   after subsection (1), there were inserted the following subsection—

        '(1A) In subsection (1), 'practice, policy or procedure' includes a provision or criterion.'.

Amendment – Inserted by Disability Discrimination Act 1995 (Amendment) Regulations 2003, SI 2003/1673, regs 3(1), 19(1).

Premises

22 Discrimination in relation to premises

(1) It is unlawful for a person with power to dispose of any premises to discriminate against a disabled person—

    (a)   in the terms on which he offers to dispose of those premises to the disabled person;

    (b)   by refusing to dispose of those premises to the disabled person; or

    (c)   in his treatment of the disabled person in relation to any list of persons in need of premises of that description.

(2) Subsection (1) does not apply to a person who owns an estate or interest in the premises and wholly occupies them unless, for the purpose of disposing of the premises, he—

    (a)   uses the services of an estate agent, or

    (b)   publishes an advertisement or causes an advertisement to be published.

(3) It is unlawful for a person managing any premises to discriminate against a disabled person occupying those premises—

    (a)   in the way he permits the disabled person to make use of any benefits or facilities;

(b)   by refusing or deliberately omitting to permit the disabled person to make use of any benefits or facilities; or

(c)   by evicting the disabled person, or subjecting him to any other detriment.

(4) It is unlawful for any person whose licence or consent is required for the disposal of any premises comprised in, or (in Scotland) the subject of, a tenancy to discriminate against a disabled person by withholding his licence or consent for the disposal of the premises to the disabled person.

(5) Subsection (4) applies to tenancies created before as well as after the passing of this Act.

(6) In this section—

'advertisement' includes every form of advertisement or notice, whether to the public or not;

'dispose', in relation to premises, includes granting a right to occupy the premises, and, in relation to premises comprised in, or (in Scotland) the subject of, a tenancy, includes—

(a)   assigning the tenancy, and

(b)   sub-letting or parting with possession of the premises or any part of the premises;

and 'disposal' shall be construed accordingly;

'estate agent' means a person who, by way of profession or trade, provides services for the purpose of finding premises for persons seeking to acquire them or assisting in the disposal of premises; and

'tenancy' means a tenancy created—

(a)   by a lease or sub-lease,

(b)   by an agreement for a lease or sub-lease,

(c)   by a tenancy agreement, or

(d)   in pursuance of any enactment.

(7) In the case of an act which constitutes discrimination by virtue of section 55, this section also applies to discrimination against a person who is not disabled.

(8) This section applies only in relation to premises in the United Kingdom.

23   Exemption for small dwellings

(1) Where the conditions mentioned in subsection (2) are satisfied, subsection (1), (3) or (as the case may be) (4) of section 22 does not apply.

(2) The conditions are that—

(a)   the relevant occupier resides, and intends to continue to reside, on the premises;

(b)   the relevant occupier shares accommodation on the premises with persons who reside on the premises and are not members of his household;

(c)   the shared accommodation is not storage accommodation or a means of access; and

(d)   the premises are small premises.

(3) For the purposes of this section, premises are 'small premises' if they fall within subsection (4) or (5).

(4) Premises fall within this subsection if—

(a)   only the relevant occupier and members of his household reside in the accommodation occupied by him;

(b)   the premises comprise, in addition to the accommodation occupied by the relevant occupier, residential accommodation for at least one other household;

(c)   the residential accommodation for each other household is let, or available for letting, on a separate tenancy or similar agreement; and

(d)   there are not normally more than two such other households.

(5) Premises fall within this subsection if there is not normally residential accommodation on the premises for more than six persons in addition to the relevant occupier and any members of his household.

(6) For the purposes of this section 'the relevant occupier' means—

(a)   in a case falling within section 22(1), the person with power to dispose of the premises, or a near relative of his;

(b)   in a case falling within section 22(4), the person whose licence or consent is required for the disposal of the premises, or a near relative of his.

(7) For the purposes of this section—

'near relative' means a person's spouse [*or* civil partner], partner, parent, child, grandparent, grandchild, or brother or sister (whether of full or half blood or *by affinity*) [by marriage or civil partnership]; and

'partner' means the other member of a couple consisting of a man and a woman who are not married to each other but are living together as husband and wife.

['partner' means the other member of a couple consisting of—

(a)   a man and a woman who are not married to each other but are living together as husband and wife, or

(b)   two people of the same sex who are not civil partners of each other but are living together as if they were civil partners].

Amendment – Prospective amendment by Civil Partnership Act 2004, s 261(1), Sch 27, para 150(1), (2)(a), (b), 3.

24   Meaning of 'discrimination'

(1) For the purposes of section 22, a person ('A') discriminates against a disabled person if—

(a)   for a reason which relates to the disabled person's disability, he treats him less favourably than he treats or would treat others to whom that reason does not or would not apply; and

(b)   he cannot show that the treatment in question is justified.

(2) For the purposes of this section, treatment is justified only if—

(a)   in A's opinion, one or more of the conditions mentioned in subsection (3) are satisfied; and

(b)   it is reasonable, in all the circumstances of the case, for him to hold that opinion.

(3) The conditions are that—

(a)   in any case, the treatment is necessary in order not to endanger the health or safety of any person (which may include that of the disabled person);

(b) in any case, the disabled person is incapable of entering into an enforceable agreement, or of giving an informed consent, and for that reason the treatment is reasonable in that case;

(c) in a case falling within section 22(3)(a), the treatment is necessary in order for the disabled person or the occupiers of other premises forming part of the building to make use of the benefit or facility;

(d) in a case falling within section 22(3)(b), the treatment is necessary in order for the occupiers of other premises forming part of the building to make use of the benefit or facility.

(4) Regulations may make provision, for purposes of this section, as to circumstances in which—

(a) it is reasonable for a person to hold the opinion mentioned in subsection 2(a);

(b) it is not reasonable for a person to hold that opinion.

(5) Regulations may make provision, for purposes of this section, as to circumstances (other than those mentioned in subsection (3)) in which treatment is to be taken to be justified.

Enforcement, etc

25 Enforcement, remedies and procedure

(1) A claim by any person that another person—

(a) has discriminated against him in a way which is unlawful under this Part; or

(b) is by virtue of section 57 or 58 to be treated as having discriminated against him in such a way,

may be made the subject of civil proceedings in the same way as any other claim in tort or (in Scotland) in reparation for breach of statutory duty.

(2) For the avoidance of doubt it is hereby declared that damages in respect of discrimination in a way which is unlawful under this Part may include compensation for injury to feelings whether or not they include compensation under any other head.

(3) Proceedings in England and Wales shall be brought only in a county court.

(4) Proceedings in Scotland shall be brought only in a sheriff court.

(5) The remedies available in such proceedings are those which are available in the High Court or (as the case may be) the Court of Session.

(6) Part II of Schedule 3 makes further provision about the enforcement of this Part and about procedure.

(7) Subsection (1) does not apply in relation to a claim by a person that another person—

(a) has discriminated against him or subjected him to harassment in relation to the provision of employment services in a way which is unlawful under this Part; or

(b) is by virtue of section 57 or 58 to be treated as having discriminated against him or subjected him to harassment in such a way.

(8) A claim of the kind referred to in subsection (7) may be presented as a complaint to an employment tribunal.

(9) Section 17A(1A) to (7) and paragraphs 3 and 4 of Schedule 3 apply in relation to a complaint under subsection (8) as if it were a complaint under section 17A(1) (and paragraphs 6 to 8 of Schedule 3 do not apply in relation to such a complaint).

Amendment – Inserted by Disability Discrimination Act 1995 (Amendment) Regulations 2003, SI 2003/1673, regs 3(1), 19(2).

26   Validity and revision of certain agreements

(1) Any term in a contract for the provision of goods, facilities or services or in any other agreement is void so far as it purports to—

(a)   require a person to do anything which would contravene any provision of, or made under, this Part,
(b)   exclude or limit the operation of any provision of this Part, or
(c)   prevent any person from making a claim under this Part.

(1A) Subsection (1) does not apply to any term in a contract, or other agreement, for the provision of employment services.

(2) Paragraphs (b) and (c) of subsection (1) do not apply to an agreement settling a claim to which section 25 applies.

(3) On the application of any person interested in an agreement to which subsection (1) applies, a county court or a sheriff court may make such order as it thinks just for modifying the agreement to take account of the effect of subsection (1).

(4) No such order shall be made unless all persons affected have been—

(a)   given notice of the application; and
(b)   afforded an opportunity to make representations to the court.

(5) Subsection (4) applies subject to any rules of court providing for that notice to be dispensed with.

(6) An order under subsection (3) may include provision as respects any period before the making of the order.

Amendment – Inserted by Disability Discrimination Act 1995 (Amendment) Regulations 2003, SI 2003/1673, regs 3(1), 19(3).

27   Alterations to premises occupied under leases

(1) This section applies where—

(a)   a provider of services ('the occupier') occupies premises under a lease;
(b)   but for this section, he would not be entitled to make a particular alteration to the premises; and
(c)   the alteration is one which the occupier proposes to make in order to comply with a section 21 duty.

(2) Except to the extent to which it expressly so provides, the lease shall have effect by virtue of this subsection as if it provided—

   (a)   for the occupier to be entitled to make the alteration with the written consent of the lessor;

   (b)   for the occupier to have to make a written application to the lessor for consent if he wishes to make the alteration;

   (c)   if such an application is made, for the lessor not to withhold his consent unreasonably; and

   (d)   for the lessor to be entitled to make his consent subject to reasonable conditions.

(3) In this section—

'lease' includes a tenancy, sub-lease or sub-tenancy and an agreement for a lease, tenancy, sub-lease or sub-tenancy; and

'sub-lease' and 'sub-tenancy' have such meaning as may be prescribed.

(4) If the terms and conditions of a lease—

   (a)   impose conditions which are to apply if the occupier alters the premises, or

   (b)   entitle the lessor to impose conditions when consenting to the occupier's altering the premises,

the occupier is to be treated for the purposes of subsection (1) as not being entitled to make the alteration.

(5) Part II of Schedule 4 supplements the provisions of this section.

28 Conciliation of disputes

(1) The Commission may make arrangements with any other person for the provision of conciliation services by, or by persons appointed by, that person in relation to disputes arising under this Part.

(2) In deciding what arrangements (if any) to make, the Commission shall have regard to the desirability of securing, so far as reasonably practicable, that conciliation services are available for all disputes arising under this Part which the parties may wish to refer to conciliation.

(3) No member or employee of the Commission may provide conciliation services in relation to disputes arising under this Part.

(4) The Commission shall ensure that any arrangements under this section include appropriate safeguards to prevent the disclosure to members or employees of the Commission of information obtained by a person in connection with the provision of conciliation services in pursuance of the arrangements.

(5) Subsection (4) does not apply to information relating to a dispute which is disclosed with the consent of the parties to that dispute.

(6) Subsection (4) does not apply to information which—

   (a)   is not identifiable with a particular dispute or a particular person; and

   (b)   is reasonably required by the Commission for the purpose of monitoring the operation of the arrangements concerned.

(7) Anything communicated to a person while providing conciliation services in pursuance of any arrangements under this section is not admissible in evidence in any proceedings except with the consent of the person who communicated it to that person.

(8) In this section 'conciliation services' means advice and assistance provided by a conciliator to the parties to a dispute with a view to promoting its settlement otherwise than through the courts.

Amendment – Substituted by Disability Rights Commission Act 1999, s 10.

PART 4

EDUCATION

Chapter 1
Schools

Duties of responsible bodies

28A   Discrimination against disabled pupils and prospective pupils

(1) It is unlawful for the body responsible for a school to discriminate against a disabled person—

- (a)   in the arrangements it makes for determining admission to the school as a pupil;
- (b)   in the terms on which it offers to admit him to the school as a pupil; or
- (c)   by refusing or deliberately omitting to accept an application for his admission to the school as a pupil.

(2) It is unlawful for the body responsible for a school to discriminate against a disabled pupil in the education or associated services provided for, or offered to, pupils at the school by that body.

(3) The Secretary of State may by regulations prescribe services which are, or services which are not, to be regarded for the purposes of subsection (2) as being—

- (a)   education; or
- (b)   an associated service.

(4) It is unlawful for the body responsible for a school to discriminate against a disabled pupil by excluding him from the school, whether permanently or temporarily.

(5) The body responsible for a school is to be determined in accordance with Schedule 4A, and in the remaining provisions of this Chapter is referred to as the 'responsible body'.

(6) In the case of an act which constitutes discrimination by virtue of section 55, this section also applies to discrimination against a person who is not disabled.

Amendment – Section and preceding Chapter heading and cross-heading inserted by Special Educational Needs and Disability Act 2001, s 11(1).

28B   Meaning of 'discrimination'

(1) For the purposes of section 28A, a responsible body discriminates against a disabled person if—

(a)   for a reason which relates to his disability, it treats him less favourably than it treats or would treat others to whom that reason does not or would not apply; and

(b)   it cannot show that the treatment in question is justified.

(2) For the purposes of section 28A, a responsible body also discriminates against a disabled person if—

(a)   it fails, to his detriment, to comply with section 28C; and

(b)   it cannot show that its failure to comply is justified.

(3) In relation to a failure to take a particular step, a responsible body does not discriminate against a person if it shows—

(a)   that, at the time in question, it did not know and could not reasonably have been expected to know, that he was disabled; and

(b)   that its failure to take the step was attributable to that lack of knowledge.

(4) The taking of a particular step by a responsible body in relation to a person does not amount to less favourable treatment if it shows that at the time in question it did not know, and could not reasonably have been expected to know, that he was disabled.

(5) Subsections (6) to (8) apply in determining whether, for the purposes of this section—

(a)   less favourable treatment of a person, or

(b)   failure to comply with section 28C,

is justified.

(6) Less favourable treatment of a person is justified if it is the result of a permitted form of selection.

(7) Otherwise, less favourable treatment, or a failure to comply with section 28C, is justified only if the reason for it is both material to the circumstances of the particular case and substantial.

(8) If, in a case falling within subsection (1)—

(a)   the responsible body is under a duty imposed by section 28C in relation to the disabled person, but

(b)   it fails without justification to comply with that duty,

its treatment of that person cannot be justified under subsection (7) unless that treatment would have been justified even if it had complied with that duty.

Amendment – Inserted by Special Educational Needs and Disability Act 2001, s 12.

28C   Disabled pupils not to be substantially disadvantaged

(1) The responsible body for a school must take such steps as it is reasonable for it to have to take to ensure that—

(a)   in relation to the arrangements it makes for determining the admission of pupils to the school, disabled persons are not placed at a substantial disadvantage in comparison with persons who are not disabled; and

(b)   in relation to education and associated services provided for, or offered to, pupils at the school by it, disabled pupils are not placed at a substantial disadvantage in comparison with pupils who are not disabled.

(2) That does not require the responsible body to—

(a)   remove or alter a physical feature (for example, one arising from the design or construction of the school premises or the location of resources); or

(b)   provide auxiliary aids or services.

(3) Regulations may make provision, for the purposes of this section—

(a)   as to circumstances in which it is reasonable for a responsible body to have to take steps of a prescribed description;

(b)   as to steps which it is always reasonable for a responsible body to have to take;

(c)   as to circumstances in which it is not reasonable for a responsible body to have to take steps of a prescribed description;

(d)   as to steps which it is never reasonable for a responsible body to have to take.

(4) In considering whether it is reasonable for it to have to take a particular step in order to comply with its duty under subsection (1), a responsible body must have regard to any relevant provisions of a code of practice issued under section 53A.

(5) Subsection (6) applies if, in relation to a person, a confidentiality request has been made of which a responsible body is aware.

(6) In determining whether it is reasonable for the responsible body to have to take a particular step in relation to that person in order to comply with its duty under subsection (1), regard shall be had to the extent to which taking the step in question is consistent with compliance with that request.

(7) 'Confidentiality request' means a request which asks for the nature, or asks for the existence, of a disabled person's disability to be treated as confidential and which satisfies either of the following conditions—

(a)   it is made by that person's parent; or

(b)   it is made by that person himself and the responsible body reasonably believes that he has sufficient understanding of the nature of the request and of its effect.

(8) This section imposes duties only for the purpose of determining whether a responsible body has discriminated against a disabled person; and accordingly a breach of any such duty is not actionable as such.

Amendment – Inserted by Special Educational Needs and Disability Act 2001, s 13.

28D   Accessibility strategies and plans

(1) Each local education authority must prepare, in relation to schools for which they are the responsible body—

(a)   an accessibility strategy;

(b)   further such strategies at such times as may be prescribed.

(2) An accessibility strategy is a strategy for, over a prescribed period—

(a) increasing the extent to which disabled pupils can participate in the schools' curriculums;

(b) improving the physical environment of the schools for the purpose of increasing the extent to which disabled pupils are able to take advantage of education and associated services provided or offered by the schools; and

(c) improving the delivery to disabled pupils—

    (i) within a reasonable time, and

    (ii) in ways which are determined after taking account of their disabilities and any preferences expressed by them or their parents,

of information which is provided in writing for pupils who are not disabled.

(3) An accessibility strategy must be in writing.

(4) Each local education authority must keep their accessibility strategy under review during the period to which it relates and, if necessary, revise it.

(5) It is the duty of each local education authority to implement their accessibility strategy.

(6) *An inspection under section 38 of the Education Act 1997 (inspections of local education authorities) may extend to the performance by a local education authority of their functions in relation to the preparation, review, revision and implementation of their accessibility strategy.*[1]

(7) Subsections (8) to (13) apply to—

(a) maintained schools;

(b) independent schools; and

(c) special schools which are not maintained special schools but which are approved by the Secretary of State, or by the National Assembly, under section 342 of the Education Act 1996.

(8) The responsible body must prepare—

(a) an accessibility plan;

(b) further such plans at such times as may be prescribed.

(9) An accessibility plan is a plan for, over a prescribed period—

(a) increasing the extent to which disabled pupils can participate in the school's curriculum;

(b) improving the physical environment of the school for the purpose of increasing the extent to which disabled pupils are able to take advantage of education and associated services provided or offered by the school; and

(c) improving the delivery to disabled pupils—

    (i) within a reasonable time, and

    (ii) in ways which are determined after taking account of their disabilities and any preferences expressed by them or their parents,

of information which is provided in writing for pupils who are not disabled.

(10) An accessibility plan must be in writing.

(11) During the period to which the plan relates, the responsible body must keep its accessibility plan under review and, if necessary, revise it.

(12) It is the duty of the responsible body to implement its accessibility plan.

(13) An inspection under the School Inspections Act 1996 may extend to the performance by the responsible body of its functions in relation to the preparation, publication, review, revision and implementation of its accessibility plan.

(14) For a maintained school [or maintained nursery school][2], the duties imposed by subsections (8) to (12) are duties of the governing body.

(15) Regulations may prescribe services which are, or services which are not, to be regarded for the purposes of this section as being—

(a)   education; or
(b)   an associated service.

(16) In this section and in section 28E, 'local education authority' has the meaning given in section 12 of the Education Act 1996.

(17) In relation to Wales—

'prescribed' means prescribed in regulations; and
'regulations' means regulations made by the National Assembly.

(18) 'Disabled pupil' includes a disabled person who may be admitted to the school as a pupil.

(19) 'Maintained school' and 'independent school' have the meaning given in section 28Q(5).

Amendments – Inserted by Special Educational Needs and Disability Act 2001, s 14(1).
[1] Subsection prospectively repealed by Children Act 2004, s 64, Sch 5, Pt 3.
[2] Words inserted in relation to England by Education Act 2002, s 215(1), Sch 21, para 26, and prospectively inserted in relation to Wales as from a day to be appointed.

28E   Accessibility strategies and plans: procedure

(1) In preparing their accessibility strategy, a local education authority must have regard to—

(a)   the need to allocate adequate resources for implementing the strategy; and
(b)   any guidance issued as to—
        (i)   the content of an accessibility strategy;
        (ii) the form in which it is to be produced; and
        (iii) the persons to be consulted in its preparation.

(2) A local education authority must have regard to any guidance issued as to compliance with the requirements of section 28D(4).

(3) Guidance under subsection (1)(b) or (2) may be issued—

(a)   for England, by the Secretary of State; and
(b)   for Wales, by the National Assembly.

(4) In preparing an accessibility plan, the responsible body must have regard to the need to allocate adequate resources for implementing the plan.

(5) If the Secretary of State asks for a copy of—

(a)   the accessibility strategy prepared by a local education authority in England, or
(b)   the accessibility plan prepared by the proprietor of an independent school (other than an Academy) in England,

the strategy or plan must be given to him.

(6) If the National Assembly asks for a copy of—

(a)   the accessibility strategy prepared by a local education authority in Wales, or

(b)   the accessibility plan prepared by the proprietor of an independent school (other than an Academy) in Wales,

the strategy or plan must be given to it.

(7) If asked to do so, a local education authority must make a copy of their accessibility strategy available for inspection at such reasonable times as they may determine.

(8) If asked to do so, the proprietor of an independent school which is not an Academy must make a copy of his accessibility plan available for inspection at such reasonable times as he may determine.

Amendments – Inserted by Special Educational Needs and Disability Act 2001, s 15. Amended by Education Act 2002, s 65(3), Sch 7, Pt 2, para 5(1), (2).

Residual duty of education authorities

28F   Duty of education authorities not to discriminate

(1) This section applies to—

(a)   the functions of a local education authority under the Education Acts; and

(b)   the functions of an education authority under—
   (i)   the Education (Scotland) Act 1980;
   (ii)   the Education (Scotland) Act 1996; and
   (iii) the Standards in Scotland's Schools etc Act 2000.

(2) But it does not apply to any prescribed function.

(3) In discharging a function to which this section applies, it is unlawful for the authority to discriminate against—

(a)   a disabled pupil; or

(b)   a disabled person who may be admitted to a school as a pupil.

(4) But an act done in the discharge of a function to which this section applies is unlawful as a result of subsection (3) only if no other provision of this Chapter makes that act unlawful.

(5) In the case of an act which constitutes discrimination by virtue of section 55, this section also applies to discrimination against a person who is not disabled.

(6) In this section and section 28G, 'local education authority' has the meaning given in section 12 of the Education Act 1996.

(7) 'The Education Acts' has the meaning given in section 578 of the Education Act 1996.

(8) In this section and section 28G, 'education authority' has the meaning given in section 135(1) of the Education (Scotland) Act 1980.

Amendment – Section and preceding cross-heading inserted by Special Educational Needs and Disability Act 2001, s 16.

28G   Residual duty: supplementary provisions

(1) Section 28B applies for the purposes of section 28F as it applies for the purposes of section 28A with the following modifications—

    (a)   references to a responsible body are to be read as references to an authority; and

    (b)   references to section 28C are to be read as references to subsections (2) to (4).

(2) Each authority must take such steps as it is reasonable for it to have to take to ensure that, in discharging any function to which section 28F applies—

    (a)   disabled persons who may be admitted to a school as pupils are not placed at a substantial disadvantage in comparison with persons who are not disabled; and

    (b)   disabled pupils are not placed at a substantial disadvantage in comparison with pupils who are not disabled.

(3) That does not require the authority to—

    (a)   remove or alter a physical feature; or

    (b)   provide auxiliary aids or services.

(4) This section imposes duties only for the purpose of determining whether an authority has discriminated against a disabled person; and accordingly a breach of any such duty is not actionable as such.

(5) A reference in sections 28I, 28K(1), 28M(6) and 28P to a responsible body is to be read as including a reference to a local education authority in relation to a function to which section 28F applies.

(6) A reference in section 28N and 28P to a responsible body is to be read as including a reference to an education authority in relation to a function to which section 28F applies.

(7) 'Authority' means—

    (a)   in relation to England and Wales, a local education authority; and

    (b)   in relation to Scotland, an education authority.

Amendment – Inserted by Special Educational Needs and Disability Act 2001, s 16.

Enforcement: England and Wales

28H   Tribunals

(1) The Special Educational Needs Tribunal—

    (a)   is to continue to exist; but

    (b)   after the commencement date is to be known as the Special Educational Needs and Disability Tribunal.

(2) In this Chapter—

'the Tribunal' means the Special Educational Needs and Disability Tribunal, and 'the Welsh Tribunal' means the Special Educational Needs Tribunal for Wales.

(3) In addition to the jurisdiction of those tribunals under Part 4 of the Education Act 1996, each of them is to exercise the jurisdiction conferred on it by this Chapter.

(4) 'Commencement date' means the day on which section 17 of the Special Educational Needs and Disability Act 2001 comes into force.[2]

Amendments – Section and preceding cross-heading inserted by Special Educational Needs and Disability Act 2001, s 17(1). Amended by Education Act 2002, s 195, Sch 18, paras 7, 8(1), (2).

28I Jurisdiction and powers of the Tribunal

(1) A claim that a responsible body—

  (a) has discriminated against a person ('A') in a way which is made unlawful under this Chapter, or

  (b) is by virtue of section 58 to be treated as having discriminated against a person ('A') in such a way,

may be made to the appropriate tribunal by A's parent.

(2) But this section does not apply to a claim to which section 28K or 28L applies.

(3) If the appropriate tribunal considers that a claim under subsection (1) is well founded—

  (a) it may declare that A has been unlawfully discriminated against; and

  (b) if it does so, it may make such order as it considers reasonable in all the circumstances of the case.

(4) The power conferred by subsection (3)(b)—

  (a) may, in particular, be exercised with a view to obviating or reducing the adverse effect on the person concerned of any matter to which the claim relates; but

  (b) does not include power to order the payment of any sum by way of compensation.

(5) Subject to regulations under section 28J(8), the appropriate tribunal—

  (a) for a claim against the responsible body for a school in England, is the Tribunal,

  (b) for a claim against the responsible body for a school in Wales, is the Welsh Tribunal.

Amendments – Inserted by Special Educational Needs and Disability Act 2001, s 18. Amended by Education Act 2002, s 195, Sch 18, paras 7, 9(1)–(3).

28J Procedure

(1) Regulations may make provision about—

  (a) the proceedings of the Tribunal on a claim of unlawful discrimination under this Chapter; and

(b)   the making of a claim.

(2) The regulations may, in particular, include provision—

(a)   as to the manner in which a claim must be made;
(b)   if the jurisdiction of the Tribunal is being exercised by more than one tribunal—

(i) for determining by which tribunal any claim is to be heard, and
(ii) for the transfer of proceedings from one tribunal to another;

(c)   for enabling functions which relate to matters preliminary or incidental to a claim (including, in particular, decisions under paragraph 10(3) of Schedule 3) to be performed by the President, or by the chairman;
(d)   enabling hearings to be conducted in the absence of any member other than the chairman;
(e)   as to the persons who may appear on behalf of the parties;
(f)   for granting any person such disclosure or inspection of documents or right to further particulars as might be granted by a county court;
(g)   requiring persons to attend to give evidence and produce documents;
(h)   for authorising the administration of oaths to witnesses;
(i)   for the determination of claims without a hearing in prescribed circumstances;
(j)   as to the withdrawal of claims;
(k)   for enabling the Tribunal to stay proceedings on a claim;
(l)   for the award of costs or expenses;
(m)   for taxing or otherwise settling costs or expenses (and, in particular, for enabling costs to be taxed in the county court);
(n)   for the registration and proof of decisions and orders; and
(o)   for enabling prescribed decisions to be reviewed, or prescribed orders to be varied or revoked, in such circumstances as may be determined in accordance with the regulations.

(2A) If made with the agreement of the National Assembly, the regulations apply to the Welsh Tribunal as they apply to the Tribunal, subject to such modifications as may be specified in the regulations.

(3) Proceedings before the Tribunal or the Welsh Tribunal are to be held in private, except in prescribed circumstances.

(4) (*repealed*)

(5) The Secretary of State may pay such allowances for the purpose of or in connection with the attendance of persons at the Tribunal or the Welsh Tribunal as he may, with the consent of the Treasury, determine.

(6) In relation to the Welsh Tribunal, the power conferred by subsection (5) may be exercised only with the agreement of the National Assembly.

(7) Part 1 of the Arbitration Act 1996 does not apply to proceedings before the Tribunal or the Welsh Tribunal but regulations may make provision, in relation to such proceedings, corresponding to any provision of that Part.

(8) The regulations may make provision for a claim under this Chapter to be heard, in prescribed circumstances, with an appeal under Part 4 of the Education Act 1996, including provision—

(a)   for determining the appropriate tribunal for the purposes of section 28I for such a claim, and
(b)   for the transfer of proceedings between the Tribunal and the Welsh Tribunal.

(9) A person who without reasonable excuse fails to comply with—

(a)   a requirement in respect of the disclosure or inspection of documents imposed by the regulations by virtue of subsection (2)(f), or

(b)   a requirement imposed by the regulations by virtue of subsection (2)(g),

is guilty of an offence.

(10) A person guilty of an offence under subsection (9) is liable on summary conviction to a fine not exceeding level 3 on the standard scale.

(11) Part 3 of Schedule 3 makes further provision about enforcement of this Chapter and about procedure.

Amendments – Inserted by Special Educational Needs and Disability Act 2001, s 19(1). Amended by Education Act 2002, s 195, Sch 18, paras 7, 10(1)–(8).

28K   Admissions

(1) If the condition mentioned in subsection (2) is satisfied, this section applies to a claim in relation to an admissions decision that a responsible body—

(a)   has discriminated against a person ('A') in a way which is made unlawful under this Chapter; or

(b)   is by virtue of section 58 to be treated as having discriminated against a person ('A') in such a way.

(2) The condition is that arrangements ('appeal arrangements') have been made—

(a)   under section 94 of the School Standards and Framework Act 1998, or

(b)   under an agreement entered into between the responsible body for an Academy and the Secretary of State under section 482 of the Education Act 1996,

enabling an appeal to be made against the decision by A's parent.

(3) The claim must be made under the appeal arrangements.

(4) The body hearing the claim has the powers which it has in relation to an appeal under the appeal arrangements.

(5) 'Admissions decision' means—

(a)   a decision of a kind mentioned in section 94(1) or (2) of the School Standards and Framework Act 1998;

(b)   a decision as to the admission of a person to an Academy taken by the responsible body or on its behalf.

Amendments – Inserted by Special Educational Needs and Disability Act 2001, s 20. Amended by Education Act 2002, s 65(3), Sch 7, Pt 2, para 5(1), (3).

28L   Exclusions

(1) If the condition mentioned in subsection (2) is satisfied, this section applies to a claim in relation to an exclusion decision that a responsible body—

(a)   has discriminated against a person ('A') in a way which is made unlawful under this Chapter; or

(b)   is by virtue of section 58 to be treated as having discriminated against a person ('A') in such a way.

(2) The condition is that arrangements ('appeal arrangements') have been made—

(a)   under section 52(3)(c) of the Education Act 2002, or

(b)   under an agreement entered into between the responsible body for an Academy and the Secretary of State under section 482 of the Education Act 1996,

enabling an appeal to be made against the decision by A or by his parent.

(3) The claim must be made under the appeal arrangements.

(4) The body hearing the claim has the powers which it has in relation to an appeal under the appeal arrangements.

(5) 'Exclusion decision' means—

(a)   a decision of a kind mentioned in section 52(3)(c) of the Education Act 2002;

(b)   a decision not to reinstate a pupil who has been permanently excluded from an Academy by its head teacher, taken by the responsible body or on its behalf.

(6) 'Responsible body', in relation to a maintained school, includes the discipline committee of the governing body if that committee is required to be established as a result of regulations made under *paragraph 4 of Schedule 11 to the School Standards and Framework Act 1998* [section 19 of the Education Act 2002][1].

(7) 'Maintained school' has the meaning given in section 28Q(5).

Amendments – Inserted by Special Educational Needs and Disability Act 2001, s 21. Amended by Education Act 2002, s 65(3), Sch 7, Pt 2, para 5(1), (4), s 215(1), Sch 21, para 27(1), (2).
[1] Words in relation to England substituted by Education Act 2002, s 215(1), Sch 21, para 27(1), (3), and prospectively inserted in relation to Wales as from a day to be appointed.

28M   Roles of the Secretary of State and the National Assembly

(1) If the appropriate authority is satisfied (whether on a complaint or otherwise) that a responsible body—

(a)   has acted, or is proposing to act, unreasonably in the discharge of a duty imposed by or under section 28D or 28E, or

(b)   has failed to discharge a duty imposed by or under either of those sections,

it may give that body such directions as to the discharge of the duty as appear to it to be expedient.

(2) Subsection (3) applies in relation to—

(a)   special schools which are not maintained special schools but which are approved by the Secretary of State, or by the National Assembly, under section 342 of the Education Act 1996; and

(b)   city academies.

(3) If the appropriate authority is satisfied (whether on a complaint or otherwise) that a responsible body—

(a)   has acted, or is proposing to act, unreasonably in the discharge of a duty which that body has in relation to—
   (i) the provision to the appropriate authority of copies of that body's accessibility plan, or
   (ii) the inspection of that plan, or
(b)   has failed to discharge that duty,

it may give that body such directions as to the discharge of the duty as appear to it to be expedient.

(4) Directions may be given under subsection (1) or (3) even if the performance of the duty is contingent upon the opinion of the responsible body.

(5) Subsection (6) applies if the Tribunal or the Welsh Tribunal has made an order under section 28I(3).

(6) If the Secretary of State is satisfied (whether on a complaint or otherwise) that the responsible body concerned—

(a)   has acted, or is proposing to act, unreasonably in complying with the order, or
(b)   has failed to comply with the order,

he may give that body such directions as to compliance with the order as appear to him to be expedient.

(7) Directions given under subsection (1), (3) or (6)—

(a)   may be varied or revoked by the directing authority; and
(b)   may be enforced, on the application of the directing authority, by a mandatory order obtained in accordance with section 31 of the Supreme Court Act 1981.

(8) 'Appropriate authority' means—

(a)   in relation to England, the Secretary of State; and
(b)   in relation to Wales, the National Assembly.

(9) 'Directing authority' means—

(a)   the Secretary of State in relation to a direction given by him; and
(b)   the National Assembly in relation to a direction given by it.

Amendments – Inserted (save in so far as it gives the National Assembly for Wales power to give directions under subss (1), (3) or makes provision in relation to such a direction) by Special Educational Needs and Disability Act 2001, s 22. Amended by Education Act 2002, s 195, Sch 18, paras 7, 11.

Enforcement: Scotland

Amendment – Inserted by Special Educational Needs and Disability Act 2001, s 23.

28N   Civil proceedings

(1) A claim that a responsible body in Scotland—

(a)   has discriminated against a person in a way which is unlawful under this Chapter, or

(b)   is by virtue of section 58 to be treated as having discriminated against a person in such a way,

may be made the subject of civil proceedings in the same way as any other claim for the enforcement of a statutory duty.

(2) Proceedings in Scotland may be brought only in a sheriff court.

(3) The remedies available in such proceedings are those which are available in the Court of Session other than an award of damages.

(4) Part 3 of Schedule 3 makes further provision about the enforcement of this Chapter and about procedure.

(5) In relation to civil proceedings in Scotland, in that Part of that Schedule—

(a)   references to sections 28I, 28K and 28L, or any of them, are to be construed as a reference to this section;

(b)   references to the Tribunal are to be construed as references to the sheriff court.

Amendment – Inserted by Special Educational Needs and Disability Act 2001, s 23.

Agreements relating to enforcement

28P   Validity and revision of agreements of responsible bodies

(1) Any term in a contract or other agreement made by or on behalf of a responsible body is void so far as it purports to—

(a)   require a person to do anything which would contravene any provision of, or made under, this Chapter;

(b)   exclude or limit the operation of any provision of, or made under, this Chapter; or

(c)   prevent any person from making a claim under this Chapter.

(2) Paragraphs (b) and (c) of subsection (1) do not apply to an agreement settling a claim—

(a)   under section 28I or 28N; or

(b)   to which section 28K or 28L applies.

(3) On the application of any person interested in an agreement to which subsection (1) applies, a county court or a sheriff court may make such order as it thinks just for modifying the agreement to take account of the effect of subsection (1).

(4) No such order may be made unless all persons affected have been—

(a)   given notice of the application; and

(b)   afforded an opportunity to make representations to the court.

(5) Subsection (4) applies subject to any rules of court providing for notice to be dispensed with.

(6) An order under subsection (3) may include provision as respects any period before the making of the order.

Amendments – Section and preceding cross-heading inserted by Special Educational Needs and Disability Act 2001, s 24.

Interpretation of Chapter 1

28Q Interpretation

(1) This section applies for the purpose of interpreting this Chapter.

(2) 'Disabled pupil' means a pupil who is a disabled person.

(3) 'Pupil'—

    (a)   in relation to England and Wales, has the meaning given in section 3(1) of the Education Act 1996; and

    (b)   in relation to Scotland, has the meaning given in section 135(1) of the Education (Scotland) Act 1980.

(4) Except in relation to Scotland (when it has the meaning given in section 135(1) of the Education (Scotland) Act 1980) 'school' means—

    (a)   a maintained school;

    (b)   a maintained nursery school;

    (c)   an independent school;

    (d)   a special school which is not a maintained special school but which is approved by the Secretary of State, or by the National Assembly, under section 342 of the Education Act 1996;

    (e)   a pupil referral unit.

(5) In subsection (4)—

'maintained school' has the meaning given in section 20(7) of the School Standards and Framework Act 1998;

'maintained nursery school' has the meaning given in section 22(9) of the School Standards and Framework Act 1998;

'independent school' has the meaning given in section 463 of the Education Act 1996; and

'pupil referral unit' has the meaning given in section 19(2) of the Education Act 1996.

(6) 'Responsible body' has the meaning given in section 28A(5).

(7) 'Governing body', in relation to a maintained school, means the body corporate (constituted in accordance with *Schedule 9 to the School Standards and Framework Act 1998* [regulations under section 19 of the Education Act 2002][1]) which the school has as a result of *section 36 of that Act* [that section][1].

(8) 'Parent'—

    (a)   in relation to England and Wales, has the meaning given in section 576 of the Education Act 1996; and

    (b)   in relation to Scotland, has the meaning given in section 135(1) of the Education (Scotland) Act 1980.

(9) In relation to England and Wales 'permitted form of selection' means—

(a)   if the school is a maintained school which is not designated as a grammar school under section 104 of the School Standards and Framework Act 1998, any form of selection mentioned in section 99(2) or (4) of that Act;

(b)   if the school is a maintained school which is so designated, any of its selective admission arrangements;

(c)   if the school is an independent school, any arrangements which make provision for any or all of its pupils to be selected by reference to general or special ability or aptitude, with a view to admitting only pupils of high ability or aptitude.

(10) In relation to Scotland, 'permitted form of selection' means—

(a)   if the school is managed by an education authority, such arrangements as have been approved by the Scottish Ministers for the selection of pupils for admission;

(b)   if the school is an independent school or a self-governing school, any arrangements which make provision for any or all of its pupils to be selected by reference to general or special ability or aptitude, with a view to admitting only pupils of high ability or aptitude.

(11) In subsection (10), 'education authority', 'independent school' and 'self-governing school' have the meaning given in section 135(1) of the Education (Scotland) Act 1980.

(12) (*repealed*)

(13) 'Accessibility strategy' and 'accessibility plan' have the meaning given in section 28D.

(14) 'The National Assembly' means the National Assembly for Wales.

Amendments – Section and preceding cross-heading inserted by Special Educational Needs and Disability Act 2001, s 25. Amended by Education Act 2002, ss 65(3), 215(2), Sch 7, Pt 2, para 5(1), (5), Sch 22, Pt 3.
[1] Words in relation to England substituted by Education Act 2002, s 215(1), Sch 21, para 28, and prospectively substituted in relation to Wales as from a day to be appointed.

Chapter 2
Further and Higher Education

Duties of responsible bodies

28R Discrimination against disabled students and prospective students

(1) It is unlawful for the body responsible for an educational institution to discriminate against a disabled person—

(a)   in the arrangements it makes for determining admissions to the institution;
(b)   in the terms on which it offers to admit him to the institution; or
(c)   by refusing or deliberately omitting to accept an application for his admission to the institution.

(2) It is unlawful for the body responsible for an educational institution to discriminate against a disabled student in the student services it provides, or offers to provide.

(3) It is unlawful for the body responsible for an educational institution to discriminate against a disabled student by excluding him from the institution, whether permanently or temporarily.

(4) In the case of an act which constitutes discrimination by virtue of section 55, this section also applies to discrimination against a person who is not disabled.

(5) The body responsible for an educational institution is to be determined in accordance with Schedule 4B, and in the remaining provisions of this Chapter is referred to as the 'responsible body'.

(6) 'Educational institution', in relation to England and Wales, means an institution—

    (a)   within the higher education sector;
    (b)   within the further education sector; or
    (c)   designated in an order made by the Secretary of State.

(7) 'Educational institution', in relation to Scotland, means—

    (a)   an institution within the higher education sector (within the meaning of section 56(2) of the Further and Higher Education (Scotland) Act 1992);
    (b)   a college of further education with a board of management within the meaning of section 36 of that Act;
    (c)   a central institution within the meaning of section 135 of the Education (Scotland) Act 1980;
    (d)   a college of further education maintained by an education authority in the exercise of their further education functions in providing courses of further education within the meaning of section 1(5)(b)(ii) of that Act;
    (e)   an institution designated in an order made by the Secretary of State.

(8) Subsection (6) is to be read with section 91 of the Further and Higher Education Act 1992.

(9) The Secretary of State may not make an order under subsection (6)(c) or (7)(e) unless he is satisfied that the institution concerned is wholly or partly funded from public funds.

(10) Before making an order under subsection (7)(e), the Secretary of State must consult the Scottish Ministers.

(11) 'Student services' means services of any description which are provided wholly or mainly for students.

(12) Regulations may make provision as to services which are, or are not, to be regarded for the purposes of subsection (2) as student services.

Amendment – Section and preceding Chapter heading and cross-heading inserted by Special Educational Needs and Disability Act 2001, s 26(1).

28S Meaning of 'discrimination'

(1) For the purposes of section 28R, a responsible body discriminates against a disabled person if—

    (a)   for a reason which relates to his disability, it treats him less favourably than it treats or would treat others to whom that reason does not or would not apply; and

(b)   it cannot show that the treatment in question is justified.

(2) For the purposes of section 28R, a responsible body also discriminates against a disabled person if—

    (a)   it fails, to his detriment, to comply with section 28T; and
    (b)   it cannot show that its failure to comply is justified.

(3) In relation to a failure to take a particular step, a responsible body does not discriminate against a person if it shows—

    (a)   that, at the time in question, it did not know and could not reasonably have been expected to know, that he was disabled; and
    (b)   that its failure to take the step was attributable to that lack of knowledge.

(4) The taking of a particular step by a responsible body in relation to a person does not amount to less favourable treatment if it shows that at the time in question it did not know, and could not reasonably have been expected to know, that he was disabled.

(5) Subsections (6) to (9) apply in determining whether, for the purposes of this section—

    (a)   less favourable treatment of a person, or
    (b)   failure to comply with section 28T,

is justified.

(6) Less favourable treatment of a person is justified if it is necessary in order to maintain—

    (a)   academic standards; or
    (b)   standards of any other prescribed kind.

(7) Less favourable treatment is also justified if—

    (a)   it is of a prescribed kind;
    (b)   it occurs in prescribed circumstances; or
    (c)   it is of a prescribed kind and it occurs in prescribed circumstances.

(8) Otherwise less favourable treatment, or a failure to comply with section 28T, is justified only if the reason for it is both material to the circumstances of the particular case and substantial.

(9) If, in a case falling within subsection (1)—

    (a)   the responsible body is under a duty imposed by section 28T in relation to the disabled person, but
    (b)   fails without justification to comply with that duty,

its treatment of that person cannot be justified under subsection (8) unless that treatment would have been justified even if it had complied with that duty.

Amendment – Inserted by Special Educational Needs and Disability Act 2001, s 27.

28T   Disabled students not to be substantially disadvantaged

(1) The responsible body for an educational institution must take such steps as it is reasonable for it to have to take to ensure that—

(a) in relation to the arrangements it makes for determining admissions to the institution, disabled persons are not placed at a substantial disadvantage in comparison with persons who are not disabled; and

(b) in relation to student services provided for, or offered to, students by it, disabled students are not placed at a substantial disadvantage in comparison with students who are not disabled.

(2) In considering whether it is reasonable for it to have to take a particular step in order to comply with its duty under subsection (1), a responsible body must have regard to any relevant provisions of a code of practice issued under section 53A.

(3) Subsection (4) applies if a person has made a confidentiality request of which a responsible body is aware.

(4) In determining whether it is reasonable for the responsible body to have to take a particular step in relation to that person in order to comply with its duty under subsection (1), regard shall be had to the extent to which taking the step in question is consistent with compliance with that request.

(5) 'Confidentiality request' means a request made by a disabled person, which asks for the nature, or asks for the existence, of his disability to be treated as confidential.

(6) This section imposes duties only for the purpose of determining whether a responsible body has discriminated against a disabled person; and accordingly a breach of any such duty is not actionable as such.

Amendment – Inserted by Special Educational Needs and Disability Act 2001, s 28.

Other providers of further education or training facilities

28U Further education etc provided by local education authorities and schools

(1) Part 1 of Schedule 4C modifies this Chapter for the purpose of its application in relation to—

(a) higher education secured by a local education authority;
(b) further education—
  (i) secured by a local education authority; or
  (ii) provided by the governing body of a maintained school;
(c) recreational or training facilities secured by a local education authority.

(2) Part 2 of that Schedule modifies this Chapter for the purpose of its application in relation to—

(a) further education, within the meaning of section 1 (5) (b) (iii) of the Education (Scotland) Act 1980;
(b) facilities whose provision is secured by an education authority under section 1 (3) of that Act.

Amendment – Section and preceding cross-heading inserted by Special Educational Needs and Disability Act 2001, s 29(1).

Enforcement, etc

28V   Enforcement, remedies and procedure

(1) A claim by a person—

    (a)   that a responsible body has discriminated against him in a way which is unlawful under this Chapter,

    (b)   that a responsible body is by virtue of section 57 or 58 to be treated as having discriminated against him in such a way, or

    (c)   that a person is by virtue of section 57 to be treated as having discriminated against him in such a way,

may be made the subject of civil proceedings in the same way as any other claim in tort or (in Scotland) in reparation for breach of statutory duty.

(2) For the avoidance of doubt it is hereby declared that damages in respect of discrimination in a way which is unlawful under this Chapter may include compensation for injury to feelings whether or not they include compensation under any other head.

(3) Proceedings in England and Wales may be brought only in a county court.

(4) Proceedings in Scotland may be brought only in a sheriff court.

(5) The remedies available in such proceedings are those which are available in the High Court or (as the case may be) the Court of Session.

(6) The fact that a person who brings proceedings under this Part against a responsible body may also be entitled to bring proceedings against that body under Part 2 is not to affect the proceedings under this Part.

(7) Part 4 of Schedule 3 makes further provision about the enforcement of this Part and about procedure.

Amendment – Section and preceding cross-heading inserted by Special Educational Needs and Disability Act 2001, s 30(1).

28W   Occupation of premises by educational institutions

(1) This section applies if—

    (a)   premises are occupied by an educational institution under a lease;

    (b)   but for this section, the responsible body would not be entitled to make a particular alteration to the premises; and

    (c)   the alteration is one which the responsible body proposes to make in order to comply with section 28T.

(2) Except to the extent to which it expressly so provides, the lease has effect, as a result of this subsection, as if it provided—

    (a)   for the responsible body to be entitled to make the alteration with the written consent of the lessor;

    (b)   for the responsible body to have to make a written application to the lessor for consent if it wishes to make the alteration;

(c) if such an application is made, for the lessor not to withhold his consent unreasonably; and

(d) for the lessor to be entitled to make his consent subject to reasonable conditions.

(3) In this section—

'lease' includes a tenancy, sub-lease or sub-tenancy and an agreement for a lease, tenancy, sub-lease or sub-tenancy; and

'sub-lease' and 'sub-tenancy' have such meaning as may be prescribed.

(4) If the terms and conditions of a lease—

(a) impose conditions which are to apply if the responsible body alters the premises, or

(b) entitle the lessor to impose conditions when consenting to the responsible body's altering the premises,

the responsible body is to be treated for the purposes of subsection (1) as not being entitled to make the alteration.

(5) Part 3 of Schedule 4 supplements the provisions of this section.

Amendment – Inserted by Special Educational Needs and Disability Act 2001, s 31(1).

28X Validity and revision of agreements

Section 28P applies for the purposes of this Chapter as it applies for the purposes of Chapter 1, but with the substitution, for paragraphs (a) and (b) of subsection (2), of 'under section 28V'.

Amendment – Inserted by Special Educational Needs and Disability Act 2001, s 32.

29 (*repealed*)

Amendment – Repealed by Special Educational Needs and Disability Act 2001, ss 40(1), 42(6), Sch 9.

Duties of funding councils

Amendment – Cross-heading inserted by Special Educational Needs and Disability Act 2001, s 34(4).

30 Further and higher education of disabled persons

(1) The Further and Higher Education Act 1992 is amended as set out in subsections (2) to (6).

(2)–(4) (*repealed*)

(5) In section 62 (establishment of higher education funding councils), after subsection (7) insert—

'(7A) In exercising their functions, each council shall have regard to the requirements of disabled persons.

(7B) In subsection (7A) "disabled persons" means persons who are disabled persons for the purposes of the Disability Discrimination Act 1995.'

(6)–(9) (*repealed*)

Amendments – Subsections (1) and (5) inserted by Further and Higher Education Act 1992, s 62(7A), (7B). Amended by Education Act 1996, s 582(2), Sch 38, Pt I; Learning and Skills Act 2000, s 153, Sch 11; Special Educational Needs and Disability Act 2001, ss 34(5), 42(6), Sch 9.

---

31 Further and higher education of disabled persons: Scotland

(1) The Further and Higher Education (Scotland) Act 1992 is amended as follows.

(2) In section 37 (establishment of Scottish Higher Education Funding Council) after subsection (4) insert—

'(4A) In exercising their functions, the Council shall have regard to the requirements of disabled persons.

(4B) In subsection (4A) above, "disabled persons" means persons who are disabled persons for the purpose of the Disability Discrimination Act 1995.'

(3) (*repealed*)

Amendment – Subsections (1) and (2) inserted by Further and Higher Education (Scotland) Act 1992, s 37(4A), (4B). Amended by Special Educational Needs and Disability Act 2001, ss 34(6), 42(6), Sch 9.

Interpretation of Chapter 2

31A Interpretation

(1) Subsections (2) to (4) apply for the purpose of interpreting this Chapter.

(2) 'Disabled student' means a student who is a disabled person.

(3) 'Student' means a person who is attending, or undertaking a course of study at, an educational institution.

(4) 'Educational institution', 'responsible body' and 'student services' have the meaning given in section 28R.

Amendment – Section and preceding cross-heading inserted by Special Educational Needs and Disability Act 2001, s 33.

Chapter 3
Supplementary

31B Conciliation for disputes

(1) The Disability Rights Commission may make arrangements with any other person for the provision of conciliation services by, or by persons appointed by, that person in connection with disputes.

(2) In deciding what arrangements (if any) to make, the Commission must have regard to the desirability of securing, so far as reasonably practicable, that conciliation services are available for all disputes which the parties may wish to refer to conciliation.

(3) No member or employee of the Commission may provide conciliation services in connection with disputes.

(4) The Commission must ensure that arrangements under this section include appropriate safeguards to prevent the disclosure to members or employees of the Commission of information obtained by any person in connection with the provision of conciliation services in accordance with the arrangements.

(5) Subsection (4) does not apply to information which is disclosed with the consent of the parties to the dispute to which it relates.

(6) Subsection (4) does not apply to information which—

    (a)   does not identify a particular dispute or a particular person; and

    (b)   is reasonably required by the Commission for the purpose of monitoring the operation of the arrangements concerned.

(7) Anything communicated to a person providing conciliation services in accordance with arrangements under this section is not admissible in evidence in any proceedings except with the consent of the person who communicated it.

(8) 'Conciliation services' means advice and assistance provided to the parties to a dispute, by a conciliator, with a view to promoting its settlement otherwise than through a court, tribunal or other body.

(9) 'Dispute' means a dispute arising under Chapter 1 or 2 concerning an allegation of discrimination.

(10) 'Discrimination' means anything which is made unlawful discrimination by a provision of Chapter 1 or 2.

Amendment – Section and preceding Chapter heading inserted by Special Educational Needs and Disability Act 2001, s 37.

31C   Application to Isles of Scilly

This Part applies to the Isles of Scilly—

    (a)   as if the Isles were a separate non-metropolitan county (and the Council of the Isles of Scilly were a county council), and

    (b)   with such other modifications as may be specified in an order made by the Secretary of State.

Amendment – Inserted by Special Educational Needs and Disability Act 2001, s 39.

PART V

PUBLIC TRANSPORT

Taxis

32 Taxi accessibility regulations

(1) The Secretary of State may make regulations ('taxi accessibility regulations') for the purpose of securing that it is possible—

    (a)   for disabled persons—
        (i) to get into and out of taxis in safety;
        (ii) to be carried in taxis in safety and in reasonable comfort; and
    (b)   for disabled persons in wheelchairs—
        (i) to be conveyed in safety into and out of taxis while remaining in their wheelchairs; and
        (ii) to be carried in taxis in safety and in reasonable comfort while remaining in their wheelchairs.

(2) Taxi accessibility regulations may, in particular—

    (a)   require any regulated taxi to conform with provisions of the regulations as to—
        (i) the size of any door opening which is for the use of passengers;
        (ii) the floor area of the passenger compartment;
        (iii) the amount of headroom in the passenger compartment;
        (iv) the fitting of restraining devices designed to ensure the stability of a wheelchair while the taxi is moving;
    (b)   require the driver of any regulated taxi which is plying for hire, or which has been hired, to comply with provisions of the regulations as to the carrying of ramps or other devices designed to facilitate the loading and unloading of wheelchairs;
    (c)   require the driver of any regulated taxi in which a disabled person who is in a wheelchair is being carried (while remaining in his wheelchair) to comply with provisions of the regulations as to the position in which the wheelchair is to be secured.

(3) The driver of a regulated taxi which is plying for hire, or which has been hired, is guilty of an offence if—

    (a)   he fails to comply with any requirement imposed on him by the regulations; or
    (b)   the taxi fails to conform with any provision of the regulations with which it is required to conform.

(4) A person who is guilty of such an offence is liable, on summary conviction, to a fine not exceeding level 3 on the standard scale.

(5) In this section—

  'passenger compartment' has such meaning as may be prescribed;
  'regulated taxi' means any taxi to which the regulations are expressed to apply;
  'taxi' means a vehicle licensed under—
    (a)   section 37 of the Town Police Clauses Act 1847, or
    (b)   section 6 of the Metropolitan Public Carriage Act 1869,

but does not include a taxi which is drawn by a horse or other animal.

33   Designated transport facilities

(1) In this section 'a franchise agreement' means a contract entered into by the operator of a designated transport facility for the provision by the other party to the contract of hire car services—

(a)   for members of the public using any part of the transport facility; and

(b)   which involve vehicles entering any part of that facility.

(2) The Secretary of State may by regulations provide for the application of any taxi provision in relation to—

(a)   vehicles used for the provision of services under a franchise agreement; or

(b)   the drivers of such vehicles.

(3) Any regulations under subsection (2) may apply any taxi provision with such modifications as the Secretary of State considers appropriate.

(4) In this section—

'designated' means designated for the purposes of this section by an order made by the Secretary of State;

'hire car' has such meaning as may be prescribed;

'operator', in relation to a transport facility, means any person who is concerned with the management or operation of the facility;

'taxi provision' means any provision of—

(a)   this Act, or

(b)   regulations made in pursuance of section 20(2A) of the Civic Government (Scotland) Act 1982,

which applies in relation to taxis or the drivers of taxis; and

'transport facility' means any premises which form part of any port, airport, railway station or bus station.

34   New licences conditional on compliance with taxi accessibility regulations

(1) No licensing authority shall grant a licence for a taxi to ply for hire unless the vehicle conforms with those provisions of the taxi accessibility regulations with which it will be required to conform if licensed.

(2) Subsection (1) does not apply if such a licence was in force with respect to the vehicle at any time during the period of 28 days immediately before the day on which the licence is granted.

(3) The Secretary of State may by order provide for subsection (2) to cease to have effect on such date as may be specified in the order.

(4) Separate orders may be made under subsection (3) with respect to different areas or localities.

35   Exemption from taxi accessibility regulations

(1) The Secretary of State may make regulations ('exemption regulations') for the purpose of enabling any relevant licensing authority to apply to him for an order (an 'exemption order') exempting the authority from the requirements of section 34.

(2) Exemption regulations may, in particular, make provision requiring a licensing authority proposing to apply for an exemption order—

(a)   to carry out such consultations as may be prescribed;

(b)   to publish the proposal in the prescribed manner;

(c)   to consider any representations made to it about the proposal, before applying for the order;

(d)   to make its application in the prescribed form.

(3) A licensing authority may apply for an exemption order only if it is satisfied—

(a)   that, having regard to the circumstances prevailing in its area, it would be inappropriate for the requirements of section 34 to apply; and

(b)   that the application of section 34 would result in an unacceptable reduction in the number of taxis in its area.

(4) After considering any application for an exemption order and consulting the Disabled Persons Transport Advisory Committee and such other persons as he considers appropriate, the Secretary of State may—

(a)   make an exemption order in the terms of the application;

(b)   make an exemption order in such other terms as he considers appropriate; or

(c)   refuse to make an exemption order.

(5) The Secretary of State may by regulations ('swivel seat regulations') make provision requiring any exempt taxi plying for hire in an area in respect of which an exemption order is in force to conform with provisions of the regulations as to the fitting and use of swivel seats.

(6) The Secretary of State may by regulations make provision with respect to swivel seat regulations similar to that made by section 34 with respect to taxi accessibility regulations.

(7) In this section—

'exempt taxi' means a taxi in relation to which section 34(1) would apply if the exemption order were not in force;

'relevant licensing authority' means a licensing authority responsible for licensing taxis in any area of England and Wales other than the area to which the Metropolitan Public Carriage Act 1869 applies; and

'swivel seats' has such meaning as may be prescribed.

36   Carrying of passengers in wheelchairs

(1) This section imposes duties on the driver of a regulated taxi which has been hired—

(a)   by or for a disabled person who is in a wheelchair; or

(b)   by a person who wishes such a disabled person to accompany him in the taxi.

(2) In this section—

'carry' means carry in the taxi concerned; and

'the passenger' means the disabled person concerned.

(3) The duties are—

(a)   to carry the passenger while he remains in his wheelchair;

(b)   not to make any additional charge for doing so;

(c)   if the passenger chooses to sit in a passenger seat, to carry the wheelchair;

(d)   to take such steps as are necessary to ensure that the passenger is carried in safety and in reasonable comfort;

(e)   to give such assistance as may be reasonably required—

     (i)   to enable the passenger to get into or out of the taxi;

    (ii) if the passenger wishes to remain in his wheelchair, to enable him to be conveyed into and out of the taxi while in his wheelchair;

   (iii) to load the passenger's luggage into or out of the taxi;

   (iv) if the passenger does not wish to remain in his wheelchair, to load the wheelchair into or out of the taxi.

(4) Nothing in this section is to be taken to require the driver of any taxi—

(a)   except in the case of a taxi of a prescribed description, to carry more than one person in a wheelchair, or more than one wheelchair, on any one journey; or

(b)   to carry any person in circumstances in which it would otherwise be lawful for him to refuse to carry that person.

(5) A driver of a regulated taxi who fails to comply with any duty imposed on him by this section is guilty of an offence and liable, on summary conviction, to a fine not exceeding level 3 on the standard scale.

(6) In any proceedings for an offence under this section, it is a defence for the accused to show that, even though at the time of the alleged offence the taxi conformed with those provisions of the taxi accessibility regulations with which it was required to conform, it would not have been possible for the wheelchair in question to be carried in safety in the taxi.

(7) If the licensing authority is satisfied that it is appropriate to exempt a person from the duties imposed by this section—

(a)   on medical grounds, or

(b)   on the ground that his physical condition makes it impossible or unreasonably difficult for him to comply with the duties imposed on drivers by this section,

it shall issue him with a certificate of exemption.

(8) A certificate of exemption shall be issued for such period as may be specified in the certificate.

(9) The driver of a regulated taxi is exempt from the duties imposed by this section if—

(a)   a certificate of exemption issued to him under this section is in force; and

(b)   the prescribed notice of his exemption is exhibited on the taxi in the prescribed manner.

37   Carrying of guide dogs and hearing dogs

(1) This section imposes duties on the driver of a taxi which has been hired—

(a)   by or for a disabled person who is accompanied by his guide dog or hearing dog, or

(b)   by a person who wishes such a disabled person to accompany him in the taxi.

(2) The disabled person is referred to in this section as 'the passenger'.

(3) The duties are—

   (a)   to carry the passenger's dog and allow it to remain with the passenger; and
   (b)   not to make any additional charge for doing so.

(4) A driver of a taxi who fails to comply with any duty imposed on him by this section is guilty of an offence and liable, on summary conviction, to a fine not exceeding level 3 on the standard scale.

(5) If the licensing authority is satisfied that it is appropriate on medical grounds to exempt a person from the duties imposed by this section, it shall issue him with a certificate of exemption.

(6) In determining whether to issue a certificate of exemption, the licensing authority shall, in particular, have regard to the physical characteristics of the taxi which the applicant drives or those of any kind of taxi in relation to which he requires the certificate.

(7) A certificate of exemption shall be issued—

   (a)   with respect to a specified taxi or a specified kind of taxi; and
   (b)   for such period as may be specified in the certificate.

(8) The driver of a taxi is exempt from the duties imposed by this section if—

   (a)   a certificate of exemption issued to him under this section is in force with respect to the taxi; and
   (b)   the prescribed notice of his exemption is exhibited on the taxi in the prescribed manner.

(9) The Secretary of State may, for the purposes of this section, prescribe any other category of dog trained to assist a disabled person who has a disability of a prescribed kind.

(10) This section applies in relation to any such prescribed category of dog as it applies in relation to guide dogs.

(11) In this section—

   'guide dog' means a dog which has been trained to guide a blind person; and
   'hearing dog' means a dog which has been trained to assist a deaf person.

37A   Carrying of assistance dogs in private hire vehicles

(1) It is an offence for the operator of a private hire vehicle to fail or refuse to accept a booking for a private hire vehicle—

   (a)   if the booking is requested by or on behalf of a disabled person, or a person who wishes a disabled person to accompany him; and
   (b)   the reason for the failure or refusal is that the disabled person will be accompanied by his assistance dog.

(2) It is an offence for the operator of a private hire vehicle to make an additional charge for carrying an assistance dog which is accompanying a disabled person.

(3) It is an offence for the driver of a private hire vehicle to fail or refuse to carry out a booking accepted by the operator of the vehicle—

(a)   if the booking was made by or on behalf of a disabled person, or a person who wishes a disabled person to accompany him; and

(b)   the reason for the failure or refusal is that the disabled person is accompanied by his assistance dog.

(4) A person who is guilty of an offence under this section is liable on summary conviction to a fine not exceeding level 3 on the standard scale.

(5) If the licensing authority is satisfied that it is appropriate on medical grounds to issue a certificate of exemption to a driver in respect of subsection (3) it must do so.

(6) In determining whether to issue a certificate of exemption, the licensing authority shall, in particular, have regard to the physical characteristics of the private hire vehicle which the applicant drives or those of any kind of private hire vehicle in relation to which he requires the certificate.

(7) A certificate of exemption shall be issued—

(a)   with respect to a specified private hire vehicle or a specified kind of private hire vehicle; and

(b)   for such period as may be specified in the certificate.

(8) No offence is committed by a driver under subsection (3) if—

(a)   a certificate of exemption issued to him under this section is in force with respect to the private hire vehicle; and

(b)   the prescribed notice is exhibited on the private hire vehicle in the prescribed manner.

(9) In this section—

'assistance dog' means a dog which—
　　　(a)   has been trained to guide a blind person;
　　　(b)   has been trained to assist a deaf person;
　　　(c)   has been trained by a prescribed charity to assist a disabled person who has a disability which—
　　　　　(i)   consists of epilepsy; or
　　　　　(ii)   otherwise affects his mobility, manual dexterity, physical co-ordination or ability to lift, carry or otherwise move everyday objects;
'driver' means a person who holds a licence granted under—
　　　(a)   section 13 of the Private Hire Vehicles (London) Act 1998 (c 34) ('the 1998 Act');
　　　(b)   section 51 of the Local Government (Miscellaneous Provisions) Act 1976 (c 57) ('the 1976 Act'); or
　　　(c)   an equivalent provision of a local enactment;
'licensing authority', in relation to any area of England and Wales, means the authority responsible for licensing private hire vehicles in that area;
'operator' means a person who holds a licence granted under—
　　　(a)   section 3 of the 1998 Act;
　　　(b)   section 55 of the 1976 Act; or
　　　(c)   an equivalent provision of a local enactment;
'private hire vehicle' means a vehicle licensed under—
　　　(a)   section 6 of the 1998 Act;
　　　(b)   section 48 of the 1976 Act; or

(c)   an equivalent provision of a local enactment.

Amendment – Inserted by Private Hire Vehicles (Carriage of Guide Dogs etc) Act 2002, s 1(1).

---

38 Appeal against refusal of exemption certificate

(1) Any person who is aggrieved by the refusal of a licensing authority to issue an exemption certificate under section 36, 37 or 38A may appeal to *the appropriate* [a magistrates'] court before the end of the period of 28 days beginning with the date of the refusal.

(2) On an appeal to it under this section, the court may direct the licensing authority concerned to issue the appropriate certificate of exemption to have effect for such period as may be specified in the direction.

(3) *'Appropriate court' means the magistrates' court for the petty sessions area in which the licensing authority has its principal office.*

Amendment – Amended by Private Hire Vehicles (Carriage of Guide Dogs etc) Act 2002, s 3. Words prospectively substituted by Courts Act 2003, s 109(1), Sch 8, para 368(1), (2) and subsection (3) prospectively repealed by Courts Act 2003, s 109(1), Sch 8, para 368(1), (3), Sch 10.

---

39 Requirements as to disabled passengers in Scotland

(1) Part II of the Civic Government (Scotland) Act 1982 (licensing and regulation) is amended as follows.

(2) In subsection (4) of section 10 (suitability of vehicle for use as taxi)—

(a)   after 'authority' insert '—(a)'; and
(b)   at the end add '; and
        (b) as not being so suitable if it does not so comply.'

(3) In section 20 (regulations relating to taxis etc) after subsection (2) insert—

'(2A) Without prejudice to the generality of subsections (1) and (2) above, regulations under those subsections may make such provision as appears to the Secretary of State to be necessary or expedient in relation to the carrying in taxis of disabled persons (within the meaning of section 1(2) of the Disability Discrimination Act 1995) and such provision may in particular prescribe—

(a)   requirements as to the carriage of wheelchairs, guide dogs, hearing dogs and other categories of dog;
(b)   a date from which any such provision is to apply and the extent to which it is to apply; and
(c)   the circumstances in which an exemption from such provision may be granted in respect of any taxi or taxi driver,

and in this subsection—

"guide dog" means a dog which has been trained to guide a blind person;
"hearing dog" means a dog which has been trained to assist a deaf person; and
"other categories of dog" means such other categories of dog as the Secretary of State may prescribe, trained to assist disabled persons who have disabilities of such kinds as he may prescribe.'

Public service vehicles

40   PSV accessibility regulations

(1) The Secretary of State may make regulations ('PSV accessibility regulations') for the purpose of securing that it is possible for disabled persons—

(a)   to get on to and off regulated public service vehicles in safety and without unreasonable difficulty (and, in the case of disabled persons in wheelchairs, to do so while remaining in their wheelchairs); and

(b)   to be carried in such vehicles in safety and in reasonable comfort.

(2) PSV accessibility regulations may, in particular, make provision as to the construction, use and maintenance of regulated public service vehicles including provision as to—

(a)   the fitting of equipment to vehicles;

(b)   equipment to be carried by vehicles;

(c)   the design of equipment to be fitted to, or carried by, vehicles;

(d)   the fitting and use of restraining devices designed to ensure the stability of wheelchairs while vehicles are moving;

(e)   the position in which wheelchairs are to be secured while vehicles are moving.

(3) Any person who—

(a)   contravenes or fails to comply with any provision of the PSV accessibility regulations,

(b)   uses on a road a regulated public service vehicle which does not conform with any provision of the regulations with which it is required to conform, or

(c)   causes or permits to be used on a road such a regulated public service vehicle,

is guilty of an offence.

(4) A person who is guilty of such an offence is liable, on summary conviction, to a fine not exceeding level 4 on the standard scale.

(5) In this section—

'public service vehicle' means a vehicle which is—
(a)   adapted to carry more than eight passengers; and
(b)   a public service vehicle for the purposes of the Public Passenger Vehicles Act 1981;
'regulated public service vehicle' means any public service vehicle to which the PSV accessibility regulations are expressed to apply.

(6) Different provision may be made in regulations under this section—

(a)   as respects different classes or descriptions of vehicle;

(b)   as respects the same class or description of vehicle in different circumstances.

(7) Before making any regulations under this section or section 41 or 42 the Secretary of State shall consult the Disabled Persons Transport Advisory Committee and such other representative organisations as he thinks fit.

41   Accessibility certificates

(1) A regulated public service vehicle shall not be used on a road unless—

- (a)   a vehicle examiner has issued a certificate (an 'accessibility certificate') that such provisions of the PSV accessibility regulations as may be prescribed are satisfied in respect of the vehicle; or
- (b)   an approval certificate has been issued under section 42 in respect of the vehicle.

(2) The Secretary of State may make regulations—

- (a)   with respect to applications for, and the issue of, accessibility certificates;
- (b)   providing for the examination of vehicles in respect of which applications have been made;
- (c)   with respect to the issue of copies of accessibility certificates in place of certificates which have been lost or destroyed.

(3) If a regulated public service vehicle is used in contravention of this section, the operator of the vehicle is guilty of an offence and liable on summary conviction to a fine not exceeding level 4 on the standard scale.

(4) In this section 'operator' has the same meaning as in the Public Passenger Vehicles Act 1981.

42   Approval certificates

(1) Where the Secretary of State is satisfied that such provisions of the PSV accessibility regulations as may be prescribed for the purposes of section 41 are satisfied in respect of a particular vehicle he may approve the vehicle for the purposes of this section.

(2) A vehicle which has been so approved is referred to in this section as a 'type vehicle'.

(3) Subsection (4) applies where a declaration in the prescribed form has been made by an authorised person that a particular vehicle conforms in design, construction and equipment with a type vehicle.

(4) A vehicle examiner may, after examining (if he thinks fit) the vehicle to which the declaration applies, issue a certificate in the prescribed form ('an approval certificate') that it conforms to the type vehicle.

(5) The Secretary of State may make regulations—

- (a)   with respect to applications for, and grants of, approval under subsection (1);
- (b)   with respect to applications for, and the issue of, approval certificates;
- (c)   providing for the examination of vehicles in respect of which applications have been made;
- (d)   with respect to the issue of copies of approval certificates in place of certificates which have been lost or destroyed.

(6) The Secretary of State may at any time withdraw his approval of a type vehicle.

(7) Where an approval is withdrawn—

- (a)   no further approval certificates shall be issued by reference to the type vehicle; but
- (b)   any approval certificate issued by reference to the type vehicle before the withdrawal shall continue to have effect for the purposes of section 41.

(8) In subsection (3) 'authorised person' means a person authorised by the Secretary of State for the purposes of that subsection.

43   Special authorisations

(1) The Secretary of State may by order authorise the use on roads of—

(a)   any regulated public service vehicle of a class or description specified by the order, or

(b)   any regulated public service vehicle which is so specified,

and nothing in section 40, 41, or 42 prevents the use of any vehicle in accordance with the order.

(2) Any such authorisation may be given subject to such restrictions and conditions as may be specified by or under the order.

(3) The Secretary of State may by order make provision for the purpose of securing that, subject to such restrictions and conditions as may be specified by or under the order, provisions of the PSV accessibility regulations apply to regulated public service vehicles of a description specified by the order subject to such modifications or exceptions as may be specified by the order.

44   Reviews and appeals

(1) Subsection (2) applies where—

(a)   the Secretary of State refuses an application for the approval of a vehicle under section 42(1); and

(b)   before the end of the prescribed period, the applicant asks the Secretary of State to review the decision and pays any fee fixed under section 45.

(2) The Secretary of State shall—

(a)   review the decision; and

(b)   in doing so, consider any representations made to him in writing, before the end of the prescribed period, by the applicant.

(3) A person applying for an accessibility certificate or an approval certificate may appeal to the Secretary of State against the refusal of a vehicle examiner to issue such a certificate.

(4) An appeal must be made within the prescribed time and in the prescribed manner.

(5) Regulations may make provision as to the procedure to be followed in connection with appeals.

(6) On the determination of an appeal, the Secretary of State may—

(a)   confirm, vary or reverse the decision appealed against;

(b)   give such directions as he thinks fit to the vehicle examiner for giving effect to his decision.

45   Fees

(1) Such fees, payable at such times, as may be prescribed may be charged by the Secretary of State in respect of—

    (a)   applications for, and grants of, approval under section 42(1);

    (b)   applications for, and the issue of, accessibility certificates and approval certificates;

    (c)   copies of such certificates;

    (d)   reviews and appeals under section 44.

(2) Any such fees received by the Secretary of State shall be paid by him into the Consolidated Fund.

(3) Regulations under subsection (1) may make provision for the repayment of fees, in whole or in part, in such circumstances as may be prescribed.

(4) Before making any regulations under subsection (1) the Secretary of State shall consult such representative organisations as he thinks fit.

Rail vehicles

46 Rail vehicle accessibility regulations

(1) The Secretary of State may make regulations ('rail vehicle accessibility regulations') for the purpose of securing that it is possible—

    (a)   for disabled persons—

        (i)   to get on to and off regulated rail vehicles in safety and without unreasonable difficulty;

        (ii)   to be carried in such vehicles in safety and in reasonable comfort; and

    (b)   for disabled persons in wheelchairs—

        (i)   to get on to and off such vehicles in safety and without unreasonable difficulty while remaining in their wheelchairs, and

        (ii)   to be carried in such vehicles in safety and in reasonable comfort while remaining in their wheelchairs.

(2) Rail vehicle accessibility regulations may, in particular, make provision as to the construction, use and maintenance of regulated rail vehicles including provision as to—

    (a)   the fitting of equipment to vehicles;

    (b)   equipment to be carried by vehicles;

    (c)   the design of equipment to be fitted to, or carried by, vehicles;

    (d)   the use of equipment fitted to, or carried by, vehicles;

    (e)   the toilet facilities to be provided in vehicles;

    (f)   the location and floor area of the wheelchair accommodation to be provided in vehicles;

    (g)   assistance to be given to disabled persons.

(3) If a regulated rail vehicle which does not conform with any provision of the rail vehicle accessibility regulations with which it is required to conform is used for carriage, the operator of the vehicle is guilty of an offence.

(4) A person who is guilty of such an offence is liable, on summary conviction, to a fine not exceeding level 4 on the standard scale.

(5) Different provision may be made in rail vehicle accessibility regulations—

    (a)   as respects different classes or descriptions of rail vehicle;

    (b)   as respects the same class or description of rail vehicle in different circumstances;

(c)   as respects different networks.

(6) In this section—

'network' means any permanent way or other means of guiding or supporting rail vehicles or any section of it;

'operator', in relation to any rail vehicle, means the person having the management of that vehicle;

'rail vehicle' means a vehicle—

(a)   constructed or adapted to carry passengers on any railway, tramway or prescribed system; and

(b)   first brought into use, or belonging to a class of vehicle first brought into use, after 31st December 1998;

'regulated rail vehicle' means any rail vehicle to which the rail vehicle accessibility regulations are expressed to apply; and

'wheelchair accommodation' has such meaning as may be prescribed.

(7) In subsection (6)—

'prescribed system' means a system using a prescribed mode of guided transport ('guided transport' having the same meaning as in the Transport and Works Act 1992); and

'railway' and 'tramway' have the same meaning as in that Act.

(8) The Secretary of State may by regulations make provision as to the time when a rail vehicle, or a class of rail vehicle, is to be treated, for the purposes of this section, as first brought into use.

(9) Regulations under subsection (8) may include provision for disregarding periods of testing and other prescribed periods of use.

(10) For the purposes of this section and section 47, a person uses a vehicle for carriage if he uses it for the carriage of members of the public for hire or reward at separate fares.

(11) Before making any regulations under subsection (1) or section 47 the Secretary of State shall consult the Disabled Persons Transport Advisory Committee and such other representative organisations as he thinks fit.

47   Exemption from rail vehicle accessibility regulations

(1) The Secretary of State may by order (an 'exemption order') authorise the use for carriage of any regulated rail vehicle of a specified description, or in specified circumstances, even though that vehicle does not conform with the provisions of the rail vehicle accessibility regulations with which it is required to conform.

(2) Regulations may make provision with respect to exemption orders including, in particular, provision as to—

(a)   the persons by whom applications for exemption orders may be made;

(b)   the form in which such applications are to be made;

(c)   information to be supplied in connection with such applications;

(d)   the period for which exemption orders are to continue in force;

(e)   the revocation of exemption orders.

(3) After considering any application for an exemption order and consulting the Disabled Persons Transport Advisory Committee and such other persons as he considers appropriate, the Secretary of State may—

(a)   make an exemption order in the terms of the application;

(b)   make an exemption order in such other terms as he considers appropriate;

(c)   refuse to make an exemption order.

(4) An exemption order may be made subject to such restrictions and conditions as may be specified.

(5) In this section 'specified' means specified in an exemption order.

Supplemental

48   Offences by bodies corporate etc

(1) Where an offence under section 40 or 46 committed by a body corporate is committed with the consent or connivance of, or is attributable to any neglect on the part of, a director, manager, secretary or other similar officer of the body, or a person purporting to act in such a capacity, he as well as the body corporate is guilty of the offence.

(2) In subsection (1) 'director', in relation to a body corporate whose affairs are managed by its members, means a member of the body corporate.

(3) Where, in Scotland, an offence under section 40 or 46 committed by a partnership or by an unincorporated association other than a partnership is committed with the consent or connivance of, or is attributable to any neglect on the part of, a partner in the partnership of (as the case may be) a person concerned in the management or control of the association, he, as well as the partnership or association, is guilty of the offence.

49   Forgery and false statements

(1) In this section 'relevant document' means—

(a)   a certificate of exemption issued under section 36, 37 or 37A;

(b)   a notice of a kind mentioned in section 36(9)(b), 37(8)(b) or 37A(8)(b);

(c)   an accessibility certificate; or

(d)   an approval certificate.

(2) A person is guilty of an offence if, with intent to deceive, he—

(a)   forges, alters or uses a relevant document;

(b)   lends a relevant document to any other person;

(c)   allows a relevant document to be used by any other person; or

(d)   makes or has in his possession any document which closely resembles a relevant document.

(3) A person who is guilty of an offence under subsection (2) is liable—

(a)   on summary conviction, to a fine not exceeding the statutory maximum;

(b)   on conviction on indictment, to imprisonment for a term not exceeding two years or to a fine or to both.

(4) A person who knowingly makes a false statement for the purpose of obtaining an accessibility certificate or an approval certificate is guilty of an offence and liable on summary conviction to a fine not exceeding level 4 on the standard scale.

Amendment – Amended by Private Hire Vehicles (Carriage of Guide Dogs etc) Act 2002, s 4(1)–(3).

PART VI

THE NATIONAL DISABILITY COUNCIL

Amendment – Prospectively repealed by Disability Rights Commission Act 1999, s 14(2), Sch 5, date in force: to be appointed.

50 (*repealed*)

Amendment – Repealed by Disability Rights Commission Act 1999, s 14(2), Sch 5.

51 Codes of practice prepared by the Council

(1), (2) (*repealed*)

(3) A failure on the part of any person to observe any provision of a code does not of itself make that person liable to any proceedings.

(4) A code is admissible in evidence in any proceedings under this Act before an employment tribunal, a county court or a sheriff court.

(5) If any provision of a code appears to a tribunal or court to be relevant to any question arising in any proceedings under this Act, it shall be taken into account in determining that question.

(6) In this section and section 52 'code' means a code issued by the Secretary of State under this section and includes a code which has been altered and re-issued.

Amendments – Amended by Employment Rights (Dispute Resolution) Act 1998, s 1(2)(a); subss (1), (2) repealed and remainder prospectively repealed by Disability Rights Commission Act 1999, s 14(2), Sch 5, partly as from a day to be appointed.

52 Further provision about codes issued under section 51

(1)–(10) (*repealed*)

(11) The Secretary of State may by order revoke a code.

(12) (*repealed*)

Amendment – Subsections (1)–(10), (12) repealed and subs (11) prospectively repealed by Disability Rights Commission Act 1999, s 14(2), Sch 5, partly as from a day to be appointed.

PART VII

SUPPLEMENTAL

53A Codes of practice

(1) The Disability Rights Commission may prepare and issue codes of practice giving practical guidance on how to avoid acts which are unlawful under Parts 2, 3 or 4, or on any other matter relating to the operation of any provision of those parts, to—

(a)   employers;

(b)   service providers;

(c)   bodies which are responsible bodies for the purposes of Chapter 1 or 2 of Part 4; or

(d)   other persons to whom the provisions of Parts 2 or 3 or Chapter 2 of Part 4 apply.

(1A) The Commission may also prepare and issue codes of practice giving practical guidance to any persons on any other matter with a view to—

(a)   promoting the equalisation of opportunities for disabled persons and persons who have had a disability; or

(b)   encouraging good practice in the way such persons are treated,

in any field of activity regulated by any provision of Part 2, 3 or 4.

(1B) Neither subsection (1) nor (1A) applies in relation to any duty imposed by or under sections 28D or 28E.

(2) The Commission shall, when requested to do so by the Secretary of State, prepare a code of practice dealing with the matters specified in the request.

(3) In preparing a code of practice the Commission shall carry out such consultations as it considers appropriate (which shall include the publication for public consultation of proposals relating to the code).

(4) The Commission may not issue a code of practice unless—

(a)   a draft of it has been submitted to and approved by the Secretary of State and laid by him before both Houses of Parliament; and

(b)   the 40 day period has elapsed without either House resolving not to approve the draft.

(5) If the Secretary of State does not approve a draft code of practice submitted to him he shall give the Commission a written statement of his reasons.

(6) A code of practice issued by the Commission—

(a)   shall come into effect on such day as the Secretary of State may by order appoint;

(b)   may be revised in whole or part, and re-issued, by the Commission; and

(c)   may be revoked by an order made by the Secretary of State at the request of the Commission.

(7) Where the Commission proposes to revise a code of practice—

(a)   it shall comply with subsection (3) in relation to the revisions; and

(b)   the other provisions of this section apply to the revised code of practice as they apply to a new code of practice.

(8) Failure to observe any provision of a code of practice does not of itself make a person liable to any proceedings.

(8A) But if a provision of a code of practice appears to a court, tribunal or other body hearing any proceedings under Part 2, 3 or 4 to be relevant, it must take that provision into account.

(9) In this section—

'code of practice' means a code of practice under this section;
(*repealed*); and
'40 day period' has the same meaning in relation to a draft code of practice as it has in section 3 in relation to draft guidance.

Amendments – Inserted by Disability Rights Commission Act 1999, s 9. Amended by Special Educational Needs and Disability Act 2001, ss 36, 42(6), Sch 9; Disability Discrimination Act 1995 (Amendment) Regulations 2003, SI 2003/1673, regs 3(1), 20(a)(i), (ii). Definition 'discrimination' repealed by Disability Discrimination Act 1995 (Amendment) Regulations 2003, SI 2003/1673, regs 3(1), 20(b).

53   Codes of practice prepared by the Secretary of State

(1)–(3) (*repealed*)

(4) A failure on the part of any person to observe any provision of a code does not of itself make that person liable to any proceedings.

(5) A code is admissible in evidence in any proceedings under this Act before an employment tribunal, a county court or a sheriff court.

(6) If any provision of a code appears to a tribunal or court to be relevant to any question arising in any proceedings under this Act, it shall be taken into account in determining that question.

(7) In this section and section 54 'code' means a code issued by the Secretary of State under this section and includes a code which has been revised and re-issued.

(8), (9) (*repealed*)

Amendments – Amended by Employment Rights (Dispute Resolution) Act 1998, s 1(2)(a); subss (1)–(3), (8), (9) repealed and subss (4)–(7) prospectively repealed by Disability Rights Commission Act 1999, s 14(2), Sch 5, partly as from a day to be appointed.

54   Further provision about codes issued under section 53

(1)–(7) (*repealed*)

(8) The Secretary of State may by order revoke a code.

(9) (*repealed*)

Amendments – Subsections (1)–(7), (9) repealed and subs (8) prospectively repealed by Disability Rights Commission Act 1999, s 14(2), Sch 5, partly as from a day to be appointed.

55   Victimisation

(1) For the purposes of Part II, Part 3 or Part 4, a person ('A') discriminates against another person ('B') if—

   (a)   he treats B less favourably than he treats or would treat other persons whose circumstances are the same as B's; and
   (b)   he does so for a reason mentioned in subsection (2).

(2) The reasons are that—

   (a)   B has—

(i)   brought proceedings against A or any other person under this Act; or

(ii) given evidence or information in connection with such proceedings brought by any person; or

(iii) otherwise done anything under this Act in relation to A or any other person; or

(iv) alleged that A or any other person has (whether or not the allegation so states) contravened this Act; or

(b)   A believes or suspects that B has done or intends to do any of those things.

(3) Where B is a disabled person, or a person who has had a disability, the disability in question shall be disregarded in comparing his circumstances with those of any other person for the purposes of subsection (1)(a).

(3A) For the purposes of Chapter 1 of Part 4—

(a)   references in subsection (2) to B include references to–
      (i)   a person who is, for the purposes of that Chapter, B's parent; and
      (ii) a sibling of B; and

(b)   references in that subsection to this Act are, as respects a person mentioned in sub-paragraph (i) or (ii) of paragraph (a), restricted to that Chapter.

(4) Subsection (1) does not apply to treatment of a person because of an allegation made by him if the allegation was false and not made in good faith.

(5) In the case of an act which constitutes discrimination by virtue of this section, sections 4, 4B, 4D, 4G, 6A, 7A, 7C, 13, 14A, 14C and 16A also apply to discrimination against a person who is not disabled.

(6) For the purposes of Part 2 and, to the extent that it relates to the provision of employment services, Part 3, subsection (2)(a)(iii) has effect as if there were inserted after 'under' 'or by reference to'.

Amendment – Amended by Special Educational Needs and Disability Act 2001, s 38(1), (7), (8). Subsections (5), (6) Inserted by Disability Discrimination Act 1995 (Amendment) Regulations 2003, SI 2003/1673, regs 3(1), 21. Amended by Disability Discrimination Act 1995 (Pensions) Regulations 2003, SI 2003/2770, regs 2, 4(3).

---

56   Help for persons suffering discrimination

(1) For the purposes of this section—

(a)   a person who considers that he may have been discriminated against or subjected to harassment, in contravention of any provision of Part II or to the extent that it relates to the provision of employment services, Part 3, is referred to as 'the complainant'; and

(b)   a person against whom the complainant may decide to make, or has made, a complaint under Part II or to the extent that it relates to the provision of employment services, Part 3 is referred to as 'the respondent'.

(2) The Secretary of State shall, with a view to helping the complainant to decide whether to make a complaint against the respondent and, if he does so, to formulate and present his case in the most effective manner, by order prescribe—

(a)   forms by which the complainant may question the respondent on his reasons for doing any relevant act, or on any other matter which is or may be relevant; and

(b)   forms by which the respondent may if he so wishes reply to any questions.

(3) Where the complainant questions the respondent in accordance with forms prescribed by an order under subsection (2)—

(a)   the question, and any reply by the respondent (whether in accordance with such an order or not), shall be admissible as evidence in any proceedings under Part II or to the extent that it relates to the provision of employment services, Part 3;

(b)   if it appears to the tribunal in any such proceedings—

(i)   that the respondent deliberately, and without reasonable excuse, omitted to reply within the period of eight weeks beginning with the day on which the question was served on him, or

(ii) that the respondent's reply is evasive or equivocal,

it may draw any inference which it considers it just and equitable to draw, including an inference that the respondent has contravened a provision of Part II or to the extent that it relates to the provision of employment services, Part 3.

(4) The Secretary of State may by order prescribe—

(a)   the period within which questions must be duly served in order to be admissible under subsection (3)(a); and

(b)   the manner in which a question, and any reply by the respondent, may be duly served.

(5) This section is without prejudice to any other enactment or rule of law regulating interlocutory and preliminary matters in proceedings before an employment tribunal, and has effect subject to any enactment or rule of law regulating the admissibility of evidence in such proceedings.

Amendment – Amended by Employment Rights (Dispute Resolution) Act 1998, s 1(2)(a) and Disability Discrimination Act 1995 (Amendment) Regulations 2003, SI 2003/1673, regs 3(1), 22(a)–(c).

---

57   Aiding unlawful acts

(1) A person who knowingly aids another person to do an unlawful act is to be treated for the purposes of this Act as himself doing the same kind of unlawful act.

(2) For the purposes of subsection (1), an employee or agent for whose act the employer or principal is liable under section 58 (or would be so liable but for section 58(5)) shall be taken to have aided the employer or principal to do the act.

(3) For the purposes of this section, a person does not knowingly aid another to do an unlawful act if—

(a)   he acts in reliance on a statement made to him by that other person that, because of any provision of this Act, the act would not be unlawful; and

(b)   it is reasonable for him to rely on the statement.

(4) A person who knowingly or recklessly makes such a statement which is false or misleading in a material respect is guilty of an offence.

(5) Any person guilty of an offence under subsection (4) shall be liable on summary conviction to a fine not exceeding level 5 on the standard scale.

(6) 'Unlawful act' means an act made unlawful by any provision of this Act other than a provision contained in Chapter 1 of Part 4.

Amendment – Amended by Special Educational Needs and Disability Act 2001, s 38(1), (9), (10).

58   Liability of employers and principals

(1) Anything done by a person in the course of his employment shall be treated for the purposes of this Act as also done by his employer, whether or not it was done with the employer's knowledge or approval.

(2) Anything done by a person as agent for another person with the authority of that other person shall be treated for the purposes of this Act as also done by that other person.

(3) Subsection (2) applies whether the authority was—

(a)   express or implied; or
(b)   given before or after the act in question was done.

(4) Subsections (1) and (2) do not apply in relation to an offence under section 57(4).

(5) In proceedings under this Act against any person in respect of an act alleged to have been done by an employee of his, it shall be a defence for that person to prove that he took such steps as were reasonably practicable to prevent the employee from—

(a)   doing that act; or
(b)   doing, in the course of his employment, acts of that description.

59   Statutory authority and national security etc

(1) Nothing in this Act makes unlawful any act done—

(a)   in pursuance of any enactment; or
(b)   in pursuance of any instrument made by a Minister of the Crown under any enactment; or
(c)   to comply with any condition or requirement imposed by a Minister of the Crown (whether before or after the passing of this Act) by virtue of any enactment.

(2) In subsection (1) 'enactment' includes one passed or made after the date on which this Act is passed and 'instrument' includes one made after that date.

(2A) Nothing in—

(a)   Part 2 of this Act, or
(b)   Part 3 of this Act to the extent that it relates to the provision of employment services,

makes unlawful any act done for the purpose of safeguarding national security if the doing of the act was justified by that purpose.

(3) Nothing in any other provision of this Act makes unlawful any act done for the purpose of safeguarding national security.

Amendment – Amended by Disability Discrimination Act 1995 (Amendment) Regulations 2003, SI 2003/1673, regs 3(1), 23(a).

PART VIII

MISCELLANEOUS

60 Appointment by Secretary of State of advisers

(1) The Secretary of State may appoint such persons as he thinks fit to advise or assist him in connection with matters relating to the employment of disabled persons and persons who have had a disability.

(2) Persons may be appointed by the Secretary of State to act generally or in relation to a particular area or locality.

(3) The Secretary of State may pay to any person appointed under this section such allowances and compensation for loss of earnings as he considers appropriate.

(4) The approval of the Treasury is required for any payment under this section.

(5) In subsection (1) 'employment' includes self-employment.

(6) The Secretary of State may by order—

    (a)   provide for section 17 of, and Schedule 2 to, the Disabled Persons (Employment) Act 1944 (national advisory council and district advisory committees) to cease to have effect—
        (i) so far as concerns the national advisory council; or
        (ii) so far as concerns district advisory committees; or
    (b)   repeal that section and Schedule.

(7) At any time before the coming into force of an order under paragraph (b) of subsection (6), section 17 of the Act of 1944 shall have effect as if in subsection (1), after 'disabled persons' in each case there were inserted ', and persons who have had a disability,' and as if at the end of the section there were added—

    '(3) For the purposes of this section—
        (a)   a person is a disabled person if he is a disabled person for the purposes of the Disability Discrimination Act 1995; and
        (b)   "disability" has the same meaning as in that Act.'

(8) At any time before the coming into force of an order under paragraph (a)(i) or (b) of subsection (6), section 16 of the Chronically Sick and Disabled Persons Act 1970 (which extends the functions of the national advisory council) shall have effect as if after 'disabled persons' in each case there were inserted ', and persons who have had a disability,' and as if at the end of the section there were added—

    '(2) For the purposes of this section—
        (a)   a person is a disabled person if he is a disabled person for the purposes of the Disability Discrimination Act 1995; and
        (b)   "disability" has the same meaning as in that Act.'

61 Amendment of Disabled Persons (Employment) Act 1944

(1) Section 15 of the Disabled Persons (Employment) Act 1944 (which gives the Secretary of State power to make arrangements for the provision of supported employment) is amended as set out in subsections (2) to (5).

(2) In subsection (1)—

    (a)   for 'persons registered as handicapped by disablement' substitute 'disabled persons';

    (b)   for 'their disablement' substitute 'their disability'; and

    (c)   for 'are not subject to disablement' substitute 'do not have a disability'.

(3) In subsection (2), for the words from 'any of one or more companies' to 'so required and prohibited' substitute 'any company, association or body'.

(4) After subsection (2) insert—

    '(2A) The only kind of company which the Minister himself may form in exercising his powers under this section is a company which is—

        (a)   required by its constitution to apply its profits, if any, or other income in promoting its objects; and

        (b)   prohibited by its constitution from paying any dividend to its members.'

(5) After subsection (5) insert—

    '(5A) For the purposes of this section—

        (a)   a person is a disabled person if he is a disabled person for the purposes of the Disability Discrimination Act 1995; and

        (b)   "disability" has the same meaning as in that Act.'

(6) The provisions of section 16 (preference to be given under section 15 of that Act to ex-service men and women) shall become subsection (1) of that section and at the end insert—

    'and whose disability is due to that service.

    (2) For the purposes of subsection (1) of this section, a disabled person's disability shall be treated as due to service of a particular kind only in such circumstances as may be prescribed.'

(7) The following provisions of the Act of 1944 shall cease to have effect—

    (a)   section 1 (definition of 'disabled person');

    (b)   sections 6 to 8 (the register of disabled persons);

    (c)   sections 9 to 11 (obligations on employers with substantial staffs to employ a quota of registered persons);

    (d)   section 12 (the designated employment scheme for persons registered as handicapped by disablement);

    (e)   section 13 (interpretation of provisions repealed by this Act);

    (f)   section 14 (records to be kept by employers);

    (g)   section 19 (proceedings in relation to offences); and

    (h)   section 21 (application as respects place of employment, and nationality).

(8) Any provision of subordinate legislation in which 'disabled person' is defined by reference to the Act of 1944 shall be construed as if that expression had the same meaning as in this Act.

(9) Subsection (8) does not prevent the further amendment of any such provision by subordinate legislation.

62, 63 (*repealed*)

Amendment – Provisions repealed by Employment Tribunals Act 1996, s 45, Sch 3, Pt I.

---

64 Application to Crown etc

(1) This Act applies—

  (a) to an act done by or for purposes of a Minister of the Crown or government department, or

  (b) to an act done on behalf of the Crown by a statutory body, or a person holding a statutory office,

as it applies to an act done by a private person.

(2) Part II applies to service—

  (a) for purposes of a Minister of the Crown or government department, other than service of a person holding a statutory office, or

  (b) on behalf of the Crown for purposes of a person holding a statutory office or purposes of a statutory body,

as it applies to employment by a private person.

(2A) Subsections (1) and (2) have effect subject to section 64A.

(3) The provisions of Parts II to IV of the 1947 Act apply to proceedings against the Crown under this Act as they apply to Crown proceedings in England and Wales; but section 20 of that Act (removal of proceedings from county court to High Court) does not apply.

(4) The provisions of Part V of the 1947 Act apply to proceedings against the Crown under this Act as they apply to proceedings in Scotland which by virtue of that Part are treated as civil proceedings by or against the Crown; but the proviso to section 44 of that Act (removal of proceedings from the sheriff court to the Court of Session) does not apply.

(5) (*repealed*)

(6) (*repealed*)

(7) Part II does not apply to service in any of the naval, military or air forces of the Crown.

(8) In this section—

  'the 1947 Act' means the Crown Proceedings Act 1947;
  'Crown proceedings' means proceedings which, by virtue of section 23 of the 1947 Act, are treated for the purposes of Part II of that Act as civil proceedings by or against the Crown;
  'service for purposes of a Minister of the Crown or government department' does not include service in any office for the time being mentioned in Schedule 2 (Ministerial offices) to the House of Commons Disqualification Act 1975;
  'statutory body' means a body set up by or under an enactment;
  'statutory office' means an office so set up.

Amendment – Sub-s (2): words repealed, Sub-s (2A): inserted, Sub-ss (5), (6): repealed, Sub-s (7): words repealed, Sub-s (8): definitions 'British Transport Police', 'fire brigade', 'Ministry of Defence Police', 'prison officer', 'Royal Parks Constabulary' and 'United Kingdom Atomic Energy Authority Constabulary' repealed by Disability Discrimination Act 1995 (Amendment) Regulations 2003, SI 2003/1673, regs 3(1), 24(a)-(e).

64A   Police

(1) For the purposes of Part 2, the holding of the office of constable shall be treated as employment—

    (a)   by the chief officer of police as respects any act done by him in relation to a constable or that office;

    (b)   by the police authority as respects any act done by them in relation to a constable or that office.

(2) For the purposes of section 58—

    (a)   the holding of the office of constable shall be treated as employment by the chief officer of police (and as not being employment by any other person); and

    (b)   anything done by a person holding such an office in the performance, or purported performance, of his functions shall be treated as done in the course of that employment.

(3) There shall be paid out of the police fund—

    (a)   any compensation, costs or expenses awarded against a chief officer of police in any proceedings brought against him under Part 2, and any costs or expenses incurred by him in any such proceedings so far as not recovered by him in the proceedings; and

    (b)   any sum required by a chief officer of police for the settlement of any claim made against him under Part 2 if the settlement is approved by the police authority.

(4) Any proceedings under Part 2 which, by virtue of subsection (1), would lie against a chief officer of police shall be brought against—

    (a)   the chief officer of police for the time being, or

    (b)   in the case of a vacancy in that office, against the person for the time being performing the functions of that office;

and references in subsection (3) to the chief officer of police shall be construed accordingly.

(5) A police authority may, in such cases and to such extent as appear to it to be appropriate, pay out of the police fund—

    (a)   any compensation, costs or expenses awarded in proceedings under Part 2 of this Act against a person under the direction and control of the chief officer of police;

    (b)   any costs or expenses incurred and not recovered by such a person in such proceedings; and

    (c)   any sum required in connection with the settlement of a claim that has or might have given rise to such proceedings.

(6) Subsections (1) and (2) apply to a police cadet and appointment as a police cadet as they apply to a constable and the office of constable.

(7) Subject to subsection (8), in this section—

'chief officer of police'—
- (a)   in relation to a person appointed, or an appointment falling to be made, under a specified Act, has the same meaning as in the Police Act 1996,
- (b)   in relation to a person appointed, or an appointment falling to be made, under section 9(1)(b) or 55(1)(b) of the Police Act 1997 (police members of the National Criminal Intelligence Service and the National Crime Squad) means the Director General of the National Criminal Intelligence Service or, as the case may be, the Director General of the National Crime Squad,
- (c)   in relation to a person appointed, or an appointment falling to be made, under the Police (Scotland) Act 1967, means the chief constable of the relevant police force,
- (d)   in relation to any other person or appointment means the officer or other person who has the direction and control of the body of constables or cadets in question;

'police authority'—
- (a)   in relation to a person appointed, or an appointment falling to be made, under a specified Act, has the same meaning as in the Police Act 1996,
- (b)   in relation to a person appointed, or an appointment falling to be made, under section 9(1)(b) or 55(1)(b) of the Police Act 1997, means the Service Authority for the National Criminal Intelligence Service or, as the case may be, the Service Authority for the National Crime Squad,
- (c)   in relation to a person appointed, or an appointment falling to be made, under the Police (Scotland) Act 1967, has the meaning given in that Act,
- (d)   in relation to any other person or appointment, means the authority by whom the person in question is or on appointment would be paid;

'police cadet' means any person appointed to undergo training with a view to becoming a constable;

'police fund'—
- (a)   in relation to a chief officer of police within paragraph (a) of the above definition of that term, has the same meaning as in the Police Act 1996,
- (b)   in relation to a chief officer of police within paragraph (b) of that definition, means the service fund established under section 16 or (as the case may be) section 61 of the Police Act 1997, and
- (c)   in any other case means money provided by the police authority;

'specified Act' means the Metropolitan Police Act 1829, the City of London Police Act 1839 or the Police Act 1996.

(8) In relation to a constable of a force who is not under the direction and control of the chief officer of police for that force, references in this section to the chief officer of police are references to the chief officer of the force under whose direction and control he is, and references in this section to the police authority are references to the relevant police authority for that force.

Amendment – Inserted by Disability Discrimination Act 1995 (Amendment) Regulations 2003, SI 2003/1673, regs 3(1), 25.

65   Application to Parliament

(1) This Act applies to an act done by or for purposes of the House of Lords or the House of Commons as it applies to an act done by a private person.

(2) For the purposes of the application of Part II in relation to the House of Commons, the Corporate Officer of that House shall be treated as the employer of a person who is (or would be) a relevant member of the House of Commons staff for the purposes of section 195 of the Employment Rights Act 1996.

(3) Except as provided in subsection (4), for the purposes of the application of sections 19 to 21, the provider of services is—

   (a)   as respects the House of Lords, the Corporate Officer of that House; and
   (b)   as respects the House of Commons, the Corporate Officer of that House.

(4) Where the service in question is access to and use of any place in the Palace of Westminster which members of the public are permitted to enter, the Corporate Officers of both Houses jointly are the provider of that service.

(5) Nothing in any rule of law or the law or practice of Parliament prevents proceedings being instituted before an employment tribunal under Part II or before any court under Part III.

Amendments – Amended by Employment Rights Act 1996, s 240, Sch 1, para 69(1), (3); Employment Rights (Dispute Resolution) Act 1998, s 1(2)(a).

66   (*repealed*)

Amendment – Repealed by Disability Discrimination Act 1995 (Amendment) Regulations 2003, SI 2003/1673, regs 3(1), 26.

67   Regulations and orders

(1) Any power under this Act to make regulations or orders shall be exercisable by statutory instrument.

(2) Any such power may be exercised to make different provision for different cases, including different provision for different areas or localities.

(3) Any such power includes power—

   (a)   to make such incidental, supplemental, consequential or transitional provision as appears to the Secretary of State to be expedient; and
   (b)   to provide for a person to exercise a discretion in dealing with any matter.

(4) No order shall be made under section 50(3) unless a draft of the statutory instrument containing the order has been laid before Parliament and approved by a resolution of each House.

(5) Any other statutory instrument made under this Act, other than one made under section 3(9), 53A(6)(a), or 70(3), shall be subject to annulment in pursuance of a resolution of either House of Parliament.

(6) Subsection (1) does not require an order under section 43 which applies only to a specified vehicle, or to vehicles of a specified person, to be made by statutory instrument but such an order shall be as capable of being amended or revoked as an order which is made by statutory instrument.

(7) Nothing in section 34(4), 40(6) or 46(5) affects the powers conferred by subsections (2) and (3).

Amendment – Amended by Disability Rights Commission Act 1999, s 14(1), Sch 4, para 3(1), (2).

68   Interpretation

(1) In this Act—

'accessibility certificate' means a certificate issued under section 41(1)(a);

'act' includes a deliberate omission;

'approval certificate' means a certificate issued under section 42(4);

'conciliation officer' means a person designated under section 211 of the Trade Union and Labour Relations (Consolidation) Act 1992;

'employment' means, subject to any prescribed provision, employment under a contract of service or of apprenticeship or a contract personally to do any work, and related expressions are to be construed accordingly;

'employment at an establishment in Great Britain' is to be construed in accordance with subsections (2) to (4A);

'enactment' includes subordinate legislation and any Order in Council, and (except in section 56(5)) includes an enactment comprised in, or in an instrument made under, an Act of the Scottish Parliament;

'Great Britain' includes such of the territorial waters of the United Kingdom as are adjacent to Great Britain;

'licensing authority' except in section 37A means—

(a)   in relation to the area to which the Metropolitan Public Carriage Act 1869 applies, the Secretary of State or the holder of any office for the time being designated by the Secretary of State; or

(b)   in relation to any other area in England and Wales, the authority responsible for licensing taxis in that area;

'mental impairment' does not have the same meaning as in the Mental Health Act 1983 or the Mental Health (Scotland) Act 1984 but the fact that an impairment would be a mental impairment for the purposes of either of those Acts does not prevent it from being a mental impairment for the purposes of this Act;

'Minister of the Crown' includes the Treasury and the Defence Council;

'occupational pension scheme' has the same meaning as in the Pension Schemes Act 1993;

'premises' includes land of any description;

'prescribed' means prescribed by regulations;

'profession' includes any vocation or occupation;

'provider of services' has the meaning given in section 19(2)(b);

'public service vehicle' and 'regulated public service vehicle' have the meaning given in section 40;

'PSV accessibility regulations' means regulations made under section 40(1);

'rail vehicle' and 'regulated rail vehicle' have the meaning given in section 46;

'rail vehicle accessibility regulations' means regulations made under section 46(1);

'regulations' means regulations made by the Secretary of State;

'section 21 duty' means any duty imposed by or under section 21;

'subordinate legislation' has the same meaning as in section 21 of the Interpretation Act 1978;

'taxi' and 'regulated taxi' have the meaning given in section 32;

'taxi accessibility regulations' means regulations made under section 32(1);

'trade' includes any business;

'trade organisation' has the meaning given in section 13;

'vehicle examiner' means an examiner appointed under section 66A of the Road Traffic Act 1988.

(2) Employment (including employment on board a ship to which subsection (2B) applies or on an aircraft or hovercraft to which subsection (2C) applies) is to be regarded as being employment at an establishment in Great Britain if the employee—

(a)   does his work wholly or partly in Great Britain; or

(b)   does his work wholly outside Great Britain and subsection (2A) applies.

(2A) This subsection applies if—

(a)   the employer has a place of business at an establishment in Great Britain;

(b)   the work is for the purposes of the business carried on at the establishment; and

(c)   the employee is ordinarily resident in Great Britain—

(i) at the time when he applies for or is offered the employment, or

(ii) at any time during the course of the employment.

(2B) This subsection applies to a ship if—

(a)   it is registered at a port of registry in Great Britain; or

(b)   it belongs to or is possessed by Her Majesty in right of the Government of the United Kingdom.

(2C) This subsection applies to an aircraft or hovercraft if—

(a)   it is—

(i) registered in the United Kingdom, and

(ii) operated by a person who has his principal place of business, or is ordinarily resident, in Great Britain; or

(b)   it belongs to or is possessed by Her Majesty in right of the Government of the United Kingdom.

(2D) The following are not to be regarded as being employment at an establishment in Great Britain—

(a)   employment on board a ship to which subsection (2B) does not apply;

(b)   employment on an aircraft or hovercraft to which subsection (2C) does not apply.

(4) Employment of a prescribed kind, or in prescribed circumstances, is to be regarded as not being employment at an establishment in Great Britain.

(4A) For the purposes of determining if employment concerned with the exploration of the sea bed or sub-soil or the exploitation of their natural resources is outside Great Britain, subsections (2)(a) and (b), (2A) and (2C) of this section each have effect as if 'Great Britain' had the same meaning as that given to the last reference to Great Britain in section 10(1) of the Sex Discrimination Act 1975 by section 10(5) of that Act read with the Sex Discrimination and Equal Pay (Offshore Employment) Order 1987.

(5) (*repealed*)

Amendment – Sub-s (1): definitions – 'benefits' repealed, 'employment at an establishment in Great Britain' amended, 'Great Britain' inserted, 'Minister of the Crown' amended, 'section 6 duty' and 'section 15 duty' repealed by Disability Discrimination Act 1995 (Amendment) Regulations 2003 SI 2003/1673, regs 3(1), 27(a)(i)–(iv). Definition 'licensing authority' amended by Private Hire Vehicles (Carriage of Guide Dogs etc) Act 2002, s 5. Sub-ss (2), (2A)–(2D), (4A): amended and sub-s (5): repealed by Disability Discrimination Act 1995 (Amendment) Regulations 2003, SI 2003/1673, regs 3(1), 27(b)–(d).

69 Financial provisions

(1) There shall be paid out of money provided by Parliament—

(a) any expenditure incurred by a Minister of the Crown under this Act;

(b) any increase attributable to this Act in the sums payable out of money so provided under or by virtue of any other enactment.

70 Short title, commencement, extent etc

(1) This Act may be cited as the Disability Discrimination Act 1995.

(2) This section (apart from subsections (4), (5) and (7)) comes into force on the passing of this Act.

(3) The other provisions of this Act come into force on such day as the Secretary of State may by order appoint and different days may be appointed for different purposes.

(4) Schedule 6 makes consequential amendments.

(5) The repeals set out in Schedule 7 shall have effect.

(5A) Sections 7A and 7B extend to England and Wales only.

(5B) Sections 7C and 7D extend to Scotland only.

(6) Subject to subsections (5A) and (5B), this Act extends to England and Wales, Scotland and Northern Ireland; but in their application to Northern Ireland the provisions of this Act mentioned in Schedule 8 shall have effect subject to the modifications set out in that Schedule.

(7) (*repealed*)

(8) Consultations which are required by any provision of this Act to be held by the Secretary of State may be held by him before the coming into force of that provision.

Amendment – Sub-ss (5A), (5B) inserted, sub-s (6) amended by Disability Discrimination Act 1995 (Amendment) Regulations 2003 SI 2003/1673, regs 3(1), 28(a), (b). Sub-s (7) repealed in part by Disability Rights Commission Act 1999, s 14(2), Sch 5.

SCHEDULES

SCHEDULE 1

PROVISIONS SUPPLEMENTING SECTION 1

Section 1(1)

Impairment

1   (1) 'Mental impairment' includes an impairment resulting from or consisting of a mental illness only if the illness is a clinically well-recognised illness.

(2) Regulations may make provision, for the purposes of this Act—

    (a)   for conditions of a prescribed description to be treated as amounting to impairments;

    (b)   for conditions of a prescribed description to be treated as not amounting to impairments.

(3) Regulations made under sub-paragraph (2) may make provision as to the meaning of 'condition' for the purposes of those regulations.

Long-term effects

2   (1) The effect of an impairment is a long-term effect if—

    (a)   it has lasted at least 12 months;

    (b)   the period for which it lasts is likely to be at least 12 months; or

    (c)   it is likely to last for the rest of the life of the person affected.

(2) Where an impairment ceases to have a substantial adverse effect on a person's ability to carry out normal day-to-day activities, it is to be treated as continuing to have that effect if that effect is likely to recur.

(3) For the purposes of sub-paragraph (2), the likelihood of an effect recurring shall be disregarded in prescribed circumstances.

(4) Regulations may prescribe circumstances in which, for the purposes of this Act—

    (a)   an effect which would not otherwise be a long-term effect is to be treated as such an effect; or

    (b)   an effect which would otherwise be a long-term effect is to be treated as not being such an effect.

Severe disfigurement

3   (1) An impairment which consists of a severe disfigurement is to be treated as having a substantial adverse effect on the ability of the person concerned to carry out normal day-to-day activities.

(2) Regulations may provide that in prescribed circumstances a severe disfigurement is not to be treated as having that effect.

(3) Regulations under sub-paragraph (2) may, in particular, make provision with respect to deliberately acquired disfigurements.

Normal day-to-day activities

4   (1) An impairment is to be taken to affect the ability of the person concerned to carry out normal day-to-day activities only if it affects one of the following—

(a)   mobility;
(b)   manual dexterity;
(c)   physical co-ordination;
(d)   continence;
(e)   ability to lift, carry or otherwise move everyday objects;
(f)   speech, hearing or eyesight;
(g)   memory or ability to concentrate, learn or understand; or
(h)   perception of the risk of physical danger.

(2) Regulations may prescribe—

(a)   circumstances in which an impairment which does not have an effect falling within sub-paragraph (1) is to be taken to affect the ability of the person concerned to carry out normal day-to-day activities;
(b)   circumstances in which an impairment which has an effect falling within sub-paragraph (1) is to be taken not to affect the ability of the person concerned to carry out normal day-to-day activities.

Substantial adverse effects

5   Regulations may make provision for the purposes of this Act—

(a)   for an effect of a prescribed kind on the ability of a person to carry out normal day-to-day activities to be treated as a substantial adverse effect;
(b)   for an effect of a prescribed kind on the ability of a person to carry out normal day-to-day activities to be treated as not being a substantial adverse effect.

Effect of medical treatment

6   (1) An impairment which would be likely to have a substantial adverse effect on the ability of the person concerned to carry out normal day-to-day activities, but for the fact that measures are being taken to treat or correct it, is to be treated as having that effect.

(2) In sub-paragraph (1) 'measures' includes, in particular, medical treatment and the use of a prosthesis or other aid.

(3) Sub-paragraph (1) does not apply—

(a)   in relation to the impairment of a person's sight, to the extent that the impairment is, in his case, correctable by spectacles or contact lenses or in such other ways as may be prescribed; or

(b)   in relation to such other impairments as may be prescribed, in such circumstances as may be prescribed.

Persons deemed to be disabled

7   (1) Sub-paragraph (2) applies to any person whose name is, both on 12th January 1995 and on the date when this paragraph comes into force, in the register of disabled persons maintained under section 6 of the Disabled Persons (Employment) Act 1944.

(2) That person is to be deemed—

(a)   during the initial period, to have a disability, and hence to be a disabled person; and
(b)   afterwards, to have had a disability and hence to have been a disabled person during that period.

(3) A certificate of registration shall be conclusive evidence, in relation to the person with respect to whom it was issued, of the matters certified.

(4) Unless the contrary is shown, any document purporting to be a certificate of registration shall be taken to be such a certificate and to have been validly issued.

(5) Regulations may provide for prescribed descriptions of person to be deemed to have disabilities, and hence to be disabled persons, for the purposes of this Act.

(6) Regulations may prescribe circumstances in which a person who has been deemed to be a disabled person by the provisions of sub-paragraph (1) or regulations made under sub-paragraph (5) is to be treated as no longer being deemed to be such a person.

(7) In this paragraph—

'certificate of registration' means a certificate issued under regulations made under section 6 of the Act of 1944; and
'initial period' means the period of three years beginning with the date on which this paragraph comes into force.

Progressive conditions

8   (1) Where—

(a)   a person has a progressive condition (such as cancer, multiple sclerosis or muscular dystrophy or infection by the human immunodeficiency virus),
(b)   as a result of that condition, he has an impairment which has (or had) an effect on his ability to carry out normal day-to-day activities, but
(c)   that effect is not (or was not) a substantial adverse effect,

he shall be taken to have an impairment which has such a substantial adverse effect if the condition is likely to result in his having such an impairment.

(2) Regulations may make provision, for the purposes of this paragraph—

(a)   for conditions of a prescribed description to be treated as being progressive;
(b)   for conditions of a prescribed description to be treated as not being progressive.

SCHEDULE 2

PAST DISABILITIES

Section 2(2)

1   The modifications referred to in section 2 are as follows.

2   References in Parts II to 4 to a disabled person are to be read as references to a person who has had a disability.

2A   References in Chapter 1 of Part 4 to a disabled pupil are to be read as references to a pupil who has had a disability.

2B   References in Chapter 2 of Part 4 to a disabled student are to be read as references to a student who has had a disability.

2C   In section 3A(5), after 'not having that particular disability' insert 'and who has not had that particular disability'.

3   In sections 4A(1), 4B(4), 4E(1), 4H(1), 6B(1), 7B(1), 7D(1), 14(1), 14B(1), 14D(1) and 16A(4), section 21A(4)(a) (in the words to be read as section 19(1)(aa)) and section 21A(6)(a) (in the words to be substituted in section 21(1)), after 'not disabled' (in each place it occurs) insert 'and who have not had a disability'.

4   In sections 4A(3)(b), 4E(3)(b), 4H(3)(b), 6B(3)(b), 7B(4)(b), 7D(3)(b), 14(3)(b), 14B(3)(b), 14D(3)(b) and 16A(6), for 'has' (in each place it occurs) substitute 'has had'.

4A   In section 28B(3)(a) and (4), after 'disabled' insert 'or that he had had a disability'.

4B   In section 28C(1), in paragraphs (a) and (b), after 'not disabled' insert 'and who have not had a disability'.

4C   In section 28S(3)(a) and (4), after 'disabled' insert 'or that he had had a disability'.

4D   In subsection (1) of section 28T, after 'not disabled' insert 'and who have not had a disability'.

4E   In that subsection as substituted by paragraphs 2 and 6 of Schedule 4C, after 'not disabled' insert 'and who have not had a disability'.

5   For paragraph 2(1) to (3) of Schedule 1, substitute—

'(1) The effect of an impairment is a long-term effect if it has lasted for at least 12 months.

(2) Where an impairment ceases to have a substantial adverse effect on a person's ability to carry out normal day-to-day activities, it is to be treated as continuing to have that effect if that effect recurs.

(3) For the purposes of sub-paragraph (2), the recurrence of an effect shall be disregarded in prescribed circumstances.'

Amendment – Amended by Special Educational Needs and Disability Act 2001, s 38(1), (11)–(13), Disability Discrimination Act 1995 (Amendment) Regulations 2003, SI 2003/1673, regs 3(1), 29(1)(a)–(c) and Disability Discrimination Act 1995 (Pensions) Regulations 2003, SI 2003/2770, regs 2, 4(4)(a), (b).

SCHEDULE 3

ENFORCEMENT AND PROCEDURE

Sections 17A(8), 25(6)

Amendment – Amended by Disability Discrimination Act 1995 (Amendment) Regulations 2003, SI 2003/1673, regs 3(1), 29(2)(a).

PART I

EMPLOYMENT

Conciliation

1 (*repealed*)

Amendment – Repealed by Employment Tribunals Act 1996, s 45, Sch 3, Pt I.

Restriction on proceedings for breach of Part II

2 (1) Except as provided by Part 2, no civil or criminal proceedings may be brought against any person in respect of an act merely because the act is unlawful under that Part. (2) Sub-paragraph (1) does not prevent the making of an application for judicial review [or the investigation or determination of any matter in accordance with Part 10 (investigations) of the Pension Schemes Act 1993 by the Pensions Ombudsman.

Amendment – Amended by Disability Discrimination Act 1995 (Amendment) Regulations 2003, SI 2003/1673, regs 3(1), 29(2)(b) and Disability Discrimination Act 1995 (Pensions) Regulations 2003, SI 2003/2770, regs 2, 4(5).

Period within which proceedings must be brought

3 (1) An employment tribunal shall not consider a complaint under section 17A or 25(8) unless it is presented before the end of the period of three months beginning when the act complained of was done.

(2) A tribunal may consider any such complaint which is out of time if, in all the circumstances of the case, it considers that it is just and equitable to do so.

(3) For the purposes of sub-paragraph (1)—

    (a)   where an unlawful act is attributable to a term in a contract, that act is to be treated as extending throughout the duration of the contract;

(b)   any act extending over a period shall be treated as done at the end of that period; and

(c)   a deliberate omission shall be treated as done when the person in question decided upon it.

(4) In the absence of evidence establishing the contrary, a person shall be taken for the purposes of this paragraph to decide upon an omission—

(a)   when he does an act inconsistent with doing the omitted act; or

(b)   if he has done no such inconsistent act, when the period expires within which he might reasonably have been expected to do the omitted act if it was to be done.

Amendment – Amended by Employment Rights (Dispute Resolution) Act 1998, s 1(2)(a) and Disability Discrimination Act 1995 (Amendment) Regulations 2003, SI 2003/1673, regs 3(1), 29(2)(c).

Evidence

4   (1) In any proceedings under section 17A or 25(8), a certificate signed by or on behalf of a Minister of the Crown and certifying—

(a)   that any conditions or requirements specified in the certificate were imposed by a Minister of the Crown and were in operation at a time or throughout a time so specified, or

(b)   (*repealed*)

shall be conclusive evidence of the matters certified.

(2) A document purporting to be such a certificate shall be received in evidence and, unless the contrary is proved, be deemed to be such a certificate.

Amendment – Amended by Employment Relations Act 1999, ss 41, 44, Sch 8, para 7, and Disability Discrimination Act 1995 (Amendment) Regulations 2003, SI 2003/1673, regs 3(1), 29(2)(e).

PART II

DISCRIMINATION IN OTHER AREAS

Restriction on proceedings for breach of Part III

5   (1) Except as provided by section 25 no civil or criminal proceedings may be brought against any person in respect of an act merely because the act is unlawful under Part III.

(2) Sub-paragraph (1) does not prevent the making of an application for judicial review.

Period within which proceedings must be brought

6   (1) A county court or a sheriff court shall not consider a claim under section 25 unless proceedings in respect of the claim are instituted before the end of the period of six months beginning when the act complained of was done.

(2) Where, in relation to proceedings or prospective proceedings under section 25, the dispute concerned is referred for conciliation in pursuance of arrangements under section 28 before the end of the period of six months mentioned in sub-paragraph (1), the period allowed by that sub-paragraph shall be extended by two months.

(3) A court may consider any claim under section 25 which is out of time if, in all the circumstances of the case, it considers that it is just and equitable to do so.

(4) For the purposes of sub-paragraph (1)—

(a)   where an unlawful act of discrimination is attributable to a term in a contract, that act is to be treated as extending throughout the duration of the contract;

(b)   any act extending over a period shall be treated as done at the end of that period; and

(c)   a deliberate omission shall be treated as done when the person in question decided upon it.

(5) In the absence of evidence establishing the contrary, a person shall be taken for the purposes of this paragraph to decide upon an omission—

(a)   when he does an act inconsistent with doing the omitted act; or

(b)   if he has done no such inconsistent act, when the period expires within which he might reasonably have been expected to do the omitted act if it was to be done.

Amendment – Amended by Disability Rights Commission Act 1999, s 14(1), Sch 4, para 3(1), (3).

Compensation for injury to feelings

7   In any proceedings under section 25, the amount of any damages awarded as compensation for injury to feelings shall not exceed the prescribed amount.

Evidence

8   (1) In any proceedings under section 25, a certificate signed by or on behalf of a Minister of the Crown and certifying—

(a)   that any conditions or requirements specified in the certificate were imposed by a Minister of the Crown and were in operation at a time or throughout a time so specified, or

(b)   that an act specified in the certificate was done for the purpose of safeguarding national security,

shall be conclusive evidence of the matters certified.

(2) A document purporting to be such a certificate shall be received in evidence and, unless the contrary is proved, be deemed to be such a certificate.

PART 3

DISCRIMINATION IN SCHOOLS

Amendment – Inserted by Special Educational Needs and Disability Act 2001, s 19(2), Sch 3, para 1.

Restriction on proceedings for breach of Part 4, Chapter 1

9 (1) Except as provided by sections 28I, 28K and 28L, no civil or criminal proceedings may be brought against any person in respect of an act merely because the act is unlawful under Chapter 1 of Part 4.

(2) Sub-paragraph (1) does not prevent the making of an application for judicial review.

Amendment – Inserted by Special Educational Needs and Disability Act 2001, s 19(2), Sch 3, para 1.

Period within which proceedings must be brought

10 (1) The Tribunal [or the Welsh Tribunal][1] shall not consider a claim under section 28I unless proceedings in respect of the claim are instituted before the end of the period of six months beginning when the act complained of was done.

(2) If, in relation to proceedings or prospective proceedings under section 28I, the dispute concerned is referred for conciliation in pursuance of arrangements under section 31B before the end of the period of six months mentioned in sub-paragraph (1), the period allowed by that sub-paragraph shall be extended by two months.

(3) The Tribunal [or the Welsh Tribunal][1] may consider any claim under section 28I which is out of time if, in all the circumstances of the case, it considers that it is just and equitable to do so.

(4) But sub-paragraph (3) does not permit the Tribunal [or the Welsh Tribunal][1] to decide to consider a claim if a decision not to consider that claim has previously been taken under that sub-paragraph.

(5) For the purposes of sub-paragraph (1)—

    (a)   if an unlawful act of discrimination is attributable to a term in a contract, that act is to be treated as extending throughout the duration of the contract;

    (b)   any act extending over a period shall be treated as done at the end of that period; and

    (c)   a deliberate omission shall be treated as done when the person in question decided upon it.

(6) In the absence of evidence establishing the contrary, a person shall be taken for the purposes of this paragraph to decide upon an omission—

    (a)   when he does an act inconsistent with doing the omitted act; or

    (b)   if he has done no such inconsistent act, when the period expires within which he might reasonably have been expected to do the omitted act if it was to be done.

Amendment – Inserted by Special Educational Needs and Disability Act 2001, s 19(2), Sch 3, para 1 and amended by Education Act 2002, s 195, Sch 18, paras 7, 12.

Evidence

11 (1) In any proceedings under section 28I, 28K or 28L, a certificate signed by or on behalf of a Minister of the Crown and certifying that any conditions or requirements specified in the certificate—

(a)   were imposed by a Minister of the Crown, and
(b)   were in operation at a time or throughout a time so specified,

shall be conclusive evidence of the matters certified.

(2) A document purporting to be such a certificate shall be received in evidence and, unless the contrary is proved, be deemed to be such a certificate.

Amendment – Inserted by Special Educational Needs and Disability Act 2001, s 19(2), Sch 3, para 1.

PART 4

DISCRIMINATION IN FURTHER AND HIGHER EDUCATION INSTITUTIONS

Amendment – Inserted by Special Educational Needs and Disability Act 2001, s 19(2), Sch 3, para 2.

Restriction on proceedings for breach of Part 4, Chapter 2

12 (1) Except as provided by section 28V, no civil or criminal proceedings may be brought against any person in respect of an act merely because the act is unlawful under Chapter 2 of Part 4.

(2) Sub-paragraph (1) does not prevent the making of an application for judicial review.

Amendment – Inserted by Special Educational Needs and Disability Act 2001, s 30(2), Sch 3, para 2.

Period within which proceedings must be brought

13 (1) A county court or a sheriff court shall not consider a claim under section 28V unless proceedings in respect of the claim are instituted before the end of the period of six months beginning when the act complained of was done.

(2) If, in relation to proceedings or prospective proceedings under section 28V—

(a)   the dispute concerned is referred for conciliation in pursuance of arrangements under section 31B before the end of the period of six months mentioned in sub-paragraph (1), or
(b)   in England and Wales, in a case not falling within paragraph (a), the dispute concerned relates to the act or omission of a qualifying institution and is referred as a complaint under the student complaints scheme before the end of that period,

the period of six months allowed by sub-paragraph (1) shall be extended by two months.

(2A) In sub-paragraph (2)(b)—

'qualifying institution' has the meaning given by section 11 of the Higher Education Act 2004;

'the student complaints scheme' means a scheme for the review of qualifying complaints, as defined by section 12 of that Act, that is provided by the designated operator, as defined by section 13(5)(b) of that Act.

(3) A court may consider any claim under section 28V which is out of time if, in all the circumstances of the case, it considers that it is just and equitable to do so.

(4) For the purposes of sub-paragraph (1)—

(a)   if an unlawful act of discrimination is attributable to a term in a contract, that act is to be treated as extending throughout the duration of the contract;

(b)   any act extending over a period shall be treated as done at the end of that period; and

(c)   a deliberate omission shall be treated as done when the person in question decided upon it.

(5) In the absence of evidence establishing the contrary, a person shall be taken for the purposes of this paragraph to decide upon an omission—

(a)   when he does an act inconsistent with doing the omitted act; or

(b)   if he has done no such inconsistent act, when the period expires within which he might reasonably have been expected to do the omitted act if it was to be done.

Amendment – Inserted by Special Educational Needs and Disability Act 2001, s 30(2), Sch 3, para 2 and amended by Higher Education Act 2004, s 19(3).

Compensation for injury to feelings

14   In any proceedings under section 28V, the amount of any damages awarded as compensation for injury to feelings shall not exceed the prescribed amount.

Amendment – Inserted by Special Educational Needs and Disability Act 2001, s 30(2), Sch 3, para 2.

Evidence

15   (1) In any proceedings under section 28V, a certificate signed by or on behalf of a Minister of the Crown and certifying that any conditions or requirements specified in the certificate—

(a)   were imposed by a Minister of the Crown, and

(b)   were in operation at a time or throughout a time so specified,

is conclusive evidence of the matters certified.

(2) A document purporting to be such a certificate is to be—

(a) received in evidence; and

(b) deemed to be such a certificate unless the contrary is proved.

Amendment – Inserted by Special Educational Needs and Disability Act 2001, s 30(2), Sch 3, para 2.

SCHEDULE 3A

VALIDITY OF CONTRACTS, COLLECTIVE AGREEMENTS AND RULES OF UNDERTAKINGS

Section 17C

PART 1

VALIDITY AND REVISION OF CONTRACTS

1

(1) A term of a contract is void where—

(a) the making of the contract is, by reason of the inclusion of the term, unlawful by virtue of this Part of this Act;

(b) it is included in furtherance of an act which is unlawful by virtue of this Part of this Act; or

(c) it provides for the doing of an act which is unlawful by virtue of this Part of this Act.

(2) Sub-paragraph (1) does not apply to a term the inclusion of which constitutes, or is in furtherance of, or provides for, unlawful discrimination against, or harassment of, a party to the contract, but the term shall be unenforceable against that party.

(3) A term in a contract which purports to exclude or limit any provision of this Part of this Act is unenforceable by any person in whose favour the term would operate apart from this paragraph.

(4) Sub-paragraphs (1), (2) and (3) apply whether the contract was entered into before or after the date on which this Schedule comes into force; but in the case of a contract made before that date, those sub-paragraphs do not apply in relation to any period before that date.

2

(1) Paragraph 1(3) does not apply—

(a) to a contract settling a complaint to which section 17A(1) or 25(8) applies where the contract is made with the assistance of a conciliation officer (within the meaning of the Trade Union and Labour Relations (Consolidation) Act 1992); or

(b) to a contract settling a complaint to which section 17A(1) or 25(8) applies if the conditions regulating compromise contracts under this Schedule are satisfied in relation to the contract.

(2) The conditions regulating compromise contracts under this Schedule are that—

(a) the contract must be in writing;

(b) the contract must relate to the particular complaint;

(c)   the complainant must have received advice from a relevant independent adviser as to the terms and effect of the proposed contract and in particular its effect on his ability to pursue a complaint before an employment tribunal;

(d)   there must be in force, when the adviser gives the advice, a contract of insurance, or an indemnity provided for members of a profession or professional body, covering the risk of a claim by the complainant in respect of loss arising in consequence of the advice;

(e)   the contract must identify the adviser; and

(f)   the contract must state that the conditions regulating compromise contracts under this Schedule are satisfied.

(3) A person is a relevant independent adviser for the purposes of sub-paragraph (2)(c)—

(a) if he is a qualified lawyer;

(b)   if he is an officer, official, employee or member of an independent trade union who has been certified in writing by the trade union as competent to give advice and as authorised to do so on behalf of the trade union; or

(c)   if he works at an advice centre (whether as an employee or a volunteer) and has been certified in writing by the centre as competent to give advice and as authorised to do so on behalf of the centre.

(4) But a person is not a relevant independent adviser for the purposes of sub-paragraph (2)(c) in relation to the complainant—

(a)   if he is, is employed by or is acting in the matter for the other party or a person who is connected with the other party;

(b)   in the case of a person within sub-paragraph (3)(b) or (c), if the trade union or advice centre is the other party or a person who is connected with the other party; or

(c)   in the case of a person within sub-paragraph (3)(c), if the complainant makes a payment for the advice received from him.

(5) In sub-paragraph (3)(a) 'qualified lawyer' means—

(a)   as respects England and Wales, a barrister (whether in practice as such or employed to give legal advice), a solicitor who holds a practising certificate, or a person other than a barrister or solicitor who is an authorised advocate or authorised litigator (within the meaning of the Courts and Legal Services Act 1990); and

(b)   as respects Scotland, an advocate (whether in practice as such or employed to give legal advice), or a solicitor who holds a practising certificate.

(6) In sub-paragraph (3)(b) 'independent trade union' has the same meaning as in the Trade Union and Labour Relations (Consolidation) Act 1992.

(7) For the purposes of sub-paragraph (4)(a) any two persons are to be treated as connected—

(a)   if one is a company of which the other (directly or indirectly) has control; or

(b)   if both are companies of which a third person (directly or indirectly) has control.

(8) An agreement under which the parties agree to submit a dispute to arbitration—

(a)   shall be regarded for the purposes of sub-paragraph (1)(a) and (b) as being a contract settling a complaint if—

  (i) the dispute is covered by a scheme having effect by virtue of an order under section 212A of the Trade Union and Labour Relations (Consolidation) Act 1992, and

  (ii) the agreement is to submit it to arbitration in accordance with the scheme; but

(b) shall be regarded as neither being nor including such a contract in any other case.

3

(1) On the application of a disabled person interested in a contract to which paragraph 1(1) or (2) applies, a county court or a sheriff court may make such order as it thinks fit for—

(a) removing or modifying any term rendered void by paragraph 1(1), or
(b) removing or modifying any term made unenforceable by paragraph 1(2);

but such an order shall not be made unless all persons affected have been given notice in writing of the application (except where under rules of court notice may be dispensed with) and have been afforded an opportunity to make representations to the court.

(2) An order under sub-paragraph (1) may include provision as respects any period before the making of the order (but after the coming into force of this Schedule).

PART 2

COLLECTIVE AGREEMENTS AND RULES OF UNDERTAKINGS

4

(1) This Part of this Schedule applies to—

(a) any term of a collective agreement, including an agreement which was not intended, or is presumed not to have been intended, to be a legally enforceable contract;
(b) any rule made by an employer for application to all or any of the persons who are employed by him or who apply to be, or are, considered by him for employment;
(c) any rule made by a trade organisation (within the meaning of section 13) or a qualifications body (within the meaning of section 14A) for application to—
  (i) all or any of its members or prospective members; or
  (ii) all or any of the persons on whom it has conferred authorisations or qualifications or who are seeking the authorisations or qualifications which it has power to confer.

(2) Any term or rule to which this Part of this Schedule applies is void where—

(a) the making of the collective agreement is, by reason of the inclusion of the term, unlawful by virtue of this Part of this Act;
(b) the term or rule is included in furtherance of an act which is unlawful by virtue of this Part of this Act; or
(c) the term or rule provides for the doing of an act which is unlawful by virtue of this Part of this Act.

(3) Sub-paragraph (2) applies whether the agreement was entered into, or the rule made, before or after the date on which this Schedule comes into force; but in the case

of an agreement entered into, or a rule made, before the date on which this Schedule comes into force, that sub-paragraph does not apply in relation to any period before that date.

5

A disabled person to whom this paragraph applies may present a complaint to an employment tribunal that a term or rule is void by virtue of paragraph 4 if he has reason to believe—

(a) that the term or rule may at some future time have effect in relation to him; and
(b) where he alleges that it is void by virtue of paragraph 4(2)(c), that—
    (i) an act for the doing of which it provides, may at some such time be done in relation to him, and
    (ii) the act would be unlawful by virtue of this Part of this Act if done in relation to him in present circumstances.

6

In the case of a complaint about—

(a) a term of a collective agreement made by or on behalf of—
    (i) an employer,
    (ii) an organisation of employers of which an employer is a member, or
    (iii) an association of such organisations of one of which an employer is a member, or
(b) a rule made by an employer within the meaning of paragraph 4(1)(b),

paragraph 5 applies to any disabled person who is, or is genuinely and actively seeking to become, one of his employees.

7

In the case of a complaint about a rule made by an organisation or body to which paragraph 4(1)(c) applies, paragraph 5 applies to any disabled person—

(a) who is, or is genuinely and actively seeking to become, a member of the organisation or body;
(b) on whom the organisation or body has conferred an authorisation or qualification; or
(c) who is genuinely and actively seeking an authorisation or qualification which the organisation or body has power to confer.

8

(1) When an employment tribunal finds that a complaint presented to it under paragraph 5 is well-founded the tribunal shall make an order declaring that the term or rule is void.

(2) An order under sub-paragraph (1) may include provision as respects any period before the making of the order (but after the coming into force of this Schedule).

9

The avoidance by virtue of paragraph 4(2) of any term or rule which provides for any person to be discriminated against shall be without prejudice to the following rights (except in so far as they enable any person to require another person to be treated less favourably than himself), namely—

(a)   such of the rights of the person to be discriminated against, and

(b)   such of the rights of any person who will be treated more favourably in direct or indirect consequence of the discrimination,

as are conferred by or in respect of a contract made or modified wholly or partly in pursuance of, or by reference to, that term or rule.

PART 3

INTERPRETATION

10

In this Schedule 'collective agreement' means any agreement relating to one or more of the matters mentioned in section 178(2) of the Trade Union and Labour Relations (Consolidation) Act 1992 (meaning of trade dispute), being an agreement made by or on behalf of one or more employers or one or more organisations of employers or associations of such organisations with one or more organisations of workers or associations of such organisations.

11

Any reference in this Schedule to a contract or act which is unlawful by virtue of this Part of this Act shall be taken to include a reference to a contract or act which is unlawful by virtue of Part 3 of this Act to the extent that it relates to the provision of employment services.

Amendment – Schedule inserted by Disability Discrimination Act 1995 (Amendment) Regulations 2003, SI 2003/1673, regs 3(1), 16(2), Schedule.

SCHEDULE 4

PREMISES OCCUPIED UNDER LEASES

Sections 18A(5) and 27(5)

Amendment – Amended by Disability Discrimination Act 1995 (Amendment) Regulations 2003, SI 2003/1673, regs 3(1), 29(3)(a).

PART I

OCCUPATION BY EMPLOYER ETC

Amendment – Amended by Disability Discrimination Act 1995 (Amendment) Regulations 2003, SI 2003/1673, regs 3(1), 29(3)(b).

Failure to obtain consent to alteration

1   If any question arises as to whether the occupier has failed to comply with any duty to make reasonable adjustments, by failing to make a particular alteration to the premises, any constraint attributable to the fact that he occupies the premises under a lease is to be ignored unless he has applied to the lessor in writing for consent to the making of the alteration.

Amendment – Amended by Disability Discrimination Act 1995 (Amendment) Regulations 2003, SI 2003/ 1673, regs 3(1), 29(3)(c).

Joining lessors in proceedings under section 17A or 25(8)

2 (1) In any proceedings under section 17A or 25(8), in a case to which section 18A applies, the complainant or the occupier may ask the tribunal hearing the complaint to direct that the lessor be joined or sisted as a party to the proceedings.

(2) The request shall be granted if it is made before the hearing of the complaint begins.

(3) The tribunal may refuse the request if it is made after the hearing of the complaint begins.

(4) The request may not be granted if it is made after the tribunal has determined the complaint.

(5) Where a lessor has been so joined or sisted as a party to the proceedings, the tribunal may determine—

    (a)   whether the lessor has—
            (i) refused consent to the alteration, or
            (ii) consented subject to one or more conditions, and
    (b)   if so, whether the refusal or any of the conditions was unreasonable.

(6) If, under sub-paragraph (5), the tribunal determines that the refusal or any of the conditions was unreasonable it may take one or more of the following steps—

    (a)   make such declaration as it considers appropriate;
    (b)   make an order authorising the occupier to make the alteration specified in the order;
    (c)   order the lessor to pay compensation to the complainant.

(7) An order under sub-paragraph (6)(b) may require the occupier to comply with conditions specified in the order.

(8) Any step taken by the tribunal under sub-paragraph (6) may be in substitution for, or in addition to, any step taken by the tribunal under section 17A(2).

(9) If the tribunal orders the lessor to pay compensation it may not make an order under section 17A(2) ordering the occupier to do so.

Amendment – Amended by Disability Discrimination Act 1995 (Amendment) Regulations 2003, SI 2003/ 1673, regs 3(1), 29(3)(d)-(f).

Regulations

3 Regulations may make provision as to circumstances in which—

    (a)   a lessor is to be taken, for the purposes of section 18A of this Part of this Schedule to have—

      (i) withheld his consent;

      (ii) withheld his consent unreasonably;

      (iii) acted reasonably in withholding his consent;

(b)   a condition subject to which a lessor has given his consent is to be taken to be reasonable;

(c)   a condition subject to which a lessor has given his consent is to be taken to be unreasonable.

Amendment – Amended by Disability Discrimination Act 1995 (Amendment) Regulations 2003, SI 2003/1673, regs 3(1), 29(3)(g).

Sub-leases etc

4 The Secretary of State may by regulations make provision supplementing, or modifying, the provision made by section 18A or any provision made by or under this Part of this Schedule in relation to cases where the occupier occupies premises under a sub-lease or sub-tenancy.

Amendment – Amended by Disability Discrimination Act 1995 (Amendment) Regulations 2003, SI 2003/1673, regs 3(1), 29(3)(g).

PART II

OCCUPATION BY PROVIDER OF SERVICES

Failure to obtain consent to alteration

5 If any question arises as to whether the occupier has failed to comply with the section 21 duty, by failing to make a particular alteration to premises, any constraint attributable to the fact that he occupies the premises under a lease is to be ignored unless he has applied to the lessor in writing for consent to the making of the alteration.

Reference to court

6 (1) If the occupier has applied in writing to the lessor for consent to the alteration and—

(a)   that consent has been refused, or

(b)   the lessor has made his consent subject to one or more conditions,

the occupier or a disabled person who has an interest in the proposed alteration to the premises being made, may refer the matter to a county court or, in Scotland, to the sheriff.

(2) In the following provisions of this Schedule 'court' includes 'sheriff'.

(3) On such a reference the court shall determine whether the lessor's refusal was unreasonable or (as the case may be) whether the condition is, or any of the conditions are, unreasonable.

(4) If the court determines—

    (a)   that the lessor's refusal was unreasonable, or

    (b)   that the condition is, or any of the conditions are, unreasonable,

it may make such declaration as it considers appropriate or an order authorising the occupier to make the alteration specified in the order.

(5) An order under sub-paragraph (4) may require the occupier to comply with conditions specified in the order.

Joining lessors in proceedings under section 25

7   (1) In any proceedings on a claim under section 25, in a case to which this Part of this Schedule applies, the plaintiff, the pursuer or the occupier concerned may ask the court to direct that the lessor be joined or sisted as a party to the proceedings.

(2) The request shall be granted if it is made before the hearing of the claim begins.

(3) The court may refuse the request if it is made after the hearing of the claim begins.

(4) The request may not be granted if it is made after the court has determined the claim.

(5) Where a lessor has been so joined or sisted as a party to the proceedings, the court may determine—

    (a)   whether the lessor has—
        (i) refused consent to the alteration, or
        (ii) consented subject to one or more conditions, and
    (b)   if so, whether the refusal or any of the conditions was unreasonable.

(6) If, under sub-paragraph (5), the court determines that the refusal or any of the conditions was unreasonable it may take one or more of the following steps—

    (a)   make such declaration as it considers appropriate;
    (b)   make an order authorising the occupier to make the alteration specified in the order;
    (c)   order the lessor to pay compensation to the complainant.

(7) An order under sub-paragraph (6)(b) may require the occupier to comply with conditions specified in the order.

(8) If the court orders the lessor to pay compensation it may not order the occupier to do so.

Regulations

8   Regulations may make provision as to circumstances in which—

    (a)   a lessor is to be taken, for the purposes of section 27 and this Part of this Schedule to have—
        (i) withheld his consent;
        (ii) withheld his consent unreasonably;

     (iii) acted unreasonably in withholding his consent;
(b)   a condition subject to which a lessor has given his consent is to be taken to be
       reasonable;
(c)   a condition subject to which a lessor has given his consent is to be taken to be
       unreasonable.

Sub-leases etc

9   The Secretary of State may by regulations make provision supplementing, or
modifying, the provision made by section 27 or any provision made by or under this Part
of this Schedule in relation to cases where the occupier occupies premises under a
sub-lease or sub-tenancy.

PART 3

OCCUPATION BY EDUCATIONAL INSTITUTIONS

Failure to obtain consent

10   If any question arises as to whether a responsible body has failed to comply with the
duty imposed by section 28T, by failing to make a particular alteration to premises, any
constraint attributable to the fact that the premises are occupied by the educational
institution under a lease is to be ignored unless the responsible body has applied to the
lessor in writing for consent to the making of the alteration.

Reference to court

11   (1) If the responsible body has applied in writing to the lessor for consent to the
alteration and—

(a)   that consent has been refused, or
(b)   the lessor has made his consent subject to one or more conditions,

that body or a disabled person who has an interest in the proposed alteration to the
premises being made, may refer the matter to a county court or, in Scotland, to the
sheriff.

(2) On such a reference the court must determine whether the lessor's refusal was
unreasonable or (as the case may be) whether the condition is, or any of the conditions
are, unreasonable.

(3) If the court determines—

(a)   that the lessor's refusal was unreasonable, or
(b)   that the condition is, or any of the conditions are, unreasonable,

it may make such declaration as it considers appropriate or an order authorising the
responsible body to make the alteration specified in the order.

(4) An order under sub-paragraph (3) may require the responsible body to comply with
conditions specified in the order.

Joining lessors in proceedings under section 28V

12 (1) In proceedings on a claim under section 28V, in a case to which this Part of this Schedule applies, the claimant, the pursuer or the responsible body concerned may ask the court to direct that the lessor be joined or sisted as a party to the proceedings.

(2) The request must be granted if it is made before the hearing of the claim begins.

(3) The court may refuse the request if it is made after the hearing of the claim begins.

(4) The request may not be granted if it is made after the court has determined the claim.

(5) If a lessor has been so joined or sisted as a party to the proceedings, the court may determine—

    (a)   whether the lessor has—
            (i) refused consent to the alteration, or
            (ii) consented subject to one or more conditions, and
    (b)   if so, whether the refusal or any of the conditions was unreasonable.

(6) If, under sub-paragraph (5), the court determines that the refusal or any of the conditions was unreasonable it may take one or more of the following steps—

    (a)   make such a declaration as it considers appropriate;
    (b)   make an order authorising the responsible body to make the alteration specified in the order;
    (c)   order the lessor to pay compensation to the complainant.

(7) An order under sub-paragraph (6)(b) may require the responsible body to comply with conditions specified in the order.

(8) If the court orders the lessor to pay compensation it may not order the responsible body to do so.

Regulations

13 Regulations may make provision as to circumstances in which—

    (a)   a lessor is to be taken, for the purposes of section 28W and this Part of this Schedule to have—
            (i) withheld his consent;
            (ii) withheld his consent unreasonably;
            (iii) acted reasonably in withholding his consent;
    (b)   a condition subject to which a lessor has given his consent is to be taken to be reasonable;
    (c)   a condition subject to which a lessor has given his consent is to be taken to be unreasonable.

Sub-leases etc

14 Regulations may make provision supplementing, or modifying, section 28W or any provision made by or under this Part of this Schedule in relation to cases where the premises of the educational institution are occupied under a sub-lease or sub-tenancy.

Amendment – Part inserted by Special Educational Needs and Disability Act 2001, s 31(2), Sch 6.

SCHEDULE 4A

RESPONSIBLE BODIES FOR SCHOOLS

Section 28A

1 (1) The bodies responsible for schools in England and Wales are set out in the following table.

(2) In that Table—

'the local education authority' has the meaning given by section 22(8) of the School Standards and Framework Act 1998; and

'proprietor' has the meaning given by section 579 of the Education Act 1996.

TABLE

Type of school	*Responsible body*
1 Maintained school [or maintained nursery school][1].	The local education authority or governing body, according to which has the function in question.
2 Pupil referral unit.	The local education authority.
3 Maintained nursery school.	*The local education authority.*[2]
4 Independent school.	The proprietor.
5 Special school not maintained by a local education authority.	The proprietor.

2 (1) The bodies responsible for schools in Scotland are set out in the following table.

(2) In that Table 'board of management', 'education authority', 'managers' and 'proprietor' each have the meaning given in section 135(1) of the Education (Scotland) Act 1980.

TABLE

Type of school	Responsible body
1 School managed by an education authority.	The education authority.
2 Independent school.	The proprietor.
3 Self-governing school.	The board of management.
4 School in respect of which the managers are for the time being receiving grants under section 73(c) or (d) of the Education (Scotland) Act 1980.	The managers of the school.

Amendments – Inserted by Special Educational Needs and Disability Act 2001, s 11(2), Sch 2.
[1] Words prospectively inserted by Education Act 2002, s 215(1), Sch 21, para 29(a), as from a day to be appointed.
[2] Paragraph prospectively repealed by Education Act 2002, s 215(1), (2), Sch 21, para 29(b), Sch 22, Pt 3, as from a day to be appointed.

SCHEDULE 4B

RESPONSIBLE BODIES FOR EDUCATIONAL INSTITUTIONS

Section 28R

1 (1) The bodies responsible for educational institutions in England and Wales are set out in the following table.

(2) In that Table 'governing body' has the meaning given by section 90 of the Further and Higher Education Act 1992.

TABLE

Type of institution	Responsible body
1 Institution within the further education sector.	The governing body.
2 University.	The governing body.
3 Institution, other than a university, within the higher education sector.	The governing body.
4 Institution designated under section 28R(6)(c).	The body specified in the order as the responsible body.

2 (1) The bodies responsible for relevant institutions in Scotland are set out in the following table.

(2) In that Table—

'board of management' has the meaning given in section 36(1) of the Further and Higher Education (Scotland) Act 1992 ('the 1992 Act');

'central institution', 'education authority' and 'managers' have the meaning given in section 135(1) of the Education (Scotland) Act 1980; and

'governing body' has the meaning given in section 56(1) of the 1992 Act.

TABLE

Type of institution	Responsible body
1 Designated institution within the meaning of Part 2 of the 1992 Act.	The governing body.
2 University.	The governing body.
3 College of further education with a board of management.	The board of management.
4 Institution maintained by an education authority in the exercise of their further education functions.	The education authority.
5 Central institution.	The governing body.
6 School in respect of which the managers are for the time being receiving grants under section 73(c) or (d) of the Education (Scotland) Act 1980.	The managers of the school.
7 Institution designated under section 28R(7)(e).	The body specified in the order as the responsible body.

Amendment – Inserted by Special Educational Needs and Disability Act 2001, s 26(2), Sch 4.

SCHEDULE 4C

MODIFICATIONS OF CHAPTER 2 OF PART 4

Section 28U

PART 1

MODIFICATIONS FOR ENGLAND AND WALES

1 For section 28R, substitute—

'28R Further education etc provided by local education authorities and schools

(1)   Subsections (2) and (3) apply in relation to—

- (a)   any course of higher education secured by a local education authority under section 120 of the Education Reform Act 1988;
- (b)   any course of further education—
  - (i)   secured by a local education authority; or
  - (ii)   provided by the governing body of a maintained school under section 80 of the School Standards and Framework Act 1998.

(2)   It is unlawful for the local education authority or the governing body to discriminate against a disabled person—

- (a)   in the arrangements they make for determining who should be enrolled on the course;
- (b)   in the terms on which they offer to enrol him on the course; or
- (c)   by refusing or deliberately omitting to accept an application for his enrolment on the course.

(3) It is unlawful for the local education authority or the governing body to discriminate against a disabled person who has enrolled on the course in the services which they provide, or offer to provide.

(4) "Services", in relation to a course, means services of any description which are provided wholly or mainly for persons enrolled on the course.

(5) It is unlawful for a local education authority to discriminate against a disabled person in the terms on which they provide, or offer to provide, recreational or training facilities.

(6) In this Chapter "responsible body" means—

- (a)   a local education authority, in relation to—
  - (i)   a course of further or higher education secured by them;
  - (ii)   recreational or training facilities; and
- (b)   the governing body of a maintained school, in relation to a course of further education provided under section 80 of the School Standards and Framework Act 1998.

(7) "Further education"—

- (a)   in relation to a course secured by a local education authority, has the meaning given in section 2(3) of the Education Act 1996; and
- (b)   in relation to a course provided under section 80 of the School Standards and Framework Act 1998 means education of a kind mentioned in subsection (1) of that section.

(8) In relation to further education secured by a local education authority—

"course" includes each of the component parts of a course of further education if, in relation to the course, there is no requirement imposed on persons registered for any component part of the course to register for any other component part of that course; and

"enrolment", in relation to such a course, includes registration for any one of those parts.

(9) "Higher education" has the meaning given in section 579(1) of the Education Act 1996.

(10) "Local education authority" has the meaning given in section 12 of the Education Act 1996.

(11) "Governing body" and "maintained school" have the same meaning as in Chapter 1.

(12) "Recreational or training facilities" means any facilities secured by a local education authority under subsection (1), or provided by it under subsection (1A), of section 508 of the Education Act 1996 (recreation and social and physical training).'

2   For subsection (1) of section 28T, substitute—

'(1) Each responsible body must take such steps as it is reasonable for it to have to take to ensure that—

(a)   in relation to its arrangements for enrolling persons on a course of further or higher education provided by it, and
(b)   in relation to services provided, or offered by it,

disabled persons are not placed at a substantial disadvantage in comparison with persons who are not disabled.'

3   In section 28W(1)(a) for 'by an educational institution' substitute 'by a responsible body wholly or partly for the purpose of its functions'.

4   Omit section 31A.

PART 2

MODIFICATIONS FOR SCOTLAND

5   For section 28R, substitute—

'28R   Further education etc provided by education authorities in Scotland

(1) Subsections (2) and (3) apply to any course of further education secured by an education authority.

(2) It is unlawful for the education authority to discriminate against a disabled person—

(a)   in the arrangements they make for determining who should be enrolled on the course;
(b)   in the terms on which they offer to enrol him on the course; or
(c)   by refusing or deliberately omitting to accept an application for his enrolment on the course.

(3) It is unlawful for the education authority to discriminate against a disabled person who has enrolled on the course in the services which they provide, or offer to provide.

(4) "Services", in relation to a course, means services of any description which are provided wholly or mainly for persons enrolled on the course.

(5) It is unlawful for an education authority to discriminate against a disabled person in the terms on which they provide, or offer to provide, recreational or training facilities.

(6) In this Chapter "responsible body" means an education authority.

(7) "Further education" has the meaning given in section 1(5) of the Education (Scotland) Act 1980.

(8) "Education authority" has the meaning given in section 135(1) of that Act.'

6   For subsection (1) of section 28T, substitute—

'(1) Each responsible body must take such steps as it is reasonable for it to have to take to ensure that—

    (a)   in relation to its arrangements for enrolling persons on a course of further education provided by it, and

    (b)   in relation to services provided or offered by it,

disabled persons are not placed at a substantial disadvantage in comparison with persons who are not disabled.'

7   In section 28W(1)(a) for 'by an educational institution' substitute 'by a responsible body wholly or partly for the purpose of its functions'.

8   Omit section 31A.

Amendment – Schedule inserted by Special Educational Needs and Disability Act 2001, s 29(2), Sch 5.

SCHEDULE 5

(*repealed*)

Amendment – Repealed by Disability Rights Commission Act 1999, s 14(2), Sch 5.

SCHEDULE 6

CONSEQUENTIAL AMENDMENTS

Section 70(4)

1–3   (*repealed*)

Companies Act 1985 (c. 6)

4   In paragraph 9 of Schedule 7 to the Companies Act 1985 (disclosure in directors' report of company policy in relation to disabled persons), in the definition of 'disabled person' in sub-paragraph (4)(b), for 'Disabled Persons (Employment) Act 1944' substitute 'Disability Discrimination Act 1995'.

Local Government and Housing Act 1989 (c. 42)

5 In section 7 of the Local Government and Housing Act 1989 (all staff of a local authority etc to be appointed on merit), in subsection (2)—

(a)   paragraph (a) shall be omitted;

(b)   the word 'and' at the end of paragraph (d) shall be omitted; and

(c)   after paragraph (e) insert—

'; and

  (f)   sections 5 and 6 of the Disability Discrimination Act 1995 (meaning of discrimination and duty to make adjustments).'

Enterprise and New Towns (Scotland) Act 1990 (c. 35)

6 In section 16 of the Enterprise and New Towns (Scotland) Act 1990 (duty of certain Scottish bodies to give preference to ex-service men and women in exercising powers to select disabled persons for training), in subsection (2), for 'said Act of 1944' substitute 'Disability Discrimination Act 1995'.

Amendments – Amended by Employment Rights Act 1996, s 242, Sch 3, Pt I; Employment Tribunals Act 1996, s 45, Sch 3, Pt I; Employment Rights (Northern Ireland) Order 1996, SI 1996/1919 (NI 16), art 257, Sch 3.

SCHEDULE 7

REPEALS

Section 70(5)

Chapter	Short title	Extent of repeal
7 & 8 Geo. 6 c. 10.	The Disabled Persons (Employment) Act 1944.	Section 1. Sections 6 to 14. Section 19. Section 21. Section 22(4).
6 & 7 Eliz. 2 c. 33.	The Disabled Persons (Employment) Act 1958.	Section 2.
1970 c. 44.	The Chronically Sick and Disabled Persons Act 1970.	Section 16.
1978 c. 44.	The Employment Protection (Consolidation) Act 1978.	In Schedule 13, in paragraph 20(3), the word 'or' in the definitions of 'relevant complaint of dismissal' and 'relevant conciliation powers'.

Chapter	Short title	Extent of repeal
1989 c. 42.	The Local Government and Housing Act 1989.	In section 7(2), paragraph (a) and the word 'and' at the end of paragraph (d).
1993 c. 62.	The Education Act 1993.	In section 161(5), the words from 'and in this subsection' to the end.

SCHEDULE 8

MODIFICATIONS OF THIS ACT IN ITS APPLICATION TO NORTHERN IRELAND

Section 70(6)

1 In its application to Northern Ireland this Act shall have effect subject to the following modifications.

2 (1) In section 3(1) for 'Secretary of State' substitute 'Department'.

(2) In section 3 for subsections (4) to (12) substitute—

'(4) In preparing a draft of any guidance, the Department shall consult such persons as it considers appropriate.

(5) Where the Department proposes to issue any guidance, the Department shall publish a draft of it, consider any representations that are made to the Department about the draft and, if the Department thinks it appropriate, modify its proposals in the light of any of those representations.

(6) If the Department decides to proceed with any proposed guidance, the Department shall lay a draft of it before the Assembly.

(7) If, within the statutory period, the Assembly resolves not to approve the draft, the Department shall take no further steps in relation to the proposed guidance.

(8) If no such resolution is made within the statutory period, the Department shall issue the guidance in the form of its draft.

(9) The guidance shall come into force on such date as the Department may by order appoint.

(10) Subsection (7) does not prevent a new draft of the proposed guidance being laid before the Assembly.

(11) The Department may—
  (a) from time to time revise the whole or any part of any guidance and re-issue it;
  (b) by order revoke any guidance.

(12) In this section—

"the Department" means the Office of the First Minister and Deputy First Minister;

"guidance" means guidance issued by the Department under this section and includes guidance which has been revised and re-issued;

"statutory period" has the meaning assigned to it by section 41(2) of the Interpretation Act (Northern Ireland) 1954.'

3 In section 4(6) for 'Great Britain' substitute 'Northern Ireland'.

4 (1) In section 7(2) for 'Secretary of State' substitute 'Office of the First Minister and Deputy First Minister'.

(2) In section 7(4) to (10) for 'Secretary of State' wherever it occurs substitute 'Office of the First Minister and Deputy First Minister', for 'he' and 'him' wherever they occur substitute 'it' and for 'his' wherever it occurs substitute 'its'.

(3) In section 7(9) for 'Parliament' substitute 'the Assembly'.

5 (1) In section 8(3) omit 'or (in Scotland) in reparation'.

(2) In section 8(7) for 'paragraph 6A of Schedule 9 to the Employment Protection (Consolidation) Act 1978' substitute 'Article 16 of the Industrial Tribunals (Northern Ireland) Order 1996'.

Amendment – Amended by Industrial Tribunals (Northern Ireland) Order 1996, SI 1996/1921, art 26, Sch 1, para 12.

---

6 (1) In section 9(2)(a) for 'a conciliation officer' substitute 'the Agency'.

(2) In section 9(4) in the definition of 'qualified lawyer' for the words from 'means' to the end substitute 'means a barrister (whether in practice as such or employed to give legal advice) or a solicitor of the Supreme Court who holds a practising certificate.'.

7 (1) In section 10(1)(b) omit 'or recognised body'.

(2) In section 10(2)(b) for 'Secretary of State' substitute 'Department of Higher and Further Education, Training and Employment'.

(3) In section 10(3) in the definition of 'charity' for '1993' substitute '(Northern Ireland) 1964', omit the definition of 'recognised body' and in the definition of 'supported employment' for 'Act 1944' substitute 'Act (Northern Ireland) 1945'.

(4) In section 10(4) for 'England and Wales' where it twice occurs substitute 'Northern Ireland'.

(5) Omit section 10(5).

8 In section 12(5) for 'Great Britain' where it twice occurs substitute 'Northern Ireland'.

9 (1) In section 19(3)(g) for 'section 2 of the Employment and Training Act 1973' substitute 'sections 1 and 2 of the Employment and Training Act (Northern Ireland) 1950'.

(2) In section 19(5) for paragraph (a) substitute—

'(a) education which is funded, or secured, by a relevant body or provided at—
  (i) an establishment which is funded by such a body or by the Department of Education for Northern Ireland; or
  (ii) any other establishment which is a school within the meaning of the Education and Libraries (Northern Ireland) Order 1986;'.

(3) For section 19(6) substitute—

'(6) In subsection (5) "relevant body" means—
    (a)   an education and library board;
    (b)   a voluntary organisation; or
    (c)   a body of a prescribed kind.'.

10   In section 20(7) for paragraphs (b) and (c) substitute '; or

   (b)   functions conferred by or under Part VIII of the Mental Health (Northern Ireland) Order 1986 are exercisable in relation to a disabled person's property or affairs.'.

11   In section 22(4) and (6) omit 'or (in Scotland) the subject of'.

12   (1) In section 25(1) omit 'or (in Scotland) in reparation'.

(2) In section 25(3) for 'England and Wales' substitute 'Northern Ireland'.

(3) Omit section 25(4).

(4) In section 25(5) omit the words from 'or' to the end.

13   In section 26(3) omit 'or a sheriff court'.

14   (1) In section 28 for 'Secretary of State' wherever it occurs substitute 'Office of the First Minister and Deputy First Minister'.

(2) In section 28(3) and (4) for 'he' substitute 'it'.

(3) In section 28(5) for 'Treasury' substitute 'Department of Finance and Personnel in Northern Ireland'.

15   Omit sections 29, 30 and 31.

16   (1) In section 32(1) for 'Secretary of State' substitute 'Department of the Environment'.

(2) In section 32(5) for the definition of 'taxi' substitute—

'"taxi" means a vehicle which—
    (a)   is licensed under Article 61 of the Road Traffic (Northern Ireland) Order 1981 to stand or ply for hire; and
    (b)   seats not more than 8 passengers in addition to the driver'.

17   In section 33, for 'Secretary of State', wherever it occurs, substitute 'Department of the Environment'.

18   For section 34 substitute—

'34 New licences conditional on compliance with accessibility taxi regulations

(1) The Department of the Environment shall not grant a public service vehicle licence under Article 61 of the Road Traffic (Northern Ireland) Order 1981 for a taxi unless the vehicle conforms with those provisions of the taxi accessibility regulations with which it will be required to confirm if licensed.

(2) Subsection (1) does not apply if such a licence was in force with respect to the vehicle at any time during the period of 28 days immediately before the day on which the licence is granted.

(3) The Department of the Environment may by order provide for subsection (2) to cease to have effect on such date as may be specified in the order.'.

19   Omit section 35.

20   In section 36(7) for 'licensing authority' substitute 'Department of the Environment'.

21   (1) In section 37(5) and (6) for 'licensing authority' substitute 'Department of the Environment'.

(2) In section 37(9) for 'Secretary of State' substitute 'Department of the Environment'.

[21A

(1) In section 37A(5) and (6) for 'licensing authority' substitute 'Department of the Environment'.

(2) In section 37A(9) for the definitions of 'driver', 'licensing authority', 'operator' and 'private hire vehicle' substitute—

'driver' means a person who holds a taxi driver's licence under Article 79A of the Road Traffic (Northern Ireland) Order 1981 (SI 1981/154 (NI 1));
'operator' means a person who in the course of a business makes provision for the invitation or acceptance of bookings for a private hire vehicle;
'private hire vehicle' means a vehicle which—

(a)   seats not more than 8 passengers in addition to the driver; and
(b)   is licensed under Article 61 of the Road Traffic (Northern Ireland) Order 1981 to carry passengers for hire (but not to stand or ply for hire).'.]

Amendment – Prospectively inserted by Private Hire Vehicles (Carriage of Guide Dogs etc) Act 2002, s 1(2), from a date to be appointed.

---

22   (1) In section 38(1) for 'a licensing authority' substitute 'the Department of the Environment'.

(2) In section 38(2) for 'licensing authority concerned' substitute 'Department of the Environment'.

(3) In section 38(3) for the words from 'the magistrates' court' to the end substitute 'a court of summary jurisdiction acting for the petty sessions district in which the aggrieved person resides'.

23   Omit section 39.

24   (1) In section 40 for 'Secretary of State' wherever it occurs substitute 'Department of the Environment'.

(2) In section 40(5) for the definition of 'public service vehicle' substitute—

'"public service vehicle" means a vehicle which—
(a)   seats more than 8 passengers in addition to the driver; and
(b)   is a public service vehicle for the purposes of the Road Traffic (Northern Ireland) Order 1981;'.

(3) In section 40(7) for the words for 'the Disabled' to the end substitute 'such representative organisations as it thinks fit'.

25   (1) In section 41(2) for 'Secretary of State' substitute 'Department of the Environment'.

(2) In section 41 for subsections (3) and (4) substitute—

'(3) Any person who uses a regulated public service vehicle in contravention of this section is guilty of an offence and liable on summary conviction to a fine not exceeding level 4 on the standard scale.'.

26 (1) In section 42 for 'Secretary of State' wherever it occurs substitute 'Department of the Environment'.

(2) In section 42(1) for 'he' substitute 'it'.

(3) In section 42(6) for 'his' substitute 'its'.

27 In section 43 for 'Secretary of State' wherever it occurs substitute 'Department of the Environment'.

28 (1) In section 44 for 'Secretary of State' wherever it occurs substitute 'Department of the Environment'.

(2) In section 44(2) for 'him' substitute 'it'.

(3) In section 44(6) for 'he' substitute 'it' and for 'his' substitute 'its'.

29 (1) In section 45 for 'Secretary of State' wherever it occurs substitute 'Department of the Environment'.

(2) In section 45(2) for 'him' substitute 'it' and at the end add 'of Northern Ireland'.

(3) In section 45(4) for 'he' substitute 'it'.

30 (1) In section 46 for 'Secretary of State' wherever it occurs substitute 'Department for Regional Development'.

(2) In section 46(6) in the definition of 'rail vehicle' for the words 'on any railway, tramway or prescribed system' substitute 'by rail'.

(3) Omit section 46(7).

(4) In section 46(11) for the words from 'the Disabled' to the end substitute 'such representative organisations as it thinks fit'.

31 (1) In section 47 for 'Secretary of State' wherever it occurs substitute 'Department for Regional Development'.

(2) In section 47(3) for the words 'the Disabled Persons Transport Advisory Committee and such other persons as he' substitute 'such persons as it' and for 'he' substitute 'it'.

32 Omit section 48(3).

33 (1) In sections 50 to 52 for 'the Council' substitute, in each place, the 'Equality Commission for Northern Ireland'.

(1A) Section 50(1) shall have no effect.

(2) In section 50(2) for 'Secretary of State' in the first place where it occurs substitute 'a Northern Ireland department' and in the other place where it occurs substitute 'that department'.

(3) In section 50(3) for 'Secretary of State' substitute 'Office of the First Minister and Deputy First Minister'.

(4) In section 50(7) for 'Secretary of State' substitute 'a Northern Ireland department' and after 'Crown' insert 'or a Northern Ireland department'.

(5) In section 50(9)(a) for sub-paragraphs (i) to (iv) substitute—

    '(i)   the Disabled Persons (Employment) Act (Northern Ireland) 1945;

    (ii) the Contracts of Employment and Redundancy Payments Act (Northern Ireland) 1965;

   (iii) the Employment and Training Act (Northern Ireland) 1950;

   (iv) the Employment Rights (Northern Ireland) Order 1996; or'.

(6) In section 50(10) for the words from 'time when' to the end substitute 'time when—

    (a)   there are no committees in existence under section 17 of the Disabled Persons (Employment) Act (Northern Ireland) 1945; and

    (b)   there is no person appointed to act generally under section 60(1) of this Act.'.

Amendment – Amended by Northern Ireland Act 1998, s 99, Sch 13, para 16(1), (2)(b) and Employment Rights (Northern Ireland) Order 1996, SI 1996/1919 (NI 16), art 255, Sch 1.

---

34   (1) In section 51(1) for 'the Secretary of State' substitute 'any Northern Ireland department' and for 'the Secretary of State's' substitute 'that department's'.

(2) In section 51(2) for 'The Secretary of State' substitute 'A Northern Ireland department'.

(3) In section 51(4) for 'a county court or a sheriff court' substitute 'or a county court'.

(4) In section 51(6) for 'the Secretary of State' substitute 'a Northern Ireland department'.

35   For section 52 substitute—

'52   Further provisions about codes issued under section 51

(1) In this section—

    "proposal" means a proposal made by the Equality Commission for Northern Ireland to a Northern Ireland department under section 51;

    "responsible department"—

        (a)   in relation to a proposal, means the Northern Ireland department to which the proposal is made,

        (b)   in relation to a code, means the Northern Ireland department by which the code is issued; and

    "statutory period" has the meaning assigned to it by section 41(2) of the Interpretation Act (Northern Ireland) 1954.

(2) In preparing any proposal, the Equality Commission for Northern Ireland shall consult—

    (a)   such persons (if any) as the responsible department has specified in making its request to the Equality Commission for Northern Ireland; and

    (b)   such other persons (if any) as the Equality Commission for Northern Ireland considers appropriate.

(3) Before making any proposal the Equality Commission for Northern Ireland shall publish a draft, consider any representations made to it about the draft and, if it thinks it appropriate, modify its proposal in the light of any of those representations.

(4) Where the Equality Commission for Northern Ireland makes any proposal, the responsible department may—

(a)   approve it;
(b)   approve it subject to such modifications as that department thinks appropriate; or
(c)   refuse to approve it.

(5) Where the responsible department approves any proposal (with or without modifications) that department shall prepare a draft of the proposed code and lay it before the Assembly.

(6) If, within the statutory period, the Assembly resolves not to approve the draft, the responsible department shall take no further steps in relation to the proposed code.

(7) If no such resolution is made within the statutory period, the responsible department shall issue the code in the form of its draft.

(8) The code shall come into force on such date as the responsible department may appoint by order.

(9) Subsection (6) does not prevent a new draft of the proposed code from being laid before the Assembly.

(10) If the responsible department refuses to approve a proposal, that department shall give the Council a written statement of the department's reasons for not approving it.

(11) The responsible department may by order revoke a code.'.

Amendment – Amended by Northern Ireland Act 1998, s 99, Sch 13, para 16(1), (2)(a).

---

36   (1) In section 53 for 'Secretary of State' wherever it occurs substitute 'Office of the First Minister and Deputy First Minister'.

(2) In section 53(1) for 'he' substitute 'it'.

(3) In section 53(3) for 'a county court or a sheriff court' substitute 'or a county court'.

37   For section 54 substitute—

'54   Further provisions about codes issued under section 53

(1) In preparing a draft of any code under section 53, the Department shall consult such organisations representing the interests of employers or of disabled persons in, or seeking, employment as the Department considers appropriate.

(2) Where the Department proposes to issue a code, the Department shall publish a draft of the code, consider any representations that are made to the Department about the draft and, if the Department thinks it appropriate, modify its proposals in the light of any of those representations.

(3) If the Department decides to proceed with the code, the Department shall lay a draft of it before the Assembly.

(4) If, within the statutory period, the Assembly resolves not to approve the draft, the Department shall take no further steps in relation to the proposed code.

(5) If no such resolution is made within the statutory period, the Department shall issue the code in the form of its draft.

(6) The code shall come into force on such date as the Department may appoint by order.

(7) Subsection (4) does not prevent a new draft of the proposed code from being laid before the Assembly.

(8) The Department may by order revoke a code.

(9) In this section—
  "the Department" means the Office of the First Minister and Deputy First Minister; and
  "statutory period" has the meaning assigned to it by section 41(2) of the Interpretation Act (Northern Ireland) 1954.'.

38 In section 56(2) and (4) for 'Secretary of State' substitute 'Office of the First Minister and Deputy First Minister'.

39 In section 59(1) after 'Crown' where it twice occurs insert 'or a Northern Ireland department'.

40 (1) In section 60(1) to (3) for 'Secretary of State' wherever it occurs substitute 'Office of the First Minister and Deputy First Minister' and for 'he' and 'him' wherever they occur substitute 'it'.

(2) In section 60(4) for 'Treasury' substitute 'Department of Finance and Personnel in Northern Ireland'.

(3) For section 60(6) substitute—

  '(6) The Office of the First Minister and Deputy First Minister may by order repeal section 17 of, and Schedule 2 to, the Disabled Persons (Employment) Act (Northern Ireland) 1945 (district advisory committees).'.

(4) In section 60(7) omit 'paragraph (b) of', for '1944' substitute '1945' and omit 'in each case'.

(5) In section 60, omit subsection (8).

41 For section 61 substitute—

'61 Amendments of Disabled Persons (Employment) Act (Northern Ireland) 1945

(1) Section 15 of the Disabled Persons (Employment) Act (Northern Ireland) 1945 (which gives the Office of the First Minister and Deputy First Minister power to make arrangements for the provision of supported employment) is amended as set out in subsection (2) to (5).

(2) In subsection (1)—
  (a) for "persons registered as handicapped by disablement" substitute "disabled persons";
  (b) for "their disablement" substitute "their disability"; and
  (c) for "are not subject to disablement" substitute "do not have a disability".

(3) In subsection (2) for the words from "any of one or more companies" to "so required and prohibited" substitute "any company, association or body".

(4) After subsection (2) insert—

"(2A) The only kind of company which the Department itself may form in exercising its powers under this section is a company which is—

(a)   required by its constitution to apply its profits, if any, or other income in promoting its objects; and

(b)   prohibited by its constitution from paying any dividend to its members.".

(5) After subsection (5) insert—

"(5A) For the purposes of this section—

(a)   a person is a disabled person if he is a disabled person for the purposes of the Disability Discrimination Act 1995; and

(b)   'disability' has the same meaning as in that Act.".

(6) The provisions of section 16 of the Act of 1945 (preference to be given under section 15 of that Act to ex-service men and women) shall become subsection (1) of that section and at the end insert—

"and whose disability is due to that service.

(2) For the purposes of subsection (1) of this section, a disabled person's disability shall be treated as due to service of a particular kind only in such circumstances as may be prescribed."

(7) The following provisions of the Act of 1945 shall cease to have effect—

(a)   section 1 (definition of "disabled person");

(b)   sections 2 to 4 (training for disabled persons);

(c)   sections 6 to 8 (the register of disabled persons);

(d)   sections 9 to 11 (obligations on employers with substantial staffs to employ quota of registered persons);

(e)   section 12 (the designated employment scheme for persons registered as handicapped by disablement);

(f)   section 13 (interpretation of provisions repealed by this Act);

(g)   section 14 (records to be kept by employer);

(h)   section 19 (proceedings in relation to offences);

(j)   sections 21 and 22 (supplementary).

(8) Any statutory provision in which "disabled person" is defined by reference to the Act of 1945 shall be construed as if that expression had the same meaning as in this Act.'.

42   (*repealed*)

Amendment – Repealed by Industrial Tribunals (Northern Ireland) Order 1996, SI 1996/1921, art 28, Sch 3.

---

43   Omit section 63.

44   (1) In section 64(3) for 'England and Wales' substitute 'Northern Ireland'.

(2) Omit section 64(4).

(3) In section 64(5)(a) omit the words from ', the British' to the end.

(4) In section 64(8)—

(a)   omit the definitions of 'British Transport Police', 'Royal Parks Constabulary' and 'United Kingdom Atomic Energy Authority Constabulary';

(b) in the definition of 'the 1947 Act' at the end add 'as it applies both in relation to the Crown in right of Her Majesty's Government in Northern Ireland and in relation to the Crown in right of Her Majesty's Government in the United Kingdom';

(c) in the definition of 'fire brigade' for the words from 'means' to the end substitute 'has the same meaning as in the Fire Services (Northern Ireland) Order 1984';

(d) in the definition of 'prison officer' for the words from 'means' to the end substitute 'means any individual who holds any post, otherwise than as a medical officer, to which he has been appointed under section 2(2) of the Prison Act (Northern Ireland) 1953 or who is a prison custody officer within the meaning of Chapter III of Part VIII of the Criminal Justice and Public Order Act 1994';

(e) in the definition of 'service for purposes of a Minister of the Crown or government department' at the end add 'or service as the head of a Northern Ireland department'.

45 Omit section 65.

46 For section 67 substitute—

'67 Regulations and orders etc

(1) Any power under this Act to make regulations or orders shall be exercisable by statutory rule for the purposes of the Statutory Rules (Northern Ireland) Order 1979.

(2) Any such power may be exercised to make different provision for different cases, including different provision for different areas or localities.

(3) Any such power, includes power—
  (a) to make such incidental, supplementary, consequential or transitional provision as appears to the Northern Ireland department exercising the power to be expedient; and
  (b) to provide for a person to exercise a discretion in dealing with any matter.

(4) No order shall be made under section 50(3) unless a draft of the order has been laid before and approved by a resolution of the Assembly.

(5) Any other order made under this Act, other than an order under section 3(9), 52(8), 54(6) or 70(3), and any regulations made under this Act shall be subject to negative resolution within the meaning of section 41(6) of the Interpretation Act (Northern Ireland) 1954 as if they were statutory instruments within the meaning of that Act.

(6) Section 41(3) of the Interpretation Act (Northern Ireland) 1954 shall apply in relation to any instrument or document which by virtue of this Act is required to be laid before the Assembly as if it were a statutory instrument or statutory document within the meaning of that Act.

(7) Subsection (1) does not require an order under section 43 which applies only to a specified vehicle, or to vehicles of a specified person, to be made by statutory rule.

(8) Nothing in section 40(6) or 46(5) affects the powers conferred by subsections (2) and (3).'

47 (1) For section 68(1) substitute—

'(1) In this Act—

"accessibility certificate" means a certificate issued under section 41(1)(a);

"act" includes a deliberate omission;

"the Agency" means the Labour Relations Agency;

"approval certificate" means a certificate issued under section 42(4);

"the Assembly" means the Northern Ireland Assembly;

"benefits", in Part II, has the meaning given in section 4(4);

"the Department of Economic Development" means the Office of the First Minister and Deputy First Minister in Northern Ireland;

"the Department of the Environment" means the Department of the Environment for Northern Ireland;

"the Department of Health and Social Services" means the Office of the First Minister and Deputy First Minister for Northern Ireland;

"employment" means, subject to any prescribed provision, employment under a contract of service or of apprenticeship or a contract personally to do work and related expressions are to be construed accordingly;

"employment at an establishment in Northern Ireland" is to be construed in accordance with subsections (2) to (5);

"enactment" means any statutory provision within the meaning of section 1(f) of the Interpretation Act (Northern Ireland) 1954;

"government department" means a Northern Ireland department or a department of the Government of the United Kingdom;

"Minister of the Crown" includes the Treasury;

"Northern Ireland department" includes (except in sections 51 and 52) the head of a Northern Ireland department;

"occupational pension scheme" has the same meaning as in the Pension Schemes (Northern Ireland) Act 1993;

"premises", includes land of any description;

"prescribed" means prescribed by regulations;

"profession" includes any vocation or occupation;

"provider of services" has the meaning given in section 19(2)(b);

"public service vehicle" and "regulated public service vehicle" have the meaning given in section 40;

"PSV accessibility regulations" means regulations made under section 40(1);

"rail vehicle" and "regulated rail vehicle" have the meaning given in section 46;

"rail vehicle accessibility regulations" means regulations made under section 46(1);

"regulations" means—

(a) in Parts I and II of this Act, section 66, the definition of "employment" above and subsections (3) and (4) below, regulations made by the Department of Economic Development;

(b) in Part V of this Act, regulations made by the Department of the Environment;

(c) in any other provision of this Act, regulations made by the Department of Health and Social Services;

"section 6 duty" means any duty imposed by or under section 6;

"section 15 duty" means any duty imposed by or under section 15;

"section 21 duty" means any duty imposed by or under section 21;

"taxi" and "regulated taxi" have the meaning given in section 32;

"taxi accessibility regulations" means regulations made under section 32(1);

"trade" includes any business;

"trade organisation" has the meaning given in section 13;
"vehicle examiner" means an officer of the Department of the Environment authorised by that Department for the purposes of sections 41 and 42.'.

(2) In section 68—

(a)   for subsection (2) substitute—
'(2) Where an employee does his work wholly outside Northern Ireland, his employment is not to be treated as being work at an establishment in Northern Ireland.'; and

(b)   in subsections (3) and (4) for 'Great Britain' wherever it occurs substitute 'Northern Ireland'.

Amendment – Amended by Equal Opportunities (Employment Legislation) (Territorial Limits) Regulations (Northern Ireland) 2000, SR 2000/8, reg 3.

---

48   (1) In section 70(3) for 'Secretary of State' substitute 'Office of the First Minister and Deputy First Minister'.

(2) In section 70(8) for 'the Secretary of State' substitute 'a Northern Ireland department' and for 'him' substitute 'it'.

49   (1) In Schedule 1 in paragraph 7(1) for 'Act 1944' substitute 'Act (Northern Ireland) 1945'.

(2) In Schedule 1 in paragraph 7(7) for '1944' substitute '1945'.

50   (1) (*repealed*)

(2) In Schedule 3 for paragraph 4(1) substitute—

'(1) In any proceedings under section 8—
(a)   a certificate signed by or on behalf of a Minister of the Crown or a Northern Ireland department and certifying that any conditions or requirements specified in the certificate were imposed by that Minister or that department (as the case may be) and were in operation at a time or throughout a time so specified; or
(b)   a certificate signed by or on behalf of the Secretary of State and certifying that an act specified in the certificate was done for the purpose of safeguarding national security,
shall be conclusive evidence of the matters certified.'.

(3) In Schedule 3 in paragraph 6(1) omit 'or a sheriff court'.

(4) In Schedule 3 for paragraph 8(1) substitute—

'(1) In any proceedings under section 25—
(a)   a certificate signed by or on behalf of a Minister of the Crown or a Northern Ireland department and certifying that any conditions or requirements specified in the certificate were imposed by that Minister or that department (as the case may be) and were in operation at a time or throughout a time so specified; or
(b)   a certificate signed by or on behalf of the Secretary of State and certifying that an act specified in the certificate was done for the purpose of safeguarding national security,
shall be conclusive evidence of the matters certified.'.

Amendment – Sub-para (1) repealed by Industrial Tribunals (Northern Ireland) Order 1996, SI 1996/1921, art 28, Sch 3.

51 (1) In Schedule 4 in paragraphs 2(1) and (5) and 7(1) and (5) omit 'or sisted'.

(2) In Schedule 4 in paragraph 4 for 'Secretary of State' substitute 'Office of the First Minister and Deputy First Minister'.

(3) In Schedule 4 in paragraph 6(1) omit 'or, in Scotland, to the sheriff'.

(4) In Schedule 4 omit paragraph 6(2).

(5) In Schedule 4 in paragraph 9 for 'Secretary of State' substitute 'Office of the First Minister and Deputy First Minister'.

52 (1) Schedule 5, except paragraph 7(a) to (c), shall have no effect.

(2) In paragraph 7(a) to (c), for 'Secretary of State' wherever it occurs substitute 'Department of Health and Social Services'.

Amendment – Amended by Northern Ireland Act 1998, s 99, Sch 13, para 16(1), (2)(c).

53 For Schedules 6 and 7 substitute—

'SCHEDULE 6

CONSEQUENTIAL AMENDMENTS

The Industrial Relations (Northern Ireland) Order 1976 (NI 16)

1 In Article 68(6) of the Industrial Relations (Northern Ireland) Order 1976 (reinstatement or re-engagement of dismissed employees)—

(a)   in the definition of "relevant complaint of dismissal", omit "or" and at the end insert "or a complaint under section 8 of the Disability Discrimination Act 1995 arising out of a dismissal";

(b)   in the definition of "relevant conciliation powers" omit "or" and at the end insert "or paragraph 1 of Schedule 3 to the Disability Discrimination Act 1995";

(c)   in the definition of "relevant compromise contract" for "or Article" substitute "Article" and at the end insert "or section 9(2) of the Disability Discrimination Act 1995".

The Companies (Northern Ireland) Order 1986 (NI 6)

3 In paragraph 9 of Schedule 7 to the Companies (Northern Ireland) Order 1986 (disclosure in directors' report of company policy in relation to disabled persons) in the definition of "disabled person" in sub-paragraph (4)(b) for "Disabled Persons (Employment) Act (Northern Ireland) 1945" substitute "Disability Discrimination Act 1995".

SCHEDULE 7

REPEALS

Chapter	Short Title	Extent of repeal
1945 c. 6 (N.I.)	The Disabled Persons (Employment) Act (Northern Ireland) 1945.	Sections 1 to 4. Sections 6 to 14. In section 16 the words "vocational training and industrial rehabilitation courses and", the words "courses and" and the words from "and in selecting" to "engagement". Section 19. Section 21. Section 22.
1960 c. 4 (N.I.)	The Disabled Persons (Employment) Act (Northern Ireland) 1960.	The whole Act.
1976 NI16	The Industrial Relations (Northern Ireland) Order 1976.	In Article 68(6) the word "or" in the definitions of "relevant complaint of dismissal" and "relevant conciliation powers".'.

Appendix II

DISABILITY RIGHTS COMMISSION ACT 1999
(1999 c. 17)

ARRANGEMENT OF SECTIONS

Section		Page
1	The Disability Rights Commission	511
2	General functions	512
3	Formal investigations	512
4	Non-discrimination notices	513
5	Agreements in lieu of enforcement action	514
6	Persistent discrimination	515
7	Assistance in relation to proceedings	516
8	Recovery of expenses of providing assistance	517
9	Codes of practice	517
10	Conciliation of disputes under Part III of the 1995 Act	518
11	Procedure for amending s 7(1) of the 1995 Act	519
12	Regulations	519
13	Interpretation	520
14	Consequential amendments and repeals	520
15	Crown application	520
16	Short title, commencement and extent	520

SCHEDULES:
Schedule 1—Constitution etc		521
Schedule 2—Additional commissioners		524
Schedule 3—Formal investigations and non-discrimination notices		525
Part I—Conduct of formal investigations		525
Part II—Non-discrimination notices		528
Part III—Action plans		530
Part IV—Supplementary		533
Schedule 4—Minor and consequential amendments		535
Schedule 5—Repeals		536

An Act to establish a Disability Rights Commission and make provision as to its functions; and for connected purposes. [27th July 1999]

1 The Disability Rights Commission

(1) There shall be a body known as the Disability Rights Commission (referred to in this Act as 'the Commission').

(2) The Secretary of State shall pay to the Commission such sums as he thinks fit to enable it to meet its expenses.

(3) Schedule 1 (the Commission's constitution and related matters) has effect.

(4) (*repealed*)

Amendment – Sub-s (4): repealed by Statute Law (Repeals) Act 2004.

2   General functions

(1) The Commission shall have the following duties—

(a)   to work towards the elimination of discrimination against and harassment of disabled persons;

(b)   to promote the equalisation of opportunities for disabled persons;

(c)   to take such steps as it considers appropriate with a view to encouraging good practice in the treatment of disabled persons; and

(d)   to keep under review the working of the Disability Discrimination Act 1995 (referred to in this Act as 'the 1995 Act') and this Act.

(2) The Commission may, for any purpose connected with the performance of its functions—

(a)   make proposals or give other advice to any Minister of the Crown as to any aspect of the law or a proposed change to the law;

(b)   make proposals or give other advice to any Government agency or other public authority as to the practical application of any law;

(c)   undertake, or arrange for or support (whether financially or otherwise), the carrying out of research or the provision of advice or information.

Nothing in this subsection is to be regarded as limiting the Commission's powers.

(3) The Commission shall make proposals or give other advice under subsection (2)(a) on any matter specified in a request from a Minister of the Crown.

(4) The Commission may make charges for facilities or services made available by it for any purpose.

(5) In this section—

'disabled persons' includes persons who have had a disability;

'discrimination' means anything which is discrimination for the purposes of any provision of Part II, Part 3 or Chapter 1 or 2 of Part 4 of the 1995 Act; and

'harassment' means anything which is harassment for the purposes of any provision of Part 2 or 3 of the 1995 Act;

'the law' includes Community law and the international obligations of the United Kingdom.

Amendment – Amended by Special Educational Needs and Disability Act 2001, s 35, Sch 7, paras 1, 2 and by Disability Discrimination Act 1995 (Amendment) Regulations 2003, SI 2003/1673, regs 3(2), 30(a)(i), (ii).

3   Formal investigations

(1) The Commission may decide to conduct a formal investigation for any purpose connected with the performance of its duties under section 2(1).

(2) The Commission shall conduct a formal investigation if directed to do so by the Secretary of State for any such purpose.

(3) The Commission may at any time decide to stop or to suspend the conduct of a formal investigation; but any such decision requires the approval of the Secretary of

State if the investigation is being conducted in pursuance of a direction under subsection (2).

(4) The Commission may, as respects any formal investigation which it has decided or been directed to conduct—

 (a) nominate one or more commissioners, with or without one or more additional commissioners appointed for the purposes of the investigation, to conduct the investigation on its behalf; and

 (b) authorise those persons to exercise such of its functions in relation to the investigation (which may include drawing up or revising terms of reference) as it may determine.

(5) Schedule 2 (appointment and tenure of office of additional commissioners) and Schedule 3 (so far as relating to the conduct of formal investigations) have effect.

4 Non-discrimination notices

(1) If in the course of a formal investigation the Commission is satisfied that a person has committed or is committing an unlawful act, it may serve on him a notice (referred to in this Act as a non-discrimination notice) which—

 (a) gives details of the unlawful act which the Commission has found that he has committed or is committing; and

 (b) requires him not to commit any further unlawful acts of the same kind (and, if the finding is that he is committing an unlawful act, to cease doing so).

(2) The notice may include recommendations to the person concerned as to action which the Commission considers he could reasonably be expected to take with a view to complying with the requirement mentioned in subsection (1)(b).

(3) The notice may require the person concerned—

 (a) to propose an adequate action plan (subject to and in accordance with Part III of Schedule 3) with a view to securing compliance with the requirement mentioned in subsection (1)(b); and

 (b) once an action plan proposed by him has become final, to take any action which—

  (i) is specified in the plan; and

  (ii) he has not already taken,

 at the time or times specified in the plan.

(4) For the purposes of subsection (3)—

 (a) an action plan is a document drawn up by the person concerned specifying action (including action he has already taken) intended to change anything in his practices, policies, procedures or other arrangements which—

  (i) caused or contributed to the commission of the unlawful act concerned; or

  (ii) is liable to cause or contribute to a failure to comply with the requirement mentioned in subsection (1)(b); and

 (b) an action plan is adequate if the action specified in it would be sufficient to ensure, within a reasonable time, that he is not prevented from complying with that requirement by anything in his practices, policies, procedures or other arrangements;

and the action specified in an action plan may include ceasing an activity or taking continuing action over a period.

(5) In this section 'unlawful act' means an act which is unlawful for the purposes of any provision of Part II, Part 3 or Chapter 1 or 2 of Part 4 of the 1995 Act or any other unlawful act of a description prescribed for the purposes of this section.

(6) Schedule 3 (so far as relating to non-discrimination notices and action plans) has effect.

Amendment – Amended by Special Educational Needs and Disability Act 2001, s 35, Sch 7, paras 1, 3 and by Disability Discrimination Act 1995 (Amendment) Regulations 2003, SI 2003/1673, regs 3(2), 30(b).

---

5   Agreements in lieu of enforcement action

(1) If the Commission has reason to believe that a person has committed or is committing an unlawful act, it may (subject to section 3(3)) enter into an agreement in writing under this section with that person on the assumption that that belief is well founded (whether or not that person admits that he committed or is committing the act in question).

(2) An agreement under this section is one by which—

   (a)   the Commission undertakes not to take any relevant enforcement action in relation to the unlawful act in question; and
   (b)   the person concerned undertakes—
         (i)   not to commit any further unlawful acts of the same kind (and, where appropriate, to cease committing the unlawful act in question); and
         (ii) to take such action (which may include ceasing an activity or taking continuing action over any period) as may be specified in the agreement.

(3) Those undertakings are binding on the parties to the agreement; but undertakings under subsection (2)(b) are enforceable by the Commission only as provided by subsection (8).

(4) For the purposes of subsection (2)(a), 'relevant enforcement action' means—

   (a)   beginning a formal investigation into the commission by the person concerned of the unlawful act in question;
   (b)   if such an investigation has begun (whether or not the investigation is confined to that matter), taking any further steps in the investigation of that matter; and
   (c)   taking any steps, or further steps, with a view to the issue of a non-discrimination notice based on the commission of the unlawful act in question.

(5) The action specified in an undertaking under subsection (2)(b)(ii) must be action intended to change anything in the practices, policies, procedures or other arrangements of the person concerned which—

   (a)   caused or contributed to the commission of the unlawful act in question; or
   (b)   is liable to cause or contribute to a failure to comply with his undertaking under subsection (2)(b)(i).

(6) An agreement under this section—

   (a)   may include terms providing for incidental or supplementary matters (including the termination of the agreement, or the right of either party to terminate it, in certain circumstances); and

(b)   may be varied or revoked by agreement of the parties.

(7) An agreement under this section may not include any provisions other than terms mentioned in subsections (2) and (6)(a) unless their inclusion is authorised by regulations made by the Secretary of State for the purposes of this section; but any provisions so authorised are not enforceable by the Commission under subsection (8).

(8) The Commission may apply to a county court or by summary application to the sheriff for an order under this subsection if—

(a)   the other party to an agreement under this section has failed to comply with any undertaking under subsection (2)(b); or

(b)   the Commission has reasonable cause to believe that he intends not to comply with any such undertaking.

(9) An order under subsection (8) is an order requiring the other party to comply with the undertaking or with such directions for the same purpose as are contained in the order.

(10) Nothing in this section affects the Commission's powers to settle or compromise legal proceedings of any description.

(11) In this section 'unlawful act' means an act which is unlawful for the purposes of any provision of Part II, Part 3 or Chapter 1 or 2 of Part 4 of the 1995 Act or any other unlawful act of a description prescribed for the purposes of this section.

(12) Schedule 3 (so far as relating to agreements under this section) has effect.

Amendment – Amended by Special Educational Needs and Disability Act 2001, s 35, Sch 7, paras 1, 4 and by Disability Discrimination Act 1995 (Amendment) Regulations 2003, SI 2003/1673, regs 3(2), 30(c).

---

6   Persistent discrimination

(1) This section applies during the period of five years beginning on the date on which—

(a)   a non-discrimination notice served on a person,

(b)   a finding in proceedings under section 17A, 25, 28I, 28K, 28L, 28N or 28V of the 1995 Act that a person has committed an act which is unlawful discrimination for the purposes of any provision of Part 2, Part 3 or Chapter 1 or 2 of Part 4 of that Act, or

(c)   a finding by a court or tribunal in any other proceedings that a person has committed an unlawful act of a description prescribed under subsection (4),

has become final.

(2) If during that period it appears to the Commission that unless restrained the person concerned is likely to do one or more unlawful acts, the Commission may apply to a county court for an injunction, or to the sheriff for interdict, restraining him from doing so.

(3) The court, if satisfied that the application is well-founded, may grant the injunction or interdict in the terms applied for or in more limited terms.

(4) In this section 'unlawful act' means an act which is unlawful discrimination or harassment for the purposes of any provision of Part II, Part 3 or Chapter 1 or 2 of Part 4

of the 1995 Act or any other unlawful act of a description prescribed for the purposes of this section.

(5) A finding becomes final for the purposes of this section when an appeal against it is dismissed, withdrawn or abandoned or when the time for appealing expires without an appeal having been brought.

Amendment – Amended by Special Educational Needs and Disability Act 2001, ss 35, 42(6), Sch 7, paras 1, 5–7, Sch 9 and by Disability Discrimination Act 1995 (Amendment) Regulations 2003, SI 2003/1673, regs 3(2), 30(d)(i), (ii).

---

7   Assistance in relation to proceedings

(1) This section applies to—

    (a)   proceedings which an individual has brought or proposes to bring under section 17A, 25, 28I, 28K, 28L, 28N or 28V of the 1995 Act (complaints and claims about unlawful discrimination or harassment under Parts II to 4); and

    (b)   proceedings of a description prescribed for the purposes of this subsection, being proceedings in which an individual who has or has had a disability relies or proposes to rely on a matter relating to that disability.

(2) Where the individual concerned applies to the Commission for assistance in relation to any proceedings to which this section applies, the Commission may grant the application on any of the following grounds—

    (a)   that the case raises a question of principle;

    (b)   that it is unreasonable to expect the applicant to deal with the case unaided (because of its complexity, because of the applicant's position in relation to another party or for some other reason);

    (c)   that there is some other special consideration which makes it appropriate for the Commission to provide assistance.

(3) If the Commission grants an application, it may—

    (a)   provide or arrange for the provision of legal advice;

    (b)   arrange for legal or other representation (which may include any assistance usually given by a solicitor or counsel);

    (c)   seek to procure the settlement of any dispute;

    (d)   provide or arrange for the provision of any other assistance which it thinks appropriate.

(4) Subsection (3)(b) does not affect the law and practice as to who may represent a person in relation to any proceedings.

(5) The Commission may authorise any employee of the Commission to exercise such of its functions under this section as it may determine.

Amendment – Amended by Special Educational Needs and Disability Act 2001, s 35, Sch 7, paras 1, 8 and by Disability Discrimination Act 1995 (Amendment) Regulations 2003, SI 2003/1673, regs 3(2), 30(e)(i), (ii).

---

8 Recovery of expenses of providing assistance

(1) This section applies where—

(a) the Commission has given an individual assistance under section 7 in relation to any proceedings; and

(b) any costs or expenses (however described) have become payable to him by another person in respect of the matter in connection with which the assistance is given.

(2) A sum equal to any expenses incurred by the Commission in providing the assistance shall be a first charge for the benefit of the Commission on the costs or expenses concerned.

(3) It is immaterial for the purposes of this section whether the costs or expenses concerned are payable by virtue of a decision of a court or tribunal, an agreement arrived at to avoid proceedings or to bring them to an end, or otherwise.

(4) The charge created by this section is subject to—

(a) any charge imposed by section 10(7) of the Access to Justice Act 1999 and any provision in, or made under, Part I of that Act for the payment of any sum to the Legal Services Commission; and

(b) any charge or obligation for payment in priority to other debts under the Legal Aid (Scotland) Act 1986 and any provision in that Act for payment of any sum into the Scottish Legal Aid Fund.

(5) Provision may be made by regulations made by the Secretary of State for the determination of the expenses of the Commission in cases where this section applies.

Amendment – Amended by Access to Justice Act 1999, s 24, Sch 4, para 56.

9 Codes of practice

(1) The following section shall be inserted at the beginning of Part VII of the 1995 Act (supplemental)—

'53A Codes of practice

(1) The Disability Rights Commission may prepare and issue codes of practice giving practical guidance—

(a) to employers, service providers or other persons to whom provisions of Part II or Part III apply on how to avoid discrimination or on any other matter relating to the operation of those provisions in relation to them; or

(b) to any persons on any other matter, with a view to—

(i) promoting the equalisation of opportunities for disabled persons and persons who have had a disability, or

(ii) encouraging good practice regarding the treatment of such persons,

in any field of activity regulated by any provision of Part II or Part III.

(2) The Commission shall, when requested to do so by the Secretary of State, prepare a code of practice dealing with the matters specified in the request.

(3) In preparing a code of practice the Commission shall carry out such consultations as it considers appropriate (which shall include the publication for public consultation of proposals relating to the code).

(4) The Commission may not issue a code of practice unless—

    (a)   a draft of it has been submitted to and approved by the Secretary of State and laid by him before both Houses of Parliament; and

    (b)   the 40 day period has elapsed without either House resolving not to approve the draft.

(5) If the Secretary of State does not approve a draft code of practice submitted to him he shall give the Commission a written statement of his reasons.

(6) A code of practice issued by the Commission—

    (a)   shall come into effect on such day as the Secretary of State may by order appoint;

    (b)   may be revised in whole or part, and re-issued, by the Commission; and

    (c)   may be revoked by an order made by the Secretary of State at the request of the Commission.

(7) Where the Commission proposes to revise a code of practice—

    (a)   it shall comply with subsection (3) in relation to the revisions; and

    (b)   the other provisions of this section apply to the revised code of practice as they apply to a new code of practice.

(8) Failure to observe any provision of a code of practice does not of itself make a person liable to any proceedings, but any provision of a code which appears to a court or tribunal to be relevant to any question arising in any proceedings under Part II or Part III shall be taken into account in determining that question.

(9) In this section—

"code of practice" means a code of practice under this section;
"discrimination" means anything which is unlawful discrimination for the purposes of any provision of Part II or Part III; and
"40 day period" has the same meaning in relation to a draft code of practice as it has in section 3 in relation to draft guidance.'

(2) The Commission may treat any consultation undertaken by the National Disability Council under section 52(2) of the 1995 Act as being as effective for the purposes of section 53A(3) of that Act as if it had been undertaken by the Commission.

(3) Nothing in this section affects the Commission's powers apart from this section to give practical guidance on matters connected with its functions.

10   Conciliation of disputes under Part III of the 1995 Act

For section 28 of the 1995 Act (arrangements by the Secretary of State with a view to the settlement of disputes under Part III) there shall be substituted the following section—

'28   Conciliation of disputes

(1) The Commission may make arrangements with any other person for the provision of conciliation services by, or by persons appointed by, that person in relation to disputes arising under this Part.

(2) In deciding what arrangements (if any) to make, the Commission shall have regard to the desirability of securing, so far as reasonably practicable, that conciliation services are available for all disputes arising under this Part which the parties may wish to refer to conciliation.

(3) No member or employee of the Commission may provide conciliation services in relation to disputes arising under this Part.

(4) The Commission shall ensure that any arrangements under this section include appropriate safeguards to prevent the disclosure to members or employees of the Commission of information obtained by a person in connection with the provision of conciliation services in pursuance of the arrangements.

(5) Subsection (4) does not apply to information relating to a dispute which is disclosed with the consent of the parties to that dispute.

(6) Subsection (4) does not apply to information which—
  (a)   is not identifiable with a particular dispute or a particular person; and
  (b)   is reasonably required by the Commission for the purpose of monitoring the operation of the arrangements concerned.

(7) Anything communicated to a person while providing conciliation services in pursuance of any arrangements under this section is not admissible in evidence in any proceedings except with the consent of the person who communicated it to that person.

(8) In this section "conciliation services" means advice and assistance provided by a conciliator to the parties to a dispute with a view to promoting its settlement otherwise than through the courts.'

11   Procedure for amending s 7(1) of the 1995 Act

For subsections (3) to (10) of section 7 of the 1995 Act (exemption for small businesses) there shall be substituted the following subsections—

'(3) Before making an order under subsection (2) the Secretary of State shall consult—

  (a)   the Disability Rights Commission;
  (b)   such organisations representing the interests of employers as he considers appropriate; and
  (c)   such organisations representing the interests of disabled persons in employment or seeking employment as he considers appropriate.

(4) The Secretary of State shall, before laying an order under this section before Parliament, publish a summary of the views expressed to him in his consultations.'

12   Regulations

(1) Any power under this Act to make regulations is exercisable by statutory instrument.

(2) Any such regulations may make—

  (a)   different provision for different cases or areas;
  (b)   provision enabling a person to exercise a discretion in dealing with any matter; and

(c)   incidental, supplemental, consequential or transitional provision.

(3) A statutory instrument containing any such regulations shall be subject to annulment in pursuance of a resolution of either House of Parliament.

13   Interpretation

(1) In this Act—

'Commission' means the Disability Rights Commission;
'final', in relation to a non-discrimination notice, has the meaning given by paragraph 11 of Schedule 3;
'formal investigation' means an investigation under section 3;
'non-discrimination notice' means a notice under section 4;
'notice' means notice in writing;
'prescribed' means prescribed in regulations made by the Secretary of State; and
'the 1995 Act' means the Disability Discrimination Act 1995.

(2) Expressions used in this Act which are defined for the purposes of the 1995 Act have the same meaning in this Act as in that Act.

14   Consequential amendments and repeals

(1) Schedule 4 (minor and consequential amendments) has effect.

(2) The enactments mentioned in Schedule 5 are repealed to the extent specified.

15   Crown application

This Act binds the Crown (but does not affect Her Majesty in her private capacity or in right of Her Duchy of Lancaster or the Duke of Cornwall).

16   Short title, commencement and extent

(1) This Act may be cited as the Disability Rights Commission Act 1999.

(2) This Act (apart from this section) shall come into force on such day as the Secretary of State may by order made by statutory instrument appoint; and different days may be appointed for different purposes.

(3) An order under subsection (2) may contain transitional provisions and savings relating to the provisions brought into force by the order.

(4) The following provisions extend to Northern Ireland—

(a)   section 14(1), in relation to paragraphs 1, 2 and 4 of Schedule 4; and
(b)   section 14(2), in relation to the repeal of words in the House of Commons Disqualification Act 1975, the Northern Ireland Assembly Disqualification Act 1975 and section 70(7) of the 1995 Act.

(5) Except as mentioned in subsection (4), this Act does not extend to Northern Ireland.

SCHEDULES

SCHEDULE 1

CONSTITUTION ETC

Section 1(3)

Status

1 (1) The Commission is a body corporate.

(2) The Commission is not the servant or agent of the Crown, it does not enjoy any status, immunity or privilege of the Crown and its property is not to be regarded as property of or as held on behalf of the Crown.

Membership

2 (1) The Commission shall consist of not less than 10 and not more than 15 commissioners appointed by the Secretary of State.

(1A) One of the commissioners shall be a person who appears to the Secretary of State to have special knowledge of Scotland.

(2) The Secretary of State may appoint as a commissioner a person who is not disabled and has not had a disability only if satisfied that after the appointment more than half of the commissioners will be disabled persons or persons who have had a disability.

(3) Sub-paragraph (2) shall not apply in respect of the first three appointments under this paragraph.

Amendment – Sub-para (1A) inserted by Scotland Act 1998 (Modification of Functions) Order 2000, SI 2000/1458, art 2.

Tenure of office of commissioners

3 (1) A commissioner shall hold and vacate office in accordance with the terms of his appointment.

(2) A person shall not be appointed a commissioner for less than two or more than five years; but a person who has served as a commissioner may be reappointed.

4 A commissioner may resign by notice in writing to the Secretary of State.

5 The Secretary of State may terminate the appointment of a commissioner if satisfied that—

(a) without the consent of the chairman he has failed to attend meetings of the Commission during a continuous period of six months beginning not earlier than nine months before the termination;

(b)   he has become bankrupt, has had his estate sequestrated or has made a composition or arrangement with, or granted a trust deed for, his creditors; or

(c)   he is otherwise unable or unfit to carry out his functions as a commissioner.

Tenure of office of chairman and deputy chairmen

6 (1) The Secretary of State shall appoint one commissioner as chairman of the Commission and either one or two other commissioners as deputy chairmen.

(2) The Secretary of State shall exercise his powers of appointment under this paragraph with a view to securing that at least one of the persons holding office as chairman or deputy chairman is a disabled person or a person who has had a disability.

7 A person appointed as chairman or deputy chairman—

(a)   shall hold and vacate that office in accordance with the terms of his appointment,

(b)   may resign that office by notice in writing to the Secretary of State, and

(c)   shall cease to hold that office if he ceases to be a commissioner.

Remuneration, pensions etc of commissioners

8 The Commission may—

(a)   pay to any commissioner such remuneration or expenses; and

(b)   pay, or make provision for the payment of, such sums by way of pensions, allowances or gratuities to or in respect of any commissioner,

as the Secretary of State may determine.

9 If the Secretary of State determines that there are special circumstances which make it right that a person who has ceased to be a commissioner should receive compensation, the Secretary of State may direct the Commission to pay that person such sum by way of compensation as the Secretary of State may determine.

Staff

10 (1) The Commission shall have—

(a)   a chief executive appointed by the Commission, subject to the approval of the Secretary of State; and

(b)   such other employees as the Commission may appoint, subject to the approval of the Secretary of State as to numbers and terms and conditions of service.

(2) The first appointment of a chief executive shall be made by the Secretary of State.

11 (1) Employment with the Commission shall be included among the kinds of employment to which a scheme under section 1 of the Superannuation Act 1972 may apply, and accordingly in Schedule 1 to that Act (in which those kinds of employment are listed) at the end of the list of Royal Commissions and other Commissions there shall be inserted—

'Disability Rights Commission.'

(2) The Commission shall pay to the Minister for the Civil Service, at such times as he may direct, such sums as he may determine in respect of the increase attributable to sub-paragraph (1) in the sums payable out of money provided by Parliament under that Act.

Proceedings etc

12 (1) The Commission may regulate its own procedure (including quorum).

(2) The quorum for meetings of the Commission shall in the first instance be determined by a meeting of the Commission attended by at least five commissioners.

13 The validity of any proceedings of the Commission is not affected by a vacancy among the commissioners or by a defect in the appointment of a commissioner.

Delegation

14 (1) The Commission may authorise any committee of the Commission or any commissioner to exercise such of its functions (other than functions relating to the conduct of a formal investigation) as it may determine.

(2) This paragraph does not affect any power of the Commission to authorise its employees to do anything on its behalf.

Accounts

15 (1) The Commission shall—

(a)   keep proper accounts and proper records in relation to the accounts,

(b)   prepare a statement of accounts in respect of each accounting year, and

(c)   send copies of the statement to the Secretary of State and the Comptroller and Auditor General not later than the 31st August following the end of the accounting year to which it relates.

(2) The Comptroller and Auditor General shall examine, certify and report on the statement of accounts and shall lay copies of the statement and of his report before each House of Parliament.

(3) The Commission's accounting year is the twelve months ending with 31st March.

(4) The Commission's first accounting year shall be the period of not more than 12 months beginning with the Commission's establishment and ending with 31st March.

Annual reports

16 (1) As soon as practicable after the end of each accounting year the Commission shall submit to the Secretary of State a report on its activities during that year.

(2) The report shall include (among other things)—

(a)   a report on anything done by the Commission, in the performance of its functions under section 2(1)(a) to (c), jointly or otherwise in co-operation with any other organisation;

(b) a general survey of developments in matters within the scope of the Commission's functions; and

(c) proposals for the Commission's activities in the current year.

(3) The Secretary of State shall lay a copy of the report before Parliament and arrange for such further publication of it as he considers appropriate.

List of consultees

17 (1) The Commission shall maintain a list of the organisations it has consulted generally for the purposes of any of its functions.

(2) An organisation may be removed from the list if it has not been consulted generally in the 12 months preceding its removal.

(3) For the purposes of sub-paragraphs (1) and (2), consultation is general unless it relates only—

(a) to an investigation to which paragraph 3 of Schedule 3 applies,

(b) to assistance under section 7, or

(c) otherwise to a particular individual or individuals.

(4) The Commission shall make the list available to the public in whatever way it considers appropriate (subject to any charge it may impose).

SCHEDULE 2

ADDITIONAL COMMISSIONERS

Section 3(5)

1 (1) The Commission may, with the approval of the Secretary of State, appoint one or more individuals as additional commissioners for the purposes of a formal investigation.

(2) An additional commissioner is not the servant or agent of the Crown.

2 (1) An additional commissioner shall hold and vacate office in accordance with the terms of his appointment (and may be re-appointed).

(2) The Commission may not alter the terms of appointment of an additional commissioner except with his consent and the approval of the Secretary of State.

3 The Commission may—

(a) pay such remuneration or expenses to any additional commissioner as the Secretary of State may determine, and

(b) pay, or make provision for the payment of, such sums by way of pensions, allowances or gratuities to or in respect of any additional commissioner as the Secretary of State may determine.

4 (1) An additional commissioner may resign by notice in writing to the Commission.

(2) The Commission may, with the approval of the Secretary of State, terminate the appointment of an additional commissioner if satisfied that—

(a) without reasonable excuse he has failed to carry out his duties during a continuous period of three months beginning not earlier than six months before the termination;

(b) he has become bankrupt, has had his estate sequestrated or has made a composition or arrangement with, or granted a trust deed for, his creditors; or

(c) he is otherwise unable or unfit to carry out his duties.

(3) The appointment of an additional commissioner shall otherwise terminate at the conclusion of the investigation for which he was appointed.

5   If the Secretary of State determines that there are special circumstances which make it right that a person who has ceased to be an additional commissioner should receive compensation, the Secretary of State may direct the Commission to pay that person such sum by way of compensation as the Secretary of State may determine.

SCHEDULE 3

FORMAL INVESTIGATIONS AND NON-DISCRIMINATION NOTICES

Sections 3(5), 4(6) and 5(12)

PART I

CONDUCT OF FORMAL INVESTIGATIONS

Introductory

1   (1) This Part of this Schedule applies to a formal investigation which the Commission has decided or has been directed to conduct.

(2) Any subsequent action required or authorised by this Part of this Schedule (or by Part IV of this Schedule) to be taken by the Commission in relation to the conduct of a formal investigation may be taken, so far as they are authorised to do so, by persons nominated under section 3(4) for the purposes of the investigation.

Terms of reference and preliminary notices

2   (1) The Commission shall not take any steps in the conduct of a formal investigation until—

(a) terms of reference for the investigation have been drawn up; and

(b) notice of the holding of the investigation and the terms of reference has been served or published as required by sub-paragraph (3) or (4).

(2) The terms of reference for the investigation shall be drawn up (and may be revised)—

(a) if the investigation is held at the direction of the Secretary of State, by the Secretary of State after consulting the Commission; and

(b) in any other case, by the Commission.

(3) Where the terms of reference confine the investigation to activities of one or more named persons, notice of the holding of the investigation and the terms of reference shall be served on each of those persons.

(4) Where the terms of reference do not confine the investigation to activities of one or more named persons, notice of the holding of the investigation and the terms of reference shall be published in such manner as appears to the Commission appropriate to bring it to the attention of persons likely to be affected by it.

(5) If the terms of reference are revised, this paragraph applies again in relation to the revised investigation and its terms of reference.

Investigation of unlawful acts etc

3 (1) This paragraph applies where the Commission proposes to investigate in the course of a formal investigation (whether or not the investigation has already begun) whether—

(a)   a person has committed or is committing any unlawful act;
(b)   any requirement imposed by a non-discrimination notice served on a person (including a requirement to take action specified in an action plan) has been or is being complied with;
(c)   any undertaking given by a person in an agreement made with the Commission under section 5 is being or has been complied with.

(2) The Commission may not investigate any such matter unless the terms of reference of the investigation confine it to the activities of one or more named persons (and the person concerned is one of those persons).

(3) The Commission may not investigate whether a person has committed or is committing any unlawful act unless—

(a)   it has reason to believe that the person concerned may have committed or may be committing the act in question, or
(b)   that matter is to be investigated in the course of a formal investigation into his compliance with any requirement or undertaking mentioned in sub-paragraph (1)(b) or (c).

(4) The Commission shall serve a notice on the person concerned offering him the opportunity to make written and oral representations about the matters being investigated.

(5) If the Commission is investigating whether the person concerned has committed or is committing any unlawful act (otherwise than in the course of a formal investigation into his compliance with any requirement or undertaking mentioned in sub-paragraph (1)(b) or (c)) the Commission shall include in the notice required by sub-paragraph (4) a statement informing that person that the Commission has reason to believe that he may have committed or may be committing any unlawful act.

(6) The Commission shall not make any findings in relation to any matter mentioned in sub-paragraph (1) without giving the person concerned or his representative a reasonable opportunity to make written and oral representations.

(7) The Commission may refuse to receive oral representations made on behalf of the person concerned by a person (not being counsel or a solicitor) to whom the Commission reasonably objects as being unsuitable.

(8) If the Commission refuses to receive oral representations from a person under sub-paragraph (7), it shall give reasons in writing for its objection.

(9) A notice required by sub-paragraph (4) may be included in a notice required by paragraph 2(3).

(10) In this paragraph 'unlawful act' means an act which is unlawful for the purposes of any provision of Part II, Part 3 or Chapter 1 or 2 of Part 4 of the 1995 Act or any other unlawful act of a description prescribed for the purposes of this paragraph.

Amendment – Sub-para (10) amended by Special Educational Needs and Disability Act 2001, s 35, Sch 7, paras 1, 9 and Disability Discrimination Act 1995 (Amendment) Regulations 2003, SI 2003/1673, regs 3(2), 30(f).

Power to obtain information

4 (1) For the purposes of a formal investigation the Commission may serve a notice on any person requiring him—

   (a) to give such written information as may be described in the notice; or
   (b) to attend and give oral information about any matter specified in the notice, and to produce all documents in his possession or control relating to any such matter.

(2) A notice under this paragraph may only be served on the written authority of the Secretary of State unless the terms of reference confine the investigation to the activities of one or more named persons and the person being served is one of those persons.

(3) A person may not be required by a notice under this paragraph—

   (a) to give information, or produce a document, which he could not be compelled to give in evidence, or produce, in civil proceedings before the High Court or the Court of Session; or
   (b) to attend at any place unless the necessary expenses of his journey to and from that place are paid or tendered to him.

5 (1) The Commission may apply to a county court or by summary application to the sheriff for an order under this paragraph if—

   (a) a person has been served with a notice under paragraph 4; and
   (b) he fails to comply with it or the Commission has reasonable cause to believe that he intends not to comply with it.

(2) An order under this paragraph is an order requiring the person concerned to comply with the notice or with such directions for the same purpose as may be contained in the order.

Recommendations

6 (1) The Commission may make recommendations in the light of its findings in a formal investigation.

(2) The recommendations may be—

(a) recommendations to any person for changes in his policies or procedures, or as to any other matter, with a view to promoting the equalisation of opportunities for disabled persons or persons who have had a disability, or

(b) recommendations to the Secretary of State, for changes in the law or otherwise.

(3) The Commission may make such recommendations before the conclusion of the investigation concerned.

Reports

7 (1) The Commission shall prepare a report of its findings in any formal investigation.

(2) The Commission shall exclude from such a report any matter which relates to an individual's private affairs or any person's business interests if—

(a) publication of that matter might, in the Commission's opinion, prejudicially affect that individual or person, and

(b) its exclusion is consistent with the Commission's duties and the object of the report.

(3) The report of an investigation carried out at the direction of the Secretary of State shall be published by the Secretary of State or, if the Secretary of State so directs, by the Commission.

(4) The report of any other investigation shall be published by the Commission.

(5) Nothing in this paragraph affects the Commission's power to issue a non-discrimination notice before a report is prepared or published.

PART II

NON-DISCRIMINATION NOTICES

Procedure for issuing and appealing against non-discrimination notices

8 (1) The Commission shall not issue a non-discrimination notice addressed to any person unless it has complied with the requirements of this paragraph.

(2) The Commission shall serve on the person concerned a notice—

(a) informing him that the Commission is considering issuing a non-discrimination notice and of the grounds for doing so,

(b) offering him the opportunity to make written and oral representations.

(3) The Commission shall give the person concerned or his representative the opportunity of making oral and written representations within a period specified in the notice of not less than 28 days.

(4) The Commission may refuse to receive oral representations made on behalf of the person concerned by a person (not being counsel or a solicitor) to whom the Commission reasonably objects as being unsuitable.

(5) If the Commission refuses to receive oral representations from a person under sub-paragraph (4), it shall give reasons in writing for its objection.

9 On issuing a non-discrimination notice, the Commission shall serve a copy on the person to whom it is addressed.

Appeal against non-discrimination notice

10 (1) A person on whom a non-discrimination notice is served may, within the period of six weeks beginning on the day after the day on which the notice is served on him, appeal against any requirement imposed by the notice under section 4(1)(b) or (3).

(2) An appeal under this paragraph lies—

   (a)   to an employment tribunal, so far as the requirement relates to acts within the tribunal's jurisdiction; and
   (b)   to a county court or a sheriff court, so far as the requirement relates to acts which are not within the jurisdiction of an employment tribunal.

(3) The court or tribunal may quash or, in Scotland, recall any requirement appealed against—

   (a)   if it considers the requirement to be unreasonable; or
   (b)   in the case of a requirement imposed under section 4(1)(b), if it considers that the Commission's finding that the person concerned had committed or is committing the unlawful act in question was based on an incorrect finding of fact.

(4) On quashing or recalling a requirement, the court or tribunal may direct that the non-discrimination notice shall have effect with such modifications as it considers appropriate.

(5) The modifications which may be included in such a direction include—

   (a)   the substitution of a requirement in different terms; and
   (b)   in the case of a requirement imposed under section 4(1)(b), modifications to the details given under section 4(1)(a) so far as necessary to describe any unlawful act on which the requirement could properly have been based.

(6) Sub-paragraph (1) does not apply to any modifications contained in a direction under sub-paragraph (4).

(7) If the court or tribunal allows an appeal under this paragraph without quashing or recalling the whole of the non-discrimination notice, the Commission may by notice to the person concerned vary the non-discrimination notice—

   (a)   by revoking or altering any recommendation included in pursuance of the Commission's power under section 4(2); or
   (b)   by making new recommendations in pursuance of that power.

11 For the purposes of this Act a non-discrimination notice becomes final when—

   (a)   an appeal under paragraph 10 is dismissed, withdrawn or abandoned or the time for appealing expires without an appeal having been brought; or
   (b)   an appeal under that paragraph is allowed without the whole notice being quashed or, in Scotland, recalled.

Enforcement of non-discrimination notice

12 (1) This paragraph applies during the period of five years beginning on the date on which a non-discrimination notice served on a person has become final.

(2) During that period the Commission may apply to a county court or by summary application to the sheriff for an order under this paragraph, if—

(a)   it appears to the Commission that the person concerned has failed to comply with any requirement imposed by the notice under section 4(1)(b); or

(b)   the Commission has reasonable cause to believe that he intends not to comply with any such requirement.

(3) An order under this paragraph is an order requiring the person concerned to comply with the requirement or with such directions for the same purpose as are contained in the order.

Register of non-discrimination notices

13 (1) The Commission shall maintain a register of non-discrimination notices which have become final.

(2) The Commission shall, in the case of notices which impose a requirement to propose an action plan, note on the register the date on which any action plan proposed by the person concerned has become final.

(3) The Commission shall arrange for—

(a)   the register to be available for inspection at all reasonable times, and

(b)   certified copies of any entry to be provided if required by any person.

(4) The Commission shall publish those arrangements in such manner as it considers appropriate to bring them to the attention of persons likely to be interested.

PART III

ACTION PLANS

Introductory

14 (1) This Part of this Schedule applies where a person ('P') has been served with a non-discrimination notice which has become final and includes a requirement for him to propose an action plan.

(2) In this Part 'adequate' in relation to a proposed action plan means adequate (as defined in section 4(4)(b)) for the purposes of the requirement mentioned in section 4(1)(b).

The first proposed action plan

15 (1) P must serve his proposed action plan on the Commission within such period as may be specified in the non-discrimination notice.

(2) If P fails to do so, the Commission may apply to a county court or by way of summary application to the sheriff for an order directing him to serve his proposed action plan within such period as the order may specify.

(3) If P serves a proposed action plan on the Commission in response to the non-discrimination notice, or to an order under sub-paragraph (2), the action plan shall become final at the end of the prescribed period, unless the Commission has given notice to P under paragraph 16.

Revision of first proposed action plan at invitation of Commission

16 (1) If the Commission considers that a proposed action plan served on it is not an adequate action plan, the Commission may give notice to P—

- (a) stating its view that the plan is not adequate; and
- (b) inviting him to serve on the Commission a revised action plan which is adequate, within such period as may be specified in the notice.

(2) A notice under this paragraph may include recommendations as to action which the Commission considers might be included in an adequate action plan.

(3) If P serves a revised proposed action plan on the Commission in response to a notice under this paragraph, it shall supersede the previous proposed action plan and become final at the end of the prescribed period, unless the Commission has applied for an order under paragraph 17.

(4) If P does not serve a revised action plan in response to a notice under this paragraph, the action plan previously served on the Commission shall become final at the end of the prescribed period, unless the Commission has applied for an order under paragraph 17.

Action by Commission as respects inadequate action plan

17 (1) If the Commission considers that a proposed action plan served on it is not an adequate action plan it may apply to the county court or by way of summary application to the sheriff for an order under this paragraph.

(2) The Commission may not make an application under this paragraph in relation to the first proposed action plan served on it by P (even where it was served in compliance with an order of the court under paragraph 15(2)) unless—

- (a) a notice under paragraph 16 has been served on P in relation to that proposed action plan; and
- (b) P has not served a revised action plan on the Commission in response to it within the period specified in the notice under paragraph 16(1)(b).

(3) An order under this paragraph is an order—

- (a) declaring that the proposed action plan in question is not an adequate action plan;
- (b) requiring P to revise his proposals and serve on the Commission an adequate action plan within such period as the order may specify; and
- (c) containing such directions (if any) as the court considers appropriate as to the action which should be specified in the adequate action plan required by the order.

(4) If on an application under this paragraph the court does not make an order, the proposed action plan in question shall become final at the end of the prescribed period.

18 (1) This paragraph applies where an order of the court under paragraph 17 ('the order') requires P to serve an adequate action plan on the Commission.

(2) If, in response to the order, P serves an action plan on the Commission, that action plan shall become final at the end of the prescribed period unless the Commission has applied to a county court or, in Scotland, to the sheriff to enforce the order on the ground that the plan does not comply with the order (and any directions under paragraph 17(3)(c)).

(3) Where an application is made as mentioned in sub-paragraph (2)—

     (a)   if the Commission withdraws its application, the action plan in question shall become final at the end of the prescribed period;

     (b)   if the court considers that the action plan in question complies with the order, that action plan shall become final at the end of the prescribed period.

Variation of action plans

19 An action plan which has become final may be varied by agreement in writing between the Commission and P.

Enforcement of action plans

20 (1) This paragraph applies during the period of five years beginning on the date on which an action plan drawn up by P becomes final.

(2) If during that period the Commission considers that P has failed to comply with the requirement under section 4(3)(b) to carry out any action specified in the action plan, the Commission may apply to a county court or by summary application to the sheriff for an order under this paragraph.

(3) An order under this paragraph is an order requiring P to comply with that requirement or with such directions for the same purpose as are contained in the order.

Power to obtain information

21 (1) For the purposes of determining whether—

     (a)   an action plan proposed by P is an adequate action plan; or

     (b)   P has complied or is complying with the requirement to take the action specified in an action plan which has become final,

the Commission may serve a notice on any person requiring him to give such information in writing, or copies of documents in his possession or control, relating to those matters as may be described in the notice.

(2) A person may not be required by a notice under this paragraph to give information, or produce a document, which he could not be compelled to give in evidence or produce in civil proceedings before the High Court or the Court of Session.

(3) The Commission may apply to a county court or by summary application to the sheriff for an order under this sub-paragraph if a person has been served with a notice under this paragraph and fails to comply with it.

(4) An order under sub-paragraph (3) is an order requiring the person concerned to comply with the notice or with such directions for the same purpose as may be contained in the order.

PART IV

SUPPLEMENTARY

Restriction on disclosure of information

22 (1) No information given to the Commission by any person ('the informant') in connection with—

(a)   a formal investigation; or

(b)   the exercise of any of its functions in relation to non-discrimination notices, action plans and agreements under section 5,

shall be disclosed by the Commission or by any person who is or has been a commissioner, an additional commissioner or an employee of the Commission.

(2) Sub-paragraph (1) does not apply to any disclosure made—

(a)   on the order of a court,

(b)   with the informant's consent,

(c)   in the form of a summary or other general statement published by the Commission which does not identify the informant or any other person to whom the information relates,

(d)   in a report of the investigation published by the Commission,

(e)   to a commissioner, an additional commissioner or an employee of the Commission, or, so far as is necessary for the proper performance of the Commission's functions, to other persons, or

(f)   for the purpose of any civil proceedings to which the Commission is a party, or of any criminal proceedings.

(3) A person who discloses information contrary to sub-paragraph (1) is guilty of an offence and liable on summary conviction to a fine not exceeding level 5 on the standard scale.

Enforcement of court orders

23 (1) This paragraph applies to any order made by a county court or the sheriff under section 5(8) or under any provision of this Schedule.

(2) Section 55 of the County Courts Act 1984 (penalty for failure to give evidence) shall have effect in relation to a failure to comply with an order made by a county court to which this paragraph applies with the following modifications—

(a)   for subsection (1) there shall be substituted—

'(1) Any person who fails without reasonable excuse to comply with an order made by a county court under section 5(8) of or any provision of Schedule 3 to the Disability Rights Commission Act 1999 shall forfeit such fine as the judge may direct.';

(b)   subsection (3) shall be omitted (but without prejudice to the operation of paragraph 4(3)(b) of this Schedule); and

(c)   in subsection (4), for the words 'the party injured by the refusal or neglect' there shall be substituted the words 'the Disability Rights Commission for expenses incurred or wasted in consequence of the failure to comply with the order concerned'.

(3) Where the sheriff finds a person to be in contempt of court in respect of the failure of a person to comply with an order made by the sheriff to which this paragraph applies—

(a)   notwithstanding section 15 of the Contempt of Court Act 1981, the sheriff shall not commit the person to prison; and

(b)   the sheriff may grant decree in favour of the Commission for such amount of any fine imposed for the contempt as appears to the sheriff to be appropriate in respect of the expense incurred or wasted by the Commission (including the expenses of any proceedings under this Schedule) in consequence of the failure to comply with the order.

(4) If the Commission applies to a county court or, in Scotland, to the sheriff to enforce an order to which this paragraph applies, the court may modify the order.

Offences

24   (1) A person who—

(a)   deliberately alters, suppresses, conceals or destroys a document to which a notice under paragraph 4 or 21, or an order under paragraph 5 or 21(3), relates; or

(b)   in complying with—
    (i)   a notice under paragraph 4 or 21;
    (ii) a non-discrimination notice;
    (iii) an agreement under section 5; or
    (iv) an order of a court under section 5(8) or under any provision of this Schedule,
makes any statement which he knows to be false or misleading in a material particular or recklessly makes a statement which is false or misleading in a material particular,

is guilty of an offence and liable on summary conviction to a fine not exceeding level 5 on the standard scale.

(2) Proceedings for an offence under this paragraph may (without prejudice to any jurisdiction exercisable apart from this sub-paragraph) be instituted—

(a)   against any person at any place at which he has an office or other place of business;

(b)   against an individual at any place where he resides, or at which he is for the time being.

Service of notices

25   (1) Any notice required or authorised by any provision of this Schedule to be served on a person may be served by delivering it to him, by leaving it at his proper address or by sending it by post to him at that address.

(2) Any such notice may—

(a)   in the case of a body corporate, be served on the secretary or clerk of that body;

(b)   in the case of a partnership, be served on any partner or a person having control or management of the partnership business;

(c)   in the case of an unincorporated association (other than a partnership), may be served on any member of its governing body.

(3) For the purposes of this paragraph and section 7 of the Interpretation Act 1978 (service of documents) in its application to this paragraph, the proper address of any person is—

(a)   in the case of a body corporate, its secretary or clerk, the address of its registered or principal office in the United Kingdom;

(b)   in the case of an unincorporated association (other than a partnership) or a member of its governing body, its principal office in the United Kingdom;

(c)   in any other case, his usual or last-known address (whether of his residence or of a place where he carries on business or is employed).

Regulations

26   The Secretary of State may make regulations making provision—

(a)   supplementing Part I or II of this Schedule in connection with any matter concerned with the conduct of formal investigations or the procedure for issuing non-discrimination notices; or

(b)   amending Part III of this Schedule in relation to the procedures for finalising action plans.

SCHEDULE 4

MINOR AND CONSEQUENTIAL AMENDMENTS

Section 14(1)

House of Commons Disqualification Act 1975 (c. 25)

1   In Part II of Schedule 1 to the House of Commons Disqualification Act 1975 (bodies whose members are disqualified) there shall be inserted at the appropriate place the words 'The Disability Rights Commission'.

Northern Ireland Assembly Disqualification Act 1975 (c. 26)

2   In Part II of Schedule 1 to the Northern Ireland Assembly Disqualification Act 1975 (bodies whose members are disqualified) there shall be inserted at the appropriate place the words 'The Disability Rights Commission'.

Disability Discrimination Act 1995 (c. 50)

3 (1) The Disability Discrimination Act 1995 shall be amended as follows.

(2) In section 67(5) (orders not subject to annulment) for '52(8), 54(6)' substitute '53A(6)(a)'.

(3) In Schedule 3 (enforcement and procedure under Parts II and III), in paragraph 6(2), for the words from 'a person' to 'approached' there shall be substituted 'the dispute concerned is referred for conciliation in pursuance of arrangements under section 28'.

Scotland Act 1998 (c. 46)

4 In Part III of Schedule 5 to the Scotland Act 1998 (reserved bodies), in paragraph 3(2)(c), for the words 'the National Disability Council' there shall be substituted 'the Disability Rights Commission'.

SCHEDULE 5

REPEALS

Section 14(2)

Chapter	Short title	Extent of repeal
1975 c. 24.	House of Commons Disqualification Act 1975.	In Part II of Schedule 1, the entry relating to the National Disability Council.
1975 c. 25.	Northern Ireland Assembly Disqualification Act 1975.	In Part II of Schedule 1, the entry relating to the National Disability Council.
1995 c. 50.	Disability Discrimination Act 1995.	Sections 50 to 54. In section 70(7), the words 'The National Disability Council'. Schedule 5.

INDEX

References are to paragraph numbers.

Absence
  adjustments to help minimise
    4.2.44
  dismissal for, comparator   3.2.9,
    3.2.10
ACAS   10.3.12–10.3.14, *see also*
  Conciliation
AIDS, *see* HIV
Access to education, *see* Education
  services
Access to goods and services
  see also Services, goods and facilities,
    provision of
  Code of Practice   5.1.3, 5.2.1,
    5.5.3–5.5.4, 5.5.6, 5.5.8
Access to premises
  adjustments duty   3.4.2, 4.2.28,
    5.5.7–5.5.12, 6.3.2–6.3.6, 7.4.7
  service providers   5.5.7–5.5.12
  trade organisation   4.9.11
Access to Work scheme
  cost of adjustments, support for
    3.4.6, 3.4.13
Act of Parliament
  act done in pursuance of   10.2.8–
    10.2.10
Addiction
  physical impairment issues   2.3.3
Adjustments duty   3.4, 4.2.27–4.2.43
  advice, failure to take   3.4.8
  allocation of duties, by   3.4.2
  'arrangements', as to   4.2.34, *see*
    also 'provision, criterion or
    practice' *below*
  barrister/clerk, on   4.8.7, 4.8.8
  building regulations, interaction
    with   6.3.3
  circumstances for   4.2.28, 4.2.37
  steps in making decision   4.2.41
  comparators   4.2.38
  contract workers   4.3.7–4.3.10

  circumstances for   4.3.7
  cost of adjustment   3.4.8–3.4.10,
    3.4.13, 5.5.3
  defence, *see* 'justification' *below*
  disabled employee/applicant, owed
    to   4.2.29–4.2.43, 6.3.3
  circumstances when duty owed
    4.2.28
  individual, duty owed to   4.2.38
  education services   7.4.6–7.4.9,
    7.4.17–7.4.18, 7.5.7–7.5.11
  EC Framework Directive
    requirement   3.2.42
  failure in (employment field)
    constructive dismissal case   4.2.9
    discrimination, as   3.2.45, 3.2.46,
      3.4.1, 4.2.27
    less favourable treatment, as
      3.2.46
    no justification post-Sept 2004
      3.2.47
    pre-Oct 2004 law   3.2.47
    reasonableness   3.2.47
  further and higher education
    institutions   7.5.7–7.5.11
    auxiliary aids provision   7.5.9
    leasehold premises   7.5.18–
      7.5.30
    physical features of premises,
      adjustments to   7.5.9
  guidance
    judicial   4.2.40–4.2.43
    statutory   3.4.2–3.4.6
  justification defence   4.2.41
    employment cases   3.2.3, 3.2.23,
      3.2.29, 3.2.30, 3.2.45–3.2.48,
      3.4.1
    goods and services provision
      5.6.1–5.6.3
  leasehold premises, *see* Leasehold
    premises

Adjustments duty – *cont*
    local education authority   7.4.17–
        7.4.18
    occupational pension scheme
        trustee   4.5.7
    office-holder   4.4.11
    partnership   4.7.4–4.7.6
        cost of steps   4.7.6
    performance-related pay
        arrangements   4.2.46
    planning permission/consents
        6.3.3, 6.3.17
    post-employment   3.5.3
    positive nature of   3.4.1, 4.2.43
    premises   3.4.2, 6.2.13, 6.3.1–6.3.30
        leaseholds, *see* Leasehold premises
        physical features   4.2.28, 4.2.37,
            5.5.7–5.5.12, 6.3.2, 6.3.4–6.3.6,
            7.4.7, 7.5.9
        Scotland   6.3.5–6.3.6
    private household/home   3.4.9,
        4.2.37
    'provision, criterion or practice', in
        application of   4.2.28, 4.2.34–
        4.2.36
        examples   4.2.34
        health clearance, case   4.2.35
        job-related, limited to   4.2.36
        scope   4.2.36
    reasonableness criterion   3.4.7–
        3.4.13
        account of all the circumstances
            3.4.8
        Codes of Practice   3.4.10
        co-operation   3.4.8
        cost/resources   3.4.8–3.4.10,
            3.4.13
        relevant factors   3.4.9–3.4.12
    schools   7.4.6–7.4.9
        auxiliary aids provision not
            required   7.4.7
        physical features, removal or
            alteration not required
            7.4.7
    service provider, *see* Services, goods
        and facilities, provision of
    steps to take   3.4.2–3.4.13
        examples in Code of Practice
            3.4.3
        illustrations in Statute   3.4.2
        'reasonable' steps   3.4.7 *et seq*

    substantial disadvantage   4.2.38,
        4.2.39
    trade organisations, *see* Trade
        organisation
    transport provider, position of
        8.1.2, 8.1.3, 8.1.4
    universities   7.5.7–7.5.11
        auxiliary aids provision   7.5.9
        leasehold premises   7.5.18–
            7.5.30
        physical features of premises,
            adjustments to   7.5.9
    working hours, *see* Hours of work
Admission
    school, to   7.4.7, 7.4.15
        claim procedure   10.5.4
Advertisement, discriminatory   3.6,
    4.2.2
    change proposed in Bill   1.5.5,
        3.8.1
    declaration/injunction remedies
        3.6.3
    proceedings for   3.6.3
    previous law   3.6.1
    third party publishing   3.8.1
    unlawful   3.6.2
Advisory, Conciliation and Arbitration
    Service, *see* ACAS
Advocate (Scotland)   4.8.9
Agent
    accommodation agency   6.2.5
    act of, liability for   10.2.7
    employment agency, *see* Employment
        services
Agreement in lieu of enforcement
    action   9.1.34–9.1.36, 10.5.11
Agricultural wages   4.2.47
Aid (auxiliary device/service)
    see also Equipment; Interpreter;
        Prosthesis; Wheelchair
    charge for, by airport operator
        8.5.2
    further and higher education
        institution   7.5.9
    impairment adjusted by   2.5.12–
        2.5.17
    schools, provision not required by
        7.4.7
    service provider provision
        'adjustment', as   5.5.1, 5.5.13–
            5.5.15
        aids covered   5.5.14
        employment services   5.7.3

Aiding unlawful act
employment tribunal jurisdiction
10.3.6
liability for   10.2.2–10.2.4, 10.2.7
defence to   10.2.3
Aircraft
employment on   4.2.18
non-statutory code of practice on
access for the disabled   8.5.1
wheelchair access   8.5.2
Airforce   4.2.21
non-application   4.11.1
Airport
hire car   8.2.19–8.2.20
wheelchair access   8.5.2
Alcohol abuse causing liver disease
'impairment'   2.3.3
Alcoholism
not 'impairment'   2.3.3
Allergic rhinitis   2.3.3
Alzheimer's disease   2.5.9
Anti-social disorder
not 'impairment'   2.3.4
Anxiety   2.3.6
Appeal
non-discrimination notices   9.1.24–
9.1.26
restricted reporting order for
10.3.19
routes   10.3.7
school admissions, use of procedure
for claim   10.5.4
school exclusions, use of procedure
for claim   10.5.5
Applicant (job), *see* Recruitment
Application form   4.2.2
Apprenticeship   4.2.17
Arbitration
small claim procedure   10.4.1
Armed forces   4.2.21, 9.5.3
non-application   4.11.1
Arrangement, *see* Adjustments duty
Association, *see* Club, private
Auxiliary aids and services, *see* Aid
(auxiliary device/service)
Aviation, *see* Aircraft; Airport

Banking services   5.2.1
Barrister   3.2.2, 4.8
background   4.8.1, 4.8.2–4.8.8
Council of Legal Education   4.10.1
Northern Ireland   4.8.10
pupillage/tenancy, discrimination
prohibition   4.8.4–4.8.8

adjustments duty   4.8.7, 4.8.8
definitions   4.8.3
harassment   4.8.6
offer/terms or refusal   4.8.4,
4.8.5
Scotland   4.8.9
Benefits (employment)
see also Insurance benefits;
Occupational pension scheme
discrimination in   4.2.5–4.2.7
adjustment duty   4.2.34, *see also*
Adjustments duty
exceptions   4.2.6
scope of   4.2.5
Bill, *see* Legislation
Birth mark   2.5.10
Blindness/partial sight   2.3.10, 2.3.11,
2.4.1
evidence of, and deemed disability
2.3.11, 2.7.3
guide dog in taxi   8.2.12–8.2.15
Body corporate
DRC as   9.1.2
public service vehicle offence,
liability   8.3.10
rail vehicle offence, liability   8.4.6
Body-piercing   2.5.11
Breakdown recovery services   8.1.3
Building, *see* Adjustments duty;
Leasehold premises
Building regulations
adjustment duty, relation to
employer's   6.3.3
service provider's   6.3.4–6.3.4,
5.5.11
Burden of proof   10.3.20
disability, as to   2.1.4
'disabled person', fulfilling
definition   2.1.4
justification defence
employer   3.2.23, 10.3.20
service provider   5.6.5
vicarious liability defence   10.2.6
Burns, disfigurement caused by
2.5.10
Bus, *see* Public service vehicle
Bus station
hire car   8.2.19–8.2.20

Cancer
no symptoms yet   1.5.7, 2.9.1, 2.9.4
progressive condition   2.5.7

Canine Partners for Independence
  8.2.13
Capacity, contractual
  incapacity, justification for service
    discrimination   5.6.8–5.6.9,
    6.2.15
Car hire   8.1.3, 8.2.4
  accessibility at designated transport
    facilities   8.2.19–8.2.20
Car parking
  dedicated, as 'adjustment'   3.4.6
Charity
  equipment from, fulfilling adjustments
    duty   3.4.13
  exception from employment
    provisions   4.2.24
Child
  education, *see* Education services;
    School
  impairment, and normal activities
    2.4.6
Chronic fatigue syndrome ('ME')
  2.3.9
City academy   10.5.8, *see also* School
Civil servant   9.5.2
Claim
  education cases, *see* Special
    Educational Needs and Disability
    Tribunal (SENDIST)
  employment cases, *see* Employment
    tribunal
  services, goods and facilities provision
    cases, *see* Services, goods and
    facilities, provision of
Claimant
  death of   10.3.6
  disabled person, burden of proof
    2.1.4
  employee, statutory questionnaire, *see*
    Questionnaire, statutory
  mitigation duty   10.3.25
  remedies, *see* Remedies
Club, private
  legislative proposals for   1.5.6,
    5.9.3–5.9.5
  adjustments duty   5.9.5
  guests   5.9.3, 5.9.4
  membership, relating to   5.9.3,
    5.9.4
  services, etc, provision   5.2.7
Coach, *see* Public service vehicle

Code of Practice
  admissibility in tribunal
    proceedings   3.1.4, 9.3.5
  Disability Rights Commission,
    preparation and issue by
    3.1.4, 9.3.2
  consultation   9.3.3
  draft, approval of   9.3.4
  new prohibitions and duties, on
    9.8.5
  revision, procedure for   9.3.4
  scope of powers   9.3.2
  Employment   3.2.28, 4.2.15, 5.5.3
  failure to observe   9.3.5
  Post-16 education   7.5.2, 7.5.3,
    7.5.9–7.5.10
  production, new process for   9.3.1
  Rights of Access: Goods, Facilities,
    Services and Premises   5.1.3,
    5.2.1, 5.5.3–5.5.4, 5.5.6, 5.5.8,
    6.2.13, 6.3.4
  Schools   7.4.1
Colour blindness   2.4.4
Commission for Racial Equality
  reform proposal   9.2
Commission for Equality and Human
    Rights
  proposal for   9.2
Comparator
  adjustments duty   4.2.38
  less favourable treatment, employment
    field   3.2.4, 3.2.5, 3.2.8–3.2.10
  direct discrimination, for   3.2.39
Compensation
  employment tribunal award, *see*
    Remedies
Compromise contract   10.3.14,
    10.3.15
  validity, conditions   10.3.14
    'independent adviser'   10.3.15
    insurance or indemnity cover
      10.3.14
    writing, agreement in   10.3.14
Concentration, impairment affecting
    2.4.1
Conciliation
  see also Dispute resolution
  agreement, form and effect of
    10.3.13
  conciliation officer, role   10.3.12,
    10.3.13
  education cases   10.5.12–10.5.13,
    10.6.5

Conciliation – *cont*
    employment cases   10.3.12–10.3.14
    services, etc, provision cases
        10.4.4–10.4.6
Confidentiality
    restriction on disclosure of
        information by DRC   9.1.38,
        10.4.4, 10.5.13
Confidentiality request   7.4.9, 7.5.11
Consent
    see also Licence
    adjustment to premises, *see* Planning
        permission
    leased premises, for alteration to, *see*
        Landlord
Constructive dismissal   4.2.9
    time-limit for claim   10.3.8
Continence, impairment affecting
    2.4.1
Contract of service   4.2.17
    terms and conditions   4.2.4
Contract
    claim based on, time-limit
        calculation   10.3.8, 10.4.3
    education case, void where
        contravenes law   10.5.11
    services, etc, for
        incapacity to make, discrimination
            justification   5.6.8–5.6.9,
            6.2.15
        void where contravenes or excludes
            law   10.4.7–10.4.9
Contract worker   4.3
    agency discrimination, protection
        from   4.3.1
    overlapping duties   4.3.9
    definition   4.3.2
    third party discrimination, protection
        from
        breadth of provisions   4.3.3
        'principal'   4.3.2
        public provision, exception
            where   4.3.6
        reasonable adjustments   4.3.7–
            4.3.10
        unlawful acts   4.3.4, 4.3.5
Cost
    adjustments duty, and, *see* Adjustments
        duty
    services, provision of, *see* Services,
        goods and facilities, provision of
Council of Legal Education   4.10.1

County court proceedings
    see also Proceedings
    education services, modification of
        contravening agreement
        10.5.10, 10.6.4
    further and higher education
        claim   10.6.1
    services, etc, small claim
        procedure   10.4.1, 10.4.2
Crown
    application to   4.2.21, 9.5
    liability for act of Crown servant,
        proposal for   9.8.3
    new duties proposed   9.8.1–9.8.3
    non-application   4.11.1

Damages   5.8.1, 10.3.26, 10.4.10,
    10.6.3
Danger, impairment of perception of
    risk of   2.4.1
DDA Helpline   10.4.5
Deafness, *see* Hearing impairment
Declaration of rights
    advert, discriminatory, remedy for
        3.6.3
    educational provision, claim in
        Scotland   10.5.10
    occupational pension scheme
        remedy   4.5.9
    services, goods or facilities provision
        claim   5.8.1, 10.4.11
Degenerative condition, *see* Progressive
    condition
Dependency
    physical impairment   2.3.3
Deposit
    refusal of full refund
        goods and facilities   5.6.16
        premises, for   6.2.16
Depression   2.3.6, 2.9.3
    employment case   3.4.5
    history of, discrimination for   2.8.3
    manic   2.3.7
Designers
    obligation to disabled consumers
        5.2.6
Detriment, subjection to   4.2.10
Diabetes
    justification defence case   3.2.31–
        3.2.33

Director (company)
office–holder, protection as   4.4.1
Disability   2.1 *et seq*
ability to carry out normal day-to-day
activities, affecting   2.4.1–2.4.7
burden of proof   2.1.4
definition   2.1.1–2.1.4, 2.2
amendment proposed   1.5.7
elements of   2.2.2
determination of, approach to
2.2.2
expert evidence, *see* Expert evidence
Guidance, statutory   2.1.2, 2.1.4,
2.2.2, 9.4.5
'impairment'   2.3.1–2.3.10, *see also*
Impairment
indirect discrimination   5.4.10
knowledge of, *see* Knowledge of
disability
long-term adverse effect   2.6.1–
2.6.5
date for judgment of   2.6.4
Guidance   2.6.3
meaning of 'long-term'   2.6.1
past disability and   2.6.5
recurring effects   2.6.3–2.6.4
meaning of term   2.2.1–2.2.2
medical treatment, effect of
2.5.12–2.5.17
past, *see* Past disability
progressive or degenerative
conditions, *see* Progressive
condition
recurring conditions, *see* Recurring
condition
severe disfigurement, *see*
Disfigurement
social   2.5.10
substantial adverse effect   2.5.1–
2.5.17
effect of medical treatment
2.5.12–2.5.17
meaning of 'substantial'   2.5.2–
2.5.4
progressive conditions   2.5.7–
2.5.9
recurring conditions   2.5.5–2.5.6
severe disfigurement   2.5.10–
2.5.11
terminal illness   2.6.2
Disability Access Rights Advisory
Service   10.4.5
Disability Conciliation Service   10.4.5

Disability Rights Commission   1.1.1,
9.1, 9.2
action plans   9.1.27–9.1.33
'adequate'   9.1.27–9.1.30
court action   9.1.30, 9.1.31–
9.1.32
final   9.1.27, 9.1.28, 9.1.29
first   9.1.28
inadequate   9.1.29, 9.1.30
information powers of DRC
9.1.33
revision   9.1.29
advert, bringing proceedings for
3.6.3
agreements in lieu of enforcement
action   9.1.34–9.1.36
annual report   9.1.9
assistance to individuals with
proceedings   9.1.10–9.1.12
expenses, recovery of   9.1.12
chairman and deputy   9.1.6
Codes of Practice, preparation and
issue of, *see* Code of Practice
commissioners   9.1.4–9.1.6
additional, appointment and
termination of   9.1.14
appointment and termination of
appointment   9.1.5
committees   9.1.8
conciliation service, arrangements for
the provision of   10.4.4–10.4.6,
10.5.12
court action for persistent
discrimination   9.1.37
court order enforcement   9.1.39
fine for failure to comply   9.1.39
criminal offences relating to
powers   9.1.40
disclosure of information   9.1.38,
10.4.4, 10.5.13
establishment   9.1.1
fine for failure to comply   9.1.39
formal investigations, *see* Investigation
by DRC
function   9.1.7
information, restriction on
disclosure   9.1.38, 10.4.4,
10.5.13
instruction or pressure to
discriminate, proceedings for
3.7.2
joinder as party   9.1.7

Disability Rights Commission – *cont*
  non-discrimination notices, *see* Non–
    discrimination notices
  offices   9.1.1
  powers   9.1.7–9.1.9
    advice and proposals   9.1.8
    court order enforcement   9.1.39
    criminal offences relating to
      9.1.40
    delegation   9.1.8
    judicial review, as to   9.1.7
    persistent discrimination, in cases
      of   9.1.37
  proceedings of, regulation   9.1.8
  reform proposal (new
    Commission)   9.2
  review of legislation   2.9.3
  service of notices   9.1.41
  staff   9.1.3
  status   9.1.2
  website   9.1.1
Disability Rights Task Force
  education, recommendations on
    7.1.3
  establishment   1.2.2
  recommendations for future
    reform   10.7.2
Disabled person   2.1 *et seq*
  see also Disability
  association with/perception as
    3.2.51
  burden of proof   2.1.4
  deemed status   1.5.7, 2.7.1, 2.7.2,
    2.9.3
    blind/partially sighted person
      2.3.11, 2.7.3
    certification or registration
      2.1.3, 2.7.1, 2.7.2
  definition   2.1.2, 2.2.1–2.2.4
  decision for tribunal   2.1.2, 2.1.4
  Guidance on, *see* Guidance
    (statutory)
  other statutes, weight of   2.1.3
  employee, *see* Employment cases
  preliminary hearing for determination
    of status   2.1.1
  statistics   1.1.1, 1.1.2
Disabled Persons' Transport Advisory
  Committee   8.2.2, 8.5.1
Disclosure of information
  restriction on DRC   9.1.38, 10.4.4,
    10.5.13

Discrimination
  direct   3.2.36–3.2.38
  disability ground   3.2.38
  meaning   3.2
Disfigurement   2.5.10, 2.5.11
  deliberately acquired   2.5.11
  exclusions from 'disability'   2.5.10,
    2.5.11
  Guidance   2.5.10
  matter of degree   2.5.10
Dismissal   4.2.8, 4.2.9
  see also Unfair dismissal
  constructive   4.2.9
  decision as 'arrangement on which
    employment afforded'   4.2.36
  EC Framework Directive applies
    4.1.1
  grievance procedure, use of
    10.3.11
  non-renewal of fixed–term
    contract   4.2.8
  time-limit for claim   10.3.8
Dispute resolution
  compensation adjustment   10.3.31
  precondition for claim   10.3.10,
    10.3.11
  see also Compromise contract;
    Conciliation; Employment
    tribunal; Settlement
Dog, guide, *see* Guide/hearing dog
DRC, *see* Disability Rights Commission
DRC Helpline   10.4.5
DRTF, *see* Disability Rights Task Force
Drug addiction   2.3.3
Dyslexia   4.2.2

Earnings, loss of   10.3.23, 10.3.25,
  10.3.29
Education services
  see also Further education institution;
    School; University
  accessibility strategies and plans
    7.4.12–7.4.15
  adjustments duty   7.4.6–7.4.9,
    7.4.17–7.4.18, 7.5.7–7.5.11
  limitations   7.4.7
  unjustified failure as
    discrimination   7.4.4, 7.4.6
  admission arrangements   7.4.7,
    7.4.15, 10.5.4
  agreement purporting to contravene
    law   10.5.11, 10.6.4

Education services – *cont*
  conciliation   10.5.12–10.5.13,
    10.6.5
  Disability Rights Task Force
    recommendations   7.1.3
  discrimination, meaning of   7.4.4–
    7.4.9
  enforcement for unlawful disability
    discrimination   7.4.19, 7.5.19
  exclusion decision   5.2.9, 7.1.2,
    7.2.1–7.2.3, 10.5.5
  independent school, *see* Independent
    school
  justification defence   7.4.5, 7.4.11,
    7.4.17, 7.5.6–7.5.7, 7.5.13
  less favourable treatment by   7.4.5,
    7.4.11, 7.4.17, 7.5.6, 7.5.13
  local education authorities   7.2.5,
    7.2.18, 7.4.1–7.4.19
    residual duty   7.4.16–7.4.18
  non-educational services and
    facilities   7.2.3
  Post-16 Code of Practice   7.5.2,
    7.5.3, 7.5.9–7.5.10
  post-Sept 2002 law
    further and higher education
      7.5.1–7.5.30
    schools and education
      authorities   7.4.1–7.4.19
    types of support available   7.4.1
  pre-Sept 2002 law   7.2.1–7.2.25
    exclusions and exemptions
      7.2.1–7.2.7
    further education colleges and
      institutions   7.2.12–7.2.16
    further education funding
      councils   7.2.17
    local education authorities
      7.2.18
    policy-making   7.2.8
    public use of facilities   7.2.3
    'relevant body'   7.2.1
    schools   7.2.1, 7.2.9–7.2.10
    Teacher Training Agency   7.2.11
    universities and higher education
      institutions   7.2.19–7.2.25
  remedies, *see* Special Educational
    Needs and Disability Tribunal
  research, facilities for   7.2.6
  school governors' annual report,
    information in   7.2.10, 7.4.15
  Schools Code of Practice   7.4.1
  Scotland, claim in   10.5.10
  services provision exclusion   5.2.9,
    7.1.1–7.1.5
  settlement of claim   10.5.11
  Tomlinson Committee on education
    and disability   7.2.17
  voluntary organisations, provision
    by   7.2.6

Employee
  see also Claimant; Employment cases
  act of, vicarious liability of employer,
    see Employer
  aiding unlawful act   10.2.2–10.2.4
Employee benefits, *see* Benefits
Employees' organisation, *see* Trade
    organisation
Employer
  liability   10.2.4
  vicarious liability   10.2.2, 10.2.4–
    10.2.6
    defence   10.2.6
Employers' association, *see* Trade
    organisation
Employers' Forum on Disability
  estimates on disability   1.1.2
Employment Appeal Tribunal (EAT)
  appeal to   10.3.7
  disabled person and disability,
    approach to question of   2.2.2
  mental illness as disability,
    recommendations where
    doubt   2.3.6
  restricted reporting order   10.3.19
Employment cases   3.1 *et seq*, 4.1 *et seq*
  adjustments, duty to make reasonable,
    see Adjustments duty
  advertisements, *see* Advertisement,
    discriminatory
  Codes of Practice   3.1.4
  common concepts   3.1.5
  contract workers, *see* Contract workers
  detriment, subjection to   4.2.10
  direct discrimination   3.2.3, 3.2.36–
    3.2.41
    adjustments, relevance of   3.2.40
    circumstances   3.2.36
    comparator, actual or
      hypothetical   3.2.39
    comparator's relevant
      circumstances   3.2.40
    knowledge of disability   3.2.38

Employment cases – *cont*
  direct discrimination – *cont*
    'on the ground of' disability
      3.2.37, 3.2.38
    no justification possible   3.2.36,
      3.2.41
    'discrimination'   3.2 *et seq*
    types, outline   3.2.1
    discriminator   3.2.2
    dismissal, *see* Dismissal
    'employment'   4.2.17
    establishment in GB, meaning
      4.2.18
    ship, on board   4.2.18, 4.2.19
  enforcement procedures, *see*
    Employment tribunal
  exemptions/exceptions   4.2.21,
    4.2.24–4.2.26, 9.5.3
  harassment   3.3.1, 3.3.2, 4.2.10,
    4.2.12
    conduct regarded as   3.3.2
  indirect   3.2.42, 3.2.43
    duty to take measures to eliminate,
      see Adjustments duty
  insurance benefits, *see* Insurance
    benefits
  instruction or pressure to
    discriminate   3.7
    proceedings for   3.7.2
  justification, *see* Justification defence
  less favourable treatment   3.2.3 *et*
    seq, 3.2.36
    approach of tribunal to   3.2.11,
      3.2.13
    breach of adjustments duty as
      3.2.46
    claimant proving facts sufficient
      unless disproved   3.2.6
    comparator/hypothetical
      comparator   3.2.4, 3.2.5,
      3.2.8–3.2.10
    concept   3.2.4
    direct discrimination, amounting
      to   3.2.41
    justification defence, and   3.2.3,
      3.2.23, 3.2.29, 3.2.30, 3.2.45–
      3.2.48
    knowledge of disability, relevance
      of   3.2.16–3.2.22
    reason 'relates to disability'
      3.2.12–3.2.15
    than another disabled person
      3.2.7

  legislation and amendments   3.1
    approach to concepts in   3.1.3
  opportunities and benefits   4.2.5–
    4.2.7
    exceptions   4.2.6
  pay, *see* Pay
  post-employment, etc, act   3.5,
    4.2.11
    adjustments duty   3.5.3
    explicit provision   3.5.1
    unlawful   3.5.2
  pension, occupational, *see*
    Occupational pension scheme
  practices and procedures having
    adverse effect   3.2.43
  preferential treatment   3.2.44
  public sector, *see* Public sector
  recruitment and selection, *see*
    Recruitment
  remedies, *see* Remedies
  respondents   3.2.2
  sick pay, non-payment of
    discretionary   3.2.14
  small business   4.2.20
  supported employment   4.2.25,
    4.2.26
  terms and conditions of service
    4.2.4
  victimisation   3.2.49, 3.2.50
  working conditions   3.4.2, 4.1.1
Employment services   5.7
  adjustments duty   5.7.3, 5.7.5
  contract term in contravention of
    provisions   5.7.6
  discrimination prohibition   5.7.3,
    5.7.4
  harassment prohibition   5.7.2
  meaning   5.7.1
Employment tribunal
  appeal from decision of   10.3.7
  burden of proof, *see* Burden of proof
  claim   10.3.7–10.3.11
    powers restricted to detail in
      4.2.1
  Code of Practice, account of   3.1.4
  claim procedure   10.3.6
  conciliation agreement, effect of
    10.3.13
  disability discrimination law covers
    10.3.7
  dispute resolution, precondition for
    claim   10.3.10, 10.3.11
  evidence, *see* Evidence

Employment tribunal – *cont*
  Guidance, requirement to take
      account of   2.1.2, 3.2.4
  judgment   10.3.7
  jurisdiction   10.3.6, 10.3.8, 10.3.13
  publicity restriction, *see* Restricted
      reporting order
  questionnaire, *see* Questionnaire,
      statutory
  recommendations, *see* Remedies
  remedies available to, *see* Remedies
  time-limit   10.3.7, 10.3.8
      extension of, discretion   10.3.9
      start of period   10.3.8
Enforcement
  see also Proceedings; Remedies
  agreements in lieu of   9.1.34–
      9.1.36, 10.5.11, 10.6.4
  court orders   9.1.39
      fine for failure to comply   9.1.39
  education field   7.4.19, 7.5.19
      Scotland   7.4.19, 7.5.19, 10.5.10
  employment field, *see* Employment
      tribunal
  non-discrimination notices   9.1.26
  premises, relating to   6.2.18
  goods, facilities or services
      provision   5.8.1
Epilepsy   2.3.9, 2.5.5
  medication-regulated   2.5.14
Equal Opportunities Commission
  new merged Commission
      proposed   9.2
Equipment   5.5.15
  modification of, as 'adjustment'
      3.4.2
      duty to make   4.2.37, *see also*
          Adjustments duty
  specialist, whether reasonable
      adjustment   3.4.13
European Community
  Framework Employment Directive
      1.2.2, 3.1.2, 3.2.36, 3.2.42, 4.1.1
Eviction
  protection for disabled person
      from   6.2.6. 6.2.20
Evidence
  see also Expert evidence
  conciliation communications
      inadmissible   10.4.4, 10.5.13
  publicity restriction where personal
      nature   10.3.16–10.3.19

  questionnaire answers   10.3.4
Exam board, *see* Qualifications body
Exclusion from school, *see* School
Exhibitionism
  not 'impairment'   2.3.4
Expert evidence
  ability to carry out normal day-to-day
      activities, assessment of   2.4.3
  effect of impairment on day-to-day
      activities, of   2.4.3
  medical
      compensation assessment hearing,
          at   10.3.23
      disability, as to   2.1.4, 2.2.2,
          3.2.34
      mental illness, on   2.3.5
      obtained after event, tribunal fact
          finding from   3.2.34
      rejection by tribunal,
          circumstances   2.1.4
  notice requirement   2.2.2
Eyesight, *see* Sight impairment
Facial disfigurement   2.5.10

Facilities, provision of, *see* Services, goods
  and facilities, provision of
Fire fighters   4.2.21, 9.5.3
Firm, *see* Partnership
Further Education Funding Council
  7.2.12–7.2.17
Further education institution   6.4.1,
  7.2.2, 7.2.12–7.2.16
  adjustments duty   7.5.7–7.5.11
  anticipatory and evolving duty
      7.5.8
  auxiliary aids provision   7.5.9
  leasehold premises   7.5.18–
      7.5.30
  physical features of premises,
      adjustments to   7.5.9, 7.5.18
  conciliation   10.6.5
  confidentiality request   7.5.11
  enforcement for unlawful disability
      discrimination   7.5.17
  justification defence   7.5.6–7.5.7,
      7.5.13
  knowledge of disability   7.5.12
  leasehold premises   7.5.18–7.5.30
  less favourable treatment by   7.5.6,
      7.5.13
  local education authority, secured
      by   7.5.14–7.5.16

Further education institution – *cont*
  Post-16 Code of Practice   7.5.2,
    7.5.3, 7.5.9–7.5.10
  post-Sept 2002 law on disability
    discrimination
    disability discrimination duties
      7.5.3–7.5.4
    proceedings   10.6.1–10.6.5
      time-limits   10.6.2
    remedies   10.6.3
    Scotland   7.2.13, 7.5.4, 7.5.14–
      7.5.16

General Medical Council   4.10.1, *see
    also* Qualifications body
Generic disability   2.3.9
Genetic risk   2.5.9
Goods, provision of, *see* Services, goods
    and facilities, provision of
Government department
  application to   9.5
Green Paper (1994)   5.1.1, 5.4.10,
    5.5.6, 5.5.7, 7.1.1, 8.1.1
Grievance procedure, statutory
    10.3.10, 10.3.11
Guarantee
  less favourable treatment in respect
    of   5.6.15
Guidance (statutory)
  consultation duty   9.4.3
  disability, on meaning of   2.1.2,
    9.4.1–9.4.5
  draft
    approval   9.4.4
    time-limit for approval   9.4.4
  employment tribunal to take account
    of   2.1.2, 2.1.4, 2.2.2
  impairment, meaning of   2.3.2,
    9.4.1–9.4.5
    mental   2.3.4
    sensory   2.3.10
  long-term adverse effect   2.6.3,
    9.4.1–9.4.2
  normal day-to-day activities, on
    2.9.2
  power of Secretary of State to issue
    9.4.1–9.4.5
  'substantial adverse effect', on
    2.5.1–2.5.17, 9.4.1–9.4.2
Guide/hearing dog   5.5.6, 8.2.12–
    8.2.15
  private hire vehicle operator
    duties   8.2.16–8.2.18

Halls of residence   7.2.7
Harassment prohibition   3.3
  barrister/clerk, by or relating to
    4.8.6
  employment field, in   3.3.1, 3.3.2,
    4.2.10, 4.2.12
  occupational pension scheme trustee,
    by   4.5.4
  office-holder   4.4.10
  partner/prospective partner, of
    4.7.3
  remedies, tribunal powers   10.3.21
    et seq, *see also* Remedies
  tenant, by landlord/manager of
    premises   6.2.6
  trade organisation   4.9.10
Health and safety
  adjustment involving breach
    3.4.13
  risk
    justifying less favourable
      treatment   3.2.24, 3.2.25,
      5.6.7, 6.2.15
    unjustified concerns, direct
      discrimination tackles
      3.2.38
Health care   4.2.5
Health insurance, *see* Insurance benefits
Health screening, pre-employment, *see*
    Medical examination
Hearing impairment   2.3.10, 2.4.1
  hearing dog
    private hire vehicle operator
      duties   8.2.16–8.2.18
    taxi driver duties   8.2.12–8.2.15
  improvement by hearing aid
    2.5.14
  trivial conditions   2.5.2
Higher education institution, *see*
    Education services; University
Hire car   8.1.3, 8.2.4
  accessibility at designated transport
    facilities   8.2.19–8.2.20
  guide dog, operator's duties as to
    8.2.16–8.2.18
  exemption   8.2.18
HIV
  diagnosis but no symptoms   2.5.8
  'disability', proposal   1.5.7, 2.9.1,
    2.9.4
  progressive condition, as   2.5.7

Home, work from
    'adjustment', as   3.4.5
    adjustment duty limited   4.2.37
Hours of work
    altering, as 'adjustment'   3.4.2,
        3.4.5
    costs   3.4.6
Houses of Parliament, *see* Parliament
Hovercraft, employment on   4.2.18
Human immunodeficiency virus, *see* HIV
Human rights, *see* Commission for
    Equality and Human Rights
Huntingdon's chorea   2.5.9

Impairment   2.3
    see also Disability
    ability to carry out normal day-to-day
        activities, affecting   2.4.1–2.4.7
        normal activities   2.4.5
        particular claimant, effect on
            2.4.2
        things done with difficulty   2.4.2
        treated as   2.4.1
        work, person in   2.4.3, 2.4.7
    cause not relevant   2.3.2
    child   2.4.6
    definition, WHO   2.3.1
    long-term adverse effect, having
        2.6.1–2.6.5
        meaning of 'long-term'   2.6.1
        past disability and   2.6.5
        recurring effects,   2.6.3–2.6.4
    meaning   2.3.1–2.3.10, 9.4.1–9.4.5
    Guidance   2.3.2
    medical treatment, *see* Medical
        treatment or aid
    mental   2.3.4–2.3.7, 2.4.7
    physical   2.3.3, 2.3.8
    progressive conditions, *see* Progressive
        condition
    psychiatric and psychological
        2.3.4–2.3.7
    recurring conditions, *see* Recurring
        condition
    sensory   2.3.10, 2.3.11
        guide/hearing dog in taxis
            8.2.12–8.2.15
    severe disfigurement, *see*
        Disfigurement
    substantial adverse effect   2.5.1–
        2.5.17

    cumulative effect of more than one
        impairment   2.5.3
    effect of medical treatment
        2.5.12–2.5.17
    Guidance   2.5.1, 2.5.3 *et seq*
    mitigating or coping strategies
        2.5.4
    progressive conditions   2.5.7–
        2.5.9
    'substantial'   2.5.2–2.5.4
    trivial condition   2.5.2
    World Health Organization
        definition   2.3.1
Independent school   7.2.1, 7.3.1
    accessibility plans   7.4.14
    disability discrimination duties
        7.4.3
Indirect discrimination   5.4.10
Induction programme   4.2.4
Injunction   3.6.3, 5.8.1, 10.4.11,
    10.6.3
Injury
    employment case, in
        compensation for, calculation
            10.3.26
        feelings, to   10.3.26, 10.4.10
    insurance provision for   4.6.5, *see
        also* Insurance benefits
    self-administered   2.5.11, 2.9.3
Instruction to discriminate   3.7
Insurance benefits   4.2.5, 4.6
    employer–insurer arrangement,
        discrimination prohibition
        4.6.1–4.6.3
    unlawful acts   4.6.3, 4.6.4
    employer provision, discrimination
        prohibition   4.6.1, 4.6.6
    'insurance services'   4.6.5
Insurance business
    added risk, burden of proof   5.6.14
Insurance scheme, group
    repeal of provisions proposed
        4.13.4
Interest
    compensation, on   10.3.27
International Maritime Organization
    (IMO)   8.5.1
Interpreter   3.4.2, 3.4.6, 5.5.14
Interview (job)   4.2.2, 4.2.30–4.2.33
Investigation by DRC   9.1.13–9.1.20
    circumstances for   9.1.13
    commissioners   9.1.14
    criminal offences   9.1.39

Investigation by DRC – *cont*
  failure to publish, effect of   9.1.19
  first, announcement of   9.1.21
  health inequalities   9.1.21
  information request   9.1.18
  notices, service of   9.1.15, 9.1.17,
    9.1.18, 9.1.19
  order for compliance to a notice
    9.1.18
  recommendations from findings
    9.1.20
  report of findings   9.1.20
  reporting period   9.1.19
  representations   9.1.17
  suspension of   9.1.13
  terms of reference   9.1.15, 9.1.16
  time-limit for completion   9.1.19
  website accessibility   9.1.21

Jobcentre Plus   5.7.1, *see also*
  Employment services
Job specification   4.2.2
Joinder
  Disability Rights Commission   9.1.7
  landlord   6.3.19
Judge
  office-holder, protection as   4.4.1
Judicial review
  DRC *locus standi* for   9.1.7
  education services case   10.5.6,
    10.6.1
  services and premises case   10.4.1
Justification defence
  adjustments duty   4.2.41
    failure, justification of   5.6.1–
      5.6.3
  contractual incapacity   5.6.8–5.6.9,
    6.2.15
  education services   7.4.5, 7.4.11,
    7.4.17, 7.5.6–7.5.7, 7.5.13
  employment field, in   3.2.3, 3.2.23–
    3.2.35
    adjustments duty, and, *see*
      Adjustments duty
    burden of proof   3.2.23
    Code of Practice guidance
      3.2.28
    examples   3.2.25
    knowledge of disability,
      relevance   3.2.35
    material and substantial   3.2.23,
      3.2.27–3.2.30, 7.4.17, 7.5.6

  particular, not general, defence
    3.2.26
  statutory sequence for   3.2.29
  test of, CA explanation   3.2.31–
    3.2.33
  health and safety risk   3.2.24,
    3.2.25, 5.6.7, 6.2.15
  insurance services   5.6.14
  knowledge of applicant's disability
    3.2.35, 5.4.9
  medical information   3.2.24
  premises, discrimination as to
    6.2.14–6.2.16
    deposit not refunded in full
      6.2.16
    health and safety risk   6.2.15
    incapacity to contract   6.2.15
  service provider, by   5.4.2, 5.4.8,
    5.6.1–5.6.16
    burden of proof   5.6.5
    conditions for defence   5.6.6–
      5.6.13
    deposit not refunded in full
      5.6.16
    greater cost   5.6.12–5.6.13
    guarantee, less favourable treatment
      in respect of   5.6.15
    health and safety risk   5.6.7
    standard of service   5.6.11
    subjective–objective test   5.6.4–
      5.6.5
  trade organisation discrimination, *see*
    Trade organisations

Knowledge of disability   3.2.16–3.2.22
  employment provisions   3.2.35,
    5.4.8
  further and higher institutions,
    relevance to   7.5.12
  justification defence   5.4.9
  objective test   5.4.8
  schools, relevance to   7.4.10
  service provisions   5.4.7–5.4.9

Labelling
  manufacturer and designers
    obligation   5.2.6

Landlord
  see also Leasehold premises
  adjustments duty proposed   1.5.6,
    6.5

Landlord – *cont*
  consent to alteration of leased
      premises (educational
      institution)   7.5.18–7.5.28
    conditions, making subject to
      7.5.22, 7.5.25
    enforcement of alterations duty and
      remedies   7.5.26
    reasonableness for discrimination
      purposes, and   7.5.25
    reference to county court
      7.5.26–7.5.28
    statutory term implied   7.5.19,
      7.5.22
    sub-lease   7.5.20, 7.5.24, 7.5.27
    withheld/treated as withheld
      7.5.23
  consent to alteration of leased
      premises (employment cases)
      6.3.8, 6.3.10, 6.3.13–6.3.15
    conditions, making subject to
      6.3.10, 6.3.15, 6.3.17
    enforcement of alterations duty and
      remedies   6.3.19
    failure to obtain   6.3.18
    reasonableness for discrimination
      purposes, and   6.3.14,
      6.3.17, 6.3.19
    statutory term implied   6.3.10,
      6.3.12, 6.3.15
    sub-lease   6.3.11
    third party consent also
      required   6.3.16
    withheld/treated as withheld
      6.3.15, 6.3.16, 6.3.19
  consent to alteration of leased
      premises (goods and services
      cases)   6.3.20–6.3.29
    conditions, making subject to
      6.3.24, 6.3.25
    enforcement of alterations duty and
      remedies   6.3.25–6.3.29
    reasonableness for discrimination
      purposes, and   6.3.24,
      6.3.27–6.3.29
    reference to county court
      6.3.25–6.3.29
    sub-lease   6.3.26
    withheld/treated as withheld
      6.3.22–6.3.24, 6.3.27
  discrimination by   6.1.1, 6.2.2–6.2.7
  joining as party to proceedings
      6.3.19

  'person with power to dispose', as
      6.2.8
  sub-tenancy, of   6.3.9, 6.3.11, 6.3.26
  unlawful acts   6.2.2–6.2.7
Law Society   4.10.1, *see also*
      Qualifications body
Learning and Skills Council   7.2.17
Learning difficulties
  education services   7.2.5
Learning disability   2.3.4, 2.3.7
LEAs, *see* Local education authority
Leasehold premises
  adjustments duty   6.1.2, 6.3.7–
      6.3.30
    commercial lease   6.1.2, 6.3.8,
      6.3.9
    consent of landlord, *see* Landlord
    educational institutions (FE and
      HE)   6.4.1, 7.5.18–7.5.30
    employment cases   6.3.13–6.3.19
    goods and services cases   6.3.20–
      6.3.29
    management and disposal of
      premises   6.2.13, 6.3.2,
      6.3.30
    order authorising occupier to make
      adjustment   6.3.19
    terms and conditions of lease,
      interaction with   6.3.10–
      6.3.19, 6.3.21
    university   6.4.1, 7.5.18–7.5.30
  further and higher education
      establishments   7.5.18–7.5.30
  harassment of disabled tenant
      6.2.6
  landlord and tenant law, relationship
      with   6.3.9–6.3.12
  'lease'   6.3.9
  person with power to grant right to
      occupy   6.2.8–6.2.9
  'sub-lease'   6.3.9, 6.3.11
    educational institution occupying
      under   7.5.18, 7.5.20
  universities   7.5.18–7.5.30
Leave, disability   4.2.44
Left handedness   2.4.4
Legal proceedings, *see* Proceedings
Legislation   1.2–1.5
  current Bill   1.5, 2.9, 4.13, 5.9, 6.5
    changes proposed by   1.5.2–
      1.5.7, 2.9.1, 2.9.4, 2.9.5, 3.8

Legislation – *cont*
  current Bill – *cont*
    Clubs, *see* Club, private
    Disability Task Force
      recommendations, and
      10.7.1, 10.7.2
    progress of   1.5.1
    qualification bodies   7.6
    rail vehicles   8.6
    transport services   5.9.2
  employment field   3.1
  scope   1.3
  territorial extent   1.4
Less favourable treatment
  comparator for, *see* Comparator
  concept   3.2.4
  education services, in, *see* Education
    services; Further education
    institution; School
  employment field, in, *see* Employment
    cases
  justification of, *see* Justification
    defence
  knowledge of disability   3.2.16–
    3.2.22
  premises, in respect of   6.2.14–
    6.2.16
  school pupils, of   7.4.5, 7.4.17
  school teacher, of, case   3.2.15
  service provider, by   5.4.2–5.4.9
  students in higher and further
    education   7.5.6, 7.5.13
Lessor, *see* Landlord
Liability   10.2
  agent   10.2.7
  aiding unlawful acts   10.2.2–10.2.4,
    10.2.7
  certification by Crown as evidence
    10.2.11, 10.2.12
  employer, *see* Employer
  national security, act done to
    safeguard   10.2.12
    certification by Crown   10.2.12
  principal, of   10.2.7
  statutory authority exception
    10.2.8–10.2.11
    certification by Crown   10.2.11
    example   10.2.10
    'in pursuance of any enactment'
      10.2.9
  vicarious, *see* Vicarious liability

Licence
  withholding, tenancy premises
    6.2.7
Lighting   4.2.37
Limitation, *see* Time-limit
Limited liability partnership, *see*
  Partnership
Liver disease from alcohol abuse
  impairment, as   2.3.3
Local authority
  adjustments duty, proposal   4.13.2
  discrimination in exercise of
    functions, prohibition
    proposal   4.13.1, 9.8.1
  elimination of discrimination and
    harassment, new duty
    proposed   9.8.2
Local education authority   7.2.5
  accessibility strategies and plans,
    duty   7.4.12–7.4.15
  adjustments duty   7.4.17–7.4.18
  enforcement for unlawful disability
    discrimination   7.4.19, 7.5.19
  further education or training
    facilities   7.5.14–7.5.16
  less favourable treatment by   7.4.5,
    7.4.17
  Post-16 Code of Practice   7.5.2,
    7.5.3
  post-Sept 2002 law on disability
    discrimination   7.2.18, 7.4.1–
    7.4.19
    disability discrimination duties
      7.4.2–7.4.3, 7.5.3–7.5.4
    residual duty of education
      authorities   7.4.16–7.4.18
  pre-Sept 2002 law on disability
    discrimination   7.2.18
  residual duties   7.4.16–7.4.18
  Schools Code of Practice   7.4.1
Local government, *see* Local authority

ME (chronic fatigue syndrome)   2.3.9

Manic depression, *see* Depression
Manual dexterity, impairment
  affecting   2.4.1
Manufacturers
  obligation to disabled consumers
    5.2.6
Meal voucher   4.2.5
Mediation UK   10.4.5
Medical evidence, *see* Expert evidence

Medical examination
  pre-employment   4.2.13–4.2.15
  'arrangement' for employment
    offer   4.2.15
  Code of Practice gives guidance
    4.2.15
Medical information   3.2.24
Medical treatment or aid
  impairment corrected by   2.5.12–
    2.5.17
  continuing treatment   2.5.15
  Guidance on   2.5.16
Medication
  impairment controlled by   2.5.12–
    2.5.17
Members' clubs, private
  services, goods and facilities, disabled
    persons rights of access to
    5.2.7
Memory, impairment affecting   2.4.1
Mental illness
  'clinically well-recognised'   2.3.5,
    2.4.7
  removal of requirement
    proposed   2.9.1
  damages in case of   10.3.26
  employment, and affect of   2.4.7
Mental impairment   2.3.4–2.3.7
  EAT recommendations on establishing
    proof   2.3.6
  excluded conditions   2.3.4
  meaning   2.3.4–2.3.7
  mental illness, clinical recognition
    2.3.5–2.3.7, 2.4.7
    removal of requirement
      proposed   2.9.1
  physical impairment distinguished
    2.3.8, 2.3.9
Minicabs   8.2.4
  accessibility at designated transport
    facilities   8.2.19–8.2.20
Mobility impairment   2.4.1
Mobility requirement
  adjustment duty   4.2.34
Moods   2.3.7
Multiple sclerosis   2.5.5, 2.9.3
  'disability', proposal where no
    symptoms   1.5.7, 2.9.1, 2.9.4
  progressive condition, as   2.5.7,
    2.5.9
Muscular dystrophy
  progressive condition, as   2.5.7

National Assembly in Wales
  role in schools cases   10.5.8–10.5.9
National Council for Education and
  Training for Wales   7.2.17
National security
  act done to safeguard   10.2.12
Nicotine addiction
  not 'impairment'   2.3.3
Non-discrimination notice
  action plan   9.1.27–9.1.28
  appeal   9.1.24–9.1.26
    requirement quashes   9.1.25
    revoking or altering
      recommendation   9.1.25
    time-limits   9.1.24
  details of unlawful act   9.1.23
  enforcement   9.1.26
    order   9.1.26
  final   9.1.26
  procedural requirements   9.1.21–
    9.1.23
  representations   9.1.23
  service of   9.1.22–9.1.23
Northern Ireland   1.4, 4.2.18, 4.3.2
  barrister, provisions apply   4.8.10
  Equality Commission for NI   9.1.1
  codes of practice   9.3.2
  taxi regulations, application of
    8.2.21
Nursery school, *see* School

Obesity   2.3.9
Occupational health practitioner
  agent for employer   4.2.15, 4.2.31
  clearance of applicants by   4.2.35
Occupational pension scheme   4.2.5,
  4.5
  admittance and membership
    issues   4.5–4.5.9
  declaration and compensation
    remedies   4.5.9
  employer as party to claim   4.5.8
  'non-discrimination rule'   4.5.4
    alteration to scheme for compliance
      with   4.5.6
    harassment covered by   4.5.4,
      4.5.5
  previous provisions revoked   4.5.1–
    4.5.3
  trustees
    adjustments, circumstances for
      making   4.5.7
    duties on   4.5.4–4.5.7

Occupational pension scheme – *cont*
  trustees – *cont*
    respondents   3.2.2
    unlawful acts   4.5.5
Office-holder, protection of   4.4
  adjustments duty relating to
    4.4.11, 4.4.12
  appointment, discrimination relating
    to
    approval or recommendation
      for   4.4.7
    detriment   4.4.9
    offer terms, refusal etc   4.4.6
    termination   4.4.9
    terms and opportunities   4.4.8
  conditions   4.4.3, 4.4.10
  discriminatory acts   4.4.5–4.4.14
  excluded posts   4.4.4
  harassment, from   4.4.10
  person protected   4.4.13, 4.4.14
    knowledge, relevance   4.4.14
  posts and offices covered   4.4.2
  'relevant person'   4.4.12
  scope of term   4.4.2
  'statutory office'   9.5.2
Offshore employment   4.2.19
Old age, provision for, *see* Insurance
  benefits; Occupational pension
  scheme
Omission   10.3.8, 10.4.3
Order, power to make   9.7.1

Pain, impact of   2.9.3
Pain killers, addiction to
  impairment, as   2.3.3
Parking badge
  proposal for recognition of
    foreign   1.5.3, 8.6.5
Parliament
  acts and omissions   9.6.1–9.6.2
  employer, as   9.6.2
  service provider, as   9.6.2
Partnership   3.2.2, 4.7
  protection for member/prospective
    member   4.7
  adjustments duty   4.7.4–4.7.6
  expulsion   4.7.3
  harassment   4.7.3
  limited liability partnership
    4.7.1
  offer of partnership/benefits
    4.7.2

  unlawful acts   4.7.2, 4.7.3
  respondent, as   3.2.2
Part-time work
  'adjustment', as   3.4.5
Past disability
  discrimination protection   2.8.1–
    2.8.3
  'disability', proof of   2.8.3
  history of disability, person with
    2.8.3
  'long-term adverse effect'   2.6.5
Pay
  agricultural   4.2.47
  EC Framework Directive applies
    4.1.1
  performance-related   4.2.39, 4.2.46
Pension trustees, *see* Occupational
  pension scheme
Pension, occupational, *see* Occupational
  pension scheme
Performance-related pay   4.2.39,
    4.2.46
Personnel officer
  aiding unlawful act, liability for
    10.2.2
  knowledge of disability as agent
    4.2.31
Physical barriers
  adjustments duty of service
    providers   5.5.1–5.5.12
Physical coordination, impairment
  affecting   2.4.1
Physical impairment   2.3.3, 2.3.8
  mental impairment distinguished
    2.3.8, 2.3.9
Place of work
  alteration as 'adjustment'   2.4.2,
    2.4.5
Planning permission
  adjustment, for   6.3.3
  condition for landlord's consent
    6.3.17
Police
  employment provisions extended
    to   4.2.21–4.2.23, 9.5.3
Police Federation   4.9.4
Positive discrimination   4.2.43,
    10.3.34
Possession order
  mental impairment as issue
    6.2.19–6.2.21
Post-employment act, *see* Employment
  cases

Post-16 Code of Practice   7.5.2, 7.5.3,
     7.5.9–7.5.10
Power of attorney   5.6.9
Pre-menstrual tension   2.3.9
Premises, adjustments duty, *see*
     Adjustments duty
Premises, management and disposal
   see also Leasehold premises
   alterations, position of manager
        6.2.13, 6.3.2, 6.3.30
      changes proposed   6.5
   deposit not refunded in full   6.2.16
   discrimination in relation to   6.2.1–
        6.2.18
      person with power to dispose
           6.2.8–6.2.9
      person with power to grant right to
           occupy   6.2.8–6.2.9
      unlawful acts   6.2.2–6.2.7
   'discrimination', definition for
        6.2.13–6.2.16
   disposal by owner-occupier by private
        agreement   6.2.9
   enforcement and remedies for
        unlawful disability
        discrimination   6.2.18
   eviction, additional protection
        6.2.6, 6.2.20
   justification defence   6.2.14–6.2.16
      health and safety risk   6.2.15
      incapacity to contract   6.2.15
      less favourable treatment   6.2.14–
           6.2.16
   'person with power to dispose'
        6.2.8
   possession order against person with
        mental impairment   6.2.19–
        6.2.21
   Rights of Access Code of Practice
        6.2.13, 6.3.4
   scope of 'premises'   6.2.10
   small dwelling exemption, *see* Small
        dwelling
   victimisation   6.2.17
Pressure to discriminate   3.7
Prison officer
   employment as   4.2.21, 9.5.3
Prison Officers' Association   4.9.4
Private health insurance, *see* Insurance
     benefits (employment)
Private household/home   3.4.9,
     4.2.37

Private members' club, *see* Club, private
Private schools, *see* Independent schools
Proceedings
   adjustments duty, county court
        reference for leased premises
        educational institution   7.5.26–
           7.5.28
      goods and service provider
           6.3.25–6.3.29
   assistance of the Disability Rights
        Commission   9.1.10–9.1.12
   Disability Rights Commission order,
        enforcement in county court
        9.1.39
   employment tribunal, *see* Employment
        tribunal
   further and higher education
        10.6.1–10.6.5
      Scotland   10.6.2
      time-limits   10.6.2
   schools   10.5.1–10.5.13
      Scotland   10.5.10
      time-limits   10.5.7
      see also Special Educational Needs
           and Disability Tribunal
           (SENDIST)
   services and premises, cases
        10.4.1–10.4.3
   time-limits   10.3.7–10.3.9, 10.4.2–
        10.4.3, 10.5.7
   universities   10.6.1–10.6.5
   victimisation for bringing/
        involvement in   10.1.3, 10.16
Professional organisation   4.9.4,
     4.10.1
Progressive condition   2.5.7–2.5.9,
     2.6.3
   adverse effect, when 'substantial'
        2.5.7
   asymptomatic condition   2.5.8
   Bill proposals for   2.9.4,
        2.9.5
   future effects, protection from
        2.5.9
   genetic risk   2.5.9
   scope   2.5.7
Promotion (at work)   4.2.34
Property
   see also Leasehold premises; Premises,
        management and disposal
   adjustment to, *see* Adjustments duty

Property – *cont*
sale or disposal   6.1.1, 6.2.1, 6.2.8–
6.2.9
owner-occupier disposal by private
agreement   6.2.9
Property management agency   6.2.5
Prosthesis   2.5.12–2.5.13, 5.5.12
Psychiatric impairment   2.3.4–2.3.7
Psychological impairment   2.3.4–2.3.7
Psychotic disorder   2.3.7
Public authority
see also Local authority
Bill proposals   5.9.1, 9.8
Public body, member of   4.4.2, *see also*
Office-holder
Public sector
application to   9.5
amendments   1.5.2, 9.5.2, 9.5.3
EC Framework Directive, of
4.1.1
Public service vehicle   8.1.5, 8.3.1–
8.3.19
accessibility
construction, use and maintenance
provisions   8.3.5
new vehicles, limited to   8.3.1,
8.3.5
regulations   8.3.3–8.3.10
standards   8.1.5
accessibility certificates   8.3.11–
8.3.16
approval of vehicle type   8.3.13
requirement   8.3.11
review of decision to refuse
application   8.3.14
criminal offences   8.3.9–8.3.10,
8.3.11, 8.3.17
body corporate, by   8.3.10
definition   8.3.2
exemptions   8.3.18–8.3.19
authorisation order   8.3.19
special authorisation   8.3.18
implementation of regulations
dates for various vehicles   8.3.5
timetable   8.3.5
lifts   8.3.7
ramps   8.3.7
'regulated public service vehicle'
8.3.4
sensory impaired travellers   8.3.8
type approval
certificate   8.3.15–8.3.16

certificate withdrawal   8.3.16
'type vehicle'   8.3.13
wheelchair users   8.3.4, 8.3.5,
8.3.7–8.3.8
Public transport, *see* Public service
vehicle; Transport
Publicity restriction, *see* Restricted
reporting order
Pupil, *see* Education services; School

Qualifications body   1.5.6, 3.2.2, 4.10
educational qualifications,
proposals   7.6
adjustments duty   7.6.3
unlawful discrimination or
harassment   7.6.2
jurisdiction restriction on employment
tribunal   10.3.6
trade or professional qualifications
adjustments duty   4.10.6–4.10.9
background   4.10.1, 4.10.2
'competence standard'   4.10.5
definition   4.10.3
unlawful discrimination or
harassment   4.10.4
Qualifications, job
discriminatory requirement   4.2.2
Questionnaire (services, etc, provision
case)
proposal for   10.7.2
Questionnaire, statutory (employment
case)   10.3.1–10.3.5
admissibility as evidence   10.3.4
failure to reply/evasive answers
10.3.5
form   10.3.2, 10.3.3
service   10.3.3

Racial discrimination
compared   5.4.10
positive discrimination not
prohibited   4.2.43, 10.3.34
statutory authority defence   10.2.9
Rail vehicle   8.1.5, 8.4.1–8.4.11
accessibility   8.4.2–8.4.11
construction, use and
maintenance   8.4.3
exemption   8.4.10–8.4.11
exemption applications and
revocations   8.4.11
new vehicles, limited to   8.4.9

Rail vehicle – *cont*
  accessibility – *cont*
    reform proposals (Bill)   8.6–
      8.6.4
    regulations   8.4.2–8.4.5
    standards   8.1.5
  criminal offences   8.4.6
    body corporate, by   8.4.6
    civil enforcement regime to
      replace   8.6.4
  'rail vehicle'   8.4.8
    amendment proposed   1.5.4
  'railway'   8.4.8
  'regulated rail vehicle'   8.4.7, 8.6.2
    compliance certificate proposed
      8.6.3
  tramcars   8.4.5
  underground   8.4.5
  wheelchair users   8.4.2–8.4.4
Ramp
  public service vehicles, in   8.3.7
  taxis, in   8.2.3
Recommendations, *see* Remedies
Recreational facilities
  local education authority, secured
    by   7.5.14–7.5.16
Recruitment   4.2.2 *et seq*
  adjustments duty to job applicants
    4.2.29–4.2.33
  arrangements, discrimination in
    4.2.2, 4.2.34
  disability-related questions   4.2.32
  EC Framework Directive applies
    4.1.1
  health screening, *see* Medical
    examination
  induction procedure   4.2.4
  refusal to offer employment   4.2.2
  terms of offer   4.2.3
Recurring condition   2.5.5, 2.5.6,
    2.6.3
  approach of tribunal to   2.5.6
  Guidance   2.5.6
  past disability   2.6.4, 2.8.1
  steps to prevent recurrence   2.5.6
Reform
  Bill, *see* Legislation
  Disability Rights Task Force, *see*
    Disability Rights Task Force
  proposals, DRC powers   9.1.8
Remedies   10.3.21–10.3.31
  compensation   10.3.23–10.3.31,
    10.3.35

additional award   10.3.30
aggravated and exemplary
  damages   10.3.26
assessment of   10.3.23
calculation principles   10.3.24,
  10.3.25
dispute resolution failure,
  adjustment for   10.3.31
hearing for   10.3.23
injury to feelings   10.3.26,
  10.4.10
interest   10.3.27
loss of earnings   10.3.23, 10.3.25,
  10.3.29
maximum   10.3.24, 10.3.29
medical evidence   10.3.23,
  10.3.25
mitigation of loss   10.3.25
services and premises cases
  10.4.11–10.4.12
unfair dismissal, act also is
  10.3.28–10.3.31
damages, *see* Damages
declaration of rights   10.3.21,
  10.3.22, 10.4.11
  Scotland, in   10.5.10
educational institution cases, *see*
  Special Educational Needs and
  Disability Tribunal (SENDIST)
recommendations   10.3.32–10.3.35
  action related to claimant
    10.3.32
  examples   10.3.33
  failure to comply   10.3.35
  use in disability cases   10.3.34
schools, *see* Special Educational Needs
  and Disability Tribunal
  (SENDIST)
services and premises cases   6.2.18,
  10.4
  county court   10.4.1
  injuries to feelings   10.4.11
  time-limits   10.4.2
Rent   6.2.2
Repetitive strain injury   2.3.9
Resignation in response to employer's
  conduct, *see* Constructive dismissal
Respondent   3.2.2, *see also* Remedies
Restricted reporting order   10.3.16–
  10.3.19
  appeal, on   10.3.19
  breach, offence   10.3.18

Restricted reporting order – *cont*
  duration   10.3.18
Risk of physical danger
  impairment affecting perception
    of   2.4.1

Schizophrenia   2.3.7, 3.2.25
School
  see also Education services
  accessibility strategies and plans
    7.4.12–7.4.15
  adjustments duty   7.4.6–7.4.9
    anticipatory and evolving duty
      7.4.7
    auxiliary aids provision not
      required   7.4.7
    physical features, removal or
      alteration not required
      7.4.7
  admission decision   7.4.7, 7.4.15
    claim relating to   10.5.4
  autistic child, failure to provide
    support for   7.4.2
  Code of Practice   7.4.1
  conciliation   10.5.12–10.5.13
  confidentiality request   7.4.9,
    7.5.11
  discrimination by   7.4.4 *et seq*
  enforcement   10.5, *see also* Special
    Educational Needs and Disability
    Tribunal (SENDIST)
  exclusion from   5.2.9, 7.1.2, 7.2.1–
    7.2.3
    claim relating to   10.5.5
  governors' annual report, information
    in   7.2.10, 7.4.15
  independent, *see* Independent schools
  justification defence   7.4.5, 7.4.11
  knowledge of disability   7.4.10
  less favourable treatment by
    3.2.15, 7.4.5
  nursery school   7.4.3, 7.4.14
  post-Sept 2002 law   7.4.1–7.4.19
    disability discrimination duties
      7.4.2–7.4.3
  pre-Sept 2002 law   7.2.9–7.2.10
  private, *see* Independent schools
  proceedings   10.5.1–10.5.13
  remedies   10.5, *see also* Special
    Educational Needs and Disability
    Tribunal

selection   7.4.5, 7.4.11, 7.4.17
special educational needs   7.2.9–
  7.2.10, 7.4.1
special school   7.4.3, 10.5.8
Scotland
  accessibility strategies   7.4.12
  advocate   4.8.9
  Disability Rights Commissioners
    9.1.4
  education services, enforcement in
    7.4.19, 7.5.19, 10.5.10
  further education colleges and
    institutions   7.2.13, 7.5.4,
    7.5.14–7.5.16
  premises adjustments duty   6.3.5–
    6.3.6
  sheriff court
    further/higher education case claim
      in   10.6.2
    schools case in   10.5.10
    services, etc, provision claim in
      10.4.2
  taxi regulations, application of
    8.2.21
Seasonal allergic rhinitis
  DDA 1995, not impairment for
    purposes of   2.3.3, 2.5.5
Secretary of State
  Code of Practice approval   9.3.4
  direction in schools cases   10.5.8–
    10.5.9
  Guidance, issue of   9.4.1–9.4.5
    approval by Parliament   9.4.4
    consultation duty   9.4.3
    disability, on meaning of   2.1.2,
      2.1.4, 2.2.2, 9.4.5
  regulations and orders, power to
    make   9.7.1
Selection for employment, *see*
  Recruitment
Selection in education   7.4.5, 7.4.11,
  7.4.17
Self-administered injury   2.5.11, 2.9.3
Self-employment
  contract worker in, protection of
    4.3.2
  services assisting   5.7.1
Sensory impairment   2.3.10
  guide/hearing dogs in taxis
    8.2.12–8.2.15
  public service vehicles provision
    for   8.3.8

Services, goods and facilities, provision
of
   adjustments to premises, duty
        5.5.1–5.5.15, 6.3.2, 6.3.4–6.3.6
      anticipatory and evolving duty
           5.5.4
      auxiliary aids provision   5.5.1,
           5.5.13–5.5.15
      building regulations   6.3.4–6.3.6
      cost factor   5.5.3
      exemption from duty, power of
           5.5.11
      failure   5.1.4, 5.3.5, 5.5.2, 6.3.2
      leased premises, and consent of
           lessor   6.3.20–6.3.29, *see also*
           Landlord
      physical features   5.5.7–5.5.12,
           6.3.2, 6.3.4–6.3.6
      'practice, policy and procedure'
           5.5.5–5.5.6
   claim   10.4.1–10.4.3
      county court   10.4.2
      time-limit   10.4.2, 10.4.3
   Code of Practice on rights of
        access   5.1.3, 5.2.1, 5.5.3–5.5.4,
        5.5.6, 5.5.8
   conciliation   10.4.4–10.4.6
   contract for
      incapacity to make   5.6.8–5.6.9,
           6.2.15
      invalidated terms, and effect of
           10.4.7–10.4.9
   costs
      compliance   5.6.13
      justifying discrimination   5.6.12–
           5.6.13
   deposit not refunded in full   5.6.16
   disabled persons as consumers
        requirement of DDA 1995
        5.2.8
   discrimination, meaning of   5.4.1–
        5.4.10
   excluded services   5.2.9
   facilities, what constitutes   5.2.3
   goods, what constitutes   5.2.3
   group insurance scheme treated as
        4.13.4
   guarantee, less favourable treatment
        in respect of   5.6.15
   indirect discrimination   5.4.10
   insurance services   5.6.14
   justification   5.4.2, 5.4.8, 5.6.1–
        5.6.16
      burden of proof   5.6.5
      conditions for defence   5.6.6–
           5.6.13
      greater cost   5.6.12–5.6.13
      health and safety risk   5.6.7
      incapacity to contract   5.6.8–
           5.6.9
      standard of service   5.6.11
      subjective-objective test   5.6.4–
           5.6.5
   labelling and instructions   5.2.6
   legislation
      background to   5.1.1–5.1.4
      implementation timetable   5.1.2
   less favourable treatment   5.4.2–
        5.4.9
      justification   5.4.2, 5.4.8, 5.6.1–
           5.6.16
   manufacturers and designers,
        obligation of   5.2.6
   physical features of premises impeding
        access, *see* 'adjustments to
        premises, duty' *above*
   private members' club, *see* Club,
        private
   questionnaire, proposal for   10.7.2
   refusal to provide   5.3.2
   remedies   10.4.10, 10.4.11
      damages   10.4.10
      declaration or injunction   5.8.1,
           10.4.11
   Scotland, proceedings in   10.4.1,
        10.4.2
   service providers   5.2.4–5.2.5
      manufacturers and designers,
           obligation of   5.2.6
      meaning and scope   5.2.4
      more than one   5.2.4
      private members' clubs   5.2.7
      United Kingdom, based in   5.2.5
      United Kingdom, provision in
           5.2.5
   services, what constitutes   5.2.1–
        5.2.9
      examples   5.2.1–5.2.2
      exclusions   5.2.9
   settlement   10.4.7–10.4.9
   standard or manner of service
        5.3.3
   terminally ill   2.6.2
   terms of provision   5.3.4
   unlawful discriminatory acts   5.1.4,
        5.3.1–5.3.5

Settlement   10.4.7–10.4.9, 10.5.11, *see also* Compromise contract; Conciliation

Severe disfigurement   2.5.10–2.5.11
    deliberately acquired   2.5.11
    exclusions from provisions   2.5.11

Sex discrimination
    compared   5.4.10

Sexual abuse tendency
    not 'impairment'   2.3.4

Shared accommodation   6.2.11–6.2.12

Sheriff court proceedings, *see* Scotland

Ship, employment on   4.2.18, 4.2.19

Shipping
    guidance on access for the disabled   8.5.1

Sickness
    insurance provision   4.6.5, *see also* Insurance benefits
    sick pay
        non-payment/part payment   3.2.14
        payment, as 'adjustment'   3.4.5

Sight impairment   2.3.10, 2.3.11, 2.4.1
    correctable   2.5.17
    guide dog in taxi   8.2.12–8.2.15
    trivial condition   2.5.2

Sign language interpreter   3.4.6

Small business
    exclusion repealed   4.2.20

Small claim procedure
    arbitration   10.4.1
    court   10.4.10

Small dwelling
    exemption from disposal/management provisions   6.2.11–6.2.12
    modification proposed   1.5.6

Smoking
    DDA 1995, not impairment for purposes of   2.3.3

Solicitor
    see also Law Society
    discrimination relating to instructing barrister   4.8.6

Special educational needs   7.2.9–7.2.10, 7.4.1

Special Educational Needs and Disability Tribunal (SENDIST)   7.4.19, 10.5

claim procedure, regulation of   10.5.1
claimant   10.5.3
    order   10.5.3
    non-compliance, Secretary of State role   10.5.9
    remedies   10.5.3
    private hearing   10.5.2
    time-limits   10.5.7

Special school   7.4.3, 10.5.8

Speech impairment   2.3.10, 2.4.1

Statistics
    disabled people   1.1.1, 1.1.2

Statutory authority, *see* Liability

Statutory body
    see also Office-holder
    'statutory office'   4.2.21, 9.5.2

Stress   2.3.6, 2.3.9

Student, *see* Education services; University

Substance abuse
    not 'impairment' per se   2.3.3

Support Dogs   8.2.13

Supported employment   4.2.25, 4.2.26

Task Force, *see* Disability Rights Task Force

Tattoo, disfigurement caused by   2.5.11

Taxi
    accessibility   8.1.3, 8.2.1–8.2.8
        failure to comply   8.2.3
        Government policy   8.2.22, 8.2.23
        implementation   8.2.22, 8.2.23
        regulations   8.2.2–8.2.3, 8.2.22
        standards   8.1.5
        wheelchair access   8.2.1–8.2.3
    criminal offences by driver   8.2.3, 8.2.9, 8.2.14
    definition   8.2.4
    drivers' duties
        assistance to passenger   8.2.9
        exemptions   8.2.10–8.2.11, 8.2.15
        guide dogs   8.2.12–8.2.15
        medical exemption   8.2.11, 8.2.15
        wheelchair user, to   8.2.9–8.2.11
    exemptions   8.2.7, 8.2.8

Taxi – *cont*
  hire car at transport terminus
    8.2.19–8.2.20
  newly licensed vehicles   8.2.1, 8.2.5
  ramps   8.2.3
  relicensing   8.2.5
  Scotland and Northern Ireland,
    application of statutory
    provisions   8.2.21, 8.2.23
  swivel-seats   8.2.8
  viability of trade   8.2.5–8.2.7
  wheelchair users   8.2.1–8.2.3,
    8.2.9–8.2.11
Teacher Training Agency   7.2.11
Tenancy   6.2.10, *see also* Leasehold
  premises
Terminal illness   2.6.2
Terms of employment, *see* Employment
  cases
Time-limit
  claim, for
    education cases   10.5.7, 10.6.2
    employment cases   10.3.7–10.3.9
    services and premises cases
      10.4.2–10.4.3
  investigation by DRC, for   9.1.19
Tomlinson Committee on education and
    disability   7.2.17
Tort, statutory   4.2.17
Trade organisation   4.9
  adjustments duty   4.9.11–4.9.14
  background   4.9.1
  definition   4.9.3
  discrimination prohibition   4.9.8,
    4.9.9
  EC Framework Directive applies
    4.1.1
  employer, as   4.9.1
  employers, organisation of   4.9.3,
    4.9.6
  harassment prohibition   4.9.10
  membership
    application   4.9.8, 4.9.12
    benefits of   4.9.9
  premises   4.9.11
  respondent, as   3.2.2
  scope of term   4.9.3–4.9.7
  services provision by   4.9.2
  workers, organisation of   4.9.3,
    4.9.4, *see also* Trade union
Trade union   4.9.4, 4.9.5, 4.9.8–4.9.14
  adjustments duty   4.9.11, 4.9.12

ballot and election arrangements
    4.9.13, 4.9.14
  discrimination prohibitions   4.9.8,
    4.9.9
  employee of   4.9.1
  harassment prohibition   4.9.10
Training
  'adjustment', as   3.4.2, 3.4.5
    costs   3.4.6
    duty to make   4.2.34
    see also Adjustments duty
  EC Framework Directive applies
    4.1.1
  local education authority, secured
    by   7.5.14–7.5.16
  vocational   5.7.1
Training of staff
  defence to vicarious liability   10.2.6
Train, *see* Rail vehicle
Tramcar   8.4.5
Transfer to vacancy
  'adjustment', as   3.4.2, 3.4.4
  duty to make adjustment to
    arrangements   4.2.34
Transport
  see also Public service vehicle
  accessibility   8.1.3, 8.1.5
  adjustments   8.1.2, 8.1.3, 8.1.4
  air, *see* Aircraft; Airport
  amendments proposed   1.5.3
  Disabled Persons' Transport Advisory
    Committee   8.22, 8.5.1
  employment   8.1.4
  exclusion from provisions   5.2.9,
    8.1.2–8.1.3
  hire car   8.1.3, 8.2.4
    accessibility at designated transport
      facilities   8.2.19–8.2.20
  minicabs   8.2.4
    accessibility at designated transport
      facilities   8.2.19–8.2.20
  rail, *see* Rail vehicle
  recovery services   8.1.3
  services provision exclusion   5.2.9,
    8.1.2–8.1.3
    Bill proposal to remove   5.9.2
  ships, *see* Shipping
  taxis, *see* Taxi
  tramcars   8.4.5
  work, to, employee benefit   4.2.5
Tribunal proceedings, *see* Employment
  tribunal

Trustees, pension, *see* Occupational
  pension scheme

Underground railway   8.4.5
Understanding, impairment
  affecting   2.4.1
Unfair dismissal
  adjustments considerations before
    dismissal   4.2.44
  compensation, interaction with
    disability discrimination
    10.3.28–10.3.31
    additional award   10.3.30
    loss of earnings   10.3.29
  continuous employment   4.2.45
  dual claim   4.2.45, 10.3.28–10.3.31
    reinstatement/re-engagement order
      not obeyed   10.3.30
  grievance procedure, statutory
    10.3.10, 10.3.11
  relationship with disability law
    4.2.44, 4.2.45
University   6.4.1, 7.2.2, 7.2.19–7.2.25
  adjustments duty   7.5.7–7.5.11
    anticipatory and evolving duty
      7.5.8
    auxiliary aids provision   7.5.9
    leasehold premises, and consent
      7.5.18–7.5.30, *see also* Landlord
    physical features of premises,
      adjustments to   7.5.9, 7.5.18
  conciliation   10.6.5
  confidentiality request   7.5.11
  disability statements   7.2.20–7.2.25
  enforcement for unlawful disability
    discrimination   7.5.17
  justification defence   7.5.6–7.5.7,
    7.5.13
  knowledge of disability   7.5.12
  leasehold premises   7.5.18–7.5.30
  less favourable treatment by   7.5.6,
    7.5.13
  Post-16 Code of Practice   7.5.2,
    7.5.3, 7.5.9–7.5.10
  post-Sept 2002 law on disability
    discrimination
    disability discrimination duties
      7.5.3–7.5.4
  proceedings   10.6.1–10.6.5
    time-limits   10.6.2
    remedies   10.6.3

Vicarious liability
  employer   10.2.2, 10.2.4–10.2.6
    defence   10.2.6
  principal   10.2.7
Victimisation   10.1
  causal link with protected act
    10.1.7
  circumstances for   10.1.3–10.1.6
  education field   10.1.1
  employment field, in   3.2.49,
    3.2.50, 10.1
  goods and services   10.1.1
  premises, relating to   6.2.17, 10.1
  separate nature of   10.1.2
Vision impairment   2.3.10, 2.4.1
  correctable by spectacles or contact
    lenses   2.5.17
  guide dogs, carrying in taxis
    8.2.12–8.2.15
  trivial conditions   2.5.2
Vocational guidance/training   5.7.1
Voyeurism
  DDA 1995, not impairment for
    purposes of   2.3.4

Wages, *see* Pay
Website
  accessibility, DRC investigation
    9.1.21
  DRC   9.1.1
Welsh Assembly
  role in schools cases   10.5.8–10.5.9
Wheelchair
  aeroplane access, provision by airport
    operator   8.5.2
  impairment 'aid'   2.5.14
    adverse treatment of user
      recognised   2.5.12
  public service vehicle, use on
    8.3.4, 8.3.5, 8.3.7–8.3.8
  rail vehicle, on   8.4.2–8.4.4
    requirements covered   8.4.4
  service provider
    adjustments duty   5.5.6, 5.5.12
    discrimination against user
      5.3.3, 5.5.6
  taxi access   8.2.1–8.2.3
  taxi drivers' duties towards
    passengers   8.2.9–8.2.11
    exemptions   8.2.10–8.2.11
White Paper   5.1.1, 5.4.10, 5.5.1,
  5.5.6, 7.1.1, 8.1.1

Work experience or placement   4.11
  adjustment duty on provider
    4.11.3–4.11.5
  definitions and scope   4.11.1
  unlawful discrimination or
    harassment   4.11.12
Workers' organisation, *see* Trade
  organisation
Workstep scheme   4.3.1

World Health Organization (WHO)
  impairment, definition of   2.3.1
  International Classification of Diseases,
    reference to   2.3.6

Zimmer frame
  medical aid, as   2.5.14